Principles
of Microeconomics

Principles
of Microeconomics

Roy J. Ruffin
University of Houston

Paul R. Gregory
University of Houston

Scott, Foresman and Company

Glenview, Illinois

Dallas, Texas   Oakland, New Jersey
Palo Alto, California   Tucker, Georgia   London, England

To Roy Ruffin, Sr., Blanche Ruffin, and Annemarie Gregory

Library of Congress Cataloging in Publication Data

Ruffin, Roy, 1938–
    Principles of microeconomics.

    Includes index.
    1. Economics. I. Gregory, Paul. R. II. Title.
HB171.5.R82 1983   330   82–16946
ISBN 0-673-15857-8

123456-RRW-86 85 84 83 82

Credit Lines

Table 4 on p. 132: From "Fortune's Directory of the 500 Largest Industrial Corporations," *Fortune* 105, 9 (May 3, 1982): 260. Copyright © 1982 Time, Inc. All rights reserved.

Figure on p. 150: Copyright © 1967, 1971 by John Wiley & Sons, Inc.

Table on p. 224: Copyright © 1970 by Random House, Inc.

Table 4 on p. 230: Copyright © 1974 by the University of Chicago Law School.

Table 3 on p. 322: Reprinted with permission from the *Journal of Economic Literature*.

Tables 4 and 5 on pp. 325 and 326: Copyright © 1979 by National Affairs, Inc.

Table 2 on p. 427: Copyright © Basil Blackwell, 1977.

To the Instructor

The presentation of microeconomics is far more concrete in this book than in most textbooks. Real-world examples, rather than fanciful or hypothetical ones, illustrate concepts like comparative advantage, increasing returns, increasing-cost industries, or U-shaped cost curves. Microeconomic theory is brought even closer to the real world by including a chapter on information costs and by drawing upon the research of industrial-organization economists to enrich the price-theory discussions. The chapter on information or transactions costs (13) includes a discussion of futures markets, the economics of search, speculation, intermediaries or "middlemen," and problems of product quality. This book also introduces the modern microeconomic topics of adverse selection, moral hazard, signaling, and unions as a voice mechanism at an elementary level.

Organization

This book is organized into four parts. Part I (Chapters 1–4) introduces the basic concepts of economics that must be learned before proceeding to the study of microeconomics.

The microeconomics core begins with the ten-chapter unit (Part II) on the product market

(Chapters 5–14). Chapter 5 teaches price elasticities of demand and supply as well as income and cross-price elasticities of demand. Chapter 6 deals with demand and utility (with an appendix on indifference curves). Business organization and corporate finance are discussed in Chapter 7, and short-run and long-run costs are explained in Chapter 8 (with an appendix on equal-output curves, or isoquants). The standard market models—perfect competition, monopoly, monopolistic competition, and oligopoly—are covered in Chapters 9–12, with a special chapter (11) devoted to comparing monopoly and competition. Chapter 13 introduces the role of information costs, and Chapter 14 deals with government/business relations, particularly government regulation and antitrust law. Factor markets are taught as a five-chapter unit in Part III (Chapters 15–19). Chapter 15 gives a theoretical overview of the workings of factor markets, and Chapters 16 and 18 discuss specific factor markets. Chapter 17 considers the role of labor unions, and Chapter 19 considers the determinants of income distribution and poverty.

Microeconomic issues are the focus of Part IV (Chapters 20–23). Chapter 20 examines the issues of public finance and taxation; Chapter 21 explains the economics of exhaustible resources and of market failure (public goods and externalities); Chapter 22 discusses modern theories of public choice; Chapter 23 explores comparative economic systems (with an appendix on the economics of Marx).

Suggestions for Course Planning

This book is intended for a one-semester course in microeconomics that is traditionally taught as a first- or second-year college course. The text for the macroeconomics course is also available in a softbound volume, and a hardbound volume is available that contains both microeconomics and macroeconomics chapters.

The instructor teaching a quarter course in microeconomics can build a course around the 19 core chapters listed below, incorporating material from the remaining 4 chapters in this book as time and interest allow.

1   The Nature of Economics
2   The Economic Problem
3   The Price System
4   The Mechanics of Supply and Demand
5   Elasticity of Supply and Demand
6   Demand and Utility
7   Business Organization
8   Costs and Productivity
9   Perfect Competition
10   Monopoly and Monopolistic Competition
12   Oligopoly
13   The Economics of Information
14   Antitrust Law and Regulation
15   Factor Markets
16   Labor Markets
19   Income Distribution and Poverty
20   Public Finance
21   Market Failure: Energy and the Environment
22   Public Choice

Supplements

This book has a complete package of supplements, which includes an *Instructor's Manual, Study Guide, Test Bank,* and *Transparency Masters.*

The *Instructor's Manual* was written by the authors. Each of the 41 chapters contains sections on: points to learn in the chapter, chapter organization, special approaches, optional material, teaching hints and special projects, bad habits to unlearn, additional essay questions, answers to end-of-chapter "Questions and Problems," and answers to the "Review Quiz" for that chapter in the *Study Guide.*

The *Instructor's Manual* is a valuable teaching aid because it supplies the instructor with additional numerical examples not contained in the text and additional real-world illustrations not discussed in the text. A chapter outline gives a brief overview of the material in the chapter that assists the instructor in preparing lecture outlines and in seeing the logical development of the chapter. The special-approaches section tells the instructor how this chapter is different from other textbooks and explains why a topic was treated differently in this text or why an entirely new topic not covered by other texts was introduced in the chapter. The optional-material section gives the instructor a ranking of priorities for the topics in the chapter and enables the instructor to trim the size of each chapter (if necessary).

The *Study Guide* was written by John Vahaly of the University of Louisville. Because the *Study Guide* is quite analytical, it will challenge the student and help him or her to better prepare for exams. The *Study Guide* supplements the text by providing summaries of the crucial elements. It contains multiple-choice and true/false questions, but unlike other study guides, it contains not only the answers to the multiple-choice and true/false questions but also *explanations for the answers.* Instead of just giving lists of the correct, *a, b, c* responses or a list of *T*s and *F*s, the *Study Guide*'s answer sections explain *why* a particular objective answer is the correct one. In addition to objective questions, each chapter of the *Study Guide* also contains analytical problems and questions. Again, the *Study Guide* provides not only the answers to the questions, but the step-by-step process for arriving at the answer.

At the back of the *Study Guide* is a "Review Quiz" for each chapter that contains multiple-choice questions the answers for which do *not* appear in the *Study Guide* but do appear in the *Instructor's Manual.* These quizzes can be used by the instructor as homework or as chapter quizzes.

The authors have also prepared a *Test Bank* that contains nearly 1,800 multiple-choice questions—most of which have already been class tested. The answers have been checked and double checked to minimize the chances that any of the questions have more than one answer. For each chapter in the text, the *Test Bank* contains 4 different tests (coded A, B, C, or D). Whether the instructor is trying to compose a one-chapter quiz or a 23-chapter final exam, that instructor can choose from among the questions in the *Test Bank,* the questions in the "Review Quizzes" at the back of the *Study Guide,* or the additional essay questions in the *Instructor's Manual*—more than 2,300 questions in all. The *Test Bank* is available both on perforated paper in book form and on computer tape.

Transparency Masters suitable for overhead projectors are available for all key figures and tables (about 150 items).

To the Student

How to Understand Economics

Many students find economics a difficult subject because, unlike many other courses a college student takes, economics cannot be mastered through memorization. Economics relies on economic theories to explain real-world occurrences—like why people tend to buy less when prices rise or why increased government spending may reduce unemployment. An economic theory is simply a logical explanation of why the facts fit together in a particular way. If the theory were not logical, or if the theory failed to be confirmed by real-world facts, it would be readily discarded by economists.

The successful student will be the one who learns that economics is built upon a number of fairly simple and easy-to-understand propositions. These propositions and assumptions—that businesses seek to maximize profits or that consumers base their expenditure decisions on disposable income, for example—form the building blocks upon which economics is based. These propositions are typically little more than common sense and should not intimidate a student. If a major building block is missing, however, the whole structure can fall apart. To prevent the student from overlooking or forgetting a crucial building block, we frequently engage in pedagogical review. In other words, when a new proposition is added to a theoretical structure, the underlying propositions are reviewed.

Another factor that can make economics difficult for a student is that economics—like other academic disciplines—has its own specific vocabulary. Unlike the physical sciences, however, where the student may be encountering a certain term for the first time, much of the vocabulary of economics—terms like *efficiency, capital, stock, unemployment*—has a common usage that is already familiar to the student. Economists, however, use the vocabulary of economics in a very exact way, and often the common usage of a term is not the same as the economic usage. In this book, each key term appears in boldface type where it is first discussed in text. Immediately following the paragraph where the term first appears in boldface type, the formal, economic definition of the term is set off in color. At the end of each chapter is a list of all the key terms that have been boldfaced and given formal definitions in that chapter; a glossary at the end of the book contains all the definitions of key terms and gives the chapter number in which the term was defined.

The modern developments in economics are simply new attempts to explain in a logical manner how the facts bind together. Modern developments have occurred because of the realization that established theories were not doing a good job of explaining the world around us. Fortunately, the major building blocks of modern theory—that people attempt to anticipate the future, that rising prices motivate wealth holders to spend less, that people and businesses gather information and make decisions in a rational manner—rely on common-sense logic.

Economics is only valuable if it explains the real world. Economics should be able to answer very specific questions like: Why are there three major domestic producers of automobiles and hundreds or even thousands of producers of textiles? Why is there a positive association between the growth of the money supply and inflation? Why does the United States export computers and farm products to the rest of the world? Why do restaurants rope off space during less busy hours? If Iowa corn land is the best land for growing corn, why is corn also grown in Texas while some land stands idle in Iowa? Why do interest rates rise when people expect the inflation rate to increase? Why did the price of petroleum rise so rapidly in the 1970s? The successful student will be able to apply the knowledge he or she gains of real-world economic behavior to explain any number of events that have already occurred or are yet to occur.

In writing this book, we have made a conscious effort to present arguments and evidence on both sides of every economic controversy. We attempt to make a case for each distinct viewpoint, even if it would be more interesting and less complicated to come out strongly in one camp. Although we are aware of our own free-market bias, we believe it is best to allow the student to keep an open mind at this very early stage in the study of economics.

Learning Aids

This book contains a number of important learning aids.

1. The *Chapter Preview* that precedes each chapter provides a brief overview of the important points to be learned in that chapter.
2. *Definitions of Key Terms* are set off in color following the paragraphs in which the terms are introduced in context.
3. *Key Ideas,* or important economic principles or conclusions, are set off in color in bold, italicized type.
4. *Boxed Examples* allow the student to appreciate how economic concepts apply in real-world settings without disrupting the flow of the text and supplement the numerous examples already found in the text discussions.
5. A *Chapter Summary* of the main points of each chapter is found at the end of each chapter.
6. *Key Terms* that were defined in color in the chapter are listed at the end of each chapter.

7. *Questions and Problems* that test the reader's understanding of the chapter follow each chapter.

8. A *Glossary,* containing all key terms defined in color in chapters and listed in chapter "Key Terms" sections, appears at the end of the book. Each entry contains the complete economic definition as well as the number of the chapter where the term was first defined.

9. The *Index* of all the names, concepts, terms, and topics covered in the book is one of the most thorough indexes ever compiled for an introductory economics text.

10. Statistical data on the major economic variables are found on the front and back inside covers for easy reference.

11. *Suggested Readings* are listed for each chapter at the back of the book.

Acknowledgments

We are deeply indebted to our colleagues at the University of Houston who had to bear with us in the writing of this book. Richard Bean, Joel Sailors, Thomas DeGregori, James Griffin, Peter Mieszkowski, Peter Zadrozny, Art DeVany, Louis Stern, Oded Palmon, and Thomas Mayor gave their time freely on an incredible number of pedagogical points in the teaching of elementary economics.

We are also grateful for the suggestions and contributions of numerous colleagues across the country who reviewed this manuscript in various stages of its development:

David Abel	Mankato State University
Ken Alexander	Michigan Technical University
Susan Alexander	College of St. Thomas
Richard G. Anderson	Ohio State University
Richard K. Anderson	Texas A & M
Ian Bain	University of Minnesota
George Bittlingmayer	University of Michigan
Robert Borengasser	St. Mary's College
Ronald Brandolini	Valencia Community College

Wallace Broome	Rhode Island Junior College
Anthony Campolo	Columbus Technical Institute
Shirley Cassing	University of Pittsburgh
Robert E. Christiansen	Colby College
Richard Clarke	University of Wisconsin, Madison
David Denslow	University of Florida
Tim Deyak	Louisiana State University, Baton Rouge
Dan Friedman	University of California, Los Angeles (UCLA)
Janet Furman	Tulane University
Charles Gallagher	Virginia Commonwealth University
Ronald Gunderson	Northern Arizona University
Edward Howe	Siena College
James Johannes	Michigan State University
James Kahn	State University of New York, Binghamton
Chris Klisz	Wayne State University
Byung Lee	Howard University
Robert Lucas	University of Chicago
Ron Luchessi	American River College
Roger Mack	DeAnza College
Allan Mandelstamm	Virginia Polytechnic Institute
Jim McKinsey	Northeastern University
W. Douglas Morgan	University of California, Santa Barbara
Norman Obst	Michigan State University
John Pisciotta	Baylor University
John Pomery	Purdue University
Jennifer Roback	Yale University
Mark Rush	University of Florida
Robert Schmitz	Indiana University
David Spencer	Washington State University
Alan Stockman	University of Rochester
Don Tailby	University of New Mexico
Helen Tauchen	University of North Carolina
Robert Thomas	Iowa State University
Roger Trenary	Kansas State University
George Uhimchuk	Clemson University
Roberton Williams	Williams College
Gary Young	Delta State University (Mississippi)

It was a pleasure to work closely with John Vahaly who, in addition to preparing the *Study Guide,* provided valuable and insightful comments on every chapter of this book.

We wish to thank George Lobell, economics editor at Scott, Foresman, who gave us encouragement and advice throughout the writing of this book. The skillful editing of the work was in the able hands of Mary LaMont, developmental editor at Scott, Foresman, whose contributions to style and content grace every page.

Special thanks go to Janet Blackburn, Annemarie Gregory, Roselyn Kennelly, Jane Wang, and Khalil Yazdi.

Roy J. Ruffin
Paul R. Gregory

Contents in Brief

Contents in Brief

Contents

APPENDIX **1A**
Reading Graphs   14

CHAPTER **2**
The Economic Problem   23

PART **II**
Product Markets   77

CHAPTER **5**
Elasticity of Supply and Demand   78

CHAPTER **6**
Demand and Utility   98

APPENDIX **6A**
Indifference Curves   111

CHAPTER **7**
Business Organization   117

CHAPTER **8**
Costs and Productivity   135

APPENDIX **8A**
Choosing the Least-Cost Method of Production   153

CHAPTER **9**
Perfect Competition   159

CHAPTER **10**
Monopoly and Monopolistic Competition   181

CHAPTER **11**
Monopoly and Competition Compared   204

CHAPTER **12**
Oligopoly   218

CHAPTER **13**

The Economics of Information   240

CHAPTER **14**
Antitrust Law and Regulation   258

PART **III**
Factor Markets   279

CHAPTER **17**
Labor Unions   313

CHAPTER **18**
Interest, Rent, and Profit   328

CHAPTER **19**
Income Distribution and Poverty   347

PART **IV**
Microeconomic Issues   369

CHAPTER **20**
Public Finance   370

CHAPTER **21**
Market Failure: Energy and the Environment   391

CHAPTER **22**
Public Choice   406

CHAPTER **23**
Comparative Economic Systems   416

APPENDIX **23A**
Marxist Economics   429

Glossary   433

Suggested Readings   444

Index   449

I

Basic Economic Concepts

1

The Nature of Economics

Chapter Preview

Understanding economics is important to each person as an individual, as a producer, and as a voter in a democratic society. Economists study many questions, but the central issue of economics is: How does the economy work? An understanding of how the economy works helps society as well as each individual. In a nutshell, the goal of economics is to sort out the sense from the nonsense in everyday economic affairs. Better information aids decision making at all levels.

Economics is an evolving and changing field. Some parts of our economic knowledge are fairly certain; other parts are uncertain. Many areas of economics are in the process of development; many are controversial. That economics is changing shows that economics is an exciting, dynamic field in search of real answers. This book will explain the rudiments of how the economy works according to our present understanding of economics.

This chapter introduces the basic concepts and tools that economists use to understand how the economy works. The chapter explains the basic principles of scarcity, choice, specialization, and exchange and shows how economists use the scientific method to study the economy. The chapter warns about the pitfalls to avoid in studying economics and explains why (and about what) economists sometimes disagree.

WHAT IS ECONOMICS: BASIC THEMES

People are concerned with improving their standard of living; they are worried about inflation and unemployment; they may be disturbed by the poverty of the less fortunate. People are confronted with difficult personal choices: when to buy a home, whether to change jobs, whether to attend college. People are often confused by the economic claims and counterclaims of opposing political parties. People can find help in dealing with these questions and concerns in the study of **economics.**

Economics is the study of how people choose to use their limited resources (land, labor, and capital goods like trucks and machinery and buildings) to produce, exchange, and consume goods and services.

The above definition touches on several different themes of economic science. Economists agree that each theme is an essential feature of economics.

Scarcity

Scarcity is the most important fact of economics. If there were no scarcity, there would be no need to study economics. Scarcity is defined in a more formal manner in Chapter 2. For now, it is sufficient to say that scarcity occurs when a society's wants exceed the ability of the economy to meet these wants. Scarcity does not imply that people are necessarily poor or that their basic needs are not being met. It simply means that it is human nature for people to want more than they can have, which forces people to make choices.

Choice

The second theme of economics is *choice*. Choice and scarcity go together. Individuals, businesses, and societies must choose among alternatives. An individual must choose between a job and a college education, between savings and consumption, between a movie and eating out. Businesses must decide where to purchase sup-

plies, which products to offer on the market, how much labor to hire, whether to build new plants. Nations must choose between more defense or more spending for social-welfare programs; they must decide whether to grant tax reductions to business or to individuals.

Specialization

The third theme of economics is *specialization*. Economics studies how participants in the economy (people, businesses, countries) specialize in tasks to which they are particularly suited. The physician specializes in medicine, the lawyer in law, the computer scientist in data processing, Saudi Arabia in oil production, Cuba in sugar production, General Motors in automobile production, Lockheed in military hardware, the economics professor in teaching economics, the vacuum cleaner salesperson in selling vacuum cleaners. Participants in the economy specialize in those things that they do better than others. (Chapter 3 will give more exact definitions of specialization.)

The principal message of Adam Smith, the founder of modern economics, in his 1776 masterwork, *The Wealth of Nations,* was that specialization creates wealth. To use Smith's words: "The greatest improvement in the productive powers of labor . . . seems to have been the effects of the division of labor."[1] *Division of labor* was Adam Smith's term for specialization.

Exchange

The fourth theme of economics is *exchange*. Exchange complements specialization. Without exchange, specialization would be of no benefit because individuals could not trade the goods in which they specialize for those that other individuals produce. Again, using Smith's words: "[Specialization] is the necessary . . . consequence of a certain propensity in human nature: the propensity to truck, barter and exchange one thing for another."[2] How exchange is organized is a major element in the study of economics.

1. Adam Smith, *The Wealth of Nations,* ed. Edwin Cannan (New York: Modern Library, 1937), p. 3.
2. Smith, *Wealth of Nations,* p. 13.

Exchange is all around us. We exchange our specialized labor services for money and then exchange money for a huge variety of goods. A country like America exchanges its wheat for TV sets made in Japan. Entrepreneurs constantly trade their skills in marketing, advertising, or product innovation in order to put together the best total product.

MARGINAL ANALYSIS

Economics is about people going about the ordinary business of making a living. If one can remember that individuals are the main actors, much of the mystery surrounding economics evaporates. The student of economics has an enormous advantage over the physics student who cannot ask, "what would I do if I were a molecule?" because the student of economics *is* one of the "molecules" economists study. Crucial to individual behavior are the incentives (that is, the carrots and sticks) that face people in any given situation. In economics, the "carrots" are the benefits that people receive from engaging in an economic activity; the "sticks" are the costs of the activity. Individuals base their economic decisions on costs and benefits.

Scarcity forces people to make choices, and economics studies how these choices are made. The most important tool used by economists to study economic decision making is **marginal analysis.**

Marginal analysis aids decision making by examining the consequences of making relatively small changes from the current state of affairs.

For example, how would you go about deciding how much studying is "enough"? First, you would examine the benefits of a slight increase in your present amount of studying. If you study, say, 2 hours more per day, you will likely earn higher grades, the respect of your fellow students, and perhaps a better job upon graduation. All these benefits of studying 2 additional hours per day cannot be measured exactly, but you have an idea of the benefits that additional study will yield. Next, you would examine the costs of 2 more hours of studying per day. You may have to

sacrifice earnings from a part-time job; you may have to give up leisure activities that you value highly (dating, your favorite soap opera, an extra two hours of sleep).

Finally, the answer to the question of whether you are studying enough depends upon whether you feel that the benefits of the extra study outweigh the costs. If they do, then you conclude that you are not studying enough, and you study more. If the extra costs are greater than the extra benefits, you will conclude that you should not study the extra time.

How do businesses make choices? Consider the case of the selection of airline routes. How would an airline (United, Eastern, American, and so on) determine whether it is offering "enough" flights? It would do so by making decisions *at the margin*. That is, the airline would add flights so long as the expected revenues from those added flights exceed the expected costs. Let us say that United is considering adding a daily flight between Chicago and Seattle. The management of United would make an estimate of the benefits that the added flight would bring in (the additional ticket sales) and would compare these benefits with the extra costs that the new flight would create (added fuel, additional flight attendants, advertising for the new route). If the benefits of the new route are greater than the costs, then the new route would be added to United's schedule. If the costs exceed the benefits, the new route would probably be rejected.

Decisions are made at the margin when a decision maker considers what the extra (or marginal) costs and benefits of an increase or decrease in a particular activity will be. If the marginal benefits outweigh the marginal costs, the extra activity is undertaken.

MICRO AND MACRO

Microeconomics

Economics is typically divided into two main branches called *microeconomics* and *macroeconomics*. Both **microeconomics** and macroeconomics deal with economic decision making but from different vantage points.

Microeconomics studies the economic decision making of firms and individuals in a market setting; it is the study of the economy in the small.

Microeconomics focuses on the individual participants in the economy: the producers, workers, employers, and consumers. In everyday economic life, things are bought and sold, people decide where and how many hours to work. Business managers decide what to produce and how this production is to be organized. These activities result in *transactions* (business deals) that take place in markets where buyers and sellers come together. People involved in microeconomic transactions are motivated to do the best they can for themselves with the limited resources at their disposal. They use marginal analysis to determine their best course of action.

Although we could supply an endless list, here are just a few of the issues that can be addressed by microeconomic analysis: 1) how consumers behave, 2) how business firms make choices, 3) how prices are determined in markets, 4) how taxes and price controls affect consumer and producer behavior, 5) how the structure of markets affects economic performance, 6) how wages, interest rates, rent, and profits are determined, and 7) how income is distributed among families.

Macroeconomics

Instead of analyzing prices, outputs, and sales in individual markets, **macroeconomics** studies the production of the entire economy. Topics of investigation include the *general* price level (rather than individual prices), the national employment rate, government spending, and the nation's money supply.

Macroeconomics is the study of the economy in the large. Rather than dealing with individual markets and individual consumers and producers, macroeconomics deals with the economy as a whole.

Because macroeconomics studies the economy as a whole, new measures of economic activity are required. Important to macroeconomics is the definition and measurement of macroeconomic *aggregates,* such as gross national product

(GNP), the consumer price index (CPI), the unemployment rate, and the government surplus and deficit. These measures are called *aggregates* because they add together (or aggregate) individual microeconomic components.

Just as microeconomics studies the relationships between individual participants in the economy, macroeconomics studies relationships between aggregate measures. What are the determinants of inflation? What is the relationship between inflation and interest rates? Is it necessary to trade off higher employment for lower inflation? What are the consequences of government deficits? What is the relationship between the money supply and inflation?

In modern economics, there is a close relationship between microeconomics and macroeconomics. Macroeconomists have come to apply more and more microeconomic analysis to traditional macroeconomic questions such as the relationship between inflation and unemployment. The rationale behind using microeconomic tools to study macroeconomics is that the economy is made up of individuals; how these individuals behave *on the average* can explain how the economy in the large behaves.

The modern convergence of microeconomics and macroeconomics follows from the realization that macroeconomic relationships cannot be analyzed without understanding the behavior of the individuals who make up the economy.

Three areas of investigation that exemplify the modern convergence of microeconomics and macroeconomics are:

1. How do workers alter the number of hours they work in response to generally rising prices?
2. How do business output decisions respond to inflation?
3. Can unemployment be reduced by changing government policies that affect the costs of unemployment?

To answer these questions the tools of microeconomic decision making (such as marginal analysis) can be applied to what are basically macroeconomic problems.

METHODOLOGY IN ECONOMICS

Economists rely heavily on economic theories to explain how the economy works. Why don't economists just go out and collect the facts and let the facts speak for themselves? The American economy includes millions of households and firms and thousands of separate federal, state, and local governments. All of these make decisions about producing millions of goods and services using millions of resources. Gathering information about economic choices from all these various sources is an incredibly complex and unmanageable task. Logical theories explain how the economy works by showing how the facts fit together in a coherent manner.

Theories and Hypotheses

A **theory** is simply a plausible and coherent explanation of how certain facts are related. A theory typically consists of one or more *hypotheses* about how a particular set of facts is related. Normally, but not always, theories contain some hypotheses of the form, "if A, then B." Two examples of hypotheses are: "if a good's price falls, people will want to buy more of it"; "if income rises, people will consume or save more."

*A **theory** isolates those factors that may be crucial determinants of the phenomenon being explained.*

For example, economists' theories of demand hold that such things as consumer eye color, height, and IQ are relatively unimportant in explaining consumer purchases compared to such things as price and income. The process of zeroing in on a limited number of factors to explain a phenomenon is called *abstraction*.

Testing Theories: The Scientific Method

Since theories are abstractions from the real world (whatever that is!) it is necessary to test them. For example: Suppose one theorized that higher prices for coffee induce people to buy less

Table 1
Coffee Prices and Consumption

Year	Price per Pound (constant 1979 dollars)	Yearly per Capita Coffee Consumption (in pounds)
1974	$1.78	13.0
1975	1.75	12.4
1976	2.56	12.8
1977	4.22	9.4
1978	3.22	10.9
1979	2.78	11.5

Source: *Statistical Abstract of the United States* (1980), Tables 211, 802, 808.

coffee. This theory seems to make sense. But is it true? By the patient collection of data one might find the results shown in Table 1.

Clearly, as the price of coffee in *constant dollars* (dollars that have been adjusted for inflation) more than doubled between 1974 and 1977, per capita coffee consumption fell dramatically—from 13 pounds per year to less than 10 pounds per year. When the price started to fall after 1977, per capita coffee consumption rose again. Thus, the data on coffee prices and coffee consumption are consistent with our theory that higher prices for an item cause people to consume less of the item. The data *fail to refute* the theory but have not really *proved* the theory beyond any doubt. Data from another time or place may contradict the theory. When data are obtained that are *not* consistent with the theory, the theory must be reformulated or revised.

For example, Table 2 shows that egg prices fell substantially between 1974 and 1979, yet egg consumption per capita remained about the same. These data appear to contradict the theory that higher prices for an item induce people to consume less of the item. In this situation we could either say that the theory does not hold for eggs, or we could revise the theory so that it would explain why eggs were an exception to the rule. The case of eggs suggests that things other than price influence consumption. The 1970s was a period in which the egg had lost some of its popularity because of allegations that egg consumption lowers human longevity. These allegations, of course, have been debated.[3] The point is that the unfavorable publicity might have had a substantial impact on consumption. The theory can be reformulated to reflect the fact that factors other than price influence consumption. Chapter 4 will do this more precisely, but for the moment the theory could be reformulated as follows: the higher the price of an item, the less of it people will want to buy, holding other factors (like unfavorable publicity, in this case) constant. The above examples illustrate how the scientific method can be applied to a simple economic theory:

1. a theory was formulated,
2. facts were gathered (Tables 1 and 2),
3. the theory was evaluated in light of the facts and
4. when the facts failed to confirm the theory, the theory was revised.

The process of formulating theories, collecting data, testing theories, and revising theories is called **the scientific method.**

The **scientific method** is one of the truly great creations of the human mind. Hard as it is to believe, at one time people did not evaluate their beliefs in light of the facts or even formulate their beliefs in a way that could be tested by others. What makes the scientific method such a valuable tool is that it raises human thought above the level of the individual, separating the idea from the person as much as possible. Claude Bernard, a 19th century writer, once perceptively summarized the orientation of all scientific subjects in comparison to artistic ones: "Art is I; science is we."

The Uses of Economic Theories

Economic theories that use the scientific method allow us to make sense of an extremely complicated world. They enable us to understand economic relationships, to make sense of past events, and even to predict the consequences of

3. A good pro-egg discussion is found in James W. Vaupel and John D. Braham, "Egg in Your Bier?" *The Public Interest* (Winter 1980).

Table 2
Egg Prices and Consumption

Year	Price per Dozen (1979 dollars)	Yearly per Capita Consumption (number of eggs)
1974	$0.93	288
1975	0.84	279
1976	0.89	274
1977	0.75	272
1978	0.69	278
1979	0.69	283

Source: *Statistical Abstract of the United States* (1980), Tables 211, 802, 808.

actions that have yet to be taken. Economists have at their disposal well-tested theories of the relationship between product prices and the quantities purchased. For example, economists have established (largely on the basis of the experiences of other countries) that people cut back their gasoline consumption when gasoline prices rise substantially. Many government officials, consumer advocates, and politicians felt that this cutback would not happen in the United States, because Americans are so dependent on automobile transportation. The United States entered into uncharted territory when it left the age of cheap energy behind in the early 1970s, and it was comforting to have a scientifically tested theory as a guide, despite its skeptics. True enough, after the higher prices went into effect in the mid-1970s, people did indeed cut back on their gasoline purchases just as economic theory predicted. This cutback became so strong that oil-producing countries had trouble finding buyers at the higher prices in 1982.

Theory can say something about facts that have yet to be collected and about events that have yet to occur; that is, theory can be used to make **predictions.**

This discussion should lay to rest the erroneous notion that a theory can be a good one even if it does not work in practice. By the criterion of the scientific method, if a theory does not work in practice it cannot be a good theory.

COMMON FALLACIES IN ECONOMICS

False economic propositions can have substantial appeal because they may appear on the surface to be eminently reasonable. Consider the following statements drawn from various newspaper reports:

U.S. Steel today announced a 10 percent increase in the price of rolled steel products. This price increase was made necessary by the 10 percent wage increase granted the steel workers' union.

The drought of the summer of 1980 has caused a disastrous harvest of wheat and corn in the midwest and southwest. The hard-pressed farmer is being pushed closer to economic ruin.

Despite a substantial rise in home mortgage rates between 1977 and 1979, there are no signs of a slowdown in home building. This shows that rising mortgage rates have little impact on home buying.

All of these statements appear to be logical and to be based upon facts, and they will probably be accepted by the average reader without much hesitation. Yet close examination of these statements reveals that they exemplify three logical *fallacies* that plague economic thinking. These fallacies are the *false-cause fallacy,* the *fallacy of composition,* and the *ceteris paribus fallacy.*

The False-Cause Fallacy

*The **false-cause fallacy** is that because two events occur together one event has caused the other.*

The fact that Event A occurs with or precedes Event B does not mean that A has caused B. The absurdity of this proposition is illustrated by the following example: between 1970 and 1980, U.S. whiskey consumption rose by 25 percent, and the number of public-school teachers rose by 30 percent.[4] To conclude from this evidence that the increase in the number of teachers caused the increase in whiskey consumption is false.

A statistical correlation between two variables does not prove that one has caused the other or that the variables have anything whatsoever to do with one another.

How does one determine whether or not two variables that are statistically correlated are involved in a cause-and-effect relationship? Economic theory attempts to determine in a coherent manner whether a logical case of cause and effect exists. Consider this counter example: whiskey consumption increased by 25 percent between 1970 and 1980, while family take-home pay increased by 33 percent (after adjustment for inflation). In this case, a logical theory could be constructed that increases in family income will be channeled into purchases of whiskey. Thus one could argue that the rise in income is a possible cause of the rise in whiskey consumption. Economic theory supports a cause/effect relationship.

One of the most difficult problems of science is the determination of cause-and-effect relationships.

An example from medical science is the endless debate over smoking and heart disease. Does smoking "cause" heart disease? Government and the tobacco industry have spent millions of dollars trying to prove or disprove a cause-and-effect relationship. Many of the unresolved controversies of economics center on cause-and-effect relationships.

The report of the steel-price increase cited above is an example of a possible **false-cause fallacy.** Just because the wage increase preceded the price increase does not prove that the one caused the other. Whether or not the wage settlement was indeed a cause of the price increase is a matter for economic theory to settle. As later chapters will point out, the theoretical relationship between wage and price increases is not clear-cut.

The Fallacy of Composition

*The **fallacy of composition** is that what is true for each part taken separately is also*

4. *Statistical Abstract of the United States,* 101st ed. (Washington, D.C.: U.S. Government Printing Office, 1980), pp. 211, 802, 808.

true for the whole or that what is true for the whole is true for each part considered separately.

To illustrate the **fallacy of composition,** consider what would happen if the government were to print money and give each person $10,000. Clearly, this action would make each individual person better off. With the $10,000 windfall, the person could buy a new car, invest in the stock market, or finance a college education. But if the government were to give everyone a windfall of $10,000, consumer spending would increase, prices would generally rise, and it is likely society as a whole would not end up any better off. This example shows that what is true for each part taken separately—namely, that receiving money makes people better off—would not necessarily be true for the whole.

The report of the 1980 summer drought cited earlier is an example of the fallacy of composition. It is true that farmers in drought-stricken areas were made worse off by the drought, but farm income actually increased for those farmers in nonstricken areas who benefited from higher farm prices. What was true for each part taken separately was not true for the whole.

The *Ceteris Paribus* Fallacy

*The **ceteris paribus fallacy** occurs when the effects of changes in one set of variables are incorrectly attributed to another set of variables.*

For example, U.S. crude-oil consumption between 1970 and 1974 rose from 14.7 million barrels per day to 16.2 million barrels. The U.S. price of crude oil, during the same period, rose from $3.18 to $6.74.[5] Does the fact that prices and consumption were both rising mean that there is a positive relationship between energy prices and energy usage?

Ceteris paribus is a Latin term meaning "other things being equal." If the relationship between

two variables is to be established, the effects of other factors that are changing as well must not be allowed to confuse the relationship. To establish the relationship between energy prices and energy usage, the effects of "other things" must somehow be understood. What other things were happening between 1970 and 1974 that would affect oil consumption in addition to rising oil prices? The prices of other commodities were rising, although not as fast as crude oil. Money incomes of American families rose 44 percent, and rising income would allow American consumers to absorb higher energy prices. The point is that the true relationship between crude oil prices and oil consumption is difficult to discern because other things that affect oil consumption did not stand still. To simply look at the graphical relationship between two variables without sorting out the effects of other factors that are also changing leads to *ceteris paribus* fallacies. Sorting out these other effects is not a simple matter. In fact, an entire branch of economics that combines economic theory and statistics, called *econometrics,* has been developed to deal with the *ceteris paribus* problem.

The mortgage rate case cited above is an example of the *ceteris paribus* fallacy. During the period in question, other things were not equal. Home prices were rising rapidly, and home buyers were opting to buy homes before the price rose out of their reach, despite high mortgage rates. The true relationship between mortgage rates and home buying was clouded by changes in other factors that affected home buying.

WHY ECONOMISTS DISAGREE

Economists have received the unfair reputation of being unable to agree on anything. The image of economists in disagreement is part of our folklore. An English commentator wrote: "If parliament were to ask six economists for an opinion, seven answers could come back—two no doubt from the volatile Mr. Keynes." The *London Times* laments the "rise in skepticism about what economists can tell us," and *Business Week* complains about "the intellectual bankruptcy of the [economics] profession."[6]

5. James Griffin and Henry Steele, *Energy Economics and Policy* (New York Academic Press, 1980), p. 18; National Foreign Assessment Center, *Handbook of Economic Statistics 1980* (Washington, D.C.: U.S. Government Printing Office, 1980).

6. J. R. Kearl et al., "A Confusion of Economists," *American Economic Review* 69, 2 (May 1979): 28.

The image of widespread disagreement among economists is overrated. The results of a survey of 100 professional economists, reported in Table 3, confirm that there is considerable agreement among economists about *what can be done,* especially in a microeconomic context. However, there is more disagreement over *what ought to be done.* Questions of what ought to be done (Should we equalize the distribution of income? Should we increase defense spending?) require moral and political value judgments on which individuals naturally differ. Finally, disagreement among professional economists receives more publicity than other scientific professions, which contributes to the false image of economists in disaccord. In Table 3, more than 60 percent of the economists agree with each other on 23 of the 30 propositions. On only 7 of the 30 issues (5 macro issues and 2 micro issues) is there less than 60 percent agreement among the economists.

Positive Economics

Economists generally agree that rising prices reduce consumption *(ceteris paribus),* that rising income will have differential but predictable effects on different products, that wage and price controls cause shortages, that tariffs and quotas raise prices to consumers, that rent controls reduce the quantity and quality of housing, that minimum-wage laws increase unemployment among youth and unskilled workers, and so on. The easiest matters on which to achieve agreement involve the microeconomic relationships that actually prevail in an economy.

Positive economics is the study of what is *in the economy.*

The areas of disagreement in **positive economics** tend to be concentrated in the field of macroeconomics, which is, after all, a relatively young field. The points of controversy and disagreement in macroeconomics include such questions as: What are the causes of inflation and unemployment? Can we combine low unemployment and low inflation? Should activist government policy be used to achieve employment and inflation goals?

Why has economics still to resolve these vital issues? The basic answer is that the economy is an unbelievably complex organism, comprised of millions of individuals, hundreds of thousands of business firms, a myriad of local, state, and federal government offices. The economy is us, and our collective economic actions are difficult to analyze. Emotions are volatile; expectations can change overnight; relationships that held last year no longer hold today; it is costly and difficult to collect up-to-date economic facts. Unlike the physical sciences, economists are denied a laboratory setting; economists do not have the physicist's vacuum, the agronomist's experimental farm, the chemist's laboratory. In addition, many economic events are random and unpredictable. Bad weather can cause poor harvests; armed conflicts can occur without warning in different parts of the globe; oil-producing countries can form an oil price-fixing alliance; consumer spending can shift in response to changing expectations.

Normative Economics

Economists do disagree—often strongly—about **normative economics.**

Normative economics is the study of what ought to be *in the economy.*

Economists disagree on whether we should have more unemployment or more inflation (a traditional Democratic/Republican difference over the years), over whether income taxes should be lowered for the middle class, the rich, or the poor, over job programs, over government-subsidized health programs. These disagreements are not over what is; opponents in a debate may agree on what will happen if Program A is chosen over Program B, but they may disagree sharply over their personal evaluation of the desirability of those consequences.

The Visibility of Economic Disputes

While disagreements in other sciences are as strong or even stronger than in economics, these disagreements are less visible to the public eye. Theoretical physicists have disagreed about the physical nature of the universe since the foundation of physics, but this scientific controversy is understood by only a few theoretical physicists.

Table 3
Do Economists Disagree?

Propositions	Generally Agree	Agree with Provisions	Generally Disagree
1. Tariffs and import quotas reduce general economic welfare.	81	16	3
2. The government should be an employer of last resort and initiate a guaranteed job program.	26	27	47
3. The money supply is a more important target than interest rates for monetary policy.	48	23	29
4. Cash payments are superior to transfers-in-kind.	68	24	8
5. Flexible exchange rates offer an effective international monetary arrangement.	61	34	5
6. The "Corporate State," as depicted by Galbraith, accurately describes the context and structure of the U.S. economy.	18	34	48
7. A minimum wage increases unemployment among young and unskilled workers.	68	22	10
8. The government should index the income-tax rate structure for inflation.	41	27	32
9. Fiscal policy has a significant stimulative impact on a less than fully employed economy.	65	27	8
10. The distribution of income in the United States should be more equal.	40	31	29
11. National defense expenditures should be reduced from the present level.	36	30	34
12. Antitrust laws should be used vigorously to reduce monopoly power from its current level.	49	36	15
13. Inflation is primarily a monetary phenomenon.	27	30	43
14. The government should restructure the welfare system along lines of a "negative income tax."	58	34	8
15. Wage-price controls should be used to control inflation.	6	22	72
16. A ceiling on rents reduces the quantity and quality of housing available.	78	20	2
17. The Fed should be instructed to increase the money supply at a fixed rate.	14	25	61
18. Effluent taxes represent a better approach to pollution control than imposition of pollution ceilings.	50	31	19
19. The government should issue an inflation-indexed security.	33	25	42
20. The level of government spending should be reduced (disregarding expenditures for stabilization).	34	23	43
21. The Fed has the capacity to achieve a constant rate of growth of the money supply if it so desired.	35	41	34
22. Reducing the regulatory power of the ICC, CAB et al. would improve the efficiency of the U.S. ecoomy.	47	31	22
23. The federal budget should be balanced over the business cycle rather than yearly.	53	30	17
24. The fundamental cause of the rise in oil prices of the past three years is the monopoly power of the large oil companies.	11	14	75
25. The redistribution of income is a legitimate role for government in the context of the U.S. economy.	52	29	19
26. In the short run, unemployment can be reduced by increasing the rate of inflation.	31	33	36
27. The fiscal policy proposed by the Ford Administration for the coming year is too restrictive.	40	19	41
28. The ceiling on interest paid on time deposits should be removed.	76	18	6
29. "Consumer protection" laws generally reduce economic efficiency.	24	28	48
30. The economic power of labor unions should be significantly curtailed.	32	38	30

Source: J. R. Kearl et al., "A Confusion of Economists?" *American Economic Review* 69, 2 (May 1979): 30.

It does not require much disagreement to bring economic disputes to the public's attention. Everyone is interested in economic questions: Will inflation accelerate? Will I lose my job? Why is the price of gasoline rising so fast? Why are home mortgages so hard to come by? Economists do disagree, particularly on some big macroeconomic issues. But often what the public perceives as disagreements over positive economics are really disagreements over what ought to be. In general, there is more agreement than disagreement among economists.

Economics studies how people use their limited resources to produce, exchange, and consume goods and services. The next chapter will begin to use the tools of the scientific method to explain how economic choices are made in a world of scarce resources. What are the costs of making choices? What arrangements are used to resolve the problem of choice? Answering these questions requires graphical analysis. The appendix to this chapter provides a review of guidelines for reading graphs.

Summary

1. Economics is important to each person as an individual, as a voter, and as a member of society. Increased knowledge improves the quality of decision making of individuals, voters, and members of society. The four themes of economics are scarcity, choice, specialization, and exchange.
2. Marginal analysis is an important tool of the economist. It aids economic decision making by examining the extra costs and benefits of economic decisions.
3. Microeconomics studies the economic decision making of firms and individuals in a market setting; it is the study of the economy in the small. Macroeconomics studies the economy as a whole and deals with issues of inflation, unemployment, money supply, the government budget; it is the study of the economy in the large. Modern macroeconomics employs tools of microeconomics.
4. Theory allows us to make sense of the real world and to learn how the facts fit together.

There is no conflict between good theory and good practice. Economic theories are based upon the scientific method of theory formulation, collection of relevant data, and testing of theories. Economic theory makes it possible to predict the consequences of actions that have yet to be taken and about facts that are yet to be collected.

5. Three logical fallacies plague economic analysis: the false-cause fallacy (assuming that Event A has caused Event B because A is associated with B); the fallacy of composition (assuming that what is true for each part taken separately is true for the whole or, conversely, assuming that what is true for the whole is also true for each part); the *ceteris paribus* fallacy (incorrectly attributing to one variable effects that are caused by another).
6. Economists tend to agree on positive economic issues (what is) while disagreeing on normative issues (what ought to be). The major unresolved issues of positive economics tend to be concentrated in macroeconomics, an evolving field in economics. Disagreements among economists are more visible to the public eye than disagreements in other scientific professions.

Key Terms

economics
marginal analysis
microeconomics
macroeconomics
theory
scientific method
false-cause fallacy
fallacy of composition
ceteris paribus **fallacy**
positive economics
normative economics

Questions and Problems

1. Consider the following scenario: You are the manager of a movie theater considering intro-

ducing an 11 A.M. matinee. You calculate that the matinee will increase monthly ticket sales by $10,000 and that the additional cost of adding the matinee would be $11,000. What would you decide?

2. An example of how to decide whether a student is studying "enough" was given in the text. Do you feel that this is an accurate description of how students make decisions?

3. Outline how you would apply the scientific method to determine what factors cause the grade point averages of students in your class to differ.

4. "I can't stand the programs I see on television. Why can't American television produce shows that the public can enjoy?" What type of logical fallacy does this statement illustrate?

5. From your own experience, construct an example of the false-cause fallacy.

6. "For several years after the surgeon general's report that cigarette smoking was injurious to health, the sale of cigarettes increased in the United States. Therefore, the surgeon general's report had no effect on smoking habits." Evaluate this conclusion.

7. Why would economists be more likely to disagree on a national health-insurance program than on the effect of higher oil prices on the consumption of oil?

8. Why is the distinction between positive and normative economics important?

APPENDIX

1A

Reading Graphs

Appendix Preview

Graphs are an important tool in learning economics. This appendix teaches the rudiments of working with graphs. It teaches graph construction, positive and negative relationships, dependent and independent variables, and the concept of slope for both linear and curvilinear relationships. It shows how slopes can be used to find the maximum and minimum values of a relationship. Finally, three common pitfalls of using graphs are discussed: the ambiguity of slope, the improper measurement of data, and the use of unrepresentative data.

THE USE OF GRAPHS IN ECONOMICS

Economics makes extensive use of graphs. A graph is simply a visual scheme for picturing the quantitative relationship between two different variables. This book contains graphs dealing with many different economic relationships, including the relationships between:

1. consumption and income.
2. the rate of inflation and time.
3. average costs of production and the volume of production.

4. profits and business decisions.
5. oil consumption and oil prices.
6. unemployment and inflation.

Relationships such as these can be pictured and analyzed by using graphs. Not only can a graph display a great deal of data; a graph can efficiently describe the quantitative relationship that exists between the variables. As the Chinese proverb says, ''a picture is worth a thousand words.'' It is easier both to understand and remember a graph than the several hundred, or perhaps thousands of numbers that the graph represents. Graphs are important tools in learning economics. The reader must understand how to use graphs in order to master the basic economic concepts in this book.

Positive and Negative Relationships

The first important characteristic of a graph is whether the two variables are positively or negatively related.

*A **positive (or direct) relationship** exists between two variables if an increase in the value of one variable is associated with an increase in the value of the other variable.*

For example, an increase in the *horsepower* of a given car's engine will increase the *maximum speed* of the automobile. Panel (a) of Figure 1 depicts this relationship in a graph. The *vertical axis* measures the maximum speed of the car from the 0 point (called the *origin*); the *horizontal axis* measures the horsepower of the engine. When horsepower is zero (the engine is broken down), the maximum speed the car can attain is obviously 0; when horsepower is 300, the maximum speed is 100 miles per hour. Intermediate values of horsepower (between 0 and 300) are graphed. When a line is drawn through all these points, the resulting curved line describes the effect of horsepower on maximum speed. Since the picture is a line that goes from low to high speeds as horsepower increases, it is an example of an *upward-sloping curve.*

When two variables are positively related the graph of the relationship is an upward-sloping curve.

Figure 1
Graphing Positive and Negative Relationships

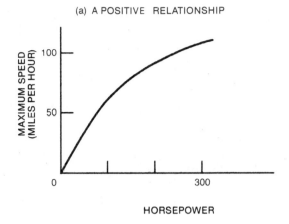

(a) A POSITIVE RELATIONSHIP

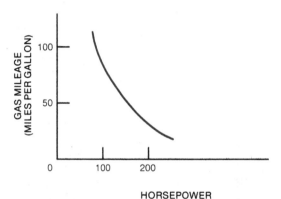

(b) A NEGATIVE RELATIONSHIP

Panel (a) shows a positive relationship. As the horizontal variable (horsepower) increases, the value of the vertical variable (maximum speed) increases. The curve rises from left to right. Panel (b) shows a negative relationship. As the horizontal variable (horsepower) increases, the vertical variable (mileage) decreases. The curve falls from left to right.

---

*A **negative (or inverse) relationship** exists between two variables if an increase in the value of one variable is associated with a reduction in the value of the other variable.*

For example, as the *horsepower* of the automobile increases, the *gas mileage* (for given driving conditions) will fall. In panel (b) of Figure 1, horsepower is still measured on the horizontal axis, but now gas mileage is measured on the vertical axis. Since the picture is a curve going from high to low values of gas mileage as horsepower increases, it is an example of a *downward-sloping curve*.

> *When two variables are negatively related the graph of the relationship is a downward-sloping curve.*

Dependent and Independent Variables

In some relationships involving two variables, one variable can be the **independent variable;** the other is the **dependent variable.**

> *A change in the value of an **independent variable** will cause the **dependent variable** to change in value.*

An increase in engine horsepower *causes* an increase in the maximum speed of the automobile in the first graph. A horsepower increase *causes* a reduction in gas mileage in the second graph. In both examples, horsepower is the independent variable. The other two variables are said to "depend upon" horsepower because the changes in horsepower bring about changes in speed and gas mileage. Maximum speed and gas mileage are dependent variables.

One goal of economic analysis is to find the independent variable(s) that explain certain dependent variables. What independent variables explain changes in inflation rates, unemployment, consumer spending, housing construction, and so on? In many cases, it is not possible to determine which variable is dependent and which is independent. Some variables are interdependent (they both affect each other). In some instances, there is no cause-and-effect relationship between the variables.

RULES FOR CONSTRUCTING GRAPHS

A glance is sufficient to tell whether a curve is positively or negatively sloped. More work is required to read all the information that a graph contains. To read a graph properly, one must know how a graph is constructed.

The data for our sample graph is given in Table 1. The numbers in this table describe the quantitative relationship between *minutes of typing* and *number of pages typed*. Let us assume that the quantitative relationship between minutes and pages is known: every 5 minutes of typing will produce 1 page of manuscript. Thus 5 minutes produces 1 page, 15 minutes produces 3 pages, and so on. Zero minutes will, of course, produce 0 pages.

Four steps are required to graph these data or any data. These steps have been carried out in Figure 2.

1. A vertical *axis* and a horizontal *axis* are drawn perpendicularly on graph paper, meeting at a point called the *origin*. The origin is labeled 0; the vertical axis is labeled $Y;$ the horizontal axis is labeled X.
2. *Minutes of typing* are marked off along the horizontal X axis in equally spaced increments of 5 minutes, and the horizontal axis is labeled "Minutes of Typing."
3. The *number of pages typed* is marked off in equally spaced increments of 1 page along the vertical Y axis, and the vertical axis is labeled "Number of Pages Typed."
4. Each pair of numbers in Table 1 is plotted at the intersection of the vertical line that corresponds to that value of X and the horizontal line that corresponds to that value of Y. Point *a* shows that 5 minutes of typing produces 1 page. Point *c* shows that 15 minutes of typing produces 3 pages, and so on.

Points *a, b, c, d,* and *e* completely describe the

Table 1
The Relationship Between Minutes of Typing and Number of Pages Typed

	Minutes of Typing (X axis)	Number of Pages Typed (Y axis)
	0	0
a	5	1
b	10	2
c	15	3
d	20	4
e	25	5

Figure 2
Constructing a Graph

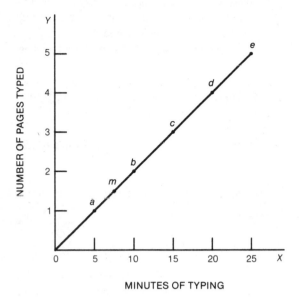

MINUTES OF TYPING

This graph reproduces the data in Table 1. Point *a* shows that 5 minutes of typing produces 1 page of typing; *b* shows that 10 minutes produces 2 pages, and so on. The upward-sloping line drawn through *a, b, c, d,* and *e* shows that the relationship between minutes of typing and number of pages typed is positive. The points between *a, b, c, d,* and *e* (such as *m*) show the number of pages typed for amounts of typing time between the 5-minute intervals.

The first advantage of graphs over tables is that it is easier to understand the relationship that exists between two variables in a graph than in a table.

Suppose that in addition to the data in Table 1, we had data for the number of pages that could be typed at all kinds of intermediate values of typing time: 6 minutes, 13 minutes, 24 minutes and 25 seconds, etc. A large table would be required to report all these numbers. In a graph, however, all these intermediate values can be represented simply by connecting points *a, b, c, d,* and *e* with a line. Thus, a second advantage of graphs is that large quantities of data can be represented in a graph more efficiently than in a table.

The second advantage of graphs over tables is that large quantities of data can be represented efficiently in a graph.

The data in Tables 1 and 2 reveal the relationship between minutes of typing and number of pages typed. This relationship was graphed in Figure 2. The relationship can change, however, if other factors that affect typing speed change. Assume that Table 1 shows minutes and pages typed on a manual typewriter. If the typist works with an IBM Selectric, a different relationship will emerge. With the IBM Selectric, perhaps the typist can type 2 pages every 5 minutes instead of one. Both relationships are graphed in Figure 3. Thus, if factors that affect speed of typing change (for example, the quality of the typewriter), the relationship between minutes and pages can shift.

data in Table 1. Indeed, a graph of the data acts as a substitute for the table from which it was constructed. This is the first advantage of graphs over tables: they provide an immediate visual understanding of the quantitative relationship between the two variables just by observing the plot of points. Since the points in this case move upward from left to right, we know that there is a *positive relationship* between the variables.

This may not seem to be a great advantage for this simple and obvious case. However, suppose the data had been arranged as in Table 2.

If one spends some time inspecting the data, it becomes clear that there is a positive relationship between X and Y; however, it is not immediately obvious. From a graph, it is easier to see the relationship between the two variables.

Table 2
The Relationship Between Minutes of Typing and Number of Pages Typed (data rearranged)

	Minutes of Typing (X axis)	Number of Pages Typed (Y axis)
b	10	2
a	5	1
	0	0
e	25	5
c	15	3
d	20	4

Figure 3
Shifts in Relationships

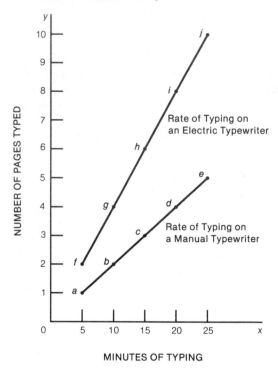

MINUTES OF TYPING

The curve *abcde* graphs the data in Table 1 that show the relationship between minutes and pages using a manual typewriter. The new (higher) curve *fghij* shows the relationship between minutes and pages with an electric typewriter. As a consequence of the change from the manual to the electric typewriter, the relationship has shifted upward.

Economists work frequently with relationships that shift, so it is important to understand shifts in graphs.

UNDERSTANDING SLOPE

The relationship between two variables is represented by a curve's **slope.** One cannot understand many central concepts of economics without understanding slope.

The slope reflects the response of one variable to changes in another. Consider the typing example. Every 5 minutes of typing on a manual typewriter produces 1 page or, equivalently, every minute of typing produces ⅕ of a page. As we shall demonstrate below, the slope of the line *abcde* is ⅕ of a page of typing per minute.

To understand slope more precisely consider in panel (a) of Figure 4 the straight-line relationship between the two variables X and Y. When $X = 5$, $Y = 3$; when $X = 7$, $Y = 6$. Suppose now that variable X is allowed to *run* (to change horizontally) from 5 units to 7 units. When this happens variable Y *rises* (increases vertically) from 3 units to 6 units.

The slope of a straight line is the ratio of the rise (or fall) in **Y** *over the run in* **X**.

The slope of the line in panel (a) of Figure 4 is:

$$\text{Slope} = \frac{\text{Rise in } Y}{\text{Run in } X} = \frac{3}{2} = 1.5$$

A *positive value of the slope signifies a positive relationship* between the two variables.

This formula works for negative relationships as well. In panel (b) of Figure 4 when X runs from 5 to 7, Y *falls* from 4 units to 1 unit. Thus the slope is:

$$\text{Slope} = \frac{\text{Fall in } Y}{\text{Run in } X} = \frac{-3}{2} = -1.5$$

A *negative* value of the slope signifies a *negative relationship* between the two variables.

Let ΔY (delta Y) stand for the change in the value of Y and ΔX (delta X) stand for the change in the value of X:

$$\text{Slope} = \frac{\Delta Y}{\Delta X}$$

This formula holds for positive or negative relationships.

Let us return to the typing example. What slope expresses the relationship between minutes of typing and number of pages? When minutes increase by 5 units ($\Delta X = 5$), pages increase by one unit ($\Delta Y = 1$). The slope is therefore $\Delta Y/\Delta X = ⅕$.

In Figures 2, 3, and 4, the points are connected by straight lines. Such relationships are called *linear relationships*. The inquisitive reader

Figure 4
Positive and Negative Slope

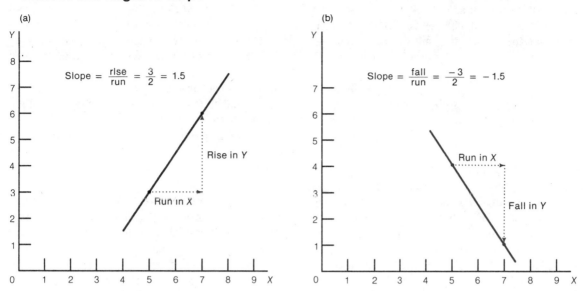

Positive slope is measured by the ratio of the rise in Y over the run in X. In panel (a), Y rises by 3 and X runs by 2, and the slope is 1.5. Negative slope is measured by the ratio of the fall in Y over the run in X. In panel (b), the fall in Y is −3, the run in X is 2, and the slope is −1.5.

will wonder how slope is measured when the relationship between *X* and *Y* is *curvilinear*.

A curvilinear example is given in Figure 5. When *X* runs from 2 units to 4 units ($\Delta X = 2$), *Y* rises by 2 units ($\Delta Y = 2$); between *a* and *b* the slope is $\frac{2}{2} = 1$. Between *a* and *c*, however, *X* runs from 2 to 6 ($\Delta X = 4$), *Y* rises by 3 units ($\Delta Y = 3$), and the slope is $\frac{3}{4}$. In the curvilinear case, the value of the slope depends on how far *X* is allowed to run. Between *b* and *c*, the slope is $\frac{1}{2}$. Thus, the slope changes as one moves along a curvilinear relationship. In the linear case, the value of the slope will *not* depend on how far *X* runs because the slope is constant and does not change as one moves from point to point.

There is no single slope of a curvilinear relationship and no single method of measuring slopes. The slope can be measured between two points (say, between *a* and *b* or between *b* and *c*) or at a particular point (say, at point *a*). Insofar as the measurement of the slope at a point depends upon the length of the run, a uniform standard must be adopted to avoid confusion. This standard is the use of *tangents* to determine the slope at a point on a curvilinear relationship.

Figure 5
Calculating Slopes of Curvilinear Relationships

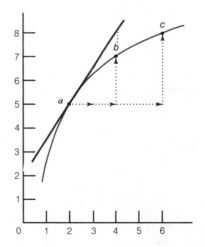

The ratio of the rise over the run yields a slope of 1 from *a* to *b* but a slope of ¾ from *a* to *c*. From *b* to *c*, the slope is ½. To compute the slope at point *a*, the slope of the tangent to *a* is calculated. The value of the slope of the tangent is ³⁄₂.

To calculate the slope at *a,* let the run of *X* be "infinitesimally small," rather than a discrete number of units such as ½, 2, 4, or whatever. An infinitesimally small change is difficult to conceive, but the graphical result of such a change can be captured simply by drawing a **tangent** to point *a.*

*A **tangent** is a straight line that touches the curve at only one point.*

If the curve is really curved at *a,* there is only one straight line that just barely touches *a* and only *a.* Any other line (a magnifying glass may be required to verify this) will cut the curve at two points or none. The tangent to *a* is drawn in Figure 5.

The slope of a curvilinear relationship at a particular point is measured using the tangent to that point:

The slope of a curvilinear relationship at a particular point is the slope of the straight line tangent at that point.

The slope of the tangent at *a* is measured by dividing the rise by the run. Because the tangent is a straight line, the length of the run does not matter. For a run from 2 to 4 ($\Delta X = 2$), the rise (ΔY) equals 3 (from 5 to 8). Thus the slope of the tangent is ³⁄₂ or 1.5.

Figure 6 shows two curvilinear relationships that have distinct high points or low points. In panel (a) the relationship between *X* and *Y* is positive for values of *X* less than 6 units and negative for values of *X* more than 6 units. The exact opposite holds for panel (b). The relationship is negative for values of *X* less than 6 and positive for *X* greater than 6. Notice that at the point where the slope changes from positive to negative (or vice versa), the slope of the curve will be exactly 0; the tangent at point $X = 6$ for both curves is a

Figure 6
Maximum and Minimum Points

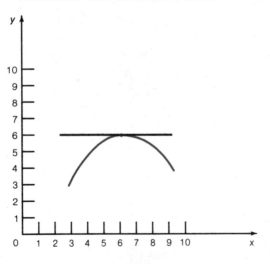

(a) *Y* Is Maximized When Slope Is Zero

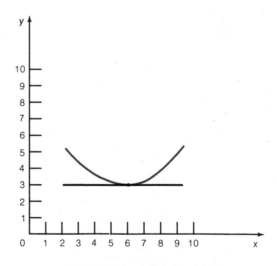

(b) *Y* Is Minimized When Slope Is Zero

Some curvilinear relationships change directions. Notice that in panel (a), when the curve changes direction at *X* = 6, the corresponding value of *Y* is *maximized*. In panel (b), when *X* = 6, *Y* is *minimized*. In either case, the slope equals zero at the maximum or minimum value.

horizontal straight line that neither rises nor falls as *X* changes.

When a curvilinear relationship has a zero slope, the value of Y *reaches either a high point—as in panel (a)—or a low point—as in panel (b)—at the value of* X *where the slope is zero.*

Economists pay considerable attention to the maximum and minimum values of relationships—as when they examine how a firm maximizes profits or minimizes costs. Suppose, for example, that *X* in panel (a) represents the 1982 *production* of automobiles by General Motors (in units of 1 million) and that the variable *Y* represents GM's *profits from automobile production* (in billions of dollars). According to this diagram, GM should settle on *X* = 6 million units of automobile production because GM's profits would be higher at *X* = 6 than at any other production level.

Suppose that in panel (b) *Y* measures GM's costs of producing an automobile while *X* still measures automobile production. Production costs per automobile are at a minimum at *X* = 6. In other words, GM will produce cars at the lowest cost per car if GM produces 6 million cars.

PITFALLS OF USING GRAPHS

When used properly, graphs illuminate the world in a convenient and efficient manner. Graphs may, however, be used to confuse or even misinform. Factions in political contests, advertisers of competing products, rivals in lawsuits can take the same set of data, apply the standard rules of graph construction, and yet offer graphs that support their own position and demonstrate the falsity of the opposition view. This is especially apparent in national political campaigns, where the incumbent party or president seeks to demonstrate how well the country's economy has been managed, while the opposition attempts to show how badly the nation's economic affairs have been bungled.

It is important to be able to form an independent judgment of what graphs say about the real world. This section warns the graph consumer about three of the many pitfalls of using graphs:

1. the ambiguity of slope,
2. the improper measurement of data, and
3. the use of unrepresentative data.

The Ambiguity of Slope

The steepness of the rise or fall of a graphed curve can be an ambiguous guide to the strength of the relationship between the two variables because the graphed slope is affected by the scale used to mark the axes and because the slope's numerical value depends upon the unit of measure.

Improper Measurement

A second pitfall in reading and evaluating graphs is *improper measurement*. Improper measurement covers a multitude of sins but does not mean simply an incorrect count of a variable (counting 20 chickens instead of 15). A variable may give the appearance of measuring one thing while in reality measuring another. Improper measurement is often subtle and difficult to detect, and the user of graphs must constantly be on the alert for this misuse.

In economics, two types of improper measurement that are encountered most often with time-series graphs are 1) inflation-distorted measures and 2) growth-distorted measures. A *time-series graph* is one in which the horizontal *X* axis measures time (in months, quarters, years, decades, etc.), and the vertical *Y* axis measures a second variable whose behavior is plotted over time.

Examples of inflation-distorted time-series graphs are not difficult to find. Consider the following misleading statement: "The American worker is better off today than three years ago; take-home pay has never been higher." Money wages alone do not measure worker living standards because inflation must be considered.

In interpreting time-series graphs, one must also be wary of *growth distortions*. An example of a growth-distorted measure is American alcohol consumption. The question is: Has alcohol abuse become a greater social problem over the past decade? The answer depends on which statistics you use. Alcohol consumption in the United States from 1965–1977 rose 38 percent, but the increase in alcohol consumption may be explained simply by the growth in population. When the figures are corrected for the increase in population, we find that alcohol expenditures *per adult* increased by only 12.5 percent.

Misinterpretations of time-series graphs can be avoided 1) by careful distinction between graphs that do and do not account for inflation and 2) by using per capita figures where appropriate or expressing graphs as percentages.

Unrepresentative Data

A final pitfall of using graphs is the problem of *unrepresentative or incomplete data*. The direction of a graphed relationship may depend upon the selection of the time period. For example, Soviet harvests have fluctuated dramatically in recent years with disastrous harvests following good harvests. If a good harvest year is chosen as the first year of a graph and a bad harvest as the last, the assessment of Soviet agricultural performance will be unfavorable. It will be more favorable if the graph starts with a bad harvest year and ends with a good one. Because the graphical relationship depends upon the choice of years covered by the graph, biased observers have the opportunity to present their version of the facts to the confusion of the user of the graph.

Summary

1. Graphs are useful for presenting positive and negative relationships between two variables.
2. A positive relationship exists between two variables if an increase in one is associated with an *increase* in the other; a negative relationship exists between two variables if an increase in one is associated with a *decrease* in the other.
3. In a graphical relationship, one variable may be an independent variable, and the other may be a dependent variable. In some relationships, it is not clear which variable is dependent and which variable is independent.
4. To construct a graph, four steps are necessary: 1) perpendicular vertical and horizontal axes are drawn on graph paper; 2) each variable is assigned to a particular axis; 3) units of measurement and scale are chosen for the X variable and for the Y variable; and 4) each related set of variables is plotted at the intersection of the appropriate grid lines on the graph. The advantages of graphs over tables are that graphs require less time to understand the relationship, and graphs can accommodate large amounts of data more efficiently.
5. For a straight line curve the slope of the curve is the ratio of the rise in Y over the run in X. The slope of the curvilinear relationship at a particular point is the slope of the straight line tangent at that point. When a curve changes slope from positive to negative as the X values increase, the value of Y reaches a *maximum* when the slope of the curve is zero; when a curve changes slope from negative to positive as the X values increase, the value of Y reaches a *minimum* when the slope of the curve is zero.
6. There are three pitfalls to avoid when using graphs: 1) choice of *units* and *scale* affects the apparent steepness or flatness of a curve; 2) the variables may be inflation-distorted or growth-distorted; and 3) omitted data or incomplete data may result in an erroneous interpretation of the relationship between two variables.

Key Terms

positive (or direct) relationship
negative (or inverse) relationship
independent variable
dependent variable
slope
tangent

2

The Economic Problem

Chapter Preview

The economic problem is how to use resources in a land of scarcity. Chapter 2 will explain how the production-possibilities frontier can show how an economy solves its economic problem and defines such crucial concepts as *resources, scarcity, scarce goods, free goods,* and *opportunity costs.* In solving its economic problem, every society must answer three questions: *What* should be produced? *How* should it be produced? *For whom* should it be produced?

UNLIMITED WANTS IN A
SANTA CLAUS WORLD

We live in what John Kenneth Galbraith has called "the affluent society."[1] Although many people in our society are poor, the standard of living of most American families is comparatively high. Is it appropriate to speak of scarcity in an affluent society?

This question underscores how important it is to understand the exact meaning of economic terms. In economics, *scarcity* has a specific meaning that differs from the one in the dictionary. Scarcity is not determined by one's standard of living, not by whether one has life's basic necessities, but by comparison of wants with those things available to satisfy wants.

Suppose there really were a Santa Claus, who every Christmas tried to bring people all the

---

1. John Kenneth Galbraith, *The Affluent Society* (Boston: Houghton Mifflin, 1957).

things that they desired. People want different things, so everyone's Christmas list would differ. Children would want all kinds of toys; teenagers would ask for motorcycles, autos, stereos, clothes. The art enthusiast would want a house full of Rembrandts and Picassos; the wine connoisseur would want a cellar full of rare French wines. The vacation traveler would want first-class air and hotel accommodations for travel throughout the world.

Consider poor Santa Claus. He would add all the requests together to determine the wants of all his clients, but he would discover rather quickly that all requests could not be met. After all, there are only a limited number of Rembrandts and Picassos and bottles of rare French wines, and they would fall far short of the number requested. Santa Claus would find that for all these goods and services, the amounts requested would exceed the amounts available.

What would Santa Claus do in this case? He would have to make choices. He would decide to meet some requests and to deny others. His decisions could be made randomly or according to some rule, like who has been good or bad. If Santa Claus is interested in maximizing his own standard of living, he may honor the requests of those who leave the best snacks by the fireplace. On the other hand, he may deliver to those in greatest need. He may appoint a committee of trusted elves to make these decisions for him.

This Santa Claus story is a useful fable because it illustrates the most basic facts of economic life: scarcity and choice. In our fable, scarcity is present because what people want far exceeds what Santa Claus could conceivably deliver. It has little to do with whether Santa's claimants are rich or poor (although he would probably run out of Rembrandts before hot dogs). Choice is necessary because Santa must decide whose wants are to be met.

The most important fact of economics is the law of scarcity: there will never be enough resources to meet everyone's wants.

THE DEFINITION OF ECONOMICS

Chapter 1 noted that **economics** is the study of four themes: scarcity, choice, specialization, and exchange:

Economics is the study of how scarce resources *are* allocated *among* competing ends.

Four terms in this definition are emphasized because their meanings must be clear if the definition is to be properly understood. What are the exact economic meanings of *scarcity, resources, allocation,* and *competing ends?*

Scarcity

In September of 1980, Air Florida announced that any tickets that were not sold 10 minutes prior to departure on all its Houston-to-Dallas/Fort Worth flights would be given away free of charge (in fact, the ticket recipients received a kiss from an attractive Air Florida employee). This offer was valid for only one week.

While these airline seats were free of charge, they were not a **free good.** Rather the seats represent a **scarce good.**

As you might have guessed, the Air Florida tickets were indeed scarce. Crowds of people gathered at the departure gate in the hope of getting one of the few available free tickets. Many disappointed travelers had to return home, after a long wait, without a ticket and without a complimentary kiss.

*An item is a **scarce** good if the amount available (offered to users) is less than the amount people want if it would be given away free of charge.*

*A **free good** is one where the amount available is greater than the amount people want at a zero price.*

The following examples will test your ability to distinguish between free goods and scarce goods:

Tumbleweeds. Along an Idaho highway, one of the authors encountered the delightful sign: "Tumbleweeds are free, take one." Like the Air Florida ticket, tumbleweeds have a price of zero, but unlike the Air Florida ticket, tumbleweeds in Idaho are a free good. Why? Tumbleweeds may give satisfaction to the Eastern tourist, who may want to take one home as a souvenir, but the number of tumbleweeds available to takers far exceeds the number people want, even though they cost nothing. This example is limited by place and circumstances. In Alaska, tumbleweeds may be such a rarity that the number people want exceeds the number available. Exotic orchids can be freely picked in some remote Hawaiian islands, while commanding a high price in New York City.

La Guardia Airport. Landing and take-off slots at major airports are not paid for by airlines. Instead, committees comprised of government officials and airline management determine which airlines will be allotted take-off and landing slots and on which days. At busy La Guardia Airport in New York City, 522 take-off slots are available on a daily basis.[2] The airlines that serve New York City collectively want more than these 522 slots and must engage in intense negotiation over which airlines get which slots. These negotiations are particularly intense for the popular 5 P.M. to 7 P.M. landing slots. Although the airlines do not pay for landing slots, they are nevertheless a scarce commodity at La Guardia Airport. Whether landing slots are scarce or free depends upon time and place. At 10 P.M., landing slots are a free good at La Guardia. At uncongested airports (say, Champaign/Urbana, Illinois) landing slots are virtually a free good.

Los Angeles Air. The early residents of Los Angeles did not have to worry about the scarcity of clean air, for prior to the automobile age and the mass migration to southern California, clean air was not scarce according to the economic definition. Now, although no one is explicitly charged for clean (or cleaner) air, it has become a scarce good. Residents are implicitly paying for clean air by purchasing homes in distant suburbs where smog is less severe, by making lengthy commutes to work, and by purchasing air-filtration systems for their homes.

Goods may be scarce even if they are free of charge, and goods may be free goods at one

time and place and scarce goods in another time and place.

Unlike landing slots and clean air, scarce goods usually command a price. The next chapter will discuss how prices help allocate scarce resources.

Resources

Resources are the natural resources (land, mineral deposits, oxygen), the capital equipment (plants, machinery, inventories), and the human resources (workers with different skills, qualifications, ambitions, managerial talents) that are used to produce scarce goods and services. Productive resources are called **factors of production.** These resources represent the economic wealth of society because they determine how much output the society can produce. Because the factors of production are limited, society's ability to produce output is limited. The limitation of resources is the fundamental source of scarcity.

*The **factors of production** can be divided into three categories—land, labor, and capital.*

Sometimes, a fourth category—*entrepreneurship*—is considered a factor of production. The economic definitions of these factors differ somewhat from the dictionary usage.

Land is a catchall term that covers all of nature's bounty—minerals, forests, land, water resources, oxygen, and so on.

Land represents those natural resources, unimproved or unaltered by inputs of the other two factors of production, that contribute to production. Desert land that had been transformed into arable land by irrigation would not be a free gift of nature. The application of the labor and capital used to build the irrigation system makes this desert land productive.

Capital refers to the equipment, plants, buildings, and inventories that are available to society.

In 1981, the total of all U.S. **capital** was approximately $11.7 trillion. Unlike land, capital is

2. "Upstarts Crack an Airline Club," *New York Times,* September 7, 1980, section 3.

not one of nature's gifts; capital is produced by combining the factors of production. Capital is long-lived: when it is used to produce output, it is not *consumed* (used up) immediately; it is consumed gradually in the process of time. An assembly plant may have a life of 40 years, a computer a life of 5 years, and a lathe a life of 10 years before it must be replaced.

When economists speak of capital, they mean physical capital goods—buildings, computers, trucks, plants. This concept of capital is distinct from *money capital*. Physical capital and money capital are related. Money capital is needed to purchase physical capital; money capital represents the ownership's claims to physical capital. The owner of 1,000 shares of AT&T owns money capital, but these shares really represent ownership of a portion of AT&T's physical capital.

One final distinction should be made between the *stock* of capital and *additions* to the stock of capital. At one point in time, there exists a stock of capital. This stock consists of all the capital (plants, equipment, inventories, buildings) that exist *at that point in time*. Each year, this stock changes; it usually grows. New plants are built, new equipment is manufactured, new homes are constructed, additions are made to inventories. Through **investment,** society adds to its stock of capital.

Investment is additions to the stock of capital.

Labor is the physical and mental talents that human beings contribute to the production process.

The ditchdigger contributes muscles; the computer engineer contributes mental abilities, the airline pilot contributes physical coordination and mental talents. Just as a society can add to the stock of physical capital, so can it add to the stock of **human capital.**

Human capital is the accumulation of past investments in schooling, training, and health that raise the productive capacity of people.

In 1981, the stock of human capital was valued at approximately $4.4 trillion. By investing in the training and education of people, society adds to the productive capacity of labor and raises the wealth of society. Investments in physical capital and human capital accomplish the same goal: they increase the capacity of society to produce output. Certain persons, called **entrepreneurs,** possess a particular talent and perform a particular role that cannot be performed by land and capital.

*An **entrepreneur** organizes, manages, and assumes the risks for an enterprise.*

Entrepreneurs are those people who organize the factors of production to produce output, who seek out and exploit new business opportunities, who introduce new technologies. The entrepreneur is the one who takes risk and bears the responsibility if the venture fails. The entrepreneur puts inventions into business practice.

Allocation

Scarcity requires that choices be made: If there is not enough of a commodity to meet unlimited wants, decisions must be made about who will receive the commodity and who will be denied it. A system of **allocation** of scarce resources must be employed. Societies cannot function unless the allocation problem is resolved in a satisfactory manner.

***Allocation** is the apportionment of resources for a specific purpose or to particular persons or groups.*

Consider what would happen if there were no organized allocation. People would have to fight or compete with one another for scarce resources. The timid would not compete effectively; the elderly or weak would have difficulty in obtaining goods, except through stronger, more aggressive benefactors. Such an allocation system was in effect for centuries in the dark and middle ages. Such free-for-all allocation is rare in modern societies, but it reappears in cases of breakdowns of the social order. Floods, natural disasters, and wars bring out looting and violent competition for scarce goods. Martial law must be declared to prevent free-for-all allocation. If there were a drastic reduction in gasoline supplies (say, to one tenth of the current level), there would probably be considerable free-for-all allocation. Individuals armed with guns, wrenches, and nasty dispositions would seek to intimidate other customers at service stations to gain access to the scarce resource, gasoline.

It is important to have an allocation system that is not based upon strong-arm tactics. Society must develop a system for orderly allocation.

Market Allocation. The allocation system that prevails in American society is the **market;** this book is devoted primarily to the study of market allocation.

*The **market** is the coming together of buyers and sellers for the purpose of determining the conditions for the exchange of resources.*

Market allocation works as follows: A commodity—let us say, a TV set—is scarce because the number desired at a zero price exceeds the number offered. Raising the price of TV sets encourages production and discourages consumption. Market allocation uses higher prices to restrict the number of buyers of the scarce commodity to the amount available. The market sets the price to encourage the *supply* of a resource (the amount offered for sale) to match actual *demand* for that resource (the amount buyers are prepared to purchase).

Market allocation and the price system are discussed in Chapter 3. Most goods and services are allocated by the market in our society—automobiles, hamburgers, computers, furniture, fresh fruits—the list is almost without end.

Government Allocation. A second allocation system is *government allocation*. Governmental agencies, officials, and administrative authorities decide who, among all those who want the scarce commodity, will be accommodated. In Communist societies, most allocation decisions are made by the government. In our economy, airport landing slots are assigned by government regulatory agencies. The regional distribution of gasoline supplies has at times been dictated by the federal government. Licenses for television and radio stations are granted by the federal government. In all these cases, access to the scarce re-

source is not determined by willingness to pay, but by some administrative authority.

In Great Britain, the government National Health Service is responsible for allocating medical care. The number of doctors, nurses, and hospital beds is not sufficient to meet wants for "free" medical care, and the National Health Service must decide who will receive medical care. Some procedures are denied to patients over 65—such as kidney dialysis or transplants. The desire for operations that are not required to save a life (elective surgery) is limited by requiring patients to wait weeks and months to see a specialist.[3] In effect, the National Health Service uses rules to allocate medical care. Of course, there is a private medical market as well that supplements the public market.

Scarce resources can be allocated by different allocation systems. There is endless controversy about which system (or combination of systems) is best. The allocation system has a substantial impact on how people live. Consider the differences between American society, which uses primarily market allocation, and Soviet society, which uses primarily government allocation. The allocation system affects personal lives, the political system, and freedom of choice.

Competing Ends

Economics is the study of competition for resources. Scarce resources must somehow be allocated among the **competing ends** of individuals, families, government agencies, and businesses according to an allocation system.

*The **competing ends** are the different purposes for which resources can be used.*

First, different individuals are in competition for resources. Which families will have a greater claim on scarce resources? Who will be rich? Who poor? How will income be distributed? There is also competition for resources between the private sector (individuals and businesses) and government. Third, there is competition for resources between current and future consumption.

3. Harry Schwartz, "What is a Life Worth?" *Wall Street Journal,* September 15, 1980, p. 22.

By investing scarce resources in physical and human capital, their current use is sacrificed to produce more goods and services in the future.

Finally, the society must choose between competing national goals when allocating resources. Is price stability, full employment, elimination of poverty, or economic growth most important? Are we prepared to achieve one goal at the expense of another?

THE ECONOMIC PROBLEM

The economic problem is how to allocate scarce resources among competing ends. Three questions must be answered: *What* products will be produced? *How* will they be produced? *For whom* will they be produced?

What?

Should society devote its limited resources to producing civilian or military goods, luxuries or necessities, goods for immediate consumption or goods that increase the wealth of society (capital goods)? Should small or large cars be produced, or should buses and subways be produced instead of cars? Should the military concentrate on strategic or conventional forces?

How?

Once the decision is made on what to produce, society must determine what combinations of the factors of production will be used. Will coal, petroleum, or nuclear power be used to produce electricity? Will bulldozers or workers with shovels dig dams? Should automobile tires be made from natural or synthetic rubber? Should Coca Cola be sweetened with sugar or corn syrup? Should tried-and-true methods of production be replaced by new technology?

For Whom?

Will society's output be divided fairly equally or will claims to society's output be unequal? Will differences in wealth be allowed to pass from one generation to the next? What role will government play in determining *for whom?* Should government intercede to change the way the economy is distributing its output?

Economic Systems

Societies must solve these economic problems of what, how, and for whom if they are to function. Different societies have different solutions. Some use private ownership and market allocation; others use public ownership and government allocation. Most use an **economic system** that is a combination of private and public ownership and a combination of market and government allocation.

*The set of organizational arrangements and institutions that are established to solve the economic problem is called an **economic system**.*

Real-world economic systems exist in almost infinite variety; the list of labels for economic systems is also long. The two major alternatives are the capitalist (market) system and the planned socialist (communist) system. How the market system solves our economic problems is discussed in Chapter 3.

OPPORTUNITY COSTS

Scarcity requires that choices be made concerning what will be produced, how it will be produced, and for whom. Choice means that some alternatives must be forgone. A sacrificed opportunity is called an **opportunity cost** by economists because the economic cost of any choice is that which must be sacrificed in order to make that choice.

*The **opportunity cost** of a particular action is the loss of the next best alternative.*

If a person buys a new car, its opportunity cost is the next best alternative that must be sacrificed. The next best alternative might have been a European trip, an investment in the stock market, or enrollment in a prestigious university. Because the person chose the car, he or she sacrificed these other things. The loss of the next best alternative is the true cost of the car. If the government increases defense spending, the opportunity cost is the best alternate government program that had to be sacrificed to make the funds available.

The notion of opportunity cost supplies a

shortcut method of differentiating between free goods and scarce goods:

Free goods have an opportunity cost of zero. Scarce goods have a positive opportunity cost.

Why does the Idaho tumbleweed have no opportunity cost? If one tumbleweed is taken, the amount available is still greater than the amount wanted. The taker has not had to give up anything as a consequence of taking the tumbleweed.

The opportunity cost of an action can involve the sacrifice of time as well as the sacrifice of goods. To gather the free tumbleweed, one would need to sacrifice time. What is the opportunity cost of attending a football game? To pay the price of the ticket, the buyer has to sacrifice the purchase of other goods, and the next best purchase is the opportunity cost of buying the ticket. Even if the buyer had received the ticket free of charge, however, there would still be an opportunity cost. The two hours spent at the game could have been devoted to alternate uses. The buyer could have slept, studied, or listened to records, for example. If a major exam were scheduled for the next day, the opportunity cost of the game could be quite high. The notion of sacrificed time as an opportunity cost is an important ingredient of economics. It explains, for example, why passenger trains and ocean liners have become relics of the past or why older residential areas close to the central city are being revived.

Every choice involving the allocation of scarce resources involves opportunity costs.

Table 1
Production-Possibilities Schedule

Combination	Tanks (in thousands)	Wheat (in tons)	Opportunity Cost of Tanks (in tons of wheat)
a	0	18	0
b	1	17	1
c	2	15	2
d	3	12	3
e	4	7	5
f	5	0	7

PRODUCTION POSSIBILITIES

The **production-possibilities frontier (PPF)** is a useful analytical tool for illustrating the concepts of scarcity, choice, and opportunity costs.

Suppose an economy produces only two types of goods: tanks and wheat. Of course, actual economies produce more than two goods, but a simple model aids our understanding. Table 1 gives the amounts of wheat and tanks that this hypothetical economy can produce with its limited factors of production and technical knowledge. These amounts are graphed in Figure 1. The table and the graph contain the same information.

Figure 1
The Production-Possibilities Frontier *(PPF)*

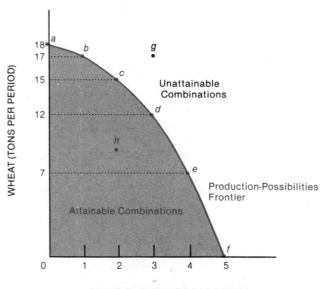

The *PPF* shows the combinations of outputs of two goods that can be produced from society's resources when these resources are utilized to their maximum potential. Point *a* shows that if 18 tons of wheat are produced, no tank production is possible. Point *f* shows that if no wheat is produced, a maximum of 5,000 tanks can be produced. Point *d* shows that if 3,000 tanks are produced, a maximum of 12 tons of wheat can be produced. Point *g* is above society's *PPF*. With its available resources, the economy cannot produce 17 tons of wheat and 3,000 tanks. Points like *h* inside the *PPF* and, therefore, attainable represent an inefficient use of the society's resources.

What do these numbers mean? How are they to be interpreted? If our hypothetical economy chose to be at point *a*, it would be producing no tanks and the *maximum* of 18 tons of wheat from the factors of production available. At point *f* the economy would be producing no wheat and the *maximum* of 5,000 tanks. The points between *a* and *f* show the combinations of wheat and tanks that the economy is capable of producing from its available resources and technology. Point *c* shows that if 2,000 tanks are produced, the maximum number of tons of wheat that can be produced is 15. Each intermediate point on the *PPF* between *a* and *f* represents a different combination of wheat and tanks that could be produced using the same resources and technology.

*The **production-possibilities frontier (PPF)** shows the combinations of goods that can be produced when the factors of production are utilized to their full potential. The production-possibilities curve reveals the economic choices open to society.*

Our hypothetical economy is capable of producing output combinations *a* through *f*. The economy is unable to produce output combination *g* (17 tons of wheat and 3,000 tanks) because *g* uses more resources than the economy has available. Point *h* is an attainable combination because it lies inside the frontier. The economy can produce any combination of outputs on or inside the *PPF*.

The Law of Increasing Cost

The production-possibilities frontier is curved like a bow; it is not a straight line. Why does it have this shape? As noted earlier, the economic cost of any action is the loss of the next best opportunity. In our example, the economy produces only two goods. The opportunity cost of increasing the production of one of those goods is the amount of the other good that must be sacrificed. In this simple case, the measurement of opportunity cost is obvious: the opportunity cost of tanks is the wheat production that must be sacrificed.

At *a,* the economy is producing 18 tons of wheat and no tanks. The opportunity cost of increasing the production of tanks from zero to

1,000 is the 1 ton of wheat that must be sacrificed in the move from *a* to *b*. The opportunity cost of 1,000 more tanks (moving from *b* to *c*) is 2 tons of wheat. The opportunity cost of the fifth thousand of tanks (moving from *e* to *f*) is a much higher 7 tons of wheat. The amounts of wheat that must be given up to increase tank production are given in the last column of Table 1. The opportunity cost per thousand of tank production rises with the production of tanks, which is consistent with the **law of increasing costs.**

*The **law of increasing costs** states that as more of a particular commodity is produced, its opportunity cost per unit will increase.*

The law of increasing costs is consistent with the bowed out shape of the *PPF*. Suppose our hypothetical economy were at peace, producing only wheat, no tanks (at *a* on the *PPF*). Its archenemy declares war, and the economy must suddenly increase its production of tanks. The amount of resources available to the economy is not altered by the declaration of war, so the increased tank production must be at the expense of wheat production. The economy *must move along* its *PPF* in the direction of more tank production.

As tank production increases, will the opportunity cost of a unit of tank production remain the same? At low levels of tank production, the opportunity cost of a unit of tank production will be relatively low. Some factors of production will be suited to producing both wheat and tanks; they can be shifted from wheat to tank production without raising opportunity cost. As tank production increases further, resources suited to wheat production but ill suited to tank production (experienced farmers make inexperienced factory workers, agricultural equipment is poorly adapted to tank factories) must be diverted into tank production. Ever-increasing amounts of these resources must be shifted from wheat to keep tank production expanding at a constant rate. The opportunity cost of a unit of tank production (the amount of wheat sacrificed) will rise, as the law of increasing costs would predict.

The law of increasing costs applies across economic systems. One of the most striking movements along a *PPF* took place in the Soviet Union between 1928 and 1937. In 1928 the Soviet leadership determined to shift most resources out of agriculture and light industry into heavy industry. This reallocation was designed to make the Soviet Union economically independent and to "build Soviet socialism." An unprecedented volume of resources was diverted to heavy industry. Untrained peasants entered into large industrial plants; major construction projects used people with shovels and wheelbarrows; light industry equipment was converted to use in heavy industry.

To the surprise of Soviet planners, the law of increasing costs applied to their economy. The economy fell far short of the cost targets set by planners for heavy industry.[4] Why did Soviet planners miscalculate costs so badly? To meet major targets, resources ill suited for heavy industry (untrained peasants, shovels and wheelbarrows, textile mills) had to be used in ever-increasing numbers. The opportunity costs of heavy industry rose, just as the law predicted.

The Law of Diminishing Returns

Underlying the law of increasing costs is the **law of diminishing returns.** Suppose that wheat is produced using land, labor, and tractors. The law of diminishing returns states that increasing the amount of labor in equal increments, holding land and tractors constant, eventually brings about smaller and smaller increases in wheat production.

*In general, the **law of diminishing returns** states that increasing the amount of one input in equal increments, holding all other inputs constant, eventually brings about ever-smaller increases in output.*

Notice that the law of diminishing returns applies in our example because the input that is being increased—labor—becomes less and less effective because more and more workers are being crowded together on a fixed amount of land and physical capital. As the number of laborers increases each laborer works with a smaller plot

4. Eugene Zaleski, *Stalinist Planning for Economic Growth* (Chapel Hill, N.C.: University of North Carolina Press, 1980).

of land and fewer tractors. Suppose 10 farm workers were employed, and they each had 100 acres to farm and one tractor with which to work. Because land and capital are fixed, increasing the number of farm workers to 20 would mean each worker would have 50 acres to farm and half of a tractor with which to work (2 workers would have to share one tractor). Increasing the number of farm workers to 1,000 would result in each worker farming $\frac{1}{10}$ of an acre and 100 workers sharing each tractor. Obviously, each worker would be less productive if each had only a fraction of an acre to farm and if each worker had to wait for 99 other workers to use the tractor.

Efficiency

The *PPF* shows the combination of goods an economy is capable of producing when its limited resources are utilized to their maximum potential. Whether an economy will indeed operate on its production-possibilities frontier depends upon whether or not the economy utilizes its resources with maximum **efficiency.**

In Figure 1, if the economy produces output combinations that lie on the *PPF* the economy is said to be *efficient*. If it operates at points inside the *PPF,* such as *h,* it is said to be *inefficient* because more wheat could be produced without cutting back on the other good.

Efficiency results when no resources are unemployed and when no resources are misallocated.

For example, if workers are unemployed or if productive machines stand idle, the economy is not operating on its *PPF* because resources are not being employed. Misallocated resources are resources that are used but not to their best advantage. For example, if a surgeon works as a ditchdigger, if cotton is planted on Iowa corn land, or if jumbo jets are manufactured in India, resources are misallocated.

Economic Growth

The production-possibilities frontier represents the economic choices open to society. It shows the maximum combinations of outputs the econ-

Figure 2
The Effect of Increasing the Stock of Capital on the *PPF*

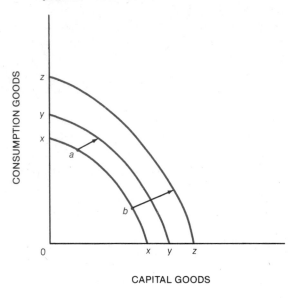

CONSUMPTION GOODS

CAPITAL GOODS

Suppose the current *PPF* is curve *XX*. If the economy chooses point *a*, allocating most resources to the production of consumption goods and few to the production of new capital goods, the *PPF* in the future will shift out to curve *YY*. But if the economy chooses point *b*, with comparatively little consumption and comparatively high production of new capital goods, the future *PPF* will shift out further—to *ZZ*.

omy is capable of producing from its scarce resources. Economies that are efficient operate on their frontier; others that are inefficient operate inside their frontier. Which combination of outputs lying on the frontier is best is a matter of economic choice.

Capital Accumulation.   Where to locate on the *PPF* may represent a choice between capital goods and consumer goods. Capital goods are the equipment, plants, and inventories that are added to society's stock of capital and can be used to satisfy wants in the future. Consumer goods are items like food, clothing, medicine, and transportation that satisfy consumer wants directly in the present. The capital goods/consumer goods choice is shown in Figure 2.

The economy on the *PPF* labeled *XX* must choose among those combinations of consumer

goods and capital goods located on *XX*. What are the implications for the future of selecting *a* or *b*? If *a* is chosen, more consumer wants are satisfied today, but additions to the stock of capital are smaller. If *b* is selected fewer wants are satisfied today, but additions to the stock of capital are greater. The creation of a larger stock of capital today means more production in the future. The society that selects *b* will therefore experience a greater outward shift of the *PPF* in the future and will be able to satisfy more wants in the future.

Economic growth occurs when the production-possibilities frontier expands outward and to the right. One source of economic growth is the expansion of capital.

The society that selects *a* will satisfy more wants today but will experience lower economic growth and will not be in as good a position to satisfy future wants.

These principles are illustrated in Figure 2. If society chooses *a*, then the *PPF* expands from *XX* now to *YY* in the future. If it locates at *b*, the *PPF* expands more, from *XX* now to *ZZ* in the future. At *ZZ*, the economy will be able to satisfy more wants than at *YY*.

Societies must choose between consumption today and consumption tomorrow. The society that devotes a greater share of its resources to producing capital sacrifices consumption now but enlarges its supply of capital and will thus have a higher rate of economic growth.

There are limits to the rule that less consumption today means more consumption tomorrow. If all resources are devoted to capital goods, the labor force would starve. If too large a share of resources is put into capital goods, worker incentives might be low and efficiency might be reduced.

Shifts in the Production-Possibilities Frontier.   The production-possibilities frontier is based on the size and productivity of the resource base. Capital accumulation is only one reason for the *PPF* to shift. Increases in labor or land or discoveries of natural resources (coal, iron, oil) will

Figure 3
Technical Progress in Wheat Production

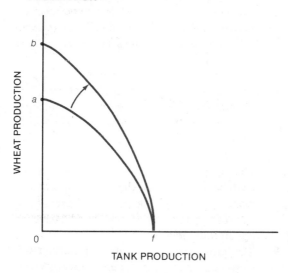

If a higher-yielding strain of wheat is discovered, a larger quantity of wheat could be produced with the same resources. Since this increase in wheat production would not influence tank production, the PPF would rotate from *af* to *bf*.

also shift the *PPF* outward. Technical progress occurs when the society learns how to get more outputs from the same inputs. Thus technical progress, or advances in productivity, will also shift the *PPF* outward.

Technical progress and accumulation of productive factors like land, labor, or capital have different effects on the *PPF*. Technical progress may affect only one industry or sector—whereas labor and capital and land can be used across all sectors. Figure 3 illustrates a technical advance in wheat production without a corresponding change in the productivity of the resources devoted to tank production. Accordingly, the *PPF* shifts from *af* to *bf*. Here the *PPF* shifts upward but not rightward. Figure 2 illustrates that a change in factor supply—illustrated in this case by capital accumulation—shifts the *PPF* both upward and rightward.

All societies must solve the economic problems of what, how, and for whom if they are to function. There are different methods of solving these problems. This book will concentrate on how market economies solve the economic prob-

Figure 4
The Economic Problem: What? How? For Whom?

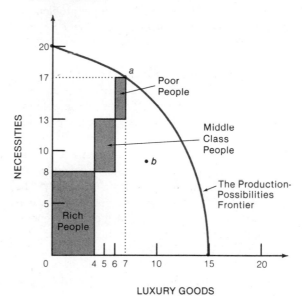

LUXURY GOODS

The *PPF* reveals the choices open to society. The *what* question is solved by the choice of where to locate on the *PPF*. Here society chooses *a*, or 7 units of luxuries and 17 units of necessities. The *how* question is solved when society decides how to combine resources to produce these outputs. Society can solve this problem efficiently and operate on the frontier (at *a*) or inefficiently and operate inside the frontier (at *b*). The *for whom* question is the division of society's output among the members of society. In this diagram, the rich get 4 units of luxuries and 8 units of necessities; the middle class get 2 units of luxuries and 5 units of necessities; the poor get one unit of luxuries and 4 units of necessities.

lems but will also discuss how planned economies and mixed economies deal with them as well.

In market economies, the *what* problem is solved when consumers decide what they want to buy and how much they are willing to pay and when voters cast their ballots for or against public spending programs. The *how* problem is solved when producers determine how to combine resources to their best advantage. The *for whom* decision depends on who owns the economy's land, labor, and capital.

A solution of the *what, how,* and *for whom* problems is shown in Figure 4. The *what* problem is nothing more than the choice of location on the

PPF. In this diagram, society chooses point *a*. The *how* problem is solved behind the scenes by decisions on how the factors of production are to be combined. How well the how problem is solved can be read directly from the *PPF* diagram. If the economy is operating *on its PPF*, such as at *a*, it is solving the how problem with maximum efficiency. If it is operating inside the *PPF*, at *b* for example, it is not solving the how problem with maximum efficiency. The solution to the *for whom* problem also takes place behind the scenes. We can show the outcome of the *for whom* problem on the *PPF* diagram. The consumer goods (necessities and luxury goods) are distributed among the members of society (the rich, the middle class, and the poor). In the diagram, the rich receive most of the luxury goods; the middle class receive some luxury goods; the poor receive negligible luxury goods.

The next chapter explains how the price system solves the *what, how,* and *for whom* problems, how it facilitates specialization and exchange, and how it provides for the future.

Summary

1. Wants are unlimited; there will never be enough resources to meet unlimited wants.
2. Economics is the study of how scarce resources are allocated among competing ends.
3. A good is *scarce* if the amount available is less than the amount people would want if it were given away free. A good is *free* if the amount people want is less than the amount available. Goods may be scarce even though they are given away free of charge.
4. The ultimate source of scarcity is the limited supply of resources. The resources that are factors of production are land, labor, and capital. Society can add to its stock of resources by investment in physical capital and in human beings.
5. Because scarcity exists, some system of allocating goods among those who want the goods is necessary. The two major allocation systems are market allocation and allocation by government plan. These two types of allocation systems can be combined to create mixed allocation systems.
6. Allocation systems must determine what resources will be made available to which individuals, how resources are to be divided between the private and public sectors, and which resources will be devoted to current use and which to future consumption.
7. Economics is the study of how societies solve the economic problems of *what* to produce, *how* to produce, and *for whom* to produce.
8. The opportunity cost of any choice is the next best alternative that was sacrificed to make the choice. Scarce goods have a positive opportunity cost; free goods have an opportunity cost of zero.
9. The production-possibilities frontier *(PPF)* shows the maximum combinations of goods that an economy is able to produce from its limited resources when these resources are utilized to their maximum potential and for a given state of technical knowledge. If societies are efficient, they will operate on the production-possibilities frontier. If they are inefficient, they will operate inside the *PPF*.
10. The law of increasing costs says that as more of one commodity is produced at the expense of others, its opportunity cost will increase. This law applies to all economic systems.
11. According to the law of diminishing returns, increasing the amount of one input in equal increments, holding all other inputs constant, eventually brings about ever smaller increases in output.
12. The two sources of economic inefficiency are unemployed resources and misallocated resources.
13. Economic growth occurs because the factors of production expand in either quantity or quality, or because technological progress raises productivity.
14. The choice of consumer goods versus capital goods affects economic growth. Generally, the greater the share of resources devoted to capital goods, the better is the economy able to meet wants in the future. The choice of consumer goods versus capi-

tal goods is really a choice between meeting wants now and meeting them in the future.

Key Terms

economics
free good
scarce good
factors of production
land
capital
labor
human capital
entrepreneur
allocation
market
competing ends
economic system
opportunity cost
production-possibilities frontier *(PPF)*
law of increasing costs
law of diminishing returns
efficiency

Questions and Problems

1. Use the Santa Claus example to illustrate how either market allocation or allocation by government planning could be used to solve Santa's allocation problem.
2. "Desert sand will always be a free good. More is available than people could conceivably want." Evaluate this statement.
3. A local millionaire buys 1000 tickets to the Super Bowl and declares that these tickets will be given away to 1000 boy scouts. Are these tickets free goods? Why or why not?
4. In Israel, desert land has been turned into farm land by irrigation. Does this example demonstrate that nature's free gifts are not fixed in supply?

5. Do you consider your time spent in college as an investment in human capital? Is it investment or consumption? Make a brief list of the opportunity costs of attending college. Do these costs equal the dollar costs listed in the college catalog?
6. The cancer drug *interferon* has received considerable attention in the press as a promising development in the search for a cancer treatment. The amount of interferon available is quite limited, while numerous cancer patients want to try it. What alternative methods could be used to allocate interferon among users?
7. Consider the following data on a hypothetical economy's production-possibilities frontier:

Hundreds of Guns	Tons of Butter
8	0
7	4
5	10
3	14
1	16
0	16.25

a. Graph the *PPF*.
b. Does it have the expected shape?
c. Calculate the opportunity cost of guns in terms of butter. Calculate the opportunity cost of butter in terms of guns. Do they illustrate the law of increasing costs?
d. If you observed this economy producing 700 guns and 3 tons of butter, what would you conclude about how this economy is solving the *how* problem?
e. If you observed this economy at some later date producing 700 guns and 12 tons of butter, what would you conclude?
8. "Economic inefficiency means wasted output no matter what type of economic system." Evaluate this statement.

3

The Price System

Chapter Preview

This chapter will examine how resources are allocated and how the decisions of the millions of people in the typical economy are coordinated. Market allocation of resources is achieved through the price system. The prices people pay for things are like a number of cleverly placed thermostats that balance the decisions of thousands of producers and millions of consumers. The price system achieves this balance by operating according to the principle of substitution, the law of comparative advantage, and the principles of supply and demand. This chapter will explain the difference between relative prices and money prices and will examine the role of property rights, specialization, and interest rates in the

working of the price system. The chapter will conclude by discussing some of the limitations of the price system.

RELATIVE PRICES AND MONEY PRICES

Prices in the Land of Ergs

Suppose you find yourself in a strange land—strange in every respect except that you are able to communicate with the inhabitants. The hospitable natives welcome you with a gift of local currency, which you learn is called the *erg*. Being in a hurry to eat breakfast, you do not have time to count how many ergs you have. You locate a diner and order coffee. A waitress brings you a cup of coffee and asks for 400 ergs. Is coffee cheap or expensive? Is the price high or low? You have no idea. Given the information you have at this point, the price of 400 ergs is meaningless.

How do you discover whether the price of coffee is high or low? You have to gather more information. You look at the menu and discover that a coke sells for 1,200 ergs, and you learn in conversation with another customer that the typical worker earns something like 24,000 ergs per hour. Now you decide that coffee is cheap by reasoning: "Back home I pay $0.40 for a cup of coffee and $0.40 for a coke, and I earn $10.00 an hour. At home, an hour's work will purchase 25 cokes or 25 cups of coffee. Here an hour of work will purchase 20 cokes and 60 cups of coffee." The moral of this parable is: A money price in isolation from other money prices is meaningless. What is important is how a particular money price stands relative to other money prices.

Calculating Relative Prices

A **relative price** indicates how one price stands in relation to other prices. A relative price is quite different from a **money price.** In the erg example, coffee sells for 400 ergs and cokes for 1,200 ergs. Three cups of coffee is the relative price of a coke, and one third of a coke is the relative price of coffee. If coffee and cokes had both sold for 400 ergs, then the relative price of a coke would have been one cup of coffee.

*A **money price** is a price expressed in monetary units (such as dollars, francs, etc.) A **relative price** is a price expressed in terms of other commodities.*

As these examples show, relative prices can be expressed in terms of anything. The relative price of coke can be expressed in terms of cups of coffee, cups of tea, hours of work, number of T-shirts, or anything else that has a money price.

Let P_A and P_B stand for the money prices of apples *(A)* and bananas *(B)*. The relative price of apples to bananas is the *ratio* of the two money prices, P_A/P_B. If the price of apples is $0.50 per pound and the price of bananas is $0.25 per pound, the relative price of one pound of apples is two pounds of bananas. Conversely, one pound

of bananas costs 0.5 pound of apples. When coffee costs 400 ergs and a coke costs 1,200 ergs, the ratio of the price of coke to the price of coffee equals 3, or the relative price of cokes equals 3 coffees.

Money prices are meaningful when they are related to prices of goods that are connected in some way with the good in question. An example of a relative price is the price of U.S. cars expressed in terms of foreign cars. It makes sense to state the price of U.S. cars relative to that of foreign cars because buyers who have decided to purchase a car must choose between U.S. and foreign cars. The money prices of U.S. cars and foreign cars are graphed in panel (a) of Figure 1 (from the data in Table 1). They show that average money prices of both U.S. and foreign cars rose substantially between 1975 and 1980. However, panel (b) shows that the relative price of U.S. cars (the price of U.S. cars divided by the price of foreign cars) fell during this same period. In 1975, the relative price of a U.S. car was 1.21 foreign cars (121 foreign cars could have been purchased with the same amount of money as 100 U.S. cars). By 1980, the relative price of a U.S. car was 0.97 foreign cars (97 foreign cars could have been purchased with the same amount of money as 100 U.S. cars). The relative price of U.S. automobiles dropped even though its money price increased.

The money price of a commodity can rise while its relative price falls. The money price can fall while its relative price rises. Money prices and relative prices need not move together.

Relative prices play a prominent role in answering the economic questions of *what, how,* and *for whom.* Money prices do not. Relative prices signal to buyers and sellers what goods are cheap or expensive. *Buying and selling decisions are made on the basis of relative prices.* If the relative price of one good goes sky high, buyers try to substitute other goods whose relative prices are lower.

The emphasis on relative prices does not mean that money prices are unimportant. Money prices tend to be fairly important in the context of macroeconomics. For example, *inflation* is not a

Table 1
Money Prices for U.S. and Foreign Cars

Year	Price of a U.S. Car (in dollars)	Price of a Foreign Car (in dollars)	Relative Price of a U.S. Car (in foreign cars)
1975	5200	4300	1.21
1976	5600	5000	1.12
1977	6200	5200	1.19
1978	6550	5850	1.12
1979	6700	6750	0.99
1980	7100	7300	0.97

Source: Merrill Lynch, Pierce, Fenner, and Smith, Inc.

movement in relative prices but a general increase in money prices. Elections are won or lost on the basis of inflation; the living standards of older people on fixed incomes are damaged by inflation. Rampant inflation can destroy the fabric of society. Inflation is important. But notice that even in the case of inflation, money prices are not considered in isolation. Instead, the level of money prices today is compared to the level of money prices yesterday. Ultimately, this is also a form of relative price.

Generally speaking, in microeconomics there is greater interest in relative prices than in money prices. In macroeconomics, there is greater interest in the level of money prices than in relative prices. In modern macroeconomics, relative prices have come to play a greater role in explaining macroeconomic events.

THE PRINCIPLE OF SUBSTITUTION

Relative prices are important because of the fundamental **principle of substitution.**

*The **principle of substitution** states that practically no good is irreplaceable in meeting demand (the amount of a good people are prepared to buy). Users are able to substitute one product for another to satisfy demand.*

Virtually no good is fully protected from the competition of substitutes. Aluminum competes with steel, coal with oil, electricity with natural gas, labor with machines, movies with TV, one brand of toothpaste with another, and so on. The only goods impervious to substitutes are such things as certain minimal quantities of water, salt, or food and certain life-saving medications, such as insulin.

To say that there is a substitute for every good does not mean that there is an *equally good* substitute for every good. One mouthwash is a close substitute for another mouthwash; a television show is a good substitute for a movie; apartments may be good substitutes for private homes. However, carrier pigeons are a poor substitute for telephone service;[1] costly insulation may be a poor substitute for fuel oil; public transportation may be a poor substitute for the private car in sprawling cities; steel is a poor substitute for aluminum in the production of jet aircraft.

Relative prices signal consumers when substitutions are necessary. If the price of one good rises relative to its substitutes, consumers will tend to switch to the relatively cheaper substitute.

Substitutions are being made all around us. As relative energy prices rise, people substitute insulation for fuel oil and natural gas, home-entertainment equipment for driving to movies, restaurants, and parties; carpools for driving one's own car. As the relative price of crude oil rises, utilities switch from oil to coal; retailers use fewer neon lights and hire more sales personnel. When

---

1.   In Buenos Aires telephone service at one time became so chaotic that businesses actually purchased carrier pigeons to substitute for telephone service.

Figure 1
Money Prices and Relative Prices for U.S. and Foreign Cars

(a) AVERAGE MONEY PRICES

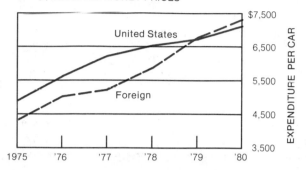

(b) RELATIVE PRICE OF U.S. CARS
IN TERMS OF FOREIGN CARS

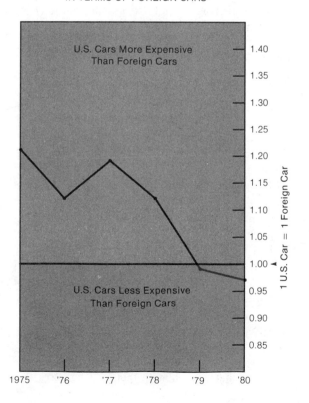

Source: Merrill Lynch, Pierce, Fenner, and Smith, Inc.

the relative price of coffee increases, people consume more tea; when beef prices rise, the consumption of poultry and fish products increases. There is no single recipe for producing a cake, a bushel of wheat, a car, comfort, recreation, or happiness. Increases in relative prices motivate consumers to search out substitutes.

PROPERTY RIGHTS

Relative prices provide information to buyers and sellers on what goods are cheap and what goods are expensive. Substitutions depend on relative prices. The manner in which buyers and sellers act on relative-price information depends on **property rights.**

> *Property rights are the rights of an owner to use and exchange property.*

Collective Ownership

There are different forms of ownership of property. In some societies, the bulk of property (capital, land, houses, etc.) is owned by the state. In the Soviet Union, virtually all plants, equipment, inventories, apartments, homes, and land are owned by the state. The state has rights to use and exchange the property that it owns. Individuals are limited in the property they are allowed to own; they may own a few head of livestock, a private home in some circumstances, a private car, a TV, and so on. In a **socialist society,** individuals have proscribed rights to use and exchange the property they own.

> *A socialist society is characterized by collective ownership of property and government allocation of resources.*

Private Ownership

Unlike in the Soviet Union with its extensive system of state ownership, in a **capitalist society,** the bulk of property is owned by private individuals.

> *A capitalist society is characterized by private ownership of property and by market allocation of resources.*

Example 1

AT&T's Picturephone

American Telephone and Telegraph (AT&T) offers a picturephone service to customers. A picturephone is a closed-circuit system where callers in different locations can view each other on a monitor as they talk to one another. Picturephone users are charged from $150 to $395 per hour. Only two customers have their own picturephone studios, but AT&T has picturephone facilities in 13 major U.S. cities. The number of picturephone customers is quite limited despite its attractive features. Why? One reason is that picturephone substitutes primarily for business travel. Rather than traveling to meet with customers, picturephone users can substitute picturephone communication. At current rates picturephone is regarded by business as having a high price relative to travel costs. If these rates were kept constant while travel costs rose, the relative price of the picturephone would fall, and video meetings would be substituted for business travel.

Source: "Picturephone Pricing Riles AT&T Rival," *Wall Street Journal*, August 28, 1980.

These two features of capitalism are intertwined. There is no such thing as a *pure* capitalist economy in which *all* property is owned privately and in which all allocation is done through the market. In the United States, local, state, and federal governments own trillions of dollars of property.

In a society where property rights are vested in private individuals, how will they exercise their property rights to solve the what, how, and for-whom problems?

The individual owner of private property (whether it be land, a house, a horse, a truck, a wheat crop, or a can of peaches) has the legal freedom (the right) to sell that property at terms mutually agreed upon between the buyer and the seller. Normally, when property is sold, the buyer and seller agree on a dollar price. In some cases, there is an exchange of property on a barter basis; for example, a high-grade stereo may be *bartered* (traded) for a low-grade car. Instead of a dollar price, the price of the car is the stereo, and the price of the stereo is the car.

The legal system protects private-property rights. It protects private property from theft, damage, and unauthorized use and defines where property rights reside. The legal system generally places some restriction on property rights. Private owners of property may not be allowed to use their property in such a manner as to inflict damage on others. For example, the owner of farmland should not be allowed to use dangerous pesticides that may poison the community's water supply; the owner of an oil tanker should not be allowed to dump excess fuel oil near beaches (see Example 2).

Unless such restrictions apply, private property gives the owner the right to use the property to the owner's best advantage and to sell the property at the best price possible. The actions of the owners of private property will be guided by relative prices. The private owner of an oil refinery will use the relative prices of gasoline, fuel oils, and kerosene to determine how much of each petroleum product to refine and will look at the relative prices of imported and domestic crude oil to determine whether to use domestic or imported crude.

The private owner of labor (that is, the individual worker) will look at the relative wage rates in different occupations to determine where to seek employment. The private owner of farmland will look at the relative prices of agricultural products to determine what mix of crops to plant.

Private owners of property are motivated to obtain the best deal possible for themselves; they are motivated by self-interest. Legal protection of private-property rights insures that owners will reap the benefits of decisions that benefit their self-interest and will suffer the consequences of decisions that don't benefit their self-interest.

THE WORKING OF THE PRICE SYSTEM

An economy consists of millions of consumers and hundreds of thousands of enterprises, and virtually every member of society owns some labor,

Example 2

Restrictions on Property Rights

Complete freedom to exercise private-property rights does not exist in any society. Complete freedom could not work. Private property cannot be used in such a way as to injure a neighbor or harm the community. The injured party has the right to petition the legal system to prevent an owner from exercising property rights in this way and to seek compensation for the damage inflicted.

In addition to this commonsense limitation on property rights, there are numerous examples of limitations on private-property rights. Most American cities have zoning laws that restrict the uses to which land can be put. The owner of land in a part of town zoned for residential use only cannot build a factory. Automobile manufacturers are subject to limitations on the exercise of their property rights. They cannot use their plant and equipment to produce any type of car they (or the public) may want; instead, they must satisfy federal safety regulations, mileage standards, and pollution-emission standards.

There are limitations on the use of labor. In the United States, workers are prohibited from selling their labor at less than the minimum wage in covered occupations. A person cannot sell work as a plumber, electrician, pharmacist, barber, dentist, or attorney without first obtaining a license from the state.

---

land, or capital resources. Each participant makes economic decisions to promote his or her self-interest. What coordinates the decisions of all these people and businesses? What prevents the economy from collapsing when all these decisions clash? If all participants are looking out for themselves, will not the end result be chaos? Is it not necessary to have someone or something in charge?

The Invisible Hand

Adam Smith describes how the price system solves economic problems efficiently without conscious direction:

> Every individual endeavors to employ his capital so that its produce may be of greatest value. He generally neither intends to promote the public interest, nor knows how much he is promoting it. He intends only his own security, only his own gain. And he is led by an *invisible hand* to promote an end which was no part of his intention. By pursuing his own interest he frequently promotes that of society more effectively than when he really intends to promote it.[2]

The invisible hand works through the **price system.** A modern economy produces millions of commodities and services, each of which has a money price. These millions of money prices form millions of relative prices that inform buyers and sellers what goods are cheap and what goods are expensive.

*The **price system** is the entire set of millions of relative prices that provides information to buyers and sellers.*

The principal function of the price system is to provide information in an efficient fashion to participants in the economy. Each participant will specialize in price information that is personally relevant. The worker will specialize in prices of those things that affect his or her well-being: wage rates in different occupations, relative prices of various consumer goods, interest rates on home mortgages. The steel-mill manager will specialize in relative prices of inputs used in the mill and in the prices of finished steel products. The investor will specialize in the relative prices of stocks, bonds, and real estate.

No *single person need know all prices to function in daily economic life*. People and enterprises need to know only the prices of those things that are significant to them.

Equilibrium

Each participant makes buying and selling decisions on the basis of relative prices. The family decides how to spend its income; the worker de-

2. Adam Smith, *The Wealth of Nations,* ed. Edwin Cannon (New York: Modern Library, 1937), p. 423.

cides where and how much to work; the factory manager decides what inputs to use and what outputs to produce. Insofar as all these decisions on what to buy and sell are being made individually in isolation, what is to guarantee that there will be enough steel, bananas, foreign cars, domestic help, steel workers, copper, lumber for homes? What is to insure that there will not be too much of one good and too little of another? Is Adam Smith's invisible hand powerful enough to prevent shortage and surplus?

Consider what would happen if U.S. automobile producers, acting on the price information in which they specialize, produce more cars than buyers want to buy *at the price asked by the automobile producers.* The automobile manufacturers will be made aware of this fact, not by a directive from the government, but by the simple fact that excess inventories of unsold cars will pile up. Dealers must pay their bills and cannot live from unsold inventories; therefore, they must sell the cars at lower prices. As the money price of cars falls, its relative price tends to fall, and customers begin to substitute automobiles for European vacations, home computers, or a remodeled kitchen. The decline in the relative price of automobiles signals automobile manufacturers to produce fewer cars. Eventually, a balance between the number of cars people are prepared to buy (the demand) and the number offered for sale (the supply) will be struck, and the price at which the balance is struck is called an **equilibrium price.**

> *The **equilibrium price** of a good or service is that price at which the amount of the good people are prepared to buy equals the amount offered for sale.*

The economy's search for equilibria through changing relative prices is not limited to a single market. The search takes place in all competitive markets simultaneously. If too much is produced, the relative price will fall; if too little is produced, the relative price will rise. As relative prices change, so do buying and selling decisions, and these changes bring markets into equilibrium. The economy is in *general equilibrium* when all markets have achieved equilibrium prices. The mechanics of equilibrium of supply and demand are discussed in Chapter 4.

Checks and Balances

The functioning of the price system is analogous to the system of checks and balances at work in an *ecological system* (the pattern of relationships between plants, animals, and their environment). These checks and balances prevent one species of plant or animal from overrunning the entire area and, in the end, extinguishing itself. Relative prices provide the checks and balances in the economic system. If one product is in oversupply, its relative price will fall; more will be purchased and less will be offered for sale. If one product is in short supply, its relative price will rise; less will be purchased and more will be offered for sale.

Just as human beings can upset nature's delicate balance, the general equilibrium of prices can be upset by interference. For example, governments can regulate and freeze prices or producer organizations may manipulate prices. When are such interventions warranted? When do they do more harm than good? Examples will be studied later in this text.

How, What, and For Whom

The price system solves the *what, how,* and *for whom* problems without conscious direction. No single participant in the economy needs to see the big picture; each participant need only know the relative prices of the goods and services of immediate interest to that person. No single person or governmental organization is required to be concerned about the economy as a whole. The millions of individual economic decisions made daily are coordinated by the price system.

Consider an economy in which all property is privately owned; property rights are vested with the owners of the property; there are no imports or exports; there is no intervention in the setting of prices. Each individual owns certain quantities of resources—land, labor, capital—that are sold or rented to business firms that produce the goods and services people want. Private-property rights are exercised; everything is sold at a price agreeable to the buyer and seller.

What is produced in the economy is determined by *dollar votes* cast by consumers for different goods and services. When consumers choose to buy a particular good or service, they are casting a dollar vote, which communicates their demand for that good or service. If many dollar votes are cast for a particular good, this means that buyers are willing to pay a high relative price for the good. Producers will exercise their property rights to produce a good with a high relative price. If few dollar votes are cast for another commodity, producers will have little incentive to produce that commodity. If consumers shift their dollar votes, producers will shift their production as well. Relative prices signal what actions to take. Relative prices signal to buyers what, where, and when to substitute and signal to producers what to produce.

The *what* problem is solved through the exercise of *consumer sovereignty* in a capitalist system. Consumers, in casting their dollar votes, determine what will be produced. If no dollar votes are cast for a particular product, it will not be produced. If enough dollar votes are cast for a product, it will be produced.

How goods are produced is determined by business firms who seek to utilize their land, labor, and capital resources as economically as possible. Business firms produce those outputs that receive high dollar votes by combining resources in the least costly way. Business firms follow the principle of substitution. If the relative price of land is increased, farmers will use less land and more tractors and labor to work the land more intensively. If the relative price of farm labor increases, farmers will use less labor and more tractors and land. If the relative price of business travel rises, businesses will travel less and use more long-distance telephoning. If the relative price of long-distance calls increases, businesses will telephone less and use more business travel. If business firms fail to reduce their costs through the use of the best available techniques and the best combination of the factors of production, the competition of other firms will drive them out of business.

For whom is determined by the dollar values the market assigns to resources owned by each separate household in the economy. The distribution of income between rich and poor reflects the prices paid for each resource and the distribution of ownership claims to scarce labor, land, and capital. People who own large quantities of land or capital will have a correspondingly large claim on the goods and services produced by the economy; those who are fortunate enough to provide high-priced labor services (doctors, lawyers, gifted athletes) will similarly receive a large share of the total output. At the other extreme, the poor are those who own few resources and furnish low-priced labor services to the market.

THE CIRCULAR FLOW OF ECONOMIC ACTIVITY

The price system, general equilibrium, the invisible hand, and market allocation are all difficult concepts to visualize. The **circular-flow diagram** is designed to illustrate how all these output and input decisions involving millions of consumers, hundreds of thousands of producers, and millions of owners of resources fit together.

*The **circular-flow diagram** summarizes the flows of goods and services from producers to households and the flows of the factors of production from households to business firms.*

Economic activity is circular. Consumers buy goods with the incomes they earn by furnishing labor, land, and capital to the business firms that produce the goods they buy. The dollars that households spend come back to them in the form of income from selling productive factors.

The circular-flow diagram in Figure 2 illustrates the circular flow of economic activity. The flows from households to firms and from firms to households are regulated by two markets: the market for goods and services and the market for the factors of production. The circular-flow diagram consists of two circles. The outer circle shows the *physical flows* of goods and services and of productive factors. The inner circle shows the *flows of money expenditures* on goods and services and on productive factors. The physical flows and the money flows go in opposite directions. When households buy goods and services, physical goods flow to the households, but the sales receipts flow to the business sector. When workers supply labor to business firms, productive factors flow to the business sector, but the wage income flows to the household sector.

For every physical flow in the economy, there is a corresponding financial transaction. To obtain consumer goods, the consumer must pay for

Figure 2
The Circular Flow of Economic Activity

Economic activity is circular. The outside circle describes the flow of physical goods and services and productive factors through the system: business furnishes goods to households who furnish land, labor, and capital to business. The inside circle describes the flow of dollars: households provide dollar sales to business, whose costs become incomes to households. These circles flow in different directions. The triangle gives a pictoral representation of the relationship of the circular flow to the solution to the *what, how,* and *for whom* questions.

---

them. When firms deliver products, they receive sales revenues. When businesses hire labor or rent land, they must pay for them. When individuals supply labor, they receive wages.

There are two pairs of supply and demand transactions in the circular flow: 1) The supply and demand for consumer goods are mediated by the market for goods and services. 2) The supply and demand for factors of production are mediated by the market for the factors of production (see Example 3).

The price system coordinates supplies and demands and insures that they match. Shortages of goods or of factors of production cause relative prices to rise; surpluses cause relative prices to fall. The predictable responses of consumers and producers to changes in relative prices are called the *laws of supply and demand.* Chapter 4 is devoted to the explanation of these laws.

SPECIALIZATION

Suppose a sailor were stranded on a desert island with no other human beings around—a modern Robinson Crusoe. While the sailor would constantly have to make decisions about whether to make fish nets or fish hooks or whether to sleep or break coconuts, the economy of the desert island would lack many features of a modern economic system. The sailor would not be *specialized;* he would have to be a jack-of-all-trades. His consumption would have to be perfectly tailored to his production. Moreover, the sailor would not use *money.* He would still have to solve the problems of *what* and *how.* The *for whom* problem would be easy. Everything he produced would be for himself. He would have to solve *what* and *how* without explicit relative prices, property rights, or markets.

Example 3

The Circular Flow as an Abstraction

The circular-flow diagram abstracts from many real-world considerations. The economy consists of more than goods, factors of production, and dollars flowing between households and businesses. The circular-flow diagram is a simplification of the real world, but it is a useful one. If you are traveling from Los Angeles to New York, you would want a road map that shows only the major interstate highways. Maps of smaller highways would not be of interest to you. The things left out of the circular flow are like the things left out of the map of the interstate highway system.

Government is left out of the circular-flow diagram. To a certain extent, government is like a business firm that provides services to the public like highways, roads, and public education in return for tax dollars. The flow of government services and tax dollars differs from other flows in several respects. There is usually no "market test" of the government service because the public typically does not have the opportunity to reject or buy the government service. Moreover, the government does not typically face competition from other business firms. The government therefore may not be forced to use the most cost-effective methods to produce its services. Government may

therefore solve the how problem differently from private firms.

Markets between firms are also abstracted out of the circular-flow diagram. It is true that the ultimate purpose of the economy is to deliver goods and services to households, and the circular flow does capture these movements. There are, however, a large number of transactions among firms that take place within the business sector. The steel industry supplies steel to the auto industry; the coal industry provides coal to electric power utilities; the lumber industry provides lumber to the construction industry. The economy consists of goods and services in various stages of production or preparation. The goods that are used within the business sector are called *intermediate goods*. They are important because how these intermediate goods are used will determine whether the economy is on its production-possibilities frontier.

The circular-flow diagram assumes a matching of what businesses *as a whole* want to sell with what consumers *as a whole* want to buy. We have shown that the price system balances the supplies and demands for individual products, but can it do this in the aggregate? This is one of the most important issues in the study of macroeconomics.

In the modern economy, it is somewhat unsettling to think about the degree to which people are specialized. The consumption of a typical household consists of thousands of articles; yet the principal breadwinner of the household may do nothing but align suspension components on an automobile production line. In short, everyone in our economy (except hermits) is dependent on the efforts of others. We produce one or two things; we consume many things.

Specialization obviously gives rise to exchange. Indeed, the exchange of one thing for another thing is the reverse side of the coin of specialization. If people consumed only those things that they produced, there would be no trade with anybody else and there would be no need for money. Money, trade, exchange, and specialization are all characteristics of a complicated economy.

Increased productivity was defined in Chapter 2 as the production of more output from the same amount of productive resources. We noted that Adam Smith began the *Wealth of Nations* with the observation that specialization is a basic source of productivity improvements. The reorganization of an acre of land, a tractor, and a hired hand to produce 75 bushels rather than the 50 bushels previously produced is a productivity advance. If freight transportation is organized so that trucks are utilized on return trips (rather than coming back empty), truck/driver combinations can haul more goods, and their productivity increases. In short, improving productivity is getting more from what's available. Specialization raises the productivity of the economy as well as the incomes of the individuals owning the resources themselves in two ways: first, resources are allocated to their best occupation or usage; second, the division of labor exploits economies of large-scale production.

Here are some examples:

1. A high level of intelligence is required to become a good lawyer or a good surgeon. It is better for intelligent people with good verbal skills to become lawyers and those with quick hands to become surgeons than vice versa. It is likewise better for those people who are talkative to be disk jockeys or sales representatives while silent, introverted people are better off in occupations such as computer programming, farming, or automobile repairing that do not require outgoing personalities.

2. Corn requires more moisture than wheat. It is better to produce wheat in Kansas's relatively dry farmland and to use Iowa's relatively wet farmland for corn. More wheat and corn can be grown if Kansas produces wheat and if Iowa produces corn than if both states produce both products.

Specialization gives rise to exchange. Lawyers must hire surgeons; surgeons must hire lawyers. Kansas and Iowa exchange wheat and corn.

Specialization means that people will produce more of particular goods than they consume and that these "surpluses" will be exchanged for the goods that they want.

The Law of Comparative Advantage

One reason for specialization is that people, land, and capital all come in different varieties. Some people are agile seven-footers, others are small and slow; some are fast-talkers, others scarcely utter a word. Some people take easily to math and computers; others are frightened by numbers and technology. Some people have quick hands; others are clumsy. Some land is moist; other land is dry. Some land is hilly; other land is flat. Some land is covered with forests; other land is populated only with mesquite bushes. Capital is different too. Some machines can move large quantities of earth; others can lift heavy loads; others can perform precision metal work; others can heat metals to high temperatures.

Because the factors of production have different characteristics and qualities, specialization offers opportunities for productivity advances.

Economists like to refer to the best employment of a resource as its *comparative advantage*. The agile seven-footer has a comparative advantage in basketball; the fast-talker can become a sales representative; the math whiz can become a computer specialist; the dextrous person might have a comparative advantage in operating a complicated machine tool. Land with high moisture content is best used in corn production; land with a relatively low moisture content is best used in wheat production. Earth-moving machinery can be used in road building: heavy-lifting equipment can be used in construction; precision tools can be used in aircraft manufacturing. Each resource has some comparative advantage.

The price system ensures that the factors of production will be used to exploit their special characteristics and skills. The Kansas farmer will make more money by growing wheat; the Iowa farmer will make more money growing corn. The agile seven-footer will make more money playing professional basketball than professional soccer. The extroverted fast-talker will earn more money as a sales representative than as a computer programmer. The person with quick hands will make more money as a surgeon than as a lawyer. The owner of the earth-moving equipment will make more money using it in roadbuilding; the owner of the heavy-lifting equipment will earn more by using it in construction. All owners of labor, land, and capital resources have to do is to use their resources in such a way as to make the most money possible, and specialization will follow naturally.

Is this an oversimplification? What about the people who have both quick minds and quick hands, the math whiz with good verbal skills, the equipment that can move large amounts of earth and lift heavy weights, or the farm land that appears suited to growing both wheat and corn? Are not some people poor at just about everything in the sense that at every task they are less efficient than other people?

In 1817, the English economist, David Ricardo, who made millions of dollars from shrewd investments, formulated the **law of comparative advantage.**

*The **law of comparative advantage** states that it is better for people to specialize in those* *activities in which their advantage over other people is greatest or in which their disadvantages compared to others are the smallest.*

The easiest way to see this principle at work is to examine two extreme cases. Suppose that you can do any and every job better than anyone else. What would you as such a superior person do? You would not want to be a jack-of-all-trades because it is likely that your *margin* of superiority will be greater in one occupation than in another. The job in which your margin of superiority over others is *the greatest* is the job you will do because it will give you the highest income.

Now examine the other extreme. Suppose there is no person in the community to whom you are superior in *any job;* you are less productive than any other person in the society in every occupation. What would you do in such an unfortunate situation? The job in which your disadvantage compared to others is the smallest would be the job that maximizes your income.

A mediocre computer programmer could possibly be the best clerk in the local supermarket. The clerks in the local supermarket may not be able to stock shelves and work a cash register as well as the computer programmer, but they have a *comparative advantage* in that occupation. An attorney may be the fastest typist in town, yet the attorney is better off preparing deeds than typing deeds. An engineering major may have verbal skills that exceed those of an English major, but his or her comparative advantage is in engineering (see Example 4).

A simple numerical example of comparative advantage will illustrate the principle in a more concrete fashion. Imagine two people, Jack and Jill, both of whom can mow lawns and type. We assume that Jack and Jill do not really care whether they type or mow lawns. Jack can type 20 pages a day or mow 2 lawns a day. Jill, on the other hand, can type 50 pages a day or mow 8 lawns a day (see Table 2). Jill is clearly more efficient in absolute terms at both tasks than Jack; she can type 250 percent (50 ÷ 20) as fast and can mow lawns 400 percent (8 ÷ 2) as fast as Jack.

Now what should Jack and Jill do? To answer this question, we must first determine the (rela-

Table 2

Computing Comparative Advantage

	Lawns per Day	Pages per Day	Opportunity Cost of Lawn Mowing (in pages)
Jack	2	20	10 pages (20 ÷ 2)
Jill	8	50	6.25 pages (50 ÷ 8)

This table illustrates the law of comparative advantage. Jill is more efficient than Jack in both typing and mowing. She can type 250 percent faster than Jack, but she can mow 400 percent faster. Jill has an absolute advantage in both lawn mowing and typing but a comparative advantage in lawn mowing. Jill will specialize in lawn mowing; Jack will specialize in typing. Note that both Jack and Jill follow the rule of specializing in that activity that has the lowest opportunity cost. Jack's opportunity cost of mowing is 10 pages; Jill's equals 6.25 pages.

tive) prices of mowing lawns and typing. Suppose typing earns $2 a page and mowing lawns pays $16 per lawn. If Jack mows lawns all day, his income would be $32 (= $16 × 2 lawns) per day; typing would earn Jack $40 (= $2 × 20 pages) per day. Thus Jack would wish to type. Jill, on the other hand, could earn $128 mowing lawns (= $16 × 8 lawns) or $100 typing ($2 × 50 pages). Thus Jill would prefer to mow lawns.

Jill has a comparative advantage in mowing lawns; Jack has a comparative advantage in typing. While Jill is better than Jack in all activities, her *greatest* advantage over Jack is in mowing lawns (she is 4 times as fast). In typing, Jill is only 2.5 times as fast. Jack's *least* disadvantage is in typing; thus Jack prefers to be a typist.

Notice that Jill will earn $128 daily mowing lawns and Jack will earn $40 a day typing. Jill's superior productivity is reflected in higher earnings. Notice that Jack in effect competes with Jill in typing by charging a lower price per unit of his time. If there are 8 hours to the work day, Jill is earning a wage of $16 per hour ($16 = $128 ÷ 8 hours) and Jack is earning only $5 an hour ($5 = $40 ÷ 8 hours). Thus Jill's hourly wage is slightly more than 3 times Jack's hourly wage. Jack's lower rate allows him to compete with Jill in typing: she is 2.5 times as efficient as a typist, but her wage is more than 3 times as high—which in the marketplace offsets her absolute advantage in typing.

Example   4

Applications of the Law of Comparative Advantage

The law of comparative advantage explains patterns of specialization both within a country and among countries. It also explains why goods will not always be produced by the "best" producer. The fastest typist may be a lawyer, the best checkout clerk may be a skilled computer programmer.

The law of comparative advantage explains a wide variety of specialization patterns that would otherwise be difficult to explain. Here are three examples.

1. *GRE Exams:* The GRE (Graduate Record Exam) is an examination for students who wish to enter graduate school. It consists of two parts: a verbal exam to test verbal ability and a quantitative exam to test math ability. During the 1975–1980 period, physics majors recorded the higher scores on the verbal exam—higher than speech majors. Why would the student who appears to be better qualified for graduate study in speech choose a career in physics?

The law of comparative advantage explains this puzzling phenomenon: Although physics majors on average have an *absolute advantage* in both physics and English (they score higher on both the verbal and quantitative GREs), they have a strong *comparative advantage* in physics. On the GRE, they score 19 percent higher than speech majors on the verbal exam, but they score 55 percent higher than speech majors on the quantitative exam. The physics major is like Jill in our numerical example; both the physics major and Jill are correct in their choice of specialization.

2. *Tobacco Growing in New England:* New England is a region poorly suited to agriculture. It is hilly, rocky, heavily wooded, and cold in the winter. New England seems an unlikely place for tobacco production, which requires a warm climate and rich, well-drained soil. Yet one of the agricultural crops of Massachusetts and Connecticut is tobacco. Why is tobacco grown in New England? Is the law of comparative advantage being violated?

Even California land would be better suited to tobacco production; an acre of land in California

---

The law of comparative advantage is nothing more than the principle that people should engage in those activities where their opportunity costs are lower than others (see Table 2).

To mow one lawn, Jack must sacrifice 10 pages of typing. Jack's opportunity cost of lawns equals 10 pages of typing. To mow one lawn, Jill must sacrifice 6.25 pages (50 ÷ 8). Jill mows lawns because her opportunity cost of lawn mowing is lower than Jack's.

Economies of Large-Scale Production

If all people were the same, if all land were identical, and if all capital were the same, would there still be specialization? Even if all people in an automobile-manufacturing plant were identical, it would still be better to have one person install the engine, another bolt down the engine, and so on in an assembly line. Individuals who focus on one task can learn their jobs better and don't waste time switching from job to job. Even if all agricultural land were identical, it would still be better to plant one farm with corn, another with wheat, and so on, than to plant smaller strips of corn and wheat on single farms because of the economies of large-scale production.

Money

Money is necessary because people are specialized and do not produce everything they need without any surpluses. Money is useful in an *exchange economy*—that is, an economy where people are specialized—because it reduces the cost of transacting with others. *Barter* is a system of exchange where products are exchanged for other products rather than for money. In barter, for example, it would be necessary for barefoot bakers to meet or exchange with hungry shoemakers. In other words, a successful barter deal requires that the two traders have matching wants. In barter, successful trades require a double coincidence of wants.

would yield much more tobacco than in New England. But New England produces tobacco, while California does not. The law of comparative advantage provides the explanation. Although California has an absolute advantage in tobacco production over New England, it has a much larger absolute advantage in alternative uses of the land (growing commercial vegetables and fruits). The alternative uses of rural New England land are limited (it is difficult to grow other crops; the land is not suited to commercial development); therefore, New England has a comparative advantage in tobacco. Stated in terms of opportunity costs: tobacco is grown in rural New England because the opportunity cost is relatively low.

3. The *Manufacture of Singer Sewing Machines in Taiwan:* The Singer Company, a U.S. company established by Isaac Singer in 1851, now manufactures many of its sewing machines in Taiwan—even though American Singer employees can produce more sewing machines per hour than their Asian counterparts. Why then did Singer shift sewing-machine manufacturing to Asia? The answer is that the American worker has a much larger productivity advantage in high-technology manufacturing, such as high-speed computers and jet aircraft. The American Singer worker may be 10 percent more productive than a Taiwanese counterpart, while the American IBM employee may be, say, 50 percent more productive than the Singer employee. Because Taiwan, on the other hand, lacks the capital resources and know-how to produce high-technology computers, the productivity of a Taiwanese worker in computer manufacturing would be less than in sewing-machine manufacturing. As in the numerical example, the American worker's superior productivity would be reflected in higher earnings, and the Taiwanese worker would compete by working at lower wages, reflecting lower productivity. The opportunity cost of an American worker producing sewing machines is high; the opportunity cost of a Taiwanese worker producing sewing machines is low.

Money is useful precisely because double coincidences of wants are rare. Money enables any person to trade with anyone else in a complicated economy. The form money takes differs from society to society. Money in a simple society will be quite different from money in a complicated society. In simple societies, things like fish hooks, sharks' teeth, beads, or cows have been used as money. In modern societies, money is issued and regulated by government, and money may (gold coins) or may not (paper money) have an intrinsic value of its own.

Money is anything that is widely accepted in exchange for goods and services and that can be used for paying debts and taxes.

PROVIDING FOR THE FUTURE

Let us return to the shipwrecked sailor. Although he would not specialize, he would at least share a common problem with modern economies: how to provide for the future. In the sailor's case, he would be confronted with a clear choice of eating more today versus eating more tomorrow. If the water were clear, he could wade out and, with patient effort, catch fish with his bare hands. He may be successful in catching enough fish to survive. However, if the sailor were to devote a few days to making a fishing net from vines, he would be able to increase his catch and reduce his effort—but at the sacrifice of having less to eat for three days. Making a net to catch the fish is an example of **roundabout production** or the production of **intermediate goods.**

Roundabout Production

Roundabout production is the production of goods that do not immediately meet consumption needs. Goods that are used to produce other goods are called intermediate goods.

There can be many stages of roundabout production. The good can be used directly to produce consumer goods. It can produce a good that produces another good that assists in the production of consumer goods, and so on.

Roundabout production means that producers are dependent on things produced in the past for the things that are produced today. In modern economies, the degree of roundabout production is striking. The wheat harvested today requires a harvesting machine produced in the past; the bread produced today is baked in ovens that were produced in the past; the shirt produced today is manufactured on a sewing machine produced in the past.

The responsibility for producing the capital goods that enable society to produce more in the future is left to the price system. Households set aside some of their income in the form of savings. Households save so that they can consume more tomorrow. They accumulate funds in savings accounts and retirement programs; they buy stocks, bonds, and life-insurance policies. How do their savings find their way into productive investments? Businesses borrow from financial institutions, sell bonds, and issue stock; they use the proceeds to build plants, to buy capital equipment, and to build up their inventories.

Interest Rates

Societies must refrain from consumption today to build capital goods. Households must sacrifice consumption today to save, but by saving the household will increase its consumption in the future. The sacrifice of current consumption is the cost of saving. The benefit of saving is that **interest** will be earned on savings. The higher the interest rate, the greater the inducement to save. The rate of interest acts not only as an inducement to save; it also signals to businesses whether they should borrow for investment.

Interest is the price of credit, usually a percentage of the amount borrowed.

Like any other price, the interest rate provides a *balance*—in this case balancing the amount people are willing to save with the amount of savings businesses want to borrow for investment. If the interest rate is low, businesses will clamor for the savings of individuals because they find it

cheap to add to their capital stock. However, when the interest rate is low, few people will be willing to save. The reverse is true at high interest rates. Few businesses will want to invest, but households will be quite willing to save.

The interest rate balances the amount of savings offered by households with the amount of investment businesses wish to undertake. The price system, operating through the interest rate, solves the **what** **problem** *of how to balance present and future consumption.*

How interest rates are determined is much more complicated than this simplified story. Interest rate determination will be examined in later chapters.

Nominal and Real Rates of Interest

So far we have been discussing the **nominal rate of interest**.

The **nominal rate of interest** *is the rate of interest expressed in terms of today's dollars.*

At a nominal interest rate of 10 percent, $100 not spent today will yield $110 that can be spent one year from today. A nominal interest rate of 5 percent means that $100 not spent today will yield only $105 that can be spent one year from today. Because lenders and borrowers are interested in how many goods and services can be purchased with money to be received in the future, they will consider both nominal interest rates and the *general rate of change of money prices*.

Suppose that the nominal rate of interest is 10 percent and that prices are rising at 5 percent per year. The *rate of inflation* measures the rate of increase in prices in general (a more exact definition of inflation will be provided in later chapters). In this case, a person lending $100 now will have $110 in one year. But $110 in one year buys only $105 worth of tomorrow's goods (approximately) because of generally rising prices (inflation). Because the $100 loaned today in reality buys only $105 worth of tomorrow's goods, the **real rate of interest** is 5 percent.

*The **real rate of interest** equals the nominal rate of interest minus the annual rate of inflation.*

It is important to distinguish between the *actual* real interest rate that is earned over a particular year and the real interest rate that is anticipated. No one knows for sure in advance what the rate of inflation will be. Therefore, no one will know in advance what the real rate of interest will be. When people borrow or lend money, they must make their best estimate of what the real rate of interest will be.

Logic tells us the general relationship between nominal interest rates and the rate of inflation. As the rate of inflation increases, people will be less willing to save at prevailing interest rates because rising prices reduce the purchasing power of tomorrow's income. Borrowers, on the other hand, will be more anxious to borrow as inflation increases. These two forces tend to drive up nominal interest rates as the rate of inflation increases.

Decisions about providing for the future are guided by what people expect the *real* rate of interest to be in the immediate future. If the real interest rate is expected to be high, people will be more willing to refrain from consumption now; they will save for the future. If the real interest rate is expected to be low, businesses will be anxious to borrow for investment purposes. Because the future is uncertain (it is difficult to know what the inflation rate will be), lenders and borrowers may guess wrong about the real rate of interest, but it nevertheless serves as a guide to saving and investment decisions.

Throughout much of the 1970s, real interest rates were negative (see Figure 3). A negative real rate of interest means that the annual inflation rate is greater than the nominal interest rate. It would not be a good idea to put money into a savings account at 6 percent interest when the annual inflation rate is 10 percent if the purpose of saving is to consume more in the future. Saving under these circumstances actually reduces one's ability to purchase goods in the future. One would be better off buying now or borrowing. If the real interest rate is negative, one can borrow to buy homes, TV sets, computers, machinery, or automobiles at, say, 8 percent and then pay back the loan in dollars that are worth 10 percent less in

Figure 3
Nominal and Real Interest Rates, United States, 1960–1980

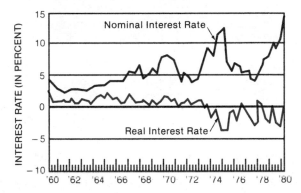

The real rate of interest equals the nominal interest rate minus the annual rate of inflation. As this figure shows, sometimes real and nominal interest rates move together; sometimes they move in opposite directions. Real interest rates can even be negative when the annual inflation rate exceeds the nominal interest rate.

Source: Mellon Bank.

one year's time, more than 20 percent less in two years' time, and so on.

LIMITS OF THE INVISIBLE HAND

This chapter has emphasized the virtues of resource allocation through the price system. The price system solves the problems of *what, how,* and *for whom* without centralized direction. It balances the actions of millions of consumers and thousands of producers, and it even solves the difficult problem of providing for the future. The price system has great strength, but it has weaknesses as well. These weaknesses must be examined to determine the costs and benefits of interfering with the workings of the price system.

Income Distribution

There is no guarantee that resource allocation through the price system will solve the *for whom* problem in such a way as to satisfy the ethical beliefs of members of society. Some people believe that income should be distributed fairly

Example 5

The Price System at Work

This chapter has surveyed how the price system solves the what, how, and for-whom problems in a capitalistic economy. Each of the following examples illustrates the principle that through voluntary exchange, the price system can coordinate the activities of many millions of people without centralized direction.

There are 12 million people living in New York city, each of whom is concerned with an infinitesimally small part of getting that city's work done. Each person is concerned—for the most part—with making a living. Imagine the numbers of trucks, airplanes, and trains moving people and goods to the right places at the right times. The logistics of these movements that keep the city going and prevent everyone from starving are enormously complicated (think of New York's well-publicized garbage-removal problems). Yet no single person or bureaucracy is in charge of the department-for-making-sure-the-city-does-not-starve. The city works by the millions of decentralized decisions of individuals responding to their own cost-benefit calculations. The price system and supply-demand coordination works so well that no one loses any sleep over the terrifying prospect of complete breakdown—no one even gives it a thought.

This classic example also shows us how something that works smoothly often goes unnoticed. Adam Smith's term, the *invisible hand,* is an apt description.

Nobel prize-winning economist Milton Friedman relates the story called, "I, Pencil: My Family Tree as Told to Leonard E. Read," in which the pencil makes the startling announcement: *"not a single person . . . knows how to make me."* If one thinks about what it takes to make a pencil—the trees that produce the wood, the saws that fell the trees, the steel to make the saws, the engines to run the saws, the hemp to make the ropes that are necessary to tie down the logs, the training of loggers, the mining of graphite in Sri Lanka for the lead, the mining of zinc and copper for making the bit of metal holding the eraser, and the rape seed oil from the Dutch East Indies used in the eraser—it is clear that the pencil is correct. No one single person knows how to make a modern pencil. The decisions of the thousands upon thousands of people involved are coordinated through the price system; that all these activities have made it possible for you to go to the bookstore and buy a pencil for, say, a mere $0.25 boggles the mind.

---

evenly; others believe that the gap between rich and poor should be large. Many believe that it is unfair for people to be rich just because they were lucky enough to inherit wealth or intelligence.

Economics can shed little light on what is a "good" or "fair" solution to the *for whom* problem, because such decisions require personal value judgments. Economics is broad enough to accommodate virtually all views on the subject of income distribution. Judgments about income distribution are in the realm of normative economics.

Nevertheless, positive economics can make a contribution to the question of income distribution. Economists can indicate what may happen to efficiency or economic growth if the income distribution is changed, but they cannot make any scientific statements about the desirability of the change in the income distribution.

The Role of Government

Another weakness of the price system is that it cannot supply certain goods—called *public goods*—that are necessary to society. Public goods include defense, the legal system, highways, and public education. In the case of private goods, there is an intimate link between costs and benefits: The one who buys a car enjoys the benefits of the car; the one who buys a loaf of bread eats that loaf. Public goods, on the other hand, are financed not by the dollar votes of consumers but by the imposition of taxes. In most cases, the benefits each individual derives from public goods will not be known. Moreover, it is difficult to prevent nonpayers from enjoying the benefits of public goods. Even if someone does not pay taxes, the national defense establishment protects that person from enemy attack just as well as it protects the payers.

The price system, therefore, breaks down in failing to provide public goods. If private individuals were left with the choice of buying and selling public goods, few public goods would be produced. Yet society must have public goods to survive.

Monopoly

The invisible hand may not function well when a single person or single group gains control over the supply of a particular commodity. What makes Adam Smith's invisible hand work so well is that individual buyers and sellers compete with one another; no single buyer or seller has control over the price. The problem with *monopoly*—a single seller with considerable control over the price—is that the monopolist can hold back the amount of goods, drive up the price, and enjoy large profits. While the monopolist would benefit from such actions, the buyer would not. Monopoly threatens the smooth functioning of the invisible hand described in this chapter.

Macroeconomic Instability

The invisible hand may solve the economic problem of scarcity but may provide a level of overall economic activity that is unstable. It is a historical fact that capitalist economies have been subject to fluctuations in output, employment, and prices—called *business cycles*—and that these fluctuations have been costly to capitalist societies.

The study of the causes of the instability of capitalism was pioneered by John Maynard Keynes during the Great Depression of the 1930s, and this theme remains a principal concern of macroeconomics.

This chapter has described in general terms how scarce resources are allocated by the price system and has explained the organization of property rights. Equilibrium prices are an invisible hand that coordinates the decisions of many different persons. The next chapter examines the detailed workings of supply and demand in an individual market and answers the questions: How is the equilibrium price set? What causes equilibrium prices to increase or decrease?

Summary

1. Relative prices guide the economic decisions of individuals and businesses. They signal to buyers and sellers what substitutions to make.

2. The principle of substitution states that no single good is irreplaceable. Users substitute one good for another in response to changes in relative prices.

3. Property can be owned by private persons, by the state, or by combinations of the two. In capitalist societies, property is owned primarily by private individuals, who are permitted to exercise property rights over the use and sale of their property subject to the restriction that such exercise does not injure other people. Socialist societies are characterized by collective ownership of property.

4. The private decisions of the millions of consumers and producers are coordinated by the price system. The "invisible hand" analogy, originated by Adam Smith in 1776, describes how a capitalist system can allow individuals to pursue their self-interest and yet provide an orderly, efficient economic system that functions without centralized direction. The price system balances supplies and demands for individual products. If too much of a product is produced, its relative price will fall. If too little of a product is produced, its relative price will rise. The balance of supply and demand is called an equilibrium. The what problem is solved by dollar votes. Consumers determine what will be produced. The how problem is solved by individual producers. Competition among producers will encourage them to combine resource inputs efficiently. The solution of the for-whom problem is determined by a) who owns productive resources and b) what the relative prices of resources are.

5. The circular-flow diagram summarizes the flows of goods and services from producers

to households and the flows of factors of production from households to producers.

6. Specialization is responsible for productivity improvements. Specialization occurs because of the differences among people, land, and capital and because of the economies of large-scale production. The law of comparative advantage states that the factors of production will specialize in those activities in which their advantage is greatest or in which their disadvantages are smallest. Money enables a person to trade with anyone else in a complicated economy. The most basic characteristic of money is that it is widely accepted in exchange.

7. The price system provides for the future by allowing people to compare costs now with benefits that will accrue in the future. The interest rate balances the amount of savings offered with the amount of investment businesses wish to undertake. Intertemporal choices are based upon real rates of interest rather than nominal rates of interest. The real interest rate equals the nominal interest rate minus the inflation rate.

8. The invisible hand can not solve the problems of income distribution, public goods, monopoly, or macroeconomic instability.

Key Terms

money price
relative price
principle of substitution
property rights
socialist society
capitalist society
price system
equilibrium price
circular-flow diagram
law of comparative advantage
money
roundabout production
intermediate goods
interest
nominal rate of interest
real rate of interest

Questions and Problems

1. Is the nominal interest rate a relative price or a money price? Is the real rate of interest a money price or a relative price? Discuss your answer.

2. "The principle of substitution states that virtually all goods have substitutes, but we all know that there are no substitutes for telephone service." Comment on this statement.

3. If you own an automobile, what property rights do you have? What restrictions are placed upon these property rights?

4. Explain why you can usually find the items you want at a grocery store without having ordered the goods in advance.

5. Assume that you have grown 50 watermelons in your backyard garden. You set up a stand alongside the highway and price them at $15 each. What do you think will happen and what will you do?

6. What determines your claim on the goods and services produced by the economy?

7. Why does your income represent someone else's costs, and why do your purchases represent someone else's sales?

8. Explain why there would be no exchange if there were no specialization, and why there would be no specialization if exchange were impossible.

9. Why is barter an inefficient means of exchange?

10. Explain why wheat is grown in Kansas while cotton is grown in Alabama.

11. Bill can prepare 50 hamburgers per hour and wait on 25 tables per hour. Mike can prepare 20 hamburgers per hour and wait on 15 tables per hour. If Bill and Mike were to open a hamburger stand, who would be the cook? Who the waiter? Would Bill do both?

12. Why would private industry find it difficult to organize national defense? How would they charge each citizen for national defense?

13. In 1974 consumer prices rose by 11 percent, and the interest rate on industrial bonds was 8.6 percent. What was the actual real interest rate?

4

The Mechanics of Supply and Demand

Chapter Preview

Chapter 3 described how capitalist economies solve the what, how, and for-whom problems by market allocation that is guided by the price system. Property is owned predominantly by private individuals who exercise private-property rights. The actions of millions of buyers and sellers are coordinated by an invisible hand. No single buyer or seller is required to know more than the prices of those things of immediate interest to that person. Each participant in the economy is motivated by self-interest. Relative prices signal to buyers and sellers what they should do. If relative prices of some goods are rising, other goods will be substituted by buyers; sellers will tend to offer more for sale. If too much of a good is produced, its

relative price will fall. If too little is produced, its relative price will rise. Through these changes in relative prices, the amounts of goods buyers are prepared to buy are brought into balance with the amounts of goods sellers are prepared to sell.

Chapter 3 provided a grand overview of how the price system works without getting into actual mechanics. This chapter will explain the workings of supply and demand and will define such terms as *demand, supply, shortage, surplus,* and *equilibrium* more exactly.

This chapter describes *how prices are determined by supply and demand*. There is a famous quip that if you teach a parrot the phrase "supply and demand," you will create a learned economist. This joke, while entertaining, does not do justice to the complexity and value of supply-and-demand analysis. An economist needs to know more than the parrot, just as the medical doctor must know more than the prescription: "Take two aspirin and call me in the morning."

The following statements (with certain details changed) were taken from two respected newspapers:

> Projections of supplies and demands reveal that there will be a large surplus of medical doctors by the end of the 1980s. The supply of M.D.s will exceed demand generally, but surpluses will be greatest in particular specialties.

> The state agriculture office reports that warm weather and sufficient moisture have produced a plentiful supply of lettuce this year. However, lettuce prices are not expected to drop because consumers usually increase their demand for lettuce when prices fall. The demand increase will offset the supply increase, so homemakers should not expect surpluses of lettuce this year.

Both of these statements may appear reasonable; they use the language of supply and demand. However, they are misleading because they confuse different supply and demand concepts; they are incorrect because they misuse the terms *supply* and *demand*.

WHAT IS A MARKET?

To develop the mechanics of supply and demand, we must narrow our vision to the study of how a *single market* works. In each **market,** buyers and sellers are guided by the price system in their buying and selling decisions.

*A **market** is an established arrangement by which buyers and sellers come together to exchange particular goods or services.*

Types of Markets

A retail store, a gas station, a farmers' market, real estate firms, the New York Stock Exchange (where stocks are bought and sold), Chicago commodity markets (where livestock, grains, and metals are traded), auctions of works of art, gold markets in London, Frankfurt, and Zurich, labor exchanges, university placement offices, and hundreds of other specialized arrangements are all markets. Markets are arrangements for bringing together buyers and sellers of a particular good or service. The New York Stock Exchange brings together by means of modern telecommunications the buyers and sellers of corporate stock. Sothebys auction in London brings together the sellers and buyers of rare works of art. The Rotterdam oil market brings together buyers and sellers of crude oil not under long-term contracts. The university placement office brings university graduates together with potential employers. The gas station brings together the buyers and sellers of gasoline. In some markets, the buyers and sellers confront each other face-to-face (roadside farm markets). In other markets, the buyer never sees the seller (the Chicago commodity markets).

Determinants of the Form of the Market

The actual form a particular market takes depends on the type of good or service being sold and on the costs of transporting the good from the point of production to the point of sale. Some markets are local (bringing together local buyers and sellers); others are national (bringing together the buyers and sellers in all parts of the nation); others are international (bringing together the buyers and sellers in all parts of the world). Real estate is traded in local markets; houses and buildings cannot be shipped from one place to another (except at great expense). College textbooks are usually exchanged in a national market. The New York Stock Exchange, the various gold exchanges, and the Chicago commodity exchanges are markets in which buyers and sellers from around the world participate.

The study of marketing arrangements is a subject area in which economics and business administration overlap. Both disciplines presume that markets develop in an orderly fashion and teach that the market form that eventually evolves will be the one that keeps the cost of delivery (or marketing cost) to a minimum.

Perfect Markets

The real world consists of an almost infinite variety of markets. This chapter deals with a very special type of market called a **perfect** (or **perfectly competitive**) **market.**

*A **perfect** (or **perfectly competitive**) **market** has the following characteristics: 1) The product's price is uniform throughout the market. 2) Buyers and sellers have perfect information about price and the product's quality. 3) There are a large number of buyers and sellers. 4) No single buyer or seller is large enough to change the price.*

The principal characteristic of a perfectly competitive market is that buyers and sellers face so much competition that no person or group has any control over the price.

The markets where most people buy and sell goods are not perfect. Buyers and sellers may not be perfectly informed about prices and qualities. Two homemakers pay different prices in adjacent grocery stores for the same national brand of cookies. Houses that are virtually identical sell at different prices. Chemically equivalent brand-name and generic drugs sell at different prices. Italy and West Germany pay different prices for the same grade of imported crude oil. Two secretaries with the same qualifications, responsibilities, and disposition in the same company earn different wages. AT&T, General Motors, and Saudi Arabia exercise some control over the prices they charge. Large buyers exercise some control over the prices they pay.

Many products, however, are exchanged in perfect markets. Stocks and bonds and commodities such as wheat, silver, copper, gold, foreign currencies, oats, pork bellies, soybeans, lumber, cotton, orange juice, cattle, cocoa, and platinum are bought and sold in perfect markets. Private investors, mutual funds, commercial banks, industrial buyers of commodities, and agricultural brokers participate in these markets. Although markets like the local grocery store, the dry cleaner, the gas station, the college placement office, or the roadside stand are not perfect, many of them function in a way that approximates perfect markets. In this respect, the behavior of perfect markets serves as a useful guide to the way many real-world markets function. The perfect market is a valuable starting point for examining economic behavior.

DEMAND

Economics is based upon the principle of *unlimited wants*. Collectively, we all want more than the economy can provide, and scarcity is the consequence of the mismatch between wants and the ability of the economy to meet these wants.

The term *wants* refers to the goods and services that consumers would claim if they were given away free. *The list of goods consumers "want" is quite different from the list of goods they* **demand.** What consumers are actually prepared to buy depends upon a variety of factors, which will be studied in this chapter.

*The **demand** for a good or service is the relationship between the amount of the good or service consumers are prepared to buy at a given price and the price of the good or service.*

The Law of Demand

A fundamental law of economics is the **law of demand.**

*The **law of demand** states that there is a negative (or inverse) relationship between the price of a good and quantity demanded, holding other factors constant.*

Thus, if prices are lowered, **quantity demanded** increases, if other factors are held constant. The importance of the *ceteris paribus* ("holding all other factors constant") restriction on the law of demand will become apparent in the course of this discussion.

*The **quantity demanded** is the amount of a good or service consumers are prepared to buy at a given price.*

The basic reason for the law of demand is that as the price of any product goes up, people will tend to find substitutes for that product. If the price of gasoline rises, drivers will cut back on less essential driving, and more people will take the bus, or walk, or ride their bicycles to work. If the price of tea rises, more people will drink coffee, or heavy tea drinkers may cut back one or two cups a day and instead buy a soft drink. The universal and natural tendency is for people who consume or use the goods to *substitute other goods or services* when the price of a good goes up. Higher prices discourage consumption.

When a price rises by enough some people may even stop consuming the good altogether. Thus as the price rises, the number of actual buyers may fall as some people *entirely* switch to other goods.

People also tend to buy less of a good as its price goes up because *they feel poorer*. If a person buys a new car every year for $5,000 (after trade-in), and the price rises to $9,000 (after trade-in), the person would need an extra $4,000 yearly income to maintain the old standard of living. The $4,000 increase in the price of the car is like a cut in income of $4,000.[1]

The law of demand shows that the everyday concept of *need* is not a very useful concept in economics. To "need" something implies that one cannot do without it. When the price of something changes, the law of demand says that quantity demanded will change. Since the word *need* implies an absolute necessity for something, this word is avoided whenever discussing demand.

The relationship between quantity demanded and price is called the *demand curve* or the *demand schedule*. The relationship is negative because of the law of demand. To avoid confusion, we shall henceforth talk about the *demand schedule* when the relationship is in tabular form and about the *demand curve* when the relationship is in graphical form.

The Demand Schedule

Table 1 shows a hypothetical demand schedule for corn. The buyers in the marketplace will demand 20 million bushels of corn per month at the price of $5 per bushel. Should the price of corn be lower—say, $4 per bushel—then the quantity demanded is higher. In this case, the quantity de-

---

1. It is preferable to raise the price of the car by $4000 than to reduce one's income by $4000, because the change in income cannot be avoided; the change in the price of the car can be avoided by spending money elsewhere on the next best alternative.

Table 1
Demand Schedule for Corn

	Price (dollars per bushel)	Quantity Demanded (millions of bushels per month)
a	5	20
b	4	25
c	3	30
d	2	40
e	1	50

manded at the lower price of $4 is 25 million bushels. By continuing to decrease the price, it is possible to induce or coax buyers to purchase more and more corn. Table 1 shows that at the price of $1, quantity demanded will be 50 million bushels. Notice that it is important to state the units of the measurement for both the price and the quantity. In this example, price is in dollars per bushel, and quantity is in millions of bushels per month. The time period, whether it be a minute, a day, a week, a month, or a year, must be specified before the demand schedule is meaningful.

The Demand Curve

The demand schedule of Table 1 can be portrayed graphically (Figure 1) as the demand curve. For demand curves, price is on the vertical axis and quantity demanded is on the horizontal axis. In this demand curve, prices are in dollars per bushel and the quantities are in millions of bushels per month. When price is $5, quantity demanded is 20 million bushels per month (point *a* in Figure 1). Point *b* corresponds to a price of $4 and a quantity of 25 million bushels. When price falls from $5 to $4, quantity demanded rises by 5 million bushels from 20 million to 25 million bushels. The remaining prices and quantities are graphed.

The curve drawn through the points *a* through *e*, labeled *D,* is the demand curve. The demand curve shows how quantity demanded responds to changes in price. Along the demand curve *D,* the price and the quantity are *negatively* related. This means the curve is downward-sloping.

Figure 1
The Demand Curve for Corn

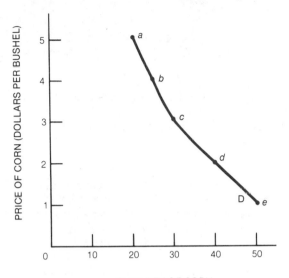

QUANTITY OF CORN
(MILLIONS OF BUSHELS PER MONTH)

Table 1 describes how the quantity of corn demanded responds to the prices of corn, holding all other factors constant. At *a*, when the price of corn *(P)* is $5 per bushel, the quantity demanded *(Q)* is 20 million bushels per month. At *e*, when the price of corn is $1, the quantity demanded is 50 million bushels. The downward-sloping curve *(D)* drawn through these points is the demand curve for corn. Graphically, it shows the amounts of corn consumers would be willing to buy at different prices in the specified time period.

Since the relationship between price and quantity demanded is downward-sloping, the law of demand is sometimes called the **law of downward-sloping demand.**

The demand curve shows that as larger quantities of corn are put on the market, lower prices are required in order to sell that quantity. The price needed to sell 25 million bushels of corn is $4 per bushel. To sell a larger quantity of corn—say, 30 million bushels—a lower price—of $3—is required.

Figure 1 is labeled "The Demand Curve for Corn." But whose demand for corn does it represent? The units of measure are in millions of bushels, so it is definitely not the demand curve of an individual family. It could be the demand curve of all American buyers of corn, or it could be the demand curve of Ralston Purina, a major American buyer of corn. It could even be the world demand curve for corn. The national demand curve for corn is simply the demand curve of all American buyers combined. The world demand curve for corn is the demand curves of all nations added together. Just as one must state the units of measure of prices and quantities, so one must state whose demand curve it is.

Normally, this book will use a **market demand curve.**

The **market demand curve** *is the demand curve of all persons participating in the market for that particular product.*

The *demand curve for corn* therefore refers to all buyers in the corn market. The corn market is essentially a national market or even an international market that brings together all American (or even world) buyers of corn. For example, the demand curve for Hawaiian real estate brings together all buyers of Hawaiian real estate; the demand curve for U.S. automobiles brings together the demand schedules of all private, corporate, and governmental buyers of U.S.-produced automobiles.

Factors That Cause the Demand Curve to Shift

Factors other than the price of the good can change the relationship between price and quantity demanded, causing the demand curve to shift left or right. A demand curve assumes that all these other factors are held constant and shows what would happen to the quantity demanded if *only the price* were to change. In the real world, these other conditions are constantly changing; therefore, it is crucial to understand how changes in factors other than price affect the demand for a good (see Example 1). The nonprice factors that can affect the demand for a good include: 1) the prices of related goods, 2) consumer income, 3) consumer preferences, 4) the number of potential buyers, and 5) expectations.

The Prices of Related Goods. Goods can be related to each other in two ways: Two goods are

Example 1

Factors That Cause a Demand Curve to Shift

Factor	Example
Change in price of substitutes	Increase in price of coffee shifts demand curve for tea to right.
Change in price of complements	Increase in price of coffee shifts demand curve for sugar to left.
Change in income	Increases in income shifts demand curve for automobiles to right.
Change in preference	Judgement that cigarettes are hazardous to health shifts demand curve for cigarettes to left.
Change in number of buyers	Increase in population of City X shifts demand curve for houses in City X to right.
Change in expectations of future prices	Expectation that prices of canned goods will increase substantially over the next year shifts demand curve for canned goods to right.

substitutes if the demand for one rises when the price of the other rises (or when the demand falls when the price of the other falls). Examples of substitutes are: coffee and tea, two brands of soft drinks, stocks and bonds, bacon and sausage, pork and beef, oats and corn, foreign and domestic cars, natural gas and electricity. Some goods are very close substitutes (two different brands of fluoride toothpaste), and others are very distant substitutes (Toyota automobiles and DC-10 aircraft).

*Two goods are **substitutes** if the demand for one rises (falls) when the price of the other rises (falls).*

Two goods are **complements** if increasing the price of one good lowers the demand for the other. Examples of complements are: automobiles and gasoline, food and drink, white dress shirts and neckties, skirts and blouses. When goods are complements there is a tendency for the two goods to be used jointly in order to achieve something more general (for example, automobiles plus gasoline equals transportation). Thus, an increase in the price of one of the goods effectively increases the price of the joint product of the two goods together. Thus an increase in the price of one of the goods will reduce the demand for the other.

*Two goods are **complements** if the demand for one rises (falls) when the price of the other falls (rises).*

Income. It is easy to understand how income influences demand. A fact of economic life is that as incomes rise, people spend more on most—but not all—goods and services.

*The demand for an **inferior good** will fall as income rises.*

To determine what goods are **inferior goods,** a person need only ask, ''What goods would I cut down on or eliminate from my budget as my income goes up?'' For some people, inferior goods might be hamburger, margarine, bus rides, second-hand clothing, day-old bread, or black-and-white TV sets. But most goods are **normal goods.**

*The demand for a **normal good** increases as income rises.*

Preferences. To the economist, the word *preferences* means what people like and dislike without regard to budgetary considerations. One may prefer a 10-bedroom mansion with servants but can only afford a 3-bedroom bungalow. One may prefer a Mercedes-Benz but may drive a

Volkswagen. One may prefer T-bone steaks but may eat hamburgers! Preferences plus budgetary considerations (price and income) determine demand. As preferences change, demand will change. If people learn that walking will increase their lifespan, the demand for walking shoes will increase. Business firms spend enormous sums trying to influence preferences by advertising on television, in newspapers, and in magazines. The goal of advertising is to shift the demand curve for the advertised product to the right.

The Number of Potential Buyers. If more buyers enter a market because of population growth or movements in the population, the demand will rise. The relaxation of trade barriers between two countries may increase the number of buyers. Lowering the legal age for alcoholic-beverage purchases will increase the number of buyers of beer.

Expectations. If people learn that the price of coffee over the next year will rise substantially (for whatever reason), they may decide to stock up on coffee today. During inflationary times, when people find prices of goods going up rapidly, they often start buying up durable goods, such as cars and refrigerators. Thus, the mere expectation of a good's price going up can induce people to buy more of it. Similarly, people can postpone the purchase of things that are expected to get cheaper. For example: during the 1980s home computers grew cheaper and cheaper. Some buyers may well have postponed their purchase of home computers on the expectation that in the future the good could be purchased for an even lower price.

Changes in any of the above factors (except the price of the good itself) will *shift the entire demand curve* for the good. Figure 2 shows the demand curve for white dress shirts. This curve, *D,* is based on a $5 price for neckties (a complement), a $10 price of sport shirts (a substitute), and fixed income, preferences, and number of buyers.

An increase in the price of neckties (a complement for white shirts) from $5 to $7.50 shifts the entire demand curve for white shirts to the left from *D* to *D'* in panel (a). White dress shirts are usually worn with neckties. If neckties increase in price, consumers will buy less of them and will

**Figure 2
Shifts in the Demand Curve: Changes in Demand**

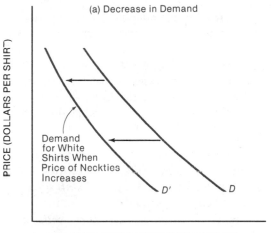

(a) Decrease in Demand

PRICE (DOLLARS PER SHIRT)

Demand for White Shirts When Price of Neckties Increases

D'   *D*

QUANTITY (NUMBER OF WHITE SHIRTS)

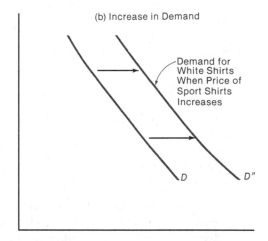

(b) Increase in Demand

PRICE (DOLLARS PER SHIRT)

Demand for White Shirts When Price of Sport Shirts Increases

D   *D"*

QUANTITY (NUMBER OF WHITE SHIRTS)

The demand for white dress shirts depends not only on the price of white dress shirts but also on the price of neckties and the price of sport shirts. When the price of neckties is $5 and the price of sport shirts is $10, the demand curve for white shirts is *D*. If the price of neckties rises to $7.50, holding the price of sport shirts at $10, then at each price for white dress shirts the demand falls. In panel (a), with a higher price of neckties the demand curve shifts to the left and depicts a decrease in demand from *D* to *D'*. In panel (b), keeping the price of neckties at $5 and raising the price of sport shirts to $15 will raise the demand for white shirts. The demand curve will shift rightward to *D"*. A rightward shift depicts an increase in demand, and a leftward shift illustrates a decrease in demand.

substitute less formal shirts for shirts that require neckties. As a result of this substitution, the demand for white dress shirts will decrease, shifting left.

An increase in the price of sports shirts (a substitute for white dress shirts) from $10 to $15 shifts the demand curve for white shirts to the right from D to D'' in panel (b). When the price of sports shirts increases, consumers substitute white dress shirts for sports shirts. As a result of this substitution, the demand for white dress shirts will increase, shifting right.

When the demand curve shifts to the left, **people wish to buy smaller quantities of the good at each price.** *A leftward shift of the demand curve indicates a* **decrease in demand.** *When the demand curve shifts to the right,* **people wish to buy larger quantities of the good at each price.** *A rightward shift of the demand curve indicates an* **increase in demand.**

Demand curves shift to the right or left when factors other than the price of the good change. If consumer income increases, and if white dress shirts are a normal good, demand will increase (D will shift to the right). If preferences change and white dress shirts fall out of fashion, demand will decrease (D will shift to the left). If buyers expect prices of white dress shirts to rise substantially in the future, demand will increase.

A change in **product price only** *will cause a movement along a demand curve. A change in a* **demand-affecting factor other than the price of the good** *(such as a related good's price, income, preferences, expectations, or the number of buyers) will cause the entire demand curve to shift.*

SUPPLY

How much corn the farmer offers for sale depends on the price of corn. Generally speaking, the higher the price, the higher the **quantity supplied.**

*The **quantity supplied** of a good or service is the amount of the good or service offered for sale at a given price.*

The relationship between quantity supplied and price is the **supply.**

*The **supply** of a good or service is the relationship between the amount of a good or service offered for sale at a given price and the price of the good or service.*

This relationship is normally—but not always—positive. A higher price for corn will induce farmers to cultivate fewer soybeans and plant more corn (this substitution occurs in production rather than consumption). A higher price for corn will make farmers more willing to put out a little extra effort to make sure that corn is not wasted during harvesting or to prevent the crop from being harmed by the weather or pests. The fundamental reason for the normally positive relationship between quantity supplied and price is the *law of diminishing returns* (see Chapter 2). The law of diminishing returns states that with other factors of production fixed, the extra output obtained by adding equal increments of a variable factor to the process of production will eventually decline. To produce more of a good under the law of diminishing returns means that as more and more obstacles are encountered, a higher price is required to overcome these obstacles. For example, farmers may find that they have to plant additional corn in areas that are rockier or that the extra harvesting requires more maintenance or more reliance on undependable labor. Whenever fixed factors are present, the productivity of the extra variable factors used to produce more output falls, and the costs of producing each additional unit of output rise.

The Supply Curve

Consider now the normal case of a positive relationship between price and quantity supplied. Table 2 shows a hypothetical supply schedule for corn that is graphed in Figure 3. When the price of corn is $5 per bushel, farmers wish to supply 40 million bushels per month (point *a*). As the price falls to $4, the quantity supplied falls to 35 million bushels (point *b*). Finally, when the price is $1 farmers wish to sell only 10 million bushels (point *e*).

The smooth curve drawn through points *a*

Table 2
Supply Schedule for Corn

	Price (dollars per bushel)	Quantity Supplied (millions of bushels per month)
a	5	40
b	4	35
c	3	30
d	2	20
e	1	10

through *e,* labeled *S,* is the supply curve. It shows how quantity supplied responds to all price variations: *it shows how much farmers offer for sale at each price*. Along the supply curve, the price of corn and the supply of corn are positively related: in order to induce farmers to offer a larger quantity of corn on the market, a higher price is required.

Factors That Cause the Supply Curve to Shift

Just as factors other than the price of the good can change the relationship between price and quantity demanded, nonprice factors can change the relationship between price and quantity supplied, causing the supply curve to shift (see Example 2). The nonprice factors that can cause the supply curve to shift include: 1) the prices of other goods, 2) the prices of relevant resources, 3) technology, 4) the number of sellers, and 5) expectations.

The Prices of Other Goods.   The resources that are used to produce any particular good can almost always be used elsewhere in the economy. Farmland can be used for corn or soybeans; engineers can work on cars or trucks; unskilled workers can pick strawberries or cotton; trains can be used to move coal or cars. As the price of a good rises, resources are naturally attracted away from other goods that use those resources. Hence, the supply of corn will fall if the price of soybeans rises; if the price of cotton rises the supply of strawberries may fall. If the price of trucks rises, the supply of cars may fall. If the price of fuel oil rises, less kerosene may be produced.

Figure 3
The Supply Curve for Corn

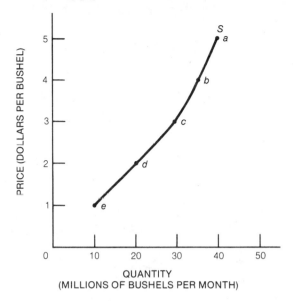

QUANTITY
(MILLIONS OF BUSHELS PER MONTH)

This graph depicts how the quantity of corn supplied responds to the price of corn. In situation *a*, when the price of corn is $5 per bushel, the quantity supplied by farmers is 40 million bushels per month. In the last situation, *e*, when the price is $1 per bushel, the quantity supplied is only 10 million bushels per month. The upward-sloping curve *(S)* drawn through these points is the supply curve of corn.

The Prices of Relevant Resources.   Goods and services require certain resources that must be purchased in resource markets. As these resource prices change, the supply conditions for the goods being produced change. An increase in the price of coffee beans will increase the costs of producing coffee and decrease the amount of coffee that coffee companies wish to sell at each price; an increase in the price of corn land, tractors, harvesters, or irrigation will tend to reduce the supply of corn; an increase in the price of cotton will tend to decrease the supply of cotton dresses; an increase in the price of jet fuel will decrease the supply of commercial aviation at each price.

Technology.   *Technology* is the knowledge that people have about how different things can be produced. If technology improves, more goods can be produced from the same resources. For example, if lobster farmers in Maine learn how to

Factors That Cause a Supply Curve to Shift

Factor	Example
Change in price of another good	Increase in price of corn shifts supply curve of wheat to left.
Change in price of resource	Decrease in wage rate of autoworkers shifts supply curve of autos to right.
Change in technology	Higher corn yields due to genetic engineering shift supply curve of corn to right.
Change in number of sellers	New sellers entering profitable field shift supply curve of product to right.
Change in expectations	Expectation of a much higher price of oil next year shifts supply curve of oil today to left. ■

feed lobsters more cheaply due to a new and cheaper combination of nutritious food, the supply of lobsters at each price will tend to increase. If a firm finds that the assembly line can be speeded up by merely rearranging the order of assembly, the supply of the good will tend to increase. If new oil-recovery procedures are discovered, the supply of oil will increase.

The Number of Sellers. If more sellers enter into the production of a particular good (perhaps because of high profits or in anticipation of high profits), the supply of the good will increase. The lowering of trade barriers may allow foreign sellers to enter the market, increasing the number of sellers.

Expectations. It takes a long time to produce many goods and services. When a farmer plants corn or wheat or soybeans, the prices that are expected to prevail at harvest time are actually more important than the current price. A college student who reads that there are likely to be too few engineers in four years may decide to major in engineering in expectation of a high wage rate. When a business firm decides to establish a plant that may take five years to build, expectations of future business conditions in that industry are crucial to that investment decision.

Changes in each of the above factors (except for the price of the good itself) *will shift the entire supply curve.* Figure 4 shows the supply curve S for corn. The supply curve is based on a $10-per-

bushel price of soybeans and a $2,000 yearly rental on an acre of corn land. If the price of soybeans rises to, say, $15 a bushel, then the supply curve for corn will shift leftward to S' in panel (a) because some land used for corn will be shifted to soybeans. If the rental price of an acre of corn land goes down from $2,000 a year per acre to $1,000 a year, the supply curve will shift to the right—to, say, S'' in panel (b). The reduction in the land rental price lowers the costs of producing a bushel of corn and makes the corn producer willing to supply more corn at the same price as before.

When the supply curve shifts to the left (for whatever reason), producers wish to **sell smaller quantities of the good at each price.** *A leftward shift (as from* S *to* S′ *in Figure 4) indicates a* **decrease in supply.** *When the supply curve shifts to the right,* **producers wish to sell larger quantities at each price.** *This rightward shift (as from* S *to* S″ *in Figure 4) indicates an* **increase in supply.**

EQUILIBRIUM OF SUPPLY AND DEMAND

Along a given demand curve, such as the one in Figure 1, there are lots of price/quantity combinations from which to choose. Along a given supply curve, there are similarly lots of different price/quantity combinations. Neither the demand

Figure 4
Shifts in the Supply Curve: Changes in Supply

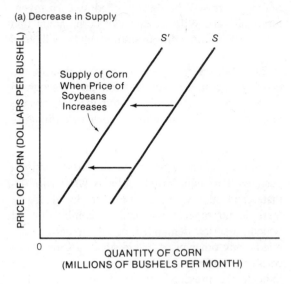

(a) Decrease in Supply

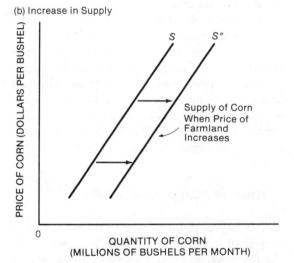

(b) Increase in Supply

The supply curve of corn depends not only on the price of corn but also on the price of soybeans and the price of farmland. When farmland is $2,000 an acre per year and soybeans are $10 per bushel, S might be the supply curve for corn. Panel (a) shows that if farmland stays at $2,000 per acre per year but soybeans fetch $15 instead of $10, profit-seeking farmers will switch farmland from corn to soybeans and cause the supply curve for corn to shift to the left from S to S' (a decrease in supply). On the other hand, panel (b) shows that if soybeans remain at $10 per bushel and farmland falls from $2,000 to $1,000 per acre, the supply curve for corn will shift to the right from S to S" (an increase in supply).

Figure 5
Market Equilibrium

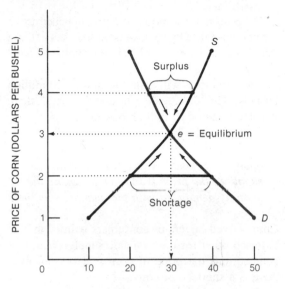

This figure shows how market equilibrium is reached. On the same diagram are drawn both the demand and the supply curves for corn. The curves are the same as in Figures 1 and 3. When the price of corn is $2, the quantity demanded is 40 million bushels, but the quantity supplied is only 20 million bushels. The result is a shortage of 20 million bushels of corn. Unsatisfied buyers will bid the price up.

Raising the price will reduce the shortage. When the price of corn is raised to $4 per bushel, the quantity demanded is 25 million bushels while the quantity supplied is 35 million bushels. The result is a surplus of 10 million bushels of corn. This surplus will cause the price of corn to fall as unsatisfied sellers bid the price down to get rid of excess inventories of corn. As the price falls the surplus will diminish. The equilibrium price is $3 because the quantity demanded equals the quantity supplied at that price. The equilibrium quantity is 30 million bushels.

curve nor the supply curve is sufficient by itself to determine the *market* price/quantity combination.

Figure 5 puts the demand curve of Figure 1 and the supply curve of Figure 3 together on the same diagram. Remember that the demand curve indicates what consumers are prepared to buy at different prices; the supply curve indicates what producers are prepared to sell at different prices. These groups of economic decision makers are (for the most part) entirely different. How much will be produced? How much will be consumed? How are the decisions of consumers and producers coordinated?

Suppose that the price of corn happened to be $2 per bushel. Figure 5 tells us the same thing that Figures 1 and 3 tell us separately: at a $2 price consumers will want to buy 40 million bushels and producers will want to sell only 20 million bushels. This discrepancy means that at $2 there is a **shortage** of 20 million bushels.

*A **shortage** results if at the current price the quantity demanded exceeds the quantity supplied; the price is too low to equate the quantity demanded with the quantity supplied.*

Corn-starved buyers or consumers will try to outbid each other for the available supply. With free competition, the price of corn will be bid up if there is a shortage of corn.

The increase in the price of corn in response to the shortage will have two main effects. On the one hand, the higher price will discourage consumption. On the other hand, the higher price will encourage production. Thus the increase in the price of corn, through the action of independent buyers and sellers, will lead both buyers and sellers in the marketplace to make decisions that will reduce the shortage of corn.

According to the demand and supply curves portrayed in Figure 5, when the price of corn is $3 per bushel, the shortage of corn disappears completely. At this price consumers want to buy 30 million bushels and producers want to sell 30 million bushels.

*The **equilibrium** (or **market-clearing**) **price** is the price at which the quantity demanded by consumers equals the quantity supplied by producers.*

What would happen if price rose above the **equilibrium price** of $3 per bushel? At the price of $4 per bushel, consumers want to buy 25 million bushels and producers want to sell 35 million bushels. Thus at $4 there is a **surplus** of 10 million bushels on the market.

*A **surplus** results if at the current price the quantity supplied exceeds the quantity demanded; the price is too high to equate the quantity demanded with quantity supplied.*

Some sellers will be disappointed as corn inventories pile up. Willing sellers of corn cannot find buyers. The competition among sellers will lead them to cut the price if there is a surplus of corn.

This fall in the price of corn will simultaneously encourage consumption and discourage production. Through the automatic fall in the price of corn, *the surplus of corn will therefore disappear*.

Again we find that the price will tend toward $3 and the quantity will tend toward 30 million bushels. This equilibrium point is where the demand and supply curves intersect. In Figure 5, there is no other price/quantity combination at which quantity demanded equals quantity supplied—any other price brings about a shortage of corn or a surplus of corn. The arrows in Figure 5 indicate the pressures on prices above or below $3 and how the amount of shortage or surplus— the size of the brackets—gets smaller.

The equilibrium of supply and demand is stationary in the sense that price will tend to remain at that price once the equilibrium price is reached. Movements away from the equilibrium price will be restored by the bidding of excess buyers or excess sellers in the marketplace. The equilibrium price is like a rocking chair in the rest position; give it a gentle push and the original position will be restored.

What the Market Accomplishes

The market coordinates the actions of a large number of independent suppliers and demanders. Their actions are brought together by the pricing of the good in a free market. The market can accomplish its actions without any participant knowing all the details. Recall the pencil example of Chapter 3: pencils get produced even though no single individual knows *all* the details for producing a pencil (from making the saw to fell the trees to making the rubber eraser).

An equilibrium price accomplishes two basic goals. First, it *rations* the scarce supply of the commodity or service among all the people who would like to have it if it were given away free. Somebody must be left out if the good is scarce.

The price, by discouraging or restraining consumption, rations the good out to the various claimants of the good.

Second, the system of equilibrium prices *economizes on the information required to match supplies and demands.* Buyers do not have to know how to *produce* the good, and sellers do not need to know why people use the good. Buyers and sellers need only be concerned with small bits of information such as price or small portions of the technological methods of production. No one person has to know everything.

Disequilibrium Prices

To understand the rationing function of equilibrium prices, let us consider what happens when prices are not allowed to reach equilibrium. For many years, the price of natural gas shipped interstate was held below equilibrium by the Federal Power Commission. During the Arab oil embargo during the summer of 1974, gasoline prices were held below market-clearing levels. In recent years, prices of consumer goods in Poland were held below equilibrium. In both cases, shortages and long lines resulted.

Rent control is an example of disequilibrium pricing. Laws are passed by municipal governments *freezing* rents (that is, preventing rents from rising).

The growing number of consumer groups demanding controls on rents is explained by a very simple fact: in the United States, the number of tenants is increasing relative to the number of homeowners.

Figure 6 shows the market for rental housing in a particular city. The supply curve is upward-sloping; the demand curve is downward-sloping. In a free market, the price of housing would settle at $500 per month for a standard rental unit. But suppose a price ceiling of $300 is established by municipal ordinance. If landlords are free to supply the number of apartments they wish, fewer units would be offered for rent: 6,000 units are supplied at a price of $300 and 8,000 units at a price of $500. The quantity demanded rises to 11,000 units as price falls. Accordingly, there will be a shortage of 5,000 units due to the rent control. If the price could rise, there would be no shortage. See Example 3 for further discussion.

Figure 6
The Effect of Rent Ceilings on the Market for Rental Housing

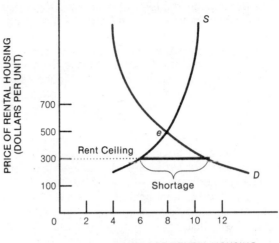

If the equilibrium price/quantity combination for the rental market is $500 per unit and 8,000 units (point e), a rent ceiling of $300 per month on a standard housing unit would lower the quantity supplied to 6,000 units and raise the quantity demanded to 11,000 units, creating a shortage of 5,000 units of rental housing.

Understanding Shortage and Surplus

The terms *shortage* and *surplus* (glut) are often misused. Earlier, the chapter quoted a newspaper report that said there will be a "glut" of doctors by 1990. One often hears reports about "shortages" of sugar or other commodities. In economics, a shortage occurs when the price is not allowed to *rise* to its equilibrium level. A surplus occurs when the price is not allowed to *fall* to its equilibrium level. If there are no impediments to these price adjustments, shortages and surpluses will disappear as prices adjust. A sugar shortage is not a shortage in the same sense as a shortage of rent-controlled apartments. By a sugar shortage writers really mean that supply and demand conditions are pushing *up* the price of sugar. By a surplus of doctors writers actually mean that supply and demand conditions push *down* the relative price of physicians' services, not that there will be doctors with no patients.

Example 3

Rent Control

The assumption that rent control breeds shortages is supported by the facts. In New York City, "temporary" rent controls were imposed in 1943. To this date, 1,250,000 apartments in that city are under rent control, and 340,000 of these remain under the controls imposed during the Second World War. New York City landlords have abandoned many thousands of buildings because they are unprofitable at controlled rental rates. To obtain a rent-controlled apartment, it is necessary to put one's name on a long waiting list or to have a friend who knows somebody. Empty units are rented immediately to whomever happens to be on the list at the right time or knows the right person or has payed a sufficient bribe. New York City is only one case of rent control. In Boston, 50,000 apartments are rent-controlled. In the District of Columbia, there are 112,000 rent-controlled units of which 5,000 have been abandoned by their owners. Rent controls are in effect in some California cities and have been proposed for Los Angeles.

Rent control offers advantages to (and is most enthusiastically supported by) people who already have a lease on a rental unit. They already have housing, and their rent cannot be raised. Unfortunately, in the long run rent controls have damaging effects on the supply of apartments and on their quality. Owners of rent-controlled apartments do not find it profitable to make necessary repairs and often decide it is better to abandon the building than to run it at a loss. Thus, a side effect of rent control is the destruction of the rental industry!

The analysis of rent control illustrates a basic fact: any effective price ceiling on a good or service will tend to cause shortages in a competitive market. Ceilings on interest rates will cause shortages of loans and mortgages. Ceilings on gasoline prices in the United States in 1974 and 1979 at times caused long gas lines in many parts of the country. In severe winters, ceilings on natural gas prices have caused shortages in northern states. In each case, the solution is the same: remove the price ceiling, and the shortage disappears!

There are both costs and benefits of shortages. When a shortage occurs, those who can get the commodity at the controlled price may be better off paying a lower price, provided they do not spend more time waiting in lines than they would in paying a comparable money price. The cost is that many who are prepared to pay the price for the controlled commodity are denied its use, even if their desire is so intense that they are willing to pay an exceptionally high price.

Source: "Reagan Leadership May Have Role in Settling Rent Control Disputes," *Christian Science Monitor*, December 19, 1980.

CHANGES IN THE EQUILIBRIUM PRICE

One important fact about the economic system is that prices always change. Sometimes prices go up, and sometimes they go down—and in relative-price terms price goes down as often as it goes up. This section will investigate the reasons why prices change. Thus far we have seen that the equilibrium price is determined by the intersection of the demand and supply curves. The only way for the price to change is for the demand or supply curves themselves to shift. The supply and demand curves can shift only if one or more of the factors besides the price of the good in question changes.

Change in Demand (or Supply) versus Change in Quantity Demanded (or Supplied)

A rise in the price of a good—as from p_1 to p_2 in panel (a) of Figure 7—induces a change in the quantity demanded but does not change the location of the demand curve. A reduction or decrease in demand occurs when a change in a factor other than the good's price shifts the entire demand curve to the left.

*A **change** (increase or decrease) **in demand** is a shift in the entire demand curve because of a change in a factor other than the good's price.*

Figure 7
Change in Demand versus Change in Quantity Demanded

(a) *Change in Quantity Demanded*

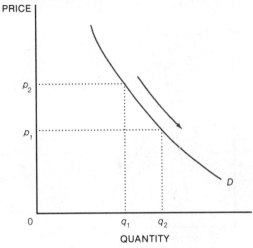

(b) *Change in Demand*

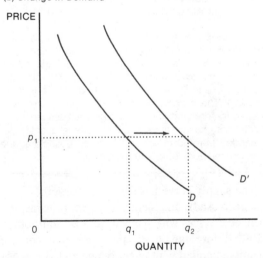

In panel (a), the increase in quantity (from q_1 to q_2) is due to the change in price (from p_2 to p_1). The change in price causes the *movement along* the demand curve (D). In panel (b), the increase in quantity (from q_1 to q_2) is due to a *shift in* the demand curve (an increase in demand) to D'. The quantity has increased due to some change that leads consumers to buy more of the product *at each price*.

A *change* (increase or decrease) *in quantity demanded* is a movement along the demand curve because of a change in the good's price (see Figure 7).

Similarly, panel (a) of Figure 8 shows that a rise in the price of a good (from p_1 to p_2) changes the quantity supplied but does not change the location of the supply curve. A reduction in supply occurs when a factor other than the good's price changes, shifting the entire supply curve to the left.

A *change* (increase or decrease) *in supply* is a shift in the entire supply curve because of a change in a factor other than the good's price.

A *change* (increase or decrease) *in quantity supplied* is a movement along the supply curve because of a change in the good's price (see Figure 8).

The Effects of a Change in Supply

Changes in supply or demand factors can influence the equilibrium price and quantity in any given market.

Consider a natural disaster, such as severe flooding, a horde of locusts, or a drought, that affects the supply of an agricultural product, such as wheat. Figure 9 illustrates the effect of a natural disaster on the wheat market. The demand curve, and the supply curve, are based on given conditions *before* the natural disaster. Suddenly, and without warning, torrential rains hit the wheat fields prior to harvest, ruining about one half of the potential wheat crop. Now at a price of $5 per bushel, instead of 50 million bushels being offered, only 25 million bushels are offered by farmers. Similarly, at all other prices smaller quantities of wheat are offered on the market. The supply curve for wheat has shifted to the left (the supply of wheat has decreased). How will this supply reduction affect the demand curve?

When the supply curve for a single good—like wheat—changes, the demand curve need not change. The factors influencing the supply of wheat *other than the price of wheat* have little or no influence on the demand for wheat. In our example, the severe rains will not shift the demand curve. Thus, in the analysis of a single market we can usually assume that the demand and supply curves are independent.

Figure 8
Change in Supply versus Change in Quantity Supplied

(a) Change in Quantity Supplied

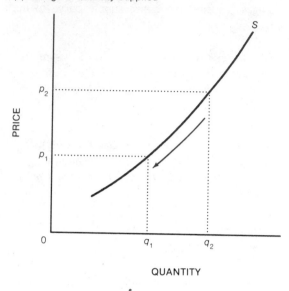

Figure 9
The Effects of a Natural Disaster on the Price of Wheat

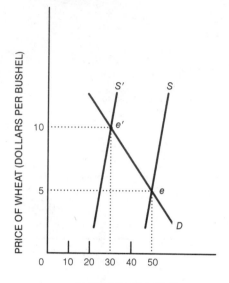

QUANTITY OF WHEAT
(MILLIONS OF BUSHELS PER YEAR)

In this graph, a natural disaster shifts the supply curve of wheat from S to S'. Where formerly $5 brought forth 50 million bushels of wheat (on S) now $5 brings forth only 25 million bushels of wheat (on S'). This decrease in supply raises the equilibrium price from $5 to $10. The movement from e to e' is a *movement along* the demand curve. Although the demand curve does not change, there is a decrease in quantity demanded from 50 million to 30 million bushels as the price rises from $5 to $10 per bushel.

(b) Change in Supply

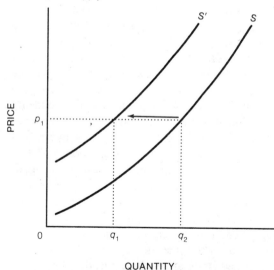

QUANTITY

In panel (a), the decrease in quantity (from q_2 to q_1) is due to a change in price (from p_2 to p_1). The change in price causes a movement along the supply curve *(S)*. In panel (b), the decrease in supply (from q_2 to q_1) is due to the shift in the supply curve (decrease in supply) from S to S'. Quantity drops without any change in price.

The supply curve has shifted to the left (supply has decreased); the demand curve remains unchanged. What will happen to the equilibrium price? Before the flood, the price that equated quantity supplied with quantity demanded was $5. After the flood, the quantity supplied at a $5 price is 25 million bushels and the quantity demanded is 50 million bushels. At the old price, there would be a shortage of wheat. Therefore, the price of wheat will be bid up until a new equilibrium price is attained (at $10), at which quantity demanded and quantity supplied are equal at 30 million bushels. As the price rises from the old equilibrium price ($5) to the new equilibrium price ($10), there is a movement up the new supply curve *(S')*. Even with a flood, a higher price will coax out more wheat.

A decrease in supply causes the price to rise and the quantity demanded to fall. An increase in supply causes the price to fall and the quantity demanded to rise.

The Effects of a Change in Demand

A change in demand is illustrated in Figure 10. The initial situation is depicted by the demand curve *D* and the supply curve *S*. The equilibrium price is $5 and the equilibrium quantity is 50 million bushels. Hence, *D* and *S* are the same curves as in Figure 9. Now imagine a change on the demand side. Medical evidence is uncovered showing that eating bread will double one's lifespan (purely hypothetical). This event would shift the demand curve for wheat sharply to the right (from *D* to *D'*). This massive increase in demand for wheat will drive the price of wheat up to $13 per bushel (from *e* to *e'*). When the price rises, the quantity supplied rises from 50 million to 58 million bushels. *There has been no increase in supply, only an increase in quantity supplied.*

Notice again that when the demand curve shifts due to some change in demand factors other than the good's price, there is no shift in the supply curve—the supply curve remains the same. The supply curve and the demand curve should be considered to be independent of one another at this level of analysis. If a market is small enough relative to the entire economy, the link between the factors that shift demand curves and those that shift supply curves (summarized in Examples 1 and 2) is weak. In our example, the change in preferences should not affect the willingness of farmers to supply wheat at different prices.

The statement by the state agriculture office quoted at the beginning of this chapter illustrates the danger of confusing changes in quantity demanded (or supplied) with changes in demand (or supply). The bad weather reported by the agriculture office shifts the supply curve to the left and causes a movement along the demand curve. The fall in supply does not cause a fall in demand but a *fall in quantity demanded.* Another example of the widespread confusion over the difference between a change in supply (or demand) and a change in quantity supplied (or demanded) is described in Example 4.

Figure 10
The Effects of an Increased Preference for Bread on the Price of Wheat

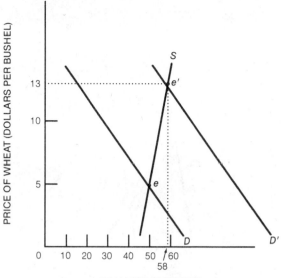

If for some reason people want to eat more bread due to a change in preferences, the demand curve for wheat will shift to the right. The shift in the demand curve from *D* to *D'* depicts an increase in demand. This increase in demand drives up the equilibrium price from $5 per bushel to $13 per bushel. As price rises from $5 to $13, there is an increase in quantity supplied from 50 million to 58 million bushels that results from the movement along the supply curve, *S*.

An increase in demand causes the price to rise and the quantity supplied to rise. A decrease in demand causes the price to fall and the quantity supplied to fall.

Simultaneous Changes in Supply and Demand

Figure 11 combines the two previous cases and illustrates what happens to price and quantity if the two events (the flood and the change in preferences) occur together. The supply curve shifts to the left from *S* to *S'* (supply falls) and the demand curve shifts to the right from *D* to *D'* (demand increases).

Prior to these changes, equilibrium price was $5, and equilibrium quantity was 50 million bush-

Figure 11
The Effects of an Increase in Demand and a Decrease in Supply on the Price of Wheat

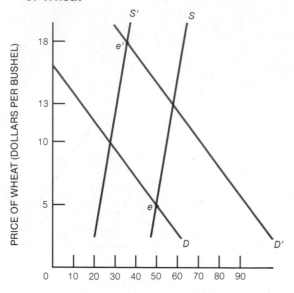

This graph combines the supply change of Figure 9 and the demand change of Figure 10. The original equilibrium was at a price of $5 and a quantity of 50 million bushels. After the shift in supply (from S to S') and the shift in demand (from D to D'), there is a shortage at the old price (quantity supplied equals 25 million bushels and quantity demanded equals 90 million bushels). The equilibrium price rises to $18 and the equilibrium quantity falls to 37.5 million bushels.

---

els. The shifts in supply and demand disrupt this equilibrium. Now at a price of $5, the quantity supplied equals 25 million bushels, and the quantity demanded equals 90 million bushels—an enormous shortage. The new equilibrium occurs at a price of $18 and a quantity of 37.5 million bushels. The two shifts magnify each other's effects. As we have shown, if there had been only the supply change, price would have risen to $10. If there had been only the demand change, price would have risen to $13. The combined effects cause the price to rise to $18. In this case the causes of the changes in supply and demand are independent.

The effects of simultaneous changes in supply and demand are sometimes indeterminate. If sup-

Figure 12
The Effect of Population Growth on the Market for Rental Housing in Los Angeles

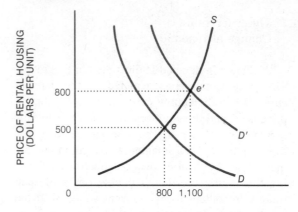

QUANTITY OF RENTAL HOUSING
(THOUSANDS OF UNITS)

When the population grows, the demand for rental housing in a city will increase, *ceteris paribus*. If the original equilibrium is point *e*, population growth will shift the demand curve from *D* to *D'* to a new equilibrium at *e'*. All those people who originally rented housing units at the lower price will find that the new population has forced up the rents they must pay.

---

ply increases (shifts right) and demand decreases (shifts left), the price will fall. If supply decreases and demand increases, the price will rise. If, however, both the demand and supply curves move in the same direction (if both increase or if both decrease), the price effect depends upon which movement dominates.

APPLICATIONS OF SUPPLY-AND-DEMAND ANALYSIS

Supply-and-demand analysis is one of the most powerful tools of economics. We have already used supply-and-demand analysis to determine the effects of decreases in supply (the natural-disaster example) and increases in demand (the change-in-preferences example) on prices and quantities. What happens when prices are not allowed to rise to equilibrium levels was examined in the discussion of rent control. Supply-and-demand analysis can also help explain why rents rise and what the effects of insecticide regulation will be.

Presidential Confusion

During his term of office, President Jimmy Carter was asked in a news conference whether or not his proposed tax on gasoline would raise the price of gasoline. The President's response was that the tax would initially push the price up, but the higher price would discourage demand and bring the price back down.

This response illustrates the common confusion of *changes in quantity demanded* with *changes in demand*. The appropriate response would be that the higher gasoline price (caused by the tax) would cause a movement up the demand curve, *reducing the quantity demanded*. It is incorrect to argue that a fall in quantity demanded can cause the price to fall.

Source: Gerald J. Lynch, "Demand or Quantity Demanded," *Collegiate Forum* (Winter 1980/81), p.5.

Why Rents Rise

One of the reasons price ceilings tend to be imposed is that many buyers perceive them to be personally beneficial; hence, any time prices rise rapidly there tends to be political pressure for price ceilings of some sort.

To the individual buyer, a high price appears to be the fault of the seller with whom he or she is dealing. There may be some cause for blaming the seller if there are not many sellers competing with one another. But in a competitive market with many buyers and sellers, the real enemy of buyers (collectively) is the existence of competing buyers. In Figure 12, the *D* and *S* curves represent the initial demand and supply curves for rental housing in a particular city—say, Los Angeles. The equilibrium is at point *e* with the average monthly rental at $500 and 800,000 units rented. If the population increases, the number of buyers increases and demand for rental housing increases. This increase in demand shifts the demand curve from *D* to *D'*. At the original price of $500 there is a shortage, so the price is bid up. As a consequence, the price goes up for the individual tenant. The individual landlords are not responsible for the increase in the price from $500 to $800 (indicated by the new equilibrium *e'*) but may get the blame from the individual tenant.

In reality, there is a larger degree of mutual interest between the buyer (tenant) and the seller (landlord) than among the individual buyers in a competitive market. Sellers gain from having many buyers to deal with and vice versa. Under a system of private property, buyers and sellers come together voluntarily because there is a presumption that both can gain from this exchange.

Unfortunately, if buyers can band together they can hurt sellers, and if sellers band together they can hurt buyers. In competitive markets, however, collusive behavior does not take place.

This example demonstrates how in those cities and parts of the country where population is rising most rapidly (the sun-belt cities and California), demand for consumer goods and housing is increasing at a faster rate than in other parts of the country. If other things are equal, we would expect prices to increase at a faster pace in these areas.

How well is this prediction of supply-and-demand analysis borne out? Los Angeles (a city that has experienced substantial population growth over the last decade) may be the next major city to institute rent control as a response to rapidly escalating rents. A more general confirmation is that consumer prices have risen much more rapidly in the sun-belt states than in those states that are declining in population.

The Effects of Insecticide Regulation

Many economic activities are regulated by government through zoning laws, occupational licensing, auto-emissions and pollution controls, safety regulations, and so on. Typically, safety,

Figure 13
The Effect of Pesticide Regulation on the Market for Raw Cotton

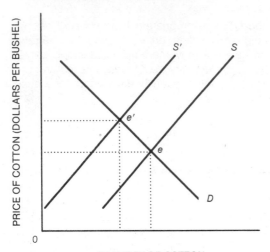

Dusting cotton crops with DDT will keep the quantity of boll weevils (a serious pest) under control. The curve S is the supply curve for cotton using DDT. The equilibrium without pesticide regulation is point e. If it is thought that DDT inflicts unacceptable ecological damage on the community, pesticide regulation (outlawing DDT) that requires a less effective insecticide will shift the supply curve to the left, raising the equilibrium price to the level indicated by point e'.

environmental, and occupational regulation affects supply and thus prices. Supply-and-demand analysis allows us to assess these effects.

Suppose a community decides to prohibit the use of DDT (Dichlorodiphenyltrichloroethane) because of its perceived ecologic damage. What would be the impact of prohibiting DDT on a single market such as cotton?

In Figure 13, the supply curve, S, shows the various quantities of cotton the market will supply at different prices when DDT can be used to control the boll weevil (a serious pest). Before DDT use is prohibited, the equilibrium price and quantity are indicated by point e. If the use of DDT (the most effective insecticide from an economic viewpoint) is prohibited, the supply curve for cotton will shift to the left: to produce cotton becomes more difficult and expensive. Prohibiting DDT has no obvious impact on the demand

curve, but is likely to raise the price of cotton and to lower the quantity of cotton produced and consumed.

Environmental and safety regulations that restrict supply (not all such regulations will limit supply) do raise prices, as supply-and-demand analysis shows. It is up to the community to decide whether the costs imposed on the community in the form of higher prices exceed the benefits imparted by a cleaner environment and by greater worker safety.

These first four chapters focused on how market economies allocate resources through the price system. The tools of supply-and-demand analysis show how equilibrium prices are established and how and why prices change. Relative prices signal to buyers what to purchase and signal to firms what and how to produce. The economic problems of *what, how,* and *for whom* are solved by the invisible hand of the market allocation system, which directs the circular flow of resources between households and businesses. The invisible hand of the market appears to work best under conditions of competition where no buyer or seller (or group thereof) can exercise control over prices.

Summary

1. A perfectly competitive market consists of many buyers and sellers in which each buyer or seller accepts the market price as given.
2. The law of demand states that as price goes up the quantity demanded falls, and vice versa; the demand curve is a graphical representation of the relationship between price and quantity demanded—other things equal. The demand curve is downward-sloping.
3. As price goes up the quantity supplied usually rises; the supply curve is a graphical representation of the relationship between price and quantity supplied. The supply curve tends to be upward-sloping because of the law of diminishing returns.
4. The equilibrium price/quantity combination occurs where the demand curve intersects the supply curve, or where quantity demanded

equals quantity supplied at the market-clearing price. Competitive pricing rations scarce economic goods and economizes on the information necessary to coordinate supply-demand decisions. A shortage results if the price is too low for equilibrium; a surplus results if the price is too high for equilibrium.

5. A change in quantity demanded means a *movement along* a given demand curve; a change in demand means the entire demand curve shifts. A change in quantity supplied means a *movement along* a given supply curve; a change in supply means the entire supply curve shifts. The demand curve will shift if a change occurs in the price of a related good (substitute or complement), income, preference, the number of buyers, or the expectation of future prices. The supply curve will shift if a change occurs in the price of another good, the price of a resource, technology, the number of sellers, or the expectation of future prices. A change in the equilibrium price/quantity combination requires a change in one of the factors held constant along the demand or supply curves.

6. Supply-and-demand analysis allows one to predict what will happen to prices and quantities when supply or demand schedules shift.

Key Terms

market
perfect (perfectly competitive) market
demand
law of demand
quantity demanded
market demand curve
substitutes
complements
inferior goods
normal goods
quantity supplied
supply
shortage
equilibrium (market-clearing) price
surplus

Questions and Problems

1. List the four characteristics of a perfectly competitive market. Explain why if any of the four conditions are not met, the principal characteristic of a perfect market (no person or group can control price) may not be met.

2. Suppose you live in a very cold climate and you pay on average 25 percent of your income for fuel. If the price of fuel rises by 15 percent, and there are no good substitutes for fuel, why would you cut back on fuel consumption?

3. Plot the supply and demand schedules in the accompanying table as supply and demand curves.

Price (dollars)	Quantity Demanded (units)	Quantity Supplied (units)
10	5	25
8	10	20
6	15	15
2	20	10
0	25	5

   a. What price would this market establish?
   b. If the state were to pass a law that the price could not be more than $2, what would happen to the equilibrium price? If the state were to pass a law that the price could not be more than $8, what effect would the law have on the equilibrium price?
   c. If preferences changed and people wanted to buy twice as much as before at each price, what will the equilibrium price be?
   d. If, in addition to the above change in preferences, there is an improvement in technology that allows firms to produce this product at lower cost than before, what will happen to the equilibrium price?

4. American baseball bats do not sell well in Japan because they do not meet the specifications of Japanese baseball officials. If the Japanese change their specifications to accommodate American-made bats, what will happen to the price of American bats?

5. ''The poor are the ones who suffer from high gas and electricity bills. We should pass a law that gas and electricity rates cannot increase by more than 1 percent annually.'' Evaluate this statement in terms of supply-and-demand analysis.

6. Much of the automobile-rental business in the United States is done at airports. What would be the predicted effect of a reduction in air fares on automobile-rental rates?

7. If both the supply and demand for coffee increase, what would happen to coffee prices? If the supply increased and the demand fell, what would happen to coffee prices?

8. a.   ''The recent fare war among the major airlines has increased the demand for air travel.''
   b.   ''The recession of 1981–82 has caused the demand for air travel to fall.''
   Which of the above statements uses incorrect terminology? Explain.

Product Markets

5

Elasticity of Supply and Demand

Chapter Preview

One of the most important tools of applied economics is the concept of elasticity. An understanding of the price elasticity of demand and the price elasticity of supply helps economists answer an enormous range of questions, such as: What will happen to the price of oranges if there is a freeze in Florida? How much will oil imports fall if the government raises the excise tax on gasoline? If a company raises its prices, will dollar sales rise or fall?

Chapter 4 distinguished between a *change in quantity demanded* (or quantity supplied) and a *change in demand* (or supply). A change in quantity demanded or quantity supplied is the *move-ment along* a demand or supply curve caused by a change in the price of that product. A change in demand or supply is a *shift in the entire* demand or supply *curve* that is caused by a change in one or more factors (other than the good's price). *Changes in demand* are due to changes in consumer preferences, consumer income, prices of related products, price expectations, or the number of buyers. *Changes in supply* are the result of changes in technology, other product prices, factor prices, price expectations, or the number of suppliers. Any change in these factors will disrupt the equilibrium and form a new equilibrium price/quantity combination.

This chapter will concentrate on what happens to equilibrium price/quantity combinations when the factors affecting supply or demand curves change.

THE PRICE ELASTICITY OF DEMAND

Remember that the demand curve shows how quantity demanded responds to different prices, *ceteris paribus;* the supply curve shows how quantity supplied responds to different prices, *ceteris paribus*. In both panels (a) and (b) of Figure 1, the equilibrium intersection of S and the demand curve (whether D or D') is at point e, where price is $10 and quantity is 100 units. The only difference between the two diagrams is in the demand. D in panel (a) is much flatter than D' in panel (b). The supply curves (S) are identical.

Suppose that the supply curve shifts leftward. The supply curve shifts if any of the factors held constant along a supply curve change. For example, the supply curve shifts to the left—as illustrated in panels (a) and (b)—if productivity falls or if the prices of factor inputs rise. Let us assume that the reduction in supply is due to rising input prices. The supply shift from S to S' is the same in both panels (a) and (b).

When there is a decrease in supply, equilibrium price rises and equilibrium quantity falls. As the supply curve shifts, price rises and quantity falls; the equilibrium point e moves in panel (a) to e' on D and in panel (b) to e" on D'. In panel (a), the price increase (from $10 to $14) that equates quantity supplied with quantity demanded is relatively small compared to the substantial reduction in quantity demanded (from 100 units to only 20 units). In panel (b), on the other hand, the price increase (from $10 to $20) that clears the market is relatively large compared to the small reduction in quantity demanded from 100 to 80 units. The difference between the two demand curves in panels (a) and (b) is in the *responsiveness of quantity demanded to a price increase*. In panel (a), quantity demanded is very responsive to the price change; in panel (b), it is less responsive to a price change. **Price elasticity of demand** is a measure of this responsiveness.

Figure 1
Response to a Reduction in Supply

(a) Quantity Demanded Is More Responsive to Price Change

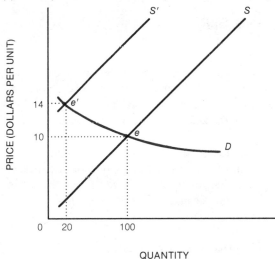

(b) Quantity Demanded Is Less Responsive to Price Change

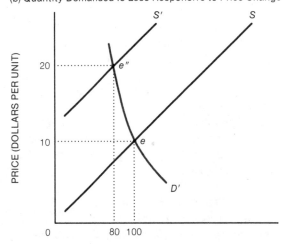

In both panels (a) and (b), S intersects the demand curve at the equilibrium price/quantity combination of $10/100 units. The supply conditions are exactly the same in each diagram, but the quantity demanded is less responsive to price changes in panel (b) than in panel (a). A decrease in supply from S to S' causes a sharper increase in the equilibrium price when quantity demanded is less responsive to price. Although the price increase in (b) from $10 to $20 is greater than the price increase in (a) from $10 to $14, quantity demanded falls more in (a) than it does in (b).

*The **price elasticity of demand** is a measure of the responsiveness of quantity demanded to a change in price.*

Calculating the Price Elasticity of Demand

Absolute changes in price or quantity demanded are inadequate measures of responsiveness. If a $1 increase in the price of coal lowers quantity demanded by 1 ton, one cannot determine whether these changes are large or small unless one knows the initial price and quantity. The measure of responsiveness of quantity demanded to price changes must therefore be the relative (or percentage) change in price or quantity demanded.

*The **price elasticity of demand** is the percentage change in the quantity demanded divided by the percentage change in price.*

Because of the law of demand, if the price rises the quantity demanded falls, and if the price falls the quantity demanded rises. Thus, since a negative number will always appear in the numerator or denominator, the sign of the price elasticity of demand will always be negative. It is a convention in economics when calculating the **coefficient of the price elasticity of demand** to drop the negative sign and to use the *absolute value* of the elasticity.

*The **coefficient of the price elasticity of demand** (E_d) is the absolute value of the percentage change in quantity demanded divided by the percentage change in price. The coefficient measures the percentage change in quantity demanded per 1 percent change in price.*

$$E_d = \left| \frac{\%\Delta Q}{\%\Delta P} \right|,$$

where %Δ stands for "percentage change."

For example, if *P* rises by 10 percent and Q *falls* by 20 percent, E_d equals 20 percent divided by 10 percent, or 2. An elasticity coefficient of 2 means that if prices were raised from the prevailing rate,

the percentage change in quantity demanded would be 2 times the percentage change in price.

The price elasticity of demand coefficient can range from a value of zero to a value that is infinitely large (as will be demonstrated shortly), but economists typically divide elasticity coefficients into three broad categories:

*1. When $E_d > 1$, demand is **elastic** (Q is strongly responsive to changes in P).*
*2. When $E_d < 1$, demand is **inelastic** (Q responds weakly to changes in P).*
*3. When $E_d = 1$, demand is **unitary elastic** (a borderline case).*

Price elasticity of demand coefficients are divided into these three categories because total revenue responds differently to price changes in each category. By looking at the behavior of total revenue as prices and quantities change, one can determine whether the response is elastic, inelastic, or unitary elastic.

Elasticity and Total Revenue

The coefficient of the elasticity of demand can be used to predict what will happen to the **total revenue** of sellers or—what is the same thing—what will happen to the total expenditures of consumers when price changes.

*The **total revenue** of sellers in a market is equal to the product of the price of the commodity times the quantity sold (TR = P × Q).*

Along a demand curve, price and quantity demanded will always move in opposite directions. Although a fall in price tends to lower total revenue, a rise in quantity demanded tends to raise total revenue. What actually happens to total revenue depends upon the responsiveness of quantity demanded to changes in price. For example, a relatively small rise in quantity demanded will not offset the decline in revenue caused by a fall in price. A substantial rise in quantity demanded could offset the loss in revenue due to a lower price. The behavior of total revenue with respect to price changes depends on the price elasticity of demand.

Elastic Demand. If $E_d > 1$, the percentage rise in quantity demanded is greater than the percentage fall in price. Revenue increases because the increase in quantity demanded more than offsets the decrease in price.

When $E_d > 1, |\%\Delta Q| > |\%\Delta P|$.
If $|\%\Delta Q| > |\%\Delta P|$, TR will move in the opposite direction of price.

Inelastic Demand. If $E_d < 1$, the percentage rise in quantity demanded is less than the percentage fall in price. Revenue falls because the decline in price is not offset by the relatively small rise in quantity.

When $E_d < 1, |\%\Delta Q| < |\%\Delta P|$.
If $|\%\Delta Q| < |\%\Delta P|$, TR will move in the same direction as price.

Unitary Elastic Demand. If $E_d = 1$, the percentage rise in quantity demanded equals the percentage fall in price. Revenue is unchanged because the decline in price is just offset by the rise in quantity.

When $E_d = 1, |\%\Delta Q| = |\%\Delta P|$.
If $|\%\Delta Q| = |\%\Delta P|$, TR will not change.

The Total Revenue Test. One can determine whether demand for a particular product is elastic, inelastic, or unitary elastic by applying the **total-revenue test,** which combines the above observations.

*The **total revenue test** is:*
1. If price and total revenue move in different directions, $E_d > 1$ (demand is elastic).
2. If price and total revenue move in the same direction, $E_d < 1$ (demand is inelastic).
3. If total revenue does not change when price changes, $E_d = 1$ (demand is unitary elastic).

There are, then, two ways to determine whether demand is elastic, inelastic, or unitary elastic. The first method is to calculate the coefficient of the price elasticity of demand from price and quantity information.

The second method is to observe what happens to total revenue when price changes and apply the total revenue test. Although this second method also indicates whether demand is elastic, inelastic, or unitary elastic, it does *not* give a value for the coefficient.

The Midpoints Formula

To calculate the price elasticity for a given segment of a demand curve, the percentage change in quantity demanded and the percentage change in price must be computed for that segment of the curve. Consider columns (1) and (2) of Table 1.

The percentage *decrease* in price from $9 to $7 could be calculated by dividing the change in price ($2) by the *initial* price ($9). In this case, the percentage decrease would be 2/9 = 22 percent (approximately).

If we had started with $7 and raised the price to $9, the percentage *increase* in price would be the increase in price ($2) divided by the *initial* price of $7, or $2/7 = 28 percent (approximately). The problem with this method is that the price elasticity is different depending on the direction of the price change.

There should not be one elasticity for price decreases and another one for price increases. This problem can be avoided by using an *average* of the initial and new prices instead of using the initial price alone as the base in calculating the percentage change. (The initial price can be added to the new price and the total can be divided by 2 to obtain the arithmetic average of the two prices.) In the present case, where $7 and $9 are the two prices, the average price is ($7 + $9)/2 = $8; thus, the percent change in price is the change in price ($2) *divided* by the average price ($8), which yields a price change of 25 percent (2/8 = 1/4). The same technique can be applied to quantity demanded. Table 1 shows that in the segment of the demand curve where price falls from $9 to $7, quantity demanded rises from 15 to 25 units. The appropriate percent increase is the change in quantity demanded (10) divided by the average of the two quantities [(15 + 25)/2 = 20]. Hence, the percent change in quantity demanded is 10/20 = 50 percent. The percent change in quantity demanded is given in column (5) and the percent change in price appears in column (6).

Table 1
Total Revenue and Elasticity

Price (dollars per unit) (1) P	Quantity (units) (2) Q	Total Revenue (3) $P \times Q = TR$	Direction of Change in Revenue (4)	Percentage Change in Quantity Demanded (5) $\dfrac{\Delta Q}{(q_1 + q_2)/2}$	Percentage Change in Price (6) $\dfrac{\Delta P}{(p_1 + p_2)/2}$	Coefficient of Price Elasticity (7) $E_d = (5) \div (6)$	Conclusion (8)
(a) 9	15	135					
7	25	175	Increase	$\dfrac{10}{20} = 50\%$	$\dfrac{2}{8} = 25\%$	$\dfrac{50}{25} = 2$	Elastic
(b) 5	35	175	No change	$\dfrac{10}{30} = 33.3\%$	$\dfrac{2}{6} = 33.3\%$	$\dfrac{33.3}{33.3} = 1$	Unitary Elastic
(c) 3	45	135	Decrease	$\dfrac{10}{40} = 25\%$	$\dfrac{2}{4} = 50\%$	$\dfrac{25}{50} = 0.5$	Inelastic

Columns (1) and (2) show a demand schedule. Column (3) is the total revenue of sellers—or the total expenditure of buyers. Column (4) shows what happens to revenue as P *falls*. Column (6) shows the percentage change in price using the midpoint between p_1 and p_2 as the base. Column (5) shows the percentage change in quantity using the midpoint between q_1 and q_2 as the base. Finally, column (7) shows the ratio of column (6) to column (5)—the elasticity of demand E_d. Notice that when demand is elastic ($E_d > 1$), revenue rises when price falls; when demand is inelastic ($E_d < 1$), revenue falls when price falls.

Once the percentage change in quantity demanded (50 percent) and the percentage change in price (25 percent) for a given segment of a demand curve are known, the price elasticity of demand can be computed using the **midpoints formula.**

The **midpoints formula** *is*[1]:

$$E_d = \frac{\textit{Percent Change in Quantity Demanded}}{\textit{Percent Change in Price}}$$

$$= \frac{\textit{Change in Quantity Demanded}}{\textit{Average of Two Quantities}}$$

$$\div \frac{\textit{Change in Price}}{\textit{Average of Two Prices}}$$

1. In symbols, if p_1 and p_2 are the two prices and q_1 and q_2 are the two quantities, the midpoints formula can be simplified as follows:

$$E_d = \frac{q_2 - q_1}{(q_1 + q_2)/2} \div \frac{p_1 - p_2}{(p_1 + p_2)/2} = \frac{q_2 - q_1}{p_1 - p_2} \times \frac{p_1 + p_2}{q_1 + q_2}$$

Dividing the percent change in quantity demanded (50 percent) by the percent change in price (25 percent) in our example yields a price elasticity of demand coefficient (E_d) of 2, as given in column (7) of Table 1. Figure 2 provides a graphical illustration of how price elasticity of demand can be determined.

Elasticity Along a Demand Curve

Total revenue (price times quantity) along the demand curve is given in column (3) of Table 1. Column (4) indicates whether total revenue rises or falls as prices decline from $9 to $7 to $5 to $3. The demand relationship from columns (1) and (2) is depicted by curve D in Figure 3. Column (4) in the table summarizes the visual information contained in the shaded areas of the graphs in Figure 3. In panel (a), the price is reduced from $9 to $7; 15 units were sold at $9, and now 25 units are sold at $7. The area shaded in black indicates the loss in revenue from having

Figure 2
The Midpoints Elasticity Formula

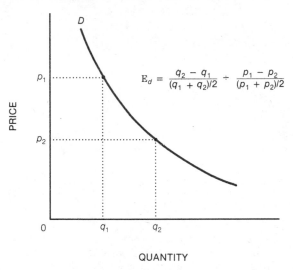

$$E_d = \frac{q_2 - q_1}{(q_1 + q_2)/2} \div \frac{p_1 - p_2}{(p_1 + p_2)/2}$$

To calculate the elasticity of demand between any two prices, p_1 and p_2, along a given demand curve, D, requires three steps: 1) calculating the percent change in quantity demanded by dividing the change in quantity by the average of the quantities, 2) calculating the percent change in price by dividing the change in price by the average of the two prices, and 3) calculating the ratio of the percent change in quantity demanded to the percent change in price.

to sell the first 15 units at the lower price of $7. But more units are sold at $7 than at $9. The color shaded area indicates the revenue gained from selling more units. Total revenue rises since the color shaded area is larger than the black shaded area when demand is *elastic*. The revenue that is lost through the lower price is more than offset by the revenue that is gained selling substantially more units. If price now falls from $7 to $5 as in panel (b), demand is now unit elastic; in this case, revenue remains constant since the revenue lost (the black area) equals the revenue gained (the color area). As price falls further, demand is inelastic. In panel (c), the revenue lost (the black area) exceeds the revenue gained (the color area) from selling a few more units, so total revenue falls.

Notice that E_d *falls* in value along the demand curve as price falls. A characteristic feature of de-

mand curves that are linear or approximately linear is that *the elasticity coefficient tends to increase as a good increases in price.*[2] In other words, consumers tend to be more responsive to price changes at high prices than at low prices for the same product. If the initial price of gasoline is $0.25 per gallon and rises by 10 percent, the elasticity coefficient would likely be lower than if the initial price were $2 per gallon and then rises by 10 percent. There are more acceptable substitutes at high prices than at low prices.

The total revenue test can be applied to the data listed in Table 1 and graphed in Figure 3:

1. Where price decreases and total revenue increases—in panel (a)—E_d (= 2) > 1.
2. Where total revenue does not change when price changes—in panel (b)—E_d = 1.
3. Where price and total revenue both decrease—in panel (c)—E_d (= 0.5) < 1.

Perfectly Elastic or Perfectly Inelastic Demand Curves

The highest degree of elasticity possible—the greatest responsiveness of quantity demanded to price—occurs when the demand curve is perfectly horizontal. In Figure 4, any amount on demand curve D can be sold at the indicated price ($5). Such a horizontal demand curve demonstrates **perfect elasticity of demand.**

The midpoints elasticity formula can be applied to the demand curve D to determine that E_d is infinitely large (E_d = ∞). In other words, the quantity demanded can be increased indefinitely without an increase in price.

Although perfectly elastic demand curves represent an extreme, they are not unknown in the real world. In perfectly competitive markets—defined in Chapter 4 as markets in which no single producer (or group of producers) is large enough to influence the market price—each seller can sell all he or she wants at the market price. Single sellers do not have to lower their prices to sell more. The price of wheat is determined in the world commodity exchanges. American corn or

2. It is possible to have demand curves that are curved in such a manner that the elasticity coefficient does not change as prices rise.

Figure 3
Elasticity Rises as Price Increases

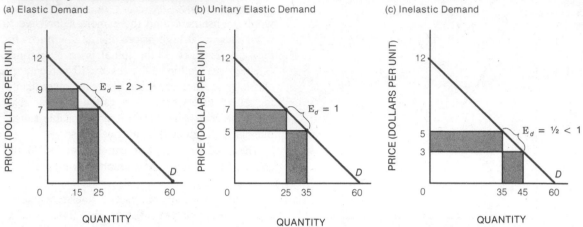

(a) Elastic Demand   (b) Unitary Elastic Demand   (c) Inelastic Demand

The linear demand curve, *D,* is the same in panels (a), (b), and (c). Between the prices of $9 and $7, the elasticity of demand (E_d) is 2; demand is elastic. Panel (a) shows that a reduction in price raises revenue. The black shaded rectangle shows the revenue lost due to the lower price, and the color shaded rectangle shows the revenue gained due to the greater number of units sold. Because the color rectangle is greater in area than the black rectangle, more revenue is gained than lost.

Between prices of $7 and $5, E_d equals 1; panel (b) shows that the reduction in price has no impact on revenue. Finally, between the prices of $5 and $3 E_d is ½; demand is inelastic. Panel (c) shows that the reduction in price lowers revenue because more revenue is lost (black shading) than gained (color shading). Thus, the elasticity of demand varies along a linear demand curve with constant slope. *Elasticity and slope are different.*

---

wheat farmers can sell all they want at that price and can't sell at a higher price.

The lowest degree of inelasticity possible—the least responsiveness of quantity demanded to price—occurs when the demand curve is perfectly vertical. In Figure 4 the vertical demand curve D' demonstrates **perfect inelasticity of demand.** With demand curve D', 75 units of the good will be sold regardless of the price. The coefficient of the elasticity of demand is zero because if the price were to rise above $5, the percentage change in the quantity demanded would be zero. When zero is divided by the percentage change in price, E_d is zero.

A perfectly inelastic demand curve suggests that no matter how high the price rises, consumers will not cut back on the quantity demanded. The closest example would be insulin for the diabetic, but even in this case if the price rose higher and higher, eventually diabetics might reduce their dosages and accept some health loss rather than pay the higher price.

Demand curves can be perfectly inelastic *within a range of prices*. If insulin prices were to

rise by 10 percent, the quantity demanded of insulin would probably not change. If the price of salt were to rise from $0.20 to $0.21 per pound, the quantity demanded would probably stay the same.

A horizontal demand curve demonstrates **perfect elasticity of demand** *($E_d = \infty$); quantity demanded is most responsive to price.*

A vertical demand curve demonstrates **perfect inelasticity of demand** *($E_d = 0$); quantity demanded is least responsive to price.*

Determinants of Price Elasticity of Demand

The price elasticity of demand measures the degree to which consumers respond to changes in prices. Price elasticity can tell producers what will happen to their sales revenue if they change their pricing strategy or if they offer more or fewer units for sale.

Figure 4
Perfectly Elastic and Perfectly Inelastic Demands

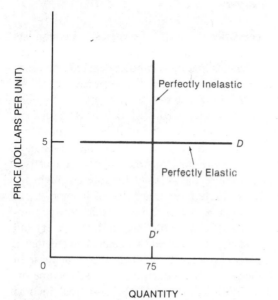

The demand curve D is perfectly elastic; it is perfectly horizontal or parallel to the quantity axis. The demand curve D' is perfectly inelastic; it is perfectly vertical or parallel to the price axis. The elasticity-of-demand coefficient of D is infinitely large along the entire demand schedule. The elasticity-of-demand coefficient of D' is zero along the entire demand curve.

The four determinants of the price elasticity of demand for a good are: 1) the availability of substitutes, 2) the relative importance of the good in the budget, 3) the amount of time available to adjust to the price change, and 4) whether the good is a necessity or luxury.

Availability of Substitutes. Telephones are the principal means of communicating with friends, neighbors, and businesses within a city or town, but they are not the only means. There are commercial messenger services, citizen-band radios, and the postal service. One could even drive or walk and talk in person. Because most of these alternatives are poor substitutes for the telephone, one would not expect a substantial percentage change in quantity demanded in response to a percentage change in price.

Next, consider movie tickets. Movies are only one form of entertainment; there are quite a few

substitutes, including subscribing to a cable TV service, watching commercial television, or going to a stage play. Because of the availability of close substitutes, the elasticity of demand for movie tickets would likely be high.

The availability of substitutes depends upon how broadly a good is defined. The elasticity of demand for automobiles will be lower than the demand for Chevrolets. The elasticity of demand for energy will be less elastic than the demand for coal. The elasticity of demand for entertainment will be less elastic than the demand for movie tickets. The more narrowly defined the product (Chevrolets vs. automobiles, coal vs. energy, movie tickets vs. entertainment), the greater the number of close substitutes (Plymouths for Chevrolets, natural gas for coal, cable TV for movies), and the higher the elasticity of demand. For example, the price elasticity of demand for lettuce has been estimated to be in the vicinity of 0.3; the demand is highly inelastic.[3] But the demand for Farmer Smith's lettuce would be very elastic because there are many perfect substitutes for the lettuce produced on Smith's farm: the lettuce of equal quality and freshness produced on any other farm.

*The greater the number of substitutes for a good, the **more elastic** is its demand. The fewer the number of substitutes for the good, the **more inelastic** is its demand.*

The Relative Importance of the Good in the Budget. Both gasoline and salt have few close substitutes. Which one would be expected to be more elastic?

Would an increase in the price of salt from $0.20 to $0.25 a package (a 22 percent increase by the midpoints method) have a substantial percentage effect on purchases of salt? The average consumer might buy two boxes of salt per year, and a 22 percent price increase would raise the family's cost of living by only $0.10 per year. A 22 percent increase in the price of gasoline, however, translates into a price increase from $1.50

3. George E. Brandow, "Interrelation Among Demands for Farm Products and Implications for Control of Market Supply," *Pennsylvania Agricultural Experimental Station Bulletin* 680, 1961, Table 1.

per gallon to $1.83 per gallon. The average family consumes about 1,000 gallons of gas per year, so the cost of living of the average family would be increased by $330 per year. Because consumers would scarcely notice the salt price increase, their purchases would be little affected. The gasoline price increase, however, would lower real income by a noticeable margin and would, therefore, depress gasoline purchases.

As this comparison shows, the price elasticity of demand will depend upon the relative importance of the good in the budget.

Goods that are a small fraction of the consumer's budget (salt, pepper, drinking water, matches) are more inelastic in demand than products that constitute a large fraction of the consumer's budget (automobiles, fuel oil, mortgage payments, television sets), other things equal.

Time to Adjust to Price Changes. Why demand is more elastic in the longer time periods than in shorter ones is explained by a number of factors. Consider the response of consumers to higher electricity prices. Immediately after electric utility rates are increased, consumers can do little more than lower their heating thermostats in the winter and raise their air-conditioning thermostats in the summer. How much they adjust their thermostats depends upon their income and their tolerance for uncomfortable temperatures. As time passes, additional substitutes for electricity become available. Extra insulation and more energy-efficient heating and air-conditioning equipment can be installed. If natural gas prices have not risen as much, the family can convert to natural gas appliances.

Some expenditures require a long period of advance planning. If transatlantic air tickets fall dramatically in price in the winter, consumers have to wait until the summer comes around to take advantage of the lower prices. Other expenditures are conditioned by habit formation. Consumers are accustomed to buying certain products, and habits are often hard to break. The family may be used to setting the thermostat at 78 degrees. If families are accustomed to having fresh vegetables and the price of fresh vegetables rises substantially, it may take a while before the habit is broken.

Generally speaking, the longer the time period in which consumers can adjust to changes in prices, the more elastic is the demand.

Necessities versus Luxuries. Economists distinguish necessities from luxuries by defining *necessities* as products whose demand increases less rapidly than income. For example, according to *Engel's Law,* there is a tendency for families to spend a smaller portion of their income on food as their income rises.[4] *Luxuries,* on the other hand, are goods whose demand increases at a more rapid rate than income. Foreign travel is a luxury because the demand for foreign travel increases at a rate three times that of income.

What is the expected relationship between necessities and luxuries (defined in this manner) and the elasticity of demand? Chapter 4 noted that a reduction in price is very much like an increase in real income. Price reductions have an income effect on quantity demanded because real income increases when prices fall. Hence, a reduction in price will stimulate the demand for luxuries more than it will stimulate the demand for necessities, if everything else (the availability of substitutes, the importance of the good in the budget, the time allowed for adjustment) is equal. The income effect is larger for luxury goods than for necessities.

There is a tendency for luxury goods to have more elastic demands than necessities.

Actual Prices Elasticities of Demand. Table 2 gives estimate of actual price elasticities. Most were compiled by Hendrick Houthakker and Lester Taylor in their noted study of consumer demand in the United States. These elasticities of demand are calculated in two variants: one is the *short-run* E_d (where the consumer has not had much time to adjust to price changes). The other is the *long-run* E_d (where the consumer has had more time to adjust to price changes).

This evidence generally supports the claim that the long-run elasticities are larger than the short-

---

4. Ernst Engel, a German statistician, in the mid-19th century conducted pioneering studies of European spending patterns.

Table 2
**Price Elasticities of Demand for U.S.
Consumers**

	E_d Short Run	E_d Long Run
Tobacco products	0.46	1.89
Jewelry	0.41	0.67
Toilet articles	0.20	3.04
Owner-occupied housing	0.04	1.22
China and glassware	1.55	2.55
Electricity	0.13	1.89
Water	0.20	0.14
Medical care and hospitaliza- tion	0.31	0.92
Tires	0.86	1.19
Auto repairs	0.40	0.38
Durable recreation equipment	0.88	2.39
Motion pictures	0.88	3.69
Foreign travel	0.14	1.77
Gasoline	0.15	0.78

Source: Hendrick S. Houthakker and Lester D. Taylor, *Consumer Demand in the United States: Analyses and Projections* (Cambridge, Mass.: Harvard University Press, 1970), pp. 166–67; James L. Sweeney, "The Demand for Gasoline: A Vintage Capital Model," Department of Engineering Economics, Stanford University.

run elasticities. In the case of electricity, E_d equals 0.13 in the short run (highly inelastic) but equals 1.89 in the long run (elastic). In the case of foreign travel, E_d rises from 0.14 in the short run to 1.77 in the long run. The elasticities tend to illustrate the important role of substitutes. Medical care has fewer good substitutes than most of the other products listed, and it has lower short-run and long-run elasticities than products, such as motion pictures, recreation equipment, gasoline, and foreign travel. In the short run, electricity has no good substitutes, and the short-run electricity E_d is low.

OTHER ELASTICITIES OF DEMAND

Consumer demand depends not only on the price of the product, but also upon consumer preferences, the prices of substitutes and complements, and consumer income. Although economists devote most of their attention to *price* elasticity of demand, the elasticity concept can also be applied to the other factors affecting demand. For example, economists try to measure

the responsiveness of demand to the prices of related goods (cross-price elasticity) and the responsiveness of demand to consumer income (income elasticity).

Cross-Price Elasticity

A change in the price of one product can cause a shift in the demand schedules of other products. This responsiveness of demand to other prices is **cross-price elasticity of demand.**

*The **cross-price elasticity of demand** (E_{xy}) is the percentage change in demand of the first product* (x) *divided by the percentage change in the price of the related product* (y).[5]

Unlike the price elasticity of demand, which will always be negative (due to the law of demand), the cross-price elasticity can be either positive or negative because the demand for *x* can increase or decrease when the price of *y* increases.

A positive cross-price elasticity of demand means that an increase in the price of one product will cause an increase in the demand for the other product. Consider beef and chicken. As the price of beef rises, the law of demand takes effect and the quantity demanded of beef falls because substitutes have been purchased in place of beef. Chicken is a substitute for beef; therefore, the beef price increase causes an increase in the demand for chicken.

A negative cross-price elasticity means that an increase in the price of one product will cause a decrease in the demand for the other product. Compare airline travel and auto rentals. The two are complements because a large proportion of auto rentals are made by airline travelers. If the price of airline tickets rises, the number of airline passengers declines. As the number of air passengers declines, so does the demand for automobile rentals.

5. The cross-price elasticity of demand is calculated by the same midpoints formula. The only difference is that instead of having the "own price" (p^x) in the denominator the price of the related product (p^y) is in the denominator:

The cross-price elasticity of demand is

$$E_{xy} = \frac{q_2^x - q_1^x}{(q_1^x + q_2^x)} \div \frac{p_2^y - p_1^y}{(p_1^y + p_2^y)}$$

Income Elasticity in Agriculture

The income elasticity of demand for a product can predict which sectors of the economy will benefit most from economic growth. Agriculture notoriously suffers relative declines as income grows. In 1950, agriculture's share of total U.S. output was 4.8 percent. By 1980, its share was only slightly above 2 percent. Since the demand for nonagricultural goods increases relative to agriculture, less total land area will be devoted to agriculture. The natural conversion of agricultural land to other uses has led to great alarm among noneconomists. Many states have passed legislation favoring the retention of land in agricultural uses. For example, in Santa Cruz county in California land is divided into various categories: 1A land is the best agricultural land and cannot be subdivided; 2D land is the worst and is open to

development. According to the president of the local farm bureau, "It would take an act of Congress and three Hail Marys to convert one acre of 1A land." A multi-agency federal team called the National Agricultural Lands Study (NALS) has been set up to study this problem. NALS claims that unless protection legislation is passed, prime farmland equivalent in number of acres to the state of Indiana will be paved over by the turn of the century. The NALS blames speculators and developers rather than the real culprits—the innocent consumer with an income elasticity of demand for farm goods less than unity.   ⊠

Source: "As World Needs Food, U.S. Keeps Losing Soil to Land Developers," *The Wall Street Journal,* October 24, 1980.

If the cross-price elasticity of demand is positive, the two products are **substitutes.** *If the cross-price elasticity is negative, the two products are* **complements.** *If the cross-price elasticity is zero, products* **x** *and* **y** *are unrelated.*

Income Elasticity of Demand

A rise or fall in consumer income will affect the demands for different products. As consumer income rises, the demand for most products increases—but not always. The responsiveness of demand to consumer income is measured by the **income elasticity of demand (E_i).**

*The **income elasticity of demand** is the percentage change in the demand for a product divided by the percentage change in income holding all prices fixed.[6]*

6. The midpoints formula for the income elasticity of demand is:

$$E_i = \frac{q_2 - q_1}{(q_1 + q_2)} \div \frac{i_2 - i_1}{(i_1 + i_2)},$$

where i denotes consumer income.

The income elasticity of demand will be positive for most goods because the higher their income, the more consumers demand of most goods. If the income elasticity equals unity, a 1 percent increase in income will lead to a 1 percent increase in the demand for the good. Hence, consumers would continue to spend the same fraction of their income on the good as before income increased. If the income elasticity exceeds 1, people will spend a larger fraction of their income on the good as income rises. If the income elasticity for some good is less than 1, people will spend a smaller fraction of their income on a good as income rises. The definitions of **necessities** and **luxuries** can be refined using the income elasticity of demand concept.

***Necessities** are those products that have an income elasticity of demand less than 1; **luxuries** are those products that have an income elasticity of demand greater than 1.*

Using this criterion, goods such as food items would be necessities, while recreational vehicles would be luxury items. Notice, though, that the economist allows the terms *luxury* and *necessity* to be defined by the market choices people make rather than by individual perceptions about what is more "necessary" than something else.

APPLICATIONS OF PRICE ELASTICITY OF DEMAND

Knowledge of price elasticity of demand guides business managers in their decisions concerning how much to charge for their products. Of course, the exact elasticity of demand can not be known with certainty. Whenever prices change, businesses enter unknown territory, especially if the price change is large by historical standards. Consider the following examples.

OPEC Oil Production

The amount of crude oil produced by OPEC (Organization of Petroleum-Exporting Countries) declined fairly steadily from 30.7 million barrels per day in 1973 to 27 million barrels per day in 1980. Yet over this period the total revenues of OPEC countries from sales rose from approximately $90 million per day to $675 million per day.[7] How is it that total revenues could rise so substantially when output was declining? The answer lies in the inelastic demand for crude oil. If E_d is low, a percentage reduction in quantity will lead to a much larger percentage increase in price. Reconsider the formula for calculating E_d. E_d is the percentage change in quantity divided by the percentage change in price. By the midpoints formula, the percentage change in quantity from 1973 to 1980 was 13 percent. The percentage increase in price was 157 percent according to the midpoints formula (the price rose from $3 to $25). From this information alone, we cannot calculate E_d accurately because many things other than oil prices and quantities were changing (worldwide inflation, rising world income, and so on). But if we stretch things a little and assume that nothing else changed, the implied E_d for OPEC oil is 0.08. With such a low price elasticity, one would expect total revenues to rise substantially when oil prices rise, which is what the numbers show.[8]

7. "The Petroleum Industry: Supply and Demand Outlook," *Bache Institutional Research*, December 31, 1979.
8. The actual price elasticity of demand for OPEC oil is probably around 0.02. *See* James Griffin and Henry Steele, *Energy Economics and Policy* (New York: Academic, 1980).

Consumer Resistance

In the financial press and in corporate reports, one frequently comes across the term *consumer resistance* or *competitive pressure*. To quote from an annual report to stockholders: "We regret that we are unable to raise prices commensurate with the increase in costs because our product would meet with increased resistance at higher prices." Another quote from an annual report of an airline: "Competitive pressure prevents us from recovering additional fuel costs by raising fares." Why is it that some industries appear to be more prone to consumer resistance or competitive pressure than others?

Consumer resistance is nothing more than high elasticity of demand. When higher prices are met by consumer resistance the product has a high elasticity of demand. If the elasticity of demand is high, consumers will resist price increases by substituting other products. *Competitive pressure* is another term for the existence of good substitutes.

THE PRICE ELASTICITY OF SUPPLY

The price elasticity of demand measures the responsiveness of *consumers* to price change. The **price elasticity of supply** measures the responsiveness of *producers* to price changes. The elasticity of supply (E_s) is calculated in the same way as the elasticity of demand, only now the qs refer to quantities *supplied,* not quantities demanded.

*The **price elasticity of supply** is defined as the percentage change in the quantity supplied divided by the percentage change in price.*

According to the midpoints formula, E_s is calculated:

$$E_s = \frac{q_2 - q_1}{(q_1 + q_2)/2} \div \frac{p_2 - p_1}{(p_1 + p_2)/2}$$

Like the elasticity of demand, the E_s coefficients are divided into three categories: elastic ($E_s > 1$), unitary elastic ($E_s = 1$), and inelastic ($E_s < 1$). The direction of movement of total revenue along a supply curve, however, will not depend upon the value of E_s. The E_s coefficient is positive ex-

Figure 5
Perfectly Elastic and Perfectly Inelastic Supply Curves

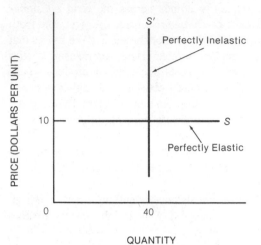

The supply curve *S* is perfectly elastic because at a price of $10 any quantity of output can be offered on the market by sellers. The supply curve *S'* is perfectly inelastic because no matter how much the price rises, the quantity supplied remains the same.

cept in rare cases; increases in price usually raise the quantity supplied. Because both price and quantity supplied are rising, total revenues rise as well.

Perfectly Elastic and Perfectly Inelastic Supply Curves

The highest degree of elasticity possible for a supply curve is a perfectly horizontal supply curve. A horizontal supply curve demonstrates **perfect elasticity of supply.** In Figure 5, the supply curve *S* is a perfectly elastic supply curve. At the price of $10, producers of the good (in the aggregate) are willing to supply any amount of the good to the market at that price.

Most of the supply curves that the average consumer deals with are perfectly elastic. The grocery store is willing to sell any person all the milk, canned goods, and dairy products that person wants to buy at the prices set. Under normal circumstances, however, all buyers together (the market) must offer higher prices to induce producers to increase the quantity supplied.

The lowest degree of elasticity occurs when the supply curve is perfectly vertical, as shown in

Figure 5 by the supply curve S'. Such a supply schedule demonstrates **perfect inelasticity of supply.** The coefficient of E_s in this case equals zero. An increase in price has no effect on quantity supplied; therefore, the percentage change in quantity supplied is always zero.

Like perfectly inelastic demand curves, supply curves can be perfectly inelastic over one range of prices but not perfectly inelastic for all prices. The supply curves of perishable agricultural products tend to be perfectly inelastic. The supply of lakefront or oceanfront locations is fixed and perfectly inelastic as is the supply of agile seven-foot tall athletes. Such supply curves will be discussed in the chapter on economic rent, interest, and profit.

Most market supply curves fall between the two extremes of perfect elasticity ($E_s = \infty$) and perfect inelasticity ($E_s = 0$).

A horizontal supply curve demonstrates **perfect elasticity of supply** *($E_s = \infty$); quantity supplied is most responsive to price.*

A vertical supply curve demonstrates **perfect inelasticity of supply** *($E_s = 0$); quantity supplied is least responsive to price.*

Elasticity of Supply in Three Time Periods

Just as the elasticity of demand depends upon the amount of time the consumer has to respond to price changes, the elasticity of supply also depends upon time.

In general, the longer the period of time the producer has to adjust to changes in prices, the greater the elasticity of supply.

When prices change, economists distinguish between three time periods during which producers adjust their supply to the new prices: **the immediate run, the short run,** and **the long run.**

The immediate run is a period of time so short that the quantity supplied cannot be changed at all. In the immediate run— sometimes called the momentary period *or* market period— *supply curves are perfectly inelastic.*

Figure 6
The Egg Market: Elasticity of Supply in the Immediate Run, the Short Run, and the Long Run

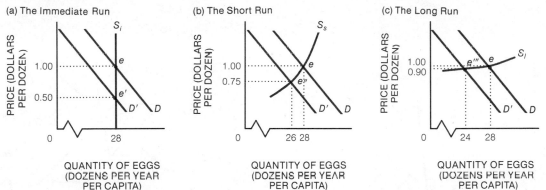

The demand curve for eggs is originally D with the equilibrium price of $1.00 per dozen. The immediate-market-period (a) supply curve S_i corresponds to a fixed supply of eggs. When the demand decreases (shifts to the left), the price falls to $0.50. In the short run (b), egg producers reduce output to trim losses by simply cutting back on feed and the number of chickens; thus, in the short run, price rises to $0.75. In the long run (c), some egg producers may leave the business altogether; the reduction in demand will cause the price to fall to only $0.90. Thus, as the egg industry moves from the immediate run to the short run to the long run, the price of eggs rises from $0.50 to $0.90.

The short run is a period of time long enough for existing firms to produce more goods but not long enough for existing firms to expand their capacity or for new firms to enter the market. Thus output can be varied but only within the limits of existing plant capacity.

The long run is a period of time long enough for new firms to enter the market, for old firms to disappear, and for existing plants to be expanded. In the long run, firms have more flexibility in adjusting to price changes.

These three time periods cannot be closely associated with calendar time. The amount of calendar time required to move from the short run to the long run varies with the type of industry. The electric power industry may require a decade to expand existing power-generating facilities and to bring new plants on line. On the other hand, the fast-food industry can construct and open a new outlet in a few months.

APPLICATIONS OF PRICE ELASTICITY OF SUPPLY

The concept of price elasticity of supply can help explain how producers respond to changes in demand. For example, price elasticity of supply can determine how the domestic oil industry responds to higher domestic energy prices or who ultimately bears the burden of a sales tax. The following two applications illustrate the power of the supply elasticity concept.

The Market for Eggs

Since 1960, per capita egg consumption in the United States has fallen about 15 percent. In 1960, people consumed on the average about 28 dozen eggs per year, but in 1979 they each consumed only about 24 dozen eggs on average. The reasons for this decline are complicated, but two important factors were the trend toward smaller breakfasts and the fear that cholesterol is a contributing factor in heart disease.[9] The U.S. demand curve for eggs thus shifted to the left during this period.

Panel (a) of Figure 6 shows what happens in the immediate run in the egg market. When the demand schedule shifts to the left from D to D', egg producers are unable to cut back on the current supply of eggs. The hens to lay these eggs

9. "Egg Prices are Likely to Climb Further as Producers Trim Output to End Losses," *Wall Street Journal*, October 7, 1980, p. 36.

Figure 7
The Elasticity of Supply of Full-Size and Economy Cars in the Short Run and Long Run

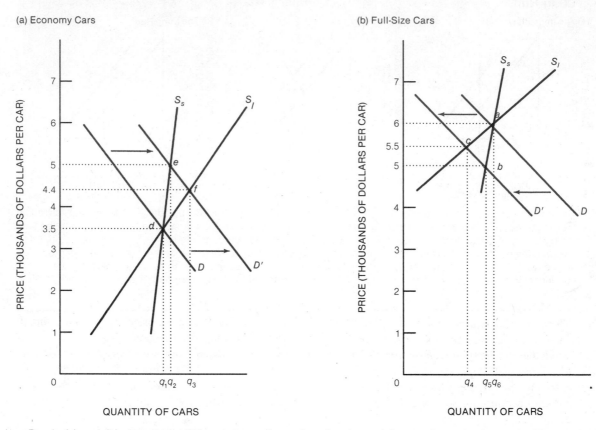

(a) Economy Cars

(b) Full-Size Cars

Panels (a) and (b) show the shift in consumer demand as the demand for economy cars increases (a) and the demand for full-size cars decreases (b). The immediate-run response is not shown. In the short run, the elasticity of supply would be low for both types of cars because of capacity limitations. Therefore, the price of economy cars would rise sharply, and the price of full-size cars would fall sharply. In the long run, the supply curves would become more elastic and the prices would be established between the original prices and the short-run prices.

have already been raised or purchased; the chicken coops have already been built; they have or are about to produce eggs for sale. When the demand reduction hits, the supply curve of eggs is perfectly inelastic. With the per capita supply fixed at 28 dozen eggs per year, the price must drop in order to induce consumers to buy all the eggs on the market. In our example, the price of eggs drops sharply, from $1 per dozen to $0.50 per dozen.

As the price of eggs falls, egg producers will find it worthwhile to start selling their laying hens. Egg prices have fallen substantially, and egg farmers find that they can reduce losses by selling their hens to slaughtering houses, where hens will be converted into canned meat, chicken soup, and pot pies. The amount of calendar time required to make this adjustment is short. All the egg growers have to do is sell their hens.

As time passes from the immediate-run period to the short run, the quantity of eggs supplied falls to 26 dozen eggs per year per capita. The supply schedule is no longer perfectly inelastic. Producers respond to lower prices by offering less output for sale. At the immediate-run price of $0.50, the quantity demanded exceeds the quantity supplied, and the price rises to $0.75 in the short run. The short-run price is lower than the original equilibrium price (of $1), but it is higher than the price in the immediate run (of $0.50).

If demand remains at D', there will be further supply adjustments as egg producers enter the long-run period. Some producers will go out of business; they will convert their chicken coops to raising minks or some other venture. Others will remain in business but will decide not to replace buildings and equipment that have worn out. These actions mean a further reduction in the quantity supplied (the supply curve pivots around the old equilibrium price), and the long-run supply curve is even more elastic than the short-run supply curve. In panel (c) of Figure 6, as the supply curve becomes more elastic, the price rises further to $0.90—still below the original price of $1 but above the immediate-run price of $0.50 and the short-run price of $0.75.

The Supply of Economy Cars

Between 1977 and 1981, the demand for small gas-efficient cars increased in the United States. At the same time, the demand for larger fuel-inefficient cars stagnated or even declined. These two trends are shown in Figure 7 by the rightward shift in demand for economy cars in panel (a) and by the leftward shift in demand for large cars in panel (b). Prior to these demand shifts, the average full-size car sold for $6,000 (point a) and the average economy car for $3,500 (point d)

What was the initial response to these differential shifts in demand? In the immediate market period, dealers found that they had too few economy cars and too many full-size cars. These cars had already been produced; the excess full-size cars therefore had to be sold at a discount; on the other hand, the economy cars could be sold at sticker or premium prices. In the short run, GM, Ford, Chrysler, and American Motors changed their production mix of economy and full-size cars in response to the changing pattern of demand. They shifted workers to economy-car plants; overtime hours were worked in these plants. Fewer hours were worked in plants that produced full-size cars; some workers were laid off. As a consequence of these actions, more

economy cars were produced and fewer full-size care were produced. New equilibrium prices were established at, say, $5,000 (point e) for economy cars and, say, $5,000 (point b) for full-size cars.

The short-run supply curves of automobile manufacturers are inelastic because in the short run, the flexibility to respond to changing relative prices is limited. The basic constraint is imposed by existing plant and equipment. Assembly lines that are tooled to turn out full-size cars cannot be converted to the production of economy cars without considerable time and investment. Automobile manufacturers have to make substantial investments in plants and design.

The American automobile industry between 1977 and 1981 undertook a costly multibillion dollar program of retooling and design to change existing capital stock. The X-cars, K-cars, and J-cars are the result of this effort. Plants that could not be converted to producing economy cars were shut down; those that could be converted were converted; new plants designed to produce economy cars were built. This investment program resulted in the growing elasticity of supply as the automobile industry went from their short-run supply curve to the long-run curve. As the quantities supplied were adjusted to long-run conditions, new relative prices were established between the original prices and the short-run prices. In Figure 7, the long-run prices (adjusted for inflation) are $5,500 (point c) for full-size cars and $4,400 (point f) for economy cars.

Tax Burdens

Local, state, and federal governments tax a variety of goods and services, including tobacco, alcohol, gasoline, and various foreign imports. Elasticity analysis can be used to determine how a tax on a particular good will affect consumers and producers. Who will pay the tax?

How the Burden is Shared.   Suppose that a tax is imposed on a luxury good like perfume. Figure 8 shows the supply curve and the demand curve for perfume before the tax is imposed. The equilibrium price is $2 per gram and the equilibrium quantity is 8 million grams per month at point e before the tax is imposed.

Titanium and Cuban Tobacco

Titanium and Cuban tobacco have one thing in common: in 1980 both shrank in supply. The supply curves for both products shifted to the left. In the titanium case, the supply reduction was the direct result of a decision by the Soviet Union (the major producer of titanium) to restrict its sales of titanium to the world market, which reduced the number of sellers (a factor that shifts a supply curve). In the Cuban case, the reduction in supply was the aftermath of a blue mold fungus that destroyed almost 90 percent of Cuba's tobacco crop.

The supply curves of titanium and Cuban tobacco both shifted to the left. In fact, the shift in the Cuban tobacco supply curve was relatively much greater than the shift in the titanium. The reduction in supply increased the market price, but the price of titanium rose from approximately $4 per pound to a high of $20 per pound while the price of Cuban tobacco rose only slightly. The Cuban economy lost almost $100 million dollars in tobacco earnings. Although the Soviets reduced their supplies of titanium to the world market, their titanium earnings actually increased.

Why did titanium prices rise so dramatically while Cuban tobacco prices scarcely rose at all? Why did Cuban earnings from tobacco sales fall while Soviet earnings rose?

The demand for titanium is very inelastic because it is used in aircraft production, and there is no known substitute that combines its lightness with its high resistance to heat and stress. If demand is highly inelastic and supply shifts to the left, the price will skyrocket. Cuban tobacco, on the other hand, has many good substitutes. Cuban refugees now grow cigar tobacco in Florida, Jamaica, and the Canary Islands the quality of which is comparable to or better than the quality of Cuban tobacco. As a consequence, the demand for Cuban tobacco is highly elastic. When the supply curve shifts to the left along an elastic demand curve, the price rises little. The total revenue test explains the behavior of revenues. Titanium is inelastic in demand; therefore, total revenue will rise as price increases. Cuban tobacco is elastic in demand; therefore, total revenue falls as price rises. ![logo]

Sources: "Titanium Pinch Felt by Aircraft Builders as Soviets Cut Shipments to World Market," *Wall Street Journal,* Wednesday, November 14, 1979; and "Funguses Attack Cuba's Tobacco Fields, Sending the Cigar Industry Up in Smoke," *Wall Street Journal,* Wednesday, March 26, 1980.

Let a tax of $1 per gram be imposed by the government. In order for sellers to earn $2, they must now charge $3; or to earn $1.25 they must charge $2.25. The tax will cause the supply curve to shift *up* by exactly $1—the amount of the tax. Before the tax, suppliers were prepared to supply 8 million grams per month at a price of $2 per gram, but after the tax, suppliers will be prepared to supply the same 8 million grams per month only if the price is $3 (because they will receive $2 per gram after the tax). Since the conditions affecting the demand curve for perfume (consumer income, other prices, consumer preferences, number of buyers) are not changed by the tax, the demand curve for perfume will remain the same. As long as buyers are charged the same price (including the tax), their quantity demanded will remain the same. The new equilibrium price must be less than $3 (the original price plus the $1 tax) because at $3, the quantity supplied is the same as without the tax but the quantity demanded is lower.

The new equilibrium point is e'. The buyers will pay $2.25 for perfume and sellers will receive $1.25, with the tax collector picking up the $1.00 difference. The equilibrium price *paid* by consumers goes up only $0.25 and the net price (price minus tax) received by producers goes down by $0.75. In this particular case, the greater burden of the tax is on the sellers who pay three quarters of the tax. Buyers pay only one quarter of the tax.

Figure 8
The Burden of a Tax

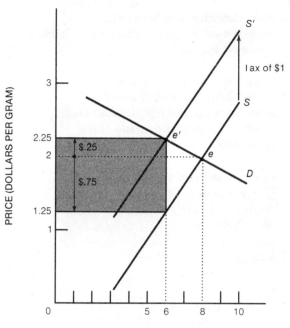

QUANTITY OF PERFUME
(MILLIONS OF GRAMS PER MONTH)

D and *S* are the demand and supply curves for perfume before the tax; the equilibrium price is $2. A tax of $1 per unit on sellers shifts the supply curve upward by exactly $1 as sellers recoup their tax payments to the state. The new equilibrium price to buyers is where the new supply curve, *S'*, intersects the old demand curve, *D*, at point *e'*; thus, the new price is $2.25 to buyers. Sellers must send $1 (per gram sold) to the tax collector; hence, sellers keep only $1.25 after paying tax. Notice that one fourth of the burden of the $1 tax ($0.25) falls on buyers and three fourths of the burden ($0.75) falls on sellers. This incidence reflects the fact that the elasticity of demand is approximately 4 times greater ($E_d = 2.4$) than the elasticity of supply ($E_s = 0.6$).

The Elasticity Determines the Tax Burden. Why is it that the producer bears a greater part of the burden than the consumer in our perfume example? The answer is found in the elasticities of demand and supply.

The demand curve in Figure 8 is more elastic than the supply curve in the vicinity of the equilibrium point *e*, as evidenced by the fact that the curve *S* is steeper than curve *D*. Consumers therefore respond more to the price than producers.

Hence, consumers have a greater opportunity to avoid the tax than producers. In fact, the elasticity of demand along *D* between $2 and $2.25 is 2.4; the elasticity of supply along *S* between $1.25 and $2 is approximately 0.6.

Had we assumed instead that the supply curve was more elastic than the demand curve, then the consumer would bear the greater burden of the tax. If consumers have a more inelastic demand, it is easier to shift the price forward to them and harder to reduce the price paid to producers. For the consumer to bear the greater burden of the tax requires that demand elasticities be significantly *smaller* than supply elasticities—which in the long run, in many industries, is likely to be true.

The concept of elasticity allows us to understand the extent to which changing prices and income affect supply and demand. The next chapter will look behind the demand curve to explain the law of demand and consumer surplus.

Summary

1. The price *elasticity* of demand is a measure of the responsiveness of consumers and producers to changes in price.
2. The price elasticity of demand (E_d) is the absolute value of the percentage change in quantity demanded divided by the percentage change in price.
3. The price elasticity of demand can be either elastic ($E_d > 1$), unitary elastic ($E_d = 1$), or inelastic ($E_d < 1$). If demand is elastic, price and total revenue move in opposite directions. If demand is inelastic, price and total revenue move in the same direction. If demand is unitary elastic, total revenue is not affected by price changes.
4. E_d can be calculated using the midpoints formula; the change in quantity is divided by the average quantity, and the change in price is divided by the average price.
5. The price elasticity of demand changes as one moves along the demand schedule. At higher prices, demand tends to become more elastic.

6. Demand is perfectly elastic when the demand curve is horizontal; demand is perfectly inelastic when the demand curve is vertical.

7. The price elasticity of demand is determined by the availability of substitutes (more substitutes mean higher elasticity), the amount of adjustment time (more time means higher elasticity), the importance in the budget (the more important the higher the elasticity), and whether the good is a necessity or a luxury (necessities tend to have lower elasticities).

8. Elasticities can also be used to measure the responsiveness of consumer demand to changes in income and the prices of other goods.

9. Cross-price elasticity is the percentage change in the quantity demanded of one good divided by the percentage change in the price of the other good. If this number is positive, the two goods are substitutes. If it is negative, the two goods are complements.

10. Income elasticity of demand is the percentage change in the quantity demanded divided by the percentage change in income. If this number is greater than one, the good is a luxury; if it is less than one, the good is a necessity.

11. The price elasticity of supply is the percentage change in quantity supplied divided by the percentage change in price.

12. Supply is perfectly elastic when the supply curve is horizontal; supply is perfectly inelastic when the supply curve is vertical.

13. The price elasticity of supply depends upon the time period of adjustment. In the immediate run, supply is fixed, and the supply schedule is perfectly inelastic. In the short run, firms can produce more or fewer goods but do not have sufficient time to alter their capital stock or enter or leave the industry. In the long run, supply can be altered through changes in capital stock and through the entry and exit of firms. Elasticity of supply is greater in the long run than in the short run.

Key Terms

price elasticity of demand (E_d)
coefficient of the price elasticity of demand
total revenue test
midpoints formula
perfect elasticity of demand
perfect inelasticity of demand
cross-price elasticity of demand (E_{xy})
income elasticity of demand (E_i)
necessities
luxuries
price elasticity of supply (E_s)
perfect elasticity of supply
perfect inelasticity of supply
immediate run
short run
long run

Questions and Problems

1. Using the demand schedule in the accompanying table, calculate the price elasticities of demand for each successive pair of rows.

Price (dollars)	Quantity (units)
$5	1
4	2
3	3
2	4
1	5

2. Suppose the price elasticity of demand for rental housing is 0.6 and the average rent increases from $250 per month to $300 per month. At $250 per month, 100,000 rental units are rented. What percentage decrease in quantity demanded would you predict from this information? How many units would be rented at $300 per month?

3. The price of gasoline rises from $1.50 per gallon to $4.00 per gallon. Why would one's short-run adjustment to this price

change be different from the long-run adjustment?

4. Currently, the basic monthly charge for a private telephone is $10.50 per month. If the rate were to rise to $11.00, would you expect a substantial reduction in the quantity demanded? Explain your answer. If, on the other hand, the basic monthly charge were $250.00 per month and the rate were to rise by the same percent as in the first case, what is your prediction about the change in quantity demanded?

5. A professional football team raises its ticket prices by 10 percent, and its sales revenues decline. From this information, what can you say about the price elasticity of demand for its tickets?

6. The price of tennis balls goes up. What impact would this price increase have on the quantity demanded of tennis rackets? What sign (+ or −) would the cross-price elasticity have? What sign would the cross-price elasticity of tennis balls and golf balls have?

7. The income elasticity of demand for services is greater than one. As the economy grows, what would you expect to happen to the share of service industries in total output?

8. Used-car sales typically rise during economic recessions while new-car sales decline during recessions. Explain why this is so.

9. Assume that you have a product called args. The elasticity of demand is 2 and the elasticity of supply is 0.2. If government imposes a tax of $1 per unit on args, who would end up paying more of the tax (bearing the larger burden of the tax): the consumer or the producer? Why? Draw a diagram illustrating your argument.

10. Evaluate the following statement: "The elasticity of demand for oranges is 0.2; therefore, California orange growers could raise their income by restricting their output."

CHAPTER

6

Demand and Utility

Nothing is more useful than water; but it will purchase scarce anything; scarce anything can be had in exchange for it. A diamond, on the contrary, has scarce any value in use; but a very great quantity of other goods may frequently be had in exchange for it.
Adam Smith, *The Wealth of Nations,* 1776.

Chapter Preview

This chapter will build a model of consumer behavior that is based on the principle that the consumer will allocate (spend) income in such a manner as to gain maximum satisfaction. The model can be used to deduce the law of demand. This chapter will also show how to combine individual demand curves to determine market demand curves and how to measure the consumer gains and losses that result from price changes.

CONSUMER WANTS, TASTES, AND PREFERENCES

Wants and *demand* are two different things in economics. *Wants* are those goods and services that households would consume if there were no budgetary limitations. *Demand* denotes those goods and services that households are prepared to buy given relative prices and the consumers' income level. The amounts of goods and services that households purchase depend not only on relative prices and income, but also on **preferences** or tastes. Some families might not want pork even if it were given away free. The individual with a fear of flying will not want free airline tickets. The opera lover would welcome a free concert ticket but might throw away a free ticket to the World Series that a baseball fan would treasure. People are different; they have different preferences.

Preferences are people's evaluations of goods and services independent of budget and price considerations.

There are two views of consumer preferences. One view, as championed by John Kenneth Galbraith, is that consumer preferences are unstable or capricious and easily manipulated. In this view, businesses can mold consumer preferences by spending large sums on advertising. Madison Avenue has the power to convince people to buy products that they never even knew they wanted. The opposing view, as represented by two prominent economists, Gary Becker and Kelvin Lancaster, is that consumer preferences are remarkably stable—when broadly defined—and are not easily manipulated by advertising.

The modern view of consumption, pioneered by Becker and Lancaster, is that the consumer wants the *services* that goods provide, not the goods themselves. Rather than wanting an automobile, the consumer wants the transportation *services* that an automobile will provide. Rather than wanting theater tickets, admission to bowling alleys, or tickets to sports events, the consumer desires the entertainment *services* that these goods provide. Rather than wanting a house or condominium, the consumer wants the shelter that these goods provide.

Stated in these terms, consumer preferences will be more stable than preferences for specific products that provide the consumption service. The taste for transportation services may be stable, but, because transportation services can be provided by a variety of goods (the private automobile, taxis, buses, trains, airplanes, one's feet), how these services are purchased will be less stable. The preference for entertainment may be quite stable, but the exact manner in which the consumer satisfies that taste can vary dramatically. One consumer watches television; another goes to a movie; another learns how to pilot an airplane; yet another buys a book.

Technology and innovations alter preferences for specific goods. For example, transportation innovations over the years have been dramatic: the consumer who used to be content to move about by horse 200 years ago may now prefer jet-powered transportation. To the casual observer, this transformation might seem like a radical change

in preferences, but economists like Becker and Lancaster would argue that the preference for the transportation service itself has remained relatively stable. Example 1 shows that preferences are basically uniform from one country to another.

THE CONCEPT OF UTILITY

At the start of the chapter, Adam Smith poses the famous *water/diamond paradox*. Smith is asking why it is that prices often fail to reflect the usefulness of goods. Goods like water and salt, without which human beings would perish, have low relative prices, while goods that have little practical value, such as diamonds, gold, and high fashion, have high relative prices. People's preferences for goods or services are based on their perception of how the goods or services add to their **utility.**

Utility is the satisfaction that people enjoy from consuming goods and services.

The Law of Diminishing Marginal Utility

It is not possible to attach a util-o-meter to a person's arm to measure the satisfaction they are experiencing from consuming goods and services. (The appendix to this chapter explains why it is not even necessary to be able to measure utility in specific units.) Suppose, however, that one could measure utility in terms of imaginary *utils,* or units of utility. From consuming 50 gallons of water per week, for example, a consumer might enjoy 3,000 utils of satisfaction. The **marginal utility** of water is the extra utility enjoyed by increasing water consumption by one gallon. If 51 gallons yields 3,010 utils, the marginal utility of the last gallon of water is 10 utils.

*The **marginal utility** of any good or service is the increase in utility that a consumer experiences when consumption of that good or service (and that good or service alone) is increased by one unit.*

The **law of diminishing marginal utility** states that, as a general rule, as more of a good

The Universality of Wants

That wants are uniform is supported by a major study of spending patterns in ten countries commissioned by the World Bank. The World Bank examined the spending patterns of ten countries and found great diversity among the individual product categories. The Japanese eat more fish; the French dine out more; the Americans spend little on public transportation (they use their private cars instead); the Indians spend a great deal on spices; the Kenyans spend little on clothing and footwear. These differences are explained in large part by differences in climate, religion, and custom. Yet if one examines broad consumption categories that satisfy basic preferences, one finds much more uniformity. The differences that remain, moreover, are primarily the consequence of differences in income levels and differences in relative prices. The World Bank study shows that as countries become more similar in income levels and relative prices, their patterns of consumption become more similar. ⌧

Source: Irving B. Kravis et al., *A System of Interventional Comparisons of Purchasing Power* (Baltimore, Md.: The Johns Hopkins Press, 1975).

---

or service is consumed, its marginal utility declines. Thus the first gallon of water (in a given week) has an enormous marginal utility because a consumer who has no water would consider 1 gallon to be very valuable. The 20th gallon of water has a relatively small marginal utility because a person who already has 19 gallons would not value a 20th very highly. The *total utility* from all 20 gallons of water would be the total of the marginal utility of all units. Why does the utility of water decline so rapidly as more water is consumed? Because the first gallon of water is essential to sustaining life, its marginal utility is astronomical. As more water becomes available, water can be applied to less urgent uses: to washing oneself, to washing one's clothes, to feeding pets, and eventually even to watering one's lawn. By the time sufficient water is available for watering the lawn, the marginal utility of the last gallon is much smaller than the marginal utility of the first gallon.

*The **law of diminishing marginal utility** states that as more of a good or service is consumed during any given time period, its marginal utility declines, holding the consumption of everything else constant.*

There are some rare exceptions (the marginal utility of the stamps of the stamp collector may rise as additional stamps are acquired), but these exceptions need not concern us here because they do not change the general pattern of consumer behavior. The law does not say how rapidly marginal utility will decline as consumption increases; this rate will vary. For some goods (food products for example), marginal utility declines rapidly. The marginal utility of the second hamburger is much less than that of the first. The marginal utility of the third hamburger will be very small. For other goods, such as women's shoes, marginal utility may decline slowly as consumption increases.

The Diamond/Water Paradox

The law of diminishing marginal utility provides the answer to the diamond/water paradox. Why do diamonds, whose total utility is much less than the total utility of water, have a higher relative price than water? The answer is that the consumption of water takes place at a low marginal utility because the supply of water is large, while the supply of diamonds is usually so limited that consumption takes place at relatively high marginal utility. Although water's total utility is high, its marginal utility will be small. Since the marginal utility of water is low no one will sacrifice very much for an additional gallon.

The diamond/water paradox holds under normal supply conditions, but what happens when normal conditions are disrupted? In the confusion at the end of the Second World War, food sup-

Table 1
The Utility of Ale and Bread

Quantity of Ale (pints) Q_A (1)	Total Utility of Ale (utils) TU_A (2)	Marginal Utility of Ale (utils) MU_A (3)	Marginal Utility of Ale per Dollar (utils) MU_A/P_A (4)	Quantity of Bread (loaves) Q_B (5)	Total Utility of Bread (utils) TU_B (6)	Marginal Utility of Bread (utils) MU_B (7)	Marginal Utility of Bread per dollar (utils) MU_B/P_B (8)
1	40	40	20	1	15	15	30
2	70	30	15	2	23	8	16
3	90	20	10	3	30	7	14
4	100	10	5	4	35	5	10
5	105	5	2.5	5	38	3	6
6	107	2	1	6	40.5	2.5	5

This table lists the quantities of ale and bread consumed by Ruffgreg along with the utility Ruffgreg attaches to each quantity. The price of ale equals $2 per pint and the price of bread equals $0.50 per loaf. The marginal utility columns illustrate the *law of diminishing marginal utility:* the marginal utility of each product falls as the amount consumed increases.

plies were interrupted, and people gladly exchanged diamonds and precious metals for bread and potatoes in parts of Europe. Supplies of food products were so limited that food products yielded a higher marginal utility (by preventing malnutrition) than did diamonds and precious metals. When the American West was being settled in the 19th century, range wars were fought (and people were killed) over the control of water holes. In arid parts of the world (Africa, Middle East), armed conflicts still break out over water.

MARGINAL UTILITY AND THE LAW OF DEMAND

The law of diminishing marginal utility explains the diamond/water paradox. Relative prices reflect marginal utility rather than total utility. The exact linkage between the law of diminishing utility and the law of demand remains to be established.

Consider an individual consumer, Mr. Ruffgreg, who purchases only two goods—ale (A) and bread (B).

Ruffgreg's preferences for both ale and bread are summarized in Table 1. They are stable and do not change as time passes and as other things change. Columns (2) and (6) show the total utility of ale (TU_A) and bread (TU_B), respectively; columns (3) and (7) show the marginal utility of ale (MU_A) and bread (MU_B), respectively.

Ruffgreg's marginal utility schedule for ale is shown in Figure 1 and is graphed from the data in column (3) of Table 1. The first pint of ale (per day) yields Ruffgreg a marginal utility of 40 utils; the second yields 30 utils; the third yields 20 utils; the fourth pint of ale yields a marginal utility of 10 utils. The total utility from consuming different quantities of ale is the sum of the bars up to the quantity of ale consumed. The total utility from consuming three pints of ale, for example, is 90 (= 40 + 30 + 20).

We cannot determine Ruffgreg's demands for ale and bread from his preferences alone. As noted in Chapter 4, demand depends not only on consumer preferences, but also on consumer income and prices. To keep our example simple, let us assume Ruffgreg has $8 to spend on ale and bread. The price of ale (P_A) is $2 per pint, and the price of bread (P_B) is $0.50 per loaf. Ruffgreg could spend the entire $8 allowance on ale, buying 4 pints of ale, or he could spend all $8 on bread, obtaining 16 loaves of bread. The most likely case, however, is that Ruffgreg will spend part of the money on ale and part on bread. For instance, he could purchase 3 pints of ale per day costing a total of $6 and 4 loaves of bread per day costing a total of $2 for a total expenditure of $8.

Figure 1
Marginal Utility

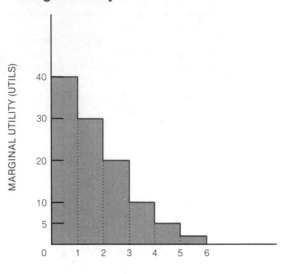

QUANTITY OF ALE (PINTS PER DAY)

This figure graphs the data in columns (1) and (3) of Table 1. The width of each bar represents one pint of ale. The vertical height and area of each bar represents marginal utility for that extra unit of ale. Total utility up to some quantity of ale is the sum of the bars to the left of that quantity of ale. For example, the total utility of 2 pints equals 70 (= 40 + 30); the total utility of 5 pints equals 105 (= 40 + 30 + 20 + 10 + 5).

Maximizing Satisfaction

How will Ruffgreg allocate his $8 between ale and bread? All consumers (if they behave rationally) will seek to obtain as much satisfaction as possible from the amount of income they have to spend.

To achieve maximum utility the consumer allocates the budget on goods in such a way that it is impossible to find a better buy by spending a bit more on one good or a bit less on the other.

We will now try to demonstrate that Ruffgreg maximizes his satisfaction when his budget is spent so that *the last dollar spent on each product (ale and bread) yields the same marginal utility.* The intuitive sense of this rule is that if the marginal utility per dollar is not the same for two products, a consumer can get more utility by switching an extra dollar to the good with the greater marginal utility per dollar.

Maximum satisfaction requires that marginal utility per extra dollar spent on A be the same as the marginal utility per extra dollar spent on B.

In columns (4) and (8) of Table 1, *marginal utility per dollar* is calculated by dividing marginal utility by the price. Since the price of ale is $2 per pint, column (4) is half of column (3); since the price of bread is $0.50 per loaf, column (8) is twice column (7). Ruffgreg is now ready to spend the $8 on ale and bread.

Note that the concept of marginal utility per dollar is a rate measure like miles per hour. Just as one can drive 50 miles per hour without driving for a full hour, marginal utility per dollar does not require the spending of a full dollar.

Table 2 shows the step-by-step process by which Ruffgreg allocates his income between bread and ale. The first loaf of bread costs $0.50 and yields a marginal utility of 15; the marginal utility *per extra dollar* spent on bread is 30 (= 15/$0.50) for the first loaf. The first pint of ale costs $2 and yields a marginal utility of 40, but the marginal utility *per dollar* is only 20 (= 40/$2) for the first pint. Because the first loaf of bread has a higher marginal utility per dollar, Ruffgreg would first buy one loaf of bread at a cost of $0.50, leaving $7.50 to spend. Ruffgreg now finds that the marginal utility per dollar is higher for the first pint of ale (20) than for the second loaf of bread (16), so he purchases a first pint of ale for $2, leaving $5.50 to spend. Marginal utility per dollar is higher for the second loaf of bread (16) than for the second pint of ale (15), so Ruffgreg's third purchase is the second loaf of bread. Ruffgreg continues to select the product with the higher marginal utility per dollar until his budget is exhausted. Ruffgreg is in **consumer equilibrium** when he buys 3 pints of ale and 4 loaves of bread, where he has spent his entire income of $8 (3 loaves at $2 each and 4 pints at $0.50 each) and where the marginal utility per dollar is 10 utils for both ale and bread.

Table 2
The Steps to Consumer Equilibrium

	Available Choices	Decision	Income Remaining
1st Purchase	1st pint of ale: $MU_A/P_A = 20$ 1st loaf of bread: $MU_B/P_B = 30$	Buy 1st loaf of bread for $0.50	$8.00 − $0.50 = $7.50
2nd Purchase	1st pint of ale: $MU_A/P_A = 20$ 2nd loaf of bread: $MU_B/P_B = 16$	Buy 1st pint of ale for $2.00	$7.50 − $2.00 = $5.50
3rd Purchase	2nd pint of ale: $MU_A/P_A = 15$ 2nd loaf of bread: $MU_B/P_B = 16$	Buy 2nd loaf of bread for $0.50	$5.50 − $0.50 − $5.00
4th Purchase	2nd pint of ale: $MU_A/P_A = 15$ 3rd loaf of bread: $MU_B/P_B = 14$	Buy 2nd pint of ale for $2.00	$5.00 − $2.00 = $3.00
5th Purchase	3rd pint of ale: $MU_A/P_A = 10$ 3rd loaf of bread: $MU_B/P_B = 14$	Buy 3rd unit of bread for $0.50	$3.00 − $0.50 = $2.50
6th Purchase and 7th Purchase	3rd pint of ale: $MU_A/P_A = 10$ 4th loaf of bread: $MU_B/P_B = 10$	Buy 3rd pint of ale for $2.00 and 4th loaf of bread for $0.50	$2.50 − $2.00 = $0.50 $0.50 − $0.50 = $0

This table shows the step-by-step process by which a consumer makes purchasing decisions that will maximize satisfaction. In choosing at each step between a unit of ale and a unit of bread, the consumer determines which commodity has the highest marginal utility per dollar and buys that commodity. Data taken from Table 1. The consumer has $8 to spend.

Consumer equilibrium occurs when the consumer has spent all income and marginal utilities per dollar spent are equal on each good purchased ($MU_A/P_A = MU_B/P_B$). At this point, the consumer is not inclined to change purchases unless some other factor (such as prices, income, or preferences) changes.

The law of demand can be deduced from this theory of consumer behavior. When the price of ale is $2, Ruffgreg purchases (demands) 3 pints of ale, given that his income is $8 and the price of bread is $0.50. The price/quantity combination of $2/3 pints of ale is one point (r in Figure 2) on the demand curve.

Other points on the demand curve can be calculated by repeating the whole process at a different price of ale, keeping income at $8 per day and the bread price at $0.50 per loaf.

If the price of ale falls from $2 to $1 per pint, the marginal utility of ale and the marginal utility per extra dollar spent on ale are the same thing ($MU_A \div 1 = MU_A$). Because of the lower price of ale, the marginal utility per dollar spent on ale is now higher than the marginal utility per dollar spent on bread at the old equilibrium of 3 pints of

Figure 2
The Demand Curve Derived from the Marginal Utility Schedule

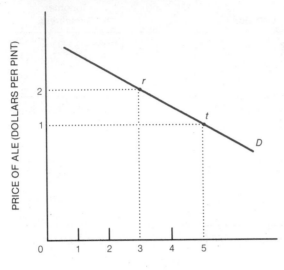

QUANTITY OF ALE (PINTS PER DAY)

This curve shows the demand curve for ale calculated from Table 1. If the price of bread is $0.50 per loaf and daily income is $8, consumer equilibrium can be calculated at the price of ale equal to $2 per pint. The equilibrium quantity of 3 pints of ale is the quantity of ale demanded when the price of ale equals $2. The equilibrium quantity can also be calculated for a price of ale equal to $1 per pint. The resulting equilibrium quantity of ale (5 pints) is the quantity of ale demanded when the price of ale equals $1.

ale and 4 loaves of bread. Ale purchases will be increased; expenditures will be reallocated between the two goods until the $8 is spent and marginal utilities per dollar are again equal—this time at 5 ales and 6 breads purchased. Thus when the price of ale is $1, the quantity demanded of ale is 5. This price/quantity combination of $1/5 pints is a second point (t) on the demand curve. As the law of demand predicts, holding all other factors constant, a decrease in the price causes an increase in the quantity demanded.[1]

1. The mathematics is simple. Start with the consumer in equilibrium with: $MU_A/P_A = MU_B/P_B$. If P_A falls, $MU_A/P_A > MU_B/P_B$. To restore equilibrium, MU_A must fall. The law of diminishing marginal utility states that MU_A will fall if consumption of A increases. From this, the negative relationship between P_A and Q_A is established.

Income and Substitution Effects

When the price of a good falls two things happen. First, consumers can buy the goods and services they used to buy plus more goods and services. A decrease in price is like an increase in income in the sense that it enables consumers to purchase more goods of any type, including more of the good whose price has fallen. The part of the increase in quantity demanded caused by such an increase in income is called the **income effect.** Second, the cheaper good now yields a higher marginal utility per dollar. Consumers bent on maximizing satisfaction will substitute this now cheaper good for other products. This part of the increase in the quantity demanded of the cheaper good is called the **substitution effect.**

When the price of a good falls people buy more of it because 1) the price reduction is like an increase in income that in itself normally leads to larger demands for all goods and services, including the one whose price has fallen (the income effect) and 2) consumers tend to substitute that good for other goods (the substitution effect).

In Table 1, before the drop in the price of ale from $2 to $1, the consumer purchased 3 pints of ale and 4 loaves of bread for a total of $8 worth of ale and bread. At the lower price of $1 per pint of ale the consumer can purchase the same 3 pints of ale and 4 loaves of bread for $5. The consumer now has $3 left over that can be spent on either ale or bread. This $3 is like an increase in income. The effect of this increase in real income on purchases of ale is the income effect.

In addition to having the extra $3, the relative price of ale has dropped (the ratio of ale price to bread price has fallen from 4 to 2). Because of the lower relative price of ale, the consumer is now getting more marginal utility *per dollar* out of ale than bread and therefore switches to buying ale. This switch from bread to ale is the substitution effect.

Consider the following real-world example: In 1979, the average American family spent almost $1,500 per annum on energy consumption (utilities, gasoline, and oil).[2] In 1980, energy prices

2. *Statistical Abstract of the United States* (101st edition, 1980).

Example 2

Marginal Utility Theory: The Terri and the Toyota

Manufacturers of paper towels are locked in a continuing competitive struggle between low-priced generic and higher-quality name-brand producers. The name brands offer the user durability and greater absorbency but at a higher price. American Can's Bolt brand, as its advertising campaign demonstrates, can even survive a machine washing. In the language of marginal utility, the name brands offer a product with higher marginal utility. But do they offer higher marginal utility *per dollar*?

Let us quote some experts on paper-towel marketing:

"Does the world really need a bulletproof paper towel?"

"Consumers don't always want the best if it costs more."

"Many people are looking for the product that simply is good enough to do the job."

"Terri's (a high quality brand) problem was that it was more than what was needed."

These quotes from manufacturers suggest that consumers do make purchasing decisions on the basis of marginal utility *per dollar,* not on the basis of marginal utility alone.

Objective comparisons of imported cars rank the Toyota Corolla well behind other foreign cars in handling, performance, styling, stability, and even gas mileage. However, the Toyota Corolla ranks highest in durability, and its price is cheap relative to other foreign imports. Durability and price are related in that the longer a car lasts, the cheaper the car. It is perhaps not surprising that the Toyota Corolla has been the best-selling imported car in the United States. Again, for many consumers the Toyota Corolla has the highest marginal utility *per dollar.*

Source: "What Happens If the Product Offers More Than Users Need," *Wall Street Journal,* September 25, 1980.

rose by 15 percent, which means the real income of the average American family declined substantially *(ceteris paribus)* as a consequence of the energy-price increase. The average family would have to spend $225 more in 1980 to buy the same amount of energy purchased in 1979. The decrease in energy consumption noted in 1980 would be the consequence of both the income effect and the substitution effect. The income effect would be the impact of the $225 reduction in real income on energy purchases. The substitution effect would be the impact of the rising price of energy that would make energy substitutes more attractive to the consumer.

Do people really behave in the mechanical fashion depicted by the model of rational consumer behavior? Few people keep marginal-utility schedules in their heads or calculate marginal utility per dollar to determine the best buys at every given moment.

But people—on the average—behave as if the above theory were more or less true. Have you ever stood at the meat counter in a supermarket and observed sharp-eyed customers pawing the packages of meat? The customer is in effect calculating *best buys*. A *best buy* at any moment is the good that yields the highest marginal utility *per extra dollar* spent. A consumer may get the most marginal utility from a delicious T-bone steak, but that consumer gets the most marginal utility *per dollar* from simple hamburger meat. The consumer may decide that: "instead of buying the T-bone steak, I'll buy the hamburger *and* take in a movie." The steak does not yield enough marginal utility per dollar compared to the hamburger and the movie.

The actual decision process of the individual is far more complicated than that described by marginal utility theory; human beings are complicated and must choose between more than just two goods. Yet when one cuts through all the apparent inconsistencies and irrationalities (like keeping up with one's neighbors), the average consumer is surprisingly rational. Individual examples cannot prove the rationality of the average consumer, but observed consumer behavior taken as a whole is

Figure 3
From Individual to Market Demand

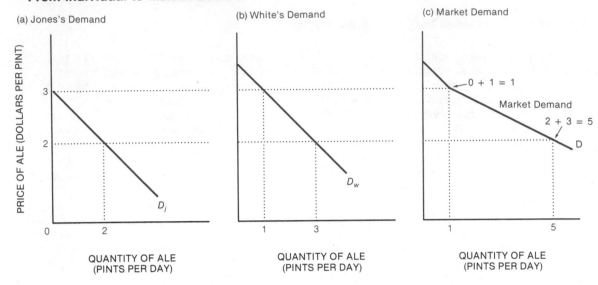

(a) Jones's Demand   (b) White's Demand   (c) Market Demand

The market demand curve is the *horizontal* summation of all individual demand curves; it is calculated by summing all individual quantities demanded at each price. Here, the market has only 2 consumers, but the principle applies to markets with any number of consumers.

consistent with the predictions of the theory. The theory of rational consumer behavior predicts that the law of demand holds.

MARKET DEMAND

The theory of consumer behavior explains how individual consumers make buying decisions. The law of diminishing marginal utility implies that rational consumers will purchase less of a product, *ceteris paribus*, if its price rises. According to the law of demand, the demand schedules of individual consumers will have negative slopes.

But prices are established in markets, and the individual consumer is only a small part of the total market. Recall from Chapter 4 that if the market is competitive, each individual participant will represent such a small share of the total that the individual will have no impact on the price. Individual demand curves must be combined to determine the **market demand curve** for a particular good.

*The **market demand** shows the total quantities demanded by all consumers in the market at each price. It is the horizontal summation of all individual demand curves in that market.*

Figure 3 shows the demand curves for ale for two consumers, Jones and White, who constitute all the buyers in the market for ale. At a price of $3 per pint, Jones demands 0 pints and White demands 1 pint. The market quantity demanded at the $3 price can be obtained by adding the two quantities demanded together ($0 + 1 = 1$ pint). At a price of $1 per pint, Jones demands 2 pints and White demands 3 pints. The market quantity demanded at the $1 price is $2 + 3 = 5$ pints.

The market demand curve in Figure 3 is downward-sloping for the same reasons that the individual demand curves are downward-sloping. In addition, as price decreases more consumers might be enticed to buy a product. In Figure 3, for example, when the price of ale is above $3 Jones is not in the market; at a price of $0.50, even more buyers may enter the market. Along the market demand curve, just as along an individual demand curve, the consumers who are purchasing the good are achieving (individually) maximum satisfaction at that price.

CONSUMER SURPLUS

We have shown that a high-priced good (diamonds) has a proportionately higher marginal utility than a low-priced good (water). When consumers maximize their satisfaction, consumption of each good is pushed to the point where marginal utility *(MU/P)* is the same for all goods. *The theory of consumer demand shows that price reflects marginal utility.*

When consumers are in equilibrium, the price of a good is a dollar measure of what the last unit of the good is worth (its marginal utility).

Figure 4 shows the market demand curve for a product. At the current market price of $5, the quantity demanded is 6 units. The demand curve shows that at a price of $10, the quantity demanded is 1 unit; at a price of $9, quantity demanded is 2 units; and so on. Similarly, the demand curve shows that if only one unit of the product were available, some consumer would have been willing to pay a price of $10 for it. If only two units of the product were available, someone would have been willing to pay $9 for the second unit. If 6 units were available, someone would have been willing to pay a price of $5 for the sixth unit. The current market price therefore reveals what consumers are willing to pay for the *last unit* of the product sold.

When the market price is $5 and the quantity demanded is 6 units (point *m*), the price reflects what the sixth unit is worth to consumers. Even though the first of those 6 units is still worth $10 to someone, the second of the 6 units is still worth $9 to someone else, and so on to the sixth unit, which is worth $5 to someone, each consumer actually pays only $5 for each of the 6 units. The total of what the 6 units combined are worth ($10 + $9 + $8 + $7 + $6 + $5 = $45) is greater than the total of what consumers pay for all 6 units (6 × $5 = $30) because each consumer pays for each of the 6 units only what the *last* unit is worth.

Consumers pay the same market price for each unit, but the market price reflects only what the *last unit sold* is worth. Because earlier units have a higher marginal value than later units, consumers enjoy a surplus on all the earlier units. The **consumer surplus** on each unit is the excess of what that unit is worth over what the consumer must pay.

At a price of $5 the first unit is worth $10 to

Figure 4
Consumer Surplus

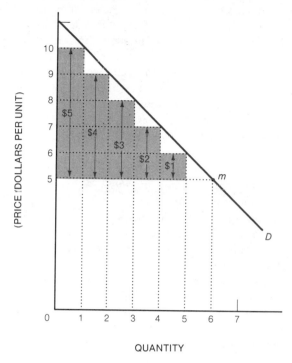

QUANTITY

The demand curve shows that consumers are prepared to buy a sixth unit of this good for $5 but were prepared to spend $10 for the first unit, $9 for the second unit, $8 for the third unit, $7 for the fourth unit, and $6 for the fifth unit. When they buy six units, however, the need pay only $5 each for all six units. Thus, they pay for each of the six units only what the sixth unit is worth to them. The difference between what each unit is worth to consumers and what the consumers actually pay is shown by the height of the shaded area for each unit. Adding these surpluses for all units yields a total consumer surplus of $5 + $4 + $3 + $2 + $1 = $15.

someone but costs $5 so that person enjoys a surplus of $5 on the first unit. Someone enjoys a surplus of $4 on the second unit, for the second unit is worth $9 to that person but costs $5. Only the last unit sold (the sixth) will yield no surplus, for its price will reflect exactly what that unit is worth to the consumer. Adding these surpluses together, one obtains the total consumer surplus of $15.

***Consumer surplus** is the excess of the total consumer benefit that a good provides over what the consumers actually have to pay.*

The consumer surplus concept provides another perspective for viewing the water/diamond paradox. Consumer surplus is a measure, to use Adam Smith's words, of the difference between the "use value" of a good and its market value. Consumer surplus on low-priced but essential goods like water will be substantial. On high-priced but nonessential goods like diamonds, consumer surplus will be low.

Consumer surplus measures how much the total benefits consumers obtain from a good or service exceed what consumers pay for the product. The lower the price of water, the higher the consumer surplus *ceteris paribus*. As consumers move along a demand curve, consumer surplus changes. If the price increases, the excess of consumer benefits over consumer costs falls; if the price falls, the excess of consumer benefits over consumer costs rises.

Consumer surplus can be used to measure consumer gains and losses from price changes along a given demand curve. If electric utility rates are raised, what have consumers lost? If airline fares are lowered, what have consumers gained? These losses and gains are the changes in consumer surplus.

Figure 5 identifies two points on a demand curve for a particular good. At *f*, the price is $15, and the quantity demanded is 1,000 units. Consumers therefore pay a total of $15,000 ($15 × 1,000 units) for the product. Consumer surplus is equal to the area of the color triangle labeled *A*. At quantities below 1,000 units, consumers are willing to pay more than the $15 they have to pay. The vertical distance between the demand curve and the horizontal line at $15 is the surplus for each unit.[3] Adding all these surpluses together yields the consumer surplus, or the area of the triangle *A*.[4]

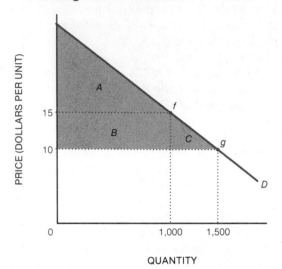

Figure 5
The Gain in Consumer Surplus Resulting from a Reduction in Price

When price is $15 and quantity demanded is 1,000 units, the consumer surplus is the area *A*, the excess of what people would be willing to pay over what they actually pay. If the price falls to $10, quantity demanded increases to 1,500 units and consumer surplus is the area *A* + *B* + *C*. Consumer surplus, therefore, increases by *B* + *C*, or by $6,250.

---

3. By changing quantity demanded in very small increments, the demand schedule approximates a smooth line. Thus, instead of a series of rectangles added together as in Figure 4, consumer surplus is measured by the smooth area of a triangle.
4. Areas of *rectangles* are computed by multiplying the horizontal width of the rectangle times the vertical height of the rectangle. The width of rectangle *B* is 1,000; the height is $5. Areas of triangles are calculated by: multiplying the width of the triangle by its height and dividing by 2 (or multiplying by ½). The area of the triangle will be ½ that of the rectangle formed by the height and width of the triangle.

What happens to consumer surplus if the market price drops to $10? Logically, it should be clear that consumer surplus will increase because now there is a surplus at all quantities less than 1,500, whereas the surplus stopped at 1,000 before. Consumer surplus at point *g*, where price is $10, is the area of the triangle formed by the demand curve and the horizontal line at $10. This new triangle is the sum of the three areas *A* + *B* + *C*. Consumer surplus at a price of $15 was area *A*; at a price of $10, consumer surplus is *A* + *B* + *C*. Therefore, the *increase* in consumer surplus as a consequence of the drop in price is *B* + *C*. The area *B* + *C* = $5,000 (area of *B*) + $1,250 (area of *C*) = $6,250.

The segment of the demand curve between *f* and *g* in this example was deliberately constructed to have an elasticity of demand of unity, so that the amount of consumer spending at the two points on the demand schedule are equal. At both prices, consumers spend $15,000 but at the lower price, consumer surplus is $6,250 greater than at the higher price.

This chapter has examined the relationship between consumer behavior and the demand curve for goods and services. The next chapter will shift to the supply side of the market for products and will examine how businesses are organized and the different types of markets in which firms operate.

Summary

1. *Preferences* are people's evaluations of goods and services independent of budget and price considerations. Consumer preferences are fairly stable when the services that the consumer goods provide are broadly defined. For example, the preference for transportation services is more stable than the demand for a particular type of transportation service.
2. The satisfaction that is obtained from consuming goods and services is called *utility*. *Marginal utility* is the increase in total utility obtained when consumption of a good is increased by one unit.
3. The law of diminishing marginal utility states that marginal utility declines as more of a good or service is consumed.
4. The fact that market prices reflect marginal utility rather than total utility explains the diamond/water paradox (why diamonds are more expensive than water).
5. The law of diminishing marginal utility is consistent with the law of demand. When the rational consumer equates marginal utility per dollar on the last purchases of each commodity, the consumer is in equilibrium. If the price of one good falls, its marginal utility per dollar initially rises and more of the commodity will be consumed.
6. Rational consumers will spend their money in a way that maximizes their satisfaction (utility).
7. When the price of a commodity drops, two effects will be set in motion: The income effect occurs when the price decrease raises the real income of the consumer and when this

increase in income is used to purchase additional goods and services. The substitution effect occurs because the fall in the relative price of the good motivates the consumer to substitute the good for other goods.
8. The market demand schedule is the horizontal summation of the demand schedules of all individuals participating in the market. The market demand schedule will have a negative slope because its individual components have negative slopes.
9. *Consumer surplus* is the excess of consumer benefits over consumer costs for a particular product. Consumer surplus follows from the law of diminishing marginal utility. Consumers pay the same market price for each unit they buy, but the market price reflects only what the last unit sold is worth. The marginal utility of earlier units exceeds the market price. Adding these surpluses together yields total consumer surplus. The consumer-surplus concept permits the measurement of consumer losses and gains from price changes.

Key Terms

preferences
utility
marginal utility
law of diminishing marginal utility
consumer equilibrium
income effect
substitution effect
market demand curve
consumer surplus

Questions and Problems

1. In some parts of Africa today, sick people go to witch doctors. In the United States, most people seek out medical doctors when they are ill; a few seek out faith healers. Are consumer preferences for medical care, then, basically unstable?
2. One of the most basic changes in consumer buying patterns in the late 1970s and early

1980s was the switch from "gas guzzlers" to fuel-efficient cars. Does this switch indicate that consumer preferences are unstable? Why is the *ceteris paribus* qualification important in this example?

3. If the marginal utility of a good *(A)* were to increase as consumption of the good increased (in opposition to the law of diminishing marginal utility), would $MU_A/P_A = MU_B/P_B$ still be the equilibrium condition?

4. Use the marginal-utility information in Table 1 to calculate the quantity demanded of ale at a price of $4. What do you do when marginal utility per dollar cannot be exactly equated on the last units sold?

5. Again using Table 1, calculate the quantity demanded of ale at the price of $2 but at a weekly income of $11. Compare this result with the answer at $8. Which is larger? Why?

6. Assume that there are 1,000 identical consumers in the market with the same income and the same preferences. When the price of *X* is $50, the typical consumer is prepared to purchase 20 units of *X*. When the price is $40, the typical consumer is prepared to purchase 25 units of *X*. Construct from this information the market demand curve for *X* (assume the demand curve is a straight line). Then calculate the loss of consumer surplus when the price rises from $40 to $50.

7. A consumer is spending an entire weekly income on goods *A* and *B*. The last penny spent on *A* yields a marginal utility of 10; the last penny spent on *B* yields a marginal utility of 20. Is it possible for the consumer to be in equilibrium? If so, what are the exact conditions?

8. *Optional Question:* Income and substitution effects can be measured. Suppose that the income elasticity of demand for housing is 1 and that the price elasticity of demand is 0.3 (these numbers are close to actual estimates). Furthermore, suppose that housing accounts for 20 percent of the households' budget. A decrease in income of 2 percent would decrease the demand for housing by 2 percent because the income elasticity is 1. Now suppose that income is held constant and that the price of housing rises by 10 percent. Since the price elasticity is 0.3, a 10 percent increase in price will lower quantity demanded by 3 percent. What portion of this 3 percent decrease in quantity demanded is due to the income effect? What portion is due to the substitution effect? (Hint: a 10 percent increase in the price of housing raises the cost of living by 2 percent since there is a 10 percent increase in 20 percent of the budget. Observe also that an increase in the cost of living of 2 percent has the same effects as a 2 percent reduction in income. Therefore, a 10 percent increase in the price of housing, holding income and other prices constant, is like a 2 percent reduction in real income.)

6A

Indifference Curves

Appendix Preview

The preceding chapter on demand and utility showed how the law of diminishing marginal utility can be used to explain the law of demand. In equilibrium, consumers will equate marginal utilities per dollar on the last unit of items consumed. If the price of good A rises, the marginal utility per dollar of A will be *less* than that of other goods. The law of diminishing marginal utility states that the marginal utility of A will increase if less of A is consumed. Therefore consumer equilibrium is reattained by consuming less of A. Because of diminishing marginal utility, there will be a negative relationship between price and quantity demanded.

The law of diminishing marginal utility does explain the law of demand but its claim to realism is limited. It requires that people be able to measure the *utility* they obtain by consuming various quantities of goods and services.

Because of skepticism about the measurement of utility, economists were forced to find an alternate approach to understanding consumer behavior. The culmination of this search is *indifference-curve theory*. This theory does not require that consumers be able to measure utility in any specific units of measurement but does assume that consumers are able to rank their preferences for combinations of goods. The consumer should be able to choose between 4 pints of ale and 5 loaves of bread on the one hand and 8 pints of ale and 1 loaf of bread on the other. If the consumer does not prefer one combination to the other, the consumer is said to be indifferent.

CONSUMER PREFERENCES

As noted above, the indifference-curve approach does not require consumers to know util values of goods in order to decide how much of each good is desired. Rather, the consumer must only be able to decide how much of one good he or she is willing to give up in trade for one unit of another good without experiencing a loss in total satisfaction. When one combination of goods yields the same satisfaction as another combination, the consumer is indifferent between the two combinations.

In Figure 1, the horizontal axis measures the quantity of ale consumed by the individual per week. The vertical axis measures the quantity of bread consumed by the individual per week. At point *a,* 6 loaves of bread and 1 pint of ale are consumed. At *a,* the consumer is willing to give up 3 loaves of bread for 1 more pint of ale. This trade-off would move the consumer to point *b* where 3 loaves of bread and 2 pints of ale are consumed. At point *b,* the consumer is no longer willing to give up 3 loaves of bread to acquire 1 more pint of ale. The consumer is now willing to give up only 1 loaf of bread to acquire 1 more

Figure 1
An Indifference Curve

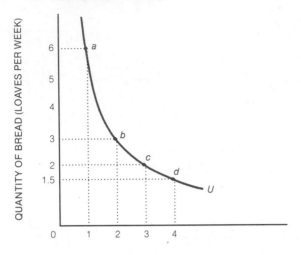

QUANTITY OF ALE (PINTS PER WEEK)

The consumer is indifferent between the commodity bundles along an indifference curve. Consumption pattern *a* yields the same satisfaction as *b, c,* or *d*. The absolute slope of an indifference curve is the marginal rate of substitution and shows—in this case—how much bread the consumer is just willing to sacrifice for one more pint of ale.

pint of ale. This trade-off would put the consumer at point *c*, consuming 2 loaves of bread and 3 pints of ale per week. Finally, to acquire 1 more pint of ale, the consumer is willing now to give up only half a loaf of bread, moving the consumer to point *d*. The consumer is indifferent between points *a, b, c,* and *d* and feels equally well off at any of these points.

A curve can be drawn, through points *a, b, c,* and *d*, which represents all possible trade-offs that keep the consumer at the same level of satisfaction. This curve is called an **indifference curve** because every point on the curve yields the same satisfaction even though the consumption pattern is different at each point.

> An **indifference curve** *is a graph of all the alternative combinations of two goods that yield the same total satisfaction and among which the consumer would be indifferent.*

An indifference curve is downward-sloping because as long as both goods yield satisfaction, more is better than less. The only way for the

consumer's satisfaction to stay the same when more of one good is consumed is to consume less of the other good.

The Law of the Diminishing Marginal Rate of Substitution

Indifference-curve analysis substitutes the concept of the **marginal rate of substitution** for the concept of marginal utility.

> The **marginal rate of substitution** *is how much of one good a person is just willing to give up to acquire one unit of another.*

Thus the marginal rate of substitution is just a fancy name for an acceptable trade-off between two goods or for the person's *valuation* of an additional unit of one good in terms of the other.

An indifference curve is always convex when viewed from below (bulges out toward the origin.) The convex curvature of the indifference curve follows from the **law of the diminishing marginal rate of substitution:** as more ale is consumed relative to bread, the consumer is willing to give up less and less bread to acquire additional units of ale. When one moves from point *a* down to point *d* and beyond, the indifference curve gets flatter and flatter since the relative valuation placed on ale is decreasing compared to bread.

> The **law of diminishing marginal rate of substitution** *is that as more of one good* (A) *is consumed, the amount of the other good* (B) *that the consumer is willing to sacrifice for one more unit of* (A) *declines.*

The flatter the slope of the indifference curve, the lower the relative valuation the consumer places on *A* (compared to *B*). The slope of the tangent at any point on the indifference curve measures the marginal rate of substitution of bread *(B)* for ale *(A)*.

Indifference curves can be drawn to represent any level of satisfaction. Figure 2 shows the same consumer at three different levels of satisfaction. Higher indifference curves for any one consumer represent higher levels of satisfaction. Each consumer has an entire map of indifference curves, one for every level of satisfaction. Figure 2 shows only three indifference curves. Whether a person

Figure 2
The Map of Indifference Curves

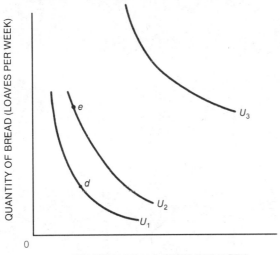

QUANTITY OF BREAD (LOAVES PER WEEK)

QUANTITY OF ALE (PINTS PER WEEK)

There is an infinite number of indifference curves for each consumer; three indifference curves for a particular consumer are shown here. The higher the indifference curve, the greater the well-being of the consumer. The indifference map shows that commodity bundle e is preferred to bundle d because the former is on a higher indifference curve. Indifference curve U_3 represents a higher level of satisfaction than U_2, and U_2 represents a higher level than U_1. The level of satisfaction along each indifference curve is constant.

is poor or well off is determined by the person's income and the relative prices of goods.

Indifference curves have five properties:

1. They are bowed out toward the origin, which reflects the law of diminishing marginal rate of substitution.
2. The consumer is better off when he or she moves to a higher indifference curve.
3. Indifference curves that show preferences between two goods from which consumers derive benefits are downward-sloping.
4. Indifference curves cannot intersect each other, because an intersection would indicate that the consumer is simultaneously worse off and better off. (Even though indifference curves do not intersect, they need not be parallel.)
5. Indifference curves do not move as a result of market circumstances (changes in income or prices).

A consumer's position on an indifference curve is determined by the consumer's budget.

Figure 3
The Budget Line

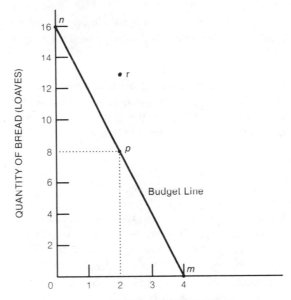

QUANTITY OF BREAD (LOAVES)

QUANTITY OF ALE (PINTS)

With a budget of $8, the consumer can buy 16 loaves of bread at a price of $0.50 a loaf or 4 pints of ale at a price of $2 a pint. Spending $4 on each good would buy 8 loaves of bread and 2 pints of ale (point p). The budget line shows the choices open to the consumer. The consumer can afford to buy any combination of goods on the budget line. Points above the budget line such as r cannot be purchased with the consumer's income. The slope of the budget line is the ratio of the price of ale to the price of bread—here 4.

The Budget Line

Suppose the price of ale is $2 a pint and the price of bread is $0.50 a loaf, as in the chapter. Assume the consumer has $8 to spend on ale and bread. If the entire $8 is spent on ale, the consumer can buy 4 pints of ale. This combination corresponds to point m in Figure 3. If the entire $8 is spent on bread, 16 loaves of bread can be purchased. this combination corresponds to point n. The **budget line** connecting points m and n represents all the other combinations of ale and bread the consumer is able to buy by spending the entire $8 income on the two goods.

*The **budget line** is all the combinations of goods the consumer is able to buy given a certain income and set prices. The budget line shows the choices of consumer goods available to the consumer.*

The budget line in Figure 3 has the slope $16/4$ = 4. This slope is the price of ale in terms of bread: P_A/P_B = $2/$0.50 = 4. The slope indicates that if the consumer wants to buy one more pint of ale, the consumer must give up 4 loaves of bread.

Algebraically, point m in Figure 3 is income divided by the price of ale because point m shows the maximum possible consumption of ale. Point n is income divided by the price of bread. The absolute slope of the line nm is then:

$$\frac{\text{Income}}{P_B} \div \frac{\text{Income}}{P_A} = \frac{P_A}{P_B}.$$

Indifference curves show what the consumer *is willing* to buy; the budget line shows what the consumer *is able* to buy. Combining the information represented by the indifference curve and the budget line shows what combination the consumer *is most likely to* buy.

CONSUMER EQUILIBRIUM

The consumer achieves equilibrium by choosing a consumption pattern that maximizes the consumer's satisfaction on the budget line. Figure 4 shows the optimal consumption pattern. The consumer is *able* to locate anywhere on the budget line, but *the rational consumer will select that consumption combination that falls on the highest attainable indifference curve*. This combination is point e: by consuming 4 loaves of bread and 3 pints of ale the consumer can reach indifference curve U_1. Any other point on the budget line will fall on a *lower* indifference curve. At the optimal consumption pattern e, the budget line is tangent to (has the same slope as) and barely touches the indifference curve.

Equivalently, consumer equilibrium occurs at that point on the highest attainable indifference curve where the marginal rate of substitution equals the price ratio. At e, the consumer's marginal rate of substitution is 4 since the consumer is willing to trade off 4 units of bread for one unit of ale. The price ratio, as we have shown, is also 4. Thus, the consumer will be in equilibrium when the marginal rate of substitution equals the price ratio.

Figure 4
Consumer Equilibrium

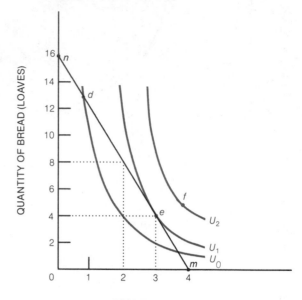

QUANTITY OF ALE (PINTS)

The consumer's optimal consumption pattern is at e. A point like d is attainable (on the budget line) but not as good as e because it places the consumer at a lower indifference curve (U_0). Point f is better than e (the consumer is on a higher indifference curve, U_2) but is not attainable with the given set of income and prices. At e, the indifference curve U_1 is tangent to the budget line. Thus the slope of the indifference curve equals the slope of the budget line. This tangency is equivalent to the marginal utility rule for maximizing utility ($MU_A/P_A = MU_B/P_B$) discussed in the chapter.

The consumer is in equilibrium when the budget line is just tangent to the highest attainable indifference curve. Two conditions are then satisfied:

1. The consumer is on the budget line.

2. The consumer's marginal rate of substitution of bread for ale equals the price ratio of ale to bread (P_A/P_B).

There is a link between indifference-curve analysis and marginal utility theory. The marginal rate of substitution of bread for ale can also be indicated by the marginal utilities of ale and bread. For example: if the marginal utility of ale (MU_A) is 20 and the marginal utility of bread (MU_B) is 5, it takes 4 extra loaves of bread to compensate the consumer for the loss of only 1

Figure 5
The Effect of a Price Change on Consumer Equilibrium: The Law of Demand

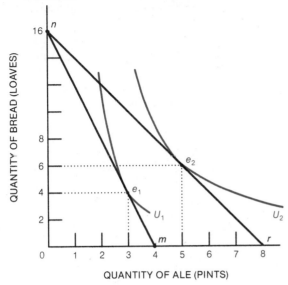

Assuming that income is $8 and the price of bread is $0.50, when the price of ale falls from $2 to $1 per pint, the budget line swings outward from *nm* to *nr* because the consumer is able to buy as many as 8 pints of ale. The consumer seeks out a new equilibrium combination, e_2, where indifference curve U_2 is tangent to the new budget line *nr*. A fall in the price of ale from $2 to $1, thus, increases the quantity of ale demanded from 3 pints at point e_1 to 5 pints at point e_2.

pint of ale. But if $MU_A = 10$ and $MU_B = 5$, the marginal rate of substitution of bread for ale is only 2. These examples show:

The marginal rate of substitution of bread for ale ($MRS_{B/A}$) equals the ratio of the ale's marginal utility to the bread's marginal utility (MU_A/MU_B).

The condition for equilibrium can now be translated into the equal-marginal-utility-per-dollar rule for consumer equilibrium described in the preceding chapter. At *e*, the slope of the indifference curve is MU_A/MU_B. The slope of the budget line is P_A/P_B. The indifference-curve equilibrium rule is equivalent to $MU_A/MU_B = P_A/P_B$. A little algebraic manipulation shows that this is equivalent to the marginal-utility-per-dollar rule for equilibrium: $MU_A/P_A = MU_B/P_B$.

THE EFFECT OF A PRICE CHANGE

The consumer's equilibrium position will be affected if income changes, if the price of ale changes, or if the price of bread changes, although the indifference curves will not move as a result of these changes. Figure 5 shows how a fall in the price of ale from $2 to $1 a pint leads to an increase in the quantity of ale demanded. The initial situation is represented by the equilibrium combination e_1, where the price of ale is $2 and the price of bread is $0.50. Reducing the price of ale to $1 will allow the consumer the option of purchasing as many as 8 pints of ale, since the income remains $8. The budget line will now swing outward from *nm* to *nr*.

When the price of one good falls, an increase in real income occurs, as shown by an outward swing of the budget line.

The new equilibrium position occurs at e_2. At this point, the consumer buys 5 pints of ale and 6 loaves of bread. Before the price change, the consumer bought 3 pints of ale and 4 loaves of bread. The law of demand is confirmed: lowering the price of ale increases the quantity of ale demanded.

The consumer is clearly made better off (moves to a higher indifference curve) by the fall in the price of ale. Clearly, the consumer gets a bonus from low prices; the lower the price of a good bought by a consumer, holding income and other prices constant, the greater the consumer's welfare.

Summary

1. Indifference-curve analysis requires only that consumers be able to state whether they prefer one combination of goods to another combination or whether they are indifferent. An indifference curve plots those combinations of goods that yield the same level of satisfaction to the consumer. Indifference curves are negatively sloped (because more is better than less), and they are convex from below.

Indifference maps show the tastes of individual consumers. If tastes differ, this will be reflected in different shapes of the indifference maps. The higher the indifference curve in the indifference map, the higher the level of satisfaction that the consumer receives.

2. In indifference-curve analysis, the law of the diminishing marginal rate of substitution replaces the law of diminishing marginal utility. It states that the greater the quantity of good X that the individual consumes relative to good Y, the smaller the quantity of good Y that the consumer will be willing to sacrifice to obtain one more unit of good X.

3. The budget line shows the choices of goods open to the consumer.

4. Maximizing satisfaction requires that the consumer seek out the highest indifference curve while remaining on the budget line. This point occurs at the tangency of the indifference curve and the budget line. The indifference curve rule for maximizing satisfaction can be translated into the marginal-utility-per dollar rule.

5. A reduction in the price of one commodity causes the budget line to swing outward. The new equilibrium takes place at the point of tangency between a higher indifference curve and the new budget line. The consumer is made better off by the price reduction because the consumer is able to locate on a higher indifference curve.

Key Terms

indifference curve
marginal rate of substitution
law of diminishing marginal rate of
    substitution
budget line

7

Business Organization

Chapter Preview

In studying consumer behavior, the previous chapter examined the demand side of the market for products. This chapter will examine the suppliers of products: firms. Firms can be owned by a single individual or by several individuals, or they can be controlled by a board of directors on behalf of stockholders. This chapter will discuss the role of business firms in the economy, the advantages and disadvantages of various forms of business organization, the elements of corporation finance (stocks and bonds), and the four market models used by economists to study the different degrees of competition in an industry.

Firms are islands of managerial coordination in a sea of market coordination. Chapters 3 and 4 described how the market coordinates economic activities and allocates resources among producers and consumers through the price system. An alternative to market coordination is **managerial coordination.**

Managerial coordination is the allocation of factors of production by a manager or central planner.

In the real world, production usually takes place by means of managerial coordination within a business firm and by means of market coordination among business firms.

THE ROLE OF BUSINESS FIRMS IN THE ECONOMY

What role do business firms play in the process of resource allocation? Why do we even need business firms? Earlier chapters discussed the role of *entrepreneurs*—individuals who combine the factors of production to produce output. It is theoretically possible for entrepreneurs to work entirely through the market without business firms. A single entrepreneur may build a home by contracting through the market with the numerous carpenters, plumbers, electricians, and lumber and glass suppliers needed to build the home. Or an entrepreneur may supply individual artisans with materials to produce goods. Such instances are, however, rare in modern economies. Most products are produced by firms that integrate operations and combine the factors of production according to the directives of an employed manager.

The construction firm builds homes by having the manager direct employees—carpenters, electricians, and unskilled laborers—to perform particular tasks. The furniture manufacturer employs skilled workers for carpentry work and unskilled workers for packing and delivery and maintains a fleet of delivery trucks.

Reasons for Managerial Allocation

Under what circumstances will managerial allocation be more effective than market allocation?

Economies of Scale.   As Adam Smith pointed out, one strong reason for business firms is the presence of **economies of scale.**

Economies of scale are present in the production process when large output volumes can be produced at a lower cost per unit than small output volumes.

Such economies are present in many production processes (Smith's example was a pin factory) in which costs per unit are reduced by the specialization of labor and equipment that is possible at a sufficiently large scale of output. The business firm brings together workers, land, and capital; the manager directs them to specialize in different tasks; output is produced in larger pro-

duction runs and at lower cost per unit than if each worker had worked alone.

Risk Bearing.   University of Chicago economist Frank Knight cited a second reason for business firms.[1] Some individuals are more willing to bear risk than others. Business ventures typically involve risk (markets can change, factor prices can fluctuate, and so on). The owner of the enterprise will be the one who is willing to bear the risks. The employees will be those individuals who dislike risk. The employer will hire workers and rent land and equipment at negotiated prices. The employer provides the suppliers of the factors of production with security, in return for which they agree to follow the owner's business directives. If the business is successful, the owner will reap the rewards; if it fails, the owner will suffer the consequences.

The Costs of Using Markets.   Ronald Coase, also of the University of Chicago, concentrates on a third reason for business firms.[2] Market coordination has its costs. The participants in market-coordinated activities must negotiate contracts, must do all sorts of paper work, must search out the best prices, and must bear the legal expenses if contracts are not fulfilled. Business firms can limit the costs of market transactions. Imagine, for example, the enormous transactions costs of using market coordination instead of managerial coordination to produce a modern commercial jet aircraft. If market coordination were used, thousands of subcontracts would have to be negotiated to produce the instruments, the hydraulic control systems, the airframe, and the interior furnishings. The expense of using market coordination would be enormous in this instance. Managerial coordination could reduce these transactions costs. Instead of negotiating thousands of market contracts, the manager simply directs employees to perform designated tasks, allocates the plant and equipment of the business enterprise, and works with fewer subcontractors.

1. Frank H. Knight, *Risk, Uncertainty, and Profit* (New York: Harper Torchbooks, 1957).
2. Ronald H. Coase, "The Nature of the Firm," *"Economica* 4 (1937): 386–405. Reprinted in George Stigler and Kenneth Boulding, eds. *Readings in Price Theory* (Homewood, Ill.: Richard D. Irwin, 1952).

In the Coase system, the dividing line between activities undertaken within the firm and those undertaken by the market would be determined by comparing the cost of market coordination with the cost of managerial coordination. As long as the marginal cost of organizing inside the firm remained below the marginal cost of organizing that activity on a market basis, the task would be carried out within the firm. When the marginal cost of organizing the activity within the firm exceeds the marginal cost of using the market, then the task will be carried out by the market.

Monitoring Team Production. UCLA economists Armen Alchian and Harold Demsetz emphasize that business enterprises are formed when there are substantial gains from team production.[3] Alchian and Demsetz believe there are situations where more output can be produced by employees working as a group than if each employee had worked alone. Where there is team production there is the problem of monitoring the performance of individual employees, because it is not easy to determine the contribution of each team member.

The role of the owner-manager, therefore, is to monitor the performance of team members and to prevent shirking of work. Because the owner of a firm is paid out of the gains to team production, the owner will be motivated to do a good job of monitoring. Moreover, the owner has the authority to change the composition of the production team by changing contractual arrangements between the business enterprise and its inputs.

Limits to Managerial Allocation

If managerial coordination is such a good idea in all the above situations, then what reasons are there *not* to have managerial coordination of all resource-allocation decisions. First, there are limits to the gains from economies of scale. If enterprises become too large, their costs of production per product may be higher than those of a smaller firm. Second, as the number and scope of managerial decisions increase, so do the costs of managerial coordination. The manager in this case is

called upon to do too many things and to have to know too much information about prices, equipment, and so on. As the business enterprise grows, an optimal size will be reached beyond which the gains to managerial coordination (in the form of reduced transactions costs) will be overwhelmed by the rising costs of managerial coordination.

The real world consists of a mixture of managerial coordination and market coordination. Some activities are carried out within firms; other activities are the result of market coordination among firms. One automobile manufacturer will produce and market automobiles entirely within the business enterprise's own plant and sales offices. Another automobile manufacturer will purchase engines and other parts from foreign and domestic manufacturers, will assemble the automobile, and will leave the marketing of the product to independent distributors. Whether the first or second mode of coordination is used depends upon economies of scale, risk, costs of arranging market transactions, and the benefits of team production.

PROFIT MAXIMIZATION

Before one can understand the behavior of business firms, one must examine what motivates a business firm. What is the goal of a business firm? Most economists have a simple answer: the objective of all business firms (other than nonprofit organizations) is **profit maximization.**

Profit maximization is the search by firms for the product quality, output, and price that give the firm the highest possible profits.

Opposing Theories

Some prominent economists disagree with the assumption that all firms seek to maximize profits. William J. Baumol argues that firms seek to maximize their sales. Robin Marris maintains that firms seek to maximize the growth of the firm after they have insured the security of the management in its position. A. A. Berle and Gardner Means argue that the separation of ownership and management has allowed managers to neglect the

3. Armen Alchian and Harold Demsetz, "Production, Information Costs, and Economic Organization," *American Economic Review* 57, 5 (December 1972): 777–95.

profit-maximization goal desired by shareholders and to concentrate on other objectives (such as the size of the firm, the number of employees reporting to them, and so on). John K. Galbraith argues in a similar vein that the separation of ownership and management has spawned a managerial elite—called the *technostructure*—whose goals are to limit risks and reduce uncertainty and surprises. Oliver Williamson maintains that managers will not pursue their own self-interests until they have kept profits and dividends at a level acceptable to shareholders. Finally, there are those like Richard Cyert, James March, and Herbert Simon who argue that managers set a goal for satisfactory profits and then pursue other goals, including perhaps what they regard as their social responsibilities.

Natural Selection

The major defense of profit maximization is the **natural selection theory.**

> According to the **natural selection theory,** if business firms do not maximize profits, they will be unable to compete with other firms and will be driven out of the market.

Obviously survival is important to all managers and owners; any firm or management that does not seek to maximize profits will not pass the "survival of the fittest" test. The natural selection argument is compelling in the case of firms that face competition. It is less compelling for monopolists who (at least in theory) do not have to deal with competition.

The ultimate test of any behavioral assumption is whether the predictions that emerge from the assumption appear to describe reality. As subsequent chapters shall demonstrate, the real power of the profit-maximization assumption is that it appears to describe the reality of business behavior quite well.

FORMS OF BUSINESS ORGANIZATION

Business enterprises are customarily classified into three categories: sole proprietorships, partnerships, and corporations. Which form a business enterprise takes determines who makes busi-

ness decisions, how capital is raised, who bears the risk of business failures, and how profits are taxed.

Sole Proprietorships

The **sole proprietorship** is the least complex form of business enterprise.

> The **sole proprietorship** is a form of business that is owned by one individual who makes all the business decisions, receives the profits that the business earns, and bears the financial responsibility for losses.

From this description, the simplicity of the individual proprietorship is apparent. Barring legal restrictions any individual can simply decide to go into business. The individual proprietor need not seek permission to enter into business except in areas of enterprise where business licenses are required, where health permits must be obtained, or where permission must be granted by zoning boards. Such restrictions aside, the individual who has accumulated or borrowed sufficient funds to set up a business can do so. No legal work is required to set up a sole proprietorship, although the individual proprietor will often seek legal and accounting advice.

Once in business, the proprietor is responsible for all business decisions. The owner determines how many employees to hire, when they should be rewarded or penalized, what products to produce, how they are to be marketed. The owner need not seek anyone's permission to make such decisions. The basic limitation upon decision making is that the owner must observe the law and honor contracts. Otherwise, the owner is free to make wise or foolish decisions.

Advantages. The first advantage of the sole proprietorship is that decision-making authority is clear-cut: it resides with the owner. In making business decisions, the owner need not consult anyone. *The owner is the sole decision maker*.

The second advantage of the sole proprietorship is that the profits of the business enterprise are *taxed only once*. The individual proprietor will receive any profits that the business earns after meeting its expenses. The proprietor pays personal income taxes on these profits.

Disadvantages.   There are three basic disadvantages of the sole proprietorship. The first is that the owner must assume *unlimited liability* (responsibility) for the debts of the company. The owner enjoys the profit of the business if it is successful, but if the business suffers a loss, the owner is personally liable. If the company borrows money, purchases materials, and incurs other bills that it cannot cover out of its revenues, the owner must personally cover the losses. The owner stands to lose personal wealth accumulated over the years in paying off the debts of the company.

The second disadvantage of the sole proprietorship is its *limited ability to raise financial capital*. This limitation makes it difficult for sole proprietorships to grow to a large size and explains why most proprietorships are small businesses. Financial capital for the expansion of the company can be raised in several ways in the case of the sole proprietorship. The owner can choose to plow profits back into the business. The owner can dip into personal wealth to invest in the company, or the owner can borrow money from relatives, friends, and lending institutions. The ability of the owner to borrow is determined by the owner's earning capacity (which will depend upon the success of the business) and personal wealth. Lending money to an individual proprietorship can be risky because the success of the business depends very much on one person, and if that person dies or becomes incapacitated, the lender will have to stand in line with other creditors.

The third disadvantage is that the business will typically die with the owner. Since the firm does not have a permanent existence, it may be difficult to find reliable employees; many employees prefer to work in firms that will be around long enough to offer employees career advancement.

Partnerships

A **partnership** is much like an individual proprietorship, but with more than one owner.

*A **partnership** is a business enterprise that is owned by two or more people (called partners), who make all the business decisions, who share the profits of the business, and who bear the financial responsibility for any losses.*

Like the individual proprietorship, partnerships are easy to establish. Most partnerships are based upon an agreement that spells out the ownership shares and duties of each partner. The partners may contribute different amounts of financial capital to the partnership; there may be an agreement on the division of responsibility for running the business; partners may own different shares of the business. One partner may make all the business decisions, while the other partner (a "silent partner") may simply provide financial capital. A partnership can be a corner gas station owned by three brothers or a nationally known bank or brokerage house.

Advantages.   The advantages of partnerships are much like those of the sole proprietorship. Partnerships are easy to set up. The profits of the company accrue to the partners and are taxed only once as personal income.

Unlike the sole proprietorship, however, there is a greater opportunity to specialize and divide managerial responsibility because the partnership consists of two or more individuals. The partner who is the better salesperson will be in charge of the sales department. The partner who is a talented mechanical engineer will be in charge of production. "Two heads are better than one," when each has different talents that are useful to the business enterprise. Second, a partnership can raise more financial capital than a sole proprietorship because the wealth and borrowing ability of more than one person can be mobilized. In fact, if a large number of wealthy partners can be assembled, such partnerships can indeed raise large sums of capital.

Disadvantages.   The ability of the partnership to raise financial capital is limited by the amount of money the partners can raise out of their personal wealth or from borrowing. The partners have unlimited liability for the debts of the partnership. A business debt incurred by any of the partners is the responsibility of the partnership. Each partner stands to lose personal wealth if the company is a commercial failure.

"Two heads are better than one" *if* the two heads agree. But if partners fail to agree, decision making can become quite complicated. In a partnership where all partners are responsible for management decisions, there is no longer one single person who is in charge. Partnerships can be immobilized when partners disagree on fundamental policy. It may be difficult to reach decisions if one partner is out of town. Partnerships involve a more complicated decision-making process that can become more complicated as the number of partners grows.

Partnerships can also be unstable. If disagreements over policy cause one partner to withdraw from the partnership, the partnership must be reorganized. When one partner dies, again the partnership agreement must be renegotiated.

Finally, partnerships can involve a considerable risk for the individual partners. The sole proprietor does bear unlimited liability for the debts of the company, but at least the owner is the one who makes the business decision that may turn out to be bad. In the case of the partnership, one partner is responsible for business debts incurred by another partner even if that partner acted without consent of the other partners. For this reason, partnerships are often made up of family members, close relatives, and close personal friends who have come to trust one another over the years. Partnerships with more partners would have a greater ability to raise capital. However, because additional partners complicate decision making and increase the likelihood of an irresponsible act being committed by a partner, many partnerships have a limited number of partners.[4]

Corporations

The **corporation** came into existence to overcome some of the disadvantages of the proprietorship and partnership noted above.

*A **corporation** is a form of business enterprise that is owned by a number of stockholders. The corporation has the legal status of a fictional individual and is authorized by law to act as a single person. The stockholders elect a board of directors that appoints the management of the corporation, usually*

headed by a president. Management is charged with the actual operation of the corporation.

Unlike sole proprietorships and partnerships that can be established with minimal paperwork, a *corporate charter* is required to set up a corporation. The laws of each state are different, but, typically, for a fee, corporations can be established (incorporated) and can become legal "persons" subject to the laws of that state. According to state and federal laws, the corporation has the legal status of a fictional individual. Officers of the corporation can act in the name of the corporation without being personally liable for its debts. If corporate officers commit criminal acts, however, they can be prosecuted as individuals.

The corporation is owned by individuals (stockholders) who have purchased shares of *stock* in the corporation. A stockholder's share of ownership of the corporation will equal the number of shares owned by that individual divided by the total number of shares *outstanding* (owned by stockholders). If a person owns 100,000 shares of AT&T stock and there are 630 million AT&T shares outstanding, then the person would only own 0.016 percent of AT&T. Owners of shares of stock have the right to vote for the board of directors and to vote on special referenda at the annual meeting of the corporation. The management of the corporation is required by law to issue periodic reports to its shareholders describing the financial and business activities of the corporation during the reporting period. The stockholders may cast their votes in person at the annual meeting (the greater the number of shares owned, the greater the weight of the individual's vote) or can vote by *proxy* (that is, turn over voting privileges to the current management or to some other group).

The stockholder who owns 1 percent of the stock of ZYX Corporation will receive 1 percent of the dividends the ZYX Corporation management chooses to pay to its shareholders out of profits and is entitled to vote on matters affecting the corporation and to vote for its board of directors. Unlike the sole proprietor who has title to 100 percent of the profits of the company or the partner who may have title to 50 percent of the profits of the company, the typical stockholder

---

4. There are partnerships in which some partners have limited liability—as in real estate and sports, for example. In these partnerships, however, there must be one or more general partners with unlimited liability.

owns a miniscule portion of the total number of shares outstanding. In the case of the sole proprietorship and partnership, the owners decide what to do with the profits. In the case of the corporate stockholder, the management determines what to do with the profits of the corporation. The shareholder who does not approve of the way these profits are handled can vote to change the current board of directors or sell the stock and buy some other asset. **Common stock, preferred stock,** and **convertible stock** are three types of corporate stock.

Common stock confers voting privileges but no prior claim on dividends. Common stock dividends are paid only if they are declared by the board of directors in any given year.

Preferred stock confers a prior claim on dividends but no voting privileges. Dividends on preferred stock must be paid before paying common stock dividends but after meeting interest obligations.

Convertible stock is a hybrid between a stock and a bond. The owner of convertible stock receives fixed interest payments but has the privilege of converting the convertible stock into common stock at a fixed rate of exchange.

Corporations often have thousands or millions of shares outstanding, and these shares are typically owned by a large number of stockholders. In the case of closely held corporations, the number of stockholders is limited, and each stockholder owns a substantial share of the corporation's stock. Unlike the sole proprietor or the partner, stockholders do not participate directly in the running of the corporation unless they happen to own a substantial share of the outstanding stock. Moreover, even if an effort were made to involve shareholders in corporate decision making, there would be too many of them, they would be geographically dispersed, and they would be too involved in their own business affairs to devote sufficient attention to corporate affairs.

For these reasons, there is usually a *separation of ownership and management* in the modern cor-

poration. The board of directors appoints a professional management team that makes decisions for the corporation. As long as the corporation is run successfully, the management team is allowed to continue. If the corporation falls on hard times, then the stockholders may vote out the current board of directors or the board of directors itself may decide to bring in a new management team.

Statistical studies of modern corporations have demonstrated the magnitude of the separation of ownership and management.[5] In most instances, the people who actually run the corporation own only a small portion of the shares. In the case of giant corporations, the officers of the corporation may own only 2 to 3 percent of the stock.

Stockholders, however, can exercise substantial indirect control over management by simply selling their stock. The sale of stock by enough unhappy stockholders will depress the price of each share and invite possible takeovers by other corporate teams.

Advantages. The first advantage of the corporation is limited liability. The owners of the corporation (the stockholders) are not personally liable for the debts of the corporation. If a corporation incurs debts that it cannot meet, its creditors can lay claim to the assets of the corporation (its bank accounts, equipment, supplies, buildings, and real estate holdings), but they cannot file claims against the stockholders. The worst thing that can happen to stockholders is that the value of their stock will decline (in extreme circumstances, it can become worthless).

Limited liability contributes to a second advantage of the corporation: corporations can raise large sums of financial capital by selling corporate bonds, by issuing stock, and by borrowing from lending institutions. (How corporations raise capital will be described in more detail later in the chapter.)

The third advantage of the corporation follows from its status as a legal individual distinct from the officers of the corporation. A change in the

5. The pioneering study of the separation of ownership and management was published in 1932 by A. A. Berle and Gardner Means, *The Modern Corporation and Private Property* (New York: Commerce Clearing House, 1932).

Table 1
Types of Business Organization

Type of Firm	Advantages	Disadvantages
Individual proprietorships	1. Simple to set up. 2. Clear-cut decision making; the owner makes the decisions 3. Earnings are taxed only once as personal income.	1. Unlimited liability; the owner's personal wealth is at risk. 2. Limited ability to raise financial capital. 3. Business dies with owner.
Partnership	1. Relatively easy to set up. 2. More management skills; two heads are better than one. 3. Earnings are taxed only once as the personal income of the partners.	1. Unlimited liability for the partners. 2. Decision making can be complicated. 3. Limited ability to raise capital. 4. Partnerships can be unstable.
Corporation	1. Limited liability for owners. 2. Able to raise large sums of capital through issuing bonds and stock. 3. Eternal life. 4. Able to recruit professional management and to change bad management.	1. Corporate income taxed twice: once as corporate profits, then as personal income (dividends). 2. Possibilities of management disagreements.

board of directors, the death or resignation of the current president, or a transfer of ownership could destroy a partnership or sole proprietorship, but these events do not alter the legal status of the corporation. The continuity of the corporation is a distinct advantage. Many major U.S. corporations are more than a century old. Few corporations have the same owners and officers that they had when the corporation was founded. Continuity is an advantage in raising financial capital. Lending institutions are willing to make long-term loans to corporations because they know the corporation will outlive its current owners and officers. In fact, U.S. corporations have loans outstanding that are not due until the 21st century. New stockholders can also be brought into the corporation because they know that the existence of the corporation is not dependent upon the individuals that currently run the corporation. Continuity also makes it easier for the firm to hire a career-minded labor force.

The fourth advantage of the corporation follows from the separation of ownership and management. Because the two functions are separated, professional managers who specialize in running different parts of the corporation's operations can be hired. Experience shows that the owners of businesses (those individuals with money to invest) do not always make the best managers. In the modern corporation, talented officers can be brought into the business who own little (or no) company stock.

Disadvantages. The major disadvantage of the corporation is the double taxation of corporate income. The profits (earnings) of the corporation can either be distributed to shareholders as *dividends* or kept as *retained earnings* to be reinvested (plowed back) in the corporation. The profits of the corporation are subject to a federal income tax. Corporations pay a tax rate of from 15 percent (on profits of $25,000 or less) to the full rate of 46 percent (on annual profits in excess of $100,000) of company earnings. In many states, corporations must also pay a state income tax. If the corporation chooses to plow back all profits into the company, corporate profits will be taxed only once, but if it distributes some of its profits to shareholders in the form of dividends, shareholders must pay personal income tax on these dividends.

The double taxation of corporate earnings is indeed a disadvantage, but the fact that the corporate form of business enterprise is so prevalent suggests that the advantages of corporations (most specifically limited liability) can compensate for double taxation.

A second (though less important) disadvantage of the corporation is its complexity. Management and ownership are typically separated; debilitating power struggles can take place between different factions of stockholders and between powerful officers of the corporation.

CORPORATE FINANCE

Limited liability and continuity give corporations an edge in raising large sums of financial capital. Corporations have options for raising capital that are not available to sole proprietorships or to partnerships. Corporations, like proprietorships and partnerships, can borrow money from banks and from other lending institutions, and they can plow profits back into the business. In addition to these traditional forms of raising capital, corporations can 1) *sell bonds* (also called *issuing debt*), or they can 2) *issue (sell) additional shares of stock.*

To raise financial capital, corporations can sell **bonds** to investors.

*Corporate **bonds** are IOUs of the corporation that bind the corporation to pay a fixed sum of money (the principal) at maturity and also to pay a fixed sum of money annually until the maturity date. This fixed annual payment is called* interest *or the* coupon *payment.*

Present Value and Discounting

Bonds are obligations to make specified payments at specific dates over a specified period of time. Bonds cannot be understood without an understanding of present and future values of money. To understand the difference between present and future payments, one must keep in mind a fundamental principle:

A dollar today is worth more than a dollar tomorrow because it can be invested.

For the sake of simplicity, assume that an annual interest rate of 10 percent is the prevailing rate of interest paid throughout the economy. In other words, if $100 is deposited in a savings account, $10 interest will be earned at the end of one year. At 10 percent interest, $100 today is worth $110 received a year from now. If the interest rate had been 20 percent, $100 today would be worth $120 received a year from now.

Looking at the process in reverse, if the bank were to offer to pay someone $110 one year from now, what would that person be willing to pay today in order to receive $110 in one year? At 10 percent interest, the most this person would be willing to pay now in order to receive $110 in one year is $100. Thus, the **present value** of a future payment of $110 is $100.

*The **present value** of money to be received in the future is the most anyone would pay today in order to receive the money in the future. The present value is sometimes called the **discounted value** because it is smaller than the amount to be received in the future.*

The price (market value) of an IOU (such as a bond) that promises to make specified payments at specified future dates will be the present value of those payments. The present value calculation can be summarized in a formula. The present value (PV) of each dollar to be paid in one year at the interest rate i (i stands for the rate of interest in decimals) is:

$$PV = \frac{\$1}{1 + i}$$

If the interest rate is 10 percent, then $i = 0.10$ and $1 + i = 1.10$. The PV of each dollar equals $0.9091. If $10,000 is the sum to be paid in one year, the PV equals $9091 ($10,000 times 0.9091).

The present value formula becomes more complicated when the time span is greater than one year. At an annual interest rate of 10 percent, how much would someone be willing to pay now to have $121 two years from now? The answer follows the same reasoning as before. In other words, at an interest rate of 10 percent, how much money would a person have to deposit today to have an account worth $121 in two years? If the sum PV were deposited at interest rate i, it would be worth $PV \times (1 + i)$ one year from now. That sum would then earn a second year's interest and by the end of the second year would be worth $PV \times (1 + i) \times (1 + i)$, or $PV(1 + i)^2$. Setting the sum, $PV(1 + i)^2$, equal to \$121 and dividing yields:

$$PV = \frac{\$121}{(1 + i)^2}$$

At a rate of interest of 10 percent, the PV of \$121 to be received two years from now is \$100 ($= \$121/1.1^2$).

This result can be generalized to show that the present value of a sum to be received in three years is that sum divided by $(1 + i)^3$; the present value of a sum to be received in four years is that sum divided by $(1 + i)^4$; and so on.

The present value (**PV**) *of a dollar to be received in* **n** *years is*

$$PV = \frac{1}{(1 + i)^n}$$

At a 10 percent interest rate, \$100 received one year from now has a present value of \$90.91; \$100 to be received five years from now has a present value of only \$62.27.

The further out in the future the money is to be paid, the lower is its present value.

The Selling of Bonds

The financial section of the newspaper usually contains a comprehensive listing of corporate bonds. By selling bonds, corporations can acquire funds to finance business expansion. Once the bond is sold, the buyer can resell it, but such trades in second-hand bonds no longer directly affect the corporation.

The interest or principal payments on corporate bonds represent a legal obligation for the corporation, just like any other debt of the corporation. The purchaser of the bond has loaned the corporation money, and in return the corporation has promised the lender fixed interest payments until maturity and payment of the principal at the date of maturity. Interest and principal payments on corporate bonds have a claim on company earnings prior to dividends. The company has no choice but to make interest payments unless it is to be declared in a state of **bankruptcy.**

A corporation can be declared in a state of bankruptcy if the corporation cannot pay its bills or its interest obligations.

Because purchasers of corporate bonds have prior claim on company earnings, bonds offer a relatively secure return on corporate investments. As long as the corporation does not become bankrupt, the bondholder will receive the promised annual coupon payment (as well as the principal payment at the date of maturity).

Nevertheless, corporate bonds are not a riskless investment. In fact, purchasing bonds can be very risky because bond prices fluctuate in the second-hand market. If the bond owner wishes to sell the bond before the date of maturity, the price received for the bond may well be less than the price paid for the bond.

Bond prices are simply the present discounted value of the coupon payments and the principal. There is an inverse relationship between interest rates and bond prices. As interest rates rise, investors will pay *less* for the stream of coupon payments offered by a bond. As interest rates fall, investors will pay *more* for the stream of coupon payments offered by the bond.

From the vantage point of the purchaser, corporate bonds have an advantage over stock in that they have a prior claim on corporate profits. The corporation must pay the annual coupon to avoid bankruptcy. The lender knows with a high degree of certainty how much money will be received from the corporation until the date of maturity. A disadvantage of bonds is that, unlike the owner of the stock of the corporation, the bondholder cannot vote for the board of directors or share in unusually high profits.

The Issue of Stock

A second means of raising financial capital is for the corporation to sell additional shares of stock. Suppose ZYX corporation has 100,000 shares of stock that is already owned by stockholders. Each share of stock currently sells for \$10 on the second-hand market for stocks. These second-hand markets for corporate stock are called *stock exchanges:* the two most prominent stock exchanges in the United States are the New York Stock Exchange (NYSE) and the American Stock Exchange (ASE), both located on Wall Street in New York City.

The corporation decides that it needs to raise $500,000 to build a new plant and arranges with an *investment bank* or an *underwriter* to sell 50,000 new shares of stock to investors. The company will prepare a *prospectus* (as required by the Securities and Exchange Commission) that describes to potential buyers of the stock the financial condition of the company and the proposed uses to which the raised funds will be put. The investment bank will charge an underwriting fee to sell the 50,000 shares.

The amount of money investors will be willing to pay for the 50,000 new shares depends upon their assessment of the impact of the proposed investment on ZYX corporation earnings. If investors expect the new plant to raise company earnings substantially, they will offer a higher price than if they expect the investment to have a small effect.

Experts believe that corporations will issue new stock only if they can avoid a decline in the price of the stock in the second-hand market. Let us suppose this is the case with ZYX corporation. When the investment bank is able to sell the 50,000 new shares at the $10-per-share price, ZYX corporation raises $500,000 through the stock issue.

The corporation now has 150,000 shares *outstanding* (owned by stockholders) rather than the previous 100,000. The owners of the new 50,000 shares are entitled to vote on corporate matters and to receive dividends. Unlike corporate bonds that legally obligate the corporation to pay fixed interest payments, there is no obligation on the part of the corporation to pay dividends. As noted earlier, the corporation cannot pay dividends before meeting its interest obligations; therefore, dividends are only paid if there are sufficient profits left over after paying interest. When corporations experience hard times, dividends are frequently cut or even omitted entirely.

Conceptually, it is easy to describe how the price of a share of stock is established:

The price of a share of stock is the perceived present value of the future earnings per share of the stock.

Stock prices fluctuate dramatically because the future is unknown. No one knows for sure what the future earnings of any company might be. There will be disagreement among those who currently own the stock and those who are considering buying the stock. No one can predict how the economy as a whole will behave in the future; no one can predict for sure whether a particular company's fortunes will improve, deteriorate, or remain the same. When a company announces the development of a new product, the investment community may become convinced that this development will raise future earnings. This event will change investors' assessments of the present value of the company, and the stock price will rise.

The **price/earnings ratio** signals whether investors believe the profits of the company will rise or fall from current profit levels.

The price/earnings ratio (PE) is the stock price divided by the earnings per share.

If the average company has a *PE* of 6, companies with a *PE* greater than 6 are expected to have profits rising at above-average rates. Companies with a *PE* less than 6 are expected to have profits rising at below-average rates.

A high PE indicates that investors believe that current profits understate the future profits of the corporation. A low PE indicates that investors believe that current profits overstate the future profits of the corporation.

Stock Prices as a Guide to Resource Allocation

The prices of stocks have an important effect on the allocation of capital resources. Consider what would happen if ZYX corporation's research and development team develops a promising anticancer drug and obtains Food and Drug Administration approval to market this drug. The inves-

Example 1

Apple Computers: Price/Earnings Ratios as a Barometer of Future Earnings

The Apple Company was founded in 1977 in Cupertino, California by two computer enthusiasts and grew quickly into the major supplier of home computers. The original owners of Apple decided to "go public" (sell shares of the company to investors), and the initial offering (sale) of Apple shares took place on December 12, 1980.

Shares of Apple were sold to the public at a price of $22 per share. For the fiscal year ending September 26, 1980, Apple earned $11.7 million, or 24 cents per share. Thus at a price of $22 per share, the price/earnings ratio of Apple stock was

almost 100. Few new issues of stock sell for more than 25 times earnings.

Why was the Apple price/earnings ratio so high? Investors obviously felt that Apple earnings would rise substantially over the next few years. If Apple's earnings were to skyrocket—like IBM's two decades earlier—then a $22 price would turn out to be a bargain. If, for example, Apple's earnings were to rise to $5 per share in a short time, the price of Apple shares would likely rise well above the $22 price.

---

tor community will realize (probably well before government approval is even granted) that ZYX corporation earnings will rise substantially, so the price of the stock will take off. In our earlier example, the price of ZYX stock was $10, and the company was able to raise $500,000 by selling 50,000 new shares of stock. If, on the other hand, the prospect of the new drug causes the price of the stock to rise to $50 (the new plant would be built to manufacture the new drug), the issue of 50,000 new shares would raise $2,500,000 instead of $500,000.

As stock prices rise, corporations find it easier to raise financial capital for expansion. Corporations with falling stock prices cannot raise large sums of money for expansion. In this sense, the second-hand markets for corporate stocks serve as barometers that signal the direction of the allocation of financial capital.

Taxation and Business Behavior

One important lesson gained from studying business enterprises is that taxes influence business behavior. The double taxation of corporate income influences whether a business will be set up as a partnership or as a corporation. If the advantages of the corporate form (limited liability, greater ability to raise capital) are not important, the business will likely be set up as a proprietorship or a partnership to avoid double taxation.

The double taxation of corporate income means that corporations must invest their financial capital in projects that offer higher rates of return than partnerships or proprietorships.

The double taxation of corporate income also affects the dividend policies of corporations. Individuals invest in corporations because stocks offer two types of returns: dividends and **capital gains.**

*A **capital gain** is the increase in the market value of any asset (stocks, bonds, houses, automobiles, art, etc.) above the price originally paid. The capital gain is realized when the asset is sold. A capital gain is short-term if the asset was held less than one year and long-term if the asset was held longer than one year.*

In the United States, realized capital gains are taxed at a much lower rate than other forms of income (wages and salaries, dividends, interest) if the asset is held for more than one year (a long-term gain). Currently, the tax on long-term capital gains is only 40 percent of the tax on other forms of income. For example, an investor in the 50 percent tax bracket in ordinary income would pay only $200 tax on a $1,000 capital gain. It is therefore argued that tax rules discourage the payment of dividends by corporations and encourage the plowing back of profits.

Figure 1
Proprietorships, Partnerships, and Corporations, 1980

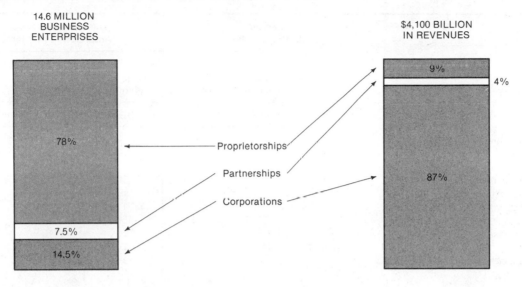

14.6 MILLION
BUSINESS
ENTERPRISES

$4,100 BILLION
IN REVENUES

78%

7.5%

14.5%

9%

4%

87%

Proprietorships

Partnerships

Corporations

Source: *Statistical Abstract of the United States,* 101st ed., 1980.

If corporate earnings are not distributed as dividends but are plowed back into the company, the earnings of the company should grow (if the money is invested wisely), and eventually the market price of the stock should rise. Investors who have held the stock for more than one year could then sell the stock and take a capital gain on which they would pay a relatively small income tax. If the company had, instead, paid out corporate profits as dividends, there would be less investment, the value of the stock would rise more slowly, and the recipient of the dividend payment would have to pay a heavy tax on the dividend.

For these reasons, it is argued that the differential taxation of capital gains encourages reinvestment of corporate earnings and discourages the payment of dividends. Roughly 80 percent of the new funds of U.S. corporations come from reinvested earnings rather than from borrowing or issuing stocks and bonds.

BIG BUSINESS

In the United States, there are roughly 15 million business enterprises (see Figure 1). The overwhelming majority of these are proprietorships (78 percent); the rest are corporations (14.5 percent) and partnerships (7.5 percent). Although proprietorships dominate in number, their share of business revenues is relatively small, accounting for only 9 percent of total revenues. Corporations, on the other hand, account for 87 percent of business revenues.

The average corporation is 12 times larger than the average partnership and 52 times larger than the average proprietorship. In 1976, the average corporation had dollar receipts of about $1.7 million.

Proprietorships are concentrated in agriculture, trade, and services, where the family farm and small family business are common (see Table 2). Corporations are especially active in manufacturing and trade. Partnerships are important in trade, finance, and services.

Large corporations (with revenues of more than $1 million) account for almost 78 percent of all business revenues (see Table 3), while large proprietorships (sales of over $100,000) account for only 5.2 percent of business revenues.

Figure 2 shows the number of industrial and commercial failures resulting in some loss to creditors for the years 1970 to 1980. Retail failures are largest in number. The post-1978 in-

Table 2
Proprietorships, Partnerships, and Corporations, by Industry, 1976

Industry	Number (in thousands)			Business Revenues (in billions of dollars)		
	Proprietor-ships	Active Partner-ships	Active Corpo-rations	Proprietor-ships	Active Partner-ships	Active Corpo-rations
Total	11,358	1,096	2,105	375.0	157.6	3,341.7
Agricutlure, forestry, and fishing	3,470	121	62	77.7	12.9	30.7
Mining	60	18	15	3.6	5.3	82.8
Construction	963	60	198	38.0	13.1	148.7
Manufacturing	223	31	214	9.4	8.0	1,400.5
Transportation, public utilities	346	17	81	11.2	2.5	274.4
Wholesale and retail trade	2,282	195	646	158.2	46.1	1,080.9
Wholesale	331	32	228	35.2	16.0	563.0
Retail	1,861	162	417	120.7	30.0	517.6
Finance, Insurance, Real Estate	827	447	414	15.3	37.6	354.7
Services	3,153	207	473	61.2	32.1	140.6

Source: *Statistical Abstract of the United States, 100th ed., 1979, p. 553.*

crease resulted from the 1980–1981 business recession and the easing of bankruptcy laws.

As noted above, the large corporation accounts for a substantial share of business sales and profits. The *absolute* size of giant corporations is awesome (see Table 4). The annual sales of certain large U.S. industrial corporations—like General Motors and Exxon—exceed the annual output of many industrial economies. The annual sales of General Motors, for example, equals the annual production of Belgium. The annual sales of the six largest U.S. industrial corporations (Ford, GM, Exxon, Mobil, Texaco, and Standard Oil of California) exceed the annual production of the United Kingdom.

THE FOUR BASIC MARKET MODELS

The classification of business enterprises into sole proprietorships, partnerships, and corporations is useful because it tells us who makes the decisions, how risks are shared, and how capital is raised. This classification does not tell us in what type of market the business enterprise is operating. How much competition does it face? How much control does it have over its prices? These are all crucial questions.

To a certain extent, business behavior is determined by the kind of market in which the firm is operating. Economists differentiate between four basic market models: **perfect competition, pure monopoly, monopolistic competition,** and **oligopoly.**

Perfect Competition

Perfect competition has the following features:

1. There are a large number of buyers and sellers in the market.

2. Each buyer and seller has perfect information about prices and product quality.

3. The product being sold is homogeneous; that is, it is not possible (or even worthwhile) to distinguish the product of one firm from that of other firms.

4. There are no barriers to entry into or exit from the market. New firms may enter the market; established firms may leave the market.

*5. All firms are **price takers**. No single seller is large enough to exert any control over the product price. Instead, the seller must accept as given the price dictated by the market.*

Table 3
Size of Business Revenues of U.S. Proprietorships, Partnerships, and Corporations, 1975

	Proprietorships			Partnerships			Corporations		
	Under $50,000	$50,000–$99,999	$100,000 or More	Under $100,000	$100,000–$499,999	$500,000 or More	Under $500,000	$500,000 $999,999	$1,000,000 or More
Number of enterprises (in thousands)	9,279	852	751	824	205	249	1,590	184	249
Average revenues of these enterprises (dollars)	9,805	66,464	251,150	22,627	214,210	335,150	119,440	703,366	11,249,000
Percent of total business revenues	2.5	1.6	5.2	0.5	1.2	2.3	5.3	3.6	77.8

Source: *Statistical Abstract of the United States,* 100th ed., p. 555.

Figure 2
Business Failures in the United States, 1970–1980

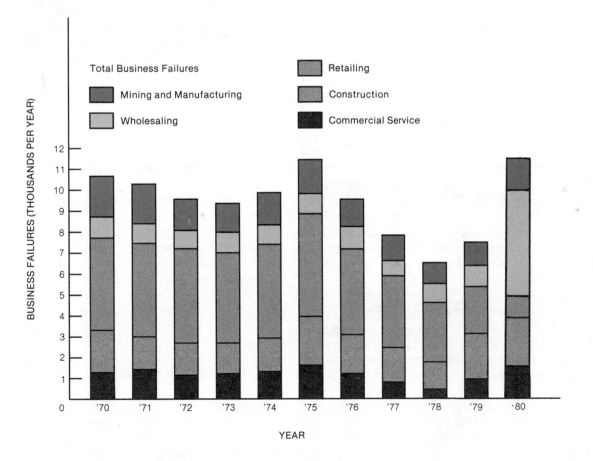

Source: *Survey of Current Business,* March 1982, p. S–6.

Table 4
The 20 Largest Industrial Corporations, Ranked by Sales, 1981

Rank	Company	Sales (thousands of dollars)
1	Exxon	108,107,688
2	Mobil	64,488,000
3	General Motors	62,698,500
4	Texaco	57,628,000
5	Standard Oil of California	44,224,000
6	Ford Motor	38,247,100
7	Standard Oil (Indiana)	29,947,000
8	International Business Machines	29,070,000
9	Gulf Oil	28,252,000
10	Atlantic Richfield	27,797,436
11	General Electric	27,240,000
12	E.I. du Pont de Nemours	22,810,000
13	Shell Oil	21,629,000
14	International Telephone & Telegraph	17,306,189
15	Phillips Petroleum	15,966,000
16	Tenneco	15,462,000
17	Sun	15,012,000
18	Occidental Petroleum	14,707,543
19	U.S. Steel	13,940,500
20	United Technologies	13,667,758

Source: *Fortune Magazine,* May 3, 1982, p. 260.

Price taking is the most important feature of perfect competition. The number of sellers is "large" if each individual firm is so small compared to the total market that no single firm can affect the market price by increasing or decreasing production. The firm can sell as much as it likes at the going market price.

In perfectly competitive markets, there are two levels of analysis: one can analyze the behavior of the individual firm as well as the behavior of the market itself. No single firm can affect the market, but all firms together do determine how the market behaves.

Pure Monopoly

Pure monopoly has the following characteristics:

1. The market consists of one producer, the pure monopolist. The industry and the firm are one; there are usually a large number of buyers.

2. The producer sells a product for which there are no close substitutes.

3. The producer is protected from the entry of competitors into the market by barriers to entry.

4. The producer is a price searcher. The producer can control the price and, therefore, must select the price that is best for the monopolist.

The first three characteristics explain why the pure monopolist is a price searcher. *Price searching is the most significant feature of monopoly.* The monopolist has competitors in the sense that there are other products that can substitute for the monopolist's product, but these products are not close substitutes. Potential competitors are kept out of the market by barriers to entry. Barriers may be technological (there is only room in the industry for one producer); there may be government restrictions on entry (an exclusive franchise granted by government); or crucial natural resources might be owned by one firm (as in the case of the nickel and diamond industries). As a consequence of these features, the monopolist is in a position to affect the price by increasing or decreasing production.

Monopolistic Competition

Monopolistic competition has the following characteristics:

1. There are a large number of firms in a market that contains many buyers.

2. These firms sell a differentiated product. The product of one firm will be different from the products of the other firms.

3. There is freedom of entry and exit. New firms can enter freely, and established firms can exit.

4. Firms exert a limited degree of control over their price but are still price searchers.

Monopolistic competition combines features of perfect competition and pure monopoly, as the name suggests. The competitive features are the large number of firms and the freedom of entry. The monopolistic features are product differentiation and price searching.

To understand monopolistic competition, one must understand why firms are price searchers but only to a very limited degree. Price searching follows from the fact that each firm produces a differentiated product. The firm can raise its price without losing all its customers because the product's special features develop some product loyalty, but this product loyalty will be weak because of the large number of close substitutes. In the language of elasticities, the monopolistic-competitive firm faces a highly elastic demand curve for its product.

The relationship between the firm and market is more complicated in the case of monopolistic competition. Each firm produces a differentiated product; therefore, the market is really not the sum of all these differentiated producers. The definition of the market in the case of monopolistic competition is not obvious.

Oligopoly

Oligopoly has the following characteristics:

1. There are a few mutually interdependent sellers in a market that contains many buyers.

2. Producers may produce homogeneous or differentiated products.

3. There are significant barriers to entry into the market.

4. Producers are price searchers.

Mutual interdependence is the most important feature of oligopoly. Firms are mutually interdependent because each firm is aware that its actions affect the other firms in the market and vice versa. If one oligopolist raises price, the sales of the other oligopolists will be affected, and they will react to this price increase. These reactions make oligopoly difficult to analyze. The presence of barriers to entry explains why there are only a few producers in the market and why there is mutual interdependence. The sources of barriers to entry are varied and can range from technological obstacles to enormous advertising expenses.

The features of the four basic market models will be discussed in great depth in the following chapters. This chapter considered business organization as the first step in the study of the supply side of product markets. The next chapter will examine the role of production costs in determining product supply.

Summary

1. Managerial coordination is an effective means of resource allocation in situations where economies of scale, risk, transactions costs, or a need for team production are present.

2. Most economists assume that the goal of business firms is the maximization of profits.

3. The three forms of business organization are the sole proprietorship (a business owned by one individual), the partnership (a business owned by two or more partners who share in making business decisions), and the corporation (a business enterprise owned by stockholders).

4. Corporations can raise capital by selling bonds or issuing more stock. Corporate bonds are IOUs that oblige the corporation to make fixed interest payments and to repay the principal at the date of maturity. The amount of money a corporation can raise will depend upon the price of its stock in the second-hand market for stocks. The stock market helps to allocate capital to various industries and firms.

5. Although there are more sole proprietorships in the United States than there are partnerships or corporations, corporations (due to their larger average size) account for the bulk of business sales and profits.

6. Economists distinguish between four basic market models: perfect competition (a market with a large number of buyers and sellers), pure monopoly (a market with one seller), monopolistic competition (a market with a large number of sellers each of which is a price searcher), and oligopoly (a market with a few mutually interdependent sellers).

Key Terms

managerial coordination
economies of scale
profit maximization
natural selection theory
sole proprietorship
partnership
corporation

common stock
preferred stock
convertible stock
bonds
present value
bankruptcy
price/earnings ratio
capital gain
perfect competition
pure monopoly
monopolistic competition
oligopoly

Questions and Problems

1. You are deciding whether to build a home yourself or whether to have an established building firm build the home. What are the transaction costs of arranging to have the home built without the use of the building company? Under what circumstances would these costs be low enough for you to decide to build the home yourself?
2. Risk bearing is one function served by business firms. What risk does the owner of a new restaurant bear?
3. The statistics on sole proprietorships reveal that they are on average smaller than partnerships and that partnerships are smaller on average than corporations. From what you know about the legal features of business organizations, explain why this is so.
4. In the real world, limited partnerships exist in which the liability of each partner for the debts of the company is limited. Explain why such partnerships may be more attractive than the traditional form of partnership.
5. Explain why corporations can issue bonds that mature in the next century while partnerships and proprietorships can borrow for only short periods of time.
6. Explain why a corporation would be reluctant to issue new shares of stock to raise capital when the price of the stock is at an all-time low.
7. One stock has a price/earnings ratio of 2; a second stock has a price/earnings ratio of 20. The average *PE* ratio is 10. What would be the investment community's best guess as to the course of future profits for each company?
8. You own 100 shares of ZYX corporation, and the management of ZYX corporation allows you to vote on whether stockholders will receive dividends on the stock or whether the management will plow earnings back into the company. How would your tax bracket affect the way you vote?
9. ZYX corporation offers to sell bonds maturing in 20 years at an interest rate of 15 percent. If you buy a $10,000 bond from ZYX, what would be the annual coupon payment? Would you be more likely to buy the bond if you expected interest rates to fall?
10. The 100 shares of ZYX corporation that you purchased two years ago for $10 per share are now selling for $20 per share. If you sell the stock, what is the profit called? How will this profit be taxed?
11. Complete the following table by entering an example in each empty box (consider local, regional, and national markets).

	Proprietorship	Partnership	Corporation
Perfect Competition			
Monopolistic Competition			
Oligopoly			
Monopoly			

8

Costs and Productivity

Chapter Preview

The preceding chapter examined the basic forms of business organization. Once a business firm has chosen its basic organizational form—whether it be single proprietorship, partnership, or corporation—it must get down to the main task of a business firm: making a profit. To make *profit* means that the business firm must earn revenues in excess of costs. Business activities may be complicated, like the production of a huge jet airliner, or simple, like the little girl or boy setting up a lemonade stand to earn money for a new bicycle. To make correct business decisions, the firm must look at both revenues and costs. If either revenue or cost is misunderstood, the firm can make incorrect or poor decisions. This chap-

ter looks at the cost side of the profit equation; the next several chapters look at the revenue side. Here we ask: What are costs? What costs are important to business decisions? How is productivity related to costs? The answers to these questions form the basis for determining how markets work.

THE NATURE OF COSTS

Opportunity Costs

Your rich aunt gives you a brand new sports car, which has a market value of $15,000. She tells you: "This car is yours. You may keep it or sell it. If you sell it, the $15,000 is yours. As long as you keep it, I'll pay for all gas, oil, maintenance, repairs, and even your insurance. The car is yours—free in every way.'' This is a nice gift. But is the car in fact free? The car would be free if it costs you nothing to *use*. What is the cost of *using* the car?

To an economist the cost of using the car under these conditions may actually be higher than the annual cost of a small car. Suppose that the $15,000 that the car is worth now could be invested at 12 percent interest per year to bring in $1,800 per year in interest income. Suppose that using the car for one year will reduce the resale value of the car from $15,000 to $11,000—a cost to you of $4,000. Hence, the total cost to you of using the car for one year is the $4,000 loss of resale value you (not your aunt) must suffer plus the $1,800 of lost interest income. The total yearly *cost* of using the car is $5,800 (= $1,800 + $4,000).[1] Thus, a "free" car is far from free if the car is used! The lesson is that *costs are not what has been paid but what has been given up by taking one action rather than another*. **Opportunity costs** are the measure of what has been given up:

> The **opportunity cost** of an action is the value of the best forgone alternative.

The concept of opportunity costs was embodied in the production-possibility curve studied in Chapter 2. When more of one good (such as tanks) is produced, a certain amount of some other good (such as wheat) must be given up. As the car example shows, opportunity costs may be **implicit costs** or **explicit costs.**

> An **explicit cost** (also called an accounting cost) is incurred when an actual payment is made. An **implicit cost** is incurred when an alternative is sacrificed.

Consider a business firm engaged in the production of some good. To produce the good re-

quires that resources be used. To acquire these resources, prices or payments must be paid to the owners of the resources because the resources have alternative uses. The minimum payments that are just necessary to attract resources into the production of the good are the opportunity costs of production. Some of these payments may be explicit (as money changes hands), and some will be implicit. The manager of the firm must consider the implicit costs (the value of those resources if used elsewhere) of the resources owned by the firm. The hired resources (labor, land, equipment) have explicit costs that must be paid to acquire them.

For example, pharmacist Smith is the owner and operator of Smith's Drugstore. Smith's managerial and pharmaceutical talents might be hired out to a chain drugstore for $2,000 per month; Smith's capital investment in the drugstore may earn $500 per month invested elsewhere. This $2,500 (= $2,000 + $500) is an *implicit* cost of doing business. (Although this $2,500 is a true opportunity cost, no money changes hands.) The explicit (accounting) costs are Smith's rent payments on the building, inventory costs, business taxes, and wage payments to clerks and other pharmacists. These explicit monthly payments add up to $37,000 per month.

Economic Profits

Economic profits are not the same as **accounting profits.** Economists do not measure profits the same way as accountants do, nor do they use the term *profits* in the way most people do.

> *Accounting profits* equal company revenues minus (explicit) accounting costs.

Accounting profits can give a misleading picture of the firm's well-being.

> *Economic profits* are the excess of revenues over total opportunity costs.

For example, Smith's Drugstore has accounting profits of $3,000 per month (that is, sales = $40,000; accounting costs = $37,000) that must be reported to the Internal Revenue Service. Smith's economic profit, however, is only $500 because accounting costs ignore the implicit costs

---

1. This $5,800 can be derived in another way. Keep the car for one year and you can sell it for $11,000. Sell the car now and you receive $15,000 today; in one year the $15,000 will grow to $16,800 at an interest rate of 12 percent. The difference between $16,800 and $11,000 is $5,800, the annual cost of using the car for the first year.

that must be paid to Smith for using Smith's entrepreneurial talents and funds. This implicit cost is $2,500—the sum of money necessary to persuade the entrepreneur/owner to commit entrepreneurial resources and financial capital to the business. In this case, if accounting profit were below $2,500, the entrepreneur would not enter the business because the entrepreneur would not be earning a normal profit. A **normal profit** is an economic profit of zero.

*A **normal profit** is the return that the time and capital of the entrepreneur would earn in the best alternative employment and is earned when total revenues equal total opportunity costs (economic profit is earned when total revenues exceed total opportunity costs).*

The Short Run and the Long Run

A business firm expands the volume of its output by hiring or using additional resources. Every good or service is produced by a combination of resources (land, labor, capital, raw materials, entrepreneurial or managerial talent). The package of resources used depends very much on three sets of factors: 1) the productivity of the resources; 2) the prices of the resources; and 3) the time available to the firm for altering output. The first two are important because the business firm will obviously try to keep costs as low as possible. The last is important because time is required to change the level of resource use. Some resources can be adjusted immediately. Other resources require considerable time to change.

A firm can work its existing labor force more intensively simply by asking each employee to work overtime. In this manner, more hours of work can be obtained quickly. The firm may also be able to acquire additional raw materials immediately. But the installation of a new piece of capital equipment or the construction of a new plant may require a significant amount of time. Economists distinguish between the **short run** and the **long run** when considering the time necessary to change input levels.

*The **short run** is a period of time so short that the existing plant or equipment cannot be varied; it is fixed in supply. Additional output can be produced only by expanding the variable inputs of labor and raw materials. The **long run** is a period of time long enough to vary all inputs.*

The long run is not a specified amount of calendar time. The long run may be as short as a few months for a fast food restaurant, a couple of years for a new automobile plant, or a decade or more for an electrical power plant. Generally speaking, engineering complexity determines whether the long run is a matter of weeks or years in actual calendar time.

Fixed and Variable Costs

In the short run there is a difference between fixed and variable costs. In the short run, some factors (such as plant and equipment) are fixed in supply to the firm; even if the firm wanted to increase or reduce them, it would not be possible in the short run. The costs of these fixed factors are **fixed costs.** In the short run, greater output is obtained by using more of the *variable inputs* (such as labor and raw materials); the costs of these variable factors are **variable costs.**

***Fixed costs** are those costs that do not vary with output.*

***Variable costs** are those costs that do vary with output.*

In the long run, all costs are variable. Thus in the long run, fixed costs are zero.

Fixed and variable costs have different effects on the behavior of the firm in the short run and in the long run. Rational firms should ignore fixed costs in the short run when making decisions because in the short run there is no way to change fixed costs; fixed costs are what people in the business world call *sunk costs*. Fixed costs are not affected by any actions the firm can take in the short run. Only variable costs affect the firm's short-run decisions. If the firm's revenues exceed variable costs in the short run, the firm has something left over to pay part or all of fixed costs. The firm that can pay fixed cost in addition to variable cost is paying its **total costs.**

***Total costs** are fixed plus variable costs.*

Table 1
Average and Marginal Relationships: Test Scores

Test	Test Score = Marginal Score	Average Test Score	Explanation
0		0	
	80		
1		80	Average and marginal values the same
	50		
2		65	Marginal below previous average; new average falls
	100		
3		76.67	Marginal above previous average; new average rises
	70		
4		75	Marginal below previous average; new average falls
	60		
5		72	Marginal below previous average; new average falls
	50		
6		68.22	Marginal below previous average; new average falls
	80		
7		70	Marginal above previous average; new average rises
	70		
8		70	Marginal equals previous average; new average unchanged

Average Costs and Marginal Costs

For the firm to make a profit, the price of the product must exceed its **average total costs.**

Average total costs are total costs divided by output.

For example, Joe's Egg Factory produces 500 dozen eggs during the week at total (opportunity) cost of $250. Average total cost is total cost ($250) divided by output (500 dozen); so a dozen eggs has an average (unit) total cost of $0.50 per dozen (= $250/500). If Joe can sell his 500 dozen eggs at $0.75 a dozen, he can make $0.25 a dozen in economic profit, which amounts to $125 (= $0.25 × 500) in economic profit for the week.

Average total costs *(ATC)* are important because the firm can tell whether a profit is being made by comparing price and average total cost. Joe's price ($0.75 a dozen) exceeds his *ATC* ($0.50 a dozen) for a $0.25 per dozen profit. Joe is making a more than normal profit because his revenue exceeds his opportunity costs of producing eggs.

How do firms decide how much output to produce? What determines whether Joe should produce 500 dozen eggs or a larger or smaller quantity? Is Joe producing the optimal quantity of eggs? To answer this question it is necessary to look at **marginal cost.**

Marginal cost is the extra cost associated with producing one more unit of output.

Suppose Joe finds that to produce another dozen eggs (501 dozen rather than 500 dozen) requires additional costs of $0.80 on feed, labor time, and egg cartons. This $0.80 is the marginal cost of a dozen eggs. But Joe can get only $0.75 a dozen for his eggs. Clearly, it would be irrational to produce a dozen more eggs if the marginal cost ($0.80) exceeds the price of eggs ($0.75). In effect, such an action would make Joe worse off by $0.05.

Marginal costs are important because they can be used to determine (together with the revenue from additional production) whether the firm is producing the optimal or profit-maximizing quantity of output. In economics, the relationship be-

Figure 1
Average and Marginal Relationships

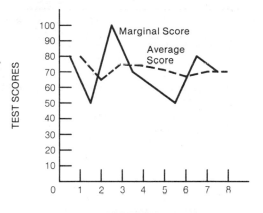

NUMBER OF EXAMS

This figure graphs the data on hypothetical test scores given in Table 1. Whenever the marginal score is less than the previous average score, the average score declines. Whenever the marginal score is greater than the previous average score, the average score rises. If the marginal score equals the previous average score, the average score will not change.

---

tween average values and marginal values comes up over and over again. There is a common arithmetical background to all average/marginal relationships.

Suppose you are taking a course in chemistry; there are eight (equally weighted) examinations. Your performance for the course is determined by your average score on all exams. Table 1 shows how the average score is computed, and Figure 1 graphs both marginal and average scores. On test number 1, you score 80 points; your average is 80. On test number 2, you score only 50; your *total* score is now 130 (= 80 + 50) and your average falls to 65 (= 130/2). Your average is the total cumulated points scored divided by the number of exams taken.

The marginal score is the increase in the total accumulated points obtained by taking one more exam. Clearly, the marginal score is simply your score on the last examination taken. On the first exam your average and marginal scores are the same: 80. The second exam score is 50, which is below the previous average of 80. What will happen to the new average? *Whenever the marginal value is below the previous average value, the new average will fall.* In this case, the average falls from 80 to 65 because it is *pulled down* by the low marginal test score. The third exam score

is 100, well above the 65 average to that point. What will happen to the new average? *When the marginal score is above the previous average test score, the new average will rise.* The average will be *pulled up* by the high marginal score.

Whenever the marginal value exceeds the previous average value, the new average value will rise. Whenever the marginal value is below the previous average value, the new average value will fall.

A second rule is illustrated by the final marginal test score. The average test score of the first seven exams is 70. The eighth exam score is 70. Because the marginal score thus *equals* the previous average score, the new average will remain the same because the marginal value will pull the average neither up nor down.

If the marginal value equals the previous average value, the new average will not be changed.

Baseball fans are also familiar with these average/marginal rules. If a batter enters a game with a batting average of 0.250 (25 hits every 100 times at bat) and goes four-for-four on that day, the average will rise because the marginal score is higher than the previous average score. If the player had gone one-for-four on that day, the average score would not have changed because the marginal equals the previous average. If the player had zero hits, the average would have fallen because the marginal was below the previous average.

COST CURVES
IN THE SHORT RUN

By definition, the short run is a period of calendar time so short that at least one fixed cost cannot be avoided.

The Family of Short-Run
Cost Curves

Table 2 supplies cost schedules of a hypothetical enterprise that has both fixed and variable costs. These schedules are graphed as cost curves in Figure 2.

Table 2
Cost Schedules in the Short Run for a Hypothetical Enterprise

(1) Quantity of Output, Q (units)	(2) Total Variable Cost, VC (dollars)	(3) Total Fixed Cost, FC (dollars)	(4) Total Cost, TC (dollars)	(5) Marginal Cost, MC (dollars)	(6) Average Variable Cost, AVC (dollars)	(7) Average Fixed Cost, AFC (dollars)	(8) Average Total Cost, ATC (dollars)
0	0	4	4		0	∞	∞
				10			
1	10	4	14		10	4	14
				6			
2	16	4	20		8	2	10
				8			
3	24	4	28		8	1.33	9.33
				10			
4	34	4	38		8.5	1	9.5
				12			
5	46	4	50		9.2	0.8	10
				14			
6	60	4	64		10	0.67	10.67

This is the family of cost schedules for a hypothetical business enterprise operating in the short run with total fixed cost of 4 (column 3). *Fixed cost* does not vary with the level of output (column 1). *Variable cost* (column 2) rises with the level of output. *Total cost* (column 4) is the sum of total fixed cost and total variable cost. *Marginal cost* (column 5) is the increase in total variable cost due to increasing output by one unit. *Average variable cost* (column 6) is total variable cost divided by the number of units produced. *Average fixed cost* (column 7) is total fixed cost divided by the number of units produced. *Average total cost* (column 8) is the sum of average fixed cost and average variable cost.

The following equations show the relationships among the various measures:

$$TC = FC + VC$$
$$TC/Q = FC/Q + VC/Q$$
$$ATC = AFC + AVC$$

Cost curves show the relationship between the level of output and the cost of producing that output. Output is on the horizontal axis, and cost is on the vertical axis. Cost curves show what happens to costs of production as the level of output changes.

The costs graphed include all opportunity costs (explicit and implicit costs). In Table 2, seven different cost measures are provided. Together, they make up the family of costs:

Variable cost (VC) *is the cost that varies with the level of output.*

Fixed cost (FC) *is the cost that does not vary with the level of output.*

Total cost (TC) *is the total of the variable and fixed costs of producing each level of output.*

$$TC = VC + FC$$

Marginal cost (MC) *is the addition to total cost (or equivalently to variable cost) of producing one more unit of output.*

Average variable cost (AVC) *is variable cost divided by output.*

$$AVC = VC \div Q$$

Average fixed cost (AFC) *is fixed cost divided by output.*

$$AFC = FC \div Q$$

Figure 2
The Family of Cost Curves

(a) Total Cost Curves

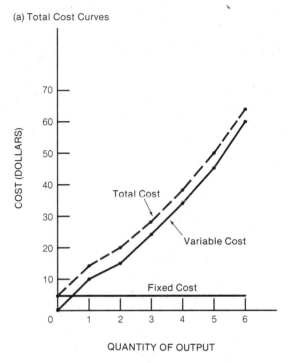

(b) Average and Marginal Cost Curves

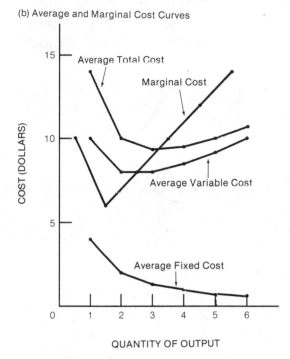

These cost curves are plotted from Table 2. In panel (a), variable cost changes with output; fixed cost does not vary with output. Total cost is the sum of variable cost and fixed cost. In panel (b), marginal cost is the change in total cost that results from producing one more unit of output. Average variable cost is variable cost divided by the number of units produced. Average fixed cost is fixed cost divided by the number of units produced and declines throughout. Average total cost is the sum of average variable cost and average fixed cost.

Average total cost (**ATC**) *is total cost divided by output, or the sum of average variable cost and average fixed cost.*

$$ATC = TC \div Q = AVC + AFC$$

In analyzing the behavior of business enterprises, the average and marginal cost curves are of greater use than the total cost curves. Note: This book graphs marginal curves at the *midpoints* between the two values on the horizontal axis. For example, the marginal cost of producing the third unit of output (going from 2 to 3 units of output) is 8. We follow the convention of graphing the marginal cost, 8, halfway between 2 and 3 (at 2.5) on the horizontal axis. In tabular form, the marginal cost figure appears in the row between the output quantities 2 and 3.

The Shape of Short-Run Cost Curves

The short-run cost curves in Figure 2 have been deliberately constructed to assume specific shapes. The average variable cost curve and the average total cost curve have *U* shapes.

Table 2 shows that as output expands from 1 to 6, the average variable and average total curves first fall in value, then reach a minimum value, and finally rise. Why short-run cost curves are expected to have this *U* shape will be discussed in the next section. The *U* shape means that there is one minimum average variable cost and one minimum average total cost.

The relationship between average and marginal costs is graphed in Figure 2. The general rule of the relationship between average and marginal values applies.

Figure 3
The Relationship Between Marginal and Average Costs

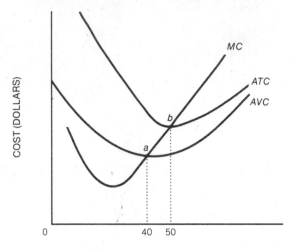

When output is less than 40 units, marginal cost *(MC)* is less than both average variable cost *(AVC)* and average total cost *(ATC)*, pulling both down. When output is between 40 and 50 units, *MC* is above *AVC* and below *ATC*, pulling *AVC* up and pulling *ATC* down. When output is greater than 50 units, *MC* pulls *ATC* up as well. The *ATC* and *AVC* curves get closer together as output increases.

The marginal cost curve will intersect the average variable cost curve and the average total cost curve at their respective minimum values. When marginal cost equals average variable cost, AVC will be at its lowest value. When marginal cost equals average total cost, ATC will be at its lowest value.

In Figure 3, the minimum point on the *AVC* curve occurs at point *a* where output quantity is 40 units; the minimum point on the *ATC* curve occurs at point *b* where output quantity is 50 units. When output is less than 40 units, marginal cost is less than both *AVC* and *ATC*—therefore both *AVC* and *ATC* are declining. When output equals 40 units, *MC* equals *AVC*, and *MC* is less than *ATC*. Therefore, *ATC* is declining, and *AVC* must reach its minimum. At output levels between 40 units and 50 units, *MC* is below *ATC* and above *AVC*, pulling *ATC* down and *AVC* up. At point *b*, *ATC* hits its minimum value when *MC* equals

Figure 4
Productivity and Costs

(a) Marginal Physical Productivity

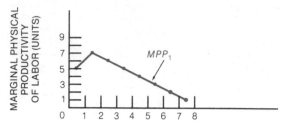

(b) Average and Marginal Costs

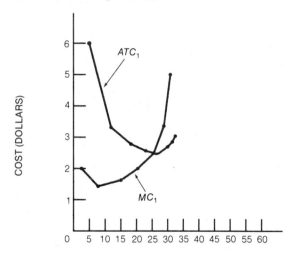

The curves shown here are plotted from data in Table 3. In panel (a), the curve (MPP_1) showing the marginal physical product of labor rising, reaching a peak, and then falling illustrates the law of diminishing returns. In panel (b), the marginal cost curve (MC_1) is a mirror image of MPP_1 in panel (a). As the marginal physical product of labor rises, the marginal cost of output falls, and vice versa.

ATC. At output levels greater than 50 units, *MC* exceeds *ATC* and pulls *ATC* up. Notice that minimum *ATC* occurs after the minimum *AVC*.

Since $ATC = AVC + AFC$, the distance between the *AVC* and *ATC* curves represents *AFC*. As a given fixed cost is spread over a larger and larger output, *AFC* gets smaller and smaller. Thus, the *AVC* and *ATC* curves get closer together as output rises.

Table 3
Production Functions and the Law of Diminishing Returns

(1) Labor Input, L (worker hours)	(2) Capital Input, K (fixed at one unit)	(3) Output, Q (units)	(4) Marginal Physical Productivity of Labor, MPP_1 (units)	(5) Fixed Cost, FC_1 (dollars)	(6) Variable Cost, VC_1 (dollars)	(7) Average Total Cost, ATC_1 (dollars)	(8) Marginal Cost, MC_1 (dollars)
0	1	0		20	0	∞	
			5				2
1	1	5		20	10	6	
			7				1.43
2	1	12		20	20	3.33	
			6				1.67
3	1	18		20	30	2.78	
			5				2
4	1	23		20	40	2.61	
			4				2.50
5	1	27		20	50	2.59	
			3				3.33
6	1	30		20	60	2.67	
			2				5
7	1	32		20	70	2.81	
			1				10
8	1	33		20	80	3.03	

The *production function* is given in the first three columns. Because the capital input is fixed at one unit, the enterprise is operating in the short run. As the variable input—labor—increases, output increases. The fourth column, marginal physical productivity, shows the increase in output as labor increases by one unit. The *law of diminishing returns* states that as variable inputs are added to a fixed input, a point will be reached beyond which the MPP will decline.

Average total cost and *marginal cost* are calculated from the production function. In this example, each unit of labor costs $10 and each unit of capital costs $20. To obtain ATC, labor (variable) costs (column 6) and capital (fixed) costs (column 5) are added together and the sum is divided by the quantity of output. Marginal cost is calculated by dividing the increase in labor costs ($10) by the increase in output *(MPP)*.

DIMINISHING RETURNS

In the study of the behavior of business enterprises, the shapes of average and marginal cost curves are quite important. In fact, the law of supply depends to a great extent upon the shapes of average and marginal cost curves. Short-run cost curves can be expected to be U-shaped because of the law of diminishing returns.

Production Functions

To understand the law of diminishing returns, it is necessary to understand what a **production function** is.

*A **production function** summarizes the relationship between labor, capital, and land inputs and the maximum output these inputs can produce.*

A production function is something like a recipe. It tells how much output can be produced from a given combination of inputs and tells by how much output will increase if one (or all) input(s) increase(s). A production function can be expressed in mathematical, graphical, or tabular form. Table 3 shows a simple production function in tabular form that is also graphed in Figure 4. The production function summarizes a production technology that uses two inputs, labor *(L)* and capital *(K)* to produce output *(Q)*

The production function in Table 3 is a *short-run production function* because at least one factor of production (in this case capital) is fixed in supply. In this example, capital is fixed at one unit, and labor is the variable input. To keep the example simple, these are the only two inputs.

Marginal Physical Product

What will happen to output as labor, the variable input, increases while capital remains fixed depends on the **marginal physical product** of labor.

*The **marginal physical product** (MPP) of a factor of production is the increase in output that results from increasing the input by one unit, holding all other inputs constant.*

The *MPP* of labor, for example, is the increase in output brought about by increasing labor by one unit ($MPP = \Delta Q/\Delta L$).

In the 19th century English economist David Ricardo noted that agricultural land was essentially fixed in supply, and, even though other factors of production such as labor and capital could be increased in supply, that the ability of an agrarian economy to expand its output would be limited. Ricardo felt that as more and more labor and capital inputs—the variable inputs—are combined with land—the fixed input—these variable inputs would yield smaller and smaller additions to output.

According to Ricardo, an economy with an expanding population, fixed agricultural land, and variable inputs that become less and less effective would soon reach a stationary state in which the growth of living standards (and of population) would cease. Ricardo's theory is known as the **law of diminishing returns.**

*The **law of diminishing returns** states that as ever larger inputs of a variable factor are combined with fixed inputs, eventually the marginal physical product of the variable input will decline.*

If variable inputs such as labor are added to a fixed input, eventually the fixed input will become overcrowded with variable inputs. When variable inputs continue to be added, each additional input has less fixed capital with which to work, and the marginal physical product of the variable input begins to decline.

In column (4) of Table 3, the marginal physical product of labor rises, reaches a peak, and then begins to fall steadily in conformity with the law of diminishing returns. Clearly, *MPP* is largest (at 7 units) when 2 units of labor are used. *MPP* then declines as labor is increased beyond 2 units of labor. Why does the *MPP* of labor at first tend to rise? The basic reason is that one person working alone cannot effectively work with the available capital. Because two workers can specialize and save the time of passing from one job to another, the *MPP* of the second worker is higher than the first. The one unit of fixed capital could be a small broom factory with two specialized machines for cutting the handles and shaping the straw. When there is only one worker, the first worker must operate both machines, moving back and forth between jobs. With two workers, each could specialize. However, six workers would overcrowd the small plant, so the *MPP* of the sixth worker would be small.

Costs and Diminishing Returns

The law of diminishing returns and the level of fixed costs determine the shape of the family of short-run cost curves. The production function shows how much output can be produced from different combinations of inputs. The cost of producing output is the cost of the inputs. In our example (Table 3), the fixed factor is capital; the fixed cost is the fixed amount of money the business must pay for this capital. One unit of capital costs $20; therefore, $FC = \$20$. Labor is the sole variable factor; therefore, the variable cost *(VC)* will be the labor cost. Given the fact that each unit of labor costs $10, the variable cost can be calculated at each level of output. Average total cost is the sum of labor costs and fixed costs divided by output. For example, the *ATC* of producing 23 units of output is $2.61—which equals $40 (the variable labor cost) plus $20 (the fixed cost) divided by 23.

Marginal cost is calculated by taking the *increase* in variable cost associated with one more

Example 1

Long-Run Costs   145

Is the Law of Diminishing Returns Realistic?

Economic laws require great regularity to deserve to be called a "law." How true is it of modern economies that marginal physical productivity will eventually decline when variable inputs are added in ever-increasing quantities to a fixed input?

1. As more variable inputs (fertilizer, corn seed, tractors, farm workers) are applied to a given acre of fertile Iowa corn land, the extra cost of an additional bushel of corn must eventually rise. On average, an acre of Iowa corn land yields more bushels of corn than an acre of Texas corn land. Why is not all corn grown in Iowa? The law of diminishing returns supplies the answer. As more variable inputs are added to Iowa corn land, the *MPP* of these inputs falls. Eventually the *MPP* will fall to the point where it is less than the *MPP* of variable resources on Texas corn land. To grow all corn in Iowa would mean using resources with very low *MPP* relative to alternate uses making it more profitable to grow corn in another state where the *MPP* would be higher.

2. Consider the large influx of small foreign cars into the United States after the price of gasoline rose dramatically from 1974 to 1981. The law of diminishing returns helps explain why Americans did not buy American small cars. Even if the American automobile manufacturer had been able to produce a small car of comparable quality as Japan and Germany, existing production facilities for manufacturing small cars were limited. If American manufacturers had attempted to substantially increase their output of small cars, they would have faced a rapidly declining *MPP* of variable inputs (or rising marginal costs of production). Rising costs would have made it difficult, if not impossible, to compete with foreign imports if larger numbers of small cars were produced.

3. The law of diminishing returns is observed on a regular basis in many restaurants. During slack periods, one or two waiters or waitresses can handle all the business more efficiently if part of the dining area is closed off. The fixed inputs are the one or two waitresses; the variable input is the dining room space. During slack times the marginal physical productivity of dining room space is not only declining but it is negative—therefore, it pays the restaurant to reduce the amount of space available!

---

unit of labor (which always equals $10 in this example) and dividing by the *increase* in output (which is the marginal physical product).[2] For example, the second unit of labor raises variable costs by $10 and raises output by 7 units (the *MPP*); the marginal cost is $10/7 units or $1.43.

When MPP is increasing, MC is declining; when MPP is falling, MC is increasing.

When marginal physical product is rising, each additional worker produces a larger addition to output than the previous worker. When each worker is paid the same wage, the addition to cost (*MC*) will decline. When *MPP* is falling, each additional worker produces a smaller addition to output; therefore, the addition to cost (*MC*) will rise. Thus, according to the law of diminishing returns, *MC* will tend to rise in the short run as output is expanded.

LONG-RUN COSTS

The basic characteristic of the long run is that enterprises do not have any fixed costs; all costs are variable. Insofar as fixed costs arise because of fixed factors of production, enterprises have no fixed factors of production in the long run.

In the long run, the business enterprise is free to choose any combination of inputs to produce output. Once long-run decisions are executed (the company completes a new plant, the commercial farming enterprise signs a 10-year lease for additional acreage), the enterprise again has fixed factors of production and fixed costs. In the long

2. The formula for calculating marginal cost from *MPP* is: $MC = W/MPP$, where W denotes the wage rate.

Table 4
Production Functions and Average and Marginal Cost

(1) Labor Input, L (worked hours)	(2) Capital Input, K (fixed at 2 units)	(3) Output, Q (units)	(4) Marginal Physical Productivity of Labor, MPP_2 (units)	(5) Average Total Cost, ATC_2 (dollars)	(6) Marginal Cost, MC_2 (dollars)
0	2	0		∞	
			9		1.11
1	2	9		5.56	
			11		0.91
2	2	20		3	
			14		0.71
3	2	34		2.06	
			8		1.25
4	2	42		1.91	
			7		1.43
5	2	49		1.84	
			5		2
6	2	54		1.85	
			3		3.33
7	2	57		1.93	
			2		5
8	2	59		2.03	

This table is constructed like Table 3 but shows what happens when the capital is fixed at 2 units instead of 1.

run, enterprises are free to select the cost-mini-mizing level of capital, labor, and land inputs. Long-run cost-minimizing decisions are based on the prices the firm must pay for land, labor, and capital.

Shifts in Cost Curves

Returning to the production function in Table 3, consider what happens when the enterprise is free to select any combination of labor and capital inputs, when capital is no longer fixed at one unit of input. Once the enterprise selects a new level of capital input, it is again in the short run, and its capital costs again become fixed costs. To keep the example simple, assume the enterprise can select either one or two units of capital in addition to its choice of labor inputs. The production function with capital fixed at one unit was given in Table 3; the production function with capital fixed at 2 units is given in Table 4. The marginal physical product and average and mar-ginal cost schedules from both tables are now graphed in Figure 5.

A different family of short-run cost curves is associated with each of the two amounts of capital input. Because MPP is higher for each level of labor input when there are two units of capital, marginal cost will be lower at each level of output (marginal cost is the mirror image of marginal physical product). What happens to average total cost as capital increases? The minimum point of the ATC_2 cost curve occurs at a higher level of output than the ATC_1 curve. In effect, the addi-tion of extra capital causes the average and mar-ginal cost curves to *shift to the right*.

For every level of fixed input, there is a different family of short-run cost curves. As the fixed input expands, the short-run cost curve shifts to the right.

Figure 5
The Effects of a Change in Plant Size

(a) Marginal Physical Product

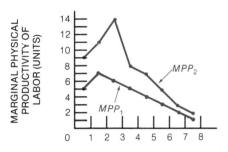

LABOR INPUT (WORKER HOURS)

(b) Marginal Cost and Average Total Cost

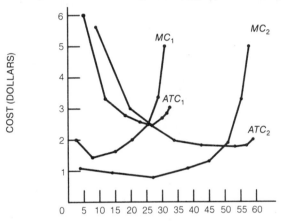

QUANTITY OF OUTPUT

Panel (a) shows that the marginal physical product of labor shifts up from MPP_1 to MPP_2 when the stock of capital increases from one unit to two units (Table 4 contains the data for the production function when two units of capital are used; Table 3 describes the production function when one unit of capital is used). Panel (b) shows the associated shifts in the cost curves resulting from the increase in capital input. The average total cost curve shifts to the right from ATC_1 to ATC_2; the marginal cost curve also shifts to the right from MC_1 to MC_2. The change in plant size represented by the increase in the capital input enables the firm to reach lower unit-cost levels.

In the long run, enterprises have the option of choosing among the different short-run cost curves by selecting the level of capital input. Once the capital input has been selected, they must operate on a new short-run cost curve. If they choose one unit of capital, this means they will operate on the first set of short-run cost curves in Figure 5. If they choose two units of capital, they will operate on the second set of short-run cost curves.

The Long-Run Cost Curve

There is a different *ATC* curve for each level of fixed input. If there are an infinite number of fixed input levels from which to choose, there would be an infinite number of associated *ATC* curves. Recall that in the long run all costs are variable; therefore, there is no distinction between long-run variable and total costs—there is only long-run average cost.

*The **long-run average cost** (**LRAC**) curve shows the minimum average cost for each level of output when all factor inputs are variable (and when factor prices are fixed).*

In the long run, the enterprise is free to select the most effective combination of factor inputs because none of the inputs is fixed. The long-run cost curve "envelopes" the short-run cost curves, forming a long-run curve that touches each short-run curve at only one point, as shown in Figure 6. In the short run, the fact that some factors of production are fixed causes the average total cost curve to be *U*-shaped. The law of diminishing returns does not apply to the long run because, in the long run, all inputs are variable.

Why the LRAC Curve is *U*-Shaped

The long-run average cost curve will also be *U*-shaped but not for the same reasons that *SRATC*s (short-run *ATC*s) are *U*-shaped. Figure 6 depicts the long-run average total cost curve as being *U*-shaped. Why would long-run average costs *(LRAC)* first decline as output expands and then later increase as output expands even further? The reason is that firms experience first economies of scale, then constant returns to scale, and finally diseconomies of scale as output expands.[3]

Economies of Scale. The declining portion of the *LRAC* curve is due to economies of scale

3. The following discussion of economies and diseconomies of scale is based on Frederic Scherer, *Industrial Market Structure and Economic Performance,* 3rd ed. (Boston: Houghton Mifflin, 1980), chap. 4.

Figure 6
The Long-Run Average Cost Curve as the Envelope of the Short-Run Average Total Cost Curves

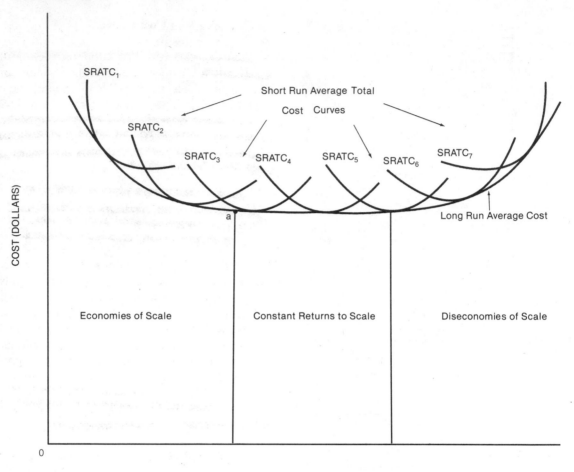

For each level of fixed input, there is a corresponding short-run average total cost curve. The long-run average cost curve is the envelope of the short-run average total cost curves. The long-run average cost curve is *U*-shaped. The declining portion shows economies of scale. The rising portion shows diseconomies of scale. The horizontal portion shows constant returns to scale. Point *a* shows the minimum efficient scale of the firm.

that arise out of the indivisibility of the inputs of labor and physical capital goods or equipment. In a large firm the division of labor will be much more specialized than in a small firm; as Adam Smith observed in his *Wealth of Nations*, workers will be able to specialize in various activities, will increase their productivity or dexterity through experience, and will save much time by "passing from one species of work to another." People are

simply indivisible; it is difficult for one person to be one part mechanic, two parts supervisor, and three parts electrician and still remain as efficient as one who specializes in just one of these tasks. The classic example of worker specialization is the assembly line of an automobile plant. The same principles apply to machines. A small firm might have to use general-purpose machine tools whereas a large firm might be able to have special equipment or machines built that will substantially lower costs when large quantities are produced. Small-scale versions of certain specialized machines simply cannot be made available.

Economies of scale can occur because of the greater productivity of specialization in any of a variety of areas, including technological equipment, marketing, research and development, and management. The optimal rate of utilization for some types of machinery may occur at high rates of output. Some workers may not be able to perfect specialized skills until a high rate of output allows them to concentrate on specific tasks. As the output of an enterprise increases with all inputs variable, average costs will decline because of the **economies of scale** associated with increased specialization of labor, management, plant, and equipment.

Economies of scale are present when equal percentage changes in the use of inputs lead to larger percentage changes in output.

Constant Returns to Scale. Economies of scale will become exhausted at some point when expanding output no longer increases productivity. The evidence suggests that for a large range of outputs there will be **constant returns to scale,** where the average costs of production remain constant.

Constant returns to scale are present when a given percent change in all inputs results in the same percent change in output.

Diseconomies of Scale. As the enterprise continues to expand its output, eventually all the economies of large-scale production will be exploited, and long-run average costs will begin to rise. The rise in long-run average costs as the capital stock of the enterprise expands is due to **diseconomies of scale.**

Diseconomies of scale are present when an equal percentage change in inputs leads to a smaller percentage change in output.

For example, managerial coordination becomes excessively complex as the scale of the firm grows. The employees of the firm become specialized as janitors, assembly-line workers, electricians, supervisors, sales managers, plant managers, vice-presidents of sales, of production, and of engineering, and even as a president or chief executive officer. When firms grow too big, it is natural and commonplace for information breakdowns to occur: messages will be misunderstood, some subordinates will understand more than their bosses, and various activities will not be properly coordinated as a "hurry up and wait" atmosphere begins to pervade the firm.

Diseconomies of scale can be caused by a series of factors. As the firm continues to expand, management skills must be spread over a larger and larger firm. Managers must assume additional responsibility, and managerial talents may eventually be spread so thin that the efficiency of management declines. The problem of maintaining communications within a large firm grows, and red tape and cumbersome bureaucracy become commonplace. Large firms may find it difficult to correct their mistakes. Employees of large firms may lose their identity and feel that their contributions to the firm are not recognized. As the output of an enterprise continues to increase average cost will eventually rise because of the diseconomies of scale associated with the growing problems of managerial coordination.

MINIMUM EFFICIENT SCALE

Cost and productivity schedules help explain a wide variety of real world phenomena, such as why some companies are more profitable than others, why some industries are more concentrated than others, or why a particular company is doing well or poorly. Actual short-run and long-run cost curves for the dairy industry, for example, show the pattern of returns to scale in dairy farming (see Example 2).

Figure 6 shows a fairly typical long-run average cost curve. Notice that the bottom portion is flat over a fairly large range. The output level associated with point *a* is called the **minimum efficient scale *(MES)*** of the firm.

*The **minimum efficient scale** (MES) is the lowest level of output at which the average costs are minimized.*

Example 2

The Cost Curves of American Dairy Farms

The adjacent figure shows actual short-run cost curves of American dairy farms ranging from large-scale farms (more than $40,000 sales annually) to small-scale farms (less than $2,500 sales annually), with figures derived from the 1964 census of agriculture. The actual short-run cost curves show that the short-run average cost curves shift downward and to the right as the scale of output increases. Economies of scale are experienced up to approximately 500,000 pounds of output, but the minimum point on the next average total cost curve (that of the largest class of dairy farm) yields virtually the same average total cost at 1.2 million pounds per year as at 500,000 pounds per year. Over the output range from 500,000 to 1.2 million pounds, returns to scale in dairy farming appear to be constant.

The long-run average cost curve of dairy farming is drawn as the envelope of the short-run average cost curves and shows a pattern of economies of scale up to 500,000 pounds, after which the LRAC curve becomes flat.

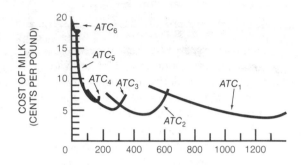

QUANTITY OF MILK
(THOUSANDS OF POUNDS PER YEAR)

The ATC curves are numbered to correspond to firms whose annual sales are: 1) more than $40,000, 2) $20,000–$39,999, 3) $10,000–$19,000, 4) $5,000–$9,999, 5) $2,500–$4,999, and 6) under $2,500.

Source: Leonard Weiss, *Case Studies of American Industry,* 2nd ed. (New York: John Wiley & Sons, 1971), p. 76.

In the real world, economies of scale differ substantially among industries. Some industries experience economies of scale up to output levels that are a high proportion of total industry sales. These industries tend to have a small number of firms. Economies of scale are an important explanation of the degree of concentration in different industries.

Economic researchers use three techniques to measure economies of scale. The first technique is *engineering estimates:* engineers are asked what the optimal scale plant is and by how much costs rise as the plant size diverges from this optimum. The second method is *statistical cost studies.* This approach examines actual cost data of firms from year to year or for different firms at the same point in time. The third approach is the *survivor technique.* The survivor technique follows firms in an industry over time to establish whether the size of firms is staying the same or increasing. If the size of firms is increasing, then firms of smaller size must not be able to *survive* (remain competitive with larger firms).[4]

Each technique has its advocates and opponents. Empirical studies of economies of scale show that some industries (electricity, automobiles) have significant economies of scale. Other industries, such as airlines, do not have any significant economies of scale. Table 5 reports the results of two studies of selected industries that show that the minimum efficient plant size is as high as 21–30 percent of sales in the case of diesel engines and as low as only 0.2 percent in the case of shoe sales.

This chapter examined how production costs behave in the short and long run. The next chapter will study how perfectly competitive firms use these costs to determine their output level.

4. These techniques for measuring economies of scale are discussed in William G. Shepherd, *The Economics of Industrial Organization* (Englewood Cliffs, N.J.: Prentice-Hall, 1979), chap. 12 and James V. Koch, *Industrial Organization and Prices,* 2nd ed. (Englewood Cliffs, N.J.: Prentice-Hall, 1980), chap. 6.

Table 5
Estimates of the Minimum Efficient Scale (MES) in U.S. Industries, 1967

Industry (1)	Minimum Efficient Scale (MES): (2)	MES as a Percentage of U.S. Demand: (3)
Diesel engines	not available	21–30
Electronic computers	not available	15.0
Refrigerators	800,000 units per year	14.1
Cigarettes	36 billion cigarettes per year	6.6
Beer brewing	4.5 million barrels per year	3.4
Bicycles	not available	2.1
Petroleum refining	200,000 barrels per day	1.9
Paints	10 million U.S. gallons per year	1.4
Flour mills	not available	0.7
Bread baking	not available	0.3
Shoes (nonrubber)	1 million pairs per year	0.2

Sources: F. M. Scherer, Alan Beckenstein, Erich Kaufer and R. D. Murphy, *The Economics of Multiplant Operation* (Cambridge, Mass.: Harvard University Press, 1975), pp. 80–94. Leonard W. Weiss, "Optimal Plant Size and the Extent of Suboptimal Capacity," in eds. Robert T. Masson and P.D. Qualls, *Essays on Industrial Organization in Honor of Joe S. Bain* (Cambridge, Mass.: Ballinger, 1975), pp. 128–31; adapted in part from C. F. Pratten, *Economies of Scale in Manufacturing Industry* (Cambridge, England: Cambridge University Press, 1971).

Summary

1. The opportunity cost of an action is the value of the best forgone alternative. Economic profit is defined as total revenue minus opportunity costs. When economic profits are zero, the firm is still earning a normal profit. In the short run the time period is so short that existing plant and equipment cannot be varied; in the long run all inputs are variable. Variable costs are those costs that vary with output; fixed costs do not vary with output. In the long run, all costs are variable. Marginal cost is the increase in cost associated with increasing output by one unit.

2. Average variable cost (AVC) is variable cost divided by output; average total cost (ATC) is total (fixed plus variable) cost divided by output. The average variable and average total cost curves tend to be U-shaped with the MC intersecting AVC and ATC at their minimum values.

3. Marginal physical product is the increase in output due to increasing an input by one unit, holding all other inputs constant. The law of diminishing returns states that as one input is increased (holding other inputs constant), the marginal physical product of the variable input labor will eventually decline. If labor were the only variable input, marginal cost in the short run would be the wage rate divided by the marginal product of labor.

4. In the long run there are different-sized plants. Associated with each sized plant is a particular short-run average total cost curve. The envelope of all such short-run average total cost curves is the *long-run average cost curve*. The long-run average cost curve gives the minimum unit cost of producing any given volume of output. Along the long-run average cost curve the firm is choosing the least-cost combination of inputs. Increasing returns to scale prevail when increasing all inputs by the same percentage increases output by a greater percentage; the long-run average cost curve is declining. Constant returns to scale prevail when increasing all inputs by the same percentage increases output by that percentage; the long-run average cost curve is constant or horizontal. Decreasing returns to scale prevail when increasing all inputs by the same percentage increases

output by a smaller percentage; the long-run average cost curve is rising.

5. A firm's minimum efficient scale *(MES)* is the lowest level of output at which average costs are minimized.

Key Terms

opportunity costs
explicit costs
implicit costs
accounting profits
economic profits
normal profits
short run
long run
fixed costs *(FC)*
variable costs *(VC)*
average total costs *(ATC)*
marginal cost *(MC)*
total costs *(TC)*
average variable cost *(AVC)*
average fixed cost *(AFC)*
production function
marginal physical product *(MPP)*
law of diminishing returns
long-run average cost *(LRAC)*
economies of scale
constant returns to scale
diseconomies of scale
minimum efficient scale *(MES)*

Questions and Problems

1. Your bank advertises a no-service-charge checking account for customers who keep a minimum of $100 in their account. Is this truly a "free" checking account?

2. Explain the distinction between accounting profits and economic profits. Why are economic profits a better guide to resource-allocation decisions?

3. Contrast the *ATC* curve of a firm that has very large fixed costs relative to variable costs with the *ATC* curve of a firm that has very small fixed costs relative to variable costs.

4. Explain why fixed costs should not affect business decisions in the short run.

5. Answer the following questions using the production-function information in the accompanying table and assuming that one unit of labor costs $5 and one unit of capital costs $10:

Labor (units)	Capital (units)	Output (units)
0	2	0
1	2	5
2	2	15
3	2	20
4	2	23
5	2	24

a. Derive the *MPP* schedule. Does it obey the law of diminishing returns?

b. Derive the short-run cost schedules.

c. Derive the *MPP* and short-run cost schedules if labor productivity doubles (with one labor unit, for example, being used to produce an output of 10 units instead of 5 units).

d. Explain why the short-run cost curves would shift if the amount of capital input changed.

6. If the previous average total cost is $25, and marginal cost is $15, what will happen to the new average total cost? To the new average variable cost? If *ATC* stays at $25 and *MC* increases to $25, what will happen to the next *ATC?*

8A

Choosing the Least-Cost Method of Production

Appendix Preview

How should the firm go about choosing the right combination of resources? The correct answer is: the firm should choose the *least-cost method* of production. This appendix will show how firms produce output using the least costly combination of resources.

THE PRODUCTION FUNCTION

Recall that the production function shows the maximum output that can be achieved by a given combination of inputs. Figure 1 shows a hypothetical firm that employs only two factors—capital and labor—to produce its output. The horizontal edge measures the labor input from 1 to 8 workers; the vertical edge measures the capital input from 1 to 8 machines. The amount of output that can be produced from any combination of labor and capital is shown in the cells corresponding to the intersection of a row of capital input and column of labor input. For example, 8 machines and 1 worker produce 50 units of output;

8 machines and 2 workers produce 71 units of output. Thus the production function shown in Figure 1 gives the possible methods of producing the outputs shown at each intersection.

Figure 1 illustrates the concept of marginal physical product, the law of diminishing returns, and the principle of substitution.

Marginal Physical Product *(MPP)*

Recall that the marginal physical product *(MPP)* of a factor is the extra output associated with increasing input of the factor by one unit, holding all other factors constant. Suppose that the amount of capital is held constant at 4 machines. With 1 worker, output is 35 units; with 2 workers, output is 50 units; and so on. Clearly the marginal product of labor is 35 for the first worker and 15 for the second worker (since output rises from 35 to 50). The *MPP* of labor can be read in the figure by simply comparing outputs along a given row. By similar reasoning, the marginal product of capital could be determined by varying the machine input, holding labor constant.

Figure 1
Production Possibilities

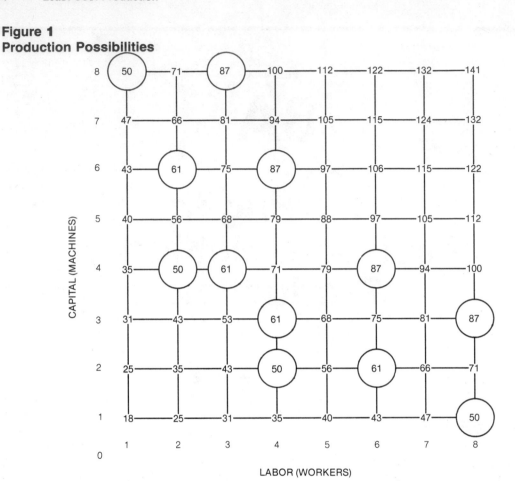

Capital inputs are measured vertically; labor inputs are measured horizontally. The number at the intersection of a row and column shows the output for that level of capital and labor input. For example: 4 machines and 2 workers produce 50 units of output. The law of diminishing returns can also be seen because when the input of machines is held constant at 4 units, additional units of labor bring about smaller additions to output; thus, along a given row output *increases* but at a *decreasing* rate.

The Law of Diminishing Returns

According to the law of diminishing returns, the marginal physical product of a factor eventually declines as more of the factor is used while holding all other productive inputs constant. In Figure 1, when capital equals 4 machines, the *MPP* of the second worker is 15 and the *MPP* for the third worker is only 11.

The production function summarized in Figure 1 assumes constant returns to scale. When there are 3 units of capital and 3 units of labor, output is 53 units; and when inputs double to 6 units of capital and 6 units of labor, output doubles to 106 units. When there are 3 units of capital and 3 units of labor, the fourth unit of labor has an *MPP* of 8 units as output rises from 53 to 61. When there are 4 units of capital and 4 units of labor, the fifth unit of labor also has an *MPP* of 8 units as output rises from 71 to 79. Thus, *the marginal physical product of labor remains the same as long as the ratio of capital to labor remains the*

Table 1
Factor Combinations for
Producing 50 Units of Output

	Output, Q (1)	Capital, C (2)	Labor, L (3)	Total Cost, TC (4)
a	50	8 machines	1 worker	$250
b	50	4 machines	2 workers	$200
c	50	2 machines	4 workers	$250
d	50	1 machine	8 workers	$425

Note: The price of capital is $25 per machine; the price of labor is $50 per worker.

same. The source of the law of diminishing returns is the varying ratio of workers to machines.

The Principle of Substitution

Figure 1 also illustrates the principle of substitution. In Figure 1, 50 units of output can be produced by four different combinations of capital and labor. These combinations are listed in columns (2) and (3) of Table 1.

The production function alone cannot tell us how to produce the 50 units of output. From the information so far provided, there is no reason for choosing the combination of 8 units of capital/1 unit of labor over the combination of 1 unit of capital/8 units of labor to produce 50 units of output.

LEAST-COST PRODUCTION

The price of labor (P_L) and the price of capital (P_C) help us determine what combination of capital and labor the firm will use. Suppose P_L = $50 and P_C = $25. Column (4) of Table 1 shows the costs of each combination of labor and capital that yields 50 units of output. For example: Combination *a* costs $250 because 8 machines cost $200 (= 8 × $25) and 1 worker costs $50. From Table 1 we can determine that the minimum cost combination is combination *b*—4 units of capital and 2 units of labor, the total cost *(TC)* of which is $200. The average cost of production is *ATC* = *TC/Q* = $200/50 = $4 per unit, which is the lowest possible cost per unit when total output is 50 units.

In going from combination *a* to combination *b*, an extra unit of labor can be substituted for 4 ma-

chines without a loss of output. Labor costs $50; but 4 machines cost $100. Thus the firm saves $100 in machine costs by substituting 1 worker for 4 machines and spends $50 on the added worker for a net gain of $50 (without a loss in output). Clearly, it pays the firm to select *b* over *a*.

Equal-Output Curve

The above principles of least-cost production can be illustrated using graphs. Figure 2 plots combinations *a, b, c,* and *d* from Table 1 and connects these points by a smooth curve. The curve *abcd* shows all the combinations of capital and labor input that produce 50 units of output; hence, it can be called the *equal-output curve* for 50 units of output.

The equal-output curve is very similar to the indifference curves studied in the appendix to the chapter on demand and utility. Just as the indifference curves were convex to the origin, so an equal-output curve is convex to the origin. The ratio of the line segment *af* to *fb* is the amount of capital that is substituted for the extra unit of labor. The slope of the curve between *a* and *b* demonstrates that the marginal physical product of labor is 4 times the marginal physical product of capital because the vertical distance *af* is 4 times the horizontal distance *fb*. The ratio of the marginal physical products measures the marginal rate of substitution, or the rate at which labor can be substituted for capital, and is measured by the slope (in absolute value) of an equal-output curve between two points or as the absolute slope of the tangent to any point on the equal-output curve.

The Marginal Rate of Substitution of Capital for Labor

$$= \frac{\textit{Marginal Physical Product of Labor}}{\textit{Marginal Physical Product of Capital}}$$

= the slope (absolute) of an equal output curve

The equal-output curve is bowed out toward the origin because when workers are substituted for machines, the *MPP* of labor falls relative to the *MPP* of capital; to keep output constant one worker will not substitute for as many machines as the number of workers increases.

Figure 2
Equal-Output Curve

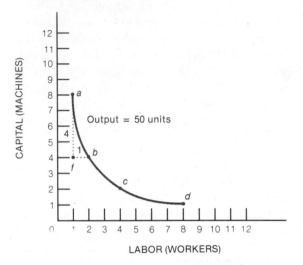

The curve shows all the combinations of labor (number of workers) and capital (number of machines) that produce the same 50 units of output. It is bowed out toward the origin because the law of diminishing returns dictates that substituting capital for labor becomes more difficult as the ratio of workers to machines increases.

Equal-Cost Curves

Assuming that the price of labor (P_L) is $50 per worker and the price of capital (P_C) is $25 per machine, the total cost *(TC)* of production is:

$$TC = (P_L \times L) + (P_C \times C) = \$50L + \$25C$$

where L = the number of workers and C = the number of machines. In Figure 3, the line TC = $300 consists of all the combinations of labor and capital that cost $300. For example, if C = 12 and L = 0, TC = $300; if C = 0 and L = 6, TC = $300; the combination 6 machines and 3 workers also costs $300.

The equal-cost line shows all the combinations of labor and capital that have the same total costs.

Figure 3 gives three illustrative equal-cost lines, but there is one for every level of total costs. These equal cost lines are parallel because each has the same slope. The absolute slope of any equal-cost line is simply P_L/P_C. In the present

Figure 3
Equal-Cost Curves

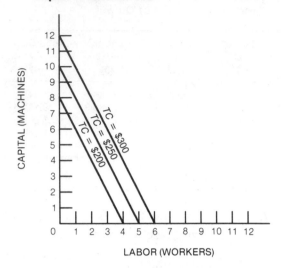

The equal-cost lines show all the combinations of labor and capital that cost the same amount. The TC = $300 shows all the combinations costing $300. The slope of each equal-cost line is measured by the ratio of the price of labor to the price of capital; in this case, labor is $50 per worker and capital is $25 per machine, so each equal-cost line has an absolute slope of 2.

case, the (absolute) slope is 2 since the price of a unit of labor is twice that of a unit of capital. If a unit of labor costs twice as much as a unit of capital, 2 units of capital can be substituted for a unit of labor without increasing or decreasing total costs.

The slope of the equal-cost line is the price of labor divided by the price of capital, which represents the rate at which firms can substitute labor for capital without affecting total costs.

THE LEAST-COST RULE

Figure 4 shows how the firm minimizes the cost of producing a given volume of output (in this case, output is 50 units). When the equal-output curve for 50 units of output and the equal-cost lines for three representative cost levels are drawn on the same graph, one can determine the least-cost combination by observing where the equal-output line *abcd* intersects the *lowest* equal-cost line (at point *b*). The lowest equal-cost line

Figure 4
Least-Cost Production

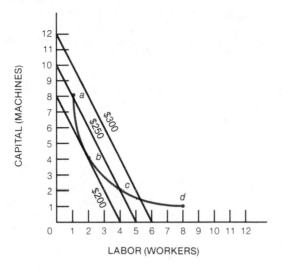

The least-cost method of producing 50 units of output can be found at the point where the equal-output curve, *abcd*, touches the lowest equal-cost line, *TC* = $200. At the point *b* the slope of the equal-product curve equals the slope of the equal-cost line. At point *b*, the two curves are tangent; here the ratio of the marginal physical product of labor to that of capital equals the ratio of the price of labor to the price of capital.

that curve *abcd* can reach is *TC* = $200. All other combinations of labor and capital on *abcd* cost more than $200. Thus, point *b* is the least-cost production point. It is the best combination of labor and capital (4 machines and 2 workers) for producing 50 units of output.

In Figure 4, it is obvious that the slope of the equal-output curve is the same as the slope of the equal-cost line since both are tangent (they touch without crossing) at that point. Thus

$$\frac{MPP_L}{MPP_C} = \frac{P_L}{P_C} \qquad (1)$$

Using a little algebra, the least-cost rule can be rewritten in a second equivalent way:

$$\frac{MPP_L}{P_L} = \frac{MPP_C}{P_C} \qquad (2)$$

In other words, least-cost production requires that the extra output from the last dollar spent on labor must equal the extra output from the last dollar

spent on capital. A third way of writing the least-cost rule (by taking the reciprocals of rule 2) is

$$\frac{P_L}{MPP_L} = \frac{P_C}{MPP_C} \qquad (3)$$

The price of labor divided by the *MPP* of labor is labor cost per unit of output, which is nothing but the marginal cost of output using labor (recall that marginal cost is the extra cost of producing one more unit of output). Similarly, the price of capital divided by the *MPP* of capital is the marginal cost of production using capital. According to the third rule, least-cost production (in the long run) requires using capital and labor in such a way that the marginal cost of production is the same whether output is increased using capital or labor. If these two weren't equal, one would be substituted for the other.

When $P_L/MPP_L = P_C/MPP_C$, the long-run marginal cost of production is the common ratio.

The Link Between the Short Run and the Long Run

The long run is a period of time so long that both workers and machines can be varied. In the short run, the number of machines is fixed. If it takes time to find the right machine, install it, and train workers to use it properly, fixed costs would be the machine costs; variable costs would be the labor costs. In the short run, marginal cost would be the ratio P_L/MPP_L. As shown in Table 2, the number of machines is fixed at 4 in the short run, and the number of workers can be varied from 0 to 5. The first four columns of Table 2 can be derived from Figure 1. Column (5) of Table 2 is the short-run marginal cost. Columns (6) through (9) show the short-run costs of production. Column (9) illustrates the average total cost *(ATC)* of production. Note that *ATC* hits its minimum at an output of 50 units where *ATC* = $4.00.

Applying the Least-Cost Rule

What would the firm do if the price of capital rises from $25 per machine to $100 per machine, while the price of labor remains the same at $50 per worker? It would of course begin to substitute the now cheaper labor for the now more expensive machinery. The price of capital is now twice

Table 2
Production Functions

Capital, C (1)	Labor, L (2)	Marginal Physical Product of Labor, MPP_L (3)	Output, Q (4)	Marginal Cost, MC (5)	Fixed Cost, FC (6)	Variable Cost, VC (7)	Total Cost, TC (8)	Average Total Cost, ATC (9)
4	0		0		0	0	0	0
		35		$1.43				
4	1		35		$100	$ 50	$150	$4.29
		15		3.33				
4	2		50		100	100	200	4.00
		11		4.54				
4	3		61		100	150	250	4.10
		10		5.00				
4	4		71		100	200	300	4.23
		8		6.25				
4	5		79		100	250	350	4.43

Note: The price of labor is $50 per worker; the price of capital is $25 per machine.

Figure 5
A change in Factor Price

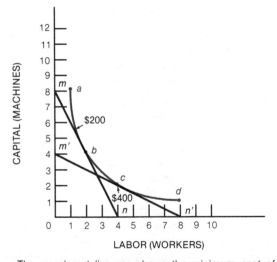

The equal-cost line *mn* shows the minimum cost of producing 50 units of output when capital is $25 per machine and labor is $50 per worker. (Line *mn* is the same as TC = 200.) If the price of capital rises to $100 per machine, the equal-cost line *m'n'* shows that the lowest cost of producting 50 units of output rises to $400 and the least-cost combination of capital and labor shifts from point *b* to point *c* as cheaper labor is substituted for machines.

as great as the price of labor, so the slope of the new equal-cost lines is ½ instead of 2. Figure 5 shows what happens. The old *TC* line was *mn*—with the minimum-cost point *b*. The new minimum *TC* line is *m'n'*, which is tangent to point *c* on the equal-output curve. The total cost of production is now $400 (4 units of capital now costs $400 and 8 units of labor costs $400). Since 50 units are still produced, the average cost of production is now $8 (= $400/50). Before capital quadrupled in price the average cost was $4. Quadrupling the price of capital causes the average cost of production to double. The optimal ratio of machines to workers is now 2 machines per 4 workers or ½ machine per worker. The production process has now become less capital-intensive and more labor-intensive.

Summary

1. An equal-output curve shows all the combinations of two factors that will produce a given level of output.
2. An equal-cost line shows all the combinations of two factors that have the same total costs.
3. The least-cost combination of two factors can be found at the point where the equal-output curve intersects the lowest equal-cost line.

CHAPTER

9

Perfect Competition

Chapter Preview

Adam Smith concluded that the "invisible hand" would lead people pursuing their own interests to serve the interest of society through the process of *competition*. Competition among the various actors on the economic stage channels the narrow and sometimes selfish interest of each person in a socially desirable direction. How this remarkable mechanism works is the subject of this chapter.

This chapter will describe how a firm facing perfect competition will make its profit-maximizing decisions in both the short run and the long run, how market prices are determined in both the short run and the long run, and how producers and consumers benefit from trading in a competitive market.

THE MEANING OF COMPETITION

In a world of scarcity, available resources are not adequate to satisfy everyone's wants. Competition for scarce resources is a necessary and unavoidable characteristic of any economy. One may dislike competition, but there is no way to avoid it. Competition can take a variety of forms. A free-for-all system of catch-as-catch-can or steal-as-much-as-one-can is one possible scheme. In such a system, there are no property rights and each person can have whatever he or she can find. It does not take much imagination to see that such a system would not work well. Another arrangement—deplored by Adam Smith—is to grant certain people special privileges *(monopolies)* to use particular scarce resources. Another system is to allow people to buy and sell property rights in all sorts of things *freely* with property rights protected by the state. If property rights were not protected by law, no person would have an incentive to buy or produce property (why produce something if somebody else can steal it?).

Individuals endowed with property rights will compete for different things. Buyers will compete with other buyers; sellers will compete with other sellers. Economists distinguish between **perfect competition** and **imperfect competition.**

> *Perfect competition between buyers or sellers exists if no single buyer or seller has a perceptible influence on the market price of the good. Imperfect competition exists if a single buyer or seller can influence the price. The less competition there is among sellers (or buyers), the more power each individual seller (or buyer) exercises over price.*

Note: we will assume in this and the following four chapters that buyers have no control over the prices they pay. This assumption holds generally for households but is less true for big business that buys from other businesses.

In the real world, almost every seller exercises some influence over price, but the more competition the seller faces the less control the individual seller can exercise over the prices charged. In the limiting case, the seller has absolutely no control over price. Each individual seller faces so much competition from other sellers that the market price is taken as a given. When the price is given to the individual seller by the market, the seller is said to be a *price taker*.

> *The five characteristics of perfect competition are: 1) a large number of sellers and buyers, 2) a homogeneous product, 3) each buyer and seller has perfect information about prices and product quality, 4) freedom of entry and exit from the industry, and 5) each seller is a price taker.*

THE FIRM AND THE MARKET

In perfect competition, all firms in the industry sell a homogeneous or identical product. No firm exercises an advantage over other firms in terms of quality, location, or other product features. If Firm A charges a higher price than Firm B for the identical product, no rational buyer will buy from A. In a perfectly competitive market, buyers have perfect information about the prices charged by different sellers. Every buyer knows that Firm B's price is lower than Firm A's price.

The difference between the perfectly competitive firm and the market (or the industry as a whole) is illustrated in Figure 1. Panel (b) shows the market demand curve *D* for the product. When the market price is $7, the quantity demanded in the market is 10,000 units. The individual firm, shown in panel (a), can sell all it wants (from a practical standpoint) at the going market price of $7. Whether the firm sells 3 units or 10 units, the price is still the $7 market price.

> *The demand curve facing the perfectly competitive firm is* **horizontal** *or* **perfectly elastic at the going market price.**

The individual firm in a perfectly competitive market produces very small amounts relative to the market as a whole. An individual firm cannot change the market price by altering the quantity of the good it offers in the marketplace. Because the individual firm faces a perfectly elastic demand schedule, the firm is a price taker. If the firm tried to sell at a price higher than the market price, it would sell nothing.

PROFIT MAXIMIZATION IN THE SHORT RUN

In the short run, a perfectly competitive firm makes its output decisions by varying the quantity of its variable inputs (such as labor, raw material, energy) that are used with its fixed plant and equipment. The fixed plant and equipment is both a burden and a blessing. It is a blessing to established firms because in the short run fixed costs prevent new firms from entering the industry. Time is needed to build more plants, install more equipment, and find new locations. Fixed plant and equipment is also a burden, because the firm in the short run is obliged to make certain contractual payments (taxes, rent payments, contractual obligations to some employees) and to forgo interest receipts that could be earned if the plant

Figure 1
Industry or Market Demand versus Firm demand

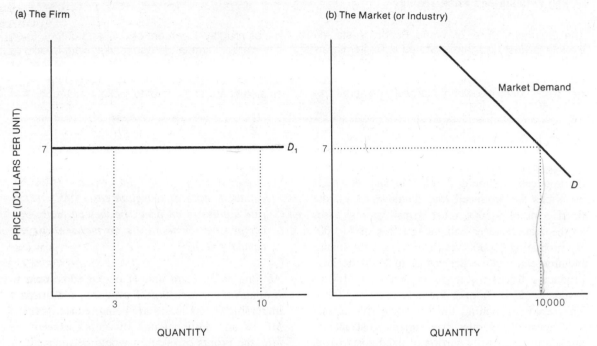

(a) The Firm

(b) The Market (or Industry)

The market demand curve D in panel (b) shows the total market demand for a homogeneous product being produced by many relatively small firms. The demand curve D_1 in panel (a) shows how the demand is perceived by the individual firm. Because the individual firm is so small relative to the market, it cannot significantly influence the market price. The firm is, thus, a price taker and can sell all it wants at the going price.

---

and equipment could be sold, even if the firm shuts down temporarily.

In the short run, the firm must make two decisions: 1) whether to temporarily shut down and produce nothing, and 2) how much to produce if it decides not to shut down. In the long run, the firm has the additional options of building more plants and acquiring more equipment or leaving the business permanently. Recall that the competitive firm does not decide the price. The firm is a *price taker;* the market sets the price.

The Rules of
Profit Maximization

The Shutdown Rule.   The firm is guided by the goal of profit maximization (or loss minimization). To maximize profit (or minimize losses), the firm will follow some simple rules.

Fixed costs should not affect decision making in the short run. In the short run, there is no way for the firm to alter fixed costs. The firm's fixed costs will continue whatever output decisions the firm makes in the short run. Even if the firm shuts down, these fixed costs must be paid. Only in the long run can fixed costs be avoided.

Thus, the first decision made by the perfectly competitive firm is: Should it shut down temporarily or should it produce some output? Surprisingly, it is not important whether or not the revenues that the firm earns cover fixed costs. Instead, the decision to shut down will depend on the relationship between revenues and *variable costs,* as the **shutdown rule** explains.

*The **shutdown rule** is: If the firm's revenues at all output levels are less than variable costs, it minimizes its losses by shutting down. If there is at least one output level at which revenues exceed variable costs, the firm should not shut down.*

For example, brick manufacturer Smith has fixed costs of $1,000 per week. She can sell

Example 1

Egg Farming and Price Taking

The Guinness Book of World Records lists the world's largest egg farm (located in California) as producing 730 million eggs per year. Total U.S. egg production averages around 70 billion eggs per year. Thus, the world's largest egg farm pro- duces roughly 1 percent of U.S. egg output. Even if the largest firm in the egg market were to double or triple its output, there would be no noticeable effect on the price. Even the largest firm is too small a share of the total to make a difference. ✕

$3,000 worth of bricks per week while incurring a variable cost *(VC)* of $2,900. Should the bricks be produced or should the plant be shut down? If no bricks are produced (the shutdown case), the fixed costs of $1,000 must be paid in any case, so the manufacturer will incur a loss of $1,000. By producing $3,000 worth of bricks, the manu- facturer can *reduce* her losses to $900 because producing bricks results in an excess of $100 of revenues ($3,000) over variable costs ($2,900). The reasoning behind the shutdown rule is that any excess of revenues over variable costs can be applied to covering a portion of fixed costs.

The Profit-Maximization Rule. Once the firm has decided not to shut down, what rule should the firm follow to maximize profits or min- imize losses? The decision about *how much* to produce is based upon marginal analysis. If at any point producing another unit of output raises the *profit of the firm (or reduces its losses),* more out- put should be produced. Adjustments in the level of output will continue to be made as long as each change adds more profit or reduces losses. As we learned in the preceding chapter, marginal cost *(MC)* is the increase in costs due to increasing output by one unit.

Once a firm decides not to shut down, the fun- damental **rule of profit maximization** is that out- put should be produced up to the point where the extra cost of an additional unit of output (mar- ginal cost) is just equal to the extra revenue de- rived from the additional unit of output **(marginal revenue).**

> *Marginal revenue* **(MR)** *is the increase in revenue brought about by increasing output by one unit.*

> *The profit-maximization rule is that a firm will maximize profits by producing that level of output at which marginal revenue* (MR) *equals or exceeds marginal costs* (MC). *(This rule applies to all firms, be they perfectly competitive, monopolistic, or monopolistic competitive.)*

As long as an extra unit of output adds more to revenues than to costs, the profits of the firm are increasing (or its losses are being reduced). If the *MC* of an additional unit of output exceeds its *MR,* the profits of the firm would be reduced (or its losses increased) if output is expanded. To a competitive firm, the price *(P)* of the product measures the extra revenue of an additional unit of output, or the marginal revenue *(MR)*. The per- fectly competitive firm can sell as much output as it wants at the prevailing market price, *P*. The increase in revenue brought about by increasing output by one unit therefore equals *P*.

> *Since* **P** *and* **MR** *are the same for a competitive firm, a profit-maximizing firm should produce that quantity of output at which* **P = MC.**

Consider the numerical example of a hypothet- ical competitive firm in Table 1. The firm must decide whether to produce 0, 1, 2, 3, or 4 units of output (see Column 1). The firm's fixed costs *(FC)* are $5. The firm's variable costs *(VC)* and marginal costs *(MC)* are given in columns (3) and (5) of Table 1.

Column (3) shows the marginal costs *(MC)* of going from one output level to the next: to pro- duce the first unit of output adds $6 to costs; to produce the second unit adds $8 to costs, and so forth.

Table 1
An Illustration of $P = MC$ Decision Making

Quantity, Q (1)	Price, $P(=MR)$ (2)	Marginal Cost, MC (3)	Revenue, R (4) = (1) × (2)	Variable Cost, VC (5)	Fixed Cost, FC (6)	Total Cost, TC (7)	Profit (loss) (8)
I. The Shutdown Case:							
0	$ 5.99		$ 0	$ 0	$5	$ 5	− $ 5.00 Best Choice
		$ 6					
1	5.99		5.99	6	5	11	−5.01
		8					
2	5.99		11.98	14	5	19	−7.02
		10					
3	5.99		17.97	24	5	29	−11.03
		12					
4	5.99		23.96	36	5	41	−17.04
II. Staying in Business with Losses:							
0	$ 6.01		$ 0:	$ 0	$5	$ 5	−$ 5.00
		$ 6					
1	6.01		6.01	6	5	11	−4.99 Best Choice
		8					
2	6.01		12.02	14	5	19	−6.98
		10					
3	6.01		18.03	24	5	29	−10.97
		12					
4	6.01		24.04	36	5	41	−16.96
III. Staying in Business with Profits:							
0	$10.01		$ 0:	$ 0	$5	$ 5	$ −5.00
		$ 6					
1	10.01		10.01	6	5	11	−0.99
		8					
2	10.01		20.02	14	5	19	+1.02
		10					
3	10.01		30.03	24	5	29	+1.03 Best Choice
		12					
4	10.01		40.04	36	5	41	−0.96

Note: numbers in boxes show output and profit (or loss) where profits are maximized (or losses are minimized).

How much output the firm will produce depends upon the price. If price is less than $6 (part I of the table), the firm will shut down (produce where output is 0) because for any level of output, revenues will not cover variable costs. Losses are minimized by shutting down.

If the price is $6.01 (part II of Table 1), the firm would then want to produce one unit of output. By producing where output is 1 unit, the firm's revenue will be $6.01 and its total costs

equal variable costs plus fixed costs (= $6 + $5 = $11). Its losses amount to $11 − $6.01, or $4.99. The firm is better off producing one unit than producing none at all because if it produced nothing its losses would equal fixed costs, or $5. It would not want to produce *more* than one unit of output because if the second unit were produced, revenues would again increase by $6.01, but costs would increase by $8.

If the price rises to $10.01 (part III of Table

1), producing the first unit now gives the firm a loss of $0.99 (because revenues are $10.01 and costs are $11). Producing the second unit adds $10.01 to revenue and only $8 to costs; hence, when output is 2 units, the firm could actually turn an economic profit of $1.02 (revenues are $20.02 and costs are $19). Producing the third unit adds $10.01 to revenues and $10 to costs, which would raise economic profit to $1.03. The firm should not produce *more* than 3 units, however, because the fourth unit of output adds $12 to costs and only $10.01 to revenues. If the fourth unit were produced, profits would fall by $1.99. Accordingly, profit is maximized at an output level of 3 units when price is $10.01.[1]

The Two Rules and the Firm's Supply Schedule

Using the shutdown rule and the profit-maximization rule[2] told us what quantities our hypothetical firm should produce at three specific prices (see Table 1). Recall that a supply curve shows quantities supplied at different prices by a seller or sellers. The three price/quantity combinations determined by using the two rules are three points on the firm's supply curve: 0 units/ $5.99, 1 unit/$6.01, and 3 units/$10.01.

Graphical Analysis of the Profit-Maximizing Firm

The cost schedules in Table 2 have been plotted in Figure 2. The *AVC* and *ATC* curves are U-shaped, and the *MC* curve intersects each average

---

1. In numerical examples involving discrete levels of output such as these, the $P = MC$ rule may not hold exactly. The reason is that going from (say) $Q = 1$ to $Q = 2$ is a discontinuous jump in output; the $MR = MC$ or $P = MC$ (for perfect competition) rule requires that the firm be able to choose not only whole numbers like $Q = 3$ but also fractional numbers like 2.5. One advantage of graphs over tables is that this problem does not arise; in graphs we can work with fractional numbers as easily as whole numbers. That the $P = MC$ rule does not hold exactly in the discrete case does not mean that it is not applied. The firm will expand output as long as P is greater than MC; it will contract output if P is less than MC. In other words, the firm will come as close as it can to observing the $P = MC$ rule.

2. Since revenue $= P \times Q$ and $VC = AVC \times Q$, the first rule will be satisfied if $P = AVC$. Thus the two rules are:
  (1) If $P < AVC$, set $Q = 0$ (shut down)
  (2) If $P > AVC$, adjust Q until $P \,(= MR) = MC$.

Figure 2
Profit Maximization for the Perfectly Competitive Firm

(a) Short-Run Loss Minimization

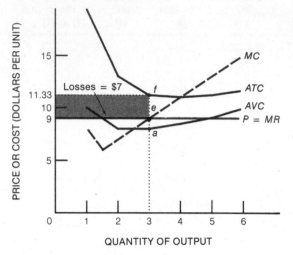

(b) Short-Run Profit Maximization

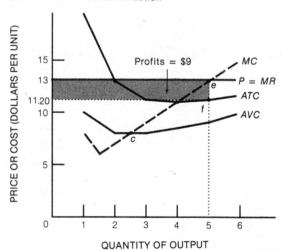

These cost curves are based on the data in Table 2. In panel (a) the market price of the good is $9; the firm's demand curve is, therefore, a horizontal line at $P = MR = 9. The firm produces 3 units of output since $MC = P$ ($9) at that point. Losses are minimized at this level of output. The black shaded area represents losses (loss per unit multiplied by total quantity). When the output level is 3 units, $AVC = 8. Since $P > AVC$ at that point, the firm has a margin of revenue over variable cost with which to defray some of the fixed costs; it should remain in production.

In panel (b), the market price is $13. The firm maximizes profits at an output level of 5 units (where $P = MC$). At $P = 13, price exceeds ATC ($11.20) by $1.80; the firm makes a profit of $1.80 times the quantity of output, or $9.

Table 2
A Numerical Example of Profit Maximization for the Perfectly Competitive Firm

Quantity, Q (1)	Variable Cost, VC (2)	Total Cost, TC (3)	Average Variable Cost, AVC (4)	Average Total Cost, ATC (5)	Marginal Cost, MC (6)	Profits when P = $7 (7)	Profits when P = $9 (8)	Profits when P = $13 (9)
0	$ 0	$10	—	—		$\boxed{-\$10}$	−$10	−$10
1	10	20	$10	$20	$10	− 13	− 11	− 7
2	16	26	8	13	6	− 12	− 8	+ 0
3	24	34	8	11.33	8	− 13	$\boxed{- \ 7}$	+ 5
4	34	44	8.50	11	10	− 16	− 8	+ 8
5	46	56	9.20	11.20	12	− 21	− 11	$\boxed{+ \ 9}$
6	60	70	10	11.67	14	− 28	− 16	+ 8

Note: numbers in boxes show output levels where profits are maximized (or losses are minimized) at different prices.

---

curve at its minimum point. Average fixed cost *(AFC)* is the vertical distance between *ATC* and *AVC*.

Loss Minimization: Price Greater than *AVC* but Less than *ATC*.   Panel (a) shows the case where the market price equals $9. At this price, the firm will not shut down because price is greater than the lowest point on the *AVC* curve ($8). By staying in operation, the firm can cover its variable costs and pay for a portion of its fixed costs. To minimize losses, the firm will produce that output (3 units) at which *P* and *MC* are equal (point *e*).

The firm's losses can be read directly from the graph. At an output quantity of 3 units, the average total cost *(ATC)* or cost per unit equals $11.33, while price is $9. The *loss per unit of output* equals $2.33, or the vertical distance *ef*. The total loss, therefore, is the area of the black rectangle, or $2.33/unit × 3 units = $7. That the firm is better off producing 3 units of output than shutting down is indicated by the vertical distance *ea* (which equals the price of $9 minus average variable cost of $8), where the market price exceeds *AVC* by $1. This $1 can be used to cover a portion of fixed costs.

Panel (a) shows one point on the firm's supply schedule. It reveals that at a market price of $9, the firm will supply 3 units of output.

Profit Maximization: Price Greater than *ATC*.   Panel (b) shows the case where the market price equals $13. Profits are maximized where *P* = *MC,* or at 5 units of output; the firm will therefore produce 5 units of output. At this output level, price ($13) exceeds *ATC* ($11.20) by $1.80, so the firm is making a profit per unit of output of $1.80 (the vertical distance *ef*). The total profit is the area of the color rectangle (= 5 units × $1.80/unit = $9). Notice that the maximum distance between the price line and the *ATC* curve occurs at 4 units of output, but 4 units is not the output level chosen by the firm because at 4 units, *MC* is less than *P*.

Perfectly competitive firms choose that level of output where *P* = *MC* or, in graphical terms, where the *P* (= *MR*) line intersects the *MC* curve—provided price is greater than the minimum level of *AVC*.

The competitive firm's supply curve (how much it is willing to sell at different prices) is that portion of the firm's MC *curve above the* AVC *curve.*

Figure 3
Competitive Equilibrium in the Short Run

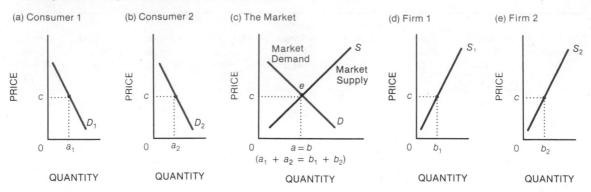

This figure depicts a competitive market with only two consumers and two producers (for simplicity). The demand curves D_1 and D_2 are the demand curves for the two consumers; the supply curves S_1 and S_2 are the supply curves for the two firms. Curve D in panel (c) is the horizontal sum of D_1 and D_2; curve S in panel (c) is the market supply curve and is the horizontal sum of S_1 and S_2. At the equilibrium price, market supply just matches market demand.

Economic Profit versus Accounting Profit

Profit equals revenue minus costs. As noted in the preceding chapter, *economic profits* equal revenues minus opportunity costs, not just dollar or accounting costs. *Opportunity costs* are the best alternatives sacrificed by the business firm when it engages in some particular production plan. *Included in these alternatives is the return that could be earned by the owner/entrepreneur if the owner's money capital, labor, and managerial time had been used elsewhere* (along with explicit payments for materials, labor, and interest). Economic losses are incurred when the return to the resources used in the business firm is less than the normal return those resources could earn in the next best alternative. When economic profits are zero, the business firm is earning a normal profit.

Industry Equilibrium in the Short Run

When one knows how the profit-maximizing (or loss-minimizing) competitive firm behaves in the short run, one can determine how a perfectly competitive industry, composed of many such firms, behaves in the short run. Recall that the short run is a period so short that old firms cannot build new plants and equipment; new firms cannot enter; old firms cannot leave. Thus, a short-run situation is one in which there are a fixed number of competitive firms of given plant sizes. Since each firm is behaving competitively, each firm's supply curve for the product is its own *MC* curve above its *AVC* curve.

How does the industry (all the firms together) behave in the short run? Figure 3 shows how the market price is determined. For simplicity, Figure 3 shows only two firms and two consumers; in reality, competitive markets have a large number of firms and consumers, but the principles are the same. Panels (d) and (e) show the supply curves S_1 and S_2 of Firms 1 and 2, respectively; these supply curves are really the firms' *MC* curves above minimum *AVC*. These two supply curves are summed horizontally to obtain the *market supply curve S* in panel (c). Panels (a) and (b) show the demand curves for Consumers 1 and 2, labeled D_1 and D_2, respectively. The two demand curves are summed horizontally to obtain the *market demand curve D* in panel (c). The market equilibrium price c clears the market and coordinates the decisions of the independent buyers and sellers.

In the short run, the market supply curve is the horizontal summation of the supply curves of each firm, which in turn are their MC curves above minimum AVC.

Figure 3 shows how price and output are determined in the short run in a perfectly competitive industry. Figure 4 shows in more detail how

Figure 4
The Firm and the Market: Short-Run Equilibrium

(a) The Representative Firm

(b) The Industry

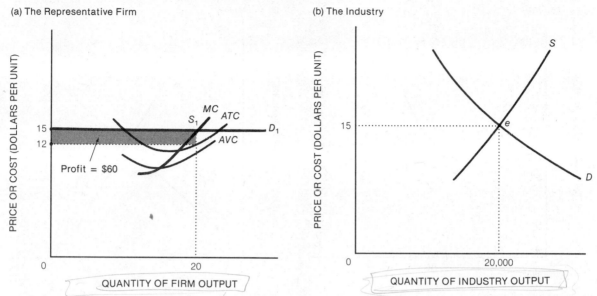

Panel (a) shows the representative firm; panel (b) shows the market. There are 1,000 firms. Firm demand is D_1 when market demand and supply are in equilibrium at point e with a $15 price and an equilibrium market output of 20,000 units. The individual firm produces 20 units of output and makes a profit of $60 ($3 × 20 units) from the pre-unit profit of $3 ($15 − $12 = $P − ATC$).

the firm's individual behavior is consistent with market behavior and vice versa.

Panel (b) of Figure 4 shows an industry consisting of 1,000 firms, and panel (a) shows a representative firm. The market supply and market demand curves in panel (b) determine the market equilibrium price of $15. This market price of $15 clears the market where a total of 20,000 units are traded. To the representative firm, the $15 price becomes the firm's horizontal demand curve. In response to this price, the firm produces 20 units of the output, where the MC curve intersects its demand curve. Since this representative firm is one of 1,000 firms in the industry, the industry as a whole will produce 20,000 units of output (20 × 1,000). Thus the profit-maximizing behavior of the individual firm is consistent with the profit-maximizing behavior of all the firms in the market. The individual firm's supply curve, S_1, is a small part of S.

Panel (a) shows a representative firm that is *making an economic profit:* ATC at the profit-maximizing output level of 20 units is $12; therefore, the firm is making a per-unit profit of $3 (= $15 − $12) on each of the 20 units for a total of

$60 economic profit. The representative firm could just as easily have made losses, since in the short run the firm will not shut down as long as it can pay part of its fixed costs.

The effect of economic profits on perfectly competitive industries is felt primarily in the long run when new firms can enter the industry and established firms can exit. As competitive firms respond to economic profits or losses, the industry short-run supply schedule shifts, and prices change.

PERFECT COMPETITION IN THE LONG RUN

The persistence of economic profits $(P > ATC)$ or economic losses $(P < ATC)$ is not a stable or equilibrium situation in the long run for a competitive industry. If losses continue to be sustained, in the long run some firms will choose to exit from the industry because the long run is a period of time long enough for firms to eliminate fixed-cost obligations by leaving the industry. If economic profits continue to be made, there will be an incentive in the long run for new firms to enter the industry to earn above-normal profits.

Figure 5
The Long-Run Equilibrium

(a) The Firm

(b) The Market

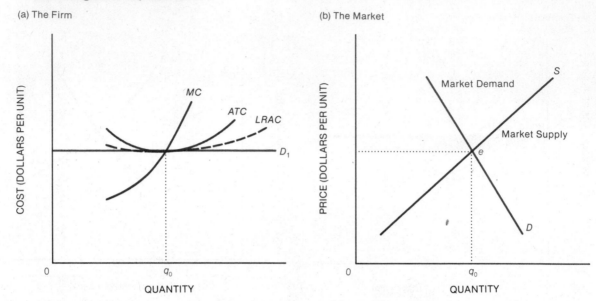

These graphs illustrate the relationship between the firm and the market in long-run equilibrium. In long-run equilibrium, three conditions are satisfied: 1) quantity supplied equals quantity demanded, 2) price equals marginal cost, and 3) price equals average total cost equals long-run average cost. (The representative firm makes zero economic profit.) The representative firm in panel (a) produces where the D_1 curve intersects the MC curve ($P = MC$), and the profits are zero because price just covers the minimum average total cost of production. The supply curve S in panel (b) is based on the number of firms in existence in long-run equilibrium.

In the long run, the number of firms in a perfectly competitive industry is not fixed. If the typical firm is making economic profits, the number of firms will expand. If the typical firm is sustaining economic losses, the number of firms will contract. In other words, if $P > ATC$, the number of firms will increase. If $P < ATC$, the number of firms will contract.

Until the number of firms stops changing, the industry is not in long-run equilibrium. In the long run, there is no incentive for new firms to enter or old firms to leave. In the long run, existing firms operate at a level of output at which average costs are minimized. Firms producing with inefficient plants cannot compete with firms producing with efficient plants.

Long-run equilibrium occurs for the competitive industry when economic profits are zero and long-run average costs are minimized.

Figure 5 shows a perfectly competitive market

in long-run equilibrium. In the long run the firm operates at an efficient scale of operation. Thus the ATC curve for the optimal plant will have a minimum average cost equal to the minimum average cost in the long-run average cost curve. The long-run equilibrium for the representative firm occurs at q_0, where $P = ATC = LRAC$.

When $P = MC$ and $P = ATC = LRAC$ at the long-run equilibrium output, and when MC intersects ATC at its minimum point, the perfectly competitive firm is producing at the lowest average cost of production in the long run.

This finding suggests that perfectly competitive firms will operate at maximum efficiency (produce at minimum $LRAC$) in the long run.

The Mechanism of Entry and Exit

A perfectly competitive industry adjusts towards a long-run equilibrium of zero economic profits through entry and exit.

Figure 6
Free Entry Drives Economic Profits to Zero and Unit Costs to a Minimum

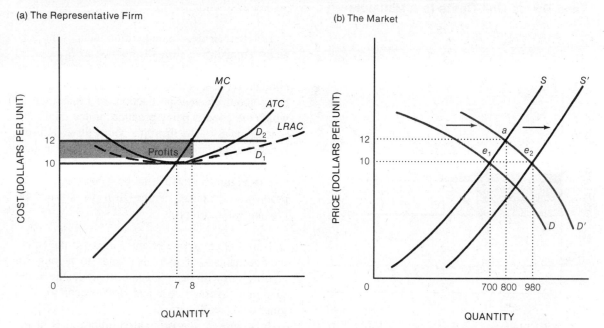

(a) The Representative Firm

(b) The Market

The initial long-run equilibrium is e_1, the intersection of D and S in panel (b). When demand shifts to D', the short-run equilibrium price rises to $12 (point a), creating economic profits for the individual firm facing the new demand curve D_2 in panel (a). In the long run, new firms enter until the supply curve shifts to S'. The long-run equilibrium is established at point e_2, where price again equals $10. The number of firms rises from 100 (700 ÷ 7) to 140 (980 ÷ 7).

Entry. The mechanism of free entry eliminates economic profits and insures that in the long run goods are produced at minimum average cost with an efficient-sized plant.

Consider the perfectly competitive industry consisting of 100 firms in panel (b) of Figure 6. Panel (a) shows the ATC and MC curves of a typical firm in this industry; we assume ATC is the short-run average cost curve in an efficient scale of plant. Panel (b) shows the market supply curve derived by summing the supply curves of 100 such firms. When the market demand curve is D, the equilibrium price is $10. At this price, the representative firm is making zero profits (a normal return). The demand curve facing the representative firm is D_1; each of the 100 firms produces 7 units of the product, making for a market output of 700 units. Equilibrium e_1 is both a short-run equilibrium and a long-run equilibrium.

Suppose that consumers increase their demand for the product, and the market-demand curve shifts from D to D'. The short-run equilibrium price rises to $12, and the short-run equilibrium output of the industry rises to 800 units.[3] At this

higher price, the firm's short-run equilibrium is now at 8 units of output, where price and marginal cost are equal. The typical firm now makes economic profits. In the short run, which may be a few months or many years, the individual firm will enjoy above-normal returns.

In the long run, above-normal profits will attract more firms. *As these new firms enter the market, the supply curve shifts to the right,* because the market supply is the sum of individual supply curves. The entry of new firms will continue as long as economic profits are positive. But as the supply curve shifts to the right (to S'), the market price falls, putting a squeeze on profits. Eventually, in the new long-run equilibrium, economic profits must again be zero. The new long-run (and short-run) equilibrium is e_2, which is at the old equilibrium price of $10. In the new long-run equilibrium, the individual firm again pro-

3. Remember in the short run, the number of firms is fixed. As market demand increases, there is a movement along the short-run supply schedule S. In the long run, new firms can enter, and there then is a rightward shift of the supply schedule to S'.

Figure 7
The Exit of Firms Eliminates Losses and Drives Unit Costs to a Minimum

(a) The Representative Firm

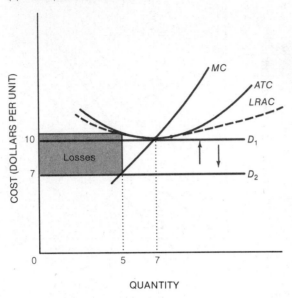

QUANTITY

(b) The Industry

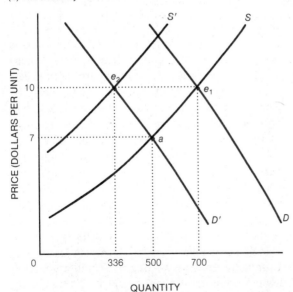

QUANTITY

The initial long-run equilibrium is e_1, the intersection of D and S. Demand drops to D', causing the short-run equilibrium price to fall to $7 (point a). The representative firm makes losses as D_1 shifts downward to D_2. The exit of firms in the long run shifts the supply curve to S', which lifts price back to $10 and eliminates losses. The number of firms falls from 100 (700 ÷ 7) to 48 (336 ÷ 7).

duces 7 units; but there are now 140 such firms producing 7 units each (or 980 total units for the market as a whole).

Efficient Scale. Competition induces the perfectly competitive firm to produce at $P = MC$; free entry causes $P = ATC = LRAC$, thereby eliminating economic profits. Both forces together bring about *efficient* production, or production in which the good is being produced at the minimum cost to society. The firm in a competitive industry cannot be inefficient in the long run; the firm cannot select an inappropriate plant size. The plant size in Figure 6 must be the best possible size for producing 7 units, or the firm would not be around in the long run.

Exit. The reverse of entry is exit. Like entry, the mechanism of exit also leads to a long-run equilibrium with the average firm producing at the minimum average cost and price equal to marginal cost (see Figure 7).

In Figure 7, the original equilibrium is at e_1, which is both a short-run and a long-run equilibrium. There are 100 firms. Point e_1 is a short-run equilibrium point because the market quantity supplied equals the market quantity demanded and because $P = MC$ for the representative firm. It is long-run equilibrium because when price is $10 (demand curve is D_1) the representative firm makes zero profits.

When the demand curve shifts from D to D' in panel (b), the short-run equilibrium shifts from e_1 to a. The short-run price falls to $7, and the short-run quantity falls to 500 units, with the representative firm producing 5 units. Since $7 is less than ATC, the representative firm makes economic losses. In the long run, firms will begin to exit (the weaker ones first). The exit of firms shifts the industry supply curve to the left until economic losses are eliminated (at S'), and price is driven back up to the original $10. The new equilibrium is at e_2, where total output is 336 units and there are now only 48 firms who again produce an average of 7 units each.

The Long-Run Industry Supply Curve

In Figures 6 and 7, increases or decreases in demand serve to raise or lower price in the short run. But in the long run, prices remain the same! In the case of Figure 6, the increase in demand is answered by an increase in supply that drives the price back down to the original level. Similarly, in Figure 7, the decrease in demand is answered by a decrease in supply that drives the price back up to the original level.

*The long-run industry supply schedule shows the quantities that the industry is prepared to supply at different prices **after** the entry or exit of firms is completed.*

Constant-Cost Industries.   The long-run industry supply curve corresponding to Figures 6 and 7 is perfectly elastic (horizontal) at the price of $10, which equals the minimum unit cost of production (minimum *LRAC*). The case of a perfectly elastic industry supply curve is illustrated in Figure 8, where S_L is the long-run industry supply curve. Shifts in demand, such as the shift from D to D', simply change the equilibrium quantity in the long run; there is no change in prices or costs. When this occurs, the industry is a **constant-cost industry.**

What determines whether an industry will be a constant-cost industry? If the individual firms' cost curves remain the same when the industry expands (or contracts), the industry will be a constant-cost industry. Firms in constant-cost industries purchase labor, raw materials, land, and the like at the same prices whether the industry is expanding or contracting. The constant-cost industry's demand for resources is a relatively small part of the total demand, and the industry's factor inputs usually are not highly specialized.

*A **constant-cost industry** is relatively small and, hence, can expand or contract without significantly affecting the terms at which factors of production used in the industry are purchased. The long-run industry supply curve is horizontal.*

Increasing-Cost Industries.   As the number of firms in an **increasing-cost industry** expands, the prices of the factors of production used by many industries are bid up. Industries whose factor purchases make up a large percentage of the market and industries that use factors of production specialized to that industry are usually in-

Figure 8
The Long-Run Supply Curve for a Constant-Cost Industry

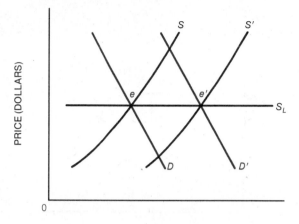

QUANTITY OF INDUSTRY OUTPUT

A constant-cost industry can buy all the inputs or productive factors it wants at constant prices; hence, the minimum average cost of production is independent of industry size. When demand increases, as from D to D', in the long run price stays the same and only quantity increases. Price must stay the same to keep economic profits at zero. Thus, the long-run supply curve, S_L, is perfectly elastic.

creasing-cost industries. Thus, when the industry is expanding the individual firms must pay higher prices for their resources—so their costs of production will rise.

*As the number of firms in an **increasing-cost industry** expands, the factor prices of resources used in the industry are bid up. As the number of firms in the industry contracts, the prices of these factors fall. Hence, the long-run industry supply curve is upward-sloping.*

The long-run adjustment in an increasing-cost industry is illustrated in Figure 9. The equilibrium is initially at e_1, with the demand curve at D. The demand curve shifts to D', causing the price to rise in the short run to the level indicated at point a. The typical firm now earns economic profits. New firms enter, the industry expands, and the price of the good itself falls, squeezing profits toward zero, as in a constant-cost industry. But factor prices are also bid up as the number of firms increases and cause the *LRAC* curve to shift up-

Figure 9
The Long-Run Supply Curve for an Increasing-Cost Industry

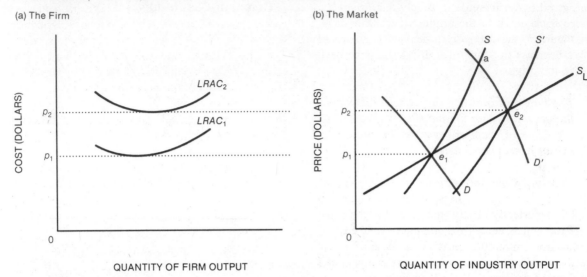

(a) The Firm   (b) The Market

The expansion of an increasing-cost industry drives up some important factor prices facing individual firms; hence, the cost curves shift up as the size of the industry increases, as illustrated in panel (a). When demand shifts from D to D', the long-run equilibrium price increases from p_1 to p_2. The cost curve $LRAC_1$ in panel (a) corresponds to the equilibrium, e_1, in panel (b); the cost curve $LRAC_2$ corresponds to e_2. The long-run supply curve, S_L, is upward-sloping but is still more elastic than the short-run supply curves, such as S or S'.

ward from $LRAC_1$ to $LRAC_2$. In the final equilibrium, indicated at e_2, profits have been squeezed to zero by the entry of new firms *and* rising costs. The long-run supply curve is shown as S_L.[4]

Differential Rents and the Representative Firm

Thus far we have assumed that perfectly competitive industries are composed of a large number of firms, all producing with *similar costs of production*. But is it not true that the production costs of competitive firms are quite different? One coal mine will offer rich veins just below the surface; another offers poor veins thousands of feet below the surface. One farm has rich fertile land; another farm has poor soil. Will these natural differences not lead to large differences in average costs among different competitive firms in the same industry? The answer is, surprisingly, no.

Consider the two different coal mines in Figure 10. The superior mine in panel (a) has lower average variable costs at each level of output than the inferior mine in panel (b) *when the cost of renting the mine from its owner is excluded.*[5] Because coal mining is a competitive industry, the coal produced from Mine A will sell for the same price as the coal from Mine B (the demand is shown as D in both cases).

The operator of Mine A will choose to produce q_A units of output and the operator of Mine B will produce q_B units. *If there were no rental payment,* the operator of Mine A would make an economic profit represented by the shaded area in (a); the operator of Mine B would make a much smaller economic profit—the shaded area in (b).

Because Mine A is a superior mine with lower production costs, however, coal operators would be willing to pay a higher *rent* for the privilege of operating A. In both cases, an economic profit

---

4. There is yet a third category of industry called the decreasing-cost industry. In decreasing-cost industries, prices paid for resources decline as the industry expands. Because decreasing-cost industries are rare and the causes of decreasing costs are complicated, we do not deal with them here.

5. Note: it does not matter whether the operator owns the mine or not. If the operator owns the mine, there is an opportunity cost in the form of sacrificing the opportunity to earn rental income from renting the mine to other operators.

Figure 10
Differential Rents on Coal Mines of Varying Richness

(a) Coal Mine A

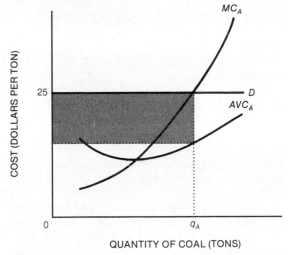

(b) Coal Mine B

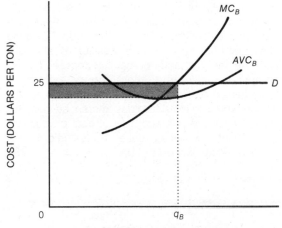

Coal Mine A depicted in panel (a) is easier to mine than Coal Mine B depicted in panel (b). Thus, AVC_A is lower than AVC_B, where the average variable cost curves exclude the costs of paying the rent on the mine itself. If the price of coal is \$25 per ton, the shaded areas correspond to the rental that will be paid on the two coal mines. It will cost more to rent Mine A than to rent Mine B.

(an above-normal return) is being earned if there were no rental payment; operators would, therefore, be willing to pay the owners of the mine property a *rent equal to the shaded area* for the privilege of using both mines. If the rent were greater than the shaded area, *ATC* would exceed price so that below-normal returns would be earned, and the operator would choose another occupation. If the rent were less than the shaded area above-normal returns would be earned, so other operators would be willing to pay a higher rent and would outbid the current operator.

The net result of paying rent for scarce resources is to equalize average costs among different competitive firms. A higher rent would be paid for Mine A than for Mine B, and this *differential rent* would equalize the average costs of production. The return from the more productive mine accrues to the owner of the scarce resource in the form of a rental payment, not to the mine operator in the form of an economic profit.

This general principle can be applied to other competitive industries in which firms are different. A farmer who is located on particularly fertile land will earn more than neighboring farmers. A particular entrepreneur who is more ingenious than other entrepreneurs in the industry will earn a higher return. These returns are included in accounting profits, but they are not considered economic profits. Economists consider these returns *rents* to scarce factors of production.

The theory of differential rent reconciles the zero-economic-profit property of perfect competition with the fact that some people earn large incomes in perfectly competitive industries in the long run. The fact that some farmers and some coal-mine owners are very rich even though their industries are competitive is not inconsistent with zero long-run economic profits. If every firm were exactly alike in a competitive industry the entrepreneurs simply could not earn more than a normal return for their effort; they would probably have incomes that were very similar to the average in the community. But all firms are not exactly alike. The fact that some firms have advantages over others simply means that the composition of opportunity costs differs from firm to firm. Part of these opportunity costs may simply be higher returns to superior resources. The superior resource (such as the rich vein of coal) means lower variable costs (such as mining the coal) and higher factor prices paid to the superior resource.

This "differential rent theory" owes its origin to David Ricardo, who, in his 1817 classic, *The*

Example 2

Constant-Cost and Increasing-Cost Industries

Retail trade is a *constant-cost industry* because it usually accounts for a relatively small share of total employment in most labor markets; it employs personnel who do not have specialized skills; the capital used in retail trade (primarily buildings) is not specialized and represents a relatively small share of total capital. These conditions mean that the output of the retail-trade industry can be expanded or contracted without affecting the factor prices that retail-trade establishments must pay.

Another example of a constant-cost industry is banking. Like retail trade, banking employment accounts for only a small percentage of total employment; banking recruits employees who do not have highly specialized skills; the equipment used by the banking industry (principally structures) represents a very small portion of the total. The expansion of the banking industry would indeed affect the prices paid for equipment specific to the banking industry (such as automated teller equipment), but this equipment would account for only a small portion of banking industry costs.

Examples of *increasing-cost industries* are not hard to find. Residential construction is an increasing-cost industry. The residential-construction industry accounts for a substantial portion of the total demand for gypsum, heating equipment, and plumbing fixtures. Moreover, the residential-construction industry is a major employer of labor with specific skills: carpenters, electricians, and plumbers. When the residential-construction industry expands, the prices of the inputs used in home building—from lumber to carpenters—will be bid up. When the industry contracts, these prices fall, as illustrated by the collapse of lumber prices in 1981 - 1982.

The petrochemicals industry—an industry that produces plastics, synthetic rubber, fertilizer, and synthetic fabrics—is another example of an increasing-cost industry. Petrochemical products are produced from crude petroleum and natural gas and are major users of petroleum and natural gas (about one quarter of these resources goes to the petrochemical industry). Therefore, expansion of petrochemicals will bid up the prices of petroleum products.

Coal mining is a third example of an increasing-cost industry. In coal-mining regions, coal mining is a major employer of labor (Pennsylvania, Kentucky, and West Virginia). As the coal industry expands, the wages of coal miners are bid up. In addition, coal mines differ in important respects. Some contain rich veins of coal that are close to the surface; others contain poor veins that are buried deep under the surface. The supply of mine sites that offer rich, easily accessible coal is limited. As the demand for coal increases, mining companies must turn to more and more of the inferior mines. As the cost of producing a ton of coal will be higher in inferior mines, increased demand will increase the average cost of coal production. As a result, the prices (called rents) paid for the superior mines will be bid up.

Principles of Political Economy and Taxation, called attention to the fact that fertile farmland paid higher rents than marginal farmland. The theory of differential rent applies to other factors of production in addition to farmland, as the above examples show.

THE GAINS FROM VOLUNTARY EXCHANGE OR TRADE

The theory of perfect competition can be used to demonstrate how both producers and consumers can gain from voluntary exchange between many independent buyers and sellers.

Figure 11 shows a market that is in equilibrium when price is $9 and output is 400 units. Since the market supply curve begins at $5, the first unit can be coaxed out of some supplier by paying just $5; anything less than $5 would yield a zero output. To coax the 100th unit out of another supplier, a price of $6 has to be paid; to coax out the 400th unit would require a price of $9. Although the market price is $9, there would have been some production of this good if its price had been less than $9. Those who would have been willing to supply the good at lower prices are getting a surplus when the market price is $9. The supplier of the first unit is receiving a surplus of $4 (= $9 − $5); the supplier of the 100th unit is receiving a surplus of $3 (= $9 − $6). All the suppliers of this good taken together are getting a total surplus equal to the area of the triangle *ceb*. Alfred Marshall, the great 19th-century British economist, called this area above the supply curve and below the price the **producers' surplus.**

*The **producers' surplus** is the excess of what producers receive over the minimum value the producer would have been willing to receive.*

In Figure 11, producers' surplus is the area *ceb* when the market price is $9. The area *ceb* equals $800.

The concept of producers' surplus is similar to the concept of consumers' surplus discussed in an earlier chapter. Recall that consumers' surplus is simply the excess of the consumer benefits (the dollar value of total utility) from consuming a good over the dollar expenditure on the good. In Figure 11, when the market price is $9, the consumers' surplus is the area *aec*. This area equals $1600.

The benefits of trade or voluntary exchange are simply those benefits represented by the consumers' surplus combined with those benefits represented by the producers' surplus. The first unit has a worth of $17 to some consumer since the demand curve intersects the vertical axis at $17. The first unit can be coaxed out of some producers for $5. Thus the first unit is worth approximately $12 to society [($17 − $9) + ($9 − $5)]. This $12 is the gain from trade between the supplier who values the first unit at only $5 and the buyer who values the first unit at $17. Similarly, the 100th unit is worth $15 to some buyer and $6 to some supplier and thus yields a net gain of $9 when the seller sells to the buyer for the market price of $9[($15 − $9) + ($9 − $6)]. The 400th unit squeezes out all the gains from trade, and a single price brings together many individual buyers and sellers.

Since the consumers' surplus *aec* = $1600, and the producers' surplus *ceb* = $800, society's net gain in the market illustrated in Figure 11 is

Figure 11
The Gains from Trade

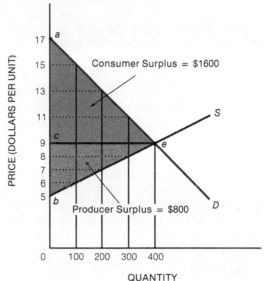

When the price is $9, producer surplus is the area *ceb* and consumer surplus is the area *cea*. The first unit is worth $17 to buyers and costs $5; it yields a gain from trade of $12 to society. All 400 units are worth the area *aeb*—the consumer surplus + the producer surplus yielded by the market equilibrium price of $9. The total of consumer and producer surplus is $2,400 (area of triangle *aeb* = ½ × base × height = ½ × $12 × 400 = $2,400).

$2400. The triangle area *aeb* can be interpreted as the potential loss to society if this market were to be eliminated.

In the real world, the gains from trade are enormous. Through the mechanism of the market, people can specialize in the production of certain goods and trade them for resources that can, in turn, be traded for the wider variety of goods people demand. The benefits to people of specializing rather than trying to produce all that they demand are represented by the triangle area formed by the combination of the producers' and consumers' surpluses in each market (the triangle area formed by the demand curve to the left of the equilibrium quantity, by the supply curve to the left of the equilibrium quantity, and by the vertical axis).

Competitive markets are the mechanism by which specialization can be coordinated. Competitive markets coordinate the specialization of different economic units and assure that goods will be provided at minimum average cost if the entry/exit mechanism is allowed to operate.

APPLICATIONS OF THE THEORY OF PERFECT COMPETITION

The theory of perfect competition describes how business firms behave in a perfectly competitive environment. These conditions of perfect competition are met in a number of markets: most agricultural markets—fibers, grains, dairy products, vegetables, oranges—are perfectly competitive. Stock markets and commodity markets are perfectly competitive as well. More important than these pure markets are industries that closely *approximate* the conditions of perfect competition. In such markets, the number of producers may not be large enough to make each firm a perfect price taker, but the amount of control over price may be negligible. Information on prices and product quality may not be perfect, but consumers have a great deal of information at their disposal. The product may not be perfectly homogeneous, but the distinctions among products may be inconsequential. An industry need not meet all the conditions of perfect competition for the theory of perfect competition about business behavior to apply.

The theory of perfect competition tells us, first, that economic profits will be squeezed out in the long run by the entry of new firms. Second, the theory tells us that when the markets are in equilibrium price and marginal cost will be equal. Third, the theory tells us that short-run behavior will differ from long-run behavior. In the short run, firms will stay in business as long as the price covers average variable cost. In the long run, if the price fails to cover average costs (remember in the long run there are no fixed costs), firms will leave the industry. In the short run, demand increases will lead to price increases; in the long run, the price will ultimately depend upon the costs of the representative firm. Fourth, theory tells us that extraordinary earnings can persist in the long run in competitive markets, but these earnings will be rental returns to the owners of scarce factors, not economic profit.

Electronic Games

The electronic-games industry was born in 1976.[6] The principal component of electronic games is the *computer chip,* a product produced by the highly competitive semiconductor industry and used in everything from computers to telephones to automobile dashboards. In addition to major toy producers such as Milton Bradley, Atari, and Mattel, the electronic-games industry is populated by a large number of smaller producers, such as Bambino Inc., Mego International, Coleco Industries, Tiger Electronic Toys, and so on.

In its formative years, the electronic-game industry experienced phenomenal growth in demand. In 1978, industry sales increased 5-fold; in 1979, they tripled; in 1980, however, they increased by only 10 to 20 percent.

In terms of supply-and-demand analysis, the electronic-games industry is one that has experienced a substantial increase in demand. With the number of electronic-game manufacturers fixed in the short run, the upward shift in demand along the short-run industry supply schedule would cause both prices and industry profits to increase. Indeed, from 1976 to 1979, the wholesale price of an average hand-held electronic game rose by approximately 55 percent. The initial profits of the various electronic-game manufacturers were substantial. Coleco Industries, for example, went from earning $0.01 per share in 1975 to $0.68 per share in 1976.

What does the theory of perfect competition predict will happen in a situation like this? If there is freedom of entry, the number of firms will increase, and this entry will drive down profits and prices in the long run. Entry into the electronic-games industry is very easy. Entry requires only a small manufacturing plant and the purchase of computer chips (that are themselves supplied by a competitive industry). Moreover, the electronic-game industry is worldwide with numerous

---

6. This discussion is based upon "A Troubled Season in Toyland," *New York Times*, December 23, 1980; "Growth of Electronic Games Slows: Oversaturation of the Market is a Factor," *Wall Street Journal*, December 17, 1980; *Standard and Poor's Stock Guide*; and telephone conversations with wholesale buyers.

manufacturers in Asia as well as the United States. The number of firms expanded between 1976 and 1980; the number of electronic games offered to the market increased. Just a few types of hand-held games were on the market in 1976. In 1979, there were approximately 100, but as many as 300 hand-held electronic games were offered to buyers in February of 1980, including 25 different varieties of electronic football games.

The theory of perfect competition predicts a squeezing of industry profits and a decline in price to the minimum average cost in the long run. Both these predictions were borne out. Most electronic-game manufacturers experienced losses in 1980. Retail prices of electronic games were heavily discounted at the retail level, and large-scale dumping of electronic games at low prices took place in early 1981. Games that sold for $25 in 1979 were discounted to $9 in 1980.

As profits fall below normal rates of return, the theory also predicts that exit from the industry will take place. Major toy manufacturers, such as Mattel, Milton Bradley, and Atari, dropped many of their product lines, and many of the newcomer firms went out of business.

Atlantic City Gambling: Entry and Rents

Gambling was legalized in Atlantic City, New Jersey in 1978, and a gambling-casino boom began.[7] Initially, there were four gambling casinos in Atlantic City—Resorts International, Caesars World, Brighton, and Bally's Park—and each earned exceptionally large profits in their first two years of operation.

Atlantic City gambling is not an example of perfect competition. There are barriers to entry in the form of the strict licensing requirements of the New Jersey casino-control commission, and substantial investments are required to open a new casino. Nevertheless, barriers to entry are not excessive, and indeed new casinos, attracted by the high profits, opened on a regular basis in Atlantic City between 1978 and 1982. Moreover, the at-

traction of high profits caused legalized gambling proposals to be offered in nearby Massachusetts and New York; if they pass, Atlantic City casinos will face additional competition.

Like the electronic-games industry, the initial high profits of casino gambling in Atlantic City caused new firms to enter the market, although with less ease than in the electronic-games industry. As predicted by theory, the entry of new firms has driven down the profits of established casinos.

What is interesting is the manner in which economic profits are converted into economic rents. As noted earlier, economic rents are returns to owners of scarce resources and should not be considered a part of economic profits. In Atlantic City, the advent of gambling created substantial economic rents for two groups of resource owners. First, the owners of oceanfront property (the best location for gambling casinos) found themselves with a scarce resource, and the operators of gambling casinos had no option but to pay exceptionally high rents for Atlantic City land. Second, New Jersey requires that pit bosses and other skilled casino employees be residents of New Jersey for six months before they can begin work and that there be a lengthy investigation of each casino employee. As a result, the competing casinos have had to bid frantically for eligible employees, and their wages have spurted upward. In economic terms, a large portion of these exceptionally high salaries can be classified as rents earned by the owners of scarce factors of production.

Why Farmers Do Not Go Out of Business

The theory of perfect competition teaches that a firm will stay in business in the short run as long as prices cover average variable costs. The reasoning is that as long as the price is above average variable costs, something will be left over to pay for a portion of fixed costs. Losses are reduced by staying in business and hoping for an improvement in prices.

Farming provides numerous examples of how this principle works in practice. Farm prices fluctuate dramatically from year to year, and the earn-

---

7. This discussion is based upon "After Lucrative Run, Atlantic City's Casinos Brace for Profit-Dampening Competition," *Wall Street Journal*, October 7, 1980.

Table 3

Cost Data for the 1980 Corn Crop of Webster Farm in Grand Island, Nebraska

(A)				
Accounting Losses (not including implicit opportunity costs)	1. Variable costs:			
	Fertilizer and herbicides		$45,279	
	Insecticides		6,240	
	Fuel		15,600	
	Seed		19,500	
	Electricity		15,600	
	Labor		19,500	
		TOTAL:		$121,719
	2. Fixed costs:			
	Depreciation and interest		$67,795	
	Repayment of land purchase loan		22,000	
	Rent on 500 leased acres		55,000	
	Taxes and insurance		17,600	
		TOTAL:		$162,395
				$284,114
	3. Output	120,000 bushels of corn		
	4. Average costs:			
	Average variable costs (per bushel)		$1.01	
	Average fixed cost (per bushel)		1.35	
	Average total cost (per bushel)		$2.36	
	5. Average price (per bushel)		$2.21	
	6. Loss per bushel		−$0.15	
(B) Economic Loss (including implicit opportunity costs)	7. Implicit costs not included above:			
	Rent on land owned by Websters		$88,000	
	Opportunity of cost of labor for 3 partners		45,000	
		TOTAL:		$123,000
	8. Average costs *including implicit costs:*			
	Average variable costs		$2.04	
	Average total cost		3.39	
	9. Economic loss per bushel		$−1.18	

Source: These figures are based on "Planting Season Arrives in the American Corn Belt," *New York Times*, Sunday, April 20, 1980.

ings of farm families vary with farm prices. In good years, farmers earn profits; in bad years they make losses.

Consider the case of the Webster family farm in Grand Island, Nebraska. The farm is a partnership of two brothers and their father; it produces corn on 800 acres owned by the partnership and on 500 rented acres.

Table 3 presents the 1980 *accounting* costs of the Webster farm. These costs are divided into variable and fixed costs. Variable costs total $121,719; fixed costs equal $162,395. 1980 output was 120,000 bushels of corn; *AVC* equals $1.01, and *AFC* equals $1.35. The Websters sold their corn for an average price of $2.21 per bushel.

Have the Websters made the right decision not to shut down? Their *ATC* (per bushel) is $2.36, but they get only $2.21 per bushel. The Websters lose $0.15 per bushel. On the basis of this *accounting* data, they have made the correct decision. If they had shut down, they would have lost their fixed costs, or $1.35 per bushel. It is obviously better to lose $0.15 per bushel than to lose $1.35 per bushel.

In order to determine whether or not staying in business is the best decision, however, the Websters must look beyond explicit costs and consider implicit costs. If the Websters had shut down, they could have worked as hired farm labor or perhaps at a factory in a nearby town. Let us say the three could have each earned $15,000 for a total of $45,000. This $45,000 is an opportunity cost of not shutting down. The Websters could also have rented out their 800 acres. They paid $110 per acre for the land they rented, so let us assume they could have rented their own land at this price. Therefore, they have an opportunity cost of $88,000 on forgone rent.

When we recalculate average variable costs *including* these implicit costs, we find that *AVC* is now $2.04. Should the Websters have shut down? According to these figures, the answer is still no. Price is still $0.17 above *AVC*. Economic losses per bushel are $1.18 if the Websters do not shut down, but they are $1.35 if the farm does shut down.

If these losses persist in the long run, the Websters would indeed leave the industry because in the long run, fixed costs can be avoided by going out of business.

Two of the most important characteristics of perfectly competitive industries are: 1) that perfectly competitive firms will operate at minimum average cost in the long run and 2) that perfectly competitive firms will produce that quantity of output at which price equals marginal cost in both the short and long run. These characteristics will be important to keep in mind when evaluating the other types of markets—monopoly, oligopoly, and monopolistic competition—that will be studied in the chapters that follow. The next chapter will examine the behavior of firms that are able to exercise some control over price. Monopolists exercise considerable control over their prices; monopolistic-competitive firms have only limited control over their prices.

Summary

1. A perfectly competitive market exists when there are a large number of sellers and buyers, when buyers and sellers have perfect information, when the product is homogeneous, and when there is freedom of entry and exit. These conditions insure that each seller will be a price taker. The price will be dictated to sellers by the market. No single seller can influence the market price.

2. The theory of perfect competition explains the behavior of perfectly competitive firms and the behavior of perfectly competitive industries.

3. In the short run, the number of firms in the industry is fixed, and the firm has fixed costs. In the long run, the number of firms can change through entry and exit, and fixed costs become variable costs. Profit-maximizing competitive enterprises make two decisions in the short-run: whether to shut down (whether to produce anything) and (if they decide not to shut down) how much to produce. If the market price covers average variable cost, the competitive firm will not shut down. The competitive firm will produce that quantity of output at which price and marginal cost are equal. The firm's supply curve is its marginal cost curve above average variable cost. The industry supply schedule is the horizontal summation of all the supply schedules of individual firms in the industry. Where the quantity supplied equals the quantity demanded determines the market price. Each firm takes this market price as given.

4. In the long run, firms enter competitive industries where economic profits are being made. They exit from industries where a below-normal profit is being earned. Economic profits must be zero for the competitive industry to be in equilibrium. In the long run, goods are produced at minimum average cost with price equal to marginal cost for the average competitive firm. Returns to scarce factors of production like land or managerial skills are called *economic rents* and are not included in economic profits.

5. The gains from voluntary exchange on trade are the sum of consumers' surplus and producers' surplus.

6. An industry need not meet all the conditions of perfect competition for the theory of perfect competition to be able to explain the behavior of firms in that industry.

Key Terms

perfect competition
imperfect competition
shutdown rule
marginal revenue
profit-maximization rule
constant-cost industry
increasing-cost industry
producers' surplus

Questions and Problems

1. Discuss why each firm may not be a price taker in an industry in which there is product differentiation among firms.

2. A firm is contemplating whether to produce its 10th unit of output and finds its marginal costs for the 10th unit are $50 and its marginal revenue for the 10th unit equals $30. What advice would you give this firm?

3. A firm has fixed costs of $100,000. It receives a price of $25 for each unit of output. Average variable costs are lowest (equal to $20) at 1,000 units of output. What advice would you give this firm? Would this advice be the same in the short run as in the long run?

4. Explain the relationships between accounting profits, normal profits, and economic profits. Will they always be different?

5. The representative firm in the widget industry, which is perfectly competitive, is making a large economic profit. What predictions can you make about what will happen in this industry in the long run?

6. "The theory of perfect competition claims that economic profits will disappear in the long run. This assumption is incorrect because I know a family that has a farm that earns more than $1 million per year." Evaluate this statement.

7. What is the difference between a constant-cost industry and constant returns to scale (where the *LRAC* curve is horizontal)?

8. Jones is an absolute genius at farming. He has an uncanny ability of knowing what to plant and when. As a result, Jones's farm consistently earns higher profits than other farms. From the economist's perspective, are these really higher profits or something else?

9. In Table 2, fixed costs are $10. If fixed costs were raised to $20, how would the supply schedule be affected in the short run? How will the supply schedule be affected in the long run?

10
Monopoly and Monopolistic Competition

Chapter Preview

Perfect competition exists when firms take the market price as given: each competitive firm is a price taker. A firm that has monopoly power has the ability to control (select) the prices of its products. Such a firm is called a **price searcher.** The greater the monopoly power, the greater the control over price.

Price searchers are firms with the ability to control the price of the goods they sell.

Most firms are price searchers. When the price searcher controls the entire market in which it operates, it is a *pure monopolist*. When the price searcher is a small firm that sells a product that is slightly differentiated from its competitors' it is a *monopolistic competitor*. When the price searcher is an industrial giant competing with a few other industrial giants, it is an oligopolist. This chapter studies monopoly and monopolistic competition; oligopoly is discussed in the chapter after the next. This chapter explains how price-searching firms go about maximizing profits, the impact of entry barriers on profits, and why price searchers engage in practices like advertising, price discrimination, and markup pricing.

CONDITIONS FOR MONOPOLY

Literally, *monopoly* means "single seller." The **pure monopoly** is one particular type of price-searching firm.

*A **pure monopoly** exists 1) when there is one seller in the market for some good or service that has no close substitutes, 2) when the seller has considerable control over price, and 3) when barriers to entry protect the seller from competition.*

Like perfect competition, examples of monopoly in this pure form are rare. The reason for studying the theory of pure monopoly is that this theory sheds light on the behavior of firms that approximate the conditions of pure monopoly.

Why Monopoly Is Not So Pure

"Pure" monopoly is hard to find for several reasons. First, substitutes of some kind exist for almost all products. Trucking substitutes for railroad freight; national magazines and TV news substitute for local newspapers; stainless steel and copper substitute for aluminum; aluminum foil substitutes for cellophane; foreign imports substitute for domestically produced goods. A pure monopoly requires that there be no good substitutes, but where does one draw the line between good and poor substitutes?

Second, modern enterprises tend to be multiproduct firms. Pharmaceutical manufacturers produce different kinds of prescription drugs; steel companies produce rolled steel and specialty steels; automobile manufacturers produce cars, trucks, and tanks; the telephone company supplies data-transmission service as well as local telephone service. It is rare for a multiproduct firm to have a pure monopoly in *all* its product lines. A drug manufacturer may have a monopoly in one drug while competing with other drug manufacturers in its other product lines.

Barriers to Entry

The basic source of pure monopoly is the presence of *barriers to entry*. The main barriers are:

1. economies of scale
2. patents
3. exclusive ownership of raw materials
4. public franchises
5. licensing.

Economies of Scale. The average costs of one large firm may be much lower than the average costs of many smaller firms. When new firms cannot compete effectively with a larger firm, it is difficult for new firms to enter the market. Large established firms are protected by economies of scale that bar the entry of new firms. A *natural monopoly* occurs when economies of scale are so large that there is room for only one firm in the industry. Competition is either unworkable or highly inefficient. Examples of natural monopolies are the local public utilities that deliver telephone services, gas services, water services, and electricity.

Patents. American *patent* laws allow an inventor the exclusive right to use the invention for a period of 17 years. During that period, the patent prohibits others from using the invention; the patent holder is protected from competition. The IBM Corporation's patents on tabulating equipment, Xerox's patents on copying equipment, the United Shoe Machinery Company's patents on shoemaking machinery, and Smith Kline's patent on the drug Tagamet are examples of this type of entry barrier. The Bell System monopoly was built on the basis of patents in the 19th century.

Exclusive Ownership of Raw Materials. Established companies may be protected from the entry of new firms by their control of raw materials. The International Nickel Company of Canada owns virtually all the world's nickel reserves; 80 percent of the world's known diamond mines are under the control of the De Beers Company of South Africa. American Metal Climax Corporation controls most of the world's supply of molybdenum.

Public Franchises. State, local, and federal governments grant to individuals or organizations exclusive *franchises* to be the sole operator in a particular business. Competitors are legally prohibited from entering the market. The U.S. post office is a classic example of a public franchise. Along tollways, the state grants exclusive franchises to operate restaurants and service stations; duty-free shops in airports and at international borders are also franchise operations.

Figure 1
Price Searching versus Price Taking

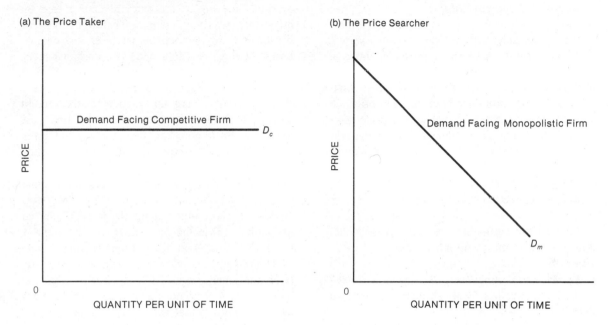

(a) The Price Taker

(b) The Price Searcher

In panel (a), the demand curve D_c facing the competitive firm is perfectly horizontal, meaning that the firm can sell additional units without lowering its price. The price taker can sell all it wants at the going market price. In panel (b), the demand curve D_m facing the monopolistic firm is downward-sloping. This firm is a price searcher.

Licensing. Entry into an industry or profession may be regulated by government agencies and by autonomous professional organizations. The American Medical Association licenses medical schools and allocates hospital staff privileges to physicians. The Federal Communications Commission licenses radio and television stations and controls entry into the broadcasting industry. Most countries license airlines and thus limit entry into the industry.

PRICE-SEARCHING BEHAVIOR

The most fundamental difference between monopoly and perfect competition is that the competitive firm must accept whatever price the market dictates. The perfectly competitive firm is literally a *price taker*. The monopolist has its own market demand curve. Thus the monopolist has the problem of searching the demand curve for the profit-maximizing price. Such price-searching behavior is not restricted to just *pure* monopolies.

Even the local grocery store has some control over price and must determine the right price.

The behavior of each price-searching firm is governed by certain general principles. First, *a price searcher faces a downward-sloping demand curve*. Unlike the perfect competitor, the price searcher cannot sell all it wants at the going market price. For the firm to sell more, it must lower the price of the product. If it raises its price, it will sell less.

Figure 1 illustrates the difference between price takers and price searchers. The price taker's demand curve is perfectly elastic, because the price is dictated by the market, and more units can be sold without lowering the price. In contrast, the price-searching firm must lower its price on all units sold in order to sell more. To determine if the revenue gains from selling more output outweigh the revenue losses of lower prices, the firm must examine the **marginal revenue** (*MR*) and marginal cost of an additional unit of output.

Marginal revenue (**MR**) *is the addition to total revenue brought about by a one-unit increase in quantity sold.*

Like price takers, price searchers also want to maximize profits. All profit-maximizing firms attempt to produce that level of output at which marginal revenue (*MR*) and marginal costs (*MC*) are equal. The main difference between price takers and price searchers is that for the price taker, price equals marginal revenue, while for the price searcher price does not equal marginal revenue.

Price, Average Revenue, and Marginal Revenue

The perfect competitor can always sell additional output at the going market price.

For perfect competitors, the market price is the extra revenue from selling one more unit (MR).

$$P = MR.$$

For price searchers, the price does not equal marginal revenue. To sell an additional unit of output, the price searcher must lower the price on the units previously sold at a higher price because the quantity of output produced before adding the marginal unit could be sold at a higher price than the quantity that results after adding the marginal unit. When a price searcher sells one more unit, the extra revenue generated equals the (new) price of the extra unit sold minus the loss in revenue from having to sell all but the marginal unit of output at a lower price. For the price searcher, price exceeds marginal revenue because of the necessity of lowering prices to sell additional output.

For a price searcher, price is greater than marginal revenue.

$$P > MR.$$

For example, suppose a price searcher faces a demand schedule in which 1 unit per week can be sold if price is $19; 2 units can be sold if price is $17. The total revenue generated is the number of units multiplied by the price per unit for that quantity. When the number of units sold is 1, rev-

enue is $19 (= $19 × 1); when the number of units sold is 2, revenue is $34 (= $17 × 2). Marginal revenue is the extra revenue raised by increasing output by one unit. Therefore, by comparing revenues at each output level, the change in revenue can be calculated. The marginal revenue of a change from 1 to 2 units is $34 − $19 = $15. Why is the price of the second unit ($17) greater than the marginal revenue for the second unit ($15)? To sell the second unit, the firm must lower price on both the first and second units from $19 to $17. The firm gains $17 in revenue on the sale of the second unit, but loses $2 on the sale of the first unit. Hence, the marginal revenue of the second unit is $17 − $2 = $15. In effect, selling one more unit "spoils the market" on the first unit because the price falls (see Example 1 for further discussion of spoiling a market).

There is another way to explain why price exceeds marginal revenue. The chapter on costs and productivity described the relationship between average and marginal values. Recall that when a new average value falls, the marginal value must be below the previous average. This relationship also exists between **average revenue** (*AR*) and marginal revenue (*MR*).

Average revenue (**AR**) *equals total revenue* (TR) *divided by output.*

In general, $TR = P \times Q$, and $TR = AR \times Q$. Hence, *AR* and *P* amount to the same thing when all units are sold at the same price. To say that the price searcher faces a downward-sloping demand schedule is to say that *AR* or *P* falls as output increases.

Whenever an average value is declining, the marginal value must be below the previous average value, pulling it down. In the case of the price searcher, *AR* is the average value; *MR* is its corresponding marginal value. If *AR* is declining, *MR* must be less than *AR*. Since $AR = P$, *P* must be greater than *MR*. Just as the demand schedule shows prices (or average revenue) for different quantities, the **marginal revenue schedule** shows the marginal revenues for different quantities.

*The **marginal revenue schedule** shows what happens to* MR *as the quantity of output changes.*

Table 1
Monopoly Equilibrium

(1) Output, Q	(2) Price or Average Revenue, P = AR	(3) Total Revenue, TR = P × Q	(4) Marginal Revenue, MR	(5) Total Cost, TC	(6) Marginal Cost, MC	(7) Profit (TR − TC)
0	$21	$ 0		10		− 10
			$19		10	
1	19	19		20		− 1
			15		6	
2	17	34		26		8
			11		8	
③	15	45		34		⑪
			7		10	
4	13	52		44		8
			3		13	
5	11	55		56		− 1
			− 1		15	
6	9	54		70		− 16
			− 5		17	
7	7	49		87		− 38
			− 9		20	
8	5	40		107		− 67
			− 13		22	
9	3	27		129		− 102
			− 15		25	
10	1	10		144		− 134

This table shows the demand and marginal revenue schedules of a price searcher. The demand schedule is given in the first two columns. Because all customers are charged the same price, price and average revenue are the same. Revenue (3) equals P × Q. Marginal revenue is the increase in total revenue brought about by increasing Q sales by one unit. (Each MR figure is placed between the two output levels.) The monopolist's profit is maximized by producing three units of output, where profit equals $11. If the monopolist had attempted to produce one more unit of output, total revenue would have increased by $7 and costs by $10, and profit would have fallen by $3. If the monopolist had produced one less unit, total revenue would have fallen by $11 and costs would have fallen by $8, reducing profit by $3. The firm expands output as long as MC does not exceed MR.

Columns (1) and (2) of Table 1 show the demand schedule facing a price-searching firm. Column (3) shows the revenue produced at each level of output (P × Q), and column (4) gives the MR schedule.

The marginal revenue figures are displayed on the lines that fall vertically between the two output levels. Thus the MR of going from 2 to 3 units of output is $11 as revenue rises from $34 to $45. Notice that MR is $11 whether output is increased from 2 to 3 units or reduced from 3 to 2 units. MR is the increase in total revenue due to

increasing output by one unit or the decrease in total revenue due to decreasing output by one unit.

The demand and marginal revenue schedules of Table 1 are graphed as demand and marginal revenue curves in Figure 2.[1] The firm's demand curve, labeled D, shows that the firm is a price searcher (it must lower price to sell more quantity).

1. The advantage of using an MR curve over a numerical schedule is that with a graph MR can be read at or between different levels of output.

Figure 2
Demand, Marginal Revenue, and Elasticity

(a) Demand and Marginal Revenue

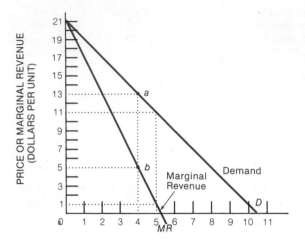

QUANTITY

(b) Elasticity

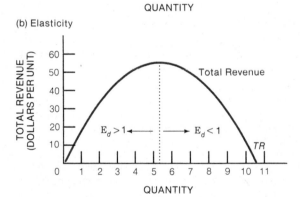

QUANTITY

In panel (a), the demand and marginal revenue schedules of Table 1 are plotted as *D* and *MR*. At an output level of 4 units, the price is $13 and the marginal revenue is $5 In other words, the value of *MR* is read vertically. If the demand curve is a straight line, the marginal revenue curve will be located horizontally halfway between the demand curve and the vertical axis. In panel (b), the total revenue schedule of Table 1 is plotted directly below the *MR* curve, showing the relationship between *MR* and total revenue. When *MR* is positive, total revenue is rising; when *MR* is negative, total revenue is falling; when *MR* is zero, total revenue reaches its highest value. The price elasticity of demand (E_d) is greater than 1 when total revenue is rising and less than 1 when total revenue is falling. When demand is elastic, reductions in price raise total revenue; when demand is inelastic, reductions in price lower total revenue.

The position of the *MR* curve below the demand curve shows graphically that price is greater than marginal revenue for any quantity of output (except for the first unit sold). Whenever the demand curve is a straight line, the *MR* curve will always be halfway between the demand curve and the vertical axis because the slope of the *MR* curve is twice as steep as the slope of the demand curve. In Table 1, when price falls by $2, marginal revenue falls by $4.

Marginal Revenue and Elasticity

Panel (b) of Figure 2 shows the behavior of total revenue ($P \times Q$) as output increases and graphs column (3) of Table 1. Revenue increases as output rises up to the quantity of 5.25 units and thereafter revenue decreases as output rises. The relationship between *MR* and total revenue is simple: when *MR* is positive, the total revenue curve is upward-sloping; when *MR* is negative, the total revenue curve is downward-sloping; when *MR* = 0, the total revenue curve reaches its highest point.

Whether *MR* is positive or negative depends on whether demand is elastic or inelastic at that point. Remember the total revenue test of elasticity from the chapter on demand and elasticity: *If demand is inelastic ($E_d < 1$), total revenue falls as the price falls. If demand is elastic ($E_d > 1$), total revenue rises as the price falls.* When demand is elastic, a reduction in price raises total revenue and *MR* is positive. When demand is inelastic, a reduction in price lowers total revenue and *MR* is negative.

When MR is positive, demand is elastic; when MR is negative, demand is inelastic.

This rule indicates that a price searcher will always operate at a level of output where demand is elastic (where $E_d > 1$). If the firm expands to the point where demand is inelastic, it is experiencing negative marginal revenue. Thus by expanding its output, the monopoly is actually driving down its revenue.

The relationship between marginal revenue and elasticity is direct: for any given price, the higher the elasticity of demand the higher the marginal

Spoiling the Market: Daimler-Benz

For the price searcher, price exceeds marginal revenue. A price searcher who attempts to increase its sales may "spoil the market" by driving prices down. If by throwing a greater quantity of goods on the market, the price of a firm's product falls, the firm has lowered the price not only of the extra production, but also of the units sold previously at a higher price. Price searchers must weigh the advantages of increased production against the risk of spoiling the market.

Daimler-Benz, located in Sindelfingen, West Germany, provides a classic example of not spoiling the market. Each year, Daimler-Benz plans a very limited production of Mercedes-Benz automobiles despite waiting lists for their cars. In other words, Daimler-Benz could easily sell more cars than it chooses to produce, but more production will "spoil the market" by driving down the price the market is prepared to pay. The result of this strategy is seen in the high premium that buyers pay for Mercedes-Benz cars over other luxury cars.

---

revenue. If demand is highly elastic, an increase in output can be sold without much of a reduction in price. The reduction in price on the previous units sold is small and MR is high (MR is close to the price). If demand is highly inelastic, an increase in output can only be sold by making a substantial reduction in price. The reduction in price on previous units sold is high and MR is negative (MR is well below P).

All price-searching firms—be they monopolies, oligopolies, or monopolistic competitors—share three common characteristics:

1. For every price searcher facing a downward-sloping demand curve, $P > MR$ (except on the first unit sold) because the price must be lowered on previous units to sell additional units.
2. MR is positive when the demand is elastic; $MR = 0$ when the elasticity of demand is unity; MR is negative when demand is inelastic.
3. The higher the elasticity of demand for a given price, the higher the marginal revenue. The more elastic the demand, the closer MR is to price.

MONOPOLY PROFITS

How Monopolies Determine Output

The monopolist maximizes profit by choosing an output level where marginal cost (MC) equals marginal revenue (MR).

Monopoly Profit = total revenue − total costs

If the MR of an additional unit of output is $10 and the MC of the additional unit is $6, $4 is added to profit by producing the additional unit. Whenever MR exceeds MC, it pays the firm to expand output. The monopoly firm will increase output—and lower its price—as long as MR exceeds MC. The monoplistic firm lowers the price as output is increased in order to sell that larger output.

If the firm finds that MR is less than MC, it pays the firm to cut output and raise price. If $MC = \$15$ and $MR = \$9$, a cut in output by one full unit would lower costs by $15 and lower revenue by only $9. Profits would rise by $6 (or losses would fall by $6).

The monopolistic firm can raise profit by expanding output (or lowering price) when **MR > MC.** *The firm can raise profit by cutting output (or raising price) when* **MR < MC.** *The monopolist—or the price searcher in general—maximizes profit by producing that quantity where* **MR = MC.**

Table 1 gives demand, revenue, and cost schedules for a monopolistic firm. What level of output will the monopolist choose to produce? Column (7) shows that profit is largest (maximized) when 3 units of output are produced. The monopolist will therefore produce 3 units of output. The monopolist will expand output as long

Example 2

Monopolies:
From Tobacco to Diamonds

Familiar examples of monopolies are the local telephone company and the local gas and electric companies. These monopolies are called *public utilities* and are typically regulated by state or local government. When public utilities are chartered by the relevant government body, they are given a legal monopoly over the market because competitors are legally prohibited from entering the market.

Public utilities, however, are not very useful examples of monopoly because their rates and services are regulated by government.

There are numerous contemporary and historical examples of monopolistic firms that are not subject to government regulation. Until 1911, the

American Tobacco Company and the Standard Oil Company controlled more than 90 percent of the output of their respective industries. Until 1945, the Aluminum Company of America controlled virtually the entire U.S. output of virgin aluminum ingots. In the 1950s, Pfizer monopolized the market for the broad spectrum antibiotic tetracycline. Currently the Smith Kline Corporation is the sole supplier of the ulcer drug Tagamet. The Boeing Corporation currently supplies 85 percent of the world's demand for commercial jet aircraft. The DeBeers Company of South Africa controls 80 percent of the world output of raw diamonds. On a smaller scale, there is typically one local newspaper and one movie theater in most small towns.

---

as MR exceeds MC. The first unit of output raises total revenue by $19 ($MR$ = $19) and raises costs by only $10 ($MC$ = $10), thus contributing $9 to paying the monopolist's $10 fixed cost—reducing a $10 loss to a $1 loss. The second unit of output raises revenue by $15 and adds $6 to costs. The second unit, therefore, changes a $1 loss to an $8 profit. The third unit adds $11 to revenue and $8 to cost, adding $3 to profit. If the fourth unit were produced, only $7 would be added to revenue while $10 would be added to cost, decreasing profit by $3.

Once the monopolist selects an output level of 3 units, the monopolist will charge the price of $15 dictated by the demand schedule. The monopolist can set either price or quantity. Once one is chosen, the other will be dictated by the market demand schedule. (Note that in Table 1, marginal revenue does not equal marginal cost because numerical examples deal with discrete jumps in output. An advantage of graphs is that they allow for continuous changes in output and thereby allow marginal revenue to equal marginal cost exactly.)

Figure 3 shows another example of profit maximization in graphical form. The demand schedule is graphed as the demand curve, D; the marginal revenue schedule is graphed as MR. When output is 7,000 units, marginal revenue exceeds marginal cost (point m is higher than point n), and

profits rise if more than 7,000 units are produced. When output is 10,000 units, marginal revenue is less than marginal cost (point r is lower than point q), and profits rise if fewer than 10,000 units are produced.

To maximize profit, the monopolist selects that output at which marginal revenue and marginal cost are equal. The MR and MC curves intersect at point a. The output level, price, and profit per unit of output can be determined by drawing a vertical line through a. Where the vertical line crosses the horizontal axis (at g) is the monopolist's output level (8,000 units); where the vertical line intersects the demand curve, D, (at c) is the price ($10); where the vertical line intersects the ATC curve (at b) shows the average total cost of producing 8,000 units ($8). The distance between c and b ($10 - $8) is economic profit per unit of output ($2). *Total* economic profit is therefore profit per unit times the number of units or the color shaded area of the rectangle *cbed*. Algebraically, total economic profit = $(P - ATC) \times Q$ = ($10 - $8) $\times$ 8,000 = $16,000.

Monopoly Profits in the Long Run

When there is competition, the distinction between the short run and the long run is crucial. In the short run, the number of firms in the industry

Figure 3
Monopoly Profit Maximization

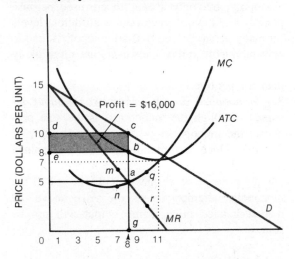

This monopolist has cost curves *ATC* and *MC* and faces the demand curve *D*. Note that *MC* intersects *ATC* at its minimum point, where marginal cost and average total cost equal $7 and output is 11,000 units. The maximum profit occurs where *MR* = *MC*. The equilibrium price/quantity combination is found by drawing a vertical line through the point *(a)* where *MR* = *MC* down to the horizontal axis. The output level represented by the point where the vertical line hits the horizontal axis (8,000 units) is the optimal output level. The point where the vertical line hits the demand curve (at *c*) is the optimal price. Profit is represented by the rectangle *cbed*, or the difference between price and *ATC* multiplied by the number of units ($2 × 8,000 = $16,000).

is fixed; in the long run, new firms can enter the industry or old firms can exit in response to economic profits or losses. This long-run entry and exit insures that economic profits will be squeezed out of perfectly competitive industries. In the case of the monopolist, the long-run/short-run distinction is not as important because barriers to entry prevent new firms from entering the industry and squeezing out monopoly profits. There is no automatic tendency for monopoly profits to be eliminated by the entry of new firms.

Unlike competitive profits, monopoly profits can persist for long periods of time.

In the real world it is difficult to find pure monopolies because of actual or potential substitutes and because absolute barriers to entry are rarely present. Most real-world monopolies are not pure monopolies; they are *near monopolies*. Near monopolies are indeed subject to the profit squeeze in the very long run, particularly if monopoly profits are exceptionally high.

Exceptional monopoly profits have historically promoted the development of closer substitutes for the monopolist's product. The railroads' monopoly over freight transportation was eventually broken by the development of trucking and air freight; the Bell System's monopoly over long-distance telephone service is being broken by the advent of microwave transmission. (For a contemporary example, see Example 3 on coal-slurry pipelines.)

Although monopoly profits will not automatically be driven down to the normal return, there is a tendency for high monopoly profits to promote the development of substitutes in the very long run.

Being a monopoly does not guarantee automatic economic profits. Monopolies can incur losses just like competitive firms. The major distinction is that monopoly profits have a tendency to persist over time, while the above normal profits of competitive firms are squeezed out by the entry of new firms.

Consider the monopolist pictured in Figure 4. The demand curve *D* passes between the average total cost *(ATC)* and the average variable cost *(AVC)* curves before it intersects *AVC*. In this example, the monopolist suffers a loss when producing the 2,000-unit output level where *MR* = *MC* because the price at 2,000 units of output is $10, which is less than the $13 *ATC*.

Like competitive firms, the monopolist must decide whether or not to shut down. The monopolist's short-run shutdown rule is the same as a competitive firm's: If price covers *AVC*, stay in business. When price is greater than *AVC*, the firm can cover all variable costs and can also recover a portion of fixed costs. If the price falls below average variable cost, the monopolist will shut down. In the long run, if price remains below average costs, the monopolist will leave the industry permanently (see the explanation of the shutdown rule in the preceding chapter).

In Figure 4, the shutdown rule says to stay in operation. When the monopolist produces 2,000 units of output (where *MC* = *MR*) the monopolist's price of $10 is greater than the *AVC* of $9

Figure 4
Monopoly Losses

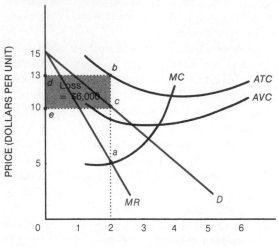

QUANTITY (THOUSANDS OF UNITS)

This monopolist minimizes losses (as long as price exceeds average variable cost) by producing 2,000 units of output (where $MC = MR$). The monopolist must charge a price of $10 at an average total cost of $13. The monopolist loses $3 per unit of output for a total loss of $6,000 (the rectangle *bced*).

but less than the *ATC* of $13. The monopolist therefore has a loss of $3 for each unit, for a total loss (the area of the shaded rectangle *bced*) of $6,000.

FACTS AND FALLACIES ABOUT MONOPOLY

Our analysis sheds light on some common facts and fallacies concerning monopoly.

Common fallacies are:

1. *Monopolists charge the highest possible price.* Monopolists must weigh the revenue gains from higher prices against the revenue loss of lower sales. They will select the price that clears the market for the output level at which $MR = MC$. In Figure 3, it is possible for the monopolist to charge a price above $10, but at these higher prices $MR > MC$ and profits are being sacrificed.

2. *Monopolies always earn profits.* Some monopolies make above-normal profits; others earn normal profits; and others suffer losses. Whether or not a monopolist makes profits depends on the

demand curve and the cost curves. (For example, every patent issued by the U.S. patent office is a monopoly, but only a handful are used because price is less than average cost at all output levels for many patent holders.) The monopolists that do earn monopoly profits, however, are more likely to keep on earning these profits in the long run than competitive firms.

3. *Monopolists do not have to worry about demand.* Although the monopolist is the sole producer, the monopolist cannot ignore the law of demand. Once the monopolist has determined how much output to produce, the market will dictate the price at which that output will sell. If the monopolist attempts to set the price above the market-dictated price, some output will not be sold.

Facts about monopoly are:

1. *Monopolists do not produce where average costs are minimized.* In the long run, perfectly competitive firms will be forced to produce that quantity of output at which average costs are minimized. Monopolists, however, both in the long run and the short run tend to produce a level of output less than necessary to minimize average costs. In Figure 3, *ATC* is minimized at an output of 11,000 units, but the monopolist produces only 8,000 units. In this sense, monopolists are less efficient than perfectly competitive firms.

2. *Monopolists charge a price higher than marginal cost.* The monopolist equates marginal revenue and marginal cost, and price is greater than marginal revenue. Thus, in the case of monopoly, $P > MC$.

3. *Monopolists produce where demand is elastic.* The profit-maximizing monopolist produces that quantity of output at which $MR = MC$. We have demonstrated that marginal revenue is only positive when demand is elastic. If the monopolist expanded into the inelastic portion of the demand schedule, total revenue would decline, and the firm's profits would fall. This characteristic of monopoly pricing can be used as a test for the existence of monopoly behavior. If the demand for a product is inelastic at the current price, the seller is not behaving like a profit-maximizing monopoly.

4. *There is no supply curve for a monopolist.* The monopolist supplies a certain quantity of out-

Example 3

Monopoly and Long-Run Competition: Coal-Slurry Pipelines

The theory of monopoly suggests that a monopolist will be able to continue to earn monopoly profits as long as potential competitors are kept out by barriers to entry. This theory, therefore, predicts that monopolists will do their best to keep entry barriers high.

A case in point is the railroads' monopoly of coal transport. Although the railroads must compete with trucking and air freight in providing transportation service, the railroads hold a virtual monopoly over coal transport. Coal is very bulky and heavy, and trucking cannot provide an economical alternative to rail transport. The hauling of coal is currently the most profitable line of business for the nation's railroads, particularly the railroads that haul coal from the Western states.

Technology has now developed an alternative form of transport for coal: the *coal-slurry pipeline*. These pipelines carry a mixture of powdered coal and water from coal fields to coal-burning utilities and ports and compete directly with the railroads. Although major companies (Bechtel Corporation, Boeing, and Texas Eastern Transmission Com-

pany) have proposed to build such pipelines (currently there is only one in existence), it is not possible to build one without government approval. Right-of-way privileges must be obtained, and only the government can grant such a privilege.

Lobbying by the railroads in Congress has blocked such legislation for 19 years. The railroads argue that coal pipelines would deprive them of their most profitable business, thereby retarding the rehabilitation of the railroad industry. Coal-burning utilities favor such legislation as a means of obtaining coal more cheaply.

The coal-slurry example illustrates that: 1) Even monopolies must worry about competition from substitutes in the very long run. These substitutes are often provided by new technology. 2) Substitutes are attracted to compete with established monopolies by the existence of monopoly profits. If coal transport did not yield monopoly profits, the railroads would not be threatened by coal-slurry pipelines. 3) Firms often rely on the government to protect the barriers to entry into their industry.

---

put given demand and cost conditions. The monopolist does not have a supply curve showing how much output will be supplied at different prices because *the monopolist sets prices*.

MONOPOLISTIC COMPETITION

All price searching firms are not monopolists. In fact, few price searchers are monopolies. Price searchers can be anything from a pure monopoly to a firm that bears a close resemblance to a perfect competitor. The characteristic common to all price searchers is that they all face a downward-sloping demand schedule for their product. In order to sell more of their product, they must lower their price.

In the real world, there is usually some basis for distinguishing between the goods and services produced by different sellers. These distinctions may be based on the physical attributes of the

product (hamburgers at one restaurant are different in some respects from hamburgers at other restaurants), on location (one gas station may be more conveniently located than another), type of service offered (one dry cleaner offers 2-hour service; another offers one-day service), and even on imagined differences (one type of aspirin is "better" than another). The point is that there are differences—real or imagined—among products. Sellers of these different products have some monopoly power over the customers who have a preference for their product. How much monopoly power they have depends upon the strength of this preference.

The theory of **monopolistic competition** was developed by the American economist Edward Chamberlin and the English economist Joan Robinson to deal with markets that produce heterogeneous products. A monopolistic-competitive industry is one that blends the features of monopoly and competition.

The four essential characteristics of
monopolistic competition *are: 1) the number*
of sellers is large enough so that each seller
acts independently of the other; 2) the product
is differentiated from seller to seller; 3) there
is free entry into and exit from the industry;
4) sellers are price searchers.

When sellers are acting independently, each seller, when deciding upon its price and output, presumes that its decisions have no discernible effect on the rest of the market. The price-searching characteristic follows from the differentiation-of-products characteristic. Because products are different (by physical traits, location, type of service, or imagined differences), the seller has some control over price. The degree of control may be quite limited, but it is there. The seller who raises the price will not lose all customers (as would the perfect competitor) because some customers will have a strong enough preference to accept the higher price. The determinants of the strength of consumer preferences are a key topic in the study of monopolistic competition. The monopolistic-competitive firm faces a downward-sloping demand curve. The firm's marginal revenue curve lies below its demand curve, just as a monopolist's does.

Profit Maximization by the Monopolistic-Competitive Firm

To maximize profits, firms produce that quantity of output at which *MR* equals *MC*. The monopolistic competitor is no exception to this rule. Like the monopolist, the monopolistic competitor faces a downward-sloping demand curve; marginal revenue will be less than average revenue (price). It therefore selects that *quantity* at which *MR* equals *MC* and charges the *price* that clears the market. Analytically, in the short run the theory of monopolistic competition is the same as the theory of the monopoly. The analysis of Table 1 and Figure 3 apply just as well to monopolistic competition as to monopoly in the short run.

Indeed, in the short run, the main difference between monopolistic competition and monopoly is the price elasticity facing the firm. Since a monopolistic competitor faces more competition

from the substitute products of other firms in the industry, its price elasticity of demand will greatly exceed that of a typical monopolist.

In the long run, however, the two types of market organization are strikingly different. Barriers to entry protect the monopolist from the entry of competitors. If a monopoly earns substantial profits, the entry of new firms will not automatically squeeze out those profits. Monopolistic competition, however, shares with perfect competition the characteristic of *freedom of entry*. Free entry means that if a monopolistic competitor earns economic profits in the short run, new firms can (and will) enter the market; new firms can gain access to these economic profits, eventually driving them down to zero.

One example of a monopolistic competitor is a service station located on a busy intersection. It earns substantial economic profits in the short run. Like the monopolist, its price is above average total cost after equating *MR* and *MC*. If the station were a monopolist (say a gas station with an exclusive franchise along a tollway), new firms could not gain access to these profits. This gas station would be protected from competition. The monopoly could keep on earning profits for a long period of time. Not so with the monopolistic competitor.

In the long run, new firms can enter the monopolistic-competitive market. Attracted by high profits, another service station will be built on the opposite corner of the intersection—a close but not a perfect substitute. The two stations will differ in terms of access, number of gas pumps, friendliness of service, operating hours, and so on. The entry of the second firm will have two effects on the demand schedule of the first: 1) When customers are attracted away from the first station, the demand schedule will shift to the left. 2) Because buyers now have more substitutes for the product of the first station, the demand schedule will become more elastic. If both stations continue to make economic profits, even more gas stations will be built—two more at the same intersection and then another at the nearest intersection. Each new entrant will reduce the demand for the other stations and make their demand schedules more elastic. As in the case of perfect competition, this process ends when economic profits have been driven down to zero.

The long-run equilibrium of a typical monopolistic-competitive firm is shown in Figure 5. In the long run, new firms will enter until economic profits are driven down to zero. Graphically, profits equal zero at a point to the left of the lowest point on the *ATC* curve, where the downward-sloping demand curve is tangent to the *ATC* curve. In Figure 5, point *b*—where output is 600 units and price is $10—is the point of zero profits and, therefore, the point of long-run equilibrium. In Figure 5, 600 units is the quantity that equates marginal cost and marginal revenue, and $10 is the price that corresponds to 600 units on the demand curve. Therefore, point *b* is the point of maximum profit. Notice that since the demand curve is tangent to *ATC* at point *b*, price is less than *ATC* to the left or to the right of point *b*. Profit is zero at point *b* and negative elsewhere. For example, at an output of 300 units, price is $13 and *ATC* is $14, resulting in a $1 loss per unit. We have already shown that profits are maximized where marginal cost equals marginal revenue. Accordingly, the *MC* and *MR* curves intersect directly below the tangency of the demand curve and the *ATC* curve at point *b*.

Product Differentiation and Advertising

The threat of the entry of new firms and the loss of economic profits are facts of life for monopolistic competitors. If they can erect artificial barriers to entry (by exclusive government franchises, licensing, zoning ordinances, and so on), they can delay the day when their economic profits are driven down to zero. Monopolistic competitors, by definition, produce goods and services that are different. If they can succeed in making their product more distinct from their competitors by engaging in **nonprice competition,** customer loyalty will be stronger. The stronger this customer loyalty, the smaller the loss of markets as new firms enter and the less elastic the demand for their product.

Nonprice competition is any action other than the lowering of prices that differentiates one product from the competition and delays the disappearance of economic profits.

Figure 5
The Long-Run Equilibrium of a Monopolistic-Competitive Firm

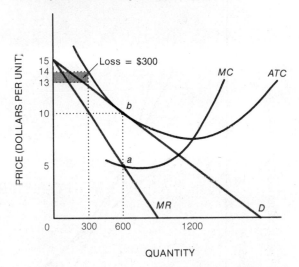

A firm engaged in monopolistic competition faces a downward-sloping demand curve, such as *D*. In the long run, because of free entry, economic profits will be driven down to zero. Thus, the long-run equilibrium must be a point such as *b* where *D* is just tangent to the *ATC* curve. For any price other than $10, profits are negative. Profits are at a maximum when price is $10 and output is 600 units. Since profits are at a maximum at 600 units of output, *MR* must equal *MC* at 600 units. Thus, the *MC* and *MR* curves must intersect directly below point *b*.

Advertising to differentiate products is encountered frequently in monopolistic-competitive markets. In fact, nonprice competition can earn considerable short-run profits for the firm and offers the potential of long-run profits if new entrants cannot copy the nonprice attribute. Profits on some brand-name products, like Bayer aspirin or Borden's condensed milk, have persisted for very long periods of time. In other cases, profits are transitory. If the gas-station owner differentiates the product by staying open all night or by offering a free car wash with fillups, then competitors can do the same.

Market Size and Efficiency

Monopolistic competition has two important characteristics in common with perfect competi-

Figure 6
Monopolistic Competition and the Size of the Market

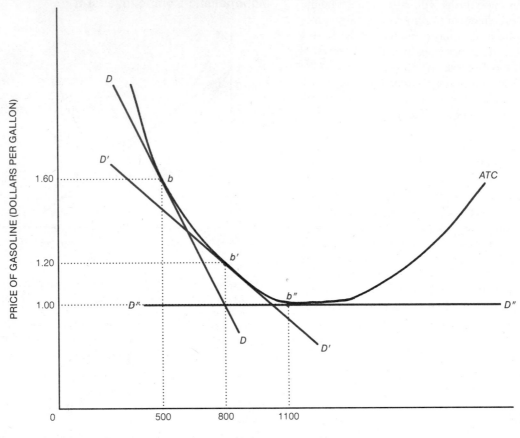

QUANTITY OF GASOLINE (GALLONS)

With a larger market for gasoline (more buyers), the demand curve is flatter because a smaller price cut is necessary to sell one more unit of the product. Thus D' would correspond to the demand curve for a larger market than the demand curve D. Since in the long run profits are zero in monopolistic competition, a larger market brings with it a smaller price (b' as opposed to b) and a greater exploitation of economies of scale within the individual firm. The bigger the market the closer is the monopolistically competitive equilibrium to the perfectly competitive (long-run) equilibrium, illustrated by the horizontal demand curve D''.

---

tion: freedom of entry and a large number of firms. In both types of industries, economic profits are driven down to zero in the long run. The major difference between the two markets is that the product is homogeneous in the case of perfect competition and heterogeneous in the case of monopolistic competition. Monopolistic competition most closely approximates perfect competition *in large markets*.

An example of a large monopolistic-competitive market would be service stations in a large metropolitan area. Service stations in a large market could be distinguished from service stations in

a small market (such as a small town) by the kinds of service available: convenient location, self-service pumps, car repairs, automatic car wash, long hours of operation.

In a small town, it may be that the service station is the only place that can offer some of these services. In a large city, each service station faces far more competition not only for gasoline but for all the other services as well. There are firms that specialize in car repair, car washing, or automobile service. In the large market, there is a greater availability of close substitutes; the large number of service stations and specialist firms makes the

Example 4

The Pros and Cons of Price Discrimination

Is price discrimination necessarily a bad thing? After all, it does not appear "fair" to charge some people more than others for the same product. Is it "fair" for the business traveler flying from New York to London to pay hundreds of dollars more than the vacation traveler in the next seat?

However, if we put aside problems of equity or fairness, price discrimination surprisingly does have positive features. Public utilities, for example, openly practice price discrimination. Price discrimination raises their revenue without necessarily raising their cost. It is quite conceivable that many public utilities could not be profitable without price discrimination. Price discrimination, by raising revenues to the firm, can make products available that would not otherwise be supplied or that would be available only with public subsidies. Thus, it is possible for price discrimination to raise monopoly output.

The main objection to price discrimination from an economic point of view is that it is not efficient to have two buyers paying different prices for the same good, given the volume of goods that is being produced by the arrangement. At the margin, the high-price buyer derives a higher marginal benefit than the low-price buyer (remember prices reflect marginal benefits). Therefore, in principle, welfare would be increased by switching goods from low-price to high-price buyers (assuming that the level of output would not be affected). In practice leveling prices to all customers may make the industry unprofitable if price discrimination was necessary for the existence of the industry or firm.

The fundamental difficulty with monopoly from an economic-efficiency point of view is that the monopolist restricts output; society could be made better off if the monopolist increased output. To the extent that price discrimination encourages the monopolist to produce more output, price discrimination may move the monopolist closer to the ideal output from the standpoint of society.

---

demand curves for each service station quite elastic. In the small market, because each service station faces less competition from close substitutes, the demand curves for each service station are not quite as elastic.

In Figure 6, the small-town demand curve, D, is steeper (and less elastic) than the big-city demand curve, D'. The small-market long-run equilibrium occurs at b, where price is \$1.60 per gallon and output is 500 gallons. The large-market long-run equilibrium occurs at b', where price is \$1.20 and output is 800 gallons. If the large market continues to grow and the distinctions between the products of the different firms become negligible, eventually the demand curve would become perfectly elastic. The market would become perfectly competitive, producing in the long run an output of 1,100 gallons at a price of \$1.00 per gallon.

In large markets, the distinction between monopolistic competition and perfect competition becomes less pronounced.

APPLICATIONS OF PRICE-SEARCHING THEORY

The theories of monopoly and monopolistic competition explain why price-searching firms behave the way they do. These theories explain a variety of behavior patterns encountered every day in the real world, including price discrimination, markup pricing, and discrepancies in product durability.

Price Discrimination

Thus far this chapter has assumed that the price searcher charges the same price to all buyers, but this is not always the case. Customers often pay different prices for the same product. Large users of electricity (factories, for example) pay lower rates than small users (households); movie prices are lower during the day than in the evening; doctors and lawyers often charge wealthy clients more than poor clients; airlines charge business travelers higher fares by requiring

Table 2
Long Distance Telephone Rates (in dollars)

Dial-Direct Sample Rates from City of Houston, to:	Weekday Full Rate (8 AM to 5 PM Monday thru Friday)		Evening 35% discount (5 PM to 11 PM Monday thru Friday & Sunday)		Night & Weekend 60% Discount (11 PM to 8 AM Monday thru Friday; 8 AM to 8 PM Saturday; 8 AM to 5 PM & 11 PM to 8 AM Sunday)	
	First Minute	Each Additional Minute	First Minute	Each Additional Minute	First Minute	Each Additional Minute
Atlanta	0.53	0.36	0.34	0.24	0.21	0.15
Boston	0.55	0.38	0.35	0.25	0.22	0.16
Chicago	0.53	0.36	0.34	0.24	0.21	0.15
Denver	0.53	0.36	0.34	0.24	0.21	0.15
Detroit	0.55	0.38	0.35	0.25	0.22	0.16
Little Rock	0.50	0.36	0.32	0.24	0.20	0.15
Miami	0.55	0.38	0.35	0.25	0.22	0.16
New York	0.55	0.38	0.35	0.25	0.22	0.16
Philadelphia	0.55	0.38	0.35	0.25	0.22	0.16
San Francisco	0.55	0.38	0.35	0.25	0.22	0.16
Seattle	0.55	0.38	0.35	0.25	0.22	0.16
Washington, D.C.	0.55	0.38	0.35	0.25	0.22	0.16

Source: Southwestern Bell Telephone Directory, Houston, Texas

advance ticket purchases and minimum stays for discounts. All of these situations are examples of **price discrimination.**[2]

Price discrimination exists when the same product or service is sold at different prices to different buyers.

Conditions for Price Discrimination. In order for firms to engage in price discrimination, three conditions must be met:

1. The seller must exercise some control over the price; price discrimination is possible only for price searchers.
2. The seller must be able to distinguish easily among different types of customers.
3. It must be impossible for one buyer to resell the product to other buyers.

2. For detailed discussions of price discrimination in the real world, see F. M. Scherer, *Industrial Market Structure and Economic Performance,* 2nd ed. (Boston: Houghton Mifflin, 1980), chap. 11; James V. Koch, *Industrial Organization and Price,* 2nd ed. (Englewood Cliffs, N.J.: Prentice-Hall, 1980), chap. 12.

If the firm is not a price searcher, it cannot control its price. The seller who cannot distinguish between customers will not know which buyers should be charged the low price. The electric company meters electricity usage and can readily distinguish high-volume from low-volume users; doctors and lawyers can fairly well identify wealthy clients on the basis of appearance, home address, and stated profession. By placing advance purchase requirements and minimum stay requirements on tickets, airlines can create conditions that many business travelers cannot meet. If one buyer can sell to another, low-price buyers can sell to high-price buyers, and no one will be willing to pay the high price. Midday movies cannot be resold to evening moviegoers; poor clients cannot resell legal and medical services to the wealthy; industrial users of electricity cannot sell their electricity to households. Airline tickets with a minimum-one-week-stay requirement cannot be sold to someone departing on a two-day business trip.

Long-Distance Telephone Rates. Table 2 gives sample direct-dial rates from the Houston,

Texas Southwestern Bell telephone directory. The pattern of long-distance pricing is obvious. Rates for weekdays between 8:00 A.M. and 5:00 P.M. are more than 50 percent higher than rates for evenings between 5:00 P.M. and 11:00 P.M. Rates from 11:00 P.M. at night to 8:00 A.M. the next morning are 65 percent lower than the evening rates. It is no coincidence that the highest rates are charged during normal business hours: business callers pay generally higher prices for long-distance calls than do residential callers, who can do their long-distance calling in the evening.

The telephone company divides its long-distance customers into two markets: business-hour customers and evening-and-weekend customers. The market demand curves of the two markets are different. The long-distance calls of individuals tend to be elastic; the volume of such calls will be responsive to prices. The business demand, on the other hand, is less elastic. Substantial increases in business-hour rates are required to lower the quantity of calls demanded. The residential demand curve is, therefore, relatively more elastic than the business demand curve.

Both demand curves are drawn in Figure 7. The residential demand curve is D_R, and the business demand curve is D_B. The marginal revenue curve of D_R is MR_R and that of D_B is MR_B. The marginal cost (MC) of providing one 5-minute call is constant at $0.40.

Southwestern Bell can treat the daytime and evening/weekend markets as two separate markets. It sets rates in the business market to equate marginal revenue and marginal cost. A rate of $1.40 for daytime calls equates MR_B and MC. The rate of $1.40 maximizes profits in the business market.

The evening rate is set at $0.90: the price where MR_R equals MC. This rate maximizes profits in the residential market. Profits are maximized when $MR = MC$ in each market; the monopolist charges different prices because more profit can be earned than if one uniform price were charged.[3]

Markup Pricing

If one were to ask price-searching business managers how they set prices, they would likely answer: "We just set the price x percent above our average cost." Such price searchers would be referring to the practice of **markup pricing.**

Markup pricing is the setting of prices at a given percentage above average cost.

According to this chapter, the business managers should be setting prices so that $MR = MC$ at the quantity demanded. Does the widespread use of markup pricing mean that business firms do not follow the $MR = MC$ rule? Because the amount of the markup depends upon the elasticity of demand, markup pricing is consistent with the theory of the profit-maximizing price searcher.

Retailers—supermarkets, drugstores, department stores, and specialty shops—buy their goods at wholesale prices (from the producers) and sell them at higher retail prices. In retailing, the percentage markup is the difference between the retail and wholesale prices divided by the wholesale price. Retailers face a downward-sloping demand curve. They offer a service (retailing) that is differentiated by location, hours of service, product lines, friendliness of service, and so on.

The supermarket, for example, offers a wide variety of goods ranging from basic food staples like flour, sugar, potatoes, and meats, to specialty items like toys, lightbulbs, greeting cards, and delicatessen foods. Each good is purchased at a wholesale price, and its retail price will be a markup over the wholesale price. Which items have a high percentage markup and which have a low percentage markup?

As we know, a profit-maximizing firm sets prices to equate marginal revenue and marginal costs. Retailers can typically buy one more unit of the product at the wholesale price; therefore, the wholesale price is the marginal cost of the re-

3. To see how price discrimination raises profits, assume that the telephone company charged the same price in both markets. It would soon discover that if it lowered the evening rate a little while raising the business rate by the same amount, it would increase revenues without changing costs because demand is more elastic in the residential market than in the business market. An equal reduction in the residential price and increase in the business market will raise revenue. The quantity demanded of telephone calls by businesses will fall by less than the increase in the number of calls by residential customers. Price discrimination enables the seller to exploit differences in demand elasticities in order to raise revenue without raising costs.

Figure 7
Price Discrimination: Long-Distance Telephone Calls

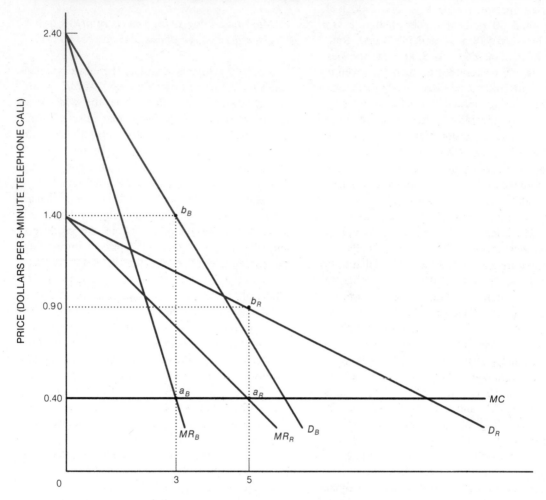

QUANTITY (THOUSANDS OF 5-MINUTE TELEPHONE CALLS PER HOUR)

The demand and marginal revenue curves of residential customers are drawn as D_R and MR_R. They are more elastic than the demand and marginal revenue curves (D_B and MR_B) of business customers. The marginal cost of providing a long-distance call *(MC)* is the same for business and residential customers and is constant. The telephone company will maximize profits in each market by equating *MR* and *MC* in each market. In the business market, $MR = MC$ at a price of $1.40; in the residential market, $MR = MC$ at a price of $0.90.

tailer. In our example, the marginal cost of flour is $0.25 and the marginal cost of a lightbulb is $0.15.

Figure 8 shows what the demand curves for flour and lightbulbs facing a particular supermarket will look like. The price elasticity of demand for food staples (flour, sugar, vegetable oils) will be quite high to each supermarket. (Remember,

the elasticity of demand facing a particular supermarket that must compete with other supermarkets is not the same thing as the elasticity of market demand for specific items like flour or lightbulbs.)These are items that are frequently purchased and well advertised. Supermarkets compete among themselves for such sales; slight changes in prices bring about large changes in sales.

Figure 8
The Theory of Markup Pricing: Flour and Lightbulbs

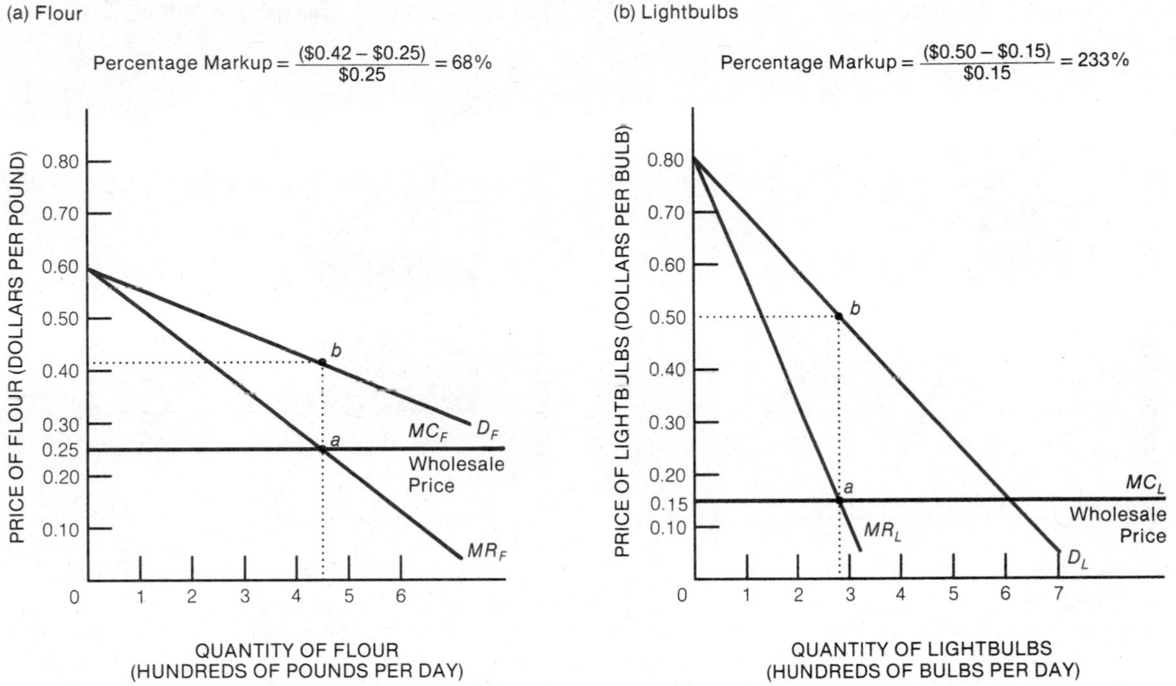

(a) Flour

Percentage Markup $= \dfrac{(\$0.42 - \$0.25)}{\$0.25} = 68\%$

(b) Lightbulbs

Percentage Markup $= \dfrac{(\$0.50 - \$0.15)}{\$0.15} = 233\%$

QUANTITY OF FLOUR
(HUNDREDS OF POUNDS PER DAY)

QUANTITY OF LIGHTBULBS
(HUNDREDS OF BULBS PER DAY)

The demand for flour, D_F, facing the supermarket is elastic. The demand for lightbulbs, D_L, is inelastic. Because the supermarket maximizes profits by equating MR and MC for each product, there will be a higher percentage markup for lightbulbs than for flour. Percentage markups tend to be higher the more inelastic is the demand for the product.

The price elasticity of demand for discretionary items (lightbulbs, stationery, and beauty aids) will be less elastic to each supermarket. These items are purchased with less frequency; they are likely to be picked up because the shopper is already in the store; the shopper tends to be less aware of the prices of these items at competitive stores. Therefore, the demand curve for flour (D_F in Figure 8) is more elastic than the demand curve for lightbulbs in each store (D_L).

The profit-maximizing supermarket manager will set prices to equate MR and MC. As Figure 8 shows, $MR = MC$ at a price of $0.42 per pound for flour and a price of $0.50 per bulb for lightbulbs. The percentage markups are 68 percent [($0.42 − $0.25)/$0.25] for flour and 233 percent [($0.50 − $0.15)/$0.15] for lightbulbs. Actual supermarket markups reveal that—as the theory predicts—the percentage markups of discretionary items tend to be higher than the percentage markups of staple items.[4]

If the price elasticity of demand is relatively high, the percentage markup will be small. If the price elasticity of demand is relatively low, the percentage markup will be high. The percentage markup is negatively related to the elasticity of demand.

Product Durability

Where is the 10-year lightbulb? Do business firms suppress ways of increasing product durability in order to maintain long-run demand? This practice is sometimes referred to as *planned obsolescence*. How many of us have heard that there

4. "Emergence of Savvy Consumers Forces Painful Rethinking by Supermarkets," *Wall Street Journal*, September 29, 1980. For instance, the percentage markups on lightbulbs and school supplies are 55 and 47 percent, respectively, while the markups on flour and coffee are 16 and 10 percent, respectively.

Figure 9
Lightbulb Durability and Monopoly Profits

(a) 1 Lightbulb = 1 Lightbulb Hour

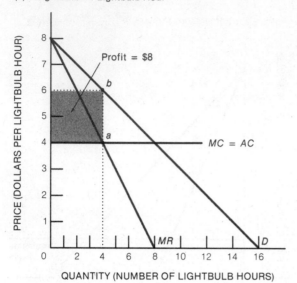

(b) 1 Lightbulb = 2 Lightbulb Hours

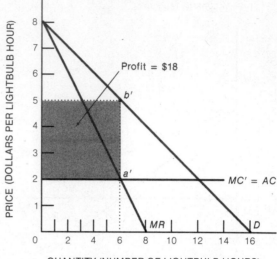

The demand curve *D* shows the demand for lightbulb hours (not lightbulbs). Panel (a) shows a situation where 1 lightbulb equals 1 lightbulb hour (each lightbulb burns only 1 hour). If the *MC* of lightbulbs is $4, monopoly profits are maximized where output is 4 bulbs, where *MC* equals $4, and where price equals $6. Monopoly profits are $8. A costless doubling of lightbulb durability (to make 1 lightbulb burn 2 lightbulb hours) is shown in panel (b). Marginal cost per lightbulb hour is now reduced to $2, but demand for lightbulb hours remains the same. The monopolist now maximizes profit at an output level of 6 lightbulb hours (= 3 bulbs). The monopoly price is now $5 per lightblub hour, and monopoly profit equals $18.

---

are tires that last twice as long, a lightbulb that lasts 10 years, more durable cars, motor oils that never have to be changed—but that these products have been suppressed so that consumers will have to buy the less durable goods more often?

The principal reason firms fail to introduce extensions in durability is because it is costly to the firm to produce more durability.

Imagine that a firm has a complete monopoly of lightbulb production. Because it need not fear competition from other producers, there is no incentive to produce a more durable product simply to differentiate the firm's product from the competition's. Because people want lightbulbs because of the light they produce, the demand for lightbulbs is derived from the demand for light or, more specifically, for *lightbulb hours*. Assume, for simplicity, that 1 lightbulb lasts exactly 1 hour; thus, 1 lightbulb = 1 lightbulb hour.

Again, for simplicity, assume that the average cost of producing a lightbulb is constant at $4. Since the average cost (*AC*) of a lightbulb is constant, the marginal cost of a lightbulb must equal *AC*; therefore, *MC* = *AC* = $4. Because we have assumed that 1 lightbulb hour equals 1 lightbulb, the *AC* or *MC* of a lightbulb hour is also $4.

Panel (a) of Figure 9 shows the initial monopoly equilibrium at point *b*. Initially, *MC* = $4, and profits are maximized at point *a*, where *MC* = *MR* = $4. At point *b* on the demand curve, the monopoly price is $6, and the monopoly quantity is 4 lightbulb hours. Monopoly profit is ($6 − $4) × 4 = $8.

Suppose that the monopolist discovers a costless method of doubling the life of a lightbulb; that is, the monopoly learns that it can continue to produce a lightbulb for $4 but the lightbulb will now last 2 hours. Will the monopolist introduce the new lightbulbs? In panel (b) 1 lightbulb = 2 lightbulb hours. If the monopoly profit in panel

(b) exceeds $8, the monopolist will introduce the more durable lightbulb.

Since the demand curve and the *MR* curve are already defined in terms of lightbulb hours (rather than lightbulbs) they are unchanged by the introduction of the more durable lightbulb. In other words, if the monopolist introduced the new 2-hour lightbulb and charged $12 (instead of the former $6 for the 1-hour lightbulb), the consumer would still want 4 lightbulb hours—but would buy only two 2-hour lightbulbs at $12 each instead of four 1-hour lightbulbs at $6 each. The demand curve remains the same, but the *MC* curve changes. To produce a lightbulb still costs $4 (because we assumed the 2-hour bulb was a costless invention), but since the lightbulb lasts for 2 hours it costs only $2 to produce a *lightbulb hour*. Thus the *MC* (= *AC*) curve in panel (b) shifts downward to *AC'* = *MC'* = $2 when the new lightbulb is introduced. With the new cost curves, the equilibrium price per lightbulb hour is $5 and the equilibrium output level is 6 lightbulb hours. If one lightbulb hour costs $5, a 2-hour lightbulb will cost $10. The new monopoly profit equals ($5 − $2) × 6, or $18. Thus the monopolist can increase profit by $10 (from $8 to $18) by introducing the new lightbulb.

In this example, we assumed that the cost of innovation was zero. In this case, monopoly profits rise from $8 to $18 as a result of the innovation. If the cost of the innovation had been greater than $10 (the increase in profit), the monopoly would not introduce the more durable lightbulb.[5]

The reason why business firms do not extend the durability of a good more than they do is that it costs firms to make goods more durable. To produce a space vehicle with virtually no chance of breaking down costs millions of dollars; the cost could be reduced dramatically if all the backup systems and safety checks were eliminated. Similarly, to produce more durable cars requires certain trade-offs; either the car must have a higher price like the Mercedes-Benz or Rolls-Royce), or other characteristics like styling and handling performance must be sacrificed (as in the Toyota Corolla).

The theory of price searching explains that both monopolists and monopolistic competitors produce that quantity of output at which marginal revenue equals marginal costs. In the long run, monopolies can maintain monopoly profits, while the profits of monopolistic competitors are squeezed out by the entry of new firms.

The chapter that follows will try to evaluate monopoly and monopolistic competition in relation to perfect competition. Characteristics that will be important in such a comparison include 1) the fact that monopolists are not pressured to produce at minimum average cost in the long run and 2) the fact that price searchers do not equate marginal cost and price.

Summary

1. A pure monopoly exists when there is one seller producing a product that has no close substitutes. Barriers to entry keep out competitors. The monopolist is a price searcher and has considerable control over price. Pure monopoly is rare in the real world because of substitutes and the absence of absolute barriers to entry, especially in the long run. Sources of monopoly are: economies of scale, patents, ownership of crucial raw materials, public franchises, and collusion.

2. Price searchers face downward-sloping demand curves; they must lower their price in order to sell more. As long as the price searcher charges all customers a uniform price, price and average revenue are the same. For price searchers, price will exceed marginal revenue. When marginal revenue is positive, demand is elastic; when marginal revenue is negative, demand is inelastic. Therefore, a profit-maximizing price searcher will never produce at an inelastic point on the demand curve.

---

5. Notice, though, that the monopoly may not introduce costly innovations that benefit society in the form of lower prices and more consumer surplus. Assume the cost of the innovation in the example above had been $11. Monopoly profit would be lowered by the introduction of the durable lightbulb from $8 to $7, so the monopolist would not introduce the durable lightbulb. But when the price of lightbulbs per hour falls from $6 to $5, consumer surplus rises by $5 (from $4 to $9); hence, the consumer would have gained more than the monopolist would have lost. The introduction of the new lightbulb would be a net gain to society.

3. Monopolists maximize profits by producing that output quantity at which marginal revenue and marginal cost are equal or by charging that price at which $MR = MC$. Once the monopolist has chosen the optimal output, the market will dictate the price. Monopolists do not always make profits. When monopolies are unprofitable, they follow the same shutdown rule as competitive firms·.

4. Popular fallacies about monopolies are:
   a) Monopolists charge the highest price possible.
   b) Monopolists do not have to be concerned with market demand.
   c) Monopolists always make a profit. Monopolists do not produce where price equals marginal cost. Monopolists do not produce in the long run where average costs are minimized. Monopolists produce where demand is elastic.

5. A monopolistic-competitive industry has many sellers, sells a differentiated product, has freedom of entry and exit, and its individual firms are price searchers. Monopolistic competitors produce where MR equals MC. In the long run, the entry of new firms will drive monopolistic-competitive profits down to zero. When profits are zero and $MR = MC$, the firm's output must be less than the minimum efficient scale; that is, unit costs are not minimized as in perfect competition. By engaging in nonprice competition—through product differentiation and advertising—monopolistic competitive firms can delay the disappearance of economic profits. In large markets, monopolistic competition approximates perfect competition.

6. Price searchers can raise their profits through price discrimination. Buyers with inelastic demand will pay higher prices than those with elastic demand. The practice of markup pricing is consistent with the MR-equals-MC rule. The percentage markup will be nega-tively related to the elasticity of demand. Product durability will depend upon the cost of supplying durability.

Key Terms

price searcher
pure monopoly
marginal revenue (MR)
average revenue (AR)
marginal revenue schedule
monopolistic competition
nonprice competition
price discrimination
markup pricing

Questions and Problems

1. Firm A can sell all it wants at a price of $5. Firm B lowers its price from $6 to $5 to sell more output. Explain why the marginal revenue of Firm A is not the same as the marginal revenue of Firm B even though they are both charging a $5 price.

2. "The shutdown rule applies only to firms operating in competitive markets. Monopolies don't use any shutdown rule." Evaluate this statement.

3. Explain why a price searcher can choose either its profit-maximizing output level or its profit-maximizing price. Why is it that when one choice is made, the firm has no choice about the other?

4. A monopolist produces 100 units of output, and the price elasticity of demand at this point on the demand curve is -0.5. What advice would you give the monopolist? From this information, what can you say about marginal revenue?

5. A price searcher produces output at a constant *MC* of $6 and has no fixed costs. The demand curve facing the price searcher is indicated in the table.

Price (dollars)	Quantity Demanded (units)
12	0
10	5
8	10
6	15
4	20

a. Determine the price searcher's profit-maximizing output, price, and profit.

b. Show that by producing more or less output, profit would decrease.

c. Explain what happens to marginal revenue when output is raised from 15 to 20 units.

6. A food concession in a sports stadium makes an economic profit of $100,000 in the first year of operation. Explain what will happen to profits in subsequent years a. if the concessionaire is granted an exclusive franchise to stadium concessions and b. if potential competitors have the freedom to set up concession stands in the stadium. In the latter case, can the concessionaire do anything to protect long-run profits?

7. Prices of movie tickets and tickets to sports events and concerts are typically lower for children than for adults. Explain why this is so using the theory of price discrimination.

8. Explain why the entry of new firms into a monopolistic-competitive market makes the demand curves of established firms more elastic.

11

Monopoly and Competition Compared

Chapter Preview

Ever since Adam Smith argued that the invisible hand of competition would lead profit-maximizing producers and utility-maximizing consumers to an efficient allocation of society's resources, economists have been captivated by its charm. In addition to the praise offered by economists, the antitrust laws of the United States, beginning with the Sherman Act of 1890 (to be discussed in a later chapter), have made a competitive order the law of the land.

This chapter explains why perfect competition is more efficient than monopoly in the absence of external costs but also describes the advantages and disadvantages of monopoly.

THE CASE FOR COMPETITION

When thinking about how competition influences the way the economy works as a whole, it is easy to commit the fallacy of composition. People might reason that because everyone in a competitive order is looking out for himself or herself, society's interests will suffer. The study of competition shows that social interests can be promoted when each person promotes his or her self-interest.

The Ideal Competitive Model

We cannot prove that competition leads to efficiency for the economy as a whole unless we can examine a situation in which all the conditions of perfect competition are met. Thus we will begin by considering an economy with no monopoly elements and with perfect information about prices and product quality. Buyers gather all the benefits of the goods they buy; sellers pay all the costs of producing the goods they sell. In other words, we are assuming well-informed consumers face many producers of shoes, shirts, housing, and so on—where property rights are well-defined and strictly enforced. How will this economy function?

Efficiency

The concept of *economic efficiency* is far from simple, but it basically means that nothing is being wasted. For example, assume that:

1. Ann and Betty live on a deserted island with only 50 apples and 100 bananas per week to subsist upon. Ann will not eat bananas and Betty will not eat apples. Each has 25 apples and 50 bananas.
2. Wheat is being grown on Iowa corn land, and corn is being grown on Kansas wheat land.
3. The price of wheat is $10 per bushel in Chicago and $2 per bushel in Kansas City. The wheat is used in the finest Illinois bakeries and as animal fodder in Kansas.

In each of these three cases, a slight rearrangement in production or consumption can make everyone better off. Both Betty and Ann will be better off if Ann gives Betty her bananas and Betty gives Ann her apples; consumers and producers of wheat and corn would benefit if wheat were grown in Kansas and corn were grown in Iowa; consumers in Illinois and producers in Kansas would benefit if wheat were shipped to Illinois. Such rearrangements would change situations characterized by economic **inefficiency** into situations characterized by economic **efficiency.**

Efficiency is present when society's resources are so organized that it is impossible to make someone better off without hurting someone else by any reallocation of resources.[1]

Inefficiency is present when resources can be reallocated to make someone better off without making someone worse off.

The above examples clearly show that inefficiency is present when profitable trading opportunities are not being exploited. Ann can trade her bananas to Betty in return for Betty's apples. Similarly, farmers will make more profits by devoting Kansas wheat land to wheat and Iowa corn land to corn. Traders can buy wheat in Kansas City and sell it for a handsome profit in Chicago. It was Adam Smith's insight that individuals, guided by their own self-interest, will eliminate any economic inefficiencies. The invisible hand operates when each person's quest for profit leads to economic efficiency for all.

Economic Efficiency and Market Equilibrium. Market equilibrium in perfectly competitive markets brings about the right balance between consumer utility and enterprise costs. When this balance is achieved, economic efficiency is the result.

Consumers buy a variety of goods—milk, shirts, cars, housing, books, and so on. Well-informed and rational consumers carry out their purchases of any particular good until the ratio of its marginal utility *(MU)* to price is the same as that ratio for all other goods. Thus individual consumers arrange consumption so that the prices of the goods they buy reflect the marginal utilities of those goods: low-priced goods have low *MUs* and high-priced goods have high *MUs*. Thus, the price of a good is a dollar measure of the good's marginal utility to the individual; indeed, we can say that the marginal benefit of the good to the consumer equals its price. But each consumer in a perfectly competitive market pays the same price.

The price of a good measures its marginal benefit to society because each utility-maximizing consumer equates the good's MU/P to that of all other goods.

---

1. This notion of efficiency was first developed by the Italian economist, Vilfredo Pareto. This concept of economic efficiency is named in his honor as *Pareto optimality.*

Now consider the other side of the market: the competitive firms that produce milk, cars, bread, shirts, and houses. Each producer will carry out production until price and marginal cost are equal. If price exceeds marginal cost, the competitive producer finds profit opportunities in expanding production until diminishing returns drive marginal cost up to the level of price. When price equals marginal cost, additional profit opportunities to each individual producer are exhausted.

In perfect competition, every producer faces the same price and, hence, produces to the point where marginal cost equals price. Each producer has the same marginal cost of production. Thus the marginal cost of bread to one producer is the same as the marginal cost of bread to society. The good is produced using a minimum of society's resources when each producer has the same marginal cost.

Market equilibrium entails producing the good at minimum cost and up to the point where marginal benefit (price) is just balanced by marginal cost. The economy is efficient when society's extra cost of producing a good equals the marginal benefit of that good. When $P = MC$ and markets clear, opportunities to increase profits have been exhausted.

Perfect Competition and Social Efficiency. The difference between price and marginal cost is not only a profit opportunity for individual producers, it also signals a social opportunity. If $P > MC$, there is a social payoff to producing more of the good. Remember that marginal cost is the opportunity cost at the margin—what is being given up elsewhere. To say that price exceeds marginal cost is to say that the resources used in the production of this particular good have a higher marginal benefit to society than those resources have elsewhere since marginal costs are measured as opportunity costs.

In Figure 1, an output of 5,000 units is 3,000 units short of the equilibrium quantity. The marginal cost to society is $70 (at point a), and the marginal benefit to society is $120 (at point b). Moving from an output of 5,000 units to an output of 8,000 units benefits society by the shaded area abc. Point c is an efficient output level.

**Figure 1
Perfect Competition and Social Efficiency**

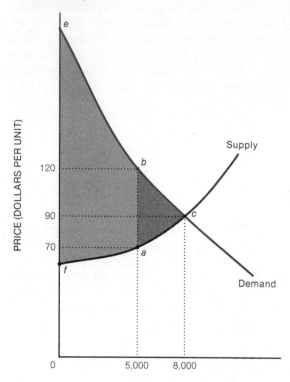

When output is restricted to 5,000 units, the marginal cost of the 5,001st unit of output is the price at point a, or $70; the marginal benefit is the price at point b, or $120. Moving to the equilibrium quantity of 8,000 units results in a net gain to society of area abc, because marginal benefits exceed marginal costs on the intervening 3,000 units. Social welfare is maximized when price is $90 and the total of consumer and producer surplus equals area ecf.

If price does not equal marginal cost for all goods, there is inefficiency in the system, and all people can be made better off (or at least some better off and none worse off) by reallocating resources until price equals marginal cost.

THE LIMITATIONS OF COMPETITION

Even in a perfectly competitive world, the invisible hand may not lead to the best of all possible worlds for at least three reasons:

1. Perfect competition may lead to inequalities in the distribution of income that are not regarded by a democratic majority as equitable.

2. When the operation of a competitive firm results in costs to someone outside the firm, perfectly competitive markets may cause inefficient resource allocation.

3. Perfect competition may not be conducive to a high rate of technological progress.

Equity and Efficiency

As demonstrated above, perfect competition leads to economic efficiency. Efficiency means nothing is being wasted. In an efficient situation, to help one person, someone else must be hurt.

Efficiency can prevail even when the resulting distribution of income is unethical, unjust, or unfair. In a perfectly efficient capitalist economy **economic equity** need not be present: some people may live in a state of grinding poverty, while those owning large quantities of scarce resources may live in luxury. In order to make the poor better off in an efficient economy, however, the rich must be made worse off because there are no extra resources around that are being wasted.

Economic equity is present when resources are distributed fairly.

In our real world of poverty and scarcity, a society that purposely enacts policies that lead to inefficiencies (or wastefulness) might be just as negligent as the efficient society that ignores those people in real need.

Externalities

A perfectly competitive allocation of resources can be economically efficient if **externalities** are absent.

Externalities are present when an economic activity results in economic costs or benefits that do not accrue to those involved in the activity.

Externalities arise when a factory belches black smoke that raises the cost of laundry or medical care for those people living in the vicinity; when the chemical plant dumps wastes that affect fishing and agricultural production; when the pulp mill pollutes the air others must breathe; or when the airport pollutes an area with deafening noise.

In order to understand the effects of an externality, it is necessary to distinguish between **private costs** and **external costs** and between **private benefits** and **external benefits.**

A private cost (or benefit) is the cost (or benefit) borne (or enjoyed) by the firm producing a good.

An external cost (or benefit) is the cost (or benefit) borne (or enjoyed) by someone other than the firm producing the good.

When externalities are present, then, the full cost to society of producing a good is determined by adding the private costs and external costs together; the full benefit to society is the sum of the private benefits and external benefits. The costs or benefits to society of producing a good are the **social costs** or **social benefits.**

Social costs = private costs + external costs

Social benefits = private benefits + external benefits

The main feature of an externality is that the marginal private cost *(MPC)* of production does not necessarily reflect the marginal social cost *(MSC)*. The marginal social cost of producing steel includes not only the marginal private costs of the steel mill but also the marginal external costs imposed on others (the extra laundry costs, medical-care costs, and so on). The steel plant does not take these external costs into account when making its economic decisions.

Externalities lead to economic inefficiency because the marginal social benefit of steel *as measured by its market price* will be less than its marginal social cost.

Figure 2 shows a competitive steel industry that imposes external costs on others. At equilibrium, 1 million tons are produced at a price of $100 per ton (point *a*). The curve *MSC* measures marginal social costs while the supply curve measures only marginal private costs *(MPC)*. With a marginal social cost of $160 per ton at equilib-

Figure 2
Externalities and Competition

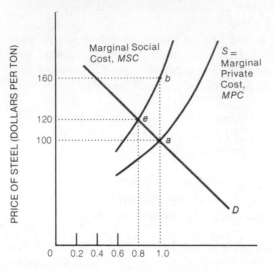

QUANTITY OF STEEL
(MILLIONS OF TONS PER PERIOD)

The supply and demand curves intersect at the price/
quantity combination of $100 per ton and 1 million
tons of steel (point a). The supply curve S reflects only
marginal *private* costs. The curve *MSC* shows marginal *social* costs. At the equilibrium point a, the marginal social cost of an extra ton of steel is $160, but
the marginal social benefit is only $100, as measured
by the height of the demand curve. Too much steel is
produced from a societal point of view.

rium, an output of 1 million tons is too much steel
production from the standpoint of society. Marginal social costs ($160) do not equal marginal
social benefits ($100) when 1 million tons are
produced because externalities are present. Too
much steel is produced when marginal social cost
is greater than price. Efficiency requires that 0.8
million tons of steel be produced (point *e*), where
both marginal social cost and price are equal to
$120.

Economic activities can have external benefits
as well as external costs. When one neighbor
plants flowers, surrounding neighbors also benefit. The person who considers only personal pleasure to be the benefit from growing flowers will
plant flowers only to the point where marginal
costs and marginal benefits are equal. The marginal costs to the person of growing the flowers
does not equal the marginal benefits enjoyed by
society (the neighborhood) because other neigh-

bors get some marginal benefits as well. Economic inefficiency is present because too few
flowers get planted. Externalities do not create
problems only under conditions of perfect competition. All systems of resource allocation—
from monopoly to planned socialism—are
plagued by externalities. Pollution is as much a
problem in the Soviet Union as it is in the United
States; externalities are not unique to competitive
capitalism. The presence of externalities simply
means that the invisible hand of perfect competition has problems when confronted with external
costs and benefits. Different economic systems
may cope better or worse with the problem of externalities.

Technological Progress

There is no guarantee that competition will be
efficient in a *dynamic* (changing) situation. Perfect competition has been shown to be efficient
when resources and technology are *static* (unchanging). Is it possible that competition is poorly
suited to creating and promoting technological
change? There is considerable controversy surrounding this question, which will be addressed
in the next section.

THE CASE AGAINST MONOPOLY

Opponents of monopoly argue that monopoly
is 1) inefficient and 2) unfair.

Sources of Inefficiency in Monopoly

Monopoly is inefficient for three reasons.
First, monopoly leads to contrived scarcities. Second, the resources used to acquire monopoly
power could have been used elsewhere in the
economy. Third, monopoly does not force efficiency in production.

Contrived Scarcity. The basic argument
against monopoly is that monopolies maximize
profit by restricting output to the scale where
price exceeds marginal cost. Remember that monopolies maximize profit where $MR = MC$, but
$P > MR$. Therefore, price will exceed marginal
cost at that output that maximizes monopoly
profit.

Price measures marginal social benefit, and marginal cost measures marginal social cost (if externalities are not present); therefore, when P > MC there is contrived scarcity in the economy.

Contrived scarcity occurs when the economy would be better off—more efficient in the sense of giving more to everyone—if more of the monopolized good were produced. When *P > MC,* one more unit of output adds more to social welfare than to social costs, and it is possible to rearrange the allocation of resources to make everyone better off.

To compare monopoly with perfect competition, consider a situation in which both are possible. Figure 3 depicts an industry where there are no economies of scale; average costs are the same for all levels of output; *AC = MC.* Either one large firm (a monopoly) or a large number of small firms (a perfectly competitive market) could satisfy consumer demand at the same average cost. Marginal cost (*= AC*) is a constant $4 per unit. The monopoly output level (300 units) is found where *MR* is also $4; the monopoly price is $7. Monopoly profits are represented by the color shaded area, which equals $900. Under perfect competition, on the other hand, free entry would squeeze out economic profits. The long-run competitive price would therefore be $4, and the competitive output would be 600 units (point *c*).

The cost of monopoly can be calculated from Figure 3. If this industry could be converted to perfect competition from monopoly, the equilibrium price/quantity combination would shift from point *b* to point *c*, and the price would fall from $7 to $4. The increase in consumer surplus resulting from the shift from monopoly to competition is the sum of the color shaded area (the monopolist's profit of $900) and grey shaded area ($450). The gain in consumer surplus would therefore equal $1350. But the monopolist, who is also a member of society, loses monopoly profits of $900 in the process. The net gain to society is simply the grey shaded triangle, which equals $450. Notice that everyone involved could be made better off as a result of the move to perfect competition. Since consumers gain $1350 in consumer surplus, they could buy off the monopolist with a payment (say, $901) greater than the orig-

Figure 3
Monopoly and Competition Compared

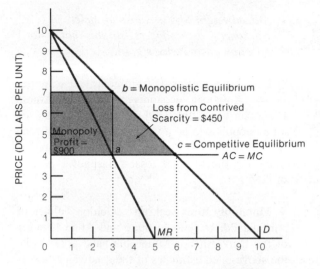

This industry has constant returns to scale where *AC = MC* = $4 for all levels of output. If the industry were perfectly competitive, price would be $4 and output would be 600 units. If this industry were a single-firm monopoly, price would be $7 and output would be 300 units with a monopoly profit of $900(= $3 × 300). Monopoly profit is the color area. The monopolist creates profits by the contrived scarcity of 300 units (the monopolist produces 300 units less than the competitive industry). The loss from contrived scarcity is the grey area, which equals $450, or the deadweight loss to society. Moving from monopoly to competition creates consumer surplus of $1,350 ($900 + $450) while destroying only $900 worth of profits for the monopolist. More is gained by all parties taken together than is lost.

inal monopoly profit—which would make the monopolist better off by $1 and the consumers better off by $449.[2] The $450 loss from monopoly is a **deadweight loss** since nothing is received in exchange for the loss. The deadweight loss of

2. When *Q* = 300 and *P* = $7, the margin between marginal social benefits and marginal social costs is $3 ($7 − $4). Hence it pays society to expand output beyond the 300th unit. In effect, the 301st unit adds $3 to social welfare. The 601st unit adds nothing to social welfare since *P = MC.* From *Q* = 300 to *Q* = 600, the extra benefit per unit declines from $3 to $0. Thus, on the average, the 300 additional units from 300 (the monopolist's *Q*) to 600 (the *Q* under perfect competition) add $1.50 each (the average of $3 and $0) or $450.

monopoly is equivalent to throwing away valuable scarce resources.

> *A **deadweight loss** is a loss to society of consumers' or producers' surplus that is not offset by anyone else's gain.*

How large are losses from contrived scarcities in the American economy? Economist Arnold Harberger has estimated the deadweight loss from all monopolies to be a very small fraction of total U.S. output.[3] A number of other researchers roughly estimate these losses at about 1 percent of GNP.

Monopoly Rent Seeking. Gordon Tullock of Virginia Polytechnic Institute and Anne Krueger of the University of Minnesota have argued that the above-cited estimates of the deadweight losses from monopoly represent lower bounds to the true loss of society from monopoly.[4] In terms of Figure 3, if the industry were perfectly competitive, the price/quantity combination would be $4/600 units, or point *c*, and there would be no deadweight losses. If someone could turn this industry into a monopoly, that person could gain the potential monopoly profit of $900 (color area). People would be willing to spend real resources on turning the industry into a monopoly to acquire the monopoly profit. The monopoly profit can be thought of as the rent received in return for expending the resources needed to turn a competitive industry into a monopoly.

> *Monopoly rent seeking is the efforts of anyone trying to turn a competitive industry into a monopoly in order to gain the monopoly profits, or "rent."*

A prime example of **monopoly rent seeking** would be lobbying costs. Monopolies can be achieved and maintained through government charters, franchises, and regulation. The preceding chapter mentioned the railroad lobby's opposition to coal-slurry pipelines. To maintain the railroads' monopoly over coal transport, real resources have to be spent on lobbying. Another prominent case is the lobbying in Congress by American automobile manufacturers for protection from foreign imports. Monopoly profits yield benefits to the monopolist, even though they harm the consumer through contrived scarcity.

If *all* monopoly profits are absorbed in monopoly rent seeking consumers would lose the grey shaded area in Figure 3 (the loss of consumer surplus) and the monopolist would *not* gain the color shaded area (monopoly profit). Monopoly rent seeking, in this extreme case, has multiplied the deadweight loss of monopoly.

Monopoly rent seeking can lead to substantial social losses. To limit monopoly rent-seeking behavior, it would be necessary to lessen substantially the possibility of "buying" monopoly through the manipulation of government. This is easier said than done.

X-Inefficiency. The third loss from monopoly power is called *X-inefficiency*, a term coined by Harvard economist Harvey Leibenstein.[5] To understand *X*-inefficiency, recall that perfect competition forces enterprises to produce as cheaply as possible to stay in business. The competitive producer that fails to minimize costs will go bankrupt in the long run. What if the firm has a monopoly? While it is beneficial to the monopolist to minimize costs of production, it is not as costly to the monopolist who fails to do so as it is to the competitor. Unlike the competitive business, the monopolist will not be driven out of business. Hence, it is likely that "organizational slack" will develop in monopolistic industries.

> *X-inefficiency is the organizational slack that results from the lack of competition in monopolies. X-inefficiency results in costs that are higher than necessary.*

3. Arnold Harberger, "Monopoly and Resource Allocation," *American Economic Review* 44 (May 1954): 77-87. We can mention only a few of the economists who have contributed to this estimate: David Schwartzman, Dean Worcester, Jr., David Kamerschen, and Michael Klass.
4. Anne Krueger, "The Political Economy of the Rent-Seeking Society," *American Economic Review* 64 (June 1974): 291–303; and Gordon Tullock, "The Welfare Cost of Tariffs, Monopolies, and Theft," *Western Economic Journal* 5 (June 1967): 224–232.

5. Harvey Leibenstein, "Allocative Efficiency vs. X-Inefficiency," *American Economic Review* 56 (June 1966): 392-415.

Example 1

The Costs to Society of OPEC

Monopoly creates a deadweight loss by destroying more consumer surplus than it creates in the form of monopoly profits. A fairly spectacular example of a deadweight loss from a monopoly is the case of OPEC (the Organization of Petroleum Exporting Countries), which emerged in 1973 as a powerful production cartel. In 1973, the price of OPEC oil was $2.91 per barrel. By 1982, this price had risen to $32 per barrel. At the $32 per barrel price, OPEC sells 20 million barrels per day. The price/quantity combination of $32 and 20 million barrels represents one point on the demand schedule (see the accompanying figure).

The question of what world oil prices would be today if there were no OPEC is difficult and controversial, but Robert Pindyck has estimated that the world oil price would be around $8 per barrel today if there were no OPEC. Supposing the price elasticity of demand for OPEC oil were -0.10 (a 100 percent price reduction leads to a 10 percent increase in quantity demanded), if the price were $8 per barrel, the quantity demanded would increase by 8 million barrels per day to 28 million barrels per day. There is no way of knowing for sure what the quantity demanded would be if the price were $8 instead of $32, but the 28 million barrels is a reasonable guess. The price quantity combination of $8 and 28 million barrels forms a second point on the demand schedule.

What are the costs of OPEC to oil consumers in terms of lost consumer surplus? As the figure shows, the loss of consumer surplus equals consumer surplus at the price of $8 per barrel minus consumer surplus at the price of $32 per barrel, or the areas $B + C$. The loss of consumer surplus in 1982 due to OPEC equals an astronomical $576 million per day.

What is the gain of OPEC to OPEC countries? Without the cartel, the price is $8 per barrel, at which price no economic profits would be earned. At the price of $32 per barrel, however, economic

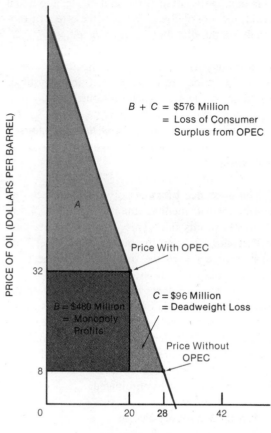

profits equal the area B, or $480 million per day. The net effect of OPEC, therefore, is to destroy $576 million per day of consumer surplus and to create $480 million per day economic profit for OPEC.

Source: Robert Pindyck, "Gains to Producers from Cartelization of Exhaustible Resources," *Review of Economics and Statistics* 60, 2 (March 1978): 238-51.

How large are monopoly *X*-inefficiencies? Estimates of *X*-inefficiency as high as 2 percent of national output have been presented by industrial-organization experts, but accurate estimates are impossible to achieve. Although X-inefficiency is a very logical concept, it is very hard to quantify with any precision.[6]

6. Walter Primeaux conducted an interesting test of X-inefficiency: Primeaux found that in 49 cities, there is competition between at least two electric companies. Primeaux found that the costs of those companies that face competition is 11 percent below those of monopoly suppliers. *See* Primeaux, "An Assessment of X-Efficiency Gained Through Competition," *Review of Economics and Statistics* 59 (February 1977): 105-108.

Monopoly and Income Distribution

Is monopoly unfair because it creates too much wealth for monopolists? What is the effect of monopoly on the distribution of income?

In Figure 3, the transformation of the industry from monopoly to perfect competition would lower the price from $7 to $4; the consumer· would pay $3 less for each unit purchased.

Income is redistributed from the monopolist to the consumer when the monopoly becomes competitive.

The existence of monopoly profits affects the distribution of income among individuals. Are monopoly profits fair? This is an ethical question that economists are ill-equiped to answer, but many people regard the transfer of income from the consumer to the monopolist as unfair.

How large an impact has monopoly had on the American distribution of income? Again, it is difficult to get reliable estimates, but one study of the wealthiest 0.25 percent of U.S. households reveals that their share of wealth would fall from 18.5 percent to between 12 and 14 percent if all monopoly power were eliminated.[7]

Taxing Monopoly Profits

A normative objection to monopolies is that they can make above-normal, or economic, profits. Since the monopolist is protected from competition, its profits are secure from the inroads of competing firms.

Recall that monopoly is inefficient because too little is being produced. What can be done about monopoly profits without making the economy more inefficient? If monopoly profits can be taxed away without affecting in any way the output decision of the monopolist, there would be no loss of efficiency and one objection to monopoly would be removed. Economists believe a **lump-sum tax** can accomplish these goals.

---

7. William Comanor and Robert Smiley, "Monopoly and the Distribution of Wealth," *Quarterly Journal of Economics* 89 (May 1975): 177-194.

Figure 4
Taxing the Monopolist: Lump-Sum Taxation

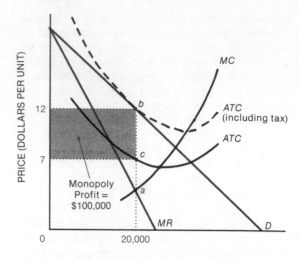

QUANTITY

This monopolist maximizes profit by producing 20,000 units of output, which are sold at a price of $12 per unit. The average cost is $7; the monopolist earns a total profit of 20,000 units × $5, or $100,000. If the government levies a lump-sum tax of $100,000, the monopolist will continue to produce the same quantity and charge the same price because this tax is a fixed cost. The *MC* curve does not shift; only the *ATC* curve shifts when the tax is included.

---

*A **lump-sum tax** is a tax that does not vary with any indicator of the firm's performance; that is, it does not vary with the firm's output, profit, or employment. It is like a fixed cost.*

The effect of lump-sum taxation on monopoly output and profits is shown in Figure 4. Figure 4 shows a monopolist making substantial economic profits. Economic profits are $100,000 per year, since the profit-maximizing output is 20,000 units and the profit per unit is $5. How can the government tax away these profits without causing the monopolist to reduce output?

The tax collector could levy a $100,000 lump-sum tax on these profits. To the monopolist, such a tax would be like a fixed cost. The monopolist would continue to produce the same output and charge the same price as before the lump-sum tax. The lump-sum tax merely reduces the monopolist's economic profit (after tax) to zero. The *ATC* curve shifts up to include the tax, and the *MC* curve remains the same because a lump-sum tax cannot affect marginal costs.

A lump-sum tax does not influence marginal costs or marginal revenue; hence, enterprise decision making is not influenced by a lump-sum tax. A lump-sum tax does not affect the productivity or efficiency of the economy as a whole. A lump-sum tax that exceeds economic (monopoly) profits would drive the monopolist out of business in the long run. The tax would drive resources into some other activity.

The main economic objection to monopoly is not that monopolists make high profits; it is always possible to tax away above-normal profits and redistribute the proceeds to the poor and to orphans. Even if all monopoly profits were taxed away and given to the most deserving members of society, monopoly would still be inefficient: if price is greater than marginal cost, society is not putting enough resources into the monopolized activity. Inefficiency is the main economic objection to monopoly.

THE CASE FOR MONOPOLY: INNOVATION

Some economists believe that monopoly is conducive to technological innovation that a competitive order would not generate. If such were the case, the disadvantages of monopoly noted above—inefficiency and unfair income distribution—might be offset by its dynamic advantages. Greater outward shifts in the production-possibilities frontier could compensate for monopoly's failure to operate on the frontier at any single point in time.

Economists have asked what type of market structure—perfect competition or monopoly—is better suited to creating significant new inventions. *Monopoly* and *big business* are not the same; as we have shown, monopolies can be relatively small. But more often than not, monopolies (or companies that possess considerable monopoly power) are giant concerns. Giant corporations like AT&T, DuPont, and IBM maintain enormous privately financed laboratories and employ thousands of scientists. Indeed, Nobel Prizes for the discovery of the laser and the tran-

sistor were awarded to scientists employed by giant corporations.

The ability of large companies to finance research and product development has caused some prominent economists to argue that big businesses are more likely to come up with significant scientific inventions than competitive businesses.

As the noted Austrian-born economist Joseph Schumpeter put it,

> As soon as we go into the details and inquire into the individual items in which progress was most conspicuous (since 1899), the trail leads not to the doors that work under conditions of comparatively free competition but precisely to the doors of the large concerns—which, as in the case of agricultural machinery, also account for much of the progress in the competitive sector—and a shocking suspicion dawns upon us that big business may have had more to do with creating (our high) standard of life than keeping it down.[8]

Why does Schumpeter refer to this conclusion as a "shocking suspicion"? Before Schumpeter's writings, economists maintained that monopolies were not especially innovative because they are not pressured by the forces of competition to innovate. Yet Schumpeter argues that monopolies are responsible for our important technological advances!

Schumpeter did not believe that innovation by monopoly would yield a permanent competitive advantage or that it would shield monopolists from long-run competition. Schumpeter believed in "creative destruction." Innovations that give a monopolist large economic profits spur economic progress, but the monopoly position will be only transitory. Eventually, another large concern will come up with a superior innovation, the original monopoly will lose out, and a new monopoly will take its place, until in turn, it is replaced by a more innovative monopoly.

Schumpeter's theme of the innovational efficiency of monopoly has been taken up by other economists. John K. Galbraith argues in a slightly different way:[9]

8. Joseph Schumpeter, *Capitalism, Socialism, and Democracy,* 2nd ed. (New York: Harper and Brothers, 1942), pp. 81-82.
9. John K. Galbraith, *American Capitalism,* Rev. ed. (Boston: Houghton Mifflin, 1956), p. 86.

A benign Providence has made modern industry of a few large firms an almost perfect instrument for inducing technological change. . . . There is no more pleasant fiction than that technological change is the product of the matchless ingenuity of the small man forced by competition to employ his wits better than his neighbor. Unhappily, it is a fiction. Technical development has long since become the preserve of the scientist and engineer. Most of the cheap and simple inventions have, to put it bluntly, been made.

What are we to make of the arguments for and against the dynamic efficiency of monopoly? On the one hand, it is argued that competition forces business firms to be innovative. On the other hand, we hear that monopoly and big business are required to create significant technological breakthroughs. Which view is correct?

What has been the actual relationship between market structure and technological innovation?[10] While the evidence is not overwhelming, it is safe to say that the evidence does not support the extreme Galbraith-Schumpeter position, despite the plausibility of their arguments.

In a major study, John Jewkes, David Sawers, and Richard Stillerman compiled case histories of 61 important 20th-century inventions.[11] They found that less than one third were discovered in large industrial laboratories. A little over one half were the product of academic investigators or of individuals working independently of any research organization. In another study, Willard F. Mueller found that of the 25 most significant inventions pioneered by DuPont, only 10 were developed in DuPont laboratories. The rest came from small independent researchers.[12]

F. M. Scherer summarizes the evidence and its bearing on public policy as follows: ''No single

firm size is uniquely conducive to technological progress. There is room for firms of all sizes. What we want, therefore, may be a diversity of sizes, each with its own special advantages and disadvantages.''[13]

Diversity can be important to technological innovation. A small firm might discover a new product or process, but a large firm may be required to put the invention on the shelf for the consumer to enjoy it. Basic ideas may come from small firms or even individuals, but a large laboratory may be required to develop the idea to the point where it can be put to practical use.

THE EXTENT OF MONOPOLY: EVIDENCE FROM PRICE CEILINGS

Earlier this chapter noted that the losses from monopoly have been estimated to be relatively small in the U.S. economy. An indirect method for appraising the extent of monopoly is to test the predictions of the two models.

Chapter 4 demonstrated how *price controls* in a competitive industry cause shortages. Without controls, the competitive industry is in equilibrium when price equals marginal cost for each firm. When a price ceiling is set below the equilibrium price, the ceiling price will be below the competitive industry's marginal cost. The lower price will drive quantity supplied down and quantity demanded up.

In a competitive industry, price ceilings below the equilibrium price cause shortages.

But the argument that price controls cause shortages depends on the existence of competition. In monopoly, there is a gap between price and marginal cost $(P > MC)$ in equilibrium.

Figure 5 shows why price ceilings do not cause shortages when monopoly prevails. The demand curve facing the monopoly is D. For simplicity, assume $MC = AC = \$4$. The monopoly price/quantity combination is $\$7/300$ units (point b). If

10. For a survey of this literature, see Morton Kamien and Nancy Schwartz, ''Market Structure and Innovation: A Survey,'' *Journal of Economic Literature* 8, 1 (March 1975): 1-38.

11. John Jewkes, David Sawers, and Richard Stillerman, *The Sources of Invention* (New York: St. Martins Press, 1959), pp. 71-85.

12. Willard F. Mueller, ''The Origins of the Basic Inventions Underlying DuPont's Major Product and Process Inventions,'' in *The Rate and Direction of Innovative Activity* (Princeton: Princeton University Press, 1962), pp. 323-46.

13. F. M. Scherer, *Industrial Market Structure and Economic Performance, 2nd ed.* (Boston: Houghton Mifflin, 1980), p. 418.

Example 2

The Patent Puzzle

Patents in the United States allow an inventor the exclusive right to use the invention for a period of 17 years. In order to be patentable, the invention must fulfill three criteria: 1) the invention must not have been obvious to a competent investigator; 2) it must not have been previously discovered; 3) it must be useful.

The main purpose of patents is to stimulate the invention or development of new products or processes. The benefit of the patent system is that it may give rise to more innovation than would otherwise occur. If an inventor could not patent an idea, the fear of imitators legally "stealing" the idea might discourage the investment of the time and energy required to make the discovery. To the private inventor, it may be impossible to capture all the profits from the innovation if others are allowed to imitate the idea. Thus, since there are costs of innovation, it is conceivable that the short-run profits from innovation might be inadequate to stimulate an appropriate degree of technical advance without patents.

The patent system sets up a temporary monopoly to make sure that the inventor is able to make enough profits from the idea to justify the costs. To reap the benefit of new inventions, society pays the cost of granting monopolies and creating monopoly distortions (*deadweight losses*).

Are patents necessary? Is it necessary to give out patents for 17 years? Can patents be used to achieve monopolies for periods longer than 17 years?

1. Economists William Nordhaus and Fritz Machlup have estimated that the best life of a patent might be substantially less than 17 years due to the losses from monopoly.

2. The short run is sometimes a long while in calendar time; the new inventor may have four to five years in which to capture spectacular profits. Moreover, without patents the inventor does not have to tell anyone what the secret is. Consider the trade secrets of Coca-Cola or Big Mac hamburgers. These companies have made large profits while being able to keep their recipes secret.

3. The patent system can be perverted by companies seeking "improvement patents" that prolong the true life of the patent indefinitely. The General Electric Company acquired many patents on improvements on the basic Edison light bulb: on the argon-filled lamp, on tungsten filaments, on tipless bulbs, on internally frosted bulbs, etc. Through this pyramiding of patents, the General Electric Company maintained a monopoly position from 1892 to the 1930s.

Some think the patent system should be scrapped; others think not. As Jewkes, Sawers, and Stillerman write: "It is almost impossible to conceive of any existing social institution so faulty in so many ways. It survives only because there seems to be nothing better."

Sources: William D. Nordhaus, *Invention, Growth, and Welfare* (Cambridge, Mass.: MIT Press, 1969), pp. 76-82; Fritz Machlup, "Patents," *International Encyclopedia of the Social Sciences,* vol 11 (London: Macmillan, 1968); John Jewkes, David Sawers, and Richard Stillerman, *The Sources of Invention* (New York: St Martin's Press, 1959), p. 253.

---

the ceiling price is set at $6, the monopoly will be able to sell 400 units. Clearly the monopolist will want to sell all 400 units because profits (= $800) would be larger than if any smaller quantity was sold at the price of $6. Thus, in a monopoly, an effective price ceiling established below the uncontrolled monopoly price but above marginal cost will not cause a shortage.

A price ceiling imposed on a monopoly below the monopoly price but above marginal cost will not cause a shortage.

Historical evidence does not support the assumption that business behavior is overall monopolistic: virtually every price control that has been instituted in history has been associated with shortages.

As far as the effects of price controls are concerned, history shows that the world behaves more like competition than like monopoly. Although the real world is often a blend of both monopoly and competition, the blend leans more toward the competitive side in this particular respect.

Figure 5
The Effect of Price Ceilings on Monopoly

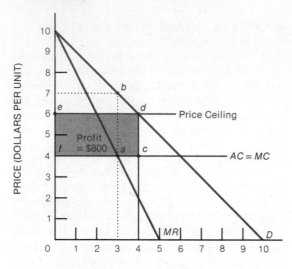

QUANTITY (HUNDREDS OF UNITS)

If there were no price ceilings, this monopolist would produce where marginal revenue and marginal cost are equal—namely, at an output level of 300 units—and would charge a price of $7 per unit. If a price ceiling is imposed below the monopoly price but above marginal cost, the monopolist will sell more. At a price of $6, the monopolist will sell 400 units because profits will be maximized (the area of the rectangle *edcf*) at that output. Price ceilings can increase output in the case of monopoly.

This chapter has compared the extremes of monopoly and competition under the assumption that both are feasible. The next chapter examines the many varieties of oligopoly behavior that combine elements of monopoly and perfect competition.

Summary

1. In an ideal world, perfect competition would exist in every industry. Consumers would be well-informed, and externalities would be absent. Efficiency is present when society's resources are so organized that it is impossible to make at least one person better off by any reallocation of resources without harming

someone else. Efficiency prevails when price and marginal cost are equal—which occurs under conditions of perfect competition.

2. Even though perfectly competitive economies are efficient, the resulting distribution of income may not be equitable from the viewpoint of society. Perfect competition is compatible with an unfair distribution of income. *Externalities* are unpriced costs and benefits of economic activities. When they exist perfect competition is not efficient.

3. Monopoly can be inefficient because of contrived scarcity, monopoly rent seeking, or X-inefficiency. Monopoly may also result in an unfair distribution of income because of monopoly profits. Monopoly profits can be taxed away by lump-sum taxation without affecting output and prices.

4. Schumpeter and Galbraith argue that large business firms or large concentrations of monopoly power are conducive to technological progress. Modern research fails to support this view.

5. A price ceiling imposed on a monopoly below the monopoly price but above *MC* will not cause a shortage. The fact that price controls have historically been associated with shortages suggests that world markets behave more like competition than monopoly.

Key Terms

efficiency
inefficiency
economic equity
• externalities
private costs
external costs
private benefits
external benefits
social costs
social benefits
deadweight loss
monopoly rent seeking
X-inefficiency
lump-sum tax

Questions and Problems

1. Restate the reasons why $P = MC$ is the condition for economic efficiency.
2. Give examples of positive external benefits and of negative external costs.
3. Why do economists say that monopolists contrive scarcity?

Price (dollars per unit)	Quantity (units)
20	0
15	500
10	1,000
5	1,500
0	2,000

4. The MC of production in Industry A is $8 and is equal to average cost. The demand schedule is linear and is given in the table. What is the deadweight loss of monopoly in this case due to contrived scarcity? What is the maximum loss due to monopoly rent seeking?
5. Explain why a lump-sum tax on monopoly profits would not affect monopoly output and prices while a tax on each unit of output would.
6. Explain the resource-allocation problem that would exist in a competitive market economy if the following had externalities: a) production of electricity by burning coal, b) immunization of children against communicable diseases. Draw a supply-and-demand diagram for each indicating both the market and the correct resource-allocation result.

12

Oligopoly

Chapter Preview

Oligopoly is an umbrella term that covers market forms between monopoly and monopolistic competition. This chapter explains why some oligopolies behave like monopolies while others act like competitive industries. Oligopoly behavior is rich and varied and presents many puzzles that require solution. This chapter will describe the characteristics of oligopoly, how oligopolies behave, and the pitfalls of collusive behavior.

OLIGOPOLY DEFINED

*An **oligopoly** is an industry characterized by:*
1. the relatively small number of firms in the industry.
2. moderate to high barriers to entry.

3. the production of either homogeneous (aluminum or steel) or differentiated products (automobiles or breakfast cereals).
4. price searching; oligopolists are able to exercise some control over price.
5. recognized mutual interdependence

The number of firms in an industry is "relatively small" if the industry is characterized by **mutual interdependence.**

Mutual interdependence is characteristic of an industry in which the actions of one firm will affect other firms in the industry and that these interrelationships will be recognized.

Mutual interdependence is the most crucial feature of oligopoly.

THE PERVASIVENESS OF OLIGOPOLY

There is no magic formula for measuring the extent of oligopoly in the American economy. Some economists believe that oligopoly is the predominant form of industrial organization; others argue that oligopoly is not so important. A tool economists use to gauge the extent of oligopoly is the **concentration ratio** (see Table 1).

*The x-firm **concentration ratio** is the percentage of industry sales (or output, or labor force, or assets) accounted for by the x largest firms.*

The 4-firm sales concentration ratio, for example, is the percentage of industry sales accounted for by the four largest firms in the industry. Concentration ratios are an imperfect guide to the extent of oligopoly for three reasons. First, competition from foreign producers or from substitute products at home. The 4-firm concentration ratio of the U.S. automobile industry is more than 93 percent—a figure that fails to measure the competition of foreign imports. The 4-firm concentration ratio in primary aluminum (79 percent) does not show the competition from stainless steel, copper, and so on.

Second, concentration ratios may not measure concentration in the relevant market. The 4-firm concentration ratio in the aircraft industry is 66 percent, but it is 97 percent in the commercial transport type aircraft industry, where Boeing and McDonnell-Douglas dominate sales.

Third, many markets, such as newspapers, cement, and real estate, are local or regional. Concentration ratios for percentages of national sales are misleading in such markets. A local or regional firm may dominate its relevant market, and this dominance would not necessarily be reflected by the national concentration ratio.

Despite these difficulties, concentration ratios—carefully used—can be useful in measuring oligopoly. A leading authority on industrial organization, F. M. Scherer, argues that a 4-firm concentration ratio of 40 percent or more indicates that the industry can be considered an oligopoly and that a 4-firm ratio of 50 percent or more is fairly conclusive evidence of oligopoly. Using

these criteria for industry classification, 50 percent of all American manufacturing industry can be characterized as oligopolistic.[1]

There is a widespread false impression that the degree of concentration of the American economy has been increasing over time. In manufacturing, this is not the case, as column (1) of Table 2 shows. The share of manufacturing output accounted for by highly concentrated industries has not changed markedly for more than 50 years.[2]

One reason for the impression of growing concentration is that the share of manufacturing output of the largest 100 companies has grown from 23 percent in 1947 to 33 percent in 1972, as shown in column (2) of Table 2. This increase has been largely due to company mergers across industries, however, not to increasing concentration within a particular industry.[3]

The nonmanufacturing sector is less concentrated than the manufacturing sector. Construction, agriculture, and many service industries are characterized by small firms and low concentration ratios. The same can be said of wholesale and retail trade, although the trade sector does have its giants like Holiday Inn, McDonald's, and Sears.

Oligopoly, as measured by concentration ratios, is therefore common in manufacturing but is less prevalent in other sectors. Unlike pure monopoly, where ideal examples are hard to locate, there is no such problem with oligopoly. Most industrial organization experts agree that steel, automobiles, breakfast cereals, cigarettes, aluminum, soaps and detergents, and drugs are among the many manufacturing industries that are oligopolies.

OLIGOPOLY VERSUS MONOPOLY

Some economists think the distinctions between oligopoly and monopoly are small. In the words of John Kenneth Galbraith, "So long as there are only a few massive firms in an industry,

---

1. F. M. Scherer, *Industrial Market Structure and Economic Performance,* 2nd ed. (Boston: Houghton Mifflin, 1980), p. 67.
2. This result has been demonstrated using a series of alternate measures of concentration for the period 1947 to 1972. See Scherer, *Industrial Market Structure,* pp. 68–70.
3. James V. Koch, *Industrial Organization and Prices,* 2nd ed. (Englewood Cliffs, N.J.: Prentice-Hall, 1980), p. 181.

Table 1
Selected Concentration Ratios in Manufacturing, 1972

Industry	4-Firm Concentration Ratio (percent)	Number of Firms
Canned bakery foods	95	n/a
Motor vehicles and car bodies	93	165
Cereal breakfast foods	90	34
Cigarettes	84	13
Photographic equipment	74	555
Tires and inner tubes	73	136
Aircraft	66	141
Metal cans	66	134
Aluminum sheets	65	24
Soaps and other detergents	62	577
Motor vehicle parts	61	1,748
Cookies and crackers	59	257
Malt beverages	52	108
Internal combustion engines	50	145
Radio and TV sets	49	343
Farm machinery	47	1,465
Blast furnaces and steel mills	45	241
Construction machinery	43	644
Toilet preparations	38	593
Hardware	35	963
Women's hosiery	35	256
Men's footwear	34	118
Gray iron foundries	34	893
Women's footwear	32	294
Confectionary products	32	917
Weaving mills (cotton)	31	190
Petroleum refining	31	152
Sporting and athletic goods	28	1,441
Pharmaceutical preparations	26	680
Periodicals	26	2,451
Mobile homes	26	352
Paper mills	24	194
Paints	22	1,318
Meat-packing plants	22	2,968
Canned fruits and vegetables	20	766
Tufted carpets	20	333
Men's and boys' suits	19	721
Radio and TV equipment	19	1,524
Corrugated and solid fiber boxes	18	709
Sawmills	18	7,664
Nuts and bolts	16	581
Wood household furniture	14	2,160
Valves and pipe fittings	11	643
Women's dresses	9	5,294
Ready mixed concrete	6	3,978
Commercial printing	4	8,160

Source: U.S. Department of Commerce, "Concentration Ratios in Manufacturing," *1972 Census of Manufacturers,* MC72 (SR)-2, October 1975.

each must act with a view of the welfare of all.''[4] While some oligopolies act like a **shared monopoly**, many do not.

*A **shared monopoly** is an oligopoly in which all the firms in the industry coordinate price and output by some means. In its extreme form, the industry behaves like one gigantic firm.*

Galbraith's view that concentrated oligopoly and monopoly are virtually equivalent is disputed by most industrial organization specialists.[5] If oligopoly were simply a complex monopoly, this chapter would be very short: it could just refer the reader back to the monopoly theory chapter. The truth is that oligopoly encompasses a broad range of market behavior and performance. The task of oligopoly theory is to study the circumstances under which oligopoly might approximate either monopoly (on the one hand) or competition (on the other hand).

Some oligopolies behave much like shared monopolies; they agree on prices, and they agree on which firms get which contracts. Other oligopolies make pricing decisions according to tradition; one acts as a price leader, and others automatically follow. Still other oligopolies engage in competitive pricing wars, behaving much like a perfectly competitive or monopolistic-competitive industry. One question oligopoly theory must answer is: why is there no single model of oligopoly behavior?

BARRIERS TO ENTRY

The prime characteristic of oligopoly is the relatively small number of firms in the industry. Barriers to entry explain the limited number of firms. A pioneering researcher in this area, Joe S. Bain, defines **barriers to entry** in the following way:[6]

---

4. John K. Galbraith, *American Capitalism*, rev. ed. (Cambridge: The Riverside Press, 1956).
5. Oliver Williamson, *Markets and Hierarchies: Analysis and Antitrust Implications* (New York: The Free Press, 1975), p. 234.
6. Joe S. Bain, *Barriers to New Competition* (Cambridge, Mass.: Harvard University Press, 1965).

Table 2

Trends in Concentration in American Manufacturing: Two Measures

Year	Percentage of Output by Firms with 4-Firm Concentration Ratio of 50 percent or Above (1)	Percentage of Output of 100 Largest Firms (2)
1895–1904	33	n.a.
1947	24	23
1954	30	30
1958	30	32
1972	29	33

Sources: G. Warren Nutter, *The Extent of Enterprise Monopoly in the United States, 1899–1939* (Chicago: University of Chicago Press, 1951), pp. 35–48, 112–150; F. M. Scherer, *Industrial Market Structure and Economic Performance* (Boston: Houghton Mifflin, 1980), pp. 68–69; *Concentration Ratios in Manufacturing, 1972 Census of Manufacturing*, Table 1.

*A **barrier to entry** is any advantage that existing firms hold over firms that might seek to enter the market.*

Economists recognize several different types of barriers to entry, including economies of scale, product differentiation, control over input supplies, government barriers to entry, large capital requirements, and technological advantages.

Economies of Scale

Economies of scale provide established firms with cost advantages over potential entrants. The established firm that produces a large volume of output will operate farther out on the general declining long-run average cost curve. New firms normally must enter the market producing small volumes of output relative to established firms.

Figure 1 depicts a situation in which a new firm's costs are higher because it must—at the beginning—have a smaller plant size than established firms. Clearly new firms will operate at less than the minimum efficient plant size and will produce at higher average cost than established firms.

Figure 1
The Cost Advantage of Established Firms over New Firms

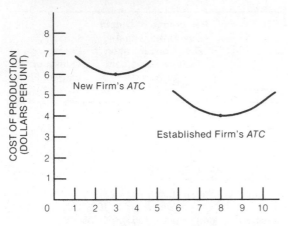

When there are economies of scale in an industry, established firms with large plants will have a lower average total cost than new firms that might operate with a smaller plant size.

Examples of oligopolistic industries protected by economies of scale barriers are automobile and tractor manufacturing and electrical power generation. Industries with low economies of scale barriers to entry are canned goods, cigarettes, meat packing, and tire manufacturing.

Product Differentiation

The more highly differentiated the product in the eyes of the consumer, the higher the barriers to entry. If the buyer is convinced that a particular brand of medication is superior to competitive brands or that a particular brand of cigarettes tastes better than others, the manufacturer has succeeded in erecting a barrier to entry.

One major means of creating product differentiation is advertising. If advertising successfully differentiates the product, higher prices can be charged without causing the entry of competitors who drive the price back down. For this reason, some economists view advertising as anticompetitive. Others stress that advertising is procompetitive because it increases the amount of product information available to the consumer.

Control over Input Supplies

If established firms control crucial inputs and can deny new firms access to these inputs, a barrier to entry has been erected.

An example of this type of entry barrier is provided by the American steel industry. The 9 largest steel producers and the 4 major iron ore merchants account for more than 95 percent of ore reserves in the nation's richest iron ore area. Moreover, only U.S. Steel Corporation has sufficient iron ore reserves, and other companies must rely on U.S. Steel for ore. The major U.S. steel producers also enjoy a commanding lead over small companies in the ownership of foreign ore reserves in Venezuela, Liberia, and Labrador.[7]

Government Barriers to Entry

If state, local, or national governments protect established firms with exclusive franchises, operating charters, and licensing arrangements that keep other firms out of the market, the entry of new firms is restricted not by economic factors, but by the force of the law.

There are numerous examples of governmental barriers to entry. Local governments grant exclusive franchises to operate concessions at municipal airports, and they often control entry into the taxicab business. The federal government for many years limited entry into the commercial airline and trucking industries, and protected the Bell System from the competition of independent long-distance companies. The Federal Communications Commission has controlled entry into radio and television broadcasting by administratively allocating broadcast frequencies.

Large Capital Requirements

In many industries, the amount of capital required to operate a firm at its efficient size is enormous. Table 3 shows the average value of capital assets for selected capital-intensive manufacturing industries in 1976. In the steel industry, the average firm equipped with blast furnaces uses

7.   Walter Adams, ed., *The Structure of American Industry*, 4th ed. (New York: Macmillan, 1971), pp. 77–78.

Product Differentiation Through Advertising: Bayer and St. Joseph's Aspirin

A classic example of product differentiation through advertising is the case of Bayer and St. Joseph's aspirin. Bayer has typically spent large sums of money advertising its adult strength aspirin, while St. Joseph has spent very little. Both companies, however, have spent equal sums on advertising their children's aspirin. The result: The Bayer adult aspirin sells at a price 60 percent above St. Joseph's, while the children's brands sell for the same price.

Source: This case study is based upon 1971 testimony before the Subcommittee on Monopoly, Select Committee on Small Business, and cited in James V. Koch, *Industrial Organization and Prices*, 2nd ed. (Englewood Cliffs, N.J.: Prentice-Hall, 1980), p. 324. ⚹

---

about $117 million in capital assets (in 1981 dollars). The average cigarette manufacturer has capital assets of $97 million. Such capital requirements may serve to protect existing firms from the competition of new firms.

Technological Advantages

Established firms may have a crucial technology that is denied to potential competitors. The exclusive right to use a technological innovation may be granted by the government in the form of a patent or it may be achieved as a result of superior research and development by an established firm.

Examples of concentrated oligopolies based upon technological advantages and patents are the prescription-drug industry, shoe manufacturing, and telephone-equipment manufacturing.

OLIGOPOLISTIC INTERDEPENDENCE

Oligopoly theory is more complicated than the theories of perfect competition, pure monopoly, and monopolistic competition because there is no one theory of oligopoly.

In **atomistic competition** there are many firms. "Many" firms are enough firms so that no individual firm can by its actions affect the market as a whole or the behavior of any of its rival firms. When there are many firms, the behavior of one firm is independent of the actual behavior of other firms or the expectation of how other firms might behave.

*To the extent that each firm is a small percentage of the total market, perfect or monopolistic competition can be referred to as **atomistic competition.***

On the other hand, there are so few firms in oligopoly that each firm's actions will influence the market as a whole and may also influence the behavior of rival firms. Oligopolistic firms are interdependent. In an oligopoly, Firm A's behavior depends on Firm B's behavior, and Firm B's behavior depends on Firm A's behavior.

Table 3

Use of Capital in Manufacturing: Value of Capital Assets Per Firm, Selected Industries, 1976

Industry	Average Value of Capital Assets per Firm (millions of 1981 dollars)
Blast furnaces, steel	116.6
Cigarettes	97.1
Alkalines and chlorine	57.7
Aluminum sheet	56.1
Primary copper	53.5
Malt beverages	38.5
Tires and tubes	31.3
Turbines, generators	26.6

Source: U.S. Department of Commerce, Bureau of the Census, *Annual Survey of Manufactures, 1976.*

Example 2

Classification of Manufacturing Industries by Barriers to Entry

When manufacturing industries are grouped according to the amount of barriers to entry, it is clear that some manufacturing industries are protected by high barriers to entry; others have very little protection from the entry of new competition.

Barriers to entry explain the fewness characteristic of some oligopolies.

Source: Based on William Shepherd, *Market Power and Economic Welfare* (New York: Random House, 1970), p. 126.

High Barriers to Entry	Moderately High Barriers to Entry	Low Barriers to Entry
Distilled liquors	Cereals	Meat packing
Wood pulp	Flour mixes	Flour
Newspapers	Bread	Canned fruits and vegetables
General periodicals	Sugar	Woolen and cotton textiles
Drugs	Soft drinks	Clothing
Soaps	Cigarettes	Brick and tile
Explosives	Lumber	Small metal products
Glass and glass products	Paper	Wooden furniture
Automobiles	Periodicals	Corrugated containers
Aircraft and parts	Gypsum products	Printing
Photographic supplies	Metal cans	Footwear
Steel	Typewriters	Cement
Copper	Books	Foundries
Tractors	Gases	
Computers	Organic chemicals	
Copying equipment	Inorganic chemicals	
Heavy electrical equipment	Synthetic rubber	
Electrical lamps	Toilet preparations	
Telephone equipment	Fertilizers	
Buses	Petroleum refining	
Locomotives	Tires and tubes	
Shipbuilding	Aluminum	
	Heavy industrial machinery	
	Large household appliances	

In oligopoly there is a mutual interdependence of actions among firms.

The Oligopolist's Demand Curve

Because of the mutual interdependence of firms in an oligopoly, the demand curve for an oligopolist's product cannot be defined until the behavior of rival firms is specified. The behavior of rival firms can range from complete independence of other oligopolists to complete coordination.

Consider the Ford Motor Company. It produces cars and competes with a handful of other automobile manufacturers around the world. Suppose that at the current price of $6000 Ford is selling 1 million units of its compact car—the Escort—with the comparable compact cars of Toyota, Volkswagen, Datsun, Chrysler, and General Motors selling for comparable prices. Point *a* in Figure 2 describes the current situation confronting an oligopolist.

Point *a* lies on Ford's demand curve, since 1 million units are being sold at a price of $6,000. What happens to Ford's demand curve if Ford reduces its price to $5,000? Figure 2 shows two extreme scenarios. Point *b* represents Ford's quantity demanded if the rest of the industry (General Motors and foreign producers) behaves *in an exactly parallel fashion,* lowering prices by the same percentage as Ford. In this case, Ford increases its sales to 1.25 million cars because auto prices in general have fallen relative to the prices of substitutes for autos. Point *b* represents the shared-monopoly effect on Ford's quantity demanded.

Point *b′* represents Ford's quantity demanded when the rest of the industry behaves *completely independently* of Ford: when Ford lowers its price, the rest of the industry continues to charge the same prices as before. In this case, there will be a large increase in Ford's sales to 1.75 million. The price of Ford cars has fallen relative to those of its closest substitutes. In Figure 2, *b* and *b′* represent the extremes of the possible positions of the demand curve. The actual position could be anywhere between *b* and *b′*, depending upon how competitors react.

If Ford raises its price to $7,000, the same range of outcomes is possible. Point *c* is a point on Ford's demand curve when there is complete coordination of pricing actions by all oligopolists. In this case, Ford sales fall to 0.75 million units. Point *c′* is a point on Ford's demand curve when there is complete independence of actions, with the other oligopolists holding the line on prices. Ford sales might then fall considerably to point *c′*, where only 0.25 million units are sold. The range of possible outcomes is represented by the line *c′c*.

In Figure 2, the demand curve for Ford's compact cars can be anywhere in the shaded region of the two triangles. The slope of the demand curve can vary from the slope of the line *cab* to the slope of *c′ab′*.

The demand curve and, hence, marginal revenue cannot be determined in oligopoly until the actions of rival firms are known.

The Kinked Demand Curve

Suppose Ford discovers its rivals tend to match Ford's price cuts but hold their prices when Ford

Figure 2
Why the Oligopolist's Demand Curve Is Indeterminant

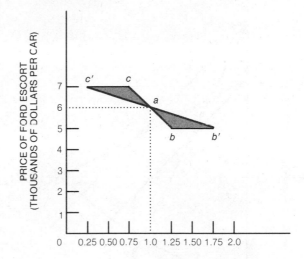

At point *a,* Ford sells 1 million cars at a price of $6,000. If Ford lowers its price to $5,000, what happens to sales depends upon how Ford's competitors react. Point *b* results when Ford's rivals match Ford's price reduction. Point *b′* results if they do not follow Ford's price reduction. If Ford raises its price to $7,000, what happens to sales again depends upon the reactions of competitors. Point *c′* results if they keep their prices constant; point *c* results when they match Ford's increase.

raises its price. In this case, Ford's demand curve would be *c′ab*. The demand curve would have a "kink" in it at point *a,* the current price.

*A **kinked demand curve** results when other firms match a firm's price decreases but don't match the firm's price increases.*

The assumptions of the **kinked demand curve** appear to be plausible in certain industries. They describe an oligopoly firm that is not the industry's **price leader** because when the firm raises its prices, the other firms keep their prices constant. There is, therefore, some independence of action when the oligopolist raises its prices. If Oligoplist A raises its price, Oligopolists B, C, and D may take the opportunity to expand their

Figure 3
An Oligopoly Firm Facing a Kinked Demand Curve

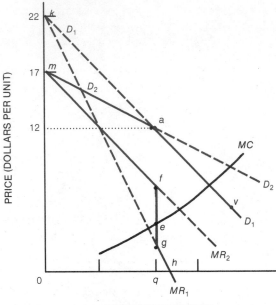

This firm's rivals will follow price reductions but will not follow price increases. Therefore, for prices below the current $12 price, the demand curve is D_1 below point a; for prices above $12, the demand curve is D_2 above point a. The marginal revenue curve corresponding to the kinked demand curve mav is mfgh. A portion of the MR curve is vertical (from f to g). MC can shift up or down (as long as it remains within this vertical portion of the MR curve) without changing the firm's price or output decisions. The kinked demand schedule is one explanation for the inflexibility of oligopoly prices.

markets by holding prices constant. On the other hand, if Oligopolist A lowers its prices, the remaining firms may fear the loss of customers and may cut their prices as well.

*A **price leader** is a firm whose price changes are consistently imitated by rival firms.*

The kinked-demand model appears to hold for some industries (and firms) but not others. In the cigarette industry, Liggett & Meyers (which accounts for 2 percent of cigarette sales) has found in the past that its price increases are not followed by other cigarette manufacturers but that its price decreases are followed. If Phillip Morris, which accounts for 31 percent of industry sales, raises its prices, however, other firms tend to follow suit. Thus Phillip Morris (the manufacturer of Marlboros) may not face a kink. A company like GM (which has lower costs than its domestic rivals) may not face a kink, but Ford and Chrysler may.

If a firm is the price leader in its industry, it will not face a kink in its demand curve because rival firms follow both price increases and price reductions. If the firm is not the industry's price leader, it is likely to face a kink unless it is so small relative to the industry that its pricing actions are ignored.[8]

Figure 3 shows an oligopoly firm facing a kinked demand curve. Since the firm faces D_1D_1 for price reductions and D_2D_2 for price increases, its demand curve is mav with the kink at point a. The firm's MR curve mfgh is discontinuous owing to the kink. The MR curve follows MR_2 from the price of $17 to point f, which is directly below the kink at $12. When the price is lowered below $12, MR follows MR_1, because other firms will match the firm's price cuts. Hence, the MR curve has a vertical segment feg, and the entire MR curve is mfgh. Because the MC curve cuts MR at point e, the firm is maximizing profits at the current price of $12.

Note: If the firm's costs changed a bit and the MC curve shifted up or down within the range f to g, MR would still equal MC at the current price! The firm would not change its output and price. Moreover, there could even be slight changes in demand conditions without altering the profit-maximizing price.

According to the kinked demand curve theory:
1. prices will be more stable in a kinked-demand oligopoly than in atomistic competition.
2. prices will be more stable in a kinked-demand oligopoly than in a pure monopoly because (as the monopoly chapter showed) monopoly prices change when costs change.

8. Scherer, *Industrial Market Structure*, p. 184.

Example 3

The Airline Industry and the Kinked Demand Curve

A recent example of a kinked-demand oligopoly is the airline industry. Since 1978, airline prices have been almost completely freed of government controls, so the airlines can set their own prices. In the early years of deregulation, some smaller airlines such as Air Florida, Southwest Airlines, and Texas International could lower their fares without the larger national airlines following. Due to the recessions of 1979 and 1981–82, the volume of air traffic fell, and the larger airlines such as Delta, TWA, and Pan American began to offer lower fares in 1981 and 1982. At this point, the demand curve became kinked. Other major airlines followed fare reductions for fear of losing market shares. Traditionally nondiscount airlines such as Delta and American matched virtually all fair reductions. When the largest American airline—United—attempted in 1981 to raise its fares and the other airlines did not follow, United abandoned its experiment with higher fares. Kinked-demand behavior for price reductions is evident in the cases where airlines offer to match the fares of competing airlines, as many did in 1982.

The kinked-demand model of oligopoly raises as many questions as it answers. The kinked demand curve applies to a limited range of situations. It does not answer the most important question of all; namely, why the kink is located where it is.

One reason for the appeal of the kinked-demand model is that it predicts that oligopoly prices will be more stable than in atomistic competition or monopoly. A number of studies have found that oligopoly prices on the average tend to change less than other prices. There is still debate among authorities who have investigated this issue, but for those who believe oligopoly prices tend to be more stable, the kinked-demand curve is a logical explanation.[9]

9. J. Fred Weston and Steven Lustgarten investigated price changes between 1954 and 1973 and found that, typically, the higher the concentration ratio the lower the annual percentage price change. This study is one of a long series that followed the 1935 studies of Gardner Means, who coined the term *administered prices* to characterize inflexible oligopoly prices. The major challenge to the administered-price notion was mounted by George Stigler and James Kindahl, who maintain that the list prices of oligopoly products like steel, automobiles, and aluminum conceal many hidden discounts that understate oligopoly price flexibility. *See:* J. Fred Weston and Steven H. Lustgarten, "Concentration and Wage-Price Changes," in eds. Harvey J. Goldschmid et al., *Industrial Concentration: The New Learning* (Boston: Little, Brown, 1974), p. 312; George Stigler and James K. Kindahl, *The Behavior of Industrial Prices* (New York: National Bureau of Economic Research, 1970).

COLLUSION AND OLIGOPOLY

The kinked demand model of oligopoly assumes there is no overt coordination among firms. Each firm knows that price increases will not be followed but that price reductions will be, and firms make their pricing decisions on the basis of this industry behavior pattern.

Other models of oligopoly assume there is collusion (secret agreements on cooperation) on pricing and output decisions. Methods of coordination range from formal agreements on price and market shares made in secret (in those countries like the United States where they are normally against the law) or openly (in cases where such agreements are legal and even sanctioned by government) to tacit coordination without any formal agreement. The effectiveness of coordination will vary. In some cases, coordination will be rigidly enforced; in other cases, it will be loosely enforced and will tend to break down.

The three major methods of oligopoly coordination are:

1. cartel agreements,
2. price leadership, and
3. conscious parallelism.

Cartel Agreements

The simplest way for an oligopoly to coordinate pricing and output policy is to enter a **cartel**

Figure 4
Collusive Oligopoly

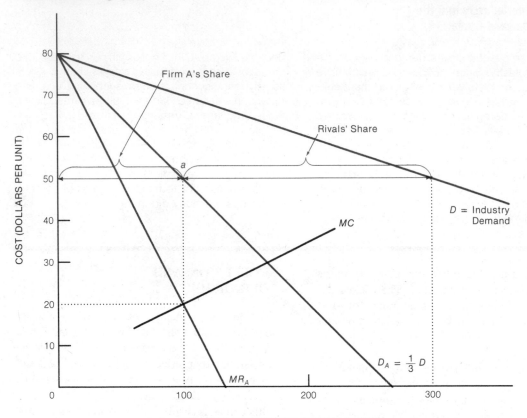

Curve *D* represents the industry demand curve. The industry consists of three oligopolistic firms who agree to share the market equally and charge the same price. D_A is the demand schedule of Firm A. It is one third of the industry demand schedule. MR_A is the marginal revenue curve of Firm A. Firm A will maximize profits by producing that output at which *MC* equals *MR*, or 100 units at $50 per unit (point *a*).

Why would Firm A be tempted to cheat on the agreement? If A lowers price a little, Firm A gains sales from its two rivals. As long as A's lower price exceeds A's *MC*, Firm A's profits will increase. The cost of cheating is that if all three firms cheat, a competitive bidding war could break out, and they could end up earning virtually no economic profits.

agreement, binding on all parties, to set the prices or market shares of each producer. Presumably, such agreements would allow the oligopolistic firms to operate their industry as a shared monopoly—to earn monopoly profits for the industry as a whole.

*A **cartel** is an arrangement that allows the participating firms to operate the industry as a shared monopoly. In effect, the participating firms coordinate their output and*

pricing decisions to yield that industry price and output combination that would have prevailed had this industry been a pure monopoly with each firm as a branch of one giant firm.

Consider an oligopolistic industry that consists of three identical firms (with the same costs and producing the same product). Assume that barriers to entry are so high that the three established firms need not worry about the attraction of new entrants should profits be high. The three identical firms agree to each share one third of the market and to charge the same monopoly price.

Joint Profit Maximization. How each firm selects its profit-maximizing price is shown in Figure 4. The industry demand curve is D. Firm A's demand and marginal revenue curves (which are the same as those of firms B and C) are shown as D_A and MR_A. Since a cartel agreement is in force to share the market equally, Firm A's demand curve is D_A ($= \frac{1}{3} \times D$). The monopoly price is determined by drawing the MR_A curve corresponding to D_A and locating its intersection with the MC curve. Firm A would maximize its profit by producing 100 units at a price of $50 per unit (point a). The other two firms also charge $50 and produce 100 units each. Industry output is 300 ($= 3 \times 100$).

The Temptation to Cheat. Notice now the position of Firm A. The two rival firms are selling 200 units at the price of $50. What would prevent Firm A from stealing some customers of the other firms by offering a slightly lower price? Firm A could charge, for instance, $49.50 and possibly obtain a great deal more business. In effect, the cartel price approximately equals the marginal revenue to the firm if it can make secret sales at slightly less than the cartel price. As long as its secret sales remain small and don't drive down the cartel price, $49.50 is now essentially the cheating firm's marginal revenue. The marginal revenue of $49.50 clearly exceeds marginal cost ($20) to each firm. Hence, substantial gains accrue to the firm that breaks the cartel agreement. Cheating on the agreement has its long-run costs, of course, since it may lead the other two firms to break the agreement. Price warfare could erupt, and economic profit would be driven down.

Cartel theory has two great and contradictory themes: 1) Every cartel member can gain through the attainment of monopoly profits if every member adheres to the cartel agreement. 2) Each cartel member can gain by cheating on the agreement if the others do not cheat.

Most cartels come and go unless they have the legal backing of governments. They have a history of instability because of the extreme difficulty of enforcing the cartel agreement. Greed leads firms into cartels; greed also leads firms to break up cartels. Very few cartels are successful over the long run.

There are numerous examples of cartel agreements on pricing. The member nations of the Organization of Petroleum Exporting Countries (OPEC) meet regularly, with full coverage by the world's press, to set (or attempt to set) the price of crude oil. The International Air Transport Association (IATA) also meets openly with the blessing of the member country governments to set airfares for travel among countries.

With some minor exceptions, formal price-setting agreements violate U.S. law, but a number of price-conspiracy cases have come to light where oligopolistic producers have met together in secret to set prices and distribute sales.

The most widely publicized case was the electrical products conspiracy case of 1961 involving top executives from General Electric, Westinghouse, Allis Chalmers, and other well-known companies. These executives met secretly to set prices and allocate contracts among companies participating in the agreement. While formal secret agreements continue to be uncovered (see Table 4), there are other less risky means of coordinating prices.

Informal agreements can also be used to coordinate pricing and output decisions. The most notable historical case of informal agreement was the so-called Gary Dinners of the early 20th century. Mr. Gary, president of U.S. Steel Corporation, would invite steel company executives representing more than 90 percent of the output of steel to dinner regularly to urge his guests to cooperate in holding prices where they were. Walter Adams describes the Gary dinners:

He exhorted them like a Methodist preacher at a camp meeting to follow the price leadership of U.S. Steel. There was no need for any formal agreements. U.S. Steel simply assumed the lead incumbent on a firm its size; its rivals followed, fully realizing the security and profitability of cooperation.[10]

10. Adams, *The Structure of American Industry,* p. 71.

Table 4
Selected Price-Fixing Conspiracies, 1961–1970

Market	Geographical Scopes	4-Firm Concentration in the Market (percent)	Number of Conspirators (and their percentage share of sales)		Number of Firms in the Market
Wrought steel wheels	National	85	5	(100)	5
Bed springs	National	<61	10		20
Metal library shelving	National	60	7	(78)	9
Self-locking nuts	National	97	4	(97)	6
Refuse collection	Local		86		102
Women's swimsuits	National	<69	9		
Steel products (wholesale)	Regional	66	5	(72)	
Gasoline	Regional	>49	12		
Milk	Local	>90	11	(>80)	13
Concrete pipe	Regional	100	4	(100)	4
Drill jig bushings	National	56	9	(82)	13
Linen supplies	Local	49	31	(90)	
Plumbing fixtures	National	76	7	(98)	15
Class rings	Regional	<100	3	(90)	5
Tickets	Regional	<78	9	(<91)	10
Baked goods (wholesale)	Regional	46	7		8
Athletic equipment	Local	>90	6	(100)	6
Dairy products	Regional	>95	3	(95)	13
Vending machines	Local	93	6	(100)	6
Ready-mix concrete	Local	86	9	(100)	9
Carbon steel sheets	National	59	10		
Liquid asphalt	Regional	56	20	(95)	

Note: The omitted figures are not available.
Source: George A. Hay and Daniel Kelly, "An Empirical Survey of Price Fixing Conspiracies," *Journal of Law and Economics* 17 (April 1974): 29–38.

Gary Dinners and their like confirm Adam Smith's perception that "people of the same trade seldom meet together, even for merriment and diversion, but the conversation ends in a conspiracy against the public, or in some contrivance to raise prices."[11]

Price Leadership

A more subtle method of collusion occurs when a recognized price leader emerges among a set of oligopolists. The price leader keeps a sharp eye on market demand and costs that are common to all firms. As noted, the price leader's price increases or decreases are followed by rival firms.

Examples of price leadership are plentiful: During the 1920s and 1930s, the "big three" cigarette manufacturers (R.J. Reynolds, American Tobacco, and Liggett & Meyers) set the classic pattern with R. J. Reynolds (Camels) serving as the price leader. In today's cigarette industry, Philip Morris has become the price leader by virtue of the market dominance of Marlboro cigarettes. The ready-to-eat breakfast-cereal industry, including Kelloggs, Post, and General Mills (the big three), has an interesting pattern of price leadership. Kelloggs leads for most product lines while General Mills and Post lead for their own best product lines. The same pattern exists for the steel industry.

Conscious Parallelism

The most subtle form of collusion is **conscious parallelism,** which uses **focal points** as a means of price setting.

11. Adam Smith, *The Wealth of Nations,* ed. Edwin Cannan (New York: Modern Library, 1937).

*A **focal point** is an obvious benchmark by which prices or output could be coordinated without an explicit agreement.*

Thomas Schelling gives the following general analogy of how focal points are discovered:

You are to meet someone in New York City. You have not been instructed where to meet; you have no prior understanding with the person on where to meet; and you cannot communicate with each other. . . . You are told the date but not the hour of this meeting; the two of you must guess the place and exact minute of the date for the meeting.[12]

According to Schelling, given these instructions, most people familiar with New York City would choose the information booth at Grand Central Station at high noon.

How do focal points apply to the economic behavior of oligopolists? Oligopolist firms will be intimately acquainted with their own industries. Business practices followed in the industry are well known. The focal points may involve certain standardized business practices—such as common percentage markups, the use of round numbers, the charging of prices like $4.95, and policies like "splitting the difference" or charging high season rates. As long as each oligopolist understands these standard practices, it can anticipate how rival firms will behave in given situations.

*Through **conscious parallelism,** the actions of producers can be coordinated within certain ranges without formal or even informal agreements. All oligopolists use their understanding of the industry to make their own decisions and anticipate the behavior of other oligopolists.*

The clearest example of conscious parallelism is the following experience of the U.S. Veterans Administration, recounted by F. M. Scherer.[13]

On June 5, 1955, five different companies submitted sealed bids to fill an order for 5,640 100-capsule bottles of the antibiotic tetracyclin, each quoting an effective net price of $19.1884 per bottle. . . . But although one can never be certain, it is probable that there was no direct collusion connected with this transaction. . . . The curious price of $19.1884 per bottle was arrived at through the application of a series of round number discounts to round number base prices: $19.1884 is the standard trade discount of 2 per cent of $19.58, which (after rounding) is 20 percent off the wholesale price of $24.48, which in turn is 20 percent off the $30.60 charged to retail druggists, which is 40 percent off the prevailing retail list price of $51.00, which in turn reflected an earlier 15 percent cut from the original list price of $60.00 per 100 capsules.

What appears to be an incredible coincidence explainable only by a secret price agreement may in fact be simply the application of focal points by the firms involved. Focal points may also help explain why oligopoly prices are sometimes inflexible. Firms accustomed to making decisions based on focal points may be reluctant to make large moves that put them outside the customary range of focal points.

THE STABILITY OF COLLUSIVE BEHAVIOR

Game Theory and the Prisoners' Dilemma

Greater insights into oligopolistic collusion can be obtained by a study of **game theory.** In 1944, mathematician John von Neumann and economist Oskar Morgenstern published *The Theory of Games and Economic Behavior.*[14]

Game theory is a way to analyze strategic decision making when the consequences of one decision maker's decisions are dependent on (and potentially adversely affected by) the decisions of other decision makers.

The Morgenstern-von Neumann book has been hailed as a great contribution to both mathematics and economics. Their idea is that in many economic situations, such as oligopoly, games of

12. Thomas Schelling, *The Strategy of Conflict* (Cambridge: Harvard University Press, 1960), p. 56.
13. Scherer, *Industrial Market Structure*, p. 191.

14. Oscar Morgenstern and John von Neumann, *Theory of Games and Economic Behavior* (Princeton: Princeton University Press, 1944).

Figure 5
Profit Payoffs to a Two-Firm Oligopoly

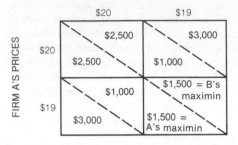

Each square (cell) shows the profits that each firm would earn when various combinations of prices are charged by the two firms. Firm A's profits are shown in color in the lower left-hand corner of each cell, and Firm B's profits are shown in black in the upper right-hand corner of each cell. For example, if A charges $19 and B charges $20, A would earn a profit of $3,000 and B would earn $1,000. The two firms do not know in advance which price the other will choose. What strategy will each pursue? There are two likely options. 1) If the two firms tacitly collude, they will charge the prices that yield them both the highest profit payoff. In this example, they would both receive the maximum benefit of $2,500 if each charged $20. 2) Each firm might decide to use a *maximin* (maximize the minimum) strategy to find the best of the worst possible outcomes. If A charges $19, the worst that can happen to A is a profit of $1,500. If A were to charge $20, the worst possible outcome for A is a profit of $1,000. By charging a $19 price, A can insure that the worst outcome will not happen. B's best of the worst possible outcomes is the $1,500 gained by charging $19. The maximin solution is for both firms to choose a price of $19.

strategy—such as poker, chess, or even sports—provide a more accurate explanation of behavior than the theory of perfect or monopolistic competition where the "players" act independently.

Consider for example the famous "prisoners' dilemma" game developed by game theorists. The prisoners' dilemma game is a way to analyze a situation much like that faced by oligopolistic producers. The setup for the game is that two bank robbers have been apprehended by the police; they are being interrogated in separate rooms. If both talk, both go to jail but with light sentences. If one talks and the other remains quiet, the one who talks gets off with a very light sentence while the silent bank robber gets a long jail sentence. If neither talks, both go free. Each prisoner is in a dilemma. Each knows that by keeping quiet both can get off free provided the other remains quiet; but keeping quiet is risky, since the other prisoner might talk. If both bank robbers take a conservative strategy of avoiding the worst possible outcome, they will both confess.

The prisoners' dilemma is much like an oligopolist's dilemma of deciding whether to collude or to act independently. In both cases the consequence of one "player's" decision depends upon the decision of another "player." Suppose Firm A and Firm B each sell a differentiated product. Suppose also that when the two products have equal prices, both firms enjoy exactly the same profit. If one charges a slightly lower price than the other, however, that firm will make large profits while the high-priced firm loses money.

Figure 5 shows the simplest possible set of outcomes. Each firm has the option of choosing a price of either $20 or $19. The *prices* Firm A might charge are shown down the left side of the figure; the prices Firm B might charge are shown along the top. The *profits* earned by each firm are the payoffs from any set of prices the *two firms together* might charge. Firm A's profit payoffs are shown in the lower-left corner of each box (in color); Firm B's profit payoffs are shown in the upper-right corner of each box (in black). As Figure 5 shows, when both charge $20, both earn $2,500; when both charge $19, both earn $1,500. When one charges $20 and the other charges $19, the lower-priced firm earns $3,000 while the higher-priced firm earns only $1,000.

If Firm A charges $20, the worst that could happen to A is if B charged $19 because A's profits would then be $1,000. If A charged $19, the worst that could happen to A would be a $1,500 profit, which would result if B also charged $19. B's worst outcome for charging $19 is a profit of $1,500. B's worst outcome for charging $20 is a profit of $1,000.

If A and B played this game repeatedly over a fairly long period of time, it is likely that A and B would somehow learn that they are both better off charging higher prices. They might learn to cooperate and choose the strategy that maximizes joint profits. In this case, both would charge $20 and earn profits of $2,500 each.

If A and B played the game only infrequently and both were charging $20, A might secretly cut its price to $19 while B continues to charge $20 in order to raise A's profit to $3,000. Firm B would be subject to the same temptation to cut its price. This type of independent strategy should lead both firms to charge $19 and to earn profits of $1,500.

The solution of both firms charging $19 is sometimes called the *maximin* (maximize the minimum) strategy. Firms following such a strategy choose the best of the worst possible outcomes. In this case, both firms will charge $19 and earn a $1,500 profit, which for each is the best of the worst possible outcomes. If the conservative maximin strategy is followed, prices are rather stable, just as in the kinked-demand-curve theory. In our example, the maximin strategy is for both firms to charge $19. If one of the firms—say Firm B—raises its price to $20 while A holds the line, B's profits will fall from $1,500 to $1,000. If each firm assumes the other will hold the line, each firm will hold prices stable at $19. Firms can cut their risk of profit losses by adopting the conservative strategy of guaranteeing the best of the worst possible outcomes.

Obstacles to Collusion

Despite the considerable gains to oligopolists from cooperation, collusion may not work. The chances for effective and lasting collusion decrease when there are 1) many sellers, 2) low entry barriers, 3) product heterogeneity, 4) high rates of innovation, 5) high fixed costs, 6) infrequent orders, 7) opportunities for cheating, and 8) legal restrictions.

Many Sellers. The more sellers or firms there are in the industry, the more difficult it is for the sellers to join in a conspiracy to raise prices. The communication network becomes much more complicated as the number of conspirators grows. When there are two sellers, there is only one communication link; when there are three sellers, there are three different information links. When there are 10 sellers, there are 45 ways information must flow! The number of information channels increases at a far greater rate than the rate at which the number of sellers in-

creases. It becomes far more difficult to coordinate collusive actions as the number of colluders grows. (The formula for the number of information flows is $n(n - 1)/2$, where n is the number of sellers.)

Low Entry Barriers. If it is easy for new firms to enter an industry, existing firms may not find it worthwhile to enter into cumbersome agreements to raise prices. Effective collusion would only bring in new firms.

High prices create profitable opportunities for new firms. For example, imagine an industry has constant returns to scale (no economies or diseconomies of scale) and only one firm. Suppose that the average cost of production—including a normal return—is $10. With complete free entry, the existing firm could not charge more than $10 in the long run. Any price above $10 would bring in new firms to capture above-normal returns. The entry of firms would eventually drive the price down to $10 where only a normal return is being earned.

Product Heterogeneity. The more heterogeneous or differentiated the product is from firm to firm, the more difficult it will be for the industry to achieve coordination or collusion. Reaching an agreement creates both costs and benefits. It is costlier to reach an agreement if the product is not homogeneous. Since steel is homogeneous, an agreement on prices and market shares between U.S. Steel and Bethlehem Steel may be fairly easy to conclude. But an agreement between McDonnell Douglas and Boeing over the relative prices of DC-10s and Boeing 747s may be quite difficult because of the differences in and the complexity of the product. An agreement between the producers of high-quality goods and low-quality goods may break down because of differences of opinion over one good's quality relative to the other good's quality.

High Rates of Innovation. If there is a high rate of innovation in an industry, collusive agreements will be more difficult to reach, as demonstrated in the prisoners' dilemma game. In unstable, quickly changing situations, players in the game have more difficulty finding the joint profit-maximizing solution. The costs of reaching an agreement are higher in relation to benefits when the industry is constantly turning out new products and developing new techniques.

High Fixed Costs.   The higher fixed costs are relative to total costs, the more likely it is that price wars or price breaks will occur in collusive agreements. Firms will ask themselves what they can gain by cheating on the pricing agreement. If fixed costs are high, variable costs are a low percentage of total costs. As long as the price covers average variable costs, there is something left over to pay fixed costs. By granting a secret price concession, a firm may gain a great deal in the short run if marginal costs are very low. Thus the benefits to secret price reductions are increased by high fixed costs.

Infrequent Orders.   If orders for the product come in infrequently, the individual firms have an incentive to break a collusive agreement. The gains to a particular firm from price cheating will be greater when orders are large and infrequent than when orders are small and frequent because the cheating will be harder to detect and more profitable per unit.

Opportunities for Cheating.   If it is easy to cheat without being detected, firms will tend to break a collusive agreement. It is easier to cheat on price agreements when actual prices charged by one party cannot be known with certainty by the other parties to the agreement. For example, barbers often can agree upon and charge uniform prices within the same city because the prices of haircuts must be posted. It is easy for rival barbers to detect barbers who are undercutting the agreed-upon price. Thus, in many cities with a strong barbers' union the price of haircuts is uniform, and there are few price wars. On the other hand, when the terms of price negotiations are not revealed (as in the cases of long-term oil-delivery contracts or purchases of commercial aircraft by the airlines), it is easier to cheat on pricing agreements.

Legal Restrictions.   In the United States, the Sherman Antitrust Act (1890) holds that combinations in restraint of trade are illegal. Such a law can obviously reduce collusion by increasing the cost of forming agreements. (Legal restrictions will be discussed in more detail in a later chapter.)

IMPLICATIONS OF OLIGOPOLY THEORY

The Diversity of Oligopoly

Oligopoly is too varied to draw general conclusions that apply to all forms of oligopoly. In less concentrated oligopolies, the number of firms is too large for formal or tacit collusion to occur, and it is difficult to prevent competitive behavior from erupting. According to Scherer, if firms supply a homogeneous product, it generally takes only 10 to 12 evenly matched suppliers for them to ignore each other's influence on price.[15]

As the number of sellers increases, the likelihood of having a maverick firm that will not hold to formal or informal pricing patterns increases. Moreover, sellers may have divergent notions on the best price for the industry. In sum, when the oligopoly is loose due to low barriers to entry, the behavior of the oligopolistic firm should not differ very much from that of monopolistically competitive or even perfectly competitive firms. Large economic profits would not be expected.

Only in highly concentrated oligopolies is coordinated action possible, but the temptations to cheat are substantial, and collusive agreements often fall apart. In its most successful form, however, a cartel arrangement yields a result that is really no different from monopoly.

Criticism of Oligopoly

The previous chapter described positive features of perfect competition—efficiency, production at minimum average cost, lower prices with higher output—and negative features of monopoly—production above minimum average cost, long-term monopoly profits, prices not equal to marginal costs, restricted output with higher prices.

15.   Scherer, *Industrial Market Structure*, p. 199.

As already noted, some oligopolies bear a strong resemblance to competitive markets while other oligopolies, especially in their collusive form, can bear a strong resemblance to monopoly. If the reader was convinced in the previous chapter that monopoly is bad and competition is good, then it is likely that same reader will conclude that less concentrated oligopolies are better than collusive oligopolies.

There has been substantial debate among industrial-organization researchers about whether or not oligopolies earn extraordinary profits. This question is difficult to study because of the difficulty of measuring economic profits (as opposed to accounting profits) and the problem of determining the degree of oligopoly, which is typically determined by measuring concentration ratios or the existence of entry barriers.

Joe S. Bain and H. Michael Mann showed that profit rates in the 1930s and 1950s tended to rise with barriers to entry and with concentration, although these results were more pronounced in the 1950s than in the 1930s.[16] More recent studies find that, particularly at high concentration ratios (70 percent and above), concentration is strongly and positively related to profits and that barriers to entry have an even stronger correlation with profits than concentration ratios. Other oligopolies (with concentration ratios below 70 percent) have profit rates that are more weakly associated with concentration or barriers to entry.[17]

Defenders of Oligopoly

Some economists defend oligopoly as an efficient form of economic market. Harold Demsetz sees the positive relationship between profit rates and concentration or barriers to entry as an indi-

**Figure 6
The Demsetz Thesis**

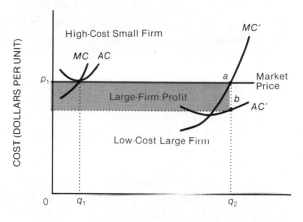

QUANTITY OF OUTPUT

The large efficient firm produces an output of q_2 units with a per-unit profit of ab. The small inefficient firm produces an output of q_1 units with a zero economic profit. According to Demsetz, perfect competition can be consistent with the positive association between concentration rates and economic profits.

cator of efficiency rather than as an indicator of market power.[18]

Demsetz maintains that higher profits are the result of the superior cost performance of larger firms in the industry. If prices are set in a competitive manner so that each firm acts more or less like a price taker (exerting no monopoly power over prices), then economic profits will accrue only to those firms that have lower costs, not to all firms in the industry. There is evidence that oligopoly profits are earned only by the largest firms in oligopolistic industries, not by all firms. Demsetz therefore concludes that oligopoly profits are not the result of the exercise of excessive market power; rather, oligopoly profits are the result of the superior efficiency of large oligopolistic firms.

Figure 6 illustrates the Demsetz argument. It assumes that a homogeneous product is being produced and that perfect competition prevails. Each

16. Joe S. Bain, *Barriers to New Competition,* pp. 192–200; H. Michael Mann, "Seller Concentration, Barriers to Entry, and Rates of Return in Thirty Industries," *Review of Economics and Statistics* (August 1966), pp. 296–307.
17. Leonard W. Weiss, "Quantitative Studies of Industrial Organization," in ed. Michael D. Intriligator, *Frontiers of Quantitative Economics* (Amsterdam: North Holland, 1971); Leonard Weiss, "Concentration-Profits Relationship and Antitrust," in eds. Goldschmid et al., *Industrial Concentration: The New Learning* (Boston: Little, Brown, 1974), pp. 184–233.
18. Harold Demsetz, "Industry Structure, Market Rivalry, and Public Policy," *Journal of Law and Economics* 16 (April 1973): 1–10.

firm equates marginal costs to the price. Figure 6 shows that when these conditions prevail, economic profits are earned by the low-cost producer. The Demsetz thesis is relatively new and has not been subjected yet to appropriate empirical testing.[19]

John K. Galbraith agrees with Demsetz that large oligopolies are much more efficient than their smaller counterparts. In fact, Galbraith argues that there is a power imbalance between the competitive sector and the oligopoly/monopoly sector.

In Galbraith's view, the competitive sector is being gradually worn down by the technically superior technostructure of the oligopoly sector. Rather than the competitive sector efficiently utilizing resources and monopoly/oligopoly underutilizing resources as theory teaches, Galbraith maintains that the reverse is true. The competitive sector cannot advertise like the large corporations, which can manipulate the demand for their products.[20]

Joseph Schumpeter argues that the large corporation is ideally equipped to generate technological progress. This technological progress is the moving force behind economic progress; it establishes some firms as dominant in their industry but not forever. Through the process of "creative destruction," Schumpeter believes that new ideas and new technologies replace the old and that the monopoly power created by technological innovation will prove to be transitory. The previous chapter raised serious questions about the validity of this argument.

19.   Scherer points out that a proper test of the oligopoly superiority hypothesis has yet to be undertaken. Such a test must take into account the interdependence between profitability, concentration, market shares, and differentiation. The superiority hypothesis would be easy to test if oligopolies produced a homogeneous good and no other. But in the real world oligopolies tend to produce many differentiated products that may be reflected in different costs. To assume that higher profits reflect the same price for the same good and thus lower unit cost remains to be demonstrated. *See* Scherer, *Industrial Market Structure*, pp. 290–91.

20.   John K. Galbraith, *The Affluent Society* (Boston: Houghton Mifflin, 1957); *American Capitalism* (Boston: Houghton Mifflin, 1956); *Economics and the Public Purpose* (Boston: Houghton Mifflin, 1973); *The New Industrial State* (Boston: Houghton Mifflin, 1967).

CASE STUDIES OF OLIGOPOLY

Production Differentiation and Breakfast Cereals

Rather than agreeing to share a market, as in the case of the cartel arrangement, oligopolists can use advertising to create submarkets wherein each oligopolist can set price to maximize profits.

Breakfast cereals provide the most notable example of a highly concentrated oligopoly based upon product differentiation. In 1950, there were 25 brands in distribution and by 1980 there were more than 80 brands. The broad evidence suggests that the minimum efficient plant size of a cereal producer is 5 percent of the market; engineering economies of scale would not lead one to expect high concentration in the breakfast-cereal industry. Yet the four largest breakfast-food manufacturers—Kellogg, General Mills, General Foods, and Quaker Oats—control 90 percent of the ready-to-eat breakfast-cereal market (see Table 5). Each spends large sums on advertising its cereals: about $0.13 of each dollar of sales is spent on advertising.

The four large breakfast-cereal manufacturers have been able to earn profit rates that are well above average for manufacturing firms and, have been able to increase their market share from 68 percent in 1940 to around 90 percent in 1980. The high concentration in breakfast cereals is not explained by economies of scale or by collusive agreements because there are too many manufacturers. The most likely explanation is that the breakfast-cereal industry is a shared monopoly created by successful product differentiation through advertising.

Will OPEC Survive as an Effective Cartel?

The most highly publicized cartel of the 1970s and 1980s is the Organization of Petroleum Exporting Countries, or OPEC. OPEC was founded in 1960 by the five major oil exporters: Iran, Iraq, Kuwait, Saudi Arabia, and Venezuela. Its founders hoped that OPEC would someday be able to set world oil prices and allocate production quotas

Table 5
Sales and Advertising Expenditures of Major Breakfast Cereals

Firm	Size Rank in *Fortune's* 500 Largest Firms	Breakfast Cereal Sales (millions of dollars)	Percentage Share of Breakfast Cereal Market	Advertising Expenditures (millions of dollars)
Kellogg	191	300	45	36
General Mills	116	141	21	19
General Foods	45	92	16	9
Quaker Oats	195	56	9	9
Nabisco	139	26	4	3
Ralston Purina	71	20	3	4

Source: The Federal Trade Commission's Complaint Against the Ready-to-Eat Breakfast Cereal Industry.

among OPEC members. By the 1970s, most of the major oil-exporting countries had joined OPEC, and the major industrial countries were no longer producing enough oil at home to cover domestic demand.

By October of 1973, OPEC found itself in a shared monopoly position. The price of OPEC oil rose from $3.01 per barrel in 1973 to $34 per barrel in 1982. The oil revenues of the OPEC countries skyrocketed, and complaints were heard that OPEC was holding the world economy hostage.

The OPEC cartel has operated by setting a uniform set of prices that its members charge oil importers. Little OPEC effort had been devoted to regulating the production of OPEC members. In this regard, each OPEC country behaves like the oligopoly firm in Figure 4. OPEC's goal is to set world price equal to the profit-maximizing price.

The OPEC cartel has already had a long life. It brought considerable prosperity to its members. But its weaknesses are becoming apparent. First, the substantial rise in oil prices has caused oil importers to search out substitutes for oil. The demand for imported oil has become more elastic in the long run. Second, the oil production of non-OPEC countries—such as Mexico—has increased. Third, the industrialized countries have suffered through three recessions since 1973. During these recessions the world demand for imported oil has stagnated. The recession of 1981–

1982 put a severe damper on the world demand for imported oil.

Under these conditions, it has become increasingly difficult to maintain a stable cartel. With demand shrinking and market shares being eaten up by noncartel producers who are not obliged to follow the cartel rules, there will be a real temptation among OPEC members to cheat. By offering discounts below the cartel price, customers can be wooed away from higher-priced producers. As long as the marginal revenue obtained from additional sales is above the marginal cost, the cheaters have benefited. If discipline were to break down and all cartel members began to cheat, then there would no longer be an effective cartel. The cartel would no longer be the one setting the price.

In 1982, some OPEC producers were indeed selling oil below the cartel price. Iran, for example, was offering $5-per-barrel discounts, and there was pressure on Nigeria to break the OPEC price. Only time will tell whether OPEC can survive as an effective cartel.

This chapter completes our study of the four basic market models. The next chapter will examine how the costs of gathering information about buyers, sellers, resources, and products affects market behavior and how markets provide information about present and future scarcity.

Summary

1. An oligopoly is an industry characterized by the relative fewness of firms, barriers to entry, and either homogeneous or differentiated products. The most basic characteristic of oligoply is mutual interdependence. The number of firms is so small that the actions of one firm will have a significant effect on other firms in the industry.

2. Even though the concentration ratio is an imperfect guide to the measurement of oligopoly, it is used to measure the extent of oligopoly. In manufacturing, oligopolistic industries account for more than 50 percent of output, but oligopoly is less prevalent in other sectors of the economy. The degree of oligopoly in manufacturing has not changed significantly over the past half century.

3. The degree of concentration in an oligopoly varies; some oligopolies act more like a monopoly than a competitive industry while others behave more competitively.

4. The presence of barriers to entry explains the small number of firms in an oligopoly. Types of barriers to entry are economies of scale, product differentiation, control over input supplies, government barriers to entry, large capital requirements, and technological advantages.

5. Because of mutual interdependence, the oligopolist's demand curve cannot be defined until the reaction pattern of rival firms is specified. The demand curve can vary from the kinked demand curve to the perfectly coordinated demand curve of a cartel arrangement. The kinked demand curve is one explanation of the apparent inflexibility of oligopoly prices. It explains how costs and demand can change without there being a change in the price. The kinked demand curve is based on the assumption that rivals will follow price decreases but will not follow price increases.

6. There are several methods of oligopoly coordination that range from formal agreements (cartels) to informal arrangements, such as price leadership or conscious parallelism.

7. Collusive agreements, if successful, allow the participating firms to earn monopoly profits. Because there are incentives to cheat on the cartel agreement, however, collusive agreements tend to be unstable. Game theory—as illustrated by the "prisoner's dilemma"—explains and analyzes the incentives to cheat on collusive agreements. Collusion is difficult when there are many sellers, low barriers to entry, heterogeneous products, high rates of innovation, high fixed costs, infrequent transactions, easy price cheating, or laws against collusion.

8. Because of the inherent instability of collusive arrangements, oligopolies often engage in nonprice competition. One important type of nonprice competition is advertising to differentiate products and create barriers to entry. Empirical studies show that at high levels of concentration, there is a positive relationship between economic profits and concentration, and between economic profits and barriers to entry. Some economists argue that the higher profits of concentrated oligopolies are the result of superior technological and cost performance of large firms (Demsetz, Galbraith, and Schumpeter), but there is substantial disagreement among industrial organization experts on this point.

9. Oligopoly theory can be used to explain product differentiation in the breakfast-cereal industry or the behavior of a cartel like OPEC.

Key Terms

oligopoly
mutual interdependence
concentration ratio
shared monopoly
barriers to entry
atomistic competition
kinked demand curve
price leader
cartel
conscious parallelism
focal point
game theory

Questions and Problems

1. According to Table 1, the 4-firm concentration ratio for aluminum sheets is 65 percent. Is this an accurate measure of the extent of oligopoly? Explain.

2. What is the relationship between fewness and mutual interdependence in oligopoly theory? Why was mutual interdependence not considered in the chapter on monopoly and monopolistic competition?

3. Firm ZYX is one of three equal-sized firms in the widget market. It currently charges $20 per widget and sells one million widgets per year. It is considering raising its price to $22 and needs some estimate of what will happen to its widget sales. Why would it be difficult to make such an estimate?

4. Firm ZYX and the two other widget manufacturers meet in secret and agree to charge a uniform price of $50 and share the market equally (each gets one third of sales). At the price of $50, each firm's marginal cost is $10. What are the rewards to cheating on the agreement if ZYX does not get caught? What happens if all three try to cheat?

5. The prisoner's dilemma is also used to explain how oligopolists devise advertising strategy. Try to apply the prisoner's dilemma to advertising in highly concentrated oligopolies.

6. Why is nonprice competition encountered frequently in oligopolistic industries?

7. In an oligopolistic industry comprised of 3 large firms and 10 small firms, the large firms earn an economic profit while the small firms earn normal profits. What do you know about the sources of economic profit in this industry?

8. How does oligopoly theory explain why there are so many different types of oligopoly behavior—collusion, nonprice competition, focal points, price leadership?

13

The Economics of Information

Chapter Preview

Perfect competition is an efficient way of organizing society's resources. If the economy is perfectly competitive, it will not be possible to raise the well-being of some without reducing the well-being of others. For this reason, perfect competition is viewed by economists as yielding an efficient allocation of resources.

Yet competition in its perfect form is rarely found in the real world for several reasons: Most products are not homogeneous; they differ according to quality, location, time, and imagined effects. Second, perfect freedom of entry and exit is hard to realize in the real world. Some barriers to entry—in the form of capital requirements, economies of scale, and so on—typically are

present even in competitive industries. Third, the condition of perfect information concerning prices and quality is met in the real world only in exceptional circumstances. Information is itself a scarce commodity; there are costs and benefits to acquiring information. This chapter focuses upon the role that information plays in our economy.

In real world markets—even those that are highly competitive—there is considerable uncertainty about prices that prevail now, prices that we must pay in the future, and even about product qualities. If information on current and future prices and product qualities were available instantaneously at no cost of time or money to individuals, such uncertainty would evaporate. But acquiring information typically does have its costs, and **information costs** have a substantial effect on real-world markets.

Information costs are the costs of acquiring information on prices and product qualities.

This chapter will examine why information is a valuable commodity; the role of intermediaries (or "middlemen"), speculators, and hedgers; and the costs of gathering information about markets and products. Information costs are also the key to understanding why it pays to shop for the lowest price and the problems of product quality and safety.

INFORMATION IS A VALUABLE COMMODITY

To carry out an economic transaction, the buyer and seller must acquire information. The buyer and seller must first find each other and then agree on the price and other terms of the contract. Knowledge of the existence and location of a willing buyer is valuable information to the seller, just as knowledge of a willing seller is valuable information to the buyer. Without this information, economic transactions cannot take place.

Information as a Scarce Good

Information is typically a scarce and valuable commodity. Information is costly because human beings have limited capacity to acquire, process, store, and retrieve facts and figures about prices, qualities, and location of products. Each person specializes in certain types of information. Chemical engineers may know a great deal about producing plastics but may know little about building houses. The produce clerks know a great deal about displaying lettuce or apples but little about how they are grown. Homemakers know a great deal about the prices of groceries in their town but little about the prices of industrial machinery. Industrial purchasing agents know more about machinery prices than about grocery prices. Information is costly to acquire because it is distributed over the population in bits and pieces.

Chapter 3 explained why no one person knows how to make a pencil from start to finish. Some people even make a profession of specializing in information—the industrial purchasing agent, the realtor, the stock-market broker—but their knowledge is limited to very specific areas.

Because information is costly, each individual accumulates information that is specific to that person's particular circumstances of time and place. This special information can be valuable. To quote the Nobel Prize laureate, Friedrich A. von Hayek:[1]

> . . . a little reflection will show that there is beyond question a body of very important but unorganized knowledge which cannot possibly be called scientific in the sense of knowledge of general rules: the knowledge of particular circumstances of time and place. It is with respect to this that every individual has some advantage over all others in that he possesses unique information of which beneficial use might be made.

By allowing people to be paid for their scarce information, the price system economizes on information costs. The auto mechanic does not have to learn nuclear physics, and the physicist does not have to know how to repair a car.

Transactions Costs

A major part of the cost of making a transaction between a buyer and a seller is the cost associated with searching for and acquiring economic information. **Transactions costs** include the costs of telephoning, shopping, and reading ads and consumer reports in order to acquire more economic information.

Transactions costs are the costs associated with bringing buyers and sellers together.

In gathering such costly information, people follow the same rule that governs most economic behavior:

People will continue to acquire economic information as long as the benefits of gathering information exceed the costs.

1. F.A. Hayek, "The Use of Knowledge in Society," *American Economic Review* 35 (1945): 510–30.

That individuals follow economic rules in gathering economic information may seem far fetched at first glance, but this notion is really quite reasonable. For example, when a person decides to buy a new car, the more information that person has on prices and on the technical qualities of various automobiles, the better the eventual choice is likely to be. But it is costly to gather such information. It is costly to drive all over town to the various dealers; it is costly to take time off from work or from leisure activities to compare prices; it may be expensive in terms of time and money to acquire and master technical information contained in the various consumer-guide reports on new automobiles. To gather all the available information about new cars would take an inordinate amount of time and money; therefore, the prospective buyer would have to draw the line somewhere. That line would be drawn approximately at the point where the person felt that the marginal benefit from acquiring more information is less than the marginal cost of acquiring more information.

"MIDDLEMEN" OR INTERMEDIARIES

"Middlemen" (or **intermediaries**) specialize in information concerning:

1. exchange opportunities between buyers and sellers.
2. the variety and qualities of different products.
3. the channels of marketing distribution of produced goods.

> *"Middlemen" or intermediaries buy in order to sell again or simply bring together a buyer and a seller.*

Real-estate brokers, grocery stores, department stores, used-car dealers, auctioneers, stock brokers, insurance agents, and travel agents are all intermediaries, or "middlemen." All these professions "intermediate" or stand between ultimate buyers and sellers in return for a profit.

Suppose that an individual is willing to sell a multimillion dollar private airplane for no less than $20 million, and a potential buyer residing in some distant country is willing to pay at most $25 million for such an airplane. How will they locate one another? Someone with information about the existence of the potential buyer and seller could act as a "middleman," or intermediary and bring the two together. It would be possible for the seller to get $20 million, for the buyer to pay $25 million, and for the intermediary to charge as much as $5 million for the service of bringing the two together.

Transactions of this sort take place all the time, although most transactions are less spectacular. The buyers and sellers of residential homes are brought together by realtors who charge a fee for this service. Stock-market brokers bring together buyers and sellers of a particular stock. Auction houses bring together sellers of rare works of art with potential buyers, and charge a fee for this service. Are such "middlemen" cheating innocent buyers and sellers, or are they providing a service that is worth the price?

The role of intermediaries in providing information to buyers and sellers is often misunderstood. The export-import agent who brings the airplane buyer and seller together and pockets $5 million may be regarded as a near-criminal by people who think that this "go between" is trading on the ignorance of others. When food prices rise, many consumers blame the intermediaries. Buyers and sellers of real estate often become upset with the high fees charged by realtors. Implicit in these complaints is the belief that the intermediaries are getting a reward for doing nothing or for doing very little.

The "middleman's" share of the price varies substantially from good to good. In real estate, the broker receives typically a 5 to 10 percent fee for bringing together the buyer and seller. This fee depends upon competitive conditions in the market. In stock-market transactions the fee varies from about 0.5 percent to about 2 percent of the price of the stock. Supermarkets charge an intermediary fee of perhaps 10 percent to 55 percent of the wholesale price at which they buy.

The fee that intermediaries charge for their services depends, like other economic activities, on the amount of competition, on the degree of freedom of entry into the business, and on the opportunity costs of bringing goods to the market. If the business is competitive, the fee will reflect in the long run a normal profit, as in any other competitive market. For example, retail grocery stores are in a very competitive business; the typical supermarket earns an accounting profit of about 1

Example 1

The Lemons Principle

Certifying quality helps prevent market breakdown. In the case of used cars, the seller knows the value of the product, but the buyer must guess the quality. Most buyers would probably assume that the car is of average quality. If every used-car dealer operated on a disreputable basis, the only used cars that would trade would be the *lemons*—those of lowest quality. If there were used cars in the market ranging from $1,000 to $6,000 in true value (a range known, say, to all potential buyers), but potential buyers could not tell the difference among them, would any rational consumer buy a used car priced at $5,000? No one would. At a price of $5,000, cars worth more than $5,000 would not be offered for sale; only those worth $5,000 or less would be put on the market—so that the average car offered for sale would be worth $3,000. Why pay $5,000 for a car that is more than likely worth much less than $5,000? At a price of $3,000, only cars worth $3,000 or less would be placed on the market (so the average car offered would be worth only $2,000). Why pay $3,000 for a car that is likely worth much less than $3,000? Indeed, any price above $1,000 would bring forth cars worth less than the price. What type of cars would therefore be traded in this fly-by-night market? Only those lemons that are worth exactly $1,000 since buyers paying more could only expect to be ripped off. In these circumstances, only when established dealers serve as certifiers of quality will nonlemons be placed on the market.

Source: Based upon George Akerlof, "The Market for 'Lemons': Quality, Uncertainty, and the Market Mechanism," *Quarterly Journal of Economics* 84 (August 1970): 488–500.

---

percent on its sales. The markups found in the supermarket are almost entirely used for paying rent, stock clerks, checkout clerks, produce specialists, and butchers. The grocery store, for example, must hire employees to prepare produce and meat for display in quantities convenient for inspection and purchase; the store must maintain inventories of products on which it must pay carrying charges. The grocery store must select a location convenient to its customers and must pay substantial rents for a good location. In return for the "middleman's" fee, consumers receive from the grocery store a convenient location, the convenience of inspecting goods before purchase, and the convenience of finding the quantity and quality of goods they want without packing, sorting, and searching for themselves.

Buyers and sellers could in most situations avoid paying the "middleman's" fee. Homemaker's could drive to farmers' markets and to wholesale distributors of meats and dairy products. They could even drive to canning factories. The intermediary, by specializing in bringing together buyers and sellers, is able to provide the service at a lower cost than if the individuals involved performed the service themselves.

Another function of Sears, Safeway, J. C. Penney, used-car lots associated with new-car dealers, and so on is to certify the quality of goods. The consumer is confronted with a vast array of goods, some of which are so complicated that the buyer is at an enormous information disadvantage relative to the producer. The number of producers is larger than the number of actual stores the consumer deals with. In such circumstances, the intermediary performs the function of certifying the quality of the good for the buyer. The customer is prepared to pay a price for this valuable service; thus the intermediary is able to charge a higher markup over costs.

The real world consists of both disreputable dealers and those who serve, at least to some degree, as certifiers of quality. Certifiers of car quality enter the market in response to profit opportunities. "Middlemen" who are better informed about the quality of cars (because they can hire skilled mechanics) than the persons who buy cars will take advantage of profit opportunities. They will buy used cars (perhaps from their new-car customers), and they will then resell them on their used-car lots. They may even provide a guarantee (usually with a time limit) that the used car is not a "lemon." Customers will be willing to pay the "middleman" a fee (in the form of a price markup) for this certifier-of-quality service (see Example 1).

Example 2

Brand Name Franchise Extention

The role of brand names as certifiers of quality can be seen in the growing practice of franchise extension. Manufacturers have found that it is costly and risky to introduce new brands. Buyers are wary and reluctant to try unproven products. Therefore, established manufacturers find ways for new products to hitch rides from existing brands by using *franchise extension*. A company enters a new business by playing on its most valuable asset—"the consumer awareness, good will and impressions conveyed by its brand name." There are numerous examples of franchise extensions: Sunkist orange soda, Bic shavers, Gerber insurance, Levi shoes, Jello pudding pops, and Del Monte Mexican foods. "A stroll down any supermarket aisle reveals many names that may have untapped value. Among them marketers cite R.T. French, Kraft, Fleischmann's, Green Giant, and Weight Watchers. Even American Telephone and Telegraph is studying products that could carry the Bell name.

Source: Adapted from "Exploiting Proven Brand Names Can Cut Risks of New Products," *Wall Street Journal*, January 22, 1981.

The same principle applies to the products sold by major grocery chains or major department stores. Customers know that the retailer serves as a certifier of quality, and, if the product happens to be defective, their money will be returned. Safeway or Sears wants its customers to come back for repeat business. Manufacturers also certify quality by identifying their products with brand names. If consumers could not distinguish the product of one manufacturer from that of all other manufacturers, there would be little incentive for the manufacturer to produce products of reasonable or uniform quality. Brand names like Sara-Lee, Levi's, Maytag, Xerox, and so on serve as certifiers of product quality.

SPECULATION

The homemaker who stocks up on peanut butter after hearing of a shortage of peanuts, the frozen-orange-juice distributor who buys oranges in response to a late frost in Florida, and the young couple that buys a house now because they fear home prices will rise beyond reach if they wait another year are all **speculators.** The professional speculator is more maligned than any other economic agent.

Speculators are those who buy or sell in the hope of profiting from market fluctuations.

Most people do not associate the term *speculator* with the family that stocks up on goods whose prices are expected to shoot up or the family that purchases a home as an inflation hedge. Most people associate the term *speculator* with the person who buys up agricultural land and holds it for future shopping-center development or the person who buys and sells foreign currencies or gold in the hopes of buying low and selling high. Such speculators buy or sell commodities in huge quantities hoping to profit from a frost, war scare, bumper crop, bad news, or good news.

The Economic Role of the Speculator

Speculators do, indeed, often profit from the misfortunes of others. They buy from the hard-pressed farmer when prices are low, and they sell later at much higher prices. Has the farm family been robbed by the speculator? Upon hearing of a frost in Florida, speculators buy oranges in large quantities, thereby driving up the prices of orange juice for the consumer. Speculators, at the first sign of international trouble, may buy gold and sell American dollars, thereby weakening the American dollar. The popular view of speculators is that they do only harm. This chapter will explain how speculators often perform a useful economic function.

The fundamental economic role of the speculator is to engage in **arbitrage** *through time*.

>*Arbitrage is buying in a market where a commodity is cheap and reselling it in a market where the commodity is more expensive.*

The arbitrageur buys wheat in Chicago at $5 per bushel and resells it for $5.10 the next minute in Kansas City. Arbitrageurs therefore serve to keep the price of wheat in Chicago and Kansas City approximately equal.

>*Arbitrage serves to equalize prices in different markets, because when price differences arise, arbitrageurs buy in the cheap market and resell in the expensive market.*

Simple arbitrage of this type is not very risky since information about prices in Chicago and Kansas City can be obtained instantly from commodity brokers. Arbitrageurs must act quickly and have sharp pencils and keen minds if they are to prosper. Unlike the arbitrageur, who buys in one location and resells in another, the speculator buys goods *at one time* and resells *at another time*. Speculation is a risky business because tomorrow's prices cannot be known with certainty.

Profitable Speculation

The objective of the speculator is to make a profit by buying low and selling high. When the speculator is making a profit—and when there are enough speculators—prices will be driven up by speculation when they are low, and they will be driven down by speculation when they are high. When speculators buy at low prices, they add to the demand and drive prices up. When speculators sell when prices are high, they drive prices down by adding to the supply.

>*Profitable speculation (that is, speculation that succeeds in buying low and selling high) stabilizes prices and consumption over time by reducing fluctuations in prices and consumption over time.*

Profitable speculation is illustrated in Figure 1. Panel (a) shows that the supply of wheat in the first period (say 1983) is S_1, or 4 million bushels. Panel (b) shows that the supply of wheat in the second period (say, 1984) is S_2, or 2 million bushels. If there were no speculation, the price of wheat would be $3 in period 1 and $5 in period 2 (we assume that demand does not change between the two periods). Thus, without speculation, prices and consumption would vary dramatically between the two periods.

If speculators correctly anticipate that next year's wheat crop will be small, they could make handsome profits by buying at $3 and selling next year at $5. But what happens as speculators begin to buy this year's wheat? When speculators buy wheat, they withdraw it from the market and place it in storage. As a result, the supply of wheat offered on the market is reduced. If speculation is profitable, the profits of the marginal speculator will be driven down to zero. When speculators buy 1 million bushels in the first period, the effective supply becomes S_s, and the price rises to $4. When speculators resell this wheat in the second period, the effective supply becomes S_s in year 2. With profitable speculation, the price would remain stable at $4 in both periods, and the quantity of wheat sold on the market would remain stable at 3 million bushels—despite substantial differences in the wheat harvest in the two periods. In this example, we assume that storage costs are zero. Had storage costs been positive, the price of wheat in the second period would have been higher by the cost of storage.

>*Profitable speculation shifts supplies from periods when supplies are relatively abundant and prices potentially low to periods when supplies are relatively scarce and prices potentially high. In this sense, profitable speculation provides the valuable economic service of stabilizing prices and consumption over time.*

Unprofitable Speculation

Speculation is risky. Speculators cannot always guess right. They may buy when they think prices are low only to find that they sink even

Figure 1
Profitable Speculation

(a) Period 1

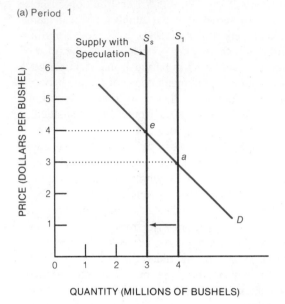

(b) Period 2

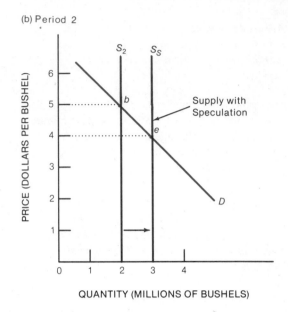

Period 1's wheat harvest is 4 million bushels, while period 2's wheat harvest is only 2 million bushels. If there were no speculation, the price would be $3 in period 1 and $5 in period 2. Perfect speculation will cause 1 million bushels of wheat to be purchased and stored by speculators in period 1, to be sold in period 2. As a result, the price is driven up to $4 in period 1 and driven down to $4 in period 2. Both prices and consumption are stabilized by speculation in this case.

lower. They may sell when they think prices are at their peak, only to watch the prices rise even further. In such cases, speculation destabilizes prices and consumption over time. When prices would otherwise be high, such speculators are buying and driving prices even higher; when prices would otherwise be low, such speculators are selling and are driving prices even lower.

Unprofitable speculation is shown in Figure 2. The supply of corn is 5 million bushels in period 1 and will also be 5 million bushels in period 2. Because demand remains the same in the two periods, the equilibrium price of corn will be $4 in both periods without speculation. Now assume speculators incorrectly guess that the supply of corn will fall in period 2 due to an anticipated poor harvest. Speculators buy 2 million bushels, which they place in storage for later sale, driving up the price to $6 in period 1 (point *a*). The speculators then wait in vain for a decline in supply that never materializes. They must sell the 2 million bushels in period 2, and they drive the price down to $2 a bushel (point *b*).

Without speculation, the price and consumption of corn would have been the same in both periods (point *e*). With unprofitable speculation, consumption is 3 million bushels in period 1 and 7 million bushels in period 2. Period 1's price is $6 and period 2's price is $2. Unprofitable speculation is inefficient for the economy as a whole.[2]

Unprofitable speculation is destabilizing because it creates artificial scarcities in some periods and artificial abundance in other periods. In this sense, speculation can be costly to society.

---

2. Because the economy is worse off, both speculators and nonspeculators together (the consumers of corn) are made worse off but consumers are made better off. The consumers of corn lose consumer surplus of $8 million in period 1 when the price rises from $4 to $6, but they gain it all back and more when consumer surplus rises $12 million above what it would have been had the price remained at $4. The gain to consumers is $4 million worth of consumer surplus. But speculators lose $8 million (the 2 million bushels bought at $6 and sold at $2). This loss exceeds the gain of consumers.

Figure 2
Unprofitable Speculation

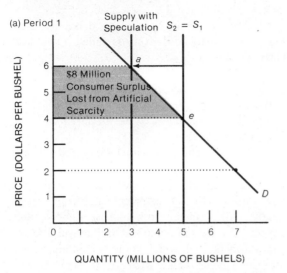

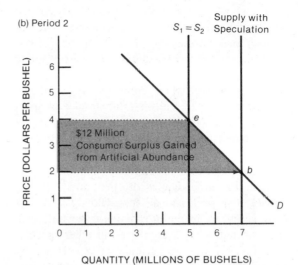

In this example, period 1 and period 2 have the same demand and supply conditions. Without speculation, the price would be $4 in both periods. Speculators guess incorrectly that the supply of corn in period 2 will be less. They buy 2 million bushels in period 1 and drive period 1's price up to $6. When they must resell the 2 million bushels in period 2, they drive the price down to $2. In the case of unprofitable speculation, price and consumption are seriously destabilized.

Ex Ante and *Ex Post* Efficiency

Speculators make guesses about future supplies and prices. Since the future is uncertain, speculators will often make wrong decisions. On balance, does society benefit from speculation?

After the event has occurred, it is easy to evaluate the prediction made by the speculator. But judging speculation on the basis of *ex post facto* (after the fact) performance is a poor way to determine whether speculation helps or hurts the economy on balance.

Most economists agree that the business of speculation is populated by a core of expert, professional speculators and a rotating periphery of nonexperts. Since decisions must be made about uncertain future events, it is better for *ex ante facto* (before the fact) decisions to be made by the best informed specialists (the professional speculators) than by poorly informed individuals.

The important question is whether the professional speculator employs *ex ante* decision rules that are efficient in the sense that they are most likely to yield the correct answer concerning future prices and quantities. A million *ex post* ex-

amples of unprofitable speculation do not prove that speculation should be abolished. Although it is difficult to prove empirically, it is probably true that the millions of *ex ante* decisions by professional speculators that turn out to be correct overwhelm the number that turn out to be incorrect.

Although no one can foresee the future, in some cases predicting future events is not as difficult as one might expect. For example, it is widely known that spring wheat is harvested in September and winter wheat is harvested in June or July. The amount of wheat harvested in other months is negligible. The seasonal pattern of wheat supply is therefore known to a rather sharp degree. What if no one were to speculate in this situation? In harvest months, farmers would harvest and sell their wheat; wheat prices would be driven down to very low levels. In the remaining months when very little wheat is harvested, wheat prices would be astronomical. Such a situation, it is obvious, would not be satisfactory. Because the pattern of wheat harvesting is well-known, speculators (who include, by the way, farmers who put their grain into storage rather than sell it immediately) purchase grain at harvest time, put it into storage, and then sell it throughout the rest of the year. This activity assures that society will not lack for wheat during the remainder of the year and that consumers will not have to pay wildly fluctuating prices. Speculators will, of course, make some errors in the process; they may incorrectly predict the size of the upcoming harvest. However, these mistakes appear to be relatively minor when compared to what the world would be like in the total absence of speculation.

In some cases, speculators do trade on the ignorance of others and thus fail to perform a useful social function even in the case of profitable speculation. In our examples of speculation, we assumed that professional speculators would not have access to inside information that would give them an unfair advantage over all other speculators. In 1977 western agricultural experts grossly underestimated the size of the Russian wheat harvest, due in part to deliberate Soviet efforts to misrepresent their forthcoming harvest. The Soviets, having inside information that the world supply of wheat would be less than most speculators thought, quietly purchased wheat through French-based companies to cover their deficit before the price of wheat began to shoot up.

THE FUTURES MARKET

The business of speculation is so highly specialized that markets have developed that separate the business of storage of the commodity being bought and sold from the business of speculation. The grain speculator does not have to worry about what the purchased grain looks like, where it is stored, and how much to take out of storage. These matters are handled by a **futures market**.

*A **futures market** is one where a buyer and seller now agree on the price of a commodity to be delivered at some specified date in the future.*

Many are familiar with futures markets only through the sensational press reports about the oil-rich Hunt family seeking to corner the silver market, about European and Asian speculators driving the price of gold to dizzying heights, or about the increase in coffee prices following a freeze in Brazil that is blamed on speculators. The type of market we are most familiar with is one in which there is an actual outlay of cash (or the arrangement of credit) for the immediate delivery of a good. The market in which a good is purchased today for immediate delivery is called a **spot (or cash) market**.

*In a **spot (or cash) market** agreements between buyers and sellers are made now for payment and delivery of the product now.*

Most of the goods consumers buy and sell are transacted in spot markets. In the grocery store, consumers pay now for goods that are delivered now. Stocks, foreign exchange, gold, and commodities like wheat, pork bellies, lumber, and copper are traded in organized exchanges. The organized markets in which commodities are traded are called *commodities markets*. In commodities markets, contracts can be made now for payment and delivery now.

Futures markets work quite differently from spot markets. *Futures contracts* are bought and sold in futures markets. In a futures contract, the terms of a future transaction (the price and the quantity) are set today. The buyer of a futures contract enters a contract today to purchase a specified quantity of a good (say, wheat) at a specified price at some specified date in the future. Both delivery and payment are to be made *in the future*. The seller is obliged to deliver the specified quantity of the good at the specified price at the specified future date. The seller of a futures contract need not even own the commodity at the time of the sale (but will in many instances).

*The **seller** of a futures contract is in a **short position** when something is sold that is not owned.*

*The **buyer** of a futures contract is in a **long position** when a claim on a good is acquired.*

When the seller agrees to sell and the buyer agrees to buy at specified prices at a specified date in the future, what guarantees that both parties live up to their ends of the bargain? The buyer and seller must each put up cash—called a *mar-*

gin requirement—equal to a small percentage of the value of the contract.[3]

The Mechanics of Futures Trading

Futures trading is different from the types of transactions most people are familiar with. Futures trading is a topsy-turvy world: traders can sell something before they buy it; traders are buying and selling obligations to buy or sell in the future a commodity they will likely never even see. Most daily newspapers supply futures prices. For example, on January 22, 1981, the price of "September 1981 wheat" was $5.07 per bushel in Chicago, while the spot price was $4.59 per bushel. The futures price is the price agreed upon now for a commodity to be paid for and delivered on some future date. Any time between now and the future date, the seller or buyer can *close out* the futures contract by engaging in an offsetting transaction. The seller offsets the transaction by simply buying another futures contract with the same delivery date; a buyer closes out by selling another futures contract with the same delivery date. Two examples of futures trading, illustrating a long position and a short position, follow.

A Long Position. George Bull thinks that wheat prices will rise in the future more than other buyers generally expect them to rise. George thinks that the September 1981 wheat price of $5.07 is too low; he expects the September price to be well above $5.07. On January 22, 1981, George buys 5,000 bushels of September 1981 wheat, paying the futures price of $5.07. George is now in a long position in wheat. George has had to put up $2,000 as a margin requirement

with his commodity broker. Time passes, and the futures price of September 1981 wheat changes. If the futures price rises above $5.07, George gains. If the price of September 1981 wheat falls below $5.07 in the future, George loses.

On February 1, the price of September wheat rises to $5.17. George has made a profit because he bought September 1981 wheat at $5.07 and can now sell it for $5.17. If George closes out his long position by selling a contract for 5,000 bushels of September 1981 wheat, he will make a profit of $500 ($0.10 × 5,000 bushels). His deposit with his commodity broker has increased from $2,000 to $2,500. Surprisingly, even if George does not close out his position by selling, his broker will automatically credit George's account for $500. If George continues his long position, he will have $2,500 on deposit with his broker (or can have the broker send him a check for $500). By continuing to hold a long position without closing out, George runs the risk that the price of September 1981 wheat will fall and that he will lose his $500 profit or more.

A Short Position. Sue Bear thinks, on the other hand, that September 1981 wheat will be lower in price than people currently anticipate. She thinks that if she sells September wheat at $5.07 per bushel, the future prices will fall, and she can make a profit. Sue Bear sells 5,000 bushels of September 1981 wheat on January 22, 1981 at the market futures price of $5.07. Sue is now in a short position in wheat (she sold something she doesn't have). While this will probably not be the case, it is convenient to think of Sue as the one who sold to George. If the price of September 1981 wheat rises above $5.07, Sue loses; if the price falls below $5.07, Sue wins. As we already indicated, on February 1, the futures price of September 1981 wheat is $5.17. If Sue closes out her short position, she loses $0.10 per bushel, or $500. Sue, who has also deposited $2,000 as a margin requirement, now has only $1,500 on deposit with her commodity broker. Even if Sue does not close out her short position, her broker will automatically debit Sue's account for $500 when the futures price rises to $5.17. If the price continues to rise and Sue keeps an open position, she will receive a *margin call* from her broker for more cash when her account balance is zero or

---

3. The actual percentage *margin requirement* varies from commodity to commodity. On January 16, 1981, "March 1981" wheat (March is the future transaction date) contracts sold at $5.025 per bushel. On a contract of 5,000 bushels (the minimum contract on the Chicago futures market), the whole contract would therefore be valued at $25,125. The buyer and seller would each have to put up approximately $1,256 to insure that the contract would be carried out. If you are wealthy and an established customer, it would have been possible to deposit some of your assets (stocks, bonds) with your commodity broker to guarantee the contract. The amount of cash put up is negligible; it basically screens out individuals who may run out on the contract if things go badly.

else the broker will automatically close out her position. Sue has the choice of closing out her short position or continuing to hold it in the hope that the price will fall and she can recoup her losses.

Hedging

The person who "hedges a bet" bets both sides in order to minimize the risks of heavy losses. Such a person might bet $5 it will rain tomorrow and $4 it won't rain. **Hedging** also takes place in futures markets.

Hedging is the temporary substitution of a futures market transaction for an intended spot or cash transaction.

Futures markets can provide an opportunity to traders of commodities in both spot and futures markets to reduce the risks of price fluctuations over time as well as to increase their profits. A futures market allows those involved in the distribution, processing, or storage of a good to concentrate on their specialized productive activities by taking advantage of the relationship between spot and futures prices.

Suppose, for example, that on July 1, 1982, the operator of a grain elevator buys 5,000 bushels of wheat from a farmer for $5 a bushel (the spot price on that date). The grain is put into storage for intended sale at some date in the future. What are the risks to the operator? If the price of wheat were to drop, the operator could incur substantial losses. Through the futures market, the elevator operator hedges by immediately selling a futures contract for 5,000 bushels of wheat to be delivered at a price of $5.15 in November 1982. The elevator operator has sold November 1982 wheat for $5.15.

If the elevator operator holds his wheat until November, the wheat purchased for $5 can be delivered on the futures contract for $5.15. The elevator operator has locked in a profit of $0.15 per bushel to cover his carrying charges.

Now suppose the spot price of wheat drops, and one month later, the elevator operator sells this wheat for $4 on the spot market to General Mills. On this spot transaction, he has lost $5,000

($1 per bushel on 5,000 bushels). But what about the November 1982 futures contract that he has previously sold? Because wheat prices are falling, the price of November 1982 wheat has dropped to $4.10. By buying a November 1982 contract for 5,000 bushels, the elevator operator would earn $1.05 × 5,000, or $5,250, by closing out the position. Remember the elevator operator had previously sold a November 1982 contract for $5,150. Through hedging, the elevator operator has not only limited the risks from falling grain prices but has made a profit. The elevator operator lost $5,000 from the spot market and gained $5,250 in the futures market and in effect, earned $250—$0.05 per bushel—by holding wheat for one month.

Large grain users such as General Mills can also hedge against the risks of fluctuating wheat prices by using the futures market. General Mills knows in July that it will require 100,000 bushels of wheat in December. It does not know what the price of wheat will be in December, but it can purchase a December 1981 futures contract for 100,000 bushels of wheat at $5 per bushel and thus protect itself against the risk that wheat will be selling well above $5 in December.

Hedgers and speculators play highly complementary roles in the economy. Hedgers are interested primarily in storing commodities or in using these commodities in their business. Hedgers are interested in their particular business and in minimizing the risks of price fluctuations. The speculator, on the other hand, does not have to be concerned with the details of storing grain or making flour and grain products. The speculator specializes in information about supply and demand in the future. There is division of labor between the hedger and the speculator.

Information and Speculation

The futures market provides information concerning the future. This information is not always accurate; sometimes it predicts that prices will rise but instead they fall, and vice versa. Prices in futures markets reveal to the economy what speculators *anticipate* will happen to the prices of different commodities in the future. If the futures price of wheat is well above the current spot price, then speculators, who attempt to anticipate future developments of supply and demand, feel that wheat prices will rise. These futures prices represent the best information available to the economy on the course of prices in the future.

Economic decisions must be made today concerning actions that must be taken in the future. Farmers must plant crops that will not be harvested for many months; mine operators must plan the expansion of mine capacity. If prices in the future were known with certainty, such planning would be grossly simplified, but the future is always uncertain. Clearly, having a futures market that establishes effective future prices today is of great benefit in an uncertain world. For those who need to know future prices, a futures market provides a summary indicator of market sentiment—a single price reflects much of what people know today about tomorrow.

THE ECONOMICS OF SEARCH

Centralized and Decentralized Markets

A market can be a highly **centralized market** or a **decentralized market.**

*A **centralized market** is one in which all buyers and sellers of a particular product make their transactions in one location.*

*A **decentralized market** is one in which buyers and sellers of a particular product make their transactions in a large number of markets with different physical locations.*

Stocks, bonds, and commodities, like wheat, gold, and soybeans, are traded in highly centralized markets. Other products, such as retail items, dry-cleaning services, real estate, and furniture are traded in decentralized markets.

Why are some markets centralized and others decentralized? Imagine what would happen if any one of our large cities (or even a medium-sized or small city) were to abolish all grocery stores and set up one central market for grocery products. Such a market, besides being hectic, would prove very inconvenient. The transactions cost of purchasing groceries would be much higher: consumers would need more time (and more gas) to drive to the centralized market, and they would need more time to purchase the desired goods once there (the centralized market could not specialize in particular products because it must service all customers). To avoid the cost and hassle, families would have to maintain much larger inventories of groceries in their homes.

A decentralized market for staple groceries is cheaper for the consumer, even though the consumer may pay lower purchase prices in the centralized market. The higher transactions costs of a centralized grocery market more than outweigh any savings in shelf prices at the centralized market.

In decentralized markets, it is more difficult for customers to know the prices charged for the same items in different stores, and even if consumers are aware of price differences, the transactions costs of going always to the cheapest store may outweigh the advantages of the lower price. As a consequence, prices in decentralized markets will differ from location to location. A *perfect market* was described in an earlier chapter as one in which all buyers paid the same price for the same product. Decentralized markets are usually imperfect because different buyers appear to pay different prices for the same product. From an economic viewpoint, however, the same good in different locations is a different product. This imperfection saves the consumer enormous transactions costs.

Information Gathering and Price Dispersion

Shopping or search costs explain why products sold in decentralized markets sell for different prices, although they are homogeneous with respect to every characteristic except location. A 19-inch Zenith color TV set may sell for different prices in stores one block apart; the same brand of milk may sell for different prices in adjacent grocery stores; the same brand of automobile may sell at different prices in two dealerships located in the same part of town.

If information about the prices charged by different retail outlets were free (assuming that no

Example 3

The Dispersion of Coffee and
Tea Prices in Houston Supermarkets

The proposition that the price dispersion on identical items would be lower the higher the total expenditure on the item was recently tested by gathering prices on two homogeneous products at five Houston supermarkets. Prices of a one-pound can of Folgers coffee and of a box of 48 Lipton tea bags were gathered at five different stores on the same day, in the same neighborhood. According to standard statistical measures, the price of the Lipton tea varied twice as much as the price of Folger's coffee. The prices are plotted in the accompanying figure. (The ratio of the standard deviation to the mean was 0.031 for coffee and 0.061 for tea).

This result is exactly what the economic theory of search predicts. It costs as much to shop for coffee as for tea, but Americans spend much more for coffee than for tea. The benefits of searching out the lowest coffee prices are, therefore, much higher than the benefits of searching out the lowest tea prices. Hence, we expect more

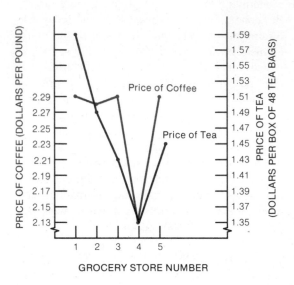

comparison shopping and far less price dispersion for coffee than for tea.

---

location is more convenient than another), the same commodity would sell for the same price, as predicted by the theory of perfect competition. But information is not free; real resources must be devoted to gathering information. Therefore, in the real world, the prices of homogeneous products sold in decentralized markets will be dispersed.

Economic theory can predict the extent of price dispersion: anything that raises the marginal benefits of search relative to the marginal costs of search will increase the amount of searching (shopping, reading, consultation of experts). The greater the volume of resources devoted to searching, the closer will be the prices of homogeneous products. The marginal benefits of search should be higher the larger the expenditures on a given item; therefore, the theory of search suggests that prices of expensive (as a percent of total expenditures) items will be less widely dispersed than those of less expensive items (see Example 3).

There is considerable evidence to support this proposition. George Stigler, in his investigation of automobile and washing-machine prices, found that prices were less widely dispersed for identical makes of automobiles than for identical brands of washing machines.[4]

An interesting paradox is that the more people search, the less the individual needs to search. If everyone devoted considerable resources to information searching, price dispersion—and the gains to further search—would be reduced because sellers would be aware of the search behavior.

PRODUCT INFORMATION

Advertising

Insofar as advertising provides information to potential buyers, one might expect advertising to reduce market imperfections by reducing price dispersion. As we have already seen in an earlier chapter, however, when advertising helps to dif-

4. George Stigler, *The Theory of Price* (New York: Macmillan, 1952), p.4.

Example 4

Uncertainty and Search Costs in the New England Fishing Market

The New England fishing market illustrates how uncertainty, information, and search costs caused real-world markets to diverge from the uniform-price feature of perfect competition. On the surface, this market appears to have the characteristics of perfect competition: there are more than 1,800 fishing vessels; there is relative freedom of entry; there are more than 400 licensed dealers who buy directly from the fishing vessels. One would expect the New England fishing market to be perfectly competitive with everyone paying the same price for the same product.

On the contrary, on the same day the same type and quality of fish sells for radically different prices. Some sellers sell at high prices; others sell at low prices. Uncertainty and high information costs explain why there is such disparity in prices.

Fishing vessels catch fish in nets and deposit their catch in their holds, never certain of the exact quantities and qualities of fish they have caught. When they arrive in port, the costs of getting alternate prices on their catch are prohibitive. The fish must be "offloaded" (at the fishing vessels expense), and the fish are likely to lose their fresh-ness in the process. Vessel owners simply are not in a position to shop from one dealer to another for alternate bids. Moreover, there is no centralized market for freshly caught fish (no spot market); fish sellers have little information on the price of fish on that particular day and are at a distinct informational disadvantage to the buyers. The result: on the same day, fish of the same type and quality sell at different prices. Sellers do not know the spot price of fish. In fact, there is no single organized spot market. Sellers cannot shop around for the highest price because the costs of such shopping around would be prohibitive. The costs of acquiring price information in such a market are very high because the fish sellers would have to have agents monitoring all the transactions taking place at different dock locations on each day to know what prices are.

Source: Based upon James Wilson, "Adaption to Uncertainty and Small Numbers Exchange: The New England Fresh Fish Market," *Bell Journal of Economics 11 (Autumn 1980): 491–504.*

---

ferentiate products, it can erect a barrier to entry that reinforces monopoly power. There are essentially two views of advertising. According to the procompetitive view of advertising, advertising provides information about prices and product qualities to buyers. As a result, advertising increases competition by making consumers aware of substitutes. Supporters of the anticompetitive view of advertising, however, believe that advertising reduces competition by giving large, established firms a competitive advantage over smaller less established firms. Advertising creates barriers to entry that limit competition and allow established firms to earn long-run profits.

Advertising can, in principle, either increase or reduce competition in an industry. Advertising's net effect on competition is therefore largely an empirical issue. If advertising's effect is largely anticompetitive, advertising would be likely to raise profit rates and industry concentration. If ad-vertising is procompetitive, advertising would be likely to reduce industry concentration and even out profit rates among firms.

What do the facts indicate? Different researchers have reached contradictory conclusions. Moreover, advertising's impact is not uniform across industries; it appears to depend upon the particular industry.[5]

1. Advertising has different effects on different products. Studies show that advertising has a greater positive effect on the profitability of non-

5. The literature on advertising has been developed by numerous economists including Lester Telser, Nicholas Kaldor, Richard Schmalensee, Phillip Nelson, William Comanor, Thomas Wilson, Michael Porter, Randall Brown, and many others. The available evidence is summarized in William Comanor and Thomas Wilson, "The Effect of Advertising on Competition," *Journal of Economic Literature* 17 (June 1979): 453–76.

durable goods than on durable goods. Durable goods (TV sets, washing machines, automobiles) are usually more expensive products where the marginal benefits to search are high. Nondurables (groceries, kitchen products, deodorant sprays, mouthwashes) are usually less expensive items where the marginal benefits of search are small. Advertising appears to have a larger positive effect on profitability in the area of convenience goods, such as paper towels and aspirin.

2. Advertising has a procompetitive effect on retail trade. This result is quite consistent with our analysis of search costs and suggests that retail advertising conveys information on prices and product qualities to consumers and reduces the cost of search. Empirical studies show that the higher the advertising intensity, the lower the profit margins of retail and service industries. The opposite result is obtained for industries that manufacture consumer goods, where advertising creates barriers to entry and increases product differentiation.

3. There are significant economies of scale of advertising present in specific industries. In the beer industry and in the cigarette industry, the advertising of large firms has a substantially greater sales impact than that of small firms. In the cigarette industry, for example, the ratio of advertising expenditures to sales declines steeply up to sales of 20 to 30 billion cigarettes, a level of sales that may take years to attain.[6]

Advertising can lead to lower prices paid by consumers when its function is to provide information on prices and quality. In this regard, consumers benefit from the advertising of retailers because advertising lowers search costs. But what of those cases where advertising reduces competition? Are consumers made worse off by advertising?

The higher price the consumer pays for advertised convenience products, such as over-the-counter drugs, children's clothes, or bleaches, may be a price willingly paid for the assurance of product quality. If, however, information were costless, and the consumer were perfectly informed about prices and product qualities, it is unlikely such price differentials would persist.

Product Quality, Durability, and Safety

Since information is costly to acquire, consumers will stop short of acquiring perfect information about the product's quality, durability, and safety. Advertising, insofar as it informs consumers about quality, durability, and safety, makes more information available to the consumer.[7] Because people are uncertain about the quality, safety, and durability of the product being purchased, consumers rely on brand names to certify the quality of the product.

Some firms guarantee that the product will meet the customer's expectations and promise to refund the customer's money or allow the customer to exchange a defective product for another one when the product fails to meet the quality, safety, or durability standards the customer expects. For example, every product sold by Quaker Oats carries such a guarantee: buyers can get their money back by sending in the label with a brief explanation of what was wrong. Firms presumably do not want to be deluged with demands to reimburse buyers for defective products, so they seek to produce a product that meets consumer expectations.

But what about cases where severe damages are inflicted upon unsuspecting buyers, even by brand-name products? Teenagers are killed in automobiles with poorly designed gas tanks (that ignite on impact). Babies are born deformed due to a drug taken by their mother during pregnancy; fingers are severed by a poorly designed lawnmower. Who should be liable for such incidents? The two basic approaches to this question are *caveat emptor* (let the consumer beware) and *caveat venditor* (let the seller beware).

---

6. Randall Brown, "Estimating Advantages to Large-Scale Advertising," *Review of Economics and Statistics* 60 (August 1978): 428–37.

7. An interesting dilemma for advertisers is whether or not to engage in negative advertising. After several air disasters involving DC-10 aircraft, one airline—TWA—advertised that it flies the "wide-bodies that most people prefer" (namely, 747s and Lockheed 1011s). American automobile manufacturers must also determine whether to exploit the poor crash performances of imported compact cars. Should they sell their cars on the basis of the *lack* of safety of foreign imports?

Example 5

The Effect of Advertising on the Prices of Eyeglasses

Economist Lee Benham studied the effect of advertising on the prices of eyeglasses in a research report published in 1972. The advertising of eyeglasses is prohibited in some states and is allowed in others. Benham compared the prices of eyeglasses in states that allowed advertising with those where advertising is not allowed.

Benham found that the average price of eyeglasses in states that barred advertising was more than double the average price in states where advertising was allowed. This study shows how advertising can promote competition. Advertising, by providing information on prices and product quality, renders the demands for the products of individual suppliers more elastic and thus lowers the prices paid by consumers.

Source: Lee Benham, "The Effect of Advertising on the Price of Eyeglasses," *The Journal of Law and Economics* 15 (October 1972): 337–52.

Caveat Emptor. There is a big difference between professional buyers employed by large enterprises and the ordinary consumer. The large enterprise employs a purchasing agent who is a specialist in the goods purchased by the firm. Such agents know as much (or more) as the seller about the products they buy. Centuries ago, the average customer may have been in roughly the same position as this specialized purchasing agent. Goods were simple, and the buyer could assess their quality rather easily. The buyer was not at an information disadvantage relative to the seller.

Under these circumstances—where the buyer and seller possess the same information—the legal doctrine of *caveat emptor* (let the buyer beware) would be efficient and would work well.

Circumstances are different today. Products are exceedingly complex. When consumers select automobiles, television sets, home furnaces, or electrical wiring, they are at an enormous information disadvantage relative to the seller. For this reason, the legal doctrine of *caveat emptor* has been modified to protect the buyer from **fraud, warranty** violations, and negligence.

Fraud is an act of deceit or misrepresentation.

Fraud occurs when the purchased product is never delivered or when a promised service is not supplied as contracted.

*A **warranty** is a guarantee of the integrity of a product and of the seller's responsibility for the repair or replacement of defective parts.*

Warranties may be expressed or implied. A good is supposed to do what it is designed to do (a washing machine is expected to wash clothes, a reclining chair is expected to recline). Whether the warranty is written or not, if the good does not perform its function, the seller has legally violated the warranty. *Negligence* occurs when the seller does not reveal to the buyer a hidden defect that later causes injury.[8]

The rule of *caveat emptor,* even in our modern world of complex products, does have some advantages. First, it provides the customer with an incentive to gain information about product quality, durability, and safety. If the user of the good is not liable for damages incurred while using the product, the consumer may not be as careful in choosing products.

Second, if the seller were liable for all damages caused by the use of a product, even by careless users, the cost of the product to the consumer could become excessive. If, for example, manufacturers of sulphuric acid were liable for all personal injuries associated with the use of the prod-

---

8. For this reason, in court cases involving personal injury due to manufacturing defects—such as a case against Ford Motors involving a fire-prone gas tank—it is very important for the claimant to establish that the company was aware of the defect.

uct, there would be little sulphuric acid supplied, and it would sell at a very high price. It is more efficient for society as a whole to require the manufacturer to simply label the product as dangerous. If the user fails to heed this warning, the manufacturer is not liable for damages.

A third argument in favor of *caveat emptor* is that products are put to different uses by different consumers. It would be impossible for the manufacturer to anticipate all these uses, and it would be prohibitively expensive to design a product that would be safe in all uses. An automobile can be used either for transportation in a quiet suburb or for high-speed stock-car racing. The car manufacturer who is held liable for brake failure when the car is racing at 130 miles per hour would be forced to produce a car that would cost the average buyer much more and would have technical characteristics of little use to the majority of users. As Roland McKean has observed:[9]

> The buyer is in a better position than anyone else to know the exact use to which he plans to put a product and what alternative qualities, or degrees of safety, in the product would mean to his costs and gains. The customer, if he is liable, has an extra incentive to acquire and make appropriate use of the information.

Caveat Venditor. *Caveat emptor* does not work well when the cost of acquiring information is very high to the consumer. Manufacturers know more than anyone else about their products. When it is very costly for consumers to acquire information, producer liability (*caveat venditor*) may be a more efficient system of assigning liability.

Information costs can be kept down for consumers by organizations like Consumers Union, which basically hires itself out to check out products scientifically for its subscribers. Government can also reduce information costs by establishing minimum standards and carrying out inspections to insure that these standards are being observed. Municipal governments usually have health inspectors to inspect public dining places and public swimming pools. There are universal standards of

weights and measures and inspections to insure that the butcher's scale is accurate. Without these governmental regulations and inspections, the costs of personal inspection and information gathering would be excessive.

Departures from perfect competition caused by information costs do not generally require government action, except to enforce contracts and to establish rules of liability. The next chapter examines departures from perfect competition that are caused by barriers to entry and oligopolistic collusion. In these cases, government has a more active role to play.

Summary

1. Information is costly because of our limited ability to process, store, and retrieve facts and figures about the economy and because real resources are required to gather information. Individuals acquire information to the point where the marginal cost of acquiring more information equals the marginal benefit of more information.
2. "Middlemen," or intermediaries, bring together buyers and sellers; they often buy in order to sell again and sometimes serve as certifiers of quality.
3. Speculators buy now in order to sell later for a profit. If speculators are profitable, they stabilize prices and consumption over time. If they are unprofitable, they destabilize prices and consumption over time. Speculators should be judged on the basis of *ex ante* rather than *ex post* efficiency.
4. A futures market is where a contract is made now for payment and delivery of a commodity in the future. Futures markets provide information about the uncertain future and allow hedging by those who wish to reduce risks.
5. Search costs explain the observed dispersion of prices. When the benefits to further search are large, price dispersion will be limited.
6. Advertising can have both procompetitive and anticompetitive effects. By providing information, advertising makes markets more perfect. Advertising can also erect barriers to

9. Roland McKean, "Product Liability: Implications of Some Changing Property Rights," *Quarterly Journal of Economics* 84 (November 1970): 611–26.

entry and thereby create monopoly power. In a complex world where the seller has more information about product quality, durability, and safety, the doctrine of *caveat emptor* (let the buyer beware) has its limitations. But even in such a world, there are still some advantages to *caveat emptor*.

Key Terms

information costs
transactions costs
"middlemen" or intermediaries
speculators
arbitrage
futures market
spot (or cash) market
hedging
centralized market
decentralized market
fraud
warranty

Questions and Problems

1. Investors can purchase shares of stock through a full-service broker (who provides information and investment advice) or through a dis- count broker. The commission charged by the full-service broker is much higher than that of the discount broker. They both pro- vide the service of buying the shares of stock ordered by the buyer. Explain why most investors use the services of the higher-priced brokers.

2. The market for wheat is highly centralized. In fact, one can say there is a world market for wheat. Why is this market centralized while other markets, like the market for au- tomobiles, are decentralized?

3. What are the transactions costs of selling a home? What effect do real estate brokers have on these costs?

4. Explain why more is spent on the advertising of deodorants than on the advertising of farm machinery.

5. If search costs in a market are zero and the market is competitively organized, what pre- dictions can you make about prices in this market?

6. Under what conditions does *caveat emptor* work well? Under what conditions would *ca- veat emptor* not work well?

7. The stock market is highly competitive with thousands of speculators trying to buy low and sell high. Using the concepts of infor- mation and search costs, explain why we all can't get rich with a little study and research by playing the stock market.

CHAPTER

14

Antitrust Law and Regulation

Chapter Preview

Public distrust of big business is not a new phenomenon. It is deeply rooted in economic theory and in the public's perception of harm done to them by monopoly power. Adam Smith's famous warning issued in 1776 about the dangers of monopoly has been reinforced by the formal theory of monopoly presented in earlier chapters. This chapter will explain why governments decide to control monopoly power and will describe how governments use public ownership, regulation, and legislation to limit monopoly power.

TO CONTROL OR NOT TO CONTROL MONOPOLY POWER

The Case Against Big Business

Opponents of ''bigness'' in business argue three points: First, a monopoly will restrict output below what would have been produced if the industry were competitive, forcing the consumer to pay a higher price for a smaller quantity of output. Monopoly, therefore, causes *deadweight*

258

losses to society that can be accentuated if there is a monopoly rent seeking. Second, if potential competition is weak, the monopolist has little incentive to innovate. Monopolists will not be motivated to introduce new products or to find new cost-saving technologies. Third, when monopoly profits increase the wealth of monopolists and of their heirs, an undesirable distribution of income can result.

The Case For Big Business

The case for big business also rests upon three points. First, if the monopolist operates in an industry where there are substantial economies of scale, a larger producer will be able to produce at lower average costs than a number of smaller producers and can, therefore, charge a lower price. Second, the monopoly power of big business is overrated. Even if a monopolist does not have immediate competitors (a railroad may offer the only rail service between two cities), monopolists must still compete with companies both at home and abroad that offer substitute products (trucking firms will compete for the railroads' customers). Moreover, if monopoly profits become too large, potential competitors may be enticed into the market. Third, only large companies can afford the enormous research and development costs required to develop modern technology. Small competitive firms simply cannot finance the laboratories and research staffs that have become essential to modern research and development.

THE NATURAL MONOPOLY

Where there is a real choice of industrial organization, government policy can be used to alter industrial structure in the desired direction. For example, a large company may be broken up into several smaller companies if the government believes that the company has used its monopoly power in a harmful way. There is no real choice of industrial structure in the case of a **natural monopoly.**

*A **natural monopoly** is a firm whose long-run average costs decline over the range of output that the industry would produce.*

Figure 1
The Natural Monopoly

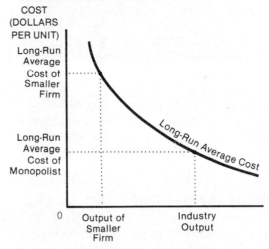

This figure shows the long-run average cost curve of a natural monopoly. As the curve shows, this firm's average costs decline until the level of industry output is reached; average total costs continue to decline until enough output is produced to satisfy the demand of the entire industry. A single producer can, therefore, produce at much lower average cost than could a number of smaller producers. For this reason, there will be only one enterprise in this industry in the long run.

The case of the natural monopoly is shown in Figure 1. The natural monopoly occurs when an enterprise experiences economies of scale until the market output of the industry is reached. Examples would be electric-power and natural-gas utilities and local telephone service. For such enterprises, long-run average costs fall as output is increased. For these reasons, long-run average costs for a natural monopoly continue to decline until the output of the entire industry is produced.

If the industry is a natural monopoly, industry output will be produced at much lower average cost than if the industry were made up of more than one producer. Imagine, for example, having three electric utilities operating in the same market with three systems of power lines and underground cables. In the case of the natural monopoly, economies of scale are so prominent that there is little choice but to operate as a single-firm industry.

Since a certain amount of monopoly power is unavoidable, government must decide *whether or not* and *how* to control monopoly power.

THE GOVERNMENT'S ARSENAL OF WEAPONS FOR CONTROL OF MONOPOLY POWER

If the government chooses to control monopoly power, what weapons does it have at its disposal? Basically, governments have three options: government ownership, regulation, and antitrust legislation.[1]

Government Ownership

The government can purchase the monopoly from private owners and run the monopoly "in the public interest." Public ownership of business in the United States is more common at the municipal and state level than at the federal level. Municipal services such as local transportation, water, sanitation, gas, and electricity are often owned and operated by state and local government. In 1979, more than 22 percent of all electrical energy was generated by government-owned enterprises.[2]

At the federal level, government enterprises are more limited. They include, among others, the Tennessee Valley Authority (a giant government-owned electrical utility), the United States Postal Service (now a semigovernmental organization), government home-mortgage programs (the Veterans Administration and Federal Housing Authority programs), various weapons-producing arsenals, and the Government Printing Office.

These activities may appear substantial, but they account for only 2 percent of American national output. The unusual feature of government policy in the United States has been the decision to leave monopolies in the hands of private owners and to control monopoly by other means.

Regulation

Regulation of monopoly prices and services is a second means of controlling monopoly. The enterprise remains in private hands, but its activities are regulated by government agencies.

In the United States, regulation at the state and local level is largely directed at monopolies—the electric, gas, water, and telephone companies. At the national level, federal regulatory commissions regulate a number of industries, ranging from long-distance telephone service to broadcasting to trucking. Federal and state regulatory agencies enforce environmental standards (the Environmental Protection Agency) and worker safety (The Occupational Safety and Health Administration, or OSHA) and license professionals. The Federal Aviation Agency (FAA) is responsible for airline safety, and the Food and Drug Administration (FDA) is responsible for the safety of foods and drugs sold in the United States. Much government regulation is also directed toward potentially competitive industries, as discussed below.

The five major federal regulatory commissions are:

1. the Interstate Commerce Commission (established in 1887), which regulates railroads, interstate oil pipelines, and interstate motor and water carriers,
2. the Federal Power Commission (established in 1920), which has jurisdiction over power projects and the interstate transmission of electricity and natural gas,
3. the Federal Communications Commission (established in 1933), which regulates interstate telephone and telegraph and broadcasting,
4. the Securities and Exchange Commission (established in 1934), which regulates securities markets, and
5. the Civil Aeronautics Board (established in 1938), which supervises domestic and international aviation.

---

1. A fourth method for controling monopoly power—not used in the United States—is to utilize state's power to tax and subsidize monopolies. This method was promoted by the English economist, A. C. Pigou, and later by American economist Arnold Harberger. The idea is to pay the monopolist a subsidy as an incentive to produce the level of output that would have been produced had this been a perfectly competitive industry. The state would then seek to tax away (by a lump-sum tax) the increase in profits resulting from the subsidy, and the consumer would be made better off by being offered more output at a lower price. In this way, the state would eliminate the deadweight loss of monopoly. See Arnold Harberger, "Monopoly and Resource Allocation," *American Economic Review*, 44 (May 1954): 77–87.

2. *Statistical Abstract of the United States*, 1980, p. 611.

Currently, a move is underway to deregulate the economy, and the responsibilities of many of these commissions are being reduced. The Civil Aeronautics Board, for example, is scheduled to go out of existence in 1984.

Regulation is supposed to ensure the availability of service, to establish standards for the quality of service, and to guarantee the public "reasonable" prices.

Antitrust Law

A third approach to monopoly control is legislation to control market structure and business conduct. The most important antitrust acts are the Sherman Act of 1890, the Clayton and Federal Trade Commission Acts of 1913, the Wheeler-Lea Act of 1938, and the Cellar-Kefauver Act of 1950. These acts prohibit general and specific business practices that increase or abuse market power. Antitrust legislation also outlaws particular market structures.

GOVERNMENT OWNERSHIP

Public ownership of monopolies is not as widespread in the United States as elsewhere, but it is one method for controlling monopoly power. Figure 2 shows a natural monopoly owned by the federal government.

How does the government operate a public enterprise in the public interest? What instructions should be given to the manager of the public enterprise? Should it produce that quantity of output at which price and marginal cost are equal (point c in Figure 2)? Point c is efficient because the marginal cost (of society's resources) is equated with the marginal benefit (received by society) as reflected in the price. But, the $P = MC$ rule means that the enterprise will be run at a loss, and taxpayers must make up that loss. Taxpayers who do not use the service will subsidize those who do.

Alternatively, the public enterprise could be instructed to *break even*—to produce where price equals average total cost (at b in Figure 2). In our example, price is almost two times greater than marginal cost, and the efficiency rule ($P = MC$) is broken. But the customer is offered a larger quantity of output q_b at a lower price p_b than if this firm were an unregulated monopoly.

Figure 2
The Dilemma of a Public Enterprise

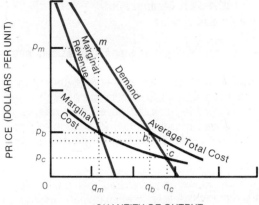

QUANTITY OF OUTPUT

This figure depicts a monopoly that is owned by the public. It is not clear which rules the manager of this public enterprise should follow to operate this public enterprise "in the public interest." The manager could equate marginal cost and price (point c), but the enterprise would be operating at a loss. The manager could attempt to break even (point b)—operate where price and average total cost are equal—but the manager would have little incentive to economize on costs as higher costs would translate into higher prices and higher revenues. Finally, the manager could attempt to maximize profits (point m), but consumers would receive a relatively small quantity of output and pay relatively high prices while monopoly profits accrued to the state.

The third option would be to instruct the public enterprise to maximize profits, just like a private unregulated monopoly. This option would yield the outcome of point m (the enterprise would choose the quantity that equates marginal revenue and marginal cost). Again, the basic efficiency rule is broken: price is more than three times marginal cost in this example. The public is offered a relatively small quantity of output q_m for which it must pay a relatively high price p_m. The only gain over a private monopoly is that the resulting monopoly profit will revert to the government, and the government can use these profits to pay for other government services.[3]

3. In the Federal Republic of Germany, the State owns the telephone company and operates it like a private unregulated monopoly. The monopoly profits from the telephone company are then used to support other government services (like the post office) that operate at a loss.

Example 1

Incentives for Managers of Public Enterprises

It is not certain that managers of public enterprises will automatically obey the rules given them by the government. The government must devise an incentive system to encourage public managers to follow the rules the government has established. Critics of public enterprise, such as Friederich von Hayek and Ludwig von Mises (both prominent Austrian economists), have argued that this is not easy.

If the government decides that public enterprises should follow the marginal-cost-equals-price rule, the manager must run the public enterprise at a loss and ask the government for subsidies. Professional managers may be reluctant to make decisions that will necessarily lead to losses. In addition, it will be virtually impossible for the manager's superior to know whether or not the manager is obeying the rules. Without extensive investigation, only the manager will know whether or not the public enterprise is producing at marginal-cost-equals-price.

If the government tells the manager to break even (produce where price equals average total cost), then there is little incentive for the public manager to hold down costs. By allowing costs to rise (through inefficient operation), the public enterprise can raise its prices and its revenues. All the manager has to do is break even; whether the manager breaks even at low or high cost is not that important.

The incentive to inflate costs will be removed if the manager is instructed to maximize profits. The professional manager would know how to do this, but this directive would cause the manager to produce at the same price/output combination as a monopoly. The public pays the same price as if this were a private monopoly, but the monopoly profits go to the state.

Source: Based on: F. A. Hayek, ed. *Collectivist Economic Planning*, 6th ed. (London: Routledge and Kegan Paul, 1963); Ludwig von Mises, "Economic Calcuation in Socialism," in ed. Morris Bornstein, *Comparative Economic Systems,* rev. ed. (Homewood, Ill.: Irwin, 1969), pp. 61–68.

REGULATION OF MONOPOLIES

The American public has chosen overwhelmingly to regulate monopolies rather than to own them. Regulation is exercised by a variety of state, local, and federal agencies. Administrative regulation is carried out by officials of the executive branch of government and by semi-independent commissions that operate under general legislative authority.

Who Is Regulated?

Natural monopolies like the gas and electric companies and local telephone service are regulated at the state and local level. However, much state and local regulation is directed at basically competitive industries (taxicab licensing, concession franchises in sports stadiums, licensing of barbers and beauticians) for the purpose of limiting competition and creating more monopoly power. Federal commissions also regulate potentially competitive industries, such as transportation and broadcasting, and often limit competition in these industries. *Government regulation is not consistent.* Some government regulation is clearly designed to combat monopoly power; other types of regulation lessen competition.

In recent years, there has been a movement toward federal *deregulation* of industries that are basically competitive, such as airlines, trucking, banking, and broadcasting. In fact, deregulation was emphasized during the Carter presidency and was an important plank in the successful 1980 presidential campaign of President Ronald Reagan.

It is difficult to estimate exactly what proportion of the U.S. economy is regulated because most businesses are regulated in one way or another. On the one hand, regulated industries could include only those industries in which rates and

Example 2

U.S. Postal Service versus United Parcel Service

The two giants of parcel-post delivery are the U.S. Postal Service and United Parcel Service (UPS). The U.S. Postal Service is a public enterprise, while UPS is a private corporation. Both operate in an industry with substantial economies of scale. These economies of scale explain why the industry has only two major competitors. By 1975, UPS had succeeded in obtaining interstate operating rights in all 48 continental states, often after protracted courtroom battles.

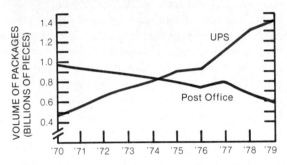

Prior to 1975, the U.S. Postal Service delivered more packages than UPS, but since then UPS has gained a much larger share of the parcel-post market than the postal service.

If the U.S. Postal Service wanted to compete with UPS to regain its lost share of the market, it would have to offer lower rates and better service than UPS. To prevent the lowering of postal rates, UPS and the Teamsters Union (UPS is the largest employer of Teamsters) have fought in Congress to keep postal rates high. UPS and the Teamsters worked hard to defeat a measure before Congress in 1978 that would have allowed the post office to set parcel-post rates without regard to cost and thus offer rates more competitive with UPS. 🔀

Source: Adapted from "The Brown Giant: UPS Delivers Profit by Expanding its Territory and Fighting to Keep Postal Rates High," *Wall Street Journal*, August 25, 1980.

---

prices are controlled by government agencies (transportation, communications, utilities, banking, and insurance). According to this criterion, some 10 percent of national output may be produced by regulated firms. If businesses that are government-supervised (such as the drug industry or meat packing) are added, the regulated sector may be as high as one quarter of national output. [4]

Any single measure of the scope of the regulated sector is misleading because some businesses are more closely supervised than others (the prescription-drug industry is more strictly supervised by the Food and Drug Administration than the automobile industry is regulated by the Environmental Protection Agency).

[4] The figure of 25 percent for 1939 comes from the studies of G. Warren Nutter, *The Extent of Enterprise Monopoly in the United States, 1899-1939* (Chicago: University of Chicago Press, 1951); and George Stigler, *Five Lectures on Economic Problems* (London: Longmans, Green and Company, 1949). Estimates of this sort for later years are not available. It is difficult to establish whether the relative magnitude of regulation has increased or decreased since then.

Objectives of Regulation

There are three basic reasons to regulate business. [5] Businesses are regulated

1. to prevent monopoly profits from being earned without preventing the firm from operating at a normal profit.
2. to encourage the regulated business to operate efficiently and safely.
3. to prevent predatory competition that would result in less competition.

The basic instrument regulators use to achieve these objectives is rate regulation, or control of the prices (rates) that regulated enterprises are allowed to charge. Regulators in some cases control

[5] For a discussion of the objectives of regulation, see William J. Baumol, "Reasonable Rules for Rate Regulation: Plausible Policies in an Imperfect World," in ed. Paul MacAvoy, *The Crisis of the Regulatory Commissions* (New York: W. W. Norton, 1970), pp. 187–206.

entry into the industry by issuing licenses and franchises. Regulators also establish rules or standards for the quality of goods or services. Although regulators do more than simply set rates, this chapter will concentrate on rate setting and its effects on the three basic objectives of regulation.

Principles of Rate Regulation

Figure 2 represents the demand and cost schedules of a privately owned natural monopoly. This monopoly is regulated by a regulatory commission, whose responsibility it is to protect the interests of users of the product. In practical terms, the regulatory commission must set "reasonable" rates for the service of the monopoly, establish standards for minimum quality of service, and guarantee access to the service to all customers without discrimination.

Regulatory commissions are bound by the safeguards of private property embodied in the Fifth and Fourteenth Amendments to the U.S. Constitution. Regulators must protect the property rights of the owners of the monopoly and are not permitted to set rates that do not cover operating costs plus a "fair" rate of return on invested capital. If regulators set rates that fail to cover operating costs and a fair rate of return, the monopoly can claim illegal seizure of private property and appeal to the courts for redress.

The Pricing Formula.   The usual regulatory pricing formula is:

Price of service = average operating cost + fair rate of return on invested capital

This pricing formula seems simple but raises as many questions as it answers. How are operating costs to be established? What constitutes a "fair" rate of return to invested capital? The formula does rule out marginal-cost pricing because marginal-cost pricing (point *c* in Figure 2) typically yields a loss and would not offer the regulated firm a fair rate of return. The fair-rate-of-return pricing formula is thought to lead to an inefficient use of resources. Increases in operating costs (whether justified or not) will be passed on to the consumer by the pricing formula in the

form of higher prices; the regulated firm need not be overly concerned with reducing its costs of production. Regulators typically do not have the information to determine whether reported costs are padded or legitimate. Regulatory commissions do have the authority to examine accounting records for extravagant costs, exorbitant managerial salaries, or excessive advertising expenditures but regulators are reluctant to substitute their judgments on what costs are reasonable for those of management.

The Rate Base.   The ability of regulated monopolies to pass cost increases on to consumers is one source of inefficiency. Rate regulation to provide a fair rate of return on invested capital creates a second type of inefficiency by encouraging the regulated monopoly to use too much capital.[6]

Suppose regulators have determined that 12 percent is a fair rate of return. The regulated firm will be allowed to earn annual profits equal to 12 percent of invested capital. The value of invested capital is the regulated firm's *rate base*.

If the company has a rate base of $10 million and the profit-rate ceiling is 12 percent, this company will be allowed to earn a maximum profit of $1.2 million per annum.

An unregulated company will add to its invested capital only if the present value of the resulting business profits exceeds the costs of acquiring the capital. The regulated monopoly, however, can increase its profits merely by expanding its rate base. By investing an additional $5 million, the rate base is expanded by $5 million (to $15 million), and the regulated company can now earn $1.8 million profit per annum. Accordingly, regulated firms have an incentive to acquire more capital than unregulated firms. According to economists, this incentive to acquire capital will lead to inefficiencies in the economic system because regulated firms will invest at the margin in projects with lower rates of return than those acceptable to unregulated firms. Therefore, regulators must decide whether certain additions to capital should be included in the rate base.

6.   The tendency of regulated monopolies to use too much capital was first analyzed by H. Averch and L. L. Johnson, "Behavior of the Firm under Regulatory Constraint," *American Economic Review* 52 (December 1962).

The Divestiture of AT&T, January 1982

In what has been termed the most important antitrust development since the dissolution of Standard Oil in 1911, American Telephone and Telegraph (AT&T) and the Justice Department settled a 7-year old antitrust suit in January 1982. The Justice Department had charged AT&T with violating the Sherman Act through its monopoly over local telephone service. Potential competitors to AT&T's long-distance service had been denied—it was charged—equal access to AT&T's network to beat down the challenge to AT&T's monopoly of long-distance telephone service. If AT&T had been found guilty, then the way would have been opened for injured parties to collect damages from AT&T. In the case of an adverse ruling, such damages may have cost AT&T some $14 billion.

The AT&T case was settled by an agreement between the Justice Department and AT&T in which AT&T did not have to admit wrongdoing. Thus injured parties would have to prove wrongdoing by AT&T—an expensive and time-consuming task. The principal provisions of the agreement are as follows: 1) AT&T agrees to divest itself of its 22 local operating companies, which account for $87 billion of AT&T's $136 billion assets. 2) AT&T keeps its long-distance telephone service, its manufacturing arm, Western Electric, and its research arm, Bell Laboratories. 3) AT&T is allowed to enter into the unregulated business it chooses.

Its long-distance rates are still to be regulated by the Federal Communications Commission as long as AT&T retains its virtual monopoly over long-distance service. The local telephone companies remain subject to regulation by state and local agencies.

Basically, the AT&T agreement allows AT&T to give up its monopoly over local telephone service in exchange for less regulation. Prior to the settlement, AT&T was restricted by a 1956 consent decree that prevented it from entering into any unregulated business. Analysts believe that the new AT&T will expand into the new high-technology areas of data transmission, electronic message services, teleconferencing, electronic blackboards, voice-generated computers, and computer programming. These computer-data-transmission activities will bring AT&T into direct competition with another industrial giant, IBM.

AT&T had to divest itself of its 22 local telephone companies within 18 months, and the local companies must provide AT&T and its long-distance competitors with equal access to local exchanges.

In agreeing to the settlement, AT&T made a bold move into the uncharted waters of the unregulated telecommunications-computer industry. No longer is AT&T operating in the safe but low-growth business of regulated local service. ■

Regulatory Lag

A fundamental problem of rate regulation is that it appears to eliminate rewards to efficiency and innovation *if regulators raise rates immediately when operating costs rise*. This rate adjustment is not necessarily very speedy, however. Regulated utilities must appeal to regulatory officials to raise rates, and the red tape and foot dragging associated with lengthy hearings can create substantial delays. If rate increases are delayed while operating costs are rising, the regulated firm will not be able to earn its fair rate or return.

Some authorities argue that **regulatory lag** does put some pressure on regulated monopolies to economize on costs and to innovate. If operating costs rise and if years are required for the approval of higher rates (called *rate relief*), company earnings fall. When rate relief is eventually granted, the new rates may already be outdated, and the incentive to hold down costs may still be present. Regulatory lag is especially harmful to utility profits during inflationary periods when costs are increasing rapidly while rate relief is slow in coming.

> *Regulatory lag occurs when government regulators adjust rates some time after operating costs and the rate base have increased.*

Regulatory lag reintroduces some of the incentives for regulated firms to use their resources efficiently, but it is only a partial (and very imperfect) solution to the fundamental problem: How can regulators encourage efficient operation when they are basically guaranteeing a fair rate of return?

The Effects of Regulation

To evaluate rate regulation of natural monopolies, one must be able to compare the rates, services, and costs that would have existed in the absence of regulation to those that result with regulation. There is no ideal method of comparing actual regulated rates with hypothetical unregulated rates, but researchers have gone back in time to periods of U.S. history when there were both regulated and unregulated utilities to determine whether regulated rates were indeed lower.

The most authoritative study of this sort was conducted by George Stigler and Claire Friedland for the period 1912 to 1937 for electric utilities in states with and without regulatory commisions.[7] After 1937, virtually all electric utilities were regulated, so there would no longer be any basis for comparison. Stigler and Friedland found that, holding other factors constant, there was no difference between the rates charged by regulated and unregulated electric utilities. Thus, regulation made no difference in rates! Writing of this controversial finding, Paul MacAvoy concludes that, despite objections to the study, "substantive results to the contrary have not yet appeared. The positions taken by Professor Stigler and Miss Friedland. . .remains relatively secure."[8]

It should be emphasized that the Stigler-Friedland results applied only to electric power; we do not know if their results can be generalized to all regulated monopolies. Nevertheless, it is important to ask why regulation has not had more of an impact on prices. Several answers have been suggested.

First, regulators are outgunned by the regulated enterprises. The legal and professional staffs of regulatory agencies are small and underpaid and cannot compete with the large and well-paid staffs of the regulated firms. Moreover, only the regulated firms know the details of the operation of the company. The regulated firms are, therefore, in a position to circumvent orders from the regulatory commission. Monopoly profits in excess of the fair rate of return can be concealed by creative accounting (in determining how the rate base is to be valued, the proper amount of depreciation, and the allocation of joint costs) without the regulators' knowledge.[9]

Second, the monopoly power of regulated monopolies is exaggerated. If there are indeed effective substitutes (natural gas for electricity) or if users (primarily industrial and commercial customers) are prepared to move to another utility region if rates become excessive, then one would not expect rate regulation to make much difference.

Third, regulators tend to be captives of the industry they regulate. Regulators often have more in common with the companies they regulate than with the public they are supposed to represent. Regulators are often recruited from the ranks of the regulated companies and often join the regulated companies upon leaving the regulatory agency.

REGULATION OF POTENTIALLY COMPETITIVE INDUSTRIES

Regulation in the United States is not limited to monopolies. There are numerous examples of the regulation of potentially competitive industries. Examples of industries that are (or have been) regulated and that have the potential for significant competition are radio and television broadcasting, trucking, passenger and freight airlines, railroads, and banking.

The Case For and Against Deregulation

The Case For Deregulation.   Over the years, most economists have favored deregulation of in-

7.   George Stigler and Claire Friedland, "What Can Regulators Regulate? The Case of Electricity," reprinted in ed. Paul MacAvoy, *The Crisis of the Regulatory Commissions* (New York: W. W. Norton, 1970), pp. 39–52.

8.   MacAvoy, *The Crisis of the Regulatory Commissions*, p. 39.

9.   For a description of how regulated companies are able to evade regulatory decrees, see Richard Posner, "Natural Monopoly and its Regulation," in ed. Paul McAvoy, *The Crisis of the Regulatory Commissions* (New York: W. W. Norton, 1970), pp. 30–38.

dustries that are potentially competitive. They argue that deregulation would permit customers to get what they pay for, would eliminate the inefficiency of setting rates that do not reflect cost differences, and would eliminate stifling bureaucratic rules. In the case of television broadcasting, deregulation would lead to more competition among the major networks, cable television, and local stations, and the viewer would have a broader choice of programming. The basic thrust of the deregulation argument is that where the potential for competition exists, it is better for professional managers to make decisions about fares and services than for government bureaucrats to make these decisions. The public will likely get better (and more diversified) service at lower cost. As Alfred Kahn, chairman of the Civil Aeronautics Board (CAB) when airline deregulation was initiated, put it: "I have more faith in greed than in regulation."[10]

Examples of the inefficiency of regulation are many.[11]

1. Regulation of transportation by the ICC (Interstate Commerce Commission) has been aimed at equalizing the prices of the different forms of ground transport (railroads and trucks) despite differences in costs and in the quality of service. Shippers, required by the ICC to pay the same price for rail or truck shipments, typically picked one that provided more convenient service— which was typically trucking—and the railroads' share in interstate freight traffic dropped from 80 percent in 1925 to 36 percent in 1979.[12]
2. The ICC regulation of trucking burdened interstate truckers with inefficient rules that forced them to travel circuitous and unprofitable routes (and often return empty from long hauls).
3. Regulation of the airlines prevented airlines from charging lower fares on high-density profitable routes (say, New York to Chicago) or higher fares on low-density unprofitable routes despite

substantial differences in costs per passenger mile. Moreover, airlines and railroads were not allowed to drop routes that made consistent losses, and routes were often awarded by administrative decree rather than on the basis of economic considerations.
4. Regulation of television by the Federal Communications Commission (FCC) has controlled access to the airwaves by limiting the number of VHF channels (channels 2-13) in a locality to three or four. The rationale for these limitations is that the public airwaves should be operated in the public interest and that the FCC could best guarantee this by regulating the three major networks. Limiting competition increased the dominance of the three major networks.

The Case Against Deregulation. The case against deregulation consists of three arguments. The first is that substantial elements of the market may be denied an essential service as a result of deregulation. For example, small communities may find themselves without rail or air service after deregulation. The second argument is that if deregulation occurs, competition may be eliminated by the emergence of a dominant producer, who will than act like a monopolist. For example, it has been argued that deregulation of banking could lead to the domination of the industry by a few large banks. The third point is that regulation permits public control of the quality of the service. For example, if access to the airwaves were not regulated, people worry that public-interest programming would disappear.[13]

Deregulation Legislation

In October 1978, President Jimmy Carter signed the Airline Deregulation Act, the first of the major deregulation acts of the 1970s and 1980s. The Airline Deregulation Act allowed the airlines, rather than the Civil Aeronautics Board, to set their own fares (within a broad range set by the CAB) and to select their own routes. Service to smaller communities was to continue for 10

10. *The New York Times,* October 7, 1980.
11. Case studies of the higher costs of regulated industries are presented in MacAvoy, *The Crisis of the Regulatory Commissions*, parts 3–5.
12. Estimates of the American Enterprise Institute are from "Deregulation is Back on Track in Congress," *New York Times*, September 7, 1980.

13. "Deregulation is Back on Track," *New York Times*, September 7, 1980; "FCC Battleground: Deregulation of TV," *New York Times*, October 20, 1980; "The U.S. Drive for Deregulation," *New York Times,* October 7, 1980.

Example 4

Has Airline Deregulation Worked?

The opponents of airline deregulation (initially the major airlines and organized labor) argued that deregulation would mean losses of service to smaller communities, increased unemployment among airline personnel, higher fares, lower airline profits, the emergence of one or two dominant airlines, compromises in airline safety, and a general breakdown in the existing airline network. What has actually happened since 1978?

Prior to deregulation, airline fares rose at only a slightly slower rate than inflation. Since deregulation, average airline fares have risen at only a small percentage of the consumer price index. In 1978, the first year of deregulation, the average fare actually fell, while consumer prices rose almost 8 percent.

After adjustment for inflation, average costs (per passenger mile) dropped substantially after deregulation despite rising fuel costs. This decline in average costs was due to greater utilization of equipment, fewer vacant seats (higher load factors), and the installation of more seats on aircrafts. Since deregulation, airline productivity has increased.

Prior to deregulation, airline profits averaged 5.4 percent of invested capital (1970–1976). From 1977 to 1979, airline profits averaged a 9.2 percent rate on invested capital despite the recession of 1979. In 1980, the recession pushed many airlines into the loss column, and in 1981 the airlines recorded their highest loss ever as an industry. The profitability performance of the airlines since deregulation has not been consistent, but it would be hard to pin the blame for recent airline losses on deregulation. In the past, recessions have also caused airline profits to drop. The airline industry has traditionally been a cyclically sensitive industry. Even the most troubled airlines do not blame their current difficulties on deregulation but on the recession and the air-traffic controllers strike of 1981.

The major airlines have indeed cut service to

---

years financed by government subsidy if necessary. The act also called for the phasing out of the CAB by 1984.

Other deregulation legislation soon followed: The Motor Carrier Act of 1980 curbed the ICC's control over interstate trucking. It allowed truckers greater freedom to set their own rates or to change their routes and permitted new firms to enter the business of interstate trucking. The Staggers Rail Act of October 1980 gave the railroads more flexibility in setting their own rates, banned the railroad industry's practice of collective rate setting, and allowed railroads to drop unprofitable routes. The year 1980 also saw the passage of the Depository Institutions Deregulation and Monetary Conrol Act, which will eventually eliminate interest-rate ceilings on bank savings deposits and allows savings and loans to offer checking accounts, car loans, and full-service credit cards. Since 1972, the FCC has been gradually deregulating the television broadcast industry by increasing the number of channels, removing barriers to direct satellite broadcasting, licensing new low-power television stations, and removing restrictions on cable television. In 1981, the number of allowable VHF channels was increased, thus creating the possibility of a fourth major network.

Deregulation is a recent phenomenon; it is too early to determine whether the optimistic predictions of better service and lower prices will prove correct. It is also too early to tell whether deregulation will lead to an upsurge in productivity growth as industries are freed from bureaucratic controls. Airline deregulation was carried out during two costly recessions and a period of escalating fuel bills (see Example 4). The deregulation of trucking has been fought by unions and by major trucking companies, and, as a result, most truckers are still subject to federal regulation. As a consequence, it is very difficult at this point in time to evaluate the effects of deregulation.

A major fear of the opponents of deregulation is that deregulation will leave customers in small, costly markets without a vital service—such as railroad, trucking, or air service. The experience of the airlines shows that these fears have not been justified. Smaller commuter airlines have replaced the major carriers and now typically offer more frequent service than the major airlines before them.

smaller communities, but this service has been replaced by commuter airlines. Commuter airlines provide smaller communities with a more varied schedule of service on smaller planes. Smaller communities have not had to pay for deregulation in the form of less service but have had to pay in terms of the higher accident rates of commuter airlines.

The fears that the airline industry would come to be increasingly dominated by a few major airlines has not come to pass. The share of the major carriers has not increased since deregulation, although there have been some mergers of airline companies (Pan Am and National, the purchase of Continental by Texas International). New airlines have appeared, and airlines that had previously operated only in intrastate markets such as Midway, Southwest, and Pacific Southwest, now compete in the interstate market with larger airlines.

The most profitable airlines appear to be the medium-sized passenger carriers like Delta, Texas International, and Southwest Airlines. The small to medium-sized airlines appear to have lower average cost and more flexibility in developing new routes. It appears that economies of scale in the airline industry are limited and that, unlike automobile manufacturing or electric power generation, small and medium-sized airlines can compete effectively with the giant airlines (such as United and American).

Although it is too early to make a final judgment on airline deregulation, Paul MacAvoy assesses the situation: "The evidence thus far is overwhelmingly on the side of the proponents of deregulation. By 1984, when the CAB is scheduled for extinction, reasoned judgment may be on the other side. But that would happen only if in the meantime the industry experienced failures of disastrous proportions."

Source: Paul MacAvoy, "Is Airline Deregulation Working:" *Wall Street Journal,* March 26, 1980.

ANTITRUST LAWS AND COURT RULINGS

The major alternative to direct regulation of monopolies is legislation to control market structure and market conduct. Rather than regulating monopolies directly by telling them what prices they can charge and what service they must offer, the government can set the legal rules of the game.

In the United States, federal legislation passed for the purpose of controlling market structure and conduct is called *antitrust law*. The cornerstone of antitrust legislation is the Sherman Antitrust Act of 1890. The Sherman Act was enacted as a reaction to the public outrage against the trust movement of the late 19th century. The 19th century railroad, steel, tobacco, and oil producers formed *trusts*.

Trusts are combinations of firms that come together to act essentially as monopolists. Trusts set common prices, agree to restrict output, and punish member firms who fail to live up to the agreement.

The Sherman Act of 1890

The Sherman Act contains two sections. Section 1 provides that

every contract, combination in the form of a trust or otherwise, or conspiracy, in restraint of trade or commerce among the several States, or with foreign nations, is hereby declared to be illegal.

Section 2 provides that

every person who shall monopolize, or attempt to monopolize, or combine or conspire with any other person or persons to monopolize any part of the trade or commerce among the several States, or with foreign nations, shall be guilty of a misdemeanor. . . .[14]

Section 1 prohibits a particular type of market conduct (conspiring to restrain trade), while sec-

14. A. D. Neale, *The Antitrust Laws of the United States of America* (Cambridge: The University Press, 1962), pp. 2–5; Eugene Singer, *Antitrust Economics* (Englewood Cliffs, N.J.: Prentice-Hall, 1968), chap. 2.

tion 2 outlaws a particular market structure (monopoly). The vague language of section 2 has led to varying court interpretations over the years. Section 2 prohibits *monopolization,* not *monopolies.* Although the act of creating a monopoly is clearly prohibited, the legality of existing monopolies is unclear.

The Clayton Act and Federal Trade Commission Act, 1914

The Sherman Act contained a general prohibition of acts in restraint of trade but did not specify actual restrictive or monopolistic practices that were in violation of the law. Moreover, the Sherman Act did not establish any agency (other than the existing Department of Justice) to enforce the provisions of the Sherman Act.

The Clayton Act of 1914 declared illegal the following four specific monopolistic practices if their "effect was to substantially lessen competition or tend to create a monopoly":

1. price discrimination (charging different prices to different customers for the same product),
2. exclusive dealing and *tying contracts* (requiring a buyer to agree not to purchase goods from competitors),
3. acquisition of competing companies, and
4. *interlocking directorates* (in which the directors of one company sit on the board of directors of another company in the same industry).

The Clayton Act gave private parties the right to sue for damages for injury to business or property as a result of violations of the antitrust laws along with other penalties.

The Federal Trade Commission Act established the Federal Trade Commission (FTC). The FTC's role was to secure compliance with the ban on "unfair methods of competition" stated in the FTC Act. It was empowered to prosecute unfair competition and also to issue cease-and-desist orders to violators.

Revisions of the Clayton Act

The Robinson-Patman Act of 1936 amended the anti–price-discrimination section of the Clayton Act to allow chain stores to sell at lower prices. Discounts and lower prices offered by large chain stores were allowed if they were justified by the lower costs of large-volume purchases or if they were necessary to meet the equally low prices of a competitor.

The Wheeler-Lea Act of 1938 extended the general ban on "unfair methods of competition" to include "unfair or deceptive" acts or practices. The FTC was empowered under this amendment to deal with false and deceptive advertising and the sale of harmful products.

The Celler-Kefauver Act of 1950 broadened the Clayton Act's ban on mergers by limiting mergers that occurred through the acquisition of one company's stock by another company. This antimerger provision applied if the acquisition served to lessen competition substantially or to create a monopoly.

Interpretation of the Sherman Act

American antitrust policy is decided in the courts as well as in Congress. The Sherman Antitrust Act, the mainstay of antitrust legislation, left unanswered a basic issue: Do antitrust laws prohibit only market *conduct* that leads to monopoly or is monopoly illegal *per se?*

The "Rule of Reason," 1911–1945.   In early court rulings, the courts interpreted the Sherman Act as outlawing market conduct in restraint of trade (mergers, price-fixing, price slashing to drive out competition), not the existence of monopoly *per se.* This interpretation became known as the **rule of reason.**[15]

*The **rule of reason** stated that monopolies were in violation of the Sherman Act if they engaged in unfair or illegal business practices. Being a monopoly* per se *was not considered a violation of the Sherman Act according to this rule.*

---

15. This discussion of court rulings is based upon the previous references and upon Frederic Scherer, *Industrial Structure and Economic Performance,* 2nd ed. (Boston: Houghton Mifflin, 1980), and Oliver Williamson, *Markets and Hierarchies: Analysis and Antitrust Implications* (New York: the Free Press, 1975).

The early landmark tests of the Sherman Act were the Standard Oil and American Tobacco Company cases, both tried in 1911. In both cases, the court ruled that these companies should be broken up into smaller companies (many of the major oil companies of today are spinoffs of Standard Oil). Both Standard Oil and American Tobacco accounted for more than 90 percent in their respective industries. The court's ruling, however, was not based upon this fact. The court ruled that Standard Oil and American Tobacco violated the Sherman Act because they had both engaged in unreasonable restraints of trade, not because they were monopolies.

The implication of the Standard Oil and American Tobacco rulings was that if a monopoly does not engage in unfair business practices, it is not in violation of the Sherman Act.

This rule of reason was upheld in the U.S. Steel Case of 1920. U.S. Steel at the time produced more than one half of the industry's output, but it had not treated its competitors unfairly or sought to control steel prices. U.S. Steel was in effect a "benevolent" monopolist. In the U.S. Steel case, the court upheld the rule of reason, stating that the law does not consider mere size or the existence of "unexerted power" to be an offense.

Questioning the Rule of Reason. The rule of reason prevailed until the Aluminum Company of America (Alcoa) Case of 1945. The courts ruled that Alcoa was in violation of the Sherman Act because it controlled more than 90 percent of the aluminum ingot market in the United States. Although Alcoa had not exercised its monopoly position to restrain trade unfairly or to drive competitors out of business, the courts (in a famous decision written by Judge Learned Hand) ruled that size alone was a violation of the Sherman Act.

The Alcoa decision appeared to overturn the rule of reason and to remove an important inconsistency. The rule of reason suggested that companies that engaged in practices that would ultimately lead to monopoly were in violation of the Sherman Act, while companies that were already monopolies, if they were well behaved, did not violate the Sherman Act. The Alcoa case appeared to reject the older "abuse theory" that required proof of the monopoly's predatory conduct. In its place a "structure test" was applied in which size was the determining factor. Actual monopolization—not the attempt to monopolize— was deemed Alcoa's offense.

Definition of Market. The Alcoa decision raised a fundamental issue: if the existence of monopoly is itself a violation of the Sherman Act, how is the market to be defined?

In the Alcoa case, the way in which the aluminum market was defined was crucial. Alcoa controlled 90 percent of the virgin aluminum ingot market, but it had to compete in the scrap ingot market and to face competition from stainless steel, lead, nickel, tin, zinc, copper, and imported aluminum. In its 1945 Alcoa decision, the court ruled that because substitutes for aluminum should not be included in Alcoa's market, Alcoa was a monopoly.

The DuPont Cellophane Case of 1956 broadened the definition of markets. DuPont in 1956 produced almost 75 percent of the *cellophane* sold in the United States but accounted for less than 20 percent of the sales of all *flexible wrapping materials*. The Justice Department filed suit against DuPont for monopolization of the cellophane market. The Supreme Court ruled that DuPont was not in violation of the Sherman Act because the market should be defined to include products that are "reasonably interchangeable" with cellophane (such as aluminum foil, waxed paper, or vegetable parchment). The court found that DuPont controlled only 20 percent of the flexible-wrapping-materials market and ruled that this share was insufficient to establish monopoly power.

In 1975, the Justice Department won an antitrust judgment against Xerox Corporation. At the time of the 1975 decision, Xerox produced more than 90 percent of plain-paper copiers and a substantial 65 percent of all copying equipment. The courts ruled that Xerox monopolized the copying-equipment market and required Xerox to make some of its patents available to competitors to increase competition in the market.

In January of 1982, the government's 13-year-old suit against IBM was dismissed by the Justice Department. In 1969, when the Justice Department filed suit against IBM for monopolizing the "general-purpose computer and peripheral-equipment industry," IBM controlled about 70 percent of the large mainframe computer market but had less than 40 percent of the office-equipment market. Again, the issue was: what constituted IBM's market?

After more than a decade of litigation involving 66 million pages of documents, the Justice Department decided in 1982 to drop the case. In the intervening years, IBM's competition in the computer industry had increased substantially. In 1982, IBM dominated only the mainframe computer industry (with 70 percent of the U.S. market). In its other lines of business, IBM's shares were relatively small: 20 percent of the minicomputer market, 18 percent of the word-processor market, and less than 5 percent of the telecommunications and computer-services markets. On the basis of these changes, the Justice Department decided that IBM did not monopolize the computer industry as broadly defined. In general, court rulings of the 1950s and 1960s appeared to move away from the Alcoa ruling by using a more liberal interpretation of what constitutes the market.

Reversing the Alcoa Decision.   Since the Alcoa case declared that size alone was a violation of the Sherman Act, business was concerned that the Alcoa decision would, in the words of Donald Baker, former head of the Justice Department's Antitrust Division, be used "to punish innovative success."[16]

Some companies gain monopoly positions not due to unfair business practices but due to superior innovation. Is a company that gains a dominant position through superior foresight, good planning, proper risk taking, and aggressive technological innovation violating the Sherman Act?[17]

An important test case of this issue was the Eastman Kodak case. In 1972, Berkey Photo Inc. filed an antitrust suit against Eastman Kodak charging that Eastman Kodak's method of introducing its pocket-sized instamatic camera and film gave Kodak an unfair advantage over Berkey and other film processors. After a lower court ruled in favor of Berkey, higher courts ruled in favor of Eastman Kodak, concluding that Kodak had earned certain advantages as a result of its superior innovation.[18]

A second test case was the charge brought by the FTC staff against DuPont Company. In a 1978 complaint, the FTC staff accused DuPont of illegally using unfair competition to overwhelm smaller rivals in the titanium dioxide market. In its ruling, the FTC dismissed antitrust charges against DuPont:

> The essence of the competitive process is to induce firms to become more efficient and to pass the benefits of the efficiency along to consumers. That process would be ill served by using antitrust to block hard, aggressive competition that is solidly based on efficiencies and growth opportunities, even if monopoly is an inevitable result.[19]

These judgments seem inconsistent with the ruling in the Alcoa case, since the apparent intent of the Alcoa ruling was to declare monopoly illegal *per se,* irrespective of how that monopoly came about. The DuPont and Eastman Kodak rulings again required the courts to weigh how a monopoly came into being—through restrictive or unfair business practices or through better management and innovation.

Price Fixing

The U.S. courts have generally interpreted price-fixing agreements as illegal restraints of trade. Exceptions have been allowed, but formal arrangements for fixing prices have consistently been ruled as illegal restraints of trade.

The United States stands virtually alone among the industrialized countries in its law that *formal* price-fixing arrangements are illegal *per se* whether or not the resulting prices are reasonable. In this way, the thorny issue of distinguishing rea-

16. The *Wall Street Journal*, November 10, 1980.
17. The Grinnel case of 1966 noted that if monopoly was the "consequence of a superior product, business acumen, or historic accident," the Sherman Act was not violated. *See* Williamson, *Markets and Hierarchies*, pp. 209–10.

18. This case is summarized in "FTC Dismisses Charges Against DuPont in Major Statement of its Antitrust Policy," *Wall Street Journal*, November 10, 1980.
19. *Wall Street Journal*, November 10, 1980.

Example 5

The Herfindahl Index: Another Measure of Concentration

In the summer of 1982, the Justice Department issued new guidelines reflecting the Reagan administration's policy on mergers. Instead of using the traditional 4-firm concentration ratio (the total of the market shares of the industry's 4 largest firms) to determine whether a merger would restrain competition beyond acceptable limits, the Justice Department now uses the *Herfindahl index* (named for the late Orris Herfindahl), which is the total of the *squared values* of the market shares of all the firms in an industry. If an industry consists of Firm 1 with a 60 percent market share and Firm 2 with a 40 percent share, the Herfindahl index *(H)* is $(60)^2 + (40)^2 = 3,600 + 1,600 = 5,200$. The general formula is:

$$H = (S_1)^2 + (S_2)^2 + (S_3)^2 + \cdots + (S_n)^2,$$

where S_1 through S_n are the market shares (totaling 100 percent) of Firms 1 through *n*.

Since the market shares are squared, large firms have a much larger impact on the index than small firms. For example, both the telephone-equipment and lightbulb industries have 4-firm concentration ratios of about 90 percent. AT&T's dominance of the telephone-equipment industry leads to a Herfindahl measure of 5,026, however, while the lightbulb industry has a Herfindahl measure of 2,036, because the dominant firms are more equal in size in the lightbulb industry.

Industrial organization experts generally agree that an industry with 10 equal-size firms would behave competitively. The Herfindahl index for an industry with 10 firms each of which has a 10 percent market share is 1,000 ($= 10^2 \times 10$). In the new Justice Department guidelines, a merger will probably not be challenged if the resulting Herfindahl index for the industry is less than 1,000.

Source: *Business Week,* May 17, 1982, p. 120; the *Wall Street Journal,* June 15, 1982. p. 3.

---

sonable from unreasonable price fixing has been avoided.

Conscious parallelism has provided the most difficult enforcement problem. (*Conscious parallelism* refers to orchestrated pricing actions taken by mutually interdependent companies—such as price leadership or uniform pricing—that appear to be the result of tacit agreement among the companies.) Prior to 1948, the courts held that clear cases of conscious parallelism were illegal even if formal price conspiracy could not be shown. After 1948, it had to be shown that the pattern of pricing could not have occurred if the company had acted alone in its own self-interest. This interpretation has established the legality of price-leadership arrangements and other forms of oligopoly pricing that result in parallel behavior without formal agreements. Some experts view this interpretation as a clear weakness in existing antitrust legislation. If no formal arrangement exists, violations are virtually impossible to prove.

Mergers

Antimerger Legislation. The antimerger legislation of the United States is provided by the Clayton Act of 1914 and the Celler-Kefauver Act of 1950. These acts prohibit the acquisition of one company by another if this action lessens competition. The courts (especially since 1950) have adopted a virtual prohibition of mergers between firms in the same industry if both have substantial market shares. Exceptions are allowed when one firm takes over another firm that is on the verge of bankruptcy (see Example 5).

Conglomerate Mergers. The major exception to the prohibition of mergers among large companies is the **conglomerate merger.**

*A **conglomerate merger** occurs when one company takes over another company in a different line of business.*

Figure 3
Mergers in the United States, 1890–1975

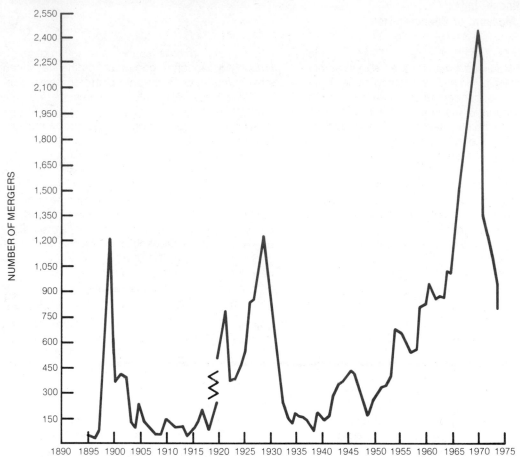

Source: The National Bureau of Economic Research and the Federal Trade Commission.

Conglomerate mergers are less likely to be opposed by the Justice Department because they do not involve mergers of competing companies. Thus, U.S. Steel was permitted to acquire Marathon Oil and DuPont was allowed to acquire Conoco because the merging companies operated in different markets.

Conglomerate mergers have led to a substantial increase in the share of corporate assets controlled by the largest U.S. corporations over the past 30 years. According to FTC statistics, the 451 largest corporations controlled 50 percent of corporate assets in 1960; by 1976, they controlled 72 percent of the corporate assets.[20]

20. These FTC statistics are from "Government May Abandon Fight to Stop Conglomerate Takeovers," *Wall Street Journal*, November 24, 1980.

The pace of mergers in the United States has been highly uneven over the years (see Figure 3). In part, this pattern reflects the fact that antimerger legislation has changed over the years as has the rigor of enforcement of antimerger legislation.

The FTC and the Justice Department have led the battle against conglomerate takeovers. In the 1960s, they were able to win about one half of the cases brought against conglomerate mergers. Prior to 1973, the government was able to fight proposed mergers on the grounds that the merger potentially threatened competition. If a steel company wanted to acquire an aluminum company, this merger could be denied because the aluminum company might have the potential to compete eventually with the parent company—whether it currently did so or not.

Since 1973, the government lost all 20 attempts to stop conglomerate takeovers. This trend can be traced to the fact that, since 1973, the government has had to prove that the proposed merger would actually (not potentially) reduce competition. Now the burden of proof is on the government to prove concretely that a conglomerate merger will indeed lessen competition.

PROPOSALS FOR GOVERNMENT CONTROL OF MONOPOLY

U.S. government control of monopoly currently takes three forms: government ownership, government regulation, and antitrust law. None of these represent ideal solutions. A variety of proposals have been made to improve government control of monopoly, including: selling monopoly franchises, requiring consumer representation in management, and repealing antitrust laws.

Selling Monopoly Franchises

Some economists argue that natural monopolies will be better managed if they are not regulated.[21] Proponents of the deregulation of natural monopolies argue that an unregulated monopoly will be motivated to minimize costs, to limit prices to keep potential competitors out of the market, and to seek out innovation. Regulated monopolies, on the other hand, are inefficient; bureaucratic decisions are less efficient than private managerial decisions.

If natural monopolies are deregulated, the government could sell *monopoly franchises* (licenses to operate the monopoly) to the highest bidder, and the government could recapture most of the monopoly profits that the private monopoly would earn, thereby avoiding most of the negative income-distribution effects of monopoly. Competitive bidding would cause private investors to pay the present value of future monopoly profits. The monopoly would continue to produce an output less than the social optimum and to charge a price higher than the optimal price.

Requiring Consumer Representation in Management

A second proposal is to place consumer representatives on the board of directors of natural monopolies or to grant consumers a voting interest in firms designated as public utilities. Important actions of the board of directors could be referred to the consumer by means of municipal elections.

If these measures were undertaken, it is argued, management would identify more closely with the interests of consumers and would refrain from abusing monopoly power.[22]

Repealing Antitrust Laws

A number of economists argue that the costs of antitrust laws outweigh the benefits to consumers. Antitrust battles cause corporations to spend billions of dollars on legal expenses, and litigation can stretch over decades. The IBM case, for example, lasted 13 years before its dismissal and cost the government more than $12 million and IBM even more.

The growth in international trade has more or less antiquated antitrust laws, which were passed in the early part of this century. Major U.S. corporations that account for substantial shares of U.S. production must now compete with foreign companies. Modern technology is able to develop substitutes for the products that monopolists sell, and the emergence of substitutes threatens all monopolies with potential competition if their monopoly profits are too high. Finally, monopolies may indeed be the result of superior innovation and better management (Eastman Kodak, DuPont, IBM, Boeing). To break these companies up may reduce rather than increase efficiency. Divestiture orders could signal other companies that aggressive innovation will be punished rather than rewarded.[23]

21. This position is associated with Milton Friedman and George Stigler. See Milton Friedman, "Monopoly and Social Responsibility of Business and Labor," in ed. Edwin Mansfield, *Monopoly Power and Economic Performance*, 3rd ed. (New York: W. W. Norton, 1974), pp. 57–68; George Stigler, "Government of the Economy," in ed. Paul Samuelson, *Readings in Economics*, 7th ed. (New York: McGraw-Hill, 1973), pp. 73–77.

22. Edward Renshaw, "Possible Alternatives to Direct Regulation" in ed. Paul MacAvoy, *The Crisis of the Regulatory Commissions* (New York: W. W. Norton, 1970), pp. 209–211.

23. For one view of why antitrust laws should be abolished, *see* Lester Thurow, "Let's Abolish the Antitrust Laws," *New York Times*, October 19, 1980.

The vacillation of antitrust policy over the years stems in the first instance from changes in the composition of the Supreme Court itself. Yet the Supreme Court justices do not live in a vacuum; they are educated people responding in part to the changing views of the economics profession. In 1945 at the time of the Alcoa decision, the economics profession had a very severe standard of a good competitive order. They wanted an economy very close to perfect competition. Today, economists are coming to realize that it is not so much the world that is imperfect but the theory of perfect competition. Because information and transactions costs exist, perfect competition in its pure form is not possible. The consequent departure of real-world industries from the assumptions of perfect competition need not represent a case for antitrust action. Economists realize that the world is complex, and efficient arrangements may take on many forms.

This chapter completes our study of product markets. The five chapters in the next section will turn to the bottom half of the circular-flow diagram: factor markets. The next chapter will give an introduction to factor markets and how they compare to product markets before examining the markets for the different kinds of factors—labor, land, capital, entrepreneurship—individually.

Summary

1. The case *against* monopolies is that a) monopolies restrict output and charge higher prices, b) monopolies have less incentive to lower costs and develop new technologies, and c) monopoly profits make the distribution of income more unequal. The case for bigness is that a) monopolies can take advantage of economies of scale, b) monopolies have less monopoly power than is commonly thought, and c) monopolies can afford to spend large sums on research and development.

2. The natural monopoly is an industry that must consist of one producer because economies of scale are experienced over the entire range of the industry's output.

3. The government uses three weapons to control monopoly: government ownership, regulation, and antitrust legislation.

4. Government ownership is not as widespread in the United States as in other countries. It is not clear how to operate government monopolies "in the public interest." Marginal-cost pricing will normally lead to losses. If the government monopoly is told to break even, there will be little incentive to reduce costs or to innovate. If the government monopoly is told to maximize profits, the consumer is no better off.

5. Regulation of natural monopolies aims at preventing monopoly profits while allowing the monopoly to operate profitably, encouraging efficient operation, and preventing predatory competition. Regulated monopolies are normally allowed to charge a price that covers operating costs plus a "fair" rate of return on invested capital. This pricing formula encourages inefficiency because higher costs can be passed on to the consumer and higher investment will automatically yield higher profits. Regulatory lag provides some incentive to minimize costs.

6. Regulation of potentially competitive industries has been criticized by economists as leading to inefficiencies and to poor service. There is now a significant deregulation movement under way to free competitive industries from government supervision.

7. Antitrust legislation seeks to control market structure and market conduct by setting the legal "rules of the game" for business. The Sherman Act outlaws actions that restrain trade and outlaws the act of monopolization. The Clayton Act specifies the business practices that illegally restrain trade (price discrimination, mergers, tying contracts). The Federal Trade Commission Act established the Federal Trade Commission and banned unfair methods of competition. The Celler-Kefauver Act toughened the antimerger provisions of the Clayton Act. The "rule of reason" that only unreasonable restraint of trade violates the Sherman Act was applied by the courts until 1945. The rule of reason was apparently overturned in 1945 with the Alcoa

decision when the courts ruled that size alone is a violation of the Sherman Act. In subsequent cases, the courts have ruled that monopolies created by superior technological achievement do not violate the Sherman Act. The courts have also ruled that market shares should be calculated to include "reasonably interchangeable" products. Formal price-fixing agreements are in violation of antitrust law. Antitrust laws are effective in preventing mergers between two companies engaged in the same line of business but are not effective in preventing conglomerate mergers.

8. Some of the alternative methods of controlling monopoly that have been proposed include a) deregulating natural monopolies and selling monopoly franchises to the highest bidder, b) placing consumer representatives on boards of directors, and c) repealing antitrust laws.

Key Terms

natural monopoly
regulatory lag
trusts
rule of reason
conglomerate merger

Questions and Problems

1. Explain why in the case of a natural monopoly, there is not enough room in the industry for more than one producer. What is meant by "not enough room"?

2. Devise a set of rules that would, in your opinion, allow a government-owned natural monopoly to operate "in the public interest." Would these rules be different if the firm were not a natural monopoly?

3. You are the president of a regulated monopoly. You know that the regulators will allow you to set rates to cover operating costs plus a "fair" rate of return on invested capital. How would you behave? Would you behave differently if you were not regulated?

4. One explanation for why regulation of electric utilities has not made much of a difference in utility rates is that electric utilities face competition. How can a monopoly like electric power utilities face competition and still be a monopoly?

5. You operate a regulated monopoly that sells in both a competitive and a monopoly market. What steps would you take to improve your position in the competitive market?

6. Deregulation of the television broadcasting industry has been opposed by the three major networks. How would deregulation affect their profits?

7. Explain the contradiction raised by the rule of reason.

8. Why would innovative and risk-taking firms such as Boeing and Eastman-Kodak oppose the Alcoa decision?

9. Evaluate the proposal to auction off monopoly franchises to the highest bidder. Why would this return most of the monopoly profits to the government?

10. "Several ill-informed people have suggested doing away with our antitrust laws. To do so would return us to the robber barons of the 19th century." Evaluate this statement.

III

Factor Markets

15

Factor Markets

Chapter Preview

The individual firm operates in two distinct markets: the product (or output) market and the factor (or input) market. The preceding chapters focused on the firm's behavior as a seller in the product market. They studied how firms determine how much output to produce, what prices to charge, and how different degrees of competition in the market affect the firm's behavior. Firms also act as buyers in the **factor market.**

The ***factor*** *(or input)* ***market*** *is the market in which firms purchase the land, labor, and capital inputs required to produce their output.*

In terms of the circular-flow diagram (see Figure 1), the activities of firms in the product or output market (the upper half of the diagram) determine the solution to the *what* problem of economics. The activities of firms in the factor market (the lower half of the diagram) determine the solutions to the *how* and *for whom* problems.

This chapter examines the *how* and *for whom* problems by explaining how factor markets work. The prices of labor, land, and capital are determined in factor markets, and these prices determine the incomes of the individuals and agents who own these productive factors.

This chapter identifies the main economic forces at work in the factor market. Rather than concentrating on one specific factor of produc-

Figure 1
The Circular Flow of Economic Activity

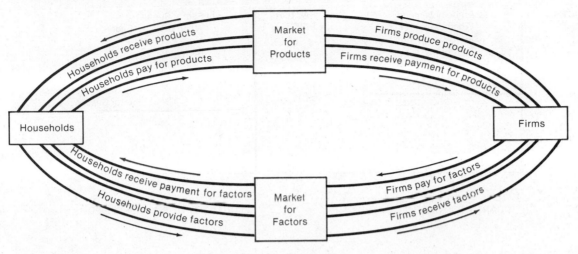

The circular-flow diagram shows that firms operate simultaneously in the product market and in the factor market. The upper half of the circular flow shows the flows of products and purchases between the business and household sectors. The bottom half shows the flows of factors from the households to business firms and the payment of factor income from business firms to households for the factors of production.

tion, like labor, this chapter will examine the general rules that govern the behavior of firms in factor markets. This chapter explains why the demand for the factors of production is a derived demand that depends upon the product market and how the prices the factor market assigns to the factors of production are the outcome of profit-maximizing decisions. Just as firms in the product market are motivated by profit maximization, the actions of firms in the factor market are also motivated by the desire to maximize profits. The rules for decisions made in product and factor markets actually boil down to a single general rule.

THE TWO FACES OF THE FIRM

The firm has two faces it displays to the outside world. One face is that of a *seller of the goods and services it produces* in product markets. As a seller, the firm can be either a price taker or a price searcher (as described in an earlier chapter). The other face is that of a *buyer of inputs* in factor markets. A firm can produce no output without factor inputs. In a factor market, the firm can again be either a **price taker** or a **price searcher.**

Price Searching and Price Taking in the Factor Market

The definitions of price searching and price taking in factor markets are analogous to the definitions of price searching and price taking given in the chapters on product markets.

*A **price taker** in a factor market is a buyer of an input whose purchases are not large enough to affect the price of the input. The price-taking firm must accept the market price as given.*

*A **price searcher** in a factor market is a buyer of inputs whose purchases are large enough to affect the price of the input.*

Figure 2 shows the four possible market conditions the firm may face in its role as either a seller of products or a buyer of factor inputs and in its role as either a price taker or a price searcher:

1. The firm may be a price taker in both the product and factor markets—panels (a) and (b).

Figure 2
The Two Faces of the Firm: Product Market and Factor Market

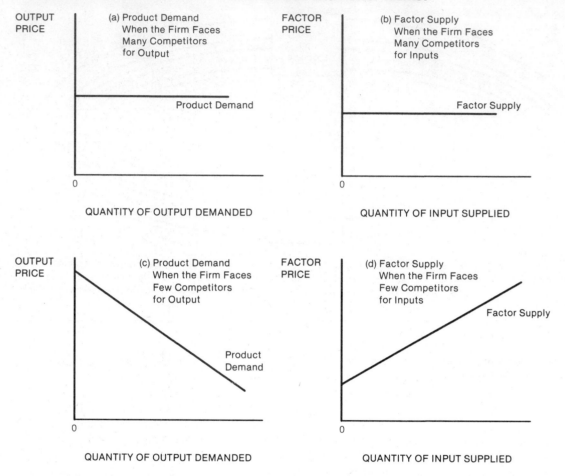

Panels (a) and (b) show a price-taking firm in the product and factor markets, respectively. Price taking on the product side means that the firm can sell all it wants at the existing market price (demand is perfectly elastic). Price taking in the factor market means that the firm can hire all the factors it wants at the prevailing factor price (factor supply is perfectly elastic).

Panels (c) and (d) show price searching in the product and factor markets, respectively. Price searching on the product side means that the firm faces a downward-sloping product demand curve—to sell more, it must lower its price. Price searching on the factor side means that the firm faces an upward-sloping factor supply curve. To hire more factor inputs, the firm must pay a higher factor price.

---

2. The firm may be a price searcher in both the product and factor markets—panels (c) and (d).
3. The firm may be a price taker in the product market and a price searcher in the factor market—panels (a) and (d).
4. The firm may be a price searcher in the product market and a price taker in the factor market—panels (b) and (c).

There is no necessary link between the amount of competition a firm faces on one side of the market and the amount it faces on the other side. A monopolist may purchase its land, labor, and capital inputs as a price taker. A perfectly competitive firm may be a price searcher in the factor market. Although there are numerous exceptions, the most likely scenario is that the firm will face more competition on the input (factor) side than on the output (product) side. In selling its products, the firm faces competition from other firms that produce either the same product or a product that serves as a substitute for the goods it produces. As demonstrated in previous chapters, such competition may be limited. The picture is different in factor markets. Factors, unless highly specialized, can typically be used by different firms and by different industries. Essentially all firms compete with one another for skilled and unskilled labor; they all compete with one another for capital and for land.

Although some factors have use in only specific industries (for example, mountainous terrain is ill-suited to wheat farming but is well-suited to grape vineyards or vacation resorts), most factors can be used by a wide variety of industries. The firm, therefore, faces competition for inputs not only from those firms with which it competes in the product market but also from firms in entirely different industries. Oil companies, universities, law offices, and retailers all compete for skilled secretaries. Restaurants, motels, gas stations, retailers, and home builders all compete for land in major cities.

A firm will usually face more competition from other firms when hiring inputs than when selling outputs.

As with most generalizations, there are exceptions to the rule that firms face more competition on the input side than the output side. A textile mill located in a small, isolated town may face little competition from other employers in its hiring of local labor, while its sales on the output side may be in a perfectly (or near perfectly) competitive product market. Certain skilled people—professional athletes, for example—are so specialized that they are suited for employment in only one industry. The employer is, therefore, likely to be a price searcher in this factor market. Certain types of capital—such as oil-drilling rigs—are suited to only one use, unlike trucks, lathes, and computers. Firms purchasing such specialized equipment are more likely to be price searchers.

When the firm has the power to influence the price at which it purchases inputs, the firm has **monopsony** power.

*A **monopsony** is a market in which there is only one buyer.*

Like pure monopoly, pure monopsony is rare. Few firms are the sole buyer of a factor of production. Even if the isolated textile mill—which appears to have a monopsony over the local labor market as the sole major employer in town—offers wages that are too low, people may move to other cities, or outside firms might be attracted into the market by the prospect of cheap labor. This textile mill faces competition from factories located in other cities (in the case where people move) and also from new firms entering the local labor market.

Marginal Factor Cost

The concepts of marginal revenue and marginal cost play a decisive role in the theory of product markets described in the preceding chapters. Profit-maximizing firms produce that level of output at which marginal revenue and marginal costs are equal. If they follow the $MC = MR$ rule, they will maximize profits or minimize losses. In the theory of factor markets, there are concepts analogous to marginal cost and marginal benefit that are applicable to the input side of the firm. Inputs have costs and benefits to the firm, just as production has costs and benefits to the firm. In making its input decisions, the most important cost the firm must consider is the additional cost of hiring more of an input, or **marginal factor cost** *(MFC)*.

Marginal factor cost (MFC) *is the extra cost to the firm of using one more unit of a factor of production.*

The marginal factor cost *(MFC)* of labor to the firm is, therefore, the extra cost of hiring one more unit of labor. The *MFC* of capital is the extra cost of using one more unit of capital.

The price of a factor of production is the wage (in the case of labor) or the rental (in the case of capital or land) that the firm must pay to hire or use the factor. Recall that, in the product market, price exceeds marginal revenue if the firm is a price searcher but that price equals marginal revenue when the firm is a price taker. In the factor market, if the firm is a price taker, marginal fac-

Figure 3
Competition versus Monopsony in the Market for Inputs

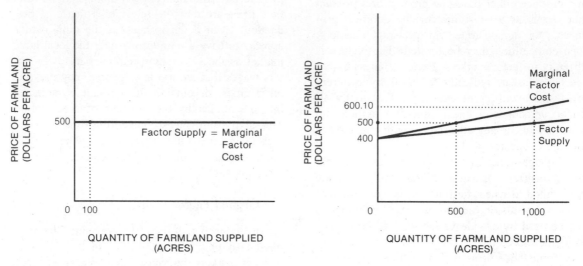

Panel (a) shows a price-taking firm that can hire all the inputs it wants at the going market price. The horizontal supply curve facing the firm is its marginal factor cost *(MFC)* curve.

Panel (b) shows a price-searching firm on the factor side that must pay higher input prices to get larger quantities of the input. Since to use more input per period requires a higher price for all quantities of the input, the extra cost of hiring one more unit of the input is the price *plus the increase in the cost of using the old input quantity*. Thus the *MFC* curve lies above the factor's supply curve.

tor cost is simply the factor's market price. The firm can hire one more unit of the factor (or more than one unit) at the going market price. The firm's actions have no effect on the input's price.

If the firm is a price searcher in the factor market, the firm's marginal factor cost will exceed the market price of the factor. As a price searcher, the firm is a large enough portion of the particular factor market so that it cannot buy more of the factor without driving up its market price. To use one more unit of the input per period, the firm must pay the same higher price for all units that it would need to pay for the last unit hired. In other words, the extra unit of the factor will cost the firm not only its market price but also the higher price paid on the previous units hired.

For example, because Firm A is a price taker, it can rent as much farmland as it wants at the market price of $500 per acre. It currently rents 100 acres. Firm B is a price searcher that currently rents 1,000 acres at $500 per acre, but B would have to pay $500.10 to rent 1,001 acres. The marginal factor cost of Firm A is the market

price of $500. The marginal cost of Firm B is the price of the 1,001st acre ($500.10) plus the $100 extra ($0.10 × 1,000) it must pay for the original 1,000 acres. Thus the marginal factor cost of Firm B is $600.10 (see Figure 3).

In panel (a), Firm A is a price taker in the factor market (it can hire all of the input it wants at the market price). For this firm, the price of the input and the marginal factor cost are equal. In panel (b), Firm B is a price searcher in the factor market. To hire more of the input, it must raise the price it pays for all previous units. Its marginal factor cost is greater than the market price. Thus B's *MFC* curve lies everywhere above the factor's supply curve.

As noted earlier, price taking is more likely in factor markets than is price searching (monopsony). The remainder of this chapter will deal with firms that are price takers in factor markets—firms in which marginal factor cost and factor price are the same. (A later chapter will examine the behavior of price-searching firms in the factor market.)

THE FIRM'S DEMAND FOR FACTORS OF PRODUCTION

The firm's demand for a factor input depends upon the input's physical productivity and upon the demand for the good the factor is being used to produce.

Marginal Physical Product

An earlier chapter analyzed the relationship between the **production function** and costs of production.

*The **production function** indicates the maximum amount of output that can be produced from different combinations of labor, capital, and land inputs.*

A factor's **marginal physical product** *(MPP)* can be determined from the production function.

*The **marginal physical product (MPP)** of a factor of production is the increase in output per period that results from increasing the factor by one unit, holding all other inputs and the level of technology fixed.*

Each factor's marginal contribution to output depends in part on how much of the the factor is being used. A fundamental law of all production functions is the **law of diminishing returns.**

*The **law of diminishing returns** states that as ever larger quantities of a variable factor are combined with fixed amounts of the firm's other factors, the marginal physical product of the variable factor will eventually decline.*

Derived Demand

Consumers buy products because they yield consumer satisfaction. The firm buys factors of production for a different reason. Inputs are purchased because they produce goods and services that create revenue for the firm. No matter how productive the input is in producing output, that input will not be hired unless it produces an output that commands a positive price in the marketplace. The garment industry buys sewing machines because they help to produce suits, shirts,

and dresses that consumers will buy. Automobile workers are hired because they help produce automobiles that people will buy. Wheat land is rented because it yields wheat that people will consume. If the most productive tailor in the world made only three-armed shirts, the demand for the tailor's services would be zero because the demand for three-armed shirts is zero. The demand for workers, the demand for wheat land, and the demand for tailors are all examples of **derived demand.**

*The demand for a factor of production is a **derived demand** because it results (is derived) from the demand for the goods and services the factor of production helps produce.*

The principle of derived demand is essential to understanding the workings of factor markets. If consumers reduce their demand for lettuce, the demand for workers employed in lettuce growing, the demand for farmland used for lettuce, and even the demand for water used in farm irrigation would also fall. When the demand for automobiles falls, there is unemployment in Detroit. When retail sales are permanently higher, rental rates paid on shopping-center land rise. When world demand for Boeing commercial aircraft is booming, employment in Seattle and Wichita (the cities where Boeing is located) rises. In short, the nature of the market for the good itself will be reflected in the derived demand for the factors used to produce it.

Joint Determination of Factor Demand

Another elementary but important fact about the demand for factors of production is that the production of a good requires the cooperation of different factors of production. Farmhands can produce no corn without corn land; corn land without farm labor is useless. Both corn land and farmhands require farm implements (ranging from hand tools to sophisticated farm machinery) to produce corn.

In general, the marginal physical product of any factor of production depends upon the quantity and quality of the cooperating factors of production.

Table 1
Marginal Revenue Product

Labor (workers) (1)	Units of Output, Q (2)	Price, P (3)	Total Revenue, TR (4)	Marginal Revenue Product, MRP (5)	Marginal Revenue, MR (6)	Units of Marginal Physical Product, MPP (7)
0	0	$24	$ 0			
				$95	$19	5
1	5	19	95			
				40	10	4
2	9	15	135			
				9	3	3
3	12	12	144			

Columns (1) and (2) give the production function (the amount of output produced by 0,1, 2, and 3 units of labor input). Columns (2) and (3) give the demand schedule facing the firm. Marginal revenue product (MRP) is calculated by taking the increase in total revenue associated with one-unit increases in the labor input. It can also be calculated by multiplying MR times MPP.

The marginal physical product of the farm worker will be less if the cooperating factor is one square yard of farmland than if it is one acre of land. The farm worker's MPP will be higher on one acre of fertile Iowa land than on one acre of rocky New England land. The MPP of the farm worker will be higher when working with modern heavy farm machinery than with hand implements. The interdependence of the marginal physical products of land, labor, and capital makes the problem of factor pricing in a market setting difficult to analyze.

Marginal Revenue Product

The demand for a factor of production—land, labor, or capital—is a derived demand. The dollar value of an extra worker, an extra unit of land, or an extra machine is the revenue from selling the marginal physical product (MPP) that the factor produces.

*The **marginal revenue product** (MRP) of any factor of production is the extra revenue generated by increasing the factor by one unit.*

There are two ways of calculating a factor's **marginal revenue product (MRP)**. Both approaches yield the same answer.

Method 1. The first method is to simply change the quantity of the factor and observe the change in revenue. According to this direct method, MRP is the change in revenue divided by the change (increase or decrease) in the factor.

$$MRP = \frac{\Delta TR}{\Delta \text{Factor}}$$

Table 1 demonstrates this process.

The different quantities of labor the firm employs are given in column (1), and the resulting output is given in column (2). Columns (1) and (2), therefore, represent the production function. Column (3) shows the market prices that clear the market for the various output levels produced. This firm is a price searcher in the product market because the price falls with higher output levels. The firm's total revenue (price times quantity of output) is given in column (4). Because marginal revenue product, in column (5), is the difference between the revenue levels at each level of labor input, it is recorded between the two input levels. The revenue generated when one worker is employed is $95; and the revenue when two workers are employed is $135. The MRP is, therefore, $135 − $95 = $40. In other words, the firm's total revenue would increase by $40 if the firm hired a second worker.

Method 2. A factor's *MRP* can be calculated indirectly as well. The marginal physical product *(MPP)* is the increase in output associated with a one unit increase in the factor but does not indicate the dollar value of this extra output. Marginal revenue *(MR)* indicates the increase in revenue associated with an increase in output of one unit. Therefore, $MRP = MPP \times MR$.[1]

That this formula works for the price searcher is shown in Table 1. Because the firm increases its output from 5 to 9 units as a consequence of adding one more unit of labor, *MPP* equals 4. The 4 extra units of output add $40 to revenue, or $10 per extra unit ($40/4); therefore, the marginal revenue is $10. Using the formula, $MRP = MR \times MPP$, one can calculate that marginal revenue product equals 10×4, or $40. Thus the indirect method of calculating *MRP* yields the same answer as the direct method. The *MRP* in column (5) is just the product of *MR* in column (6) and *MPP* in column (7).

To clarify why $MRP = MPP \times MR$, consider a corn farm that is a price taker in the output market. Because the firm must take the market price as given, price and marginal revenue are equal. On this farm, the marginal physical product of an acre of land is 500 bushels, which means that an additional acre adds 500 bushels to the total output of the firm. The dollar value of the output produced by the additional acre of land is its marginal revenue product. As a price taker, the firm receives the prevailing market price of $4 per bushel. Therefore, the extra acre adds 4×500 bushels, or $2,000, to revenue; $2,000 is the *MRP* of an additional acre.

The marginal revenue product of a factor can be calculated directly by determing the increase in revenue at different input levels or indirectly by multiplying marginal physical product times marginal revenue.

PROFIT MAXIMIZATION

In the product market, the firm maximizes profit by producing that output at which marginal

revenue and marginal cost are equal. The firm is also guided by profit maximization in the factor market. Profit-maximizing decisions in the product market are basically the same as profit-maximizing decisions in the factor market because deciding on the quantity of inputs determines the level of output.

To understand how firms choose the profit-maximizing level of factor inputs, consider the case of a firm deciding how much unskilled labor to hire. *The firm will hire one more unit of unskilled labor if the extra revenue (the extra benefit) the firm derives from the sale of the output produced by the extra unit exceeds the marginal factor cost of the extra unit of unskilled labor.* Recall that if the firm is a price taker, marginal factor cost will be the market wage. As in any other economic activity, a firm will hire inputs to the point where marginal benefits equal marginal costs.

Rule 1: $MRP = MFC$

The firm will continue to hire inputs as long as their marginal revenue product *(MRP)* exceeds their marginal factor cost *(MFC)*. For a price taker in the factor market, the market prices of the inputs the firm uses (wage rates, rental rates, interest rates) are the unchanging marginal factor costs of these inputs. The marginal benefit of an additional unit of factor input is its marginal revenue product. As long as the *MRP* exceeds the price of the input, it pays the firm to hire the factor. If the *MRP* of Factor A is $40 and its price is $20, it pays the firm to hire the factor. The firm *maximizes* its profit when the *MRP* of each factor equals its market price.

Figure 4 shows the marginal revenue product of Factor A. The *MRP* curve is downward-sloping because the more of Factor A that is used, the lower will be its marginal physical product (because of the law of diminishing returns). Also, if the firm is a price searcher in the product market, higher levels of output mean a lower marginal revenue. Thus, as the quantity of Factor A increases, both *MPP* and *MR* tend to decline, so that *MRP* (which is $MR \times MPP$) declines. The firm will hire Factor A until its price equals *MRP*.

*The **MRP** curve is the firm's demand curve for a factor because the firm hires that*

---

1. For a price taker in the product market, $P \times MPP = MR \times MPP$. For a price searcher in the product market, $P \times MPP > MR \times MPP$. In intermediate textbooks, the product $P \times MPP$ is called the *value of the marginal product*.

Figure 4
Firm Equilibrium: The Hiring of Factor Inputs

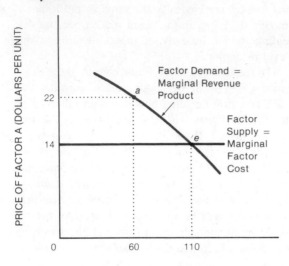

The firm's derived demand for Factor A is the marginal revenue product curve. The supply schedule of Factor A as seen by the firm is perfectly horizontal at the market price of $14. Equilibrium (e) will be reached at a price of $14 and a quantity of 110 units of Factor A. At this point, marginal revenue product equals marginal factor cost.

---

factor quantity at which the price of the factor equals the **MRP** *of the factor.*

The supply curve of Factor A to the firm is horizontal at the market price of $14. The factor price-taking firm can hire all it wants at $14. If the firm hired only 60 units of Factor A (point *a*), it would not maximize its profit: at 60 units, A's *MRP* equals $22 and A's *MFC* equals $14. The firm will continue to hire to the point where *MRP* and *MFC* are equal, which occurs at 110 units of Factor A (point *e*). The firm will be in equilibrium (earning a maximum profit or minimizing its losses) when each factor is employed up to the point where marginal factor cost (which equals the price of the factor when the input market is competitive) equals the marginal revenue product of the factor.

In equilibrium, $MRP_A = MFC_A$, $MRP_B = MFC_B$, *and so on, where* A *and* B *are specific factors.*

Rule 2: The Least-Cost Rule

The rules of profit-maximization explain the behavior of firms in the factor market. These rules predict that firms will employ that level and combination of inputs that maximizes their profit. In the product market, firms produce that level of output (and charge the associated price) that maximizes their profit.

To maximize profit, it is necessary to minimize the cost of producing a given quantity of output. Firms produce outputs with cooperating factors. How will they know when they are combining all their inputs in a least-cost fashion? For example, a firm has decided to produce 200 units of output and currently uses 15 labor hours and 25 machine hours to produce this output. The wage rate (the price of labor) is $5 per hour, and the rental rate on the machinery is $20 per hour. The marginal physical product of labor is 10 units of output, and the marginal physical product of capital is 30 units of output. Is the firm using the optimal amount of labor and capital?

The firm is using too much capital and too little labor. If the firm were to substitute 3 units of labor for one unit of capital, total output will not change, but costs will be reduced by $5. One unit of capital (at the margin) is three times as productive as one unit of labor. Adding 3 units of labor increases output by 30, and subtracting 1 machine unit decreases output by 30; there is no net change in output. However, cutting back on one machine hour saves $20, while hiring 3 more units of labor costs $15. Output remains the same, but costs have been reduced by $5.

What signals to the firm that a substitution of this sort will increase profits? The firm will look at marginal physical product *per dollar of cost*. In this example, because an extra unit of labor increases output by 10 units and increases costs by $5, an extra dollar spent on labor produces 2 units (10/$5) of output. Because an extra machine hour increases output by 30 units and increases costs by $20, an extra dollar spent on capital produces 1.5 units of output. In our example, a dollar spent on more labor is more effective than a dollar spent on more capital.

The marginal physical product per dollar is the ratio of the *MPP* of a factor to its price. The price-taking firm takes both the wage rate for la-

Table 2
Two Ways of Looking at Profit Maximization

Labor Hours (1)	Units of Marginal Physical Product, MPP (2)	Price Equals Marginal Revenue, P = MR (3)	Wage Equals Marginal Factor Cost, W = MFC (4)	Marginal Revenue Product, MRP (5)	Marginal Cost, MC (6)
0					
	5	$10	$20	$50	$ 4
1					
	4	10	20	40	5
2					
	2	10	20	20	10
3					

This firm is a price taker on both sides of the market. Column (5) equals column (2) times column (3) because the additional revenue from one more unit of labor is simply the marginal product multiplied by the price (or marginal revenue). Column (6) equals column (4) divided by column (2) because marginal cost equals the wage per unit of marginal physical product.

bor (W) and the rental rate on capital (R) as given. If the marginal physical product per dollar of labor is greater than the marginal physical product per dollar of capital, the firm is not combining inputs in a least-cost fashion. It can produce the same output at lower cost by substituting labor for capital until:

$$\frac{MPP_L}{W} = \frac{MPP_K}{R}$$

According to the least-cost rule, the firm is producing at minimum cost only if the marginal physical products per dollar of the various factors are equal.

The Two Sides of the Firm

In the product market, the rule of profit maximization is $MC = MR$. In the factor market, the rule is $MRP = MFC$ for each factor. These rules are logically the same. Recall that marginal cost is the mirror image of marginal physical product. That is:

$$MC = \frac{W}{MPP_L} \tag{1}$$

The rule for profit maximization in the product market is:

$$MR = MC \tag{2}$$

Since MC equals W/MPP_L according to equation (1), equation (2) can be rewritten as:

$$W = MR \times MPP_L \tag{3}$$

Since the wage for a factor is equal to the marginal factor cost (when a firm is a price taker in the factor market), and since $MR \times MPP$ equals MRP, equation (3) can become:

$$MFC = MRP, \tag{4}$$

which is the profit-maximizing rule in the factor market.

Table 2 provides a numerical example of how profit maximization in the product market is equivalent to profit maximization in the factor market. The firm is a price taker in both markets, so $W = MFC$ and $P = MR$. The product price is $10 and the wage rate is $20 per day. The marginal product schedule is given in columns (1) and (2) of Table 2. Column (3) shows MR (which equals P in this case), and column (4) shows

MFC (which equals *W* in this case). Marginal revenue product is simply column (2) multiplied times column (3) and is shown in column (5). Marginal cost is the wage for an additional unit of labor divided by the change in output resulting from the additional unit, or $W \div MPP$, and is shown in column (6). When $P = MC$ (both $10), it is also true that $MRP = MFC$ (both $20). When one rule is satisfied, the other rule is also satisfied.

THE MARGINAL PRODUCTIVITY THEORY OF INCOME DISTRIBUTION

Economists distinguish between **the functional distribution of income** and the **personal distribution of income.** Both are determined in the factor market.

*The **functional distribution of income** is the distribution of income among the four broad classes of productive factors—land, labor, capital, and entrepreneurship.*

*The **personal distribution of income** is the distribution of income among households, or how much income one family earns from the factors of production it owns relative to other families.*

The profit-maximizing and least-cost rules explain the *how* problem in economics. They show how firms go about combining inputs to produce output. These same rules also explain the *for whom* problem.

Factors of production, unless they are highly specialized (such as 7-foot basketball players), are demanded by many firms and by many industries. For example, the market demand for truck drivers will come from a wide cross section of American industry: the steel industry, retailers, the moving industry, the local florist will all have a derived demand for truck drivers. The demand for urban land will also come from a broad cross section of American industry: heavy industry requires land for its plant sites; motel chains require land for their motels; home builders require land to develop subdivisions. The demand for capital goods will also come from a cross section of American industry.

Figure 5
Determination of the Market Price(Wage) of Truck Drivers in a Competitive Market

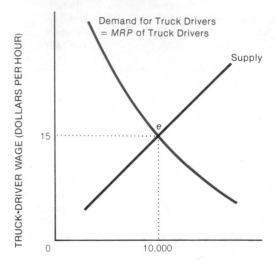

The market supply of truck drivers is upward-sloping, which indicates that individuals are prepared to work more hours as truck drivers at high wages than at low wages. The market demand curve is derived from the marginal revenue product curve of truck drivers across several industries. Equilibrium is achieved at point *e*, where the quantity supplied of truck drivers equals the quantity demanded. At the equilibrium wage of $15, there are 10,000 labor hours used in the various industries using truck drivers.

How the price (wage) of truck drivers is determined is shown in Figure 5. The wage rate of truck drivers reflects two forces: the derived demand for truck drivers as represented by their marginal revenue product and the supply of truck drivers. At equilibrium, the market wage will equate quantity supplied and quantity demanded, and the wage will equal the marginal revenue product. In other words, truck drivers will be paid their *MRP*. The same is true of the other factors of production. Skilled labor and unskilled labor will be paid their respective *MRP*s. Capital goods will be paid their *MRP*s. Land will be paid its *MRP*.

According to the marginal productivity theory of income distribution, the functional distribution of income between land, labor, and capital is determined by the relative marginal revenue products of the different factors of production. The price of each factor will equal the MRP of that factor.

Why some factors have high *MRP*s and others low *MRP*s will be discussed later in this chapter.

Marginal Productivity and Efficiency

The preceding chapters that discussed product markets were interested in the relative efficiency of different market structures, particularly perfect competition and monopoly. It was argued that monopoly is inefficient because it created contrived scarcity by failing to expand output to the point where price (the measure of the marginal benefit to society) and marginal cost (the measure of the extra cost to society) are equal.

If a firm has monopoly power in the product market, $P > MR$. Although the monopolistic firm will pay its inputs their marginal revenue products, which will equal $MR \times MPP$, the factor is actually worth $P \times MPP$ to society because each unit of output of MPP is valued at P. Because $MR \times MPP$ is less than $P \times MPP$, the monopolist is paying factors less than what they're worth to society.

Figure 6 illustrates a monopolist in the product market who is a price taker in the factor market. The curve $P \times MPP$ shows the marginal benefits to society of an additional unit of the factor. The marginal revenue product curve shows the marginal benefit to the monopolist of hiring an additional unit of the factor. When the monopolist operates at point *a* rather than at point *b*, the monopolist stops hiring workers short of their marginal worth to society (or pays them less than they're worth to society, as represented by point *c*). The fact that the monopolist hires too little of the factor from the viewpoint of society is the other side of the coin to the conclusion that monopolists produce too little output from society's viewpoint.

If the firm is perfectly competitive in the product market, marginal revenue product of a factor will be equal to the marginal benefit of the factor to society. Because price equals marginal revenue in a competitive firm, the firm will hire factors until the point where $P \times MPP$ equals the fac-

Figure 6
The Monopolist Hires Too Few Inputs

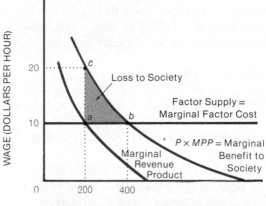

The firm is a monopolist in the product market and a price taker in the factor market. The value of the marginal product to society is $P \times MPP$ (the marginal benefit to society), and the marginal benefit to the monopolist is its marginal revenue product. If the wage rate is $10, the monopolist employs 200 labor hours because at that point marginal revenue product equals the wage. If the monopolist were forced to employ 400 labor hours, society would gain the area *abc*.

tor's price. Each factor adds a net marginal benefit to society equal to the factor's market price. This market price reflects its opportunity cost to society.

Marginal Productivity and Factor Incomes

The marginal productivity theory of income distribution suggests that productive factors are usually paid their marginal revenue products.

The marginal revenue product of one factor depends upon the quantity and quality of cooperating factors. Two textile workers, one in the United States and the other in India, may be equally skilled and diligent, but one works with a $50 sewing machine while the other works with a $100,000 advanced knitting machine. The New England farmer may be just as skilled as the Kansas farmer but may have a low *MRP* because of the low quality of the land. *MRP* also depends upon the supplies of factors. Residential land is quite limited in supply in Hawaii but abundantly supplied in Iowa. The equilibrium *MRP* of land is therefore higher in Hawaii. If women are limited to employment opportunities in only a few professions, they will *overcrowd* these professions and drive down the *MRP* and thus wages. Finally, *MRP*, as stated earlier, depends upon the demand for the product being produced. If product demand falls, so will the factor's *MRP*.

*The marginal productivity theory of income distribution states that competitively determined factor price reflects the factor's marginal revenue product. **MRP** is the result of 1) the relative supplies of the different factors, 2) the quantity and quality of cooperating factors, and 3) the market demands for the goods the factors produce.*

The Aggregate Production Function

The marginal productivity theory of income determination can be applied both widely and narrowly. In its narrow form, it can explain why one person earns more than another or why one plot of land rents for more than another. The aggregate economy is the summation of all the participants in the economy; therefore, it is possible to talk about average wages, average land rental rates, and average interest rates. The economy churns out millions of goods and services using the different quantities and qualities of labor, capital, and land inputs at its disposal. The economy as a whole can be represented by an **aggregate production function.**

*The **aggregate production function** shows the relationship between the total output produced by the economy and the total labor, capital, and land inputs used by the economy.*

The aggregate production function is a stark representation of the economy, but it is a useful tool for investigating the functional distribution of income among the broad factors of production—land, labor, and capital (see Figure 7).

To simplify the analysis, assume the economy produces only one product—corn—and that it is perfectly competitive in all markets. The demand curve for corn is the marginal physical product of labor for the entire economy. If we assume that

Figure 7
The Aggregate Production Function and the Functional Distribution of Income

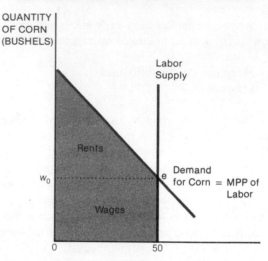

This figure represents the aggregate production function of an entire economy. The economy produces a generalized physical output at a product price of $1. All markets are assumed to be perfectly competitive. Because the price of a unit of output is $1, the demand schedule is the marginal physical product of labor, it declines according to the law of diminishing returns. The vertical supply line represents the supply of labor, which is fixed at 50 million workers. The *MPP* curve will be the demand for labor, and the market wage will be set at w_0, where labor supply equals labor demanded.

How much output has the economy produced and how much will go to labor? Each unit of labor adds to the economy's output. The area under the demand curve is the total output of the economy at that point. The 50 million workers will produce an output equal to the shaded area. Workers will receive their wage w_0, times the number of workers. Their share of output is the shaded rectangle labeled *Wages*. The cooperating nonlabor factors (land and capital) will get what is left over, or the shaded triangle labeled *Rents*.

the price of a bushel of corn is $1, then the demand curve for corn measures both the marginal physical product and marginal revenue product for the entire economy and is also the demand curve for labor. The supply of labor is fixed at 50 million workers. The equilibrium wage rate is w_0, which brings about a quantity of labor demanded of 50 million (which equals the quantity supplied).

Table 3
Percentage Distribution of Earnings in the U.S. Business Sector, 1929–1969

Year	Total (1)	Labor (2)	Nonresidential Structures and Equipment (3)	Inventories (4)	Land (5)
1929	100.00	79.38	10.80	4.46	5.36
1940	100.00	81.19	10.51	4.27	4.03
1950	100.00	77.58	12.70	5.26	4.46
1960	100.00	82.22	10.85	3.65	3.28
1965	100.00	78.33	12.94	4.33	4.40
1968	100.00	79.94	12.06	3.96	4.04

Source: Edward Denison, *Accounting for United States Economic Growth,* 1929–1969 (Washington, D.C.: The Brookings Institution, 1974), p. 260.

The total output of the economy is the area under the demand curve since the curve shows the additional corn produced by each and every worker.[2] Of this total output, labor will receive the area of the rectangle labeled *Wages* and the nonlabor factors, such as capital and land, will receive the area of the triangle labeled *Rents.* Workers are paid the dollar value of the *MPP* of the 50th unit rather than the dollar value of earlier units that have larger *MPP*s (as measured by the height of the demand curve).

The marginal productivity theory states that the factors of production will be paid their marginal revenue products. If the world is sufficiently competitive, the theory suggests that the factors of production will be paid their marginal products.

Table 3 shows the actual distribution of earnings among labor and nonlabor factors (capital structures, inventories, and land) in the American business sector (1929–1969). According to Table 3, the share of labor has remained fairly constant at around 80 percent of earnings, and the share of land has varied from 5 to 3 percent, leaving a capital (structures and inventories) share of 15 to 17 percent.

Is the marginal productivity theory consistent with these facts? Why should the labor share be

roughly constant over this 40-year period? During this period, the economy's capital stock more than doubled, while the number of hours worked increased only 20 percent.[3] Under these conditions why did not the share of capital increase?

The explanation can be found in the marginal productivity theory of income distribution. Because the cooperating factor to labor—capital—has been increasing relative to labor, we would expect the marginal physical product of labor to rise relative to the marginal physical product of capital. This rise in the *MPP* of labor, according to marginal productivity theory, would be reflected in an increase in the price of labor relative to the price of capital. Indeed, the price of labor (relative to capital) did indeed rise substantially over this period. The fact that the slower growth of labor was therefore offset by the increase in its relative price explains the constant shares of labor and capital.

This chapter sought to provide an overview of how factor markets work, but each factor market—the labor market, the capital market, and the market for land—has its own special features. In the labor market, the supply of labor is based upon individuals choosing among market work, work in the home, and leisure. These are choices

2.   The demand curve shows the *MPP* at each level of labor input. The *MPP*s for each successive unit of labor can be added together to yield total output. For 50 million workers, total output is the shaded area in Figure 7.

3.   Edward Denison, *Accounting for Economic Growth in the United States, 1929–1969* (Washington, D.C.: The Brookings Institution, 1974), pp. 32,54.

not faced by the owners of capital and land. Moreover, the labor market is affected by the organization of workers into unions and by the effect of education and training on labor's marginal physical product. In the capital market, intertemporal choices are involved. Buyers of capital can receive the benefits of capital over a long period of time. Suppliers of capital must choose between consumption today and more consumption tomorrow. The market for land is characterized by the relative fixity of the supply of land.

The next three chapters will examine each factor market in detail, but these discussions will all be based upon the general theoretical framework established in this chapter.

Summary

1. Firms operate in two markets: the product (output) market and the factor (input) market. Firms sell their output in the product market, and they buy inputs to produce output in the factor market. The *what* problem is solved in the product market. The *how* and *for whom* problems are solved in the factor market. A firm can be: a) a price taker in both the product and factor market, b) a price taker in the product market and a price searcher in the factor market, c) a price searcher in the product market and a price taker in the factor market, d) a price searcher in both markets. Firms are more likely to be price takers in the factor market because they face competition for the factors from all industries that use the factor, not just from firms that produce substitutes. Marginal factor cost *(MFC)* is the extra cost of hiring one more unit of the factor of production. A price-searching firm in the factor market will have a marginal factor cost that is greater than price. A price taker in the input market will have a marginal factor cost equal to the price of the input.

2. The firm's demand for a factor of production will depend upon the demand for the product being produced and the factor's productivity. The marginal physical product *(MPP)* of a factor of production is the increase in output that results from increasing the factor by one unit, other things equal. The demand for a factor of production is a derived demand because it depends on the demand for the goods and services the factor helps produce. Production requires the cooperation of the factors of production. The marginal physical product of one factor will depend upon the quantity and quality of cooperating factors. Marginal revenue product *(MRP)* is the increase in revenue brought about by hiring one more unit of the factor of production.

3. Profit-maximizing firms will observe the following rule in factor markets: factors of production will be hired to the point where $MFC = MRP$. The $MFC = MRP$ rule in the factor market is equivalent to the $MR = MC$ rule in the product market. If firms are perfectly competitive in the factor market, they will hire the various factors of production to the point where the MRP of each factor equals its price. The least-cost rule for firms is to hire factors of production so that MPP per dollar of one factor equals the MPP per dollar of any other factor.

4. The marginal productivity theory of income distribution explains the functional distribution of income (among the four classes of production factors) and the personal distribution of income (among households).

Key Terms

factor market
price taker
price searcher
monopsony
marginal factor cost *(MFC)*
production function
marginal physical product *(MPP)*
law of diminishing returns
derived demand
marginal revenue product *(MRP)*
functional distribution of income
personal distribution of income
aggregate production function

Questions and Problems

1. If a law were passed that prohibited the movement of people from agriculture to industry, how would wages be affected in industry and agriculture? How would this law affect the overall economic efficiency of the economy?

2. Explain how workers in Country X could earn $10 per hour while workers in the same industry in Country Y earn only $.50 per hour. Do the higher wages in Country X mean that workers in this country work harder than those in Country Y?

3. The last unit of land rented by a farmer costs $100 and increases output by 1,000 bushels. The last unit of capital costs $1,000 to rent and increases output by 20,000 bushels. Is this farmer minimizing costs? If not, what should he or she do?

4. In Soviet industry, capital has been growing about 10 times as fast as labor. What would you expect to happen to the marginal physical product of capital?

5. Evaluate the following statement: "Income distribution as explained by the marginal productivity theory is entirely fair. After all, people are simply getting back what they personally have contributed to society."

6. A manufacturing plant in a small town accounts for 85 percent of employment in the town. The plant receives a large contract and decides to expand its work force by 40 percent. What will be the relationship between marginal factor cost and the wage rate in this case? Construct a graph to illustrate your answer.

7. One type of equipment—such as specialized oil-drilling equipment—can be used only in a particular industry. Another type—such as general-purpose lathes—can be used in a wide variety of industries. How would the amount of competition differ for these two types of equipment?

CHAPTER

16

Labor Markets

Chapter Preview

This chapter will examine why some people earn more than others, why some jobs pay more than others, why wages and productivity are positively related, and why some people remain out of the labor force.

The preceding chapter showed that the profit-maximizing firm hires inputs up to the point where marginal factor costs *(MFC)* equals marginal revenue product *(MRP)*. This rule applies generally to the hiring of land, labor, and capital inputs. The labor market differs from other factor markets because of the human element. There are four special features of labor:

1. A person cannot be bought like an acre of land or a piece of equipment; slavery is against the law. Land and capital assets can be bought and sold, but the owner of labor can only rent out his or her labor services. A professional athlete may be under contract for a number of years; many workers in Japan have lifetime labor contracts. But professional athletes and Japanese workers can only be used for the specific tasks designated in the contract; a slave, a piece of land, or a machine can be used for anything the owner wants.

2. Unlike the owner of land and capital, the owner of labor services can use his or her resources for useful alternatives to labor service. If land and machines are not put to productive use, they stand idle, and the owners do not normally benefit. When the owners of labor services do not engage in market labor activity, they can spend time in work in the home or in leisure.

3. Land and capital do not care to which use they are put. The owners of labor services have preferences regarding the type of work they perform and the location of the work.

4. The existence of labor unions also differentiates labor from the other factors of production. Workers join together into labor unions in order to affect conditions in the labor market. *Labor unions* are organizations that seek to affect the supply of and demand for the workers they represent and to establish rules and procedures concerning general employee/employer relationships.

This chapter will explain how supply, demand, and market equilibrium are determined in the labor market and will examine wage structure and alternative uses of time for the owners of labor services.

THE LABOR MARKET DEFINED

A market is an arrangement that allows buyers and sellers of a particular good or service to come together for the purpose of making transactions. The **labor market** is a market in this sense of the term. Its distinguishing feature is that labor services are being bought and sold rather than inanimate goods and services.

*A **labor market** is an arrangement whereby buyers and sellers of labor services come together to agree on working conditions such as compensation, fringe benefits, and hours of work. The agreement may be a formal contract or an informal, unwritten arrangement.*

Labor markets differ in many ways. Labor markets may be national or local in scope. Examples of national and even international labor markets are the markets for some engineers, academics, airline pilots, and upper-level executives.

Examples of local labor markets are the markets for sales clerks, teenage employees, unskilled workers, and sanitation workers.

Labor markets can also vary in their formality and structure. Some labor markets are highly informal. Job openings are announced by posting notices at the factory gate, by placing "help wanted" ads in the local newspaper, or by word of mouth. Other labor markets operate according to a well-defined set of rules. Government civil-service jobs are regulated by detailed legislation and rules. In unionized industries, rules governing hiring and firing are spelled out in considerable detail. Union rules may specify which employees are the first to be laid off, which tasks a worker can or cannot perform, or how overtime work is to be compensated.

The term *labor market* therefore encompasses a wide range of market behavior. If the buyer of a labor service must pay the wage rate dictated by the market regardless of how much labor is hired, the buyer is a *price taker* in the labor market. If the buyer of a labor service raises the wage rate by buying more and lowers it by buying less of a labor service, this buyer is a price searcher in the labor market. If the buyer of a labor service must accept the market wage as given, the buyer is a perfectly competitive buyer of labor services. If the buyer affects wage rates by buying more or less of the labor service, the buyer has monopsonist power in the labor market.

The discussion that follows deals only with perfectly competitive buyers of labor. As the preceding chapter argued, competition in the labor market (and other factor markets) is a relatively more common phenomenon than competition in the product market. (The chapter on labor unions will deal explicitly with monopsony.)

To be useful, labor-market analysis must be able to explain observed trends and patterns in the labor market. Some of the empirical facts that economic analysis must account for in explaining labor market behavior are:

1. *Average hours worked per week have declined over the long run.* In 1914, workers in manufacturing worked an average of 49.4 hours per week (see Table 1). By 1980, this number had fallen to 39.7 hours per week.

Table 1
Facts About the Labor Market

Year	Average Hours Worked per Week in Manufacturing (1)	Index of Hourly Earnings in Manufacturing, 1900 = 100 (adjusted for inflation) (2)	Female Labor-Force Participation Rate (3)
1914	49.4	100	22.8 (1910)
1930	42.1	151	24.8
1940	38.1	214	27.4
1950	40.5	273	31.4
1960	39.7	348	34.8
1970	39.8	396	42.6
1975	39.4	408	45.9
1980	39.7	403	51.1

Sources: Hours and real wages are from Ronald Ehrenberg and Robert Smith, *Modern Labor Economics: Theory and Public Policy* (Glenview, Ill.: Scott, Foresman, 1982), Table 2.5. The female-participation-rate data are from *Historical Statistics of the United States: Colonial Times to the Present*, series D29–41, p. 133; and from *Statistical Abstract of the United States*, 1981, p. 388.

2. *Real wages have risen over the long run.* After adjustment for inflation, the real hourly wage rate of American manufacturing workers increased more than 4 times between 1914 and 1980 (see Table 1). In other words, an hour of work in 1980 bought about 4 times the quantity of goods and services as an hour of work in 1914.

3. *The labor-force participation rate of American women has risen dramatically over the last 50 years.* The *female labor-force participation rate* is the ratio of women 16 years or older in the labor force to the total number of women 16 years or older. Since 1930, the female labor-force participation rate has risen from 24.8 to 51.1 percent (Table 1).

4. *Some people earn more than others.* Coal miners earn $12.41 per hour on average while textile workers earn $6.00 per hour. The president of a large corporation may earn $800,000 per year, a surgeon may earn $250,000 per year, a school teacher may earn $20,000 per year, and a roustabout on an offshore drilling rig earns $45,000 per year.

5. *There is usually a close positive relationship between worker productivity and wages.* Labor *productivity* is the amount of output produced per unit of labor input. Over the years, wages rise when labor productivity rises.

The theory of labor-market behavior should be able to provide explanations for each of these facts.

THE DEMAND FOR A SINGLE GRADE OF LABOR

The wage rate for a particular type of labor is determined in the labor market. The equilibrium wage rate/labor quantity combination is determined by the forces of demand for and supply of labor of that grade, just as product price/quantity combinations are determined by supply and demand.

The Firm's Demand for Labor

How does a firm decide how much labor of a single grade to hire at different wage rates? According to the preceding chapter, profit-maximizing firms hire factors up to the point where the marginal factor cost *(MFC)* equals the marginal revenue product *(MRP)* of the factor. The firm, therefore, will continue to hire labor as long as the marginal revenue product of the additional worker exceeds that worker's marginal factor cost. The firm in Figure 1 is perfectly competitive

Figure 1
The Firm's Demand for Stenographers

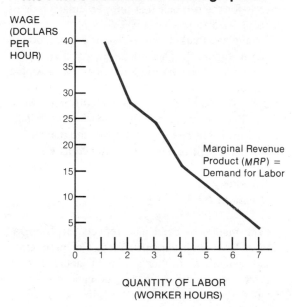

WAGE
(DOLLARS
PER
HOUR)

QUANTITY OF LABOR
(WORKER HOURS)

Marginal Revenue
Product (*MRP*) =
Demand for Labor

The labor demand curve shows the *MRP* of different quantities of labor hours. This firm is competitive in both the labor market and the product market. The firm uses 4 stenographer hours when the wage rate is $16 per hour (the *MRP* of the fourth hour is equal to the market wage of $16 per hour). If the market wage rate rises to $28 per hour, the $16 *MRP* of the fourth worker hour is well below the wage rate. The firm would not wish to employ 4 hours at a wage of $28 but would employ only 2 stenographer hours because the *MRP* of the second hour equals $28.

Table 2
The Demand for Stenographers

Labor Input (hours) (1)	Quantity of Output (pages per hour) (2)	Marginal Physical Product, MPP (3)	Marginal Revenue Product, MRP = P × MPP (4)
0	0		
		20	$40
1	20		
		14	28
2	34		
		12	24
3	46		
		8	16
4	54		
		6	12
5	60		
		4	8
6	64		
		2	4
7	33		

turns applies to the labor input. Figure 1 graphs the data from column (4) of Table 2.

This firm is a price taker in the product market as well as in the factor market; therefore, its *MRP* equals its product price, *P,* times labor's marginal physical product *(MPP)*. As the preceding chapter demonstrated, the firm will demand the quantity of labor at which $W = MRP$.

When the market wage is $28, the firm will demand that quantity of labor at which *MRP* is $28. Table 2 shows that the *MRP* of the second stenographer hour is $28; therefore, the firm will demand 2 stenographer hours. If the market wage falls to $16 per hour, the firm will no longer demand 2 stenographer hours because $28 (the *MRP* of the second hour) is greater than $16 (the wage being paid), and the firm is paying for the last hour a wage that is less than the hour's contribution to the firm's revenue. The situation offers a profit opportunity to the firm; it would react by hiring more stenographer hours. As the firm increases employment, *MRP* will fall because of the law of diminishing returns. The firm will continue to increase labor until the last hour's *MRP* just equals the market wage of $16. At a $16 wage,

in the stenographer market (it must take the market wage rate as given), and its *MFC* is the market wage rate. This firm can hire all the labor it wants at the prevailing market wage rate. Its labor supply schedule is a horizontal line (perfectly elastic) at the market wage.

Columns (1) and (2) of Table 2 show the amounts of output that are associated with various amounts of labor input for this firm. Columns (3) and (4) give the marginal physical product and marginal revenue product for each level of input. Table 2 assumes that the firm's product will sell for $2 per page and that the capital input is fixed in the short run. Column (2) shows that under these circumstances, the law of diminishing re-

Figure 2
The Market Demand for Stenographers

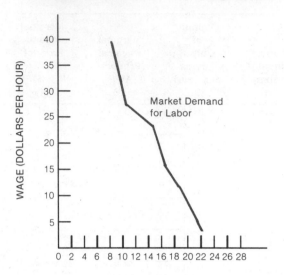

QUANTITY OF LABOR
(HUNDREDS OF WORKER HOURS)

The market demand curve for stenographers indicates the number of stenographer hours that would be demanded by all firms that hire stenographers at different wage rates. Because the demand curves of each firm are negatively sloped, the market demand curve is also negatively sloped.

the firm would use 4 stenographer hours because the *MRP* of the fourth hour is $16. If the market wage had risen (instead of fallen), the firm would have reacted by hiring less labor. The quantity of labor demanded varies inversely with the wage rate, which can be seen by comparing columns (1) and (4) or by observing the downward-sloping shape of the demand curve in Figure 1. More labor will be hired at lower wages than at higher wages, *ceteris paribus*.

The individual firm's demand curve for labor is its marginal revenue product curve.

The Market Demand for Labor

If there are 400 firms demanding stenographers, the market demand for stenographers is the summation of the demand of all 400 firms that purchase labor of that grade. The market demand curve shows how the total quantity of labor demanded varies as the wage changes.

The market demand curve for labor is a derived demand curve for labor that reflects the demands for the product that the particular grade of labor is used to produce.

A typical market demand curve for labor is given in Figure 2. This market demand curve for stenographers shows the quantities of a single grade of labor that are demanded by all 400 employers of that type of labor at different wage rates. Because the labor demand curves of individual firms are negatively sloped, the market demand curve will be negatively sloped as well.[1]

Elasticity of Demand for Labor

The market demand also reflects the cooperation of labor with the other factors of production (land, capital, and other grades of labor). Just as the price elasticity of product demand curves reflects the responsiveness of quantity demanded to changes in product prices, so the price elasticity of labor demand curves reflects the responsiveness of the quantity of labor demanded to changes in the wage rate.[2]

Three factors determine whether the market demand for labor of a single grade is elastic or inelastic: 1) the price elasticity of the product labor helps produce, 2) the substitutability of other factors, and 3) the ratio of labor costs to total costs.

The derived demand for labor will be more elastic the more price elastic is the demand for the product that labor produces. When labor costs rise, the cost of producing the product increases. Therefore, an increase in the wage rate is

---

1. The market demand curve for labor is *not* the horizontal sum of all the individual demand curves for labor. The individual-firm demand curves for labor can hold product prices constant; but, as all the firms expand output, the fall in product prices affects the *MRP*s of the individual firms. It is still true that at any given wage rate, the market demand is the sum of all the individual-firm demands (in the quantity-demanded sense). In the demand-schedule sense, the market demand curve for labor will be steeper than the simple horizontal sum of the individual demand curves since the product price must fall to sell additional industry output.

2. The *elasticity of demand for labor* is defined as the percentage change in the quantity demanded of labor divided by the percentage change in the wage rate. If this ratio is greater than unity, demand is elastic. If it equals one, demand is unitary elastic. If it is less than one, demand is inelastic.

passed on in the form of a higher product price. When price elasticity is high, the quantity of the product demanded drops sharply with each price increase, and, hence, the quantity demanded of labor and other factors used in its production drops sharply. For example, the price elasticity of demand for meat cutters by one supermarket will be higher than the price elasticity of demand for all meat cutters, simply because the price elasticity of demand for supermarket A's beef will be higher than that for beef in general.

The derived demand for labor will be more elastic the easier it is to substitute other productive factors for labor. The more substitutes there are for anything, the greater the elasticity of demand. If machines are available that can do the work of people, the demand for workers will be more price elastic than if these machines were not available. The ease of substitution is also determined by technical factors.

The derived demand for labor will tend to be more elastic the greater is the ratio of labor costs to total costs. If costs for labor of a particular grade are a large fraction of total costs, a larger fraction of wage increases will be passed on to product buyers in the form of higher prices. The higher prices will cause a larger decline in the quantity demanded of output—and, hence, of labor—than if labor were a small fraction of costs. For example, because wheat production is less labor-intensive than strawberry production, the price elasticity of demand for wheat farm labor will be less than the price elasticity of demand for strawberry farm labor, *ceteris paribus*.

Many real-world phenomena are explained by the elasticity of demand for labor. The behavior of unions is affected by the elasticity of demand for the labor of union members. Why firms substitute capital for labor more readily in some industries than in others is also explained by the elasticity of demand for labor. The elasticity of demand for labor also explains who ultimately bears the burden of the social-security payroll tax (see Example 1).

Factors That Shift the Labor Demand Schedule

Factors other than wages can affect the demand curve for a particular grade of labor. The

demand curve for labor will shift to the right (increase) if:

1. the demand for the final product produced using that grade of labor increases.
2. the price of a substitute factor of production increases.
3. the price of a complementary factor of production decreases.
4. the productivity (marginal physical product) of labor increases.

If the demand for the final product increases, there will be an increase in that product's price, *ceteris paribus*. This price increase will raise the marginal revenue product of labor, shifting the demand curve to the right. Substitute factors are those that can be substituted for the type of labor in question in the process of production. Automated equipment may be substituted for bank tellers; sophisticated word-processing equipment may be substituted for secretaries; skilled labor may be substituted for unskilled labor; the farmer may substitute chemical fertilizers for farm workers. If the prices of substitute factors increase, firms will increase their demand for labor. Complementary factors are those that are used in combination with the factor in question. Materials, such as steel, aluminum, and plastics, are used in combination with labor to make automobiles, for example. If the prices of these materials rise, the demand for labor will fall. When labor productivity increases, more output can be produced from the same amount of labor. When the marginal physical product of labor increases, *ceteris paribus,* the marginal revenue product of (and, therefore, the demand for) labor rises. The positive relationship between productivity and wages is explained by the fact that rising productivity increases the demand for labor, thereby raising wages. Competitive industries will pay a real wage *(W/P)* that equals the marginal physical product of labor because competitive firms hire to the point where $W = P \times MPP$. Accordingly, real wages should rise when the marginal physical product of labor rises. The phenomenon of increasing real wages noted in Table 1 is explained by rising labor productivity. The main causes of labor productivity improvements are increases in technological knowledge and increases in the volumn of cooperating factors (particularly capital).

Example 1

Who Pays for the Employer Payroll Tax?

In 1982, employers paid a social-security payroll tax of 6.7 percent of the first $32,400 in wages earned by an employee. Employees must pay the Social Security Administration an equivalent sum, which is deducted from their paychecks. By dividing the contribution equally between the employer and employee, it appears that employers foot at least one half of the bill for the social-security system. Is it true that the existing system splits the burden of financing social security equally between employer and employee?

A worker with a base wage of $10,718 per year is receiving only $10,000 (after deduction of the employee's share of the payroll tax), and the employer is paying $11,436 ($10,718 to the employee + $718 to the government). The total tax per employee, therefore, is $1,436 on wages of $10,000. Who bears the burden of this tax depends upon the price elasticities of demand and supply of labor.

The payroll tax causes a reduction in the demand for labor (a downward shift in the demand curve) because the firm wants fewer workers at the $11,436 wage than at the $10,000 wage. The demand curve shifts down by exactly the amount of the combined tax on the employer and employee, or by $1,436. The accompanying figure shows that as the demand for labor falls as a result of the tax, the wage rate falls below what it would have been in the absence of the tax. The tax shifts the demand curve down by the vertical distance ae', and the wage drops from w_1 to w_2 (from $11 to $6). Employers now pay $13 rather than $11 as a result of the tax.

Who ultimately pays the tax? In order for the ultimate burden of the tax to be divided evenly between employer and employee the price elasticity of demand for labor would have to equal the price elasticity of supply. The accompanying figure presupposes that the price elasticity of demand is

---

THE SUPPLY OF A SINGLE GRADE OF LABOR

Now that we've determined that the market demand curve for labor of a single grade is negatively sloped, what are the determinants of the supply of labor to buyers of a particular grade of labor?

The Labor Supply Curve

If all other factors are held constant, the amount of a single grade of labor that will be supplied will depend on the wage rate offered by employers. Workers, in making their labor-supply choices, compare the wage they can earn in one occupation with their opportunity cost (the wage they could receive from employment in another occupation). The higher the wage offered for labor of that grade, the greater will be the number of workers of that grade who offer their services.

Workers will typically be paid their opportunity cost. Employers must pay workers a wage that is at least equal to the

opportunity cost of the next best alternative that the worker sacrifices in accepting that employment.

The employer who fails to pay workers their opportunity costs will have no workers because they would all take the next best alternative (which then becomes their best alternative).

Figure 3 is a representative market supply curve that shows the number of hours stenographers are willing to work at different wage rates. The supply curve is positively sloped because at higher wages stenographic employment becomes more attractive relative to employment in other occupations. Workers will, therefore, shift hours from other occupations for which they are qualified (receptionists, office managers, grocery-store clerks) into stenographic work. The market labor supply curve is the summation of the individual labor supply curves of stenographers.

Factors That Shift the Labor Supply Curve

The labor supply curve of Figure 3 is drawn holding all factors other than wages constant.

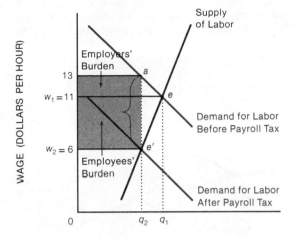

WAGE (DOLLARS PER HOUR)

QUANTITY OF LABOR (WORKER HOURS)

more than the price elasticity of supply, which means that employees are less price sensitive than employers and, hence, that they will pay more than their share.

Economists have sought to estimate what proportion of the employer's social-security contribution is passed on to employees in the form of lower wages. Although there is no unanimity, the most recent findings suggest that less than half (perhaps less than one third) of the increases in employer social-security taxes are passed on to the employee in the form of lower wages. ✂

Source: Daniel Hamermesh, "New Estimates of the Incidence of the Payroll Tax," *Southern Economic Journal* 45 (February 1979): 1208–19; Ronald Ehrenberg, Robert Hutchens, and Robert Smith, *Distribution of Unemployment Insurance Benefits and Costs,* Technical Analysis Paper, no. 58, U.S. Department of Labor, October 1978.

There are two basic factors other than wages that affect the supply of labor to a particular occupation: 1) the wages that can be earned in other occupations and 2) the nonpecuniary aspects of the occupation. The wages paid in other occupations affect the supply of labor to a particular occupation. If receptionist wages increase, the supply of stenographers should fall, for example. The supply of labor responds to different types of work conditions. Other things remaining the same, people prefer to avoid heavy, unpleasant, or dangerous work or work in harsh climates. An increase in the unpleasantness or danger associated with a particular job (for example, an increase in the risk of getting lung cancer in an asbestos factory) will cause a decrease in the supply of labor to that industry. Such an increase in the danger of the job would shift a supply curve leftward. The effect of unions on the supply of labor will be discussed in the chapter on unions.

LABOR MARKET EQUILIBRIUM

Wage rates are determined in a competitive labor market by the interaction of the forces of supply and demand. The market demand curve for

Figure 3
The Market Supply of Stenographers

This market supply curve shows the number of hours stenographers are willing to work at different wage rates, all other things remaining the same. The labor supply curve is positively sloped because at higher wages, stenographic employment is more attractive relative to other types of employment.

Example 2

Productivity and Wages

The accompanying figure shows the pattern of compensation changes and productivity changes between 1960 and 1980. It illustrates the close positive relationship between wages and labor productivity. Economic theory provides an explanation for this relationship. Increases in labor productivity should cause the demand for labor to in-

crease. As the demand for labor increases, the wage rate should rise, *ceteris paribus* (as long as the labor supply curve is upward-sloping). Thus, the close positive relationship between labor productivity and wages is predicted by theory.

Source: U.S. Bureau of the Census.

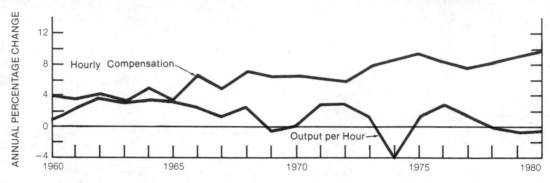

labor of a single grade is negatively sloped; the market supply curve of labor of a single grade is positively sloped.

> *The equilibrium wage rate in the labor market is that wage rate at which the quantity of labor demanded equals the quantity of labor supplied.*

The market supply and demand curves are brought together in Figure 4. The wage rate of $16 equates the quantity of stenographer hours supplied with the quantity of stenographer hours demanded, or 1,600 hours. At any wage above $16, the number of hours stenographers wish to work exceeds the number demanded. At any wage below $16, the number of hours firms wish stenographers to work exceeds the number stenographers are willing to work.

Labor Shortages and Surpluses

In a free labor market, wage rates adjust until they equal the equilibrium wage rate. If there is a **labor surplus,** some workers willing to work at the prevailing wage will be without jobs. Some

will offer their services at lower wages and thus drive down the wage rate. If there is a **labor shortage,** some firms wishing to hire workers at the prevailing wage rate will go away empty-handed. Some will offer higher wages to attract employees and thus drive up wage rates.

> *A **labor surplus** occurs when the number of workers willing to work at the prevailing wage rate exceeds the number firms wish to employ at that wage rate.*

> *A **labor shortage** occurs when the number of workers firms wish to hire at the prevailing wage rate exceeds the number willing to work at that wage rate.*

Shifts in Labor Supply and Demand

Unless something happens to prevent the labor market from seeking out the equilibrium wage, the market wage will be that wage which equates the quantity of labor demanded with the quantity of labor supplied. If any of the factors capable of shifting a demand or supply curve were to

Figure 4
Equilibrium in the Market for
Stenographers

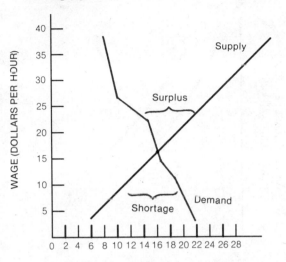

The market supply of stenographers (from Figure 3) and the market demand for stenographers (from Figure 2) are brought together in this figure. The equilibrium wage rate is $16 per hour. At the $16 wage, the quantity demanded (1,600 hours) equals the quantity supplied. At wage rates above $16, there is a surplus (quantity supplied exceeds quantity demanded); at wage rates below $16, there is a shortage of labor (quantity demanded exceeds quantity supplied).

change, the equilibrium would be disrupted and a new wage rate would be established by the market.

Changes in conditions other than the wage rate can shift the supply or demand curve. The supply curve of labor may shift to the left because of higher wages in other occupations or increased health hazards on the job. As Figure 5 shows, if the supply of labor falls (shifts left) from S to S', there would be a shortage of labor at the wage, w, that initially equated quantity supplied and quantity demanded. Therefore, the wage would rise (to w'). If the demand for labor falls (shifts left), there would be a surplus of labor at the old wage, w, and the wage rate would fall to w''. The possible causes of a demand reduction include a decline of labor productivity, a fall in the demand for the final product labor is used to produce, or

a change in the prices of other inputs that cooperate with labor.

WAGE STRUCTURE

The preceding explanation of how the wage rate for labor of a single homogeneous grade is determined did not explain why some people earn more than others or why some occupations command a higher wage than others. These wage differences occur, very simply, because people are different and because jobs are different. Under competitive conditions, if all people were the same and if all jobs were the same, then everyone would earn the same wage.

Compensating Wage Differentials

Underground coal miners are paid more than workers in manufacturing industries in both capitalist and socialist countries. For example, miners in Canada earn 20 percent more than Canadian manufacturing workers. In Hungary and the Soviet Union, the percentages are even higher. In the United States in 1982, workers in coal mining were paid an average wage of $12.41 per hour—compared to the average wage of $7.55 per hour in nonagricultural industries.[3]

Why are coal miners paid more than other production workers? Coal mining does not require highly specialized skills or training; the skills that most manufacturing workers possess could readily be used in underground coal mining. The reason for the wage difference lies on the supply side of the labor market: jobs are different.

One of the factors capable of shifting the labor supply curve is the general desirability of the job. People prefer to avoid dirty, monotonous, and dangerous jobs, other things equal. Coal mining is one of the most dangerous professions with a rate of 0.3 fatalities per million work hours. The fatality rate in minerals mining is 0.2 fatalities per million work hours (two thirds that of coal mining), and the hourly wage in minerals mining is 85 percent that of coal mining.[4]

3. U.S. Department of Labor, *Employment and Earnings* 29, 3 (March 1982):80.
4. *Statistical Abstract of the United States, 1981,* 102nd ed., p. 730.

Figure 5
Shifts in Labor Supply and Demand

(a) Labor Supply Decreases

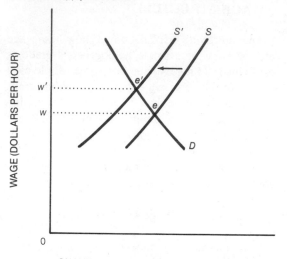

(b) Labor Demand Decreases

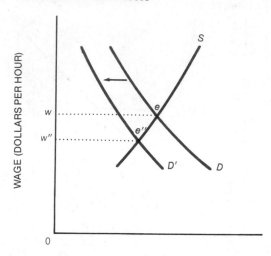

Panel (a) shows the effect of a decrease in the supply of labor. When there is a reduction in supply from S to S', there is a shortage of labor (firms want to use more worker hours than workers are willing to work) at the equilibrium wage, w. The competition among firms for labor will bid the wage up to w'. Panel (b) shows the effect of a decrease in demand. When the demand curve shifts from D to D', there is a surplus of labor (workers wish to work more hours than employers wish to use) at the original equilibrium wage. Competition among workers will drive the wage down to w".

Figure 6 shows the effect of differences in the danger of the occupation on relative wages. For simplicity, the demand curve for coal miners is assumed to be identical to the demand curve for textile workers. The labor supply curves are quite different. The position of the coal miners' supply curve (higher than the textile workers' supply curve) reflects the fact that workers prefer, *ceteris paribus*, less dangerous employment. To get an equivalent supply of coal miners, coal-mine employers must offer higher wages than textile employers.

This model can be used to explain a wide variety of **compensating wage differentials:** why welders on the Alaskan pipeline have to be paid so much (to compensate for the harsh climate and higher living costs) or why sanitation workers are usually better paid than clerical workers (to compensate for the unpleasantness and social stigma).

Compensating wage differentials are the higher rewards (wages or fringe benefits) that must be paid workers to compensate them for undesirable job characteristics.

Numerous studies by economists have demonstrated that compensating wage differentials are indeed paid to offset undesirable job characteristics. Although individuals do differ a great deal (some enjoy heavy outdoor work and would detest office work; others enjoy work in the office but hate being outdoors), almost everyone wishes to avoid injury and disease. Eight separate studies by economists all show that wages are positively associated with the risk of being killed on the job. These studies show that workers receive, depending upon the job, between $20 and $300 more per year for every 1 in 10,000 increase in the death rate associated with a job.[5] As already noted, the occupational fatality rate in other mining occupations is two thirds that of coal mining, and coal miners earn an hourly wage 17 percent above minerals miners—even though both jobs require similar skills. Improvements in safety in coal mining would lead to a narrowing of this differential, according to economic theory.

5.   Ronald Ehrenberg and Robert Smith, *Modern Labor Economics: Theory and Public Policy* (Glenview, Ill.: Scott Foresman, 1982), chap. 8.

Figure 6
Wages in Coal Mining and Textiles

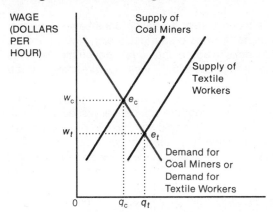

QUANTITY OF LABOR (WORKER HOURS)

For simplicity, the demand curve for coal miners is assumed to be identical to the demand curve for textile workers. Wages are higher for coal miners because the quantity supplied of coal miners is less than the quantity supplied of textile workers at each wage rate.

Noncompeting Groups

The discussion of the labor market in this chapter has assumed to this point that all labor is the same (homogeneous). The difference in the wages earned by different workers was attributed to differences in job characteristics. In reality, both jobs *and* people are different. Because people are different, firms must take the trouble to distinguish high-productivity workers from low-productivity workers. Some individuals are qualified by mental and physical skills and training for a wide variety of occupations. Others are qualified for only a few occupations. Only a limited number of people have the peculiar abilities to become brain surgeons, trial lawyers, or theoretical physicists. Surgeons must have extremely sensitive and sure hands; trial lawyers must be articulate and be able to think quickly on their feet; and theoretical physicists must have an enormous analytical aptitude. The number of individuals qualified to be professional athletes is limited to those possessing the necessary physical attributes. On the other hand, the number of individuals who are qualified to be stock clerks, management trainees, factory workers, and so on is much greater.

Adam Smith pointed out that the natural differences among people are less than commonly supposed, while training is responsible for the significant differences among people. While the philosopher and electrician may not be genetically that different, background, education, and experience differentiate them to the point where it becomes difficult for electricians to compete with philosophers. Labor suppliers are divided into **noncompeting groups,** the existence of which has a substantial effect on the distribution of income.

Noncompeting groups are groups of labor suppliers that are differentiated by natural ability and abilities acquired through education, training, and experience to the extent that they do not compete with one another for jobs.

If people were the same and had equal access to all occupations, the wage differences that would remain would be the consequence of different job conditions. The brain surgeon would earn as much as the garbage collector if the two jobs were equally desirable. In the absence of differences in people, if brain surgery was regarded as a more pleasant job (or a higher-status job) than garbage collection, it is even conceivable that garbage collectors would receive higher wages.[6]

Signaling and the Internal Labor Market

Because people are different, it is often costly for the potential employer to determine the marginal physical product of each worker. Employers typically do not know exactly how productive a potential employee will be in a particular position. The problem of gathering information on the marginal physical products of different workers is similar to the consumer's problem of gathering information on product quality and product prices discussed in an earlier chapter. Consumers solve the problem of costly information by buying brand names and by limiting searching time in the case of less expensive items. Employers have de-

6. The brain surgeon may require years of study while the garbage collector may begin work immediately after schooling. Wage differences attributable to differences in the amount of training and education would still remain, but everyone would have the "opportunity" to become brain surgeons.

Who Pays for Occupational Safety?

To protect American workers from job-related injuries and illnesses, Congress passed in 1970 the Occupational Safety and Health Act. This act established The Occupational Safety and Health Administration (OSHA) to issue and enforce safety and health standards for private employers. The passage of this act was prompted by the numerous fatalities in coal mining and the health hazards of working in asbestos and chemical plants—both of which received considerable notoriety in the press.

What are the costs and benefits to chemical workers of occupational safety legislation that enjoins a chemical manufacturer from employing women in a plant that manufactures chemicals that may cause birth defects? What about legislation that requires that miners with black lung disease be placed in above-ground jobs?

Although such legislation does serve to protect workers, it does create costs along with benefits. Economists agree that such governmental rules and regulations play a very positive role if the affected workers are unaware of the dangers they face, such as a chemical worker who is unaware of an increased risk of cancer associated with working with a particular chemical or a woman who, unknowingly, risks genetic damage to her unborn child by working with toxic chemicals. But what about those workers who are well-informed about the risks and dangers of the job, who are mobile and able to find other work but at lower wages? To what extent are they helped by federal regulations that may compel them to seek work elsewhere? Such legislation, in effect, penalizes workers who are not sensitive to risk and who willingly accept the higher wages that greater risk brings. ◢◣

---

veloped similar techniques to deal with the problem of distinguishing low-productivity workers from high-productivity workers.

Credentials or Screening. Employers must bear the costs of training employees, but they presumably want to minimize these costs by hiring the most able persons for the job. It is costly for firms to investigate intensively the backgrounds of potential employees or to administer comprehensive examinations designed to determine worker qualifications. When training costs (for example, the costs of teaching new employees how to operate sophisticated equipment) are substantial, firms will spend more on testing employees and investigating their backgrounds. Indeed, companies like IBM who must expend large sums of money to train new employees do indeed devote considerable resources to **screening** potential employees.

Screening is the process used by employers to raise the probability of selecting the most qualified workers on the basis of observable characteristics.

Employers can reduce screening costs by relying upon worker **signaling.** Employers may know from experience, for example, that college graduates in math and business are on average more productive in certain occupations than high-school graduates or college graduates from other disciplines. They, therefore, specify that a business or math degree is a requirement for the job. Employers may believe that, on the average, scholastic grades are an indicator of worker productivity. Employers may therefore specify that only students with a B average or better be hired for particular positions.

Signaling is the process by which credentials (such as education degrees, grades, specific experience, or references) are used to differentiate among prospective employees.

By requiring college degrees or minimum grade-point averages employers screen out job candidates who, on average, are not qualified for the job in question. The use of credentials allows them to reduce the costs of distinguishing qualified from unqualified job applicants. They know

Example 4

An Internal Labor Market:
The Dallas Cowboys

Professional football teams often hire football players through the external labor market. When a particular position must be staffed, the team will attempt to hire (on the basis of the player's credentials) the best available player from another team. An exception to this behavior is the Dallas Cowboys football team—a team that rarely hires in the external labor market. Players are promoted to starting positions from within the organization. Rarely will a position be staffed by hiring a player from another team. Why do the Dallas Cowboys rely so heavily on the internal labor market while other teams use the external labor market? One possible explanation is that the costs of training new players are greater in the case of the Dallas Cowboys, a team that uses a very sophisticated and hard-to-learn offense and defense. It may take one or two years for the newcomer to learn to function in his position as efficiently as a player who has been in the organization a number of years, even though the newcomer is basically a more talented athlete with better credentials in that position.

that these techniques will be correct on average. They know that not every person who holds the desired credentials will actually be suited for the job, while some individuals who do not hold the right credentials may be ideally suited for the job.

Internal Labor Markets. One way employers can resolve the problem of obtaining the best qualified persons with a minimum of hiring costs is to draw workers from an **internal labor market.**

*The firm's **internal labor market** is the hierarchy of labor—from general laborers to top-level executives—within the firm itself.*

Normally, entrance into the internal labor market is through general entry-level positions, such as management trainee, bookkeeper, or apprentice machinist. In internal labor markets, rules and established procedures determine who will be promoted and when, the role that the union organization will play, and the manner in which vacancies will be filled. Rather than screening potential employees on the basis of credentials, firms that rely on an internal labor market hire a large number of people without much testing, interviewing, or screening. A large department store will hire a large number of management trainees; a factory may hire a large number of general laborers. Once on the job, the management of the firm has the opportunity to observe job performance and to determine actual worker productivities. The major benefit of using the internal labor market to fill job vacancies is that the firm can learn a great deal about the person being considered for a job. The major cost of using the internal labor market is that the firm passes up the opportunity to hire more qualified persons from outside the firm by restricting its hiring and promotions to those already employed by the firm.

LEISURE AND HOUSEHOLD PRODUCTION

Individuals do have options other than work in the labor force. These other options have an effect upon the total supply of labor to the economy. Individuals must choose among work in the labor force, **household production,** and **leisure.**

Household production is work in the home, including such activities as meal preparation, child rearing, and cleaning.

Leisure is time spent in any activity other than work in the labor force or work in the home.

What determines how an individual will allocate his or her time among these three activities?

Figure 7
The Backward-Bending Labor Supply Curve

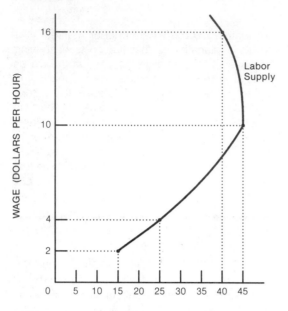

QUANTITY OF LABOR (WORKER HOURS)

The labor supply curve is upward-sloping until a wage of $10 per hour is reached. Below $10 the substitution effect of higher wages dominates the income effect of higher wages. At wage rates above $10, the quantity of labor supplied falls as the wage rate increases because the income effect dominates the substitution effect.

The theory of the allocation of time developed by Gary Becker, Jacob Mincer, Yoram Ben Porath, and others is designed to analyze this choice in the framework of rational economic decision making.

Labor/Leisure Choices

The opportunity cost of leisure is the income (or household production) that must be given up to enjoy leisure. The opportunity cost of leisure, therefore, rises when the price of market work rises. If real wages have risen over time, one would expect the quantity of market work that each person performs to have increased over time. As Table 1 shows, real wages have in fact risen while average hours worked per week have declined dramatically.

The evidence in Table 1 suggests that the labor supply curve representing the relationship between wages and hours worked per person is *backward-bending* (it has a section with a negative slope), as shown in Figure 7. When the wage rate rises, two things happen: First, leisure becomes more expensive to the individual. Second, the individual's income increases. When leisure becomes more expensive because its opportunity cost (earnings sacrificed) has increased, *leisure is discouraged;* when income rises, *leisure is encouraged*.

The chapter on demand and utility identified two effects of a price change on the consumption of goods: the *income effect* (the impact of the change in income that results from a price change) and the *substitution effect* (the substitution of cheaper goods for more expensive goods that results from a price change).

The increase in wages (or the "price" of leisure) also results in income and substitution effects. The increase in the relative price of leisure (that occurs when wages rise) motivates individuals to substitute other things—in this case market work—for leisure, thereby discouraging leisure. On the other hand, the increase in wages increases income (an income effect), making more income available for leisure. Typically, as income rises, more consumption of a good occurs—if the good is a *normal good* (a good the demand for which increases as income rises). If the substitution effect of a wage increase discourages leisure, and the income effect of a wage increase encourages leisure, what then will be the overall effect on leisure of the wage increase? The overall effect depends upon which effect is stronger, the substitution effect or the income effect.

In Figure 7, when the wage is only $2 per hour and hours worked are only 15 hours per week, a dollar increase in wages adds up to only an additional $15 per week; the income effect is weak. When wages are $4 per hour and hours worked are 25 per week, a dollar increase in wages is like an extra $25 per week; the income effect is stronger. When wages are $10 per hour and 45 hours are worked per week, the income effect is even stronger. Figure 7 assumes that the income effect begins to dominate the substitution effect after wages reach $10 per hour. Further increases in wages cause hours worked per person to actually decline, as shown by the backward-bending section of the labor supply curve.

The data presented in Table 1 suggest that in the long run the income effect is stronger than the substitution effect, which explains why average hours worked per week have been dropping despite rising real wages. The data are generally consistent with a backward-bending labor supply curve.

Wages and Household Production

One explanation for the dramatic rise in the labor-force participation rate of women reported in Table 1 is that the social roles of men and women have been changing. High divorce rates and a larger number of one-parent families also explain rising female labor-force participation.

Economic theory provides another plausible explanation. According to economic theory, whether people work in the labor force or in household production depends in part upon the value of their household production relative to the wage they could earn in market employment. If work in the home (child rearing, cleaning, food preparation) is worth, say, $10 per hour, and the market wage a woman could earn in the labor market is $8 per hour, she would not enter the labor force. If, however, the market wages of women rise more rapidly than the value of household production, then one would expect women to enter the labor force. The rise in the real wages of women in recent decades is the explanation cited by some economists for the rise in the labor-force participation rates of women. Products such as automatic dishwashers and microwave ovens also lower the value of household work relative to market work.

This chapter examined how labor markets work. The next chapter will take a look at the effect of labor unions on the labor market.

Summary

1. Labor markets operate like other factor markets, but labor is different because workers desire leisure and because workers have preferences concerning different jobs. Labor cannot be bought and sold like the other factors of production. A labor market brings buyers and sellers of labor services together. If the buyer of the labor service must accept the market wage as given, this buyer is perfectly competitive in the labor market. If the buyer affects wage rates, the buyer has some monopsonist power. Labor-market analysis must explain why average hours worked have fallen, why the labor-force participation rates of women have increased, why wage differentials exist, why real wages have risen, and why there is a close positive relationship between labor productivity and wages.

2. Individual firms hire labor to the point where $MFC = MRP$. The firm's MRP schedule is its labor demand schedule. The labor demand curve will be negatively sloped both for firms and for the market. The labor demand curve will shift if demand for the firm's final product changes, if the price of either substitute or complementary factors changes, or if the productivity of labor changes.

3. The labor supply curve will be positively sloped because workers must be paid their opportunity costs. The labor supply curve will shift if job conditions or wages in other industries change.

4. The market wage rate is typically that wage at which the quantity demanded of labor of a single grade equals the quantity supplied. A shortage exists when the quantity demanded exceeds the quantity supplied at that wage. A surplus exists when the quantity supplied exceeds the quantity demanded at that wage. A new equilibrium wage/quantity combination will result when either the market supply or market demand curve shifts because of changes in productivity, product prices, the prices of other factors, or job conditions.

5. The theory of labor markets explains why workers in dangerous occupations are paid more. Noncompeting groups are workers with different abilities who do not compete for the same jobs. In the real world, it is costly for employers to determine the real productivities of potential employees. They therefore use signaling, credentials, and internal labor markets to distinguish high productivity workers.

6. When wage rates in general rise, the opportunity cost of leisure increases as does income. Whether the aggregate labor-supply

curve will be backward-bending depends upon the relative strengths of the income and substitution effects. Whether people work in household production or in the market labor force depends upon the value of time in the home compared to their market wage.

Key Terms

labor market
labor surplus
labor shortage
compensating wage differentials
noncompeting groups
screening
signaling
internal labor market
household production
leisure

Questions and Problems

1. Explain why labor's special features cause the labor market to work differently from the other factor markets.

2. A logging company employs 90 percent of those working in a small mining community. Why is this company likely to be a price searcher? Because of its dominant position, could this company get away permanently with offering wages that are 30 percent of the state average.

3. A price-taking firm in both its product and factor markets is currently employing 25 workers. The 25th worker's *MRP* is $300 per week and the worker's wage is $200 per week. Is this firm maximizing its profits? If not, what would you advise the company to do?

4. This chapter has shown that there is a close positive association between labor productivity and wages. Using the theory presented in this chapter, explain this relationship.

5. State law in New Jersey requires that employees in licensed gambling casinos be residents of New Jersey for a specified period of time. What effect does this legislation have upon the elasticity of demand for casino employees in New Jersey? What effect does this legislation have upon the incidence of the employee payroll tax?

6. During recessions and periods of falling wages, the number of volunteers for the all-volunteer army rises. Using the economic theory of this chapter, explain why this supply of labor rises.

7. Explain why a worker in India earns much less than a worker in West Germany.

8. "If all jobs were the same, everyone would earn the same wage." Evaluate this statement.

9. "If all people were the same, everyone would earn the same wage." Evaluate this statement.

10. You are a surgeon earning $200,000 per year. When the demand for your services increases, the charge for each operation increases by 25 percent. What effect will this increase have on the number of operations you perform?

17

Labor Unions

Chapter Preview

Labor unions are an integral part of modern capitalist economies. Some people view labor unions as a positive force for justice, equality, and even economic efficiency and believe unions protect workers from the monopsony power of employers. Others see labor unions as monopolistic and often corrupt organizations that benefit their own members while imposing costs on nonmembers and on society as a whole. Some economists argue that the economic role of labor unions is substantial, while others maintain that the power of unions to affect wages and employment has been exaggerated.

This chapter will examine the role of **labor unions** in the labor market, and will discuss how

unions affect wages and employment, trends in union membership, and empirical studies of the impact of unions on wages, employment, and economic efficiency.

*A **labor union** is a collective organization of workers and employees.*

DEFINITIONS

The labor union's primary objectives are to improve the pecuniary and nonpecuniary conditions of employment of its members. Labor unions are traditionally one of three types: 1) a **craft union,** 2) an **industrial union,** or 3) an **employee association.**

313

Figure 1
Union and Employee Association Membership as Percent of Labor Force, 1870-1980

About one out of five members of the labor force in the United States belongs to unions. Union membership rose from 6.7 percent in the 1930s to a peak of 25 percent in the 1950s before declining to recent levels.

Source: *Statistical Abstract of the United States,* 102nd ed. (1981), Table 691; *Handbook of Labor Statistics* (U.S. Department of Labor, Bureau of Labor Statistics, December 1980), Table 165; *Historical Statistics of the United States, Colonial Times to 1970,* 1976, part I, series D.

---

*A **craft union** is a union that represents workers of a single occupation.*

A craft union could be an electricians' union or a plumbers' union.

*An **industrial union** is a union that represents employees of an industry or a firm regardless of their specific occupation.*

Examples of industrial unions are the United Automobile Workers (a union that represents automobile workers of all types) and the United Mine Workers (a union that represents all types of workers engaged in mining).

*An **employee association** is an organization that represents employees in a particular profession.*

Historically, employee associations, such as the National Education Association, the American Association of University Professors, and state employee associations, were primarily concerned

with maintaining professional standards, but in recent years they have become increasingly involved in the primary union function of improving the pecuniary and nonpecuniary conditions of employment of their members.

Unions perform a variety of functions. Their most visible function is to engage in *collective bargaining* with the employers of their members. Instead of each employee negotiating individually with the employer concerning wages, fringe benefits, and work conditions, the union represents all employees in negotiations or discussions with employers. Unions may bargain collectively about a number of issues, ranging from wage rates, vacation pay, and group health insurance to job-security provisions, lay-off rules, and safety conditions.

FACTS AND FIGURES

In the United States, there are about 22 million union members; one out of five members of the labor force belongs to unions (see Figure 1). If members of employee associations that engage in collective bargaining are included, the percentage of unionized workers rises from 20 to 22 percent. In the 1930s, union members accounted for between 6 and 7 percent of the labor force. This percentage rose in the late 1930s and 1940s and peaked at 25 percent in the mid-1950s. Since then, the share of union members has fallen steadily to the current 20 percent figure.

Union membership as a percentage of employment has declined in recent years for several reasons. The percentage of women in the labor force has been rapidly increasing, and women have tended historically not to join unions. The share of white-collar workers in total employment has been rising as well; white-collar employees also tend not to join unions. Moreover, there has been a well-publicized shift in population from the northeastern and midwestern states to the southern and southwestern states, which are the states where union membership has been weakest. The rapid unionization of public employees after 1963 has kept the percentage of union members from falling even more. In 1964, only 7.7 percent of state- and local-government employees belonged to unions. By 1978, the proportion had risen to 17.4 percent.

Most American unions are affiliated with the AFL–CIO (American Federation of Labor–Congress of Industrial Organizations). Unions affiliated with the AFL-CIO account for 78 percent of union members. The Teamsters and the United Automobile Workers are the two largest unions not affiliated with the AFL-CIO, and constitute 16 percent of union membership (see Table 1).

HISTORY AND LEGISLATION

The Growth of the AFL–CIO

As Figure 1 shows, unions were not a powerful force in American life until the late 1930s, although the first national conventions of labor unions met as early as 1869 to lobby for restrictions on Chinese immigration. Union membership expanded rapidly after 1886 when the traditional craft unions banded together in the American Federation of Labor (AFL) under the leadership of Samuel Gompers, the "father of the American labor movement." Gompers made a lasting imprint on the American labor-union movement through

Table 1
Membership in Large Unions

Union	Membership (in thousands)
Teamsters	1,889
Automobile workers	1,358
Steelworkers	1,300
Electrical (IBEW)	924
Machinists	917
Carpenters	820
State, county (AFSCME)	750
Retail clerks (RCIA)	699
Laborers (LIUNA)	627
Service employees (SEIU)	575
Meat cutters	510
Clothing and textile workers	502
Communications workers	483
Teachers (AFT)	446
Hotel and restaurant	432
Engineers, operating	420
Garment, ladies' (ILGWU)	365
Musicians	330
Paperworkers	300
Mine workers	277
United transportation	265
Government (AFGE)	260
Postal workers	252
Electrical (IUE)	238
Plumbers	228
Letter carriers	227
Railway, steamship clerks	211
Rubber	211
Retail, wholesale	200
Painters	195
Iron workers	179
Oil, chemical workers	177
Firefighters	174
Electrical (UE)	165
Sheet metal workers	153
Government (NAGE)	150
Transit union	150
Transport workers	150
Boilermakers	145
Bakery, confectionery	135
Bricklayers	135
Maintenance of way	119
Printing and graphic (IPGCU)	109
Woodworkers	109
Typographical	100
Graphic arts	93
Federal government (NFFE)	(NA)

Source: U.S. Bureau of Labor Statistics, *Directory of National Unions and Employee Associations*, 1975.

his espousal of a nonpolitical, nonsocialist approach to unionism. Gompers believed that unions should be organized by craft and should not include unskilled workers.

Unskilled and semiskilled workers joined the Knights of Labor (organized in 1869), which experienced phenomenal growth in the early 1880s. Unlike the AFL, the Knights of Labor was committed as much or more to political goals as to wage increases. When violence in Chicago's Haymarket Square in 1887 stiffened employer resistance to the Knights of Labor and turned public opinion against organized labor, the Knights of Labor suffered a fatal collapse.

One reason for the difficulty in organizing the American labor force into unions is the unfavorable political climate that prevailed until the 1930s. Antitrust laws (the Sherman Antitrust Act of 1890) were applied against "monopolistic" labor unions; companies used private police forces, threats, and intimidation to prevent the formation of labor unions. It was not until 1932 that the government adopted a conscious policy favoring the free organization of unions. Prior to 1932, management was often able to obtain court orders that prohibited union activity, and employers were allowed to require new employees to sign "yellow dog" contracts in which the employee had to agree not to join a union as a condition of employment.[1]

Industrial unionism (which suffered a severe setback with the collapse of the Knights of Labor) made a comeback in the 1930s under the leadership of John L. Lewis. The failure of the AFL to organize unskilled and semiskilled workers in assembly-line production caused conflicts within the AFL organization. As a consequence, the Congress of Industrial Organizations (CIO) was formed in 1936 to organize workers on an industrial rather than a craft basis.

In 1955, the AFL and CIO merged to form the combined AFL–CIO, to which 78 percent of all union members now belong. At this point, no one can tell whether continuing efforts to bring major non-AFL–CIO unions—the Teamsters, the United Auto Workers—back into the AFL–CIO will succeed.

1. For a history of the American labor movement, see Lance E. Davis et al., *American Economic Growth* (New York: Harper and Row, 1972), pp. 219–27.

Legislation

Two pro-union laws passed during the Great Depression paved the way for the growth of the organized labor movement in the 1930s and 1940s. The Norris-LaGuardia Act of 1932 restricted the use of court orders and injunctions to combat union organizing drives and prohibited "yellow dog" contracts. The National Labor Relations Act (The Wagner Act) of 1935 defined specific unfair labor practices. Employers were required to bargain with unions representing a majority of employees, and it became illegal to interfere with employees' rights to organize into unions. The National Labor Relations Board (NLRB) was established and given the authority to investigate unfair labor practices. The NLRB was also authorized to conduct elections to determine which union the employees wanted, if any, to represent them.

The Norris-LaGuardia Act of 1932 and the Wagner Act of 1935 encouraged union growth. Table 1 makes it clear that until these laws were passed, labor unions were relatively insignificant in size. After World War II, unions lost some of their popular support. The Taft-Hartley and Landrum Griffin Acts were the result of anti-union sentiment. The Taft-Hartley Act of 1947 gave states the right to pass *right-to-work laws* that prohibited the requirement that union membership be a condition for employment. *Closed-shop agreements* that required firms to hire only union members were outlawed for firms engaged in interstate commerce. Major strikes that could disrupt the economy could be delayed by an 80-day cooling-off period if ordered by the President.

The Landrum-Griffin Act of 1959 was designed to protect the rights of union members and to increase union democracy. It included provisions for periodic reporting of union finances and for regulating union elections.

UNION OBJECTIVES

What are the objectives of labor unions? Surprisingly, the answer to this question is not as obvious as it appears. Unions would like to obtain higher wages, better fringe benefits, and safer working conditions for their members. They would also like to prevent the unemployment of

Figure 2
The Trade-Off Between Wages and Employment: The Competitive Case

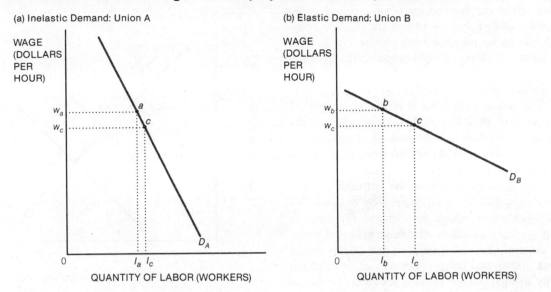

(a) Inelastic Demand: Union A

(b) Elastic Demand: Union B

The demand curve for the members of Union A is relatively inelastic, while the demand curve for the members of Union B is relatively elastic. If both unions, in the collective-bargaining process, push for the same wage increases, more jobs will be lost in Union B (where demand is elastic) than in Union A.

their members. Are the two objectives of higher wages and lower unemployment compatible—given the fact (demonstrated in the previous chapter) that the firm will hire more labor at low wages than at high wages, *ceteris paribus?*

Assume that two different unions—A and B—collectively bargain about wages with management. For simplicity, we assume that the average worker in each union is earning the same wage w_c and that employment is the same in both cases (at l_c). The derived demand curve for each union's labor force is shown in Figure 2. The demand in the case of Union A is inelastic: moving from point c to point a in panel (a) results in a large percentage increase in the wage (to w_a) compared to the percentage reduction in the quantity of labor demanded (from l_c to l_a). The demand is elastic in the case of Union B: moving from c to b in panel (b) results in a small percentage increase in the wage compared to the percentage reduction in the quantity of labor demanded (from l_c to l_b).

The leadership of Union B is faced with a dilemma. If it pushes for wages higher than w_c,

such as w_b, the number of jobs available to union members will decline from l_c to l_b. Jobs will be traded off for higher wages, and the rank and file of the union will likely be dissatisfied with the current union leadership. This **wage/employment trade-off** is less acute in the case of Union A because the same increase in wages causes the loss of fewer jobs (because of the difference in elasticity between A and B).

*The **wage/employment trade-off** is the situation confronted by any labor union that faces a downward-sloping demand curve: higher wages can be obtained only by sacrificing the number of jobs; lower unemployment can be obtained only by sacrificing higher wages.*

Union Behavior

The wage/employment trade-off explains a great deal of observed union behavior. First, it allows economists to predict which types of industries will be most easily unionized: one would expect unions to be formed first in those industries where the demand for labor is relatively inelastic. Indeed, history shows that the first occupations to be unionized were those crafts—carpenters, printers, glassblowers, and shoemakers—where the demand for labor was relatively inelastic.

The demand for labor is relatively inelastic in the case of skilled labor because the availability of close substitutes is limited. It is not easy to substitute unskilled for skilled labor or to substitute a skilled printer for a skilled glassblower. The occupations that were the last (and presumably most difficult to organize) were the unskilled occupations in which the demand for labor is highly elastic, such as wholesale and retail trade.

Second, the model suggests that unions should seek to do two things: they should attempt not only to increase the demand for labor, but to reduce the elasticity of demand for labor. By increasing the demand for labor, labor unions can obtain both higher wages and higher employment. By reducing the elasticity of demand for labor, unions can raise wages with a smaller cost in lost employment.

Unions attempt to increase the demand for union labor and lower its elasticity of demand in a variety of ways. Unions lobby for tariffs and quotas on foreign-produced products to increase the demand for the products produced by union workers. Unions conduct advertising campaigns telling the public to "look for the union label" or to "buy American." Unions oppose relaxation of immigration laws and support the repatriation of illegal aliens. Unions have traditionally supported raising the minimum wage—an act that makes unskilled labor more expensive relative to the more skilled workers that tend to belong to unions.

Unions lobby for minimum staffing requirements, such as the rule that the new DC-9 aircraft be staffed by three cockpit personnel (two pilots and a flight engineer) rather than the two pilots that airline management may want. Staffing requirements that call for the use of additional labor for jobs that have become redundant (such as fire stokers on diesel-powered locomotives) are called *featherbedding*. Unions may also bargain for rules that make it difficult or impossible to substitute

Figure 3
Craft Unions and Wages: Limiting Supply

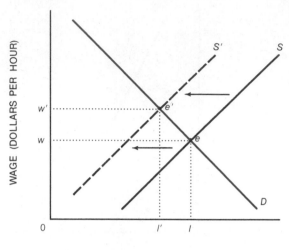

By limiting entry into the profession, a craft union shifts the labor supply curve to the left (from S to S'), and the wage rate of union members is raised above what it would have been without the union.

other grades of labor for union labor. In construction, unions specify in detail which jobs can be performed only by electricians and by no one else, and there are sanctions against builders who hire nonunion employees.

Limitations of Labor Supply

Some unions seek to drive up the wage by limiting the supply of union labor. The union typically controls who will be allowed to work in a particular occupation by means of certification and qualification requirements. In craft unions, the number of union members can be limited by long apprenticeships, by rules limiting entry into the union, by difficult qualifying exams, and by state licensing. In the process of limiting labor supply, the union screens out unqualified workers but may also exclude some qualified people who are prepared to work in that occupation.

Figure 3 shows the effect of limiting labor supply on wages. The decrease in supply (from S to S') moves the equilibrium wage/employment combination from e to e'; at e' wages are higher, but the number of jobs is fewer. When unions seek to control wages through limitations on the supply of union labor, it is especially important to prevent employers from substituting nonunion labor. For this reason, craft unions favor rigid certification requirements and rules prohibiting nonunion workers from performing certain tasks.

Strikes and Collective Bargaining

Industrial unions that represent all the workers in a particular industry have a more difficult time limiting the supply of labor. Such unions can indeed affect overall labor-supply conditions by favoring restrictions on immigration, mandatory retirement, shorter work weeks, and laws against teenage employment. But they, unlike plumbers, electricians, and physicians, find it difficult to control the number of union members. Industrial unions, therefore, use **collective bargaining** to raise the wages of union members.

Collective bargaining is the process whereby the union bargains with management as the representative of all union employees.

Collective bargaining gives workers a stronger voice than they would have if each worker bargained separately with management.

The threat of **strike** is the union's most effective weapon in collective bargaining. The effect of the collective bargaining process (with threat of strike) is represented in Figure 4. The supply curve, S, represents the supply of labor to the industry if each individual were to bargain separately with management. When the union threatens to strike, the union is, in effect, telling management that: at wages less than w_c, no labor will be supplied; at the wage of w_c, management can hire as much labor as it wants up to l_c of labor; as wages increase above w_c, management can hire ever-increasing amounts of labor beyond l_c. Thus, the new labor supply curve with the threat of a strike is indicated by the heavy line that connects w_c on the vertical axis with point c and then continues up the original supply curve above point c. Without the threat of strike, the supply curve would be the original curve S, and point e would be the equilibrium wage/employment combination. With the threat of a strike, the demand curve would meet the new supply curve

Figure 4
Collective Bargaining with the Threat of Strike

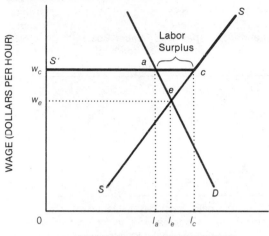

QUANTITY OF LABOR (WORKERS)

The supply curve, S, represents the labor supply if each worker were to bargain separately with the employer. The heavy black supply curve that is S' to the left of point c and S above c is the supply curve with collective bargaining because no union labor will be supplied at a wage below w_c. Point e is the equilibrium wage/employment combination without collective bargaining or the threat of a strike; point a is the equilibrium wage/employment combination with collective bargaining. The *benefit* to union members of collective bargaining is that a wage higher than the one that would have prevailed is achieved (w_c is higher than w_e). The *cost* is that the number of jobs available to union members is reduced. Some union members who are willing to work at w_c are without jobs in the industry (the number represented by the difference between l_c and l_a is the number left without jobs); however, l_c workers minus l_e workers is the number of workers attracted by the higher wages.

at point a, and the firm would hire l_a workers at a wage of w_c.

*A **strike** occurs when all unionized employees cease to work until management agrees to specific union demands.*

From the standpoint of union members, collective bargaining has its costs and benefits. The benefits are the higher wages that collective bargaining brings (w_c is higher than w_e). If the industry is entirely unionized, the costs are that some union members who are willing to work at the negotiated wage will not be employed in this

Table 2
The Monopsonist's Labor Cost

Labor (workers) (1)	Wage (dollars per hour) (2)	Labor Cost (dollars) (3) = (1) × (2)	Marginal Factor Cost, MFC (dollars) (4)
1	5	5	
			9
2	7	14	
			13
3	9	27	
			21
4	12	48	

The monopsonist must pay a higher wage to employ more workers. The marginal factor cost of an extra worker is, therefore, greater than the wage. For example, the wage of the second worker is $7 per hour, but the marginal factor cost is $9 (or $7 plus the $2 difference between the wage necessary to hire one worker and the wage necessary to hire two workers).

industry. Although l_c workers are willing to work at w_c, only l_a workers will be hired. The unemployment effects of collective bargaining are softened by numerous rules within the union (an internal labor market) governing which members will be laid off first. Typically, union members who have *seniority* (have been in the union the longest time) are laid off last.

FIRM MONOPSONY

If employers have monopoly power over their labor market, the trade-off between higher wages and union employment does not hold. An employer has monopsony power if the employer accounts for a large enough portion of total hiring in the labor market to affect the market wage. The labor supply curve to a monopsonistic firm is not horizontal at the market wage because the employer cannot hire all the labor it wants at the market wage. Instead, to hire more labor, the monopsonistic firm will have to offer higher wages to all its employees.

Consider a monopsonist faced with the labor supply schedule given in Table 2. As demonstrated in an earlier chapter, the wage rate is not the marginal factor cost *(MFC)* in the case of the

Figure 5
Monopsony and Collective Bargaining

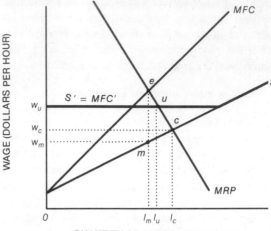

Because this industry is a monopsonist, *MFC* is greater than the wage at each quantity. The monopsonist will hire that quantity of labor at which *MFC* = *MRP*. Without unions, *MFC* = *MRP* at point *e;* the monopsonist will hire l_m workers and pay the wage of w_m. If a union collectively bargains for a wage of w_u, the monopsonist's *MFC* curve shifts to *MFC'* because of the change in labor supply and becomes a horizontal line at w_u; *MFC* will now equal *MRP* at point *u*. In this case, collective bargaining actually increased both wages (from w_m to w_u) and union employment (from l_m to l_u).

monopsonist. To hire one more unit of labor, the monopsonist must pay a higher wage not only to the new worker but also to workers previously hired. To hire the second worker, the monopsonist must pay a higher wage ($7 rather than the previous $5) to the first worker. The *MFC* of the second worker is, therefore, the wage paid the second worker ($7) plus the increase in the wage of the first worker ($2) for a total of $9. The *MFC* for each additional worker is shown in the fourth column.

The marginal factor cost of the monopsonist is greater than the wage rate paid by the monopsonist.

The relationship between *MFC* and wages is shown in Figure 5. The monopsonist will hire that quantity of labor at which *MFC* and *MRP* are equal. In the absence of collective bargaining,

$MFC = MRP$ at point e, so the monopsonist will hire l_m workers. The wage required to induce l_m workers to work is only w_m; therefore, the monopsonist will operate at point m in the absence of collective bargaining, hiring l_m workers at a wage of w_m.

Since MFC exceeds the wage rate, the monopsonist will hire less labor than would be the case if the industry were competitive in the labor market and each firm treated the wage rate as its MFC. In Figure 5, the competitive industry would operate at point c, where S (which equals the competitive firm's MFC) equals MRP.

If a union collectively bargains for a wage of w_u in Figure 5, the monopsonist's MFC curve becomes a horizontal line at w_u (MFC' in Figure 5). Collective bargaining makes the supply of union labor perfectly elastic (horizontal) at the union wage. By demanding w_u the union makes this wage the MFC of the monopsonist. In this case, $MRP = MFC$ at point u, where the monopsonist hires l_u of labor. Collective bargaining has succeeded in raising both wages and union employment when the firm is a monopsonist.

The wage/employment trade-off *need not exist when the employer is a monopsonist.*

There are no measures of the degree of monopsony in the labor markets of our economy. Earlier it was argued that monopsony in factor markets is less likely than monopoly in product markets. Although important cases of monopsony can be found, the observed behavior of labor unions—the obvious efforts of unions to soften the wage/employment trade-off—suggests that monopsony is not prevalent and that in most cases unions must trade off jobs for higher wages.

THE EFFECT OF UNIONS ON WAGES

Unions can affect the wages of their members by limiting the supply of union labor, by increasing the demand for union labor through staffing requirements and programs to increase the demand for the product, and through collective bargaining. Considerable effort of labor economists has gone into estimating the extent to which unions have been able to raise the wages of their members relative to comparable nonunion workers.

Union Effect on Union Wages

Empirical studies of the effect of unions on wages yield different results for different industries and time periods (see Table 3), but there is general agreement on the following points:[2]

1. Overall, unions have succeeded in raising the wages of their members relative to comparable nonunionized workers by 10 to 20 percent in recent years.
2. The union wage advantage tends to be larger during recessions because unionized wages have been found to be less responsive to a declining labor market.
3. Unions have succeeded in raising the wages of black males more than those of white males or females.
4. In specific industries (such as construction) and specific craft occupations, the union wage differential is quite large, perhaps as high as 50 percent.

Union Effect on Nonunion Wages

It is more difficult to establish the effect of unions on the general level of wages, or on the wages of nonunion workers. Theory suggests that unions could either depress or increase the wage rates of nonunion workers.

According to economic theory, the labor market in any given industry consists of a union sector and a nonunion sector. For example, Figure 1 showed that 1 U.S. worker out of 5 is a union member. The economy's labor force is indeed made up of both unionized and nonunionized sectors. If unions in the unionized sector bargain for substantial increases in the union wage and trade off jobs for large wage increases, some union members who are willing to work at the union wage are unemployed, and they "spill over" into the nonunion sector. The young union members with low seniority are the ones most likely laid

2. The pioneering study of the effects of unions on wage rates is by H. G. Lewis, *Unionism and Relative Wages in the United States* (Chicago: University of Chicago Press, 1963). A survey of this literature is provided by C. J. Paisley, "Labor Union Effects on Wage Gains: A Survey of Recent Literature," *Journal of Economic Literature* 18, 1 (March 1980): 1–31.

Table 3
Effects of Unions on Wages in the United States

Author	Time Period	Subject of Study	Percentage by Which Unions Raise Wages
Lewis	1923–29	Industrial	15–20
	1931–33		25+
	1939–41		10–20
	1945–49		0–5
	1957–58		10–15
Throop	1950	Selected industries	25.0
	1960		29.7
Weiss	1959	Craftspersons	7–8
		Operatives	6–8
Ashenfelter	1961–66	Firefighters	6–16
Schmenner	1962–70	Teachers	12–14
		Firefighters/police (in eleven cities)	15
Stafford	1966	Craftspersons	24
		Operatives	26
		Laborers	52
		Clerical	18
		Professional	−8
Boskin	1967	Professional	19.0
		Managers	−5.3
		Clerical	9.1
		Sales	2.3
		Craftspersons	15.5
		Operatives	15.2
		Service	7.4
		Laborers	24.7
Personick	1972	Construction industry:	35–50
		carpenters	40–65
		laborers	55–70
		electricians/plumbers	35–50
		cement masons	
Personick and Schwenk	1971	Shirt manufacturing:	
		all production workers	12.5–16
		sewing-machine operators	
		(women)	10–13
		sewing machine repair (men)	7–9
Ryscavage	1973	All workers	12
		White men	8
		Black men	27
		White women	22
		Black women	19
Ashenfelter	1975	All workers	17.0
		White men	16.0
		Black men	22.5
		White women	17.0
		Black women	17.0

Source: C. J. Parsley, "Labor Union Effects on Wage Gains," *Journal of Economic Literature* 18, 1 (March 1980): 7.

Figure 6
The Effect of Unions on Nonunion Wages

(a) Unionized Industry A

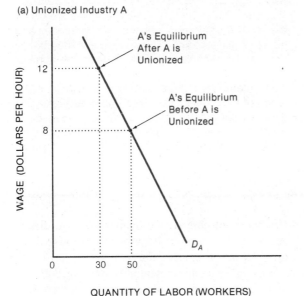

(b) Nonunion Industry B

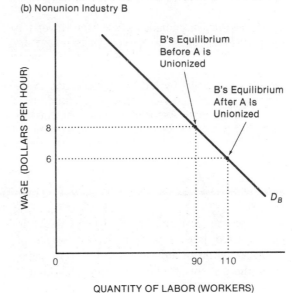

Before Industry A is unionized, wages are $8 per hour in both A and B; 50 workers are employed in A and 90 are employed in B. After A is unionized, workers in A earn a new wage of $12, and 20 workers lose their jobs and must be absorbed into Industry B. A's unionization drives the wage down to $6 in the nonunionized industry by increasing the supply of workers to industry B. This example assumes that the employer is perfectly competitive, that workers have perfect information about jobs, and that labor is homogeneous.

off in the unionized sector. When they seek employment in the nonunionized sector, the labor supply curve in the nonunionized sector shifts to the right (increases), and wages in the nonunionized sector are bid down. This *spill-over effect* is one reason why unions may depress the wages of nonunion workers.

A highly simplified view of the spill-over effect is shown in Figure 6. Before Industry A is unionized, both industries pay $8 per hour; A uses 50 workers, and B uses 90 workers. When A is unionized, employment in A falls to 30 workers and employment in B rises to 110 workers. The wage rate in A rises to $12, and wages in B fall to $6 as a result of A's unionization. This example assumes perfect competition in the firm's product market, perfect information about jobs, and homogeneous labor. Here the 30 original members of Industry A benefit at the expense of the 20 workers who move to Industry B and must take lower wages.

On the other hand, unions could possibly raise wages in the nonunionized sector in two ways. First, employers of nonunion workers may fear that if they do not match union wage increases, pressure will build among their workers to form a union. Second, when a unionized worker is laid off, there is a possibility that that worker will not spill over into the nonunionized sector but will wait until he or she is recalled to a job in the union sector. The probability of such *wait unemployment* is greatest when there is a substantial wage differential between the nonunion and union job, when the likelihood of recall is high, and when the costs of unemployment are low (because of the availability of unemployment benefits or union unemployment funds). If unemployed union workers do not spill over into nonunionized jobs, the downward pressure on nonunion wages would be removed.

The empirical evidence on the question of union effects on nonunion wages is not extensive,

Example   1

Work Rules: Safety or More Employment?

Unions and management have clashed over the years on the issue of work rules. Often unions argue that work rules are required for greater work safety. The new "Super" DC-9 aircraft, for example, was designed by McDonnel-Douglass to be flown by a 2-person flight crew. The Flight Engineers' International Association, however, has argued that the third crew member—the flight engineer—is essential to the crew's safety. The flight engineer, they argue, determines the worthiness of the aircraft, maintains anticollision vigilance, and monitors all systems. The third crew member is considered especially important given the number of near misses near congested airports. Because work rules can increase the demand for specific types of labor—such as flight engineers—they do keep wages above what they would have been without the rules. It is, therefore, in the union's interest to retain work rules.

---

but it does suggest that unions depress wages in nonunionized jobs. For example, the wages of nonunion workers are typically lower in cities where the percent of unionized workers is high.[3]

THE EFFECT OF UNIONS ON EFFICIENCY

The Traditional View

The traditional view of the effect of unions on economic efficiency is that unions have a negative effect on efficiency and productivity. The reasons for this view include the following:

1. Unions tend to bargain for staffing requirements *(featherbedding)* that prevent employers from using labor and capital in the most efficient manner. If union rules prevent carpenters from turning a screw on any electrical fixture, for example, the economy will operate below its potential.

2. Union strikes disrupt output and cause the economy to produce below its production potential. Strikes in major industries, like steel and rail transportation, can disrupt other sectors of the economy and cause losses of real output.

3. Unions drive a wedge between the wages of comparable workers in union and nonunion employment.

If workers of comparable quality are paid different wages because one belongs to a union and the other is in nonunion employment, the economy has again lost some potential output. In both the unionized and nonunionized sectors, workers will be employed to the point where their wage equals their *MRP,* but the *MRP*s of union workers will be higher than those of comparable nonunion workers. The economy could have increased its output by reallocating workers from the nonunionized sector (where *MRP* is lower) into the union sector (where *MRP* is higher). But the task of unions is to raise the wages of their members above what they would have been without the union. Whenever significant spillover effects occur, *MRP*s will be different.

Economists have attempted to estimate the loss of output due to the presence of unions. Economist Albert Rees, for example, has estimated this loss at approximately 0.8 percent of gross national product from the 1930s to the 1960s.[4] This loss has to be balanced against the perceived benefits that unions have brought workers.

Unions as a Voice Institution

Economists Albert Hirschman, Richard Freeman, and James Medoff maintain that unions actually improve productivity rather than reduce efficiency, as has been traditionally suggested. In

---

3. Lawrence Kahn, "The Effect of Unions on the Earnings of Nonunion Workers," *Industrial and Labor Relations Review* 31 (Janary 1978): 205–16.

4. Albert Rees, "The Effects of Unions on Resource Allocation," *Journal of Law and Economics* 6 (October 1963): 69–78.

their view, unions improve productivity by acting as a collective voice for union members. Without unions, if workers are dissatisfied with their employer, their only recourse is to use the *exit mechanism,* or to revolt against bad employers and bad work conditions by quitting and seeking another job. In this way, bad employers are penalized, good employers are rewarded, and the efficiency of the social system is improved. However, the exit mechanism results in heavy job turnover, which costs the economy lost output as employees must learn new jobs and spend time in often lengthy job searches.

Unions offer an alternative to the exit mechanism by making it possible for workers to discuss with an employer conditions that must be changed. In other words, unions give workers a voice. As individuals, workers will not have an effective voice at the workplace for two reasons. First, there is a limited incentive for an individual worker to seek to improve important aspects of work conditions such as safety, grievance procedures, and work sharing. Few individuals want to run all the risks and devote the time to issues that affect other workers' welfare as much as their own. Each individual would prefer to let someone else do the protesting and wait for the benefits. Because of the *free rider effects* of improvement efforts, unions oppose right-to-work laws that, by allowing workers the choice of union membership, allow nonunion workers to take advantage of benefits the union has gained. Second, there are risks to individual workers in expressing their true feelings to their employers; employers may seek to get rid of activists. In order for unions to have an effective voice, activists must be protected by the union organization. This fact is recognized in the National Labor Relations Act, which protects collective (but not individual) actions at the workplace.

Unions can have a positive effect on productivity in three ways. First, when worker grievances are handled by the union, workers need not leave the firm in order to bring about an improvement in their work conditions. If fewer workers quit because the union gives them a voice for their protests or complaints, the firm can reduce its hiring and training costs, and the functioning of work groups is smoother. Second, senior workers (who are most important politically in the union orga-

Table 4
Effects of Unions on Quit Rates

Sample	Percentage by Which Quits Are Reduced by Unionism
All workers, Michigan panel study, 1968–1978	45
All workers, current population surveys, 1973–1975	86
Male workers, national longitudinal survey	
Men 48–62 in 1969	107
Men 17–27 in 1969	11
Manufacturing workers, BLS statistics	34–48

Source: Richard Freeman and James Medoff, "The Two Faces of Unionism," *The Public Interest* 57 (Fall 1979): 79.

nization) are more likely to provide informal training and assistance in enterprises where unions give them a voice. When the union provides a channel of communication between workers and management, the improved information flows between workers and managers can improve the efficiency of the enterprise.

Evidence

What does the empirical evidence suggest about the effect of unions on productivity? First, there is strong evidence that the presence of unions causes a dramatic reduction in employee turnover (see Table 4). Although the quit rates of young workers (who happen to be the first laid off in unions) are only slightly reduced by unionization, all other workers' quit rates are reduced by the presence of unions from 34 to 107 percent.

The view of unions as a positive factor in labor productivity is fairly new to the economics literature and remains to be subjected to careful scrutiny and debate. The final word on whether unions raise or lower economic efficiency remains to be written.

The evidence that unions reduce quit rates does not necessarily prove that unions do improve labor productivity. The evidence cited by Freeman and Medoff (see Table 5) does suggest that unions have increased output per worker in those indus-

Table 5
Effect of Unions on Productivity

Industry	Percentage Increase in Output per Worker Due to Unions
Manufacturing	20–25
Wooden furniture	15
Cement	6–8
Underground coal, 1965	25–30
Underground coal, 1975	−20– −25

Source: Richard Freeman and James Medoff, "The Two Faces of Unionism," *The Public Interest* 57 (Fall 1979): 80.

tries studied with the exception of underground bituminous coal mining. The negative effect of unions in underground bituminous coal mining may be due to deteriorating industrial relations in that industry in the late 1960s that prevented the United Mine Workers from being an effective union voice.

This chapter continued the discussion of labor markets begun in the preceding chapter by examining how unions affect wages and economic efficiency. The next chapter will turn to the nonlabor factors of production: land, capital, and entrepreneurship.

Summary

1. A union is a collective organization of workers and employees whose objective is to improve the pecuniary and nonpecuniary conditions of its members. A craft union represents workers of a particular occupation. An industrial union represents workers of a particular industry.

2. Currently 20 percent of the labor force belongs to unions—a decline from the high of 25 percent in the 1950s. The declining percentage is due to the rise of white-collar employment, the rising share of women in the work force, and the shift of industry to the south and southwest. The most substantial gains in union membership in recent years have been in public employment.

3. The formation of unions was aided by prolabor legislation beginning with the Norris-LaGuardia Act of 1932, which facilitated union organizing drives. The National Labor Relations Act of 1935 made it illegal for employers to interfere with the rights of employees to organize. The Taft-Hartley Act of 1947 was a reaction against the pro-union legislation of the 1930s.

4. Unions must weigh the advantages of higher wages against the disadvantages of less union employment. Unions respond to the trade-off between jobs and employment by increasing the demand for union labor and by promoting measures to reduce the elasticity of demand for union labor. In collective bargaining, the most potent weapon of the union is the threat of strike.

5. In the case of labor monopsony, the trade-off between higher wages and employment may not be present. That unions do attempt to reduce this trade-off suggests that monopsony is not prevalent.

6. Unions are able to raise the wages of union members relative to comparable nonunion members. The amount wages are raised varies by industry and union. Unions can have both a positive and a negative effect on nonunion wages. When unions raise wages in the union sector, the workers who are laid off spill over into the nonunion sector, and the increase in labor supply lowers nonunion wages; however, when unions raise wages in the union sector nonunion employers may raise wages because they fear the formation of a union if they do not raise wages. The empirical evidence suggests that the net effect of unions on nonunion wages is negative.

7. There are two views on the effect of unions on productivity. The traditional view maintains that unions adversely affect labor productivity. The new view argues that unions serve as a voice institution that raises labor productivity of union workers.

Key Terms

labor union
craft union
industrial union
employee association
wage/employment trade-off
collective bargaining
strike

Questions and Problems

1. Assume that the elasticity of demand for labor (the percentage change in quantity of labor demanded divided by the percentage change in the wage) is 1.5 in the widget industry and is 0.5 in the ratchet industry. Which industry would be easier to unionize? In which industry is the trade-off between employment and higher wages more costly?

2. If you were the president of a major industrial union, what would your attitude be towards free immigration into the United States? Toward the minimum-wage law? Explain your answer.

3. Explain why the employment/wage trade-off does not exist for a monopsonistic industry.

4. Explain why both the automobile unions and the management of the automobile industry favor import restrictions on imported cars.

5. Assume that you belong to a union of bank tellers. What would your attitude be towards automated bank tellers? Explain.

6. Explain why the impact of higher union wages on nonunion wages might depend upon the extent of wait unemployment.

18

Interest,
Rent, and Profit

Chapter Preview

Interest, rent, and profit account for approximately 25 percent of national income; wages and salaries constitute the remaining 75 percent (see Table 1). The last two chapters described wages, or the payments to labor; this chapter will describe the income earned by the remaining factors of production: land, capital, and entrepreneurship. The owner of each of these three factors of production offers the use of the factor in return for payment.

The payment for the use of capital is *interest*. The supply of capital is the accumulation of saving by households and firms. The payment for the use of land and other natural resources is *rent*. The supply of land or natural resources is rela-

tively fixed. The payment for the use of an entrepreneur's services is *profit*. The supply of entrepreneurship is heavily dependent on the detailed social, educational, and economic characteristics of the society from which entrepreneurs are drawn. This chapter will identify the principal forces determining interest, rent, and profit.

INTEREST

Interest is the price paid for capital. Capital goods are required for the indirect or roundabout production of consumer goods. Chapter 2 noted that roundabout production is typically more productive than direct production. For example, productivity is raised when a net is used instead of bare hands in catching fish. Capital goods such as

Table 1
Shares of National Income by Type, 1980

Type of Income	Share (percent)
Compensation of employees	75.3
Proprietors' income	6.2
Rental income of persons	1.5
Corporate profits	8.5
Net interest	8.5

Source: *Statistical Abstract of the United States, 1981* (Washington, D.C.: U.S. Government Printing Office, 1981), p. 425.

trucks, conveyors, buildings, lathes, cranes, hammers, and computers enlist the mechanical, electrical, and chemical powers of nature to expand the production possibilities of society far beyond what otherwise could be accomplished by unaided human hands or minds. Interest is determined by the forces of supply of and demand for capital.

The Supply of Capital

Economists distinguish between *tangible capital* and *intangible capital*. Tangible capital differs from the other factors of production in that in its concrete form (from trucks and computers to fish nets and shovels) it has already been produced. Land that has been improved by irrigation, the clearing of forests, and the draining of swamps is also "produced" and as such is a capital good just like machines and factories.

Intangible capital takes two general forms: *research and development* (R & D) *capital* is accumulated investments in technology, productive knowledge, and know-how; *human capital* is accumulated investments in human beings—investments in training, education, and improved health that improve the productive capacities of human beings. Human-capital investments, which are an important determinant of the distribution of income, will be discussed in more detail in the next chapter. Human-capital theory suggests that the human capital embodied in trained labor is "produced" in the same economic sense as a truck or factory.

The inventory or stock of capital that exists in an economy at any moment of time depends on 1) the accumulated saving and investment deci-

sions that have been made in the past and 2) the extent to which old capital goods have undergone **depreciation** through use or obsolescence.

Depreciation is the wearing down of the economic value of capital goods as they are used in the production process.

Each year, the consumer decides how much to save; each year, the firm decides how much to invest in new capital goods. Each year, new capital goods are added to the stock of capital depending on how much consumers are saving and how much firms are investing. Over time, capital goods (broadly defined to include human capital and investments in land improvements) accumulate and depreciate. If the rate of accumulation exceeds the rate of depreciation, the stock of capital will grow.

The current stock of capital is the result of past saving and investment decisions. The stock of capital grows if the rate of capital accumulation exceeds the rate of depreciation. The stock of capital declines if the rate of accumulation is less than the rate of depreciation.

Credit Markets

The production of capital goods for use in roundabout production is made possible in a modern society through **credit markets,** which are also called *capital markets*.

Credit markets are markets for borrowing and lending.

Robinson Crusoe, living alone on a deserted island, had no need for credit markets. Crusoe would simply *save* (give up some present consumption) so he could *invest* (engage in roundabout production to increase his future consumption). When Crusoe took three days off from fishing to weave a net, he was both saving and investing. Simultaneous saving and investing is also characteristic of primitive agricultural societies. Farmers both save and invest by taking time off from current production to drain a swamp or to build an earthen dam. In a modern economy, however, financial assets—stocks, bonds, bank credit, and trade credit—are used to finance the accumulation of capital goods. In a modern economy, investors and savers are often separate. Credit markets make possible the separation of the act of saving from the act of investing.

Credit or capital markets are necessary because of specialization. A business firm that has the foresight to increase future production by investing today (building a larger plant, installing new equipment) usually needs to borrow funds in credit markets in order to be able to make the investment.

Households specialize in saving because they do not have the information to act on profitable investment opportunities. Business firms that specialize in production are able to seek out and take advantage of profitable investment opportunities. There is, therefore, a natural trade that can be set up between households and businesses. In credit markets firms wishing to invest in capital goods borrow from households (and other businesses); similarly, savers (households and businesses) lend to investors.

The growth of the stock of tangible capital is paralleled by the growth of the financial assets of those individuals or firms who accumulate savings. These financial assets (stocks, bonds, and various IOUs) are specific types of claims on the net productivity of real capital. The owners of such capital receive **interest** (or dividend) **income** from investors as payment for the use of the capital.

Interest income is income earned from the direct or indirect ownership of capital.

The Rate of Interest

As a convention, the **interest rate** is usually expressed as an annual percentage rate.

*The **interest rate** measures the cost of borrowing over a specified period of time.*

If $1,000 is borrowed on January 1 and $1,100 (the $1,000 borrowed plus $100 interest) is repaid on December 31, the $100 interest represents a 10 percent rate of interest on an annual percentage basis. If the loan were for only six months, and

$1,050 were repaid on June 30, the $50 interest still represents a 10 percent annual rate.

Referring to the rate of interest as the "price of money" is confusing and misleading because of the problem of interpreting the word *money*. Strictly speaking, in economics *money* is the medium of exchange used by an economy. Interest was defined earlier as the payment for capital. Since capital is financed through borrowing and lending, interest can also be considered the *price of credit*. The "price of credit" is a better definition than the "price of money" because the term *credit* assumes the passage of time between borrowing and repayment. The rate of interest represents the terms of trade between the present and future. A high interest rate means that future goods are cheap relative to present goods; a low interest rate means present goods are cheap relative to future goods. If ice cream is $1 a gallon both this year and next year, a 0 percent interest rate means that to give up 1 gallon of ice cream today (saving $1) will yield only 1 gallon next year; a 50 percent interest rate means that to give up 1 gallon of ice cream today will yield 1.5 gallons next year.

As a price of credit or borrowing, the interest rate indicates the terms of trade between things today and things tomorrow. The interest rate is the price that links the present and the future. Money, on the other hand, is the medium of exchange *for present transactions*.

Present Values.   Since the interest rate can be used to link the present and future, it can be used to convert future values into present values. The simplest case of present values is that of a perpetual income stream. Suppose someone has an *asset* (an income-producing property) that yields $100 per year *in perpetuity* (forever). What is such an asset worth today? What would its price be if it were to exchange hands?

If the interest rate were 10 percent, a $1,000 interest-yielding asset would generate $100 per year in interest income. This $1,000 is the **present value** of the $100 perpetual income stream. If the interest rate doubled to 20 percent, a $500 investment would earn $100 a year in perpetuity. Hence, $500 would be the present value of an asset that yielded $100 per year at a 20 percent rate of interest.

*The **present value** of an asset yielding a stream of future returns is the most anyone is willing to pay today to be able to receive those returns in the future.*

The general formula for calculating the present value *(PV)* of an asset that yields a perpetual income stream is:

$$PV = \frac{R}{i} \qquad (1)$$

where R = the annual income stream, and i = the rate of interest expressed in decimal form. At an interest rate of 10 percent, the present value of $100 a year in perpetuity is $100 ÷ 0.10, or $1,000.

Typically, financial assets do not yield perpetual income streams. Instead, financial assets typically make payments of specified amounts for a limited number of years. How does one compute the present value of such an asset? The general formula for computing the present value of a sum of money to be paid in n years in the future is:

$$PV = \frac{R_n}{(1 + i)^n}, \qquad (2)$$

where R_n is the sum of money to be paid in n years and i is the interest rate in decimal form. For example, if $121 is the amount to be paid in 2 years and i = 0.10, PV = $121/(1.1 × 1.1) = $100. In other words, $100 invested today will yield $121 in 2 years.

Bond Prices. The present value formula reveals that *there is an inverse relationship between present values and interest rates*. The higher the interest rate, the lower the present value, and vice versa.

The prices that savers are willing to pay for a financial asset that promises payments in the future—such as bonds—will equal the asset's present value. Thus, bonds that promise a specific sequence of dollar payments in the future will fall in price whenever interest rates rise. If the price of a long-term bond is $1,000 when the interest rate is 10 percent, the market price will fall if the interest rate rises to 15 percent because at an interest rate of 15 percent, a new bond pays 15 percent. To compete with the new bonds, the old bonds must be sold at a discount from their orig-

inal price. The increase in the interest rate causes the present value of the future interest payments to fall. If the bond is sold after the interest rate rises, the owner will suffer a capital loss (the price at which the owner sells will be less than the price at which the owner bought). Thus substantial capital losses can be incurred on bond holdings as interest rates rise. Conversely, if interest rates fall, the prices of bonds rise. Owners of such bonds can then sell them at a profit (that is, they can experience capital gains).

The Structure of Interest Rates

Although the interest rate is the price of credit, this price is not the same for all borrowers. Some borrowers pay higher interest rates than others. Savings and loan associations may pay as little as 5¼ percent when they borrow from their depositors. Individuals who borrow from the savings and loan may be charged interest rates of 15 percent for automobile and home-mortgage loans. The U.S. treasury may pay 14 percent to purchasers of its six-month treasury bill and 10 percent on a three-year treasury bond, while a near-bankrupt company must pay 21 percent on a six-month bank loan. *Different interest rates are paid on different financial assets*. Interest rates differ because of differences in the conditions of *risk, liquidity,* and *maturity* associated with a loan.

Risk. Borrowers with high credit ratings will pay lower interest rates than borrowers with low credit ratings. Lenders must be compensated for the extra risk associated with lending to borrowers with low credit ratings if they are to be competitive and earn a normal profit. If a certain type of borrower fails to repay bank loans 1 percent of the time, banks will require such a borrower to pay an interest rate at least 1 percent above the *prime rate* (the interest rate charged borrowers with the highest credit rating). The extra 1 percent is called a *risk premium*.

Liquidity. A financial asset that can be turned into cash quickly or with a small penalty is characterized by liquidity. People are willing to hold savings accounts paying 5.5 percent interest when six-month certificates of deposits pay 12 percent simply because the former can be turned into cash (the medium of exchange) quickly and without penalty. The general rule is that interest rates will vary inversely with liquidity, *ceteris paribus.*

Maturity. Interest rates will also vary with the term of maturity. A corporation borrowing $1,000 for one year may pay a lower rate of interest than if it borrows the same $1,000 for two years because credit-market conditions during the second year are expected to differ from conditions in the first year. If the credit market expects the interest rate on one-year loans to be 10 percent during the first year and 14 percent during the second year of a two-year loan, the interest rate on a two-year loan will be 12 percent. If $1,000 were invested for one year at 10 percent, it would yield $1,100 in one year; if the $1,100 were then reinvested at 14 percent it would yield $1,254. On the other hand, if $1,000 were invested at 12 percent for two years, it would also yield $1,254. Thus $1,000 invested at 10 percent for one year with the proceeds invested for one more year at 14 percent is the same thing as investing $1,000 for two years at 12 percent. Roughly speaking, the two-year interest rate (expressed on an annual basis) will be an average of the one-year interest rates the credit market anticipates over the two years.

The Level of Interest Rates

If all funds were loaned out for the same period of time and all the credit instruments were of the same risk and liquidity, all borrowers would pay the same rate of interest. Whether this single interest rate is high or low is determined by the interaction of the supply of and demand for loanable funds.

The Supply of Loanable Funds. The rate of interest is determined in the market for **loanable funds.**

Loanable funds are the amount of lending from all households, governments, and businesses, or the bank credit made available to borrowers in credit markets.

Figure 1
The Market for Loanable Funds

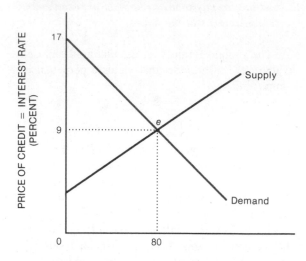

QUANTITY OF LOANABLE FUNDS
(BILLIONS OF DOLLARS)

The supply curve shows the quantity of loanable funds offered by lenders at different interest rates; lenders will offer more at high interest rates. The demand curve shows the quantity of loanable funds demanded by borrowers at different interest rates; less will be demanded at high interest rates. The market for loanable funds is in equilibrium at an interest rate of 9 percent, where the quantity demanded equals the quantity supplied.

For credit markets as a whole, the supply of loanable funds during a given period comes primarily from the net savings of businesses and households during that period. The supply curve in Figure 1 shows the quantity of loanable funds savers are willing to save (and thereby make available to lenders) at each interest rate. This supply curve is positively sloped to show that a larger quantity of loanable funds will be saved (made available to lenders) at high interest rates than at low interest rates, *ceteris paribus.*

The Demand for Loanable Funds. The demand for loanable funds is principally the demand for new investments in capital goods of businesses. Households also demand loanable funds for automobile loans, consumer credit, and home mortgages, but this chapter will concentrate primarily on business investment.

What determines the demand for capital goods? New capital raises the output (and therefore the revenue) of the firm for a number of years because capital goods are in use for more than one year. For example, a machine will be used for 8 years on average, and a plant will be used for 35 years on average. Capital's *marginal revenue product* (the amount an extra unit of capital will contribute to a firm's revenues) must be calculated over each year of the capital's useful life in order to determine **the rate of return of a capital good.**

> *The rate of return on a capital good is that rate of interest which makes the present value of the stream of marginal revenue products for each year of the good's life equal to the cost of the capital good.*

Business firms will increase the use of capital as long as marginal benefits exceed marginal cost.

> *The cost of additional capital is usually the interest rate that firms must pay for credit. The marginal benefit of capital is its rate of return. The equilibrium amount of capital for the firm will be that amount at which the rate of interest and the rate of return on the last investment project are equal.*

For example, a firm may purchase for $200 a typewriter that will be used for only two years. The firm estimates that the typewriter will have a marginal revenue product of $110 in the first year and $121 the second year. After the second year it will be retired from service and will have a $0 salvage value. The typewriter costs $200. What is its anticipated rate of return?

As noted above, the rate of return of a capital good is that rate of interest that makes the present value of the stream of *MRP*s for each year of the life of the capital good equal to the cost of the capital good, or that value of r (denoting rate of interest or rate of return in decimal form) that solves the equation:

$$\$200 = \frac{\$110}{(1 + r)} + \frac{\$121}{(1 + r)^2}$$

Solving for r yields $r = 0.10$, or 10 percent. The firm will not undertake this investment project unless the rate of interest on the $200 necessary to buy the typewriter is less than 10 percent (the rate of return on the typewriter).

The law of diminishing returns applies to capital just as it applies to labor. Additional capital investment projects will yield successively lower rates of return. In making their investment plans, businesses will consider a variety of investment projects. By adding on a new wing of their plant, they may achieve a high rate of return. By acquiring new equipment to replace older-generation equipment, they may achieve a substantial but lower rate of return. Successive projects bring lower and lower rates of return due to the law of diminishing returns.

The demand curve for loanable funds in Figure 1 is downward-sloping. The demand curve reflects the rate of return on capital investment projects because business firms will be willing to add to their capital stock as long as the rate of return of the investment projects exceeds the rate of interest (the cost of borrowing finance capital). In Figure 1, the demand curve shows the quantity of loanable funds investors are prepared to borrow at each interest rate.

> *The demand curve for loanable funds is negatively sloped because at high interest rates there are fewer investment projects that have a rate of return equal to or greater than the interest rate. At low interest rates, there are more investment projects with rates of return equal to or greater than the interest rate.*

The Equilibrium Interest Rate. Like any other price, the equilibrium (market) rate of interest established by the credit market is that rate at which the quantity of loanable funds supplied equals the quantity demanded.

In Figure 1, when the interest rate is 9 percent, there are $80 billion worth of investment projects that yield a rate of return of 9 percent or above. Since the quantity supplied of loanable funds equals the quantity demanded of loanable funds at that point, the equilibrium rate of interest is 9 percent.

The equilibrium interest rate equates the quantity demanded and quantity supplied for loanable funds so that investment projects yielding rates of return less than the equilibrium rate are choked off. Only those investments yielding the market interest rate or above are financed.

The Productivity of Capital. The demand for loanable funds reflects the basic productivity of capital. Anything that makes capital more productive will shift the demand curve to the right and cause the interest rate to rise. The supply curve of loanable funds reflects the basic thriftiness of the population. Anything that causes the population to be more thrifty (that is, to save more at each interest rate) will shift the supply curve to the right and cause the interest rate to fall.

If an important technological breakthrough raises the productivity of capital, the demand curve would shift to the right and would drive up the interest rate, *ceteris paribus*. If there were a change in tax laws to reward those families that save, the supply curve would shift right and lower the market rate of interest, *ceteris paribus*.

Real versus Nominal Interest Rates

Inflation occurs when the money prices of goods, on the average, rise over time. How does inflation affect interest rates? Anticipated inflation affects both the demand for and supply of loanable funds. Loans are repaid in dollars over the course of the loan. Inflation causes these dollars to become cheaper over time. Lenders will become less anxious to lend and the borrower more anxious to borrow if the rate of inflation is expected to increase. As a result, anticipated inflation causes the demand curve for loanable funds to shift to the right and the supply curve of loanable funds to shift to the left (see Figure 2).

In Figure 2, the initial equilibrium interest rate is 9 percent when there is 0 percent inflation. If borrowers and lenders anticipate a 5 percent rate of inflation, lenders will want to be compensated for the declining value of the dollars in which the loan is repaid, and borrowers will be willing to pay a higher interest rate because they can repay the loan in cheaper dollars.

Figure 2
Anticipated Inflation and Interest Rates

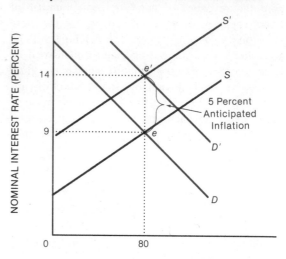

QUANTITY OF LOANABLE FUNDS
(BILLIONS OF DOLLARS)

When there is a 0 percent rate of inflation, the original equilibrium is at point e. When a 5 percent inflation rate is anticipated, borrowers will be willing to pay an interest rate 5 percent higher than before, and lenders must be paid an interest rate 5 percent higher because repayments are in cheaper dollars. Both S and D shift upward by 5 percent. The new equilibrium is e' at a 14 percent interest rate. The real interest rate is still 9 percent (equal to the nominal rate minus the anticipated rate of inflation).

What matters to borrowers and lenders is not so much the *nominal* (or stated) *interest rate* but the **real interest rate.**

*The **real interest rate** equals the nominal interest rate minus the anticipated rate of inflation.*[1]

A 14 percent nominal rate of interest with a 5 percent rate of inflation yields the same real rate of interest as a 9 percent interest rate with 0 percent inflation. In Figure 2, the supply and demand curves for loanable funds at 14 percent nominal

1. This formula holds approximately. Where r = the real interest rate, p = the inflation rate, and i = the nominal interest rate, the actual formula is:

$$r = i - p - rp$$

When r and p are small, rp is close to zero.

interest intersect at the same quantity of loanable funds (in constant dollars) as at 9 percent nominal interest, or $80 billion worth of loanable funds.

Interest-Rate Ceilings

Usury laws (that place ceilings on interest rates charged by lenders) are in effect in many states and countries. An interest-rate ceiling is considered to be effective if the legislated rate is below the market interest rate that would have prevailed without the usury law.

Usury laws have considerable popular support because they claim to protect the poor from excessive interest rates charged by the rich. Insofar as the rich are the large lenders and the poor are the ones who must borrow, usury laws are thought to redistribute wealth from the rich to the poor. However, most economists agree that effective interest-rate ceilings may redistribute wealth differently.

Wealth Redistributions. If the interest-rate ceiling lowers the interest rate, the quantity of loans demanded will rise and the quantity supplied will fall. Thus, the ceiling causes an excess demand for loans. The interest rate cannot rise sufficiently to ration the scarce supply of loanable funds.

Figure 3 shows how interest-rate ceilings create shortages of loanable funds. The interest-rate ceiling of 7 percent means there will be an excess of $50 billion in loanable funds demanded by borrowers over what lenders are willing to supply. The excess demand means that some potential borrowers will be unable to get the financing they desire at the interest-rate ceiling. Lenders will be made worse off by the ceiling (at least those lenders that abide by the law) because they are able to lend fewer funds at lower interest rates. The borrowers who actually obtain financing at lower rates are made better off because they will be earning high rates of return on their investment projects but need pay back their loans at the lower ceiling rate of interest. Those shut out of the loan market lose the returns they could have gained if they had had funds for investment. Ceilings therefore redistribute wealth from the unlucky (those who are unable to obtain financing at the ceiling rate) to the lucky (those who are able to get financing at the ceiling rate). Interest-rate ceilings

tend to redistribute loanable funds from those who can earn lower rates of return to those that can earn higher returns because the ones who can earn higher returns are better risks. Unfortunately, a larger fraction of poor people are bad credit risks, and they will be the ones who suffer the major burden of the ceiling. In many cases, the only alternative of poor people driven out of the legal loan markets is to find a loan shark charging much more than what the interest rate would be in the absence of ceilings. The loan shark is an entrepreneur taking risks and must be compensated for breaking the law and dealing with people, who through self selection, reveal themselves to have inferior credit ratings.[2]

Economic Efficiency. Credit rationing reduces economic efficiency because there is no guarantee that scarce loanable funds will go to finance those investment projects yielding the highest rates of return. Under credit rationing with a 7 percent interest ceiling, for example, a borrower with a 17 percent project may not receive credit while one with a 7 percent project does receive credit. When this happens—as it will under credit rationing—society loses economic output. This loss of output is a deadweight loss to society. In Figure 3, the loans could just as easily go to the borrowers in segment *bc* of the demand curve as to the borrowers in segment *ab,* resulting in lower returns on investments.

> *When there is an excess demand for loanable funds that cannot be eliminated by higher interest rates, there is no guarantee that available loanable funds will be allocated to their highest and best use.*

In Figure 3, there are $50 billion worth of investment projects that yield from 17 percent to 12 percent rate of return (along segment *ab* of the demand curve.). There are also $50 billion worth of projects that yield from 12 percent to 7 percent rate of return (along segment *bc* of the demand curve). Efficient credit rationing would ensure

2. It was probably through the usury laws that the early economists such as Adam Smith were alerted to the unfortunate effects of interfering with the market mechanism. Adam Smith realized that what legislators intended was often quite different than the actual impact of laws such as interest-rate ceilings.

Figure 3
Interest Ceilings and Credit Rationing

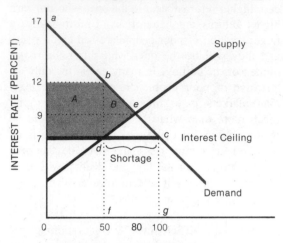

QUANTITY OF LOANABLE FUNDS
(BILLIONS OF DOLLARS)

The equilibrium interest rate at point *e* is 9 percent, where $80 billion worth of loanable funds are borrowed. When an interest ceiling of 7 percent is imposed, $100 billion worth of investment projects are demanded with returns ranging from 17 percent to 7 percent. At an interest rate of 7 percent, only $50 billion worth of these projects can be financed (point *d*). If rationing is efficient, the best half of all the desirable projects—those with returns ranging from 17 percent to 12 percent along segment *ae* of the demand curve—would receive financing. If only these high-return projects are financed, society loses the welfare represented by triangle *B*. If only those projects that earn the lowest rates of return—those represented by segment *bc* of the demand curve, earning 12 to 7 percent rates of return—are financed, society loses area *A*, which is the maximum loss from interest ceilings.

that the $50 billion worth of available funds would go to the high-yielding (17 percent to 12 percent) projects. In this case, society would only lose area *B*. But nothing would prevent the low-yielding projects (12 percent to 7 percent) from getting financed. Switching from the first $50 billion (along *ab*) to the second $50 billion (along *bc*) would lower total returns from 0*abf* to *fbcg*, in which case society would lose area *A*.

The highest and best use of scarce loanable funds (or resources in general) can be secured by a credit market that sets equilibrium interest rates. An interest-rate ceiling can result in credit ration-

ing that reallocates scarce loanable funds from high-yielding investment projects to low-yielding investment projects.

RENT

The rent on land is a relatively small proportion—about 2 or 3 percent—of the total of all payments to factors of production in the United States. This figure includes payments based on the natural fertility of the land and its locational advantages but excludes the returns to investments erected on the land or capital improvements in the land (such as irrigation). The crucial feature of land and other natural resources is that they are relatively inelastic in supply. They are nature's bounty, and the quantity supplied is not affected by the price received as a factor payment.

Even though land rents account for such a small portion of factor payments, relative inelasticity of supply can characterize productive factors other than land and natural resources. Because other types of factor payments resemble land rents, the study of rents for land and natural resources is much more important than the small percentages of factor payments to land suggests.

''Rents'' paid for apartments, cars, tools, or moving trucks should not be confused with the *economic rents* studied in this section. ''Rental payments'' for the temporary use of a particular piece of property owned by someone else can be returns to land, labor, or capital. Apartment rent is a payment both to land (for the land on which the apartment resides) and to capital (for the structure itself). Thus, the common term *rent* is simply a price or rental rate rather than a payment to a specific factor of production.

Pure Economic Rent

Figure 4 shows the determination of the competitive price paid for a fixed amount of land. The market demand curve is generated from the demand curves of all firms for the land; its height at any point equals the marginal revenue product of different amounts of land inputs. The supply curve is completely inelastic: more land is not forthcoming at higher prices. The competitive rent paid to land is that price which equates the fixed quantity supplied with the quantity de-

Figure 4
Pure Economic Rent

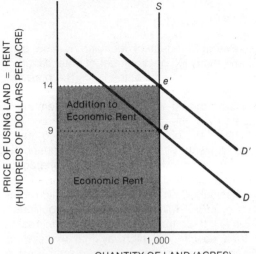

QUANTITY OF LAND (ACRES)

Because the supply of land is fixed at 1,000 acres, the supply curve *S* is perfectly inelastic. The equilibrium rent of $900 per acre at *e* gives rise to pure economic rents, since the land has no alternative uses. The entire rental payment is a surplus over opportunity costs. In this case, opportunity costs are zero. If the demand curve for land increases from *D* to *D'*, due to an increase in the demand for the product the land is used to produce, the economic rent will rise from $900 to $1,400 per acre at *e'*. Changes in economic rents are demand determined because supply is fixed.

manded. As such, the equilibrium price rations the fixed supply of land among the various claimants for the land.

The main economic role of **pure economic rent** is to assure that the factors of production that are fixed in supply are used in the highest and best use.

*A **pure economic rent** is the price paid to a productive factor that is completely inelastic in supply. Land is the classic example.*

Figure 4 illustrates the concept of pure economic rent. If the price of land were $0, the same quantity of land would be supplied as if the price were $900 or $1,400 per acre, as signified by the vertical supply curve. The quantity demanded, however, at a zero price would likely be very large. Even if the land were prime agricultural

land, at a zero price, instead of being used to produce food, the land might be used as a garbage dump or as a dumpyard for old cars. A higher price of land will cut off the various demands for the land that have a low *MRP*. If the price is too high, the land will not be fully used, and there will be an excess supply. If the price is too low, the land may not be put to its best use. Just as interest-rate ceilings may allow investments with relatively low rates of return to be financed, so land rents that are below equilibrium can allow land to be put to uses that yield relatively low *MRP*s. Efficiency requires that the price be set where the quantity supplied equals the quantity demanded of land.

The pure economic rent that is paid to a productive factor does not serve the incentive function to increase the quantity supplied of the scarce factor because the supply is perfectly inelastic. Pure economic rent in a competitive market serves as a guide to efficient resource use by rationing the available supply to the most efficient use.

Is Economic Rent a Cost?   When something is perfectly inelastic in supply, price incentives cannot lead to an increase in its supply. The price of a good or factor that is perfectly inelastic in supply must, therefore, be demand-determined. If the demand curve in Figure 4 shifts from *D* to *D'* due to technological advances in the use of the land or increases in the final demands for goods that the land is used to produce, competitive economic rents will be bid up.

From the standpoint of an individual firm using agricultural land, economic rent is most certainly a cost of production. In order to bid the land away from other uses, the individual firm must pay the competitive price. From the standpoint of the economy as a whole, however, rent is not a true opportunity cost to society. The amount of available land and other resources that are fixed in supply is a free gift of nature. In the case of pure rent, the payment to the factor of production exceeds the payment required to keep the resource available to the economy by the entire amount of the rental payment. The land is fixed in supply; the economy has use of the land whether it pays

Example 1

Economic Rents and Sites Along Interstate Highways

Pure economic rents on land are by no means limited to agriculture. Pure rents are generated when limited-access interstate highways are constructed. Once the highway is completed, there are only a fixed number of entry and exit roads. Therefore, the number of locations suitable for commercial development (gas stations, restaurants, gift shops) is fixed in supply. Even if very high prices are offered for such locations, the quantity supplied will not change. Conversely, if very low (or even zero) prices are offered the quantity available to society will not diminish. Given the highway, therefore, the opportunity cost to society of these sites is zero.

For commercial establishments renting these locations, the price will not be zero. If there is heavy traffic along the interstate highway, the marginal revenue product of the land will be quite high, and there will be a number of potential users willing to bid for the use of the land. The pure rent that firms with successful bids must pay for this land will be that at which the quantity demanded is equated with the fixed quantity supplied.

Whether land rents will rise or fall along the interstate highway will be largely a consequence of changes in demand for the products offered by commercial establishments. If there is an energy crisis that cuts down on automobile traffic on the interstate, MRPs will decline, and the equilibrium rent will fall. If, on the other hand, traffic increases due to a new feeder highway into the system, MRPs will rise, and the equilibrium rent will rise. Thus, economic rents are demand-determined, not supply-determined.

---

something or nothing. But the individual firm does not have use of the land unless it is willing to bid the land away from alternate users. For the economy as a whole, the opportunity cost of land that is fixed in supply is zero. For the individual user of that land, the equilibrium economic rent is a real cost of production that must be paid in order to prevent the land from being used in an alternative way.

Land Taxes and Efficiency. A tax on the natural fertility or locational advantages of a piece of land will have no impact on the supply of the land. The same amount of land is offered for rent on the market even if the economic rent received by the owner is lowered. Therefore, the market-clearing price will not change if a tax (to be paid by the owner) is levied. This feature of land makes it an attractive target of taxation because it means that a tax on land will not harm economic efficiency. The tax does not affect the quantity of land supplied, unlike a tax on labor and capital that would reduce the quantity supplied.

Suppose the government institutes a 50 percent tax on land rents and that prior to the tax, land was renting for $1,000 per acre. What effect will the tax have on land rents? Who will "pay" the tax? From the perspective of businesses renting the land, the tax does not affect the MRP of the land, so the demand curve for the land will remain the same. In order for the land owner to pass the tax on to the user, the supply of land would have to be reduced, thereby raising the rental price to the user. In the case of land, the individual landowner gains no advantage from withdrawing the land from use, since rental income would fall to zero. Thus the rental price would remain as it was before the tax, and the landowner would "pay" the entire tax. Land would continue to rent for $1,000 per acre, but the landowner would receive only $500 after paying the tax to the government. Economic efficiency has not been impaired because the quantity of land in use has remained the same.

The distribution of the burden of a 50 percent tax on land rents is illustrated in Figure 5. Since the tax does not affect the marginal revenue product of the land (as measured by the height of the demand curve before the tax), the rent the market is willing to pay per acre for any given total quantity of land will remain the same. The tax collector, however, will take 50 percent of the rental

Figure 5
The Incidence of a Land Tax

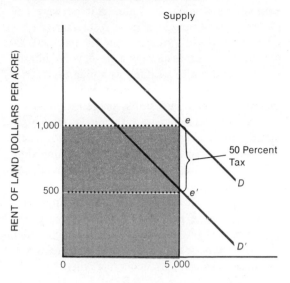

A 50 percent tax shifts the demand curve facing land-owners from *D* to *D′* because the tax collector takes half the rental price land users are willing to pay. The net price received by landowners falls from $1,000 per acre to $500 per acre. The landowners bear the entire burden of the tax.

price. The equilibrium rental price remains at $1,000 per acre, but the price received by the landowners falls to $500 per acre. The entire tax falls on the shoulders of the owners of land.

Quasi Rents

Naturally productive land and land located in prime urban and manufacturing areas is inelastic in supply in the long run. No matter what is done, no matter what economic rents are paid, such land cannot be increased in supply. Payments to such land are *pure economic rents*. Because the opportunity cost to society of this land is zero in both the long and short runs, the entire factor payment is a payment of economic rent. Many factors that are fixed in supply in the short run, however, are more elastic in supply in the long run.

There are many examples of factors that are fixed in supply in the short run. In a booming sunbelt city, the amount of space in office buildings is fixed in supply in the short run; when the demand for office space increases, office rental rates rise dramatically. The demand curve moves up along a vertical supply curve. In the long run, however, developers will respond to soaring office rents by constructing new office buildings, but it may take two to five years to plan and complete significant additions to the stock of office buildings. In the long run, as these office buildings are completed, the supply curve becomes more elastic and office rents are reduced.

The supply of professional tennis players is essentially fixed in the short run, for it takes years of training and practice to develop players of professional caliber. If the demand for professional tennis players increases due to an increase in the popularity of the sport, the earnings of the fixed number of tennis professionals will increase. In the short run, they will be able to earn extraordinary salaries. In the long run, however, new professional-caliber players who are attracted by high prize earnings will enter the profession; the supply becomes more elastic and the extraordinary earnings of tennis professionals will be bid down.

As these examples show, the owners of resources that are fixed in supply in the short run will receive economic rents. But such a payment is not a pure economic rent but a **quasi rent** because it cannot be maintained in the long run.

*A **quasi rent** is a payment over and above the short-run opportunity cost necessary to induce the owners of the resources to offer their resources for sale or rent in the short run.*

In the long run, quasi rents will disappear as the supply curve becomes more elastic. In the long run, the supply curve will become more and more elastic until quasi rents have been dissipated. At this point, the factor of production will be paid its opportunity cost.

Economic Rent and Other Factors of Production

Pure economic rents represent an extreme case of factor payment. At the other extreme is a payment to a factor that justs equals its opportunity cost. A factor of production that is perfectly elastic in supply earns no economic rents because the factor is paid its *opportunity costs* (its earnings in its next best alternative use). For example, a small farmer must compete with other farmers and potential users of the land. If the farmer does not pay what the land could earn in its next best use, the land will be used elsewhere.

In between factors of production that are perfectly elastic in supply and those that are perfectly inelastic are numerous cases where factors of production earn some surplus return over their opportunity costs, or **economic rent**.

Economic rent is the excess of the payment to the factor over its opportunity cost.

The major distinction between *economic rent* and *pure economic rent* is that a factor that earns pure economic rent has an opportunity cost of zero. A factor that earns economic rent has an opportunity cost that is positive but smaller than the payment to the factor.

The amount of economic rent earned by a factor depends upon the perspective from which the factor is viewed. The corn land rented by an Iowa farmer does not earn economic rent—because the *individual* farmer is paying the land's opportunity cost—but Iowa corn land in *general* does earn economic rent. In other words, *rents accrue to factor owners, not factor users*. The economic rent of John Smith as an engineer differs from the economic rent of John Smith as an engineer *for General Motors*. Smith can earn $30,000 per year working for GM, $29,000 working for Ford, and $20,000 working in his best nonengineering job. Smith's economic rent as a GM engineer is $1,000 (the excess of his earnings over his opportunity cost); his economic rent as an engineer is $10,000 (the excess of his earnings as an engineer over his next best nonengineering alternative).

The prices paid to an attractive movie star, a late-night talk-show host, the winningest pitcher in major league baseball, Iowa farm land, and offices in New York City surprisingly have much in common: a large fraction of the factor's income is economic rent. These factors receive payments in excess of their opportunity cost (their earnings in alternative uses). The factor payment serves the function of assuring that the factor is employed efficiently in its highest and best use. Baseball star Reggie Jackson's million-dollar contracts serve the important economic function of assuring that his assets are efficiently utilized; the utility of baseball fans would be reduced if he were employed as a waiter at a local restaurant. Paying one of the world's most talented tenors $40,000 per performance assures that he devotes himself to opera and not to working as a plumber.

Although people often resent individuals with inherited talents, rare skills, or good looks who earn substantial salaries, it should be recognized that oil-drilling rigs, Hawaii real estate, Iowa corn land, and high-speed computers are earning similar rewards; namely, payments in excess of their opportunity costs. Although land rents account for only a small portion of total factor earnings, economic rents are paid to a wide variety of economic factors. Actors, professional athletes, musicians, surgeons, professors, and television repair persons can earn economic rents.

PROFITS

When corporate profits are high, newspaper headlines shriek about soaring profits and the billions of dollars earned by company XYZ. In general, the public tends to be suspicious of the ethics of those individuals and companies who earn high profits. In the Middle Ages, high profits were seen as a sure sign that a pact had been made with the devil, who would soon get another lost soul for Hades' fire.

Profits that are headlined on the business pages are *accounting profits* that often have little to do with *economic profit*. From an economist's point of view, **accounting profits** have little meaning because they do not take into account the firm's *opportunity costs*, which include actual payments to factors of production as well as the costs of the next best alternative that the firm has sacrificed. Economists prefer to evaluate a firm's profitability on the basis of **normal profits** and **economic profits**.

Accounting profits are simply enterprise revenues minus explicit enterprise costs.

Normal profits are the profits required to keep resources in that particular business. Normal profits are earned when revenues equal opportunity costs.

Example 2

Economic Rents and Classical Musicians

Symphony orchestras complain that their financial difficulties are caused by the soaring fees that the top concert artists are now earning. In 1981, the top fees per performance earned by musicians were: Luciano Pavarotti (tenor) and Vladimir Horowitz (pianist)—$40,000; Rudolf Serkin (pianist) and Joan Sutherland (soprano)—$25,000; M. Rostropovich (cellist), Leonard Bernstein (conductor), and George Solti (conductor)—$15,000.

How much economic rent these performers are earning as musicians would depend upon their next best alternative earnings as nonmusicians. Some may have good options outside of music. Leonard Bernstein, for example, could perhaps be a politician or TV announcer, earning, say, $5,000 per appearance. Bernstein's economic rent would therefore be $10,000 per performance ($15,000-$5,000). Others of these musicians may have limited earning potential outside of music. Their economic rent would be even more substantial.

Why are these extraordinary economic rents being paid? From the viewpoint of the symphony orchestra, music society, or opera company, these fees must be paid because others are paying these fees. Opera companies, for example, bid among themselves for top stars. Although the Metropolitan Opera of New York attempted to maintain a top fee of $6,000, the company found that other companies were paying $10,000 and even more. If the Met is to attract top performers, it simply must pay the going rate.

The supply of musical superstars is inelastic because the superstars offer something other performers cannot match, an ingredient that sells out every concert. Other musicians may have equal skill, but they do not have the charisma and attraction of the superstar.

Source: "Soaring Fees for Star Musicians Are Disrupting the Concert World," *New York Times,* November 30, 1980.

Economic profits are the excess of revenues over total opportunity costs (which include both actual payments and sacrificed alternatives). Economic profits are profits in excess of normal profits.

Sources of Economic Profits

There are three basic sources of economic profits. The first source is the existence of barriers to entry in an industry or business. Such economic profits, called *monopoly profits,* are the basis of popular misgivings about profits. The second source of profits is the dynamic and ever-changing nature of the economic system. Such profits arise from the uncertain or risky nature of economic activity. The third source of economic profits is innovation. The individual (or group of individuals) who engage in risk taking and innovation are called *entrepreneurs.* For this reason, economic profits that are not the result of monopoly restrictions are often considered the reward to entrepreneurship.

Entry Restrictions. As we have shown, monopolies can earn a profit rate in excess of normal profits. Moreover, unlike competitive profits, which are transitory in nature, monopoly profits can persist over a long period of time. In other words, under conditions of monopoly, businesses can earn revenues that exceed the opportunity costs of the factors they employ. In this sense, monopoly profits are like economic rents; for this reason, economists often refer to monopoly profits as *monopoly rents.* Monopoly profits can also be earned in a potentially competitive industry where entry is restricted by government licensing or franchising. If monopoly profits cannot be competed away by the entry of new firms, existing firms can enjoy monopoly rents. The source of these monopoly rents is the restriction on supply caused by entry restrictions.

Examples of monopoly profits due to entry restrictions are not hard to find. Cable-television franchises are granted by municipal authorities and by local governments. Once the franchise is granted, the cable-television company is protected by law from the entry of competitors. In many

Example 3

Monopoly Profits and New York Cabs

Over the years, a New York City cab *medallion* (taxi license) has entitled the original owner to earn economic profits. If the license entitles the bearer to earn economic profits of $5,000 per year in perpetuity, the market price of the medallion should be the capitalized value of the perpetual stream of economic profits, which will depend upon the interest rate. If the market interest rate is 10 percent, the capitalized value is $5,000/0.10, or $50,000. The purchaser of the medallion does not earn economic profits because the normal operating costs plus the interest costs of purchasing the medallion yield only a normal rate of profit. The monopoly profit accrues to the original owner of the license who has received the monopoly profit in a lump-sum payment. It is difficult to detect economic profits when they must be traced back to the original monopolist.

---

cities, taxicab drivers must be licensed, and entry into the business is controlled by the high cost of the license. Monopoly profits in the prescription-drug industry are protected by patents. Economies of scale also limit the entry of competitors into power generation, telecommunication services, and parcel deliveries.

Monopoly profits are often difficult to detect because they will be *capitalized* (converted to their present value) when the firm is sold to a new owner. For example, in New York City, when taxicab drivers sell their licenses (called *medallions*) to others, the market price that the license brings will be the present value of the cab's monopoly profits. The cab driver who purchases the license is earning no economic profit because the economic profit has gone to the original owner of the license (see Example 3 for a more detailed discussion).

Risk Taking. If there were no entry restrictions, if people could predict the future perfectly, and if there were no costs to obtaining information about current market opportunities, there would be no economic profit. All businesses would earn normal profits. If an opportunity arose to earn economic profits, it would be anticipated and the free entry of new firms would serve to keep profits down to a normal return.

Unfortunately, no one can predict the future. Industry is unprepared for wars, changes in fashions and preferences, weather, and new inventions. Even with free entry, at any given time, some industries will earn economic profits and,

others will suffer negative economic profits. Unanticipated shifts in demand or costs cause economic profits to rise and fall. The majority of people wish to limit their exposure to the ups and downs of the economy; they want a steady income. Therefore, there must be rewards to those who are willing to risk the ups and downs of economic fortunes. Just as those who lend money to poor credit risks require risk premiums, so those who desire economic profits must be willing to reward risk bearing. In his book, *Risk, Uncertainty, and Profit* (1921), economist Frank Knight emphasized that uncertainty and risk taking are the ultimate source of profit. Knight noted that there will be a large element of luck in the fortunes of different enterprises. Economic profits cannot be assured in an uncertain world; the outcome of the profit game will be to a large extent random.

Uncertainty turns the quest for profits into something resembling a game of chance in which there will be winners and losers even in the long run. Entrepreneurs are the ones who bear this risk. The winners will earn economic profits; the losers will make losses. Like games of chance, there will be some big winners and some big losers. Most business firms will earn either more or less than the average return to risk bearing. Some firms will have extreme good luck and experience large returns; others will experience large misfortunes. All is not fair in love, war, and . . . business. As in a game of chance, profits will average out to a normal return over all firms but there will be a wide range of profit outcomes with a few big

Example 4

An Entrepreneur: Louis Marx

For decades the Louis Marx Company was the most profitable toy-making company in the United States. Generations of children from the mid-1950s to the 1970s grew up playing with Marx toys. Marx's toys include the Uncle Wiggley car, the Milton Berle car, the Rock-em Sock-em Robots, and the Big Wheel. Louis Marx, who sold his business in 1972, is described by his former associates as a creative genius. Marx worked 18 hours a day, creating the toys himself and testing them on his children and friends. Marx's first successful toy was a metal monkey that climbed up and down a string. Marx was called the "Henry Ford of the toy industry." He was the first to use advanced mass-production techniques to make toys inexpensively to sell in a broad market; he was one of the first toymakers to concentrate on selling to major retailers such as Woolworths and Sears. Marx was one of the first big toy manufacturers to import toys from the Orient. Under Marx's leadership, the company always made consistent profits.

What happens to a company after an entrepreneurial genius retires? In the case of Marx toys, Marx sold the company to Quaker Oats for $51 million and retired. Four years later, the unprofitable toy company was sold for a $23 million loss. Since Marx's departure, the company has been unable (with the exception of the Big Wheel) to come up with spectacularly successful toys. It failed to anticipate the success of space dolls and electronic games, concentrating instead on hunters, animals, and jungle accessories that did not catch on with children. According to one toy buyer: "Marx lost its innovation."

Source: Adapted from "Successors Couldn't Match his Genius, So Louis Marx's Toy Empire Crumbled," *Wall Street Journal,* February 8, 1980.

---

winners, a few big losers, and a larger number of intermediate winners and losers.

Innovation. Blind luck cannot explain all economic profits. The economy is in a constant state of flux. New technologies are developing, consumer tastes are changing, new markets are being discovered. Resource availabilities are changing. To be an innovator requires ability, foresight, luck, and the willingness to bear risk.

Austrian-born economist Joseph Schumpeter (1883–1950) maintained that profits were primarily the return to the entrepreneur and innovator, but that these entrepreneurial profits were temporary. Economic progress requires a succession of new innovations to replace the old. A successful entrepreneur will earn substantial economic profits only temporarily until another entrepreneur with a newer and better idea comes along to take customers and profits away.

Business history is replete with success stories of business geniuses—Henry Ford and the Model-T, Edwin Land and the Polaroid camera, Richard Sears and Alvah Roebuck and mass retailing, and Louis Marx and his children's toy empire (see Example 4). It is difficult to believe that ability and entrepreneurial genius did not lead to the success of each of these companies. More was involved than a game of chance with an uncertain outcome. Yet even ability does not guarantee success. Many able people are trying to become the next Henry Ford or the next Sears or Roebuck, but few succeed.

Empirical Evidence

According to economic theory, profits arise from monopoly restrictions and barriers, uncertainty and risk, and entrepreneurial innovation. Does the factual record support these propositions? It is very difficult for economists to test the relationship between economic profit and these three factors. It is virtually impossible to measure economic profit. Although it is easier to measure accounting profit—a measure that includes elements of normal returns to land, labor, and capital—accounting profit is less valuable as an economic measure. Empirical studies typically assume that rates of return based on accounting profits are indicative of rates of return based on economic profits.

Figure 6
Compensation of Employees and Corporate Profits, 1960-1981

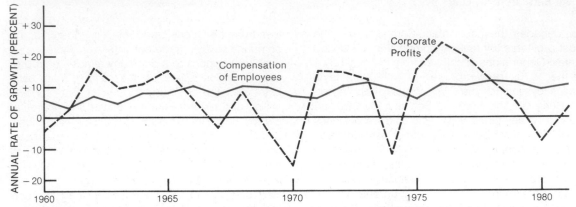

This graph shows that corporate profits are characterized by greater variability than wage income over time—suggesting that it is more risky to be dependent on profits than it is to be dependent on wage income.

Source: *Economic Report of the President,* 1982 (Washington, D.C.: U.S. Government Printing Office, 1982), pp. 254-55.

Barriers to Entry and Profits. There is some support in the empirical literature that economic profits are strongly associated with monopoly barriers to entry. For example, prescription drugs protected by patents sell at 60 to 100 times average costs, and price-fixing conspiracies have been shown to create extraordinary profits. Other examples of the correlation between barriers to entry and profit rates can be found in the chapter on oligopoly.

Risk and Profits. The problem in determining the relationship between risk and profit rates is that it is very difficult to measure the amount of risk a firm or an industry faces. In empirical studies, risk is typically measured by the variability of profits. If there are considerable ups and downs in profits over time or among firms in a particular industry, substantial risk is said to be present.

Figure 6 plots annual growth in wage income (employee compensation) and corporate profits over time. The most striking differences between the two series is the much greater variability of profits. Unlike earnings from labor, which tend to rise smoothly from year to year, profits rise and fall—sometimes with very substantial declines from one year to the next. If risks are indeed measured by ups and downs, it is definitely more

risky to be dependent upon profits than on wages, at least as far as the aggregate economy is concerned. The annual ups and downs of profits may not be an accurate guide to risk, however, because more serious risk stems from longer-run dangers from new technology and new competition that can cause a permanent decline in profits.

Economists that have studied the relationship between the rate of profit and risk (as measured by the variability of profits) find (although there is some dispute on this matter) that profit rates are indeed higher in risky industries. Firms and industries that are subject to greater risk earn *risk premiums*. Entrepreneurs and stockholders are compensated in the form of higher average profits for being called upon to bear more risk than others.[3]

3. Empirical studies of the relationship between risk and profitability have been conducted by I. N. Fisher and G. R. Hall, "Risk and Corporate Rates of Return," *Quarterly Journal of Economics* 83 (February 1969): 79–92 and P. Cootner and D. Holland, "Rate of Return and Business Risk," *Bell Journal of Economics* 1 (Fall 1970): 211–16. Both studies found a positive association between risk and corporate profit rates. A different interpretation of these findings has been suggested by Richard Caves and Basil Yamey, "Risk and Corporate Returns: Comment," *Quarterly Journal of Economics* 85 (August 1971): 513–17 and by W. G. Shepherd, *The Treatment of Market Power* (New York: Columbia University Press, 1975), who argue that these higher rates of return are the result of oligopoly structure rather than greater risk.

Innovation and Profits. The association between entrepreneurial activity and profit rates is difficult to establish empirically because it is difficult to find measurements of trends in entrepreneurial activity to associate with the ups and downs of profits. Although statistical tests remain to be conducted, economic history shows that great fortunes (the fortunes of the Rockefeller, Carnegie, Mellon, and Ford families) have been amassed by great entrepreneurs. Although good fortune may have played a role in the accumulation of these fortunes, a more likely interpretation is that the fortunes were the consequence of entrepreneurial innovation.

The last three chapters surveyed how the economy determines wages, rents, interest, and profit—the payments to the productive factors of labor, land, capital, and entrepreneurship. The next chapter will turn from the functional distribution of income to the personal distribution of income and will address questions like: How equally or unequally is income distributed among persons? What has happened to the personal distribution of income? How does America's income distribution compare to that of other countries? What can be done about poverty?

Summary

1. Interest, rent, and profits account for some 25 percent of factor payments in the United States.
2. Interest is payment for the use of capital. The supply of capital is the result of past saving and investment decisions. Interest rates are determined in credit markets, which make possible the specialization of savings and investment decisions. The structure of interest rates depends upon risk, liquidity, and maturity. Interest rates are determined in the market for loanable funds by the demand and supply of loanable funds. The real rate of interest is the nominal interest rate minus the anticipated rate of inflation.
3. Rent is payment for the use of land or natural resources. Pure economic rent is the payment to a factor of production that is completely inelastic in supply and is demand-deter-

mined. A quasi rent is a payment to a factor of production above short-run opportunity costs. In the long run, quasi rents tend to disappear. Economic rent is the excess of the payment to a factor over its opportunity cost.
4. Economic profits are the excess of revenues over total opportunity costs. The sources of economic profits are: restrictions to entry into an industry, uncertainty, and entrepreneurship. Empirical evidence supports the relationship between profits and entry barriers, between profits and risk taking, and between profits and innovation.

Key Terms

depreciation
credit markets
interest income
interest rate
present value
loanable funds
the rate of return of a capital good
real interest rate
pure economic rent
quasi rent
economic rent
accounting profits
normal profits
economic profits

Questions and Problems

1. Why is it incorrect to call interest the price of money?
2. This chapter emphasized that the credit market is another example of specialization in economics. Explain how this specialization works and its effect on economic efficiency.
3. If you borrow $10,000 from the bank and repay the bank $12,000 in one year, what is the annual rate of interest?
4. A business earns $1,000 per year in economic profits and is expected to earn these annual profits in perpetuity. The current market interest rate is 10 percent. What is

the present value of this business? How is the present value related to the rate of interest?

5. A machine that costs $1,000 will last two years, after which it must be scrapped with no salvage value. If the machine is purchased it will raise profits by $0 the first year and $1800 the second. What is the rate of return on this investment? Would the firm invest if the interest rate were 20 percent?

6. A company has four investment projects that yield returns of 20 percent, 15 percent, 10 percent, and 5 percent. Explain how the company will decide which of these projects to carry out.

7. The interest rate is currently 10 percent, and the inflation rate is 5 percent. If people anticipate that the inflation rate will rise to 10 percent, what effect will this expectation have on interest rates?

8. Distinguish between pure economic rents and quasi rents.

9. "Pure economic rents play no useful role in the economy because the supply of the factor in question is fixed. The factor will be supplied no matter what rent is paid." Evaluate this statement.

10. Why should the profit rate be higher in businesses that are risky? How do we measure risk?

19

Income Distribution and Poverty

Chapter Preview

This chapter will consider why some people are poor and others are rich. The distribution of personal income among households and among private individuals is determined first in factor markets. One's factor income equals the sum of the earnings of one's factors of production—one's land, labor, capital, and entrepreneurship. These earnings will be high if one owns relatively large quantities of factors that command relatively high prices in factor markets. The one who owns only one factor of production—say, unskilled labor—that commands a very low price in the labor market will have a low factor income. Government can change the distribution of income received from the ownership of the factors of production

through differential taxes, through the unequal distribution of government services, and through transfer payments. The government's role in determining the distribution of income is an important topic in this chapter. Previous chapters have already described how factor markets operate—how wage rates, interest payments, and rents are determined; this knowledge is necessary to understand income distribution.

MEASUREMENT OF INCOME INEQUALITY

The Lorenz Curve

The most common measure of the degree of inequality in the distribution of income is the **Lorenz curve**.

Figure 1
The Lorenz Curve

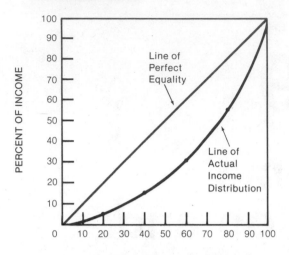

PERCENT OF HOUSEHOLDS

The Lorenz curve measures the cumulative percentage of households (ranked from lowest to highest incomes) on the horizontal axis and the cumulative percentage of income earned by these households on the vertical axis. If all households earned the same income (perfect equality), the Lorenz curve would be a 45-degree line. The 45-degree line is called the *line of perfect equality.* The bowed out Lorenz curve shows an unequal distribution of income. The more the Lorenz curve for a society is bowed away from the line of perfect equality, the greater the inequality in the distribution of income in that society.

The **Lorenz curve** *shows the percentage of all income earned by households at successive income levels. The cumulative share of households (ranked from lowest to highest incomes) is plotted on the horizontal axis of the Lorenz curve, and the cumulative share of income earned by the cumulative percent of households is plotted on the vertical axis.*

Typically Lorenz curves are plotted in *quintiles,* or fifths. A household in the top fifth of the income distribution earns more than at least 80 percent of all households. A household in the bottom fifth earns less than at least 80 percent of all households. A hypothetical Lorenz curve is drawn in Figure 1 and plots the cumulative percentage of households against their cumulative share of income, given in column (3) of Table 1. For example, the cumulative share of income for the first four quintiles is 55 percent. That is, the bot-

Table 1
A Hypothetical Lorenz Curve

Quintile (1)	Share of Income (percent) (2)	Cumulative Share of Income (percent) (3)
Lowest fifth	5	5
Second fifth	10	15
Third fifth	15	30
Fourth fifth	25	55
Highest fifth	45	100

tom 80 percent of households accounts for 55 percent of all income. The bottom 20 percent of households earns only 5 percent of all income, and the top 20 percent earns 45 percent of all income.

A 45-degree line can be drawn to show absolute equality in the distribution of income: if income were equal, the bottom 20 percent of households would receive 20 percent of all income; the bottom 40 percent of households would receive 40 percent of all income; and so on. When the Lorenz curve deviates from the 45-degree line, which is called the *line of perfect equality,* the income distribution departs from perfect equality. The more bowed the Lorenz curve is from the line of perfect equality, the more unequal is the distribution of income.[1]

Facts and Figures

Table 2 gives some facts about the American distribution of income before taxes in 1929 and 1979. The corresponding Lorenz curves are drawn in Figure 2. Over the past 50 years, there

---

1. Another measure of the inequality of income distribution is the Gini Coefficient. The *Gini coefficient* is a numerical measure of inequality. The Gini coefficient is defined as the area between the 45-degree line and the Lorenz curve divided by the total area under the 45-degree line. If there is perfect equality, the Lorenz curve and the 45-degree line coincide, and the Gini coefficient is zero. If there is perfect inequality (one household gets all the income), then the difference between the Lorenz curve and the 45-degree line equals the entire area under the 45-degree line, and the Gini coefficient equals 1. In between these two extremes, the Gini coefficient can measure whether one income distribution is more or less unequal than another.

Table 2
The U.S. Distribution of Income (before taxes)

Quintile of Households	1929		1979	
	Share of Income (percent)	Cumulative Share of Income (percent)	Share of Income (percent)	Cumulative Share of Income (percent)
Lowest fifth	3.9	3.9	5.3	5.3
Second fifth	8.6	12.5	11.6	16.9
Third fifth	13.8	26.3	17.5	34.4
Fourth fifth	19.3	45.6	24.1	58.5
Highest fifth	54.4	100	41.5	100
Top 5 percent	30.0		15.7	

Source: *Historical Statistics of the United States, Part 1*, p. 300; *Statistical Abstract of the United States*, 1981, p. 438.

has been a noticeable leveling in the American distribution of income—a distinct trend towards more equality. Households in the top fifth accounted for 54.4 percent of all income in 1929 but for only 41.5 percent in 1979. The top 5 percent accounted for 30 percent of all income in 1929 but for only 15.7 percent in 1979. The share of the lowest 40 percent of households rose from 12.5 percent in 1929 to 16.9 percent in 1979. The *middle class* (households in the third and fourth quintiles) increased its relative standing most over the past half century: its share of income rose from 33.1 percent to 41.6 percent.

Despite the long-term trend toward a more equal distribution of income before taxes, there is still considerable inequality in the distribution of income. The top 5 percent of U.S. households accounts for 15.7 percent of all income, while the bottom 20 percent accounts for only 5.3 percent of all income. Since the top 20 percent earns 41.5 percent of all income, households in the top 20 percent earn on average about 8 times as much as those in the bottom 20 percent.

Why do some individuals and households earn a great deal more than others? Why is it that actual distribution of income departs so much from the line of perfect equality?

SOURCES OF INEQUALITY

To determine what can be done (or should be done) about the distribution of income, it is im-

portant to understand the causes of inequality, including differences in ability, chance and luck, discrimination, occupational differences, human-capital investment choices, and inheritance.

Figure 2
Lorenz Curves of the U.S. Distribution of Income, 1929 and 1979

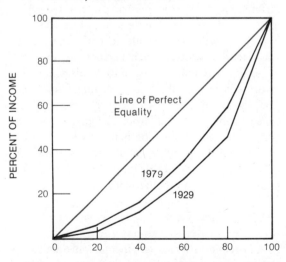

Over the past 50 years, there has been a distinct trend toward more equality in the U.S. distribution of income.

Source: *Historical Statistics of the United States*, 1976, part 2, p. 300; *Statistical Abstract of the United States*, 1981, p. 438.

Differences in Ability

People have different mental and physical abilities that they are born with or acquire during their childhood years. Because of differences in ability, individuals are limited in their choice of occupation. Not everyone has the ability (mental skills and manual dexterity) to become a surgeon; few have the physical endowments to become professional athletes or high-paid fashion models. On the other hand, many possess the necessary skills to perform unskilled labor, to do typing, or to serve as bank tellers or store clerks. Because people are different, the labor market segregates them into noncompeting groups, as mentioned in the chapter on labor markets. The limited numbers of individuals with high IQs compete among themselves for jobs as physicians, lawyers, and engineers. The limited numbers of individuals with superb athletic ability compete among themselves for jobs as professional athletes. Those individuals with extroverted personalities and glib tongues compete among themselves for jobs as sales representatives, public-relations agents, politicians, and union organizers. Because people are segregated into noncompeting groups, substantial wage differentials may emerge that can persist over a long period of time. Workers from a noncompeting group will not be able to enter the higher-wage market because such persons are excluded by ability, strength, or just outright discrimination from working in the higher-paying profession. The six-figure earnings of the surgeon will not cause people to switch from ditchdigging to surgery. The requirement of being able to lift 100 pounds will keep many people from seeking employment on offshore-drilling rigs even though high wage rates are being paid.

Chance and Luck

A second source of income inequality is chance (random occurrences) and luck. Accidents and poor health can unexpectedly destroy one's earning capacity. Choosing a profession (such as teaching English or modern languages) in which there is an unexpected decline in demand can lead to low earnings. Likewise, having the good fortune to select a profession (such as petroleum engineering in the late 1970s) in which there is an unexpected increase in demand can have a significant positive and unplanned effect on one's lifetime earnings. Luck determines whether individuals earn the economic rents discussed in the preceding chapter. Having the good fortune to be in the right place at the right time can have a marked impact on relative income. Having the bad fortune to be in the wrong profession or industry during downswings in the business cycle can also harm earnings. Involuntary unemployment not only reduces current earnings but also cuts down on the amount of work experience and training an individual accumulates. This loss will affect earnings even after the individual is employed again.

Discrimination

Discrimination according to age, sex, skin color, or national origin can also contribute to income inequality. If individuals are denied equal access to education and training, they will be unable through no fault of their own to accumulate the same amounts of human capital as those who are not subject to discrimination. If individuals are denied access to jobs in craft unions or industrial unions for reasons of race, color, or creed, then these individuals will be the ones who spill over into the nonunionized sector, creating a favorable wage differential for unionized workers. If individuals are restricted by employers in their choice of occupation even though they may possess the necessary qualifications, then they will be forced into noncompeting groups, unable to compete for the higher-paying positions for which they may be qualified.

Occupational Differences

Other things being the same, most people prefer to work in occupations that are not dangerous, that offer pleasant surroundings, and that do not involve heavy and dirty work. The supply of labor to attractive occupations and jobs will be greater than the supply of labor to dangerous, dirty, and unattractive jobs, *ceteris paribus*. Even though the coal miner and the garbage collector earn more than many others with the same physical and mental skills, labor does not move automatically into these higher-paying jobs to wipe

Example   1

Women's Pay and "Comparable Worth"

In 1963, Congress passed the Equal Pay Act, which requires employers to pay men and women equally when they perform equal jobs. In 1964, Congress passed the Civil Rights Act, which prohibits bias in employment based on sex or race. These two laws form the foundation of protection against discrimination in the job market.

On the surface, these two laws appear clear, but in reality, the issues involved are extremely complex. For example, women matrons in a jail in Hillsboro, Oregon sued the county because they were paid $200 per month less than men performing comparable work. The women matrons guarded women prisoners on the jail's third floor while male corrections officers guarded male prisoners on the second floor. Were the women matrons performing work comparable to the men's work? The lower court rejected the matrons' plea on the ground that the work was not comparable, but the case is pending before the Supreme Court. In another case, city nurses in Denver argued that they were underpaid in comparison to other city workers. The trial judge ruled against the nurses on the grounds that comparable worth could not be proved in this case. Finally, in Pittsburgh, a federal judge ruled against Charley Brothers groceries on the grounds that women were paid less for handling beauty and health aids than men were paid for handling perishable foods. As these cases show, it is very difficult to determine what is comparable work.

Source: Based on "High Court Looks at Women's Pay in Dispute on 'Comparable Worth,'" *Wall Street Journal,* May 14, 1980.

---

out the wage differential. Compensating wage differentials exist because people require a reward for working in unpleasant jobs.

The existence of compensating wage differences means that some inequality is in fact a matter of conscious choice. The low-paid high-school dropout who switches from a job as a grocery clerk to a job on a drilling rig in the Alaskan permafrost or to a job as a garbage collector can improve his or her relative income position. The fact that an individual chooses to forgo compensating wage differences means that his or her utility or satisfaction is greater at the lower level of earnings. The nonpecuniary advantages of one type of occupation may outweigh the compensating wage differences offered by another occupation.

Some people may value leisure more than others. One person may work a 60-hour week, while another (who earns the same hourly wage) works a 30-hour week. The first person will have weekly earnings twice those of the second, but the second will have twice as much leisure. This extra leisure is worth something to the recipient that is not reflected in his or her money income.

Inequality through individual choice applies as well to occupational choices under conditions of uncertain income prospects. Different occupations involve different degrees of risk. The small-business owner has more uncertain income prospects than the tenured university professor. The wheat farmer, whose crops may be destroyed by blights and droughts, has a more uncertain income than the union employee with seniority. The real-estate speculator stands to make a fortune if lucky but will go bankrupt if unlucky.

Society is comprised of individuals with differing attitudes towards risk. *Risk seekers* are more willing to incur risks than others, while *risk avoiders* are reluctant to take on risks.[2] If society consists largely of risk avoiders and has only a small number of risk seekers, the distribution of income would be unequal for this reason alone. Some of those willing to incur risks will strike it rich and rise to the top income level. Other risk seekers will be less fortunate and will be at the bottom of the totem pole. The vast majority—the risk avoiders—will be in the middle, earning steadier incomes.

2. The theory of individual choice of inequality was formulated by Milton Friedman in the article "Choice, Chance, and the Personal Distribution of Income," *Journal of Political Economy* 61,4 (August 1953): 277–90.

Example 2

Compensating Wage Differentials: Arctic Drillers

What high-school graduate would not want to earn $90,000 per year? All a person has to do to earn this salary is work as an arctic driller. An arctic driller works on an offshore drilling rig in arctic temperatures of 40 degrees below zero. On some days, the temperature falls to 90 degrees below zero. Drillers work 14 consecutive 12-hour days before taking 7 days off. Dropping a wrench down the drilling hole is grounds for immediate dis-missal. Drillers live in a camp of connected trailers; they have no living expenses and the food is good. The job is dangerous. A wrong move with one lever will result in injuries. Frost bite is common. Drinking, gambling, drugs, and fighting are not allowed. Drillers with a few years' experience are paid more than $90,000 per year. The one who helps the cook is paid $40,000.

Human-Capital Investment Choices

Human-capital theory suggests that inequality can be the consequence of choice, not chance. This theory, pioneered by Theodore W. Schultz, Gary Becker, and Jacob Mincer, is based on the premise that individuals are faced with the choice of different lifetime-earnings streams.[3] Individuals will make rational personal optimizing decisions based upon the costs and benefits of the different earnings streams.

Just as businesses invest in plant and equipment to increase the firm's productive capacity, so human beings invest in themselves to raise their own productivity and, hence, their future earning capacity. They (and their parents) can invest in extra schooling and technical education. They can pay the costs of migrating to areas where job opportunities are better. They can invest in medical care to improve their health.

These activities are regarded as investment because any activity that raises productive capacity can be classified as investment. Building a new plant, acquiring a new assembly line, installing an irrigation system are all forms of investment in tangible capital. All of these activities are designed to raise the productive capacity of the firm undertaking the investment. The same holds true for individuals: by acquiring more training and education, individuals can increase their own productivity.

If human-capital investment translates into higher lifetime productivity and, therefore, higher lifetime earnings, why does not everyone demand the same amounts of human-capital investment? Although human investment yields benefits, it also has its costs. To acquire a college degree requires paying not only for tuition and books but also for the loss of current earnings due to prolonging formal education. To move to another city to seek a better job means the payment of moving costs, the loss of income between jobs, and the personal costs of leaving family and friends behind. Each form of human-capital investment has its costs and benefits. Confronted with these costs and benefits, individuals (and their parents) are assumed to make rational investment decisions; that is, they will acquire more human capital as long as the marginal benefits exceed the marginal costs. Insofar as the benefits from human-capital investment will be spread out over a number of years in the form of higher earnings in the future, the appropriate measure of benefits is the present value of the increase in future earnings.

The human-capital theorists view inequalities in the distribution of income as partly the result of conscious and rational decision making. Individuals must select between more money now (going to work after high school for example) and more money later (going to college and not earning money now). This decision will depend upon

---

3. The pioneering articles in human capital theory are: Gary Becker, "Investment in Human Capital: A Theoretical Analysis," *Journal of Political Economy* 70, 5 (October 1962): 9–49; Theodore W. Schultz, "Capital Formation by Education," *Journal of Political Economy* 68, 6 (December 1960): 571–83.

the anticipated rate of return to additional human-capital investment, and this rate of return will depend upon the interest rate used to capitalize future earnings and the anticipated increase in future earnings. Individuals who place a high value on having money *now* (a high implicit interest rate) are less likely to acquire human capital.[4]

Inheritance

Thus far, the chapter has offered several explanations for inequalities in the distribution of labor income. But income from other factors of production—land, capital, and entrepreneurship—is also unequally distributed. In fact, income from the ownership of land, mineral, and capital property is distributed more unequally than income from labor. Most nonlabor income derives from the ownership of **wealth** (stocks, bonds, real estate).

*Personal **wealth** (or net worth) is the value of one's total assets minus one's liabilities.*

The distribution of income from wealth can be inferred from the distribution of wealth (see Table 3). In 1972, the top 1 percent of wealth holders in the United States accounted for 24.1 percent of all wealth. The top 0.5 percent accounted for 18.9 percent of all wealth. On the income side, the top 5 percent of households accounted for 15.7 percent of all income; thus, wealth is distributed more unequally than income. Like the distribution of income, the distribution of wealth has become more equal over the years. In 1929, the top 1 percent had 36.3 percent of all wealth compared to 24.1 percent in 1972.

Table 3

Percentage of Wealth Held by Top 1 Percent of Wealth Holders, 1972

Type of Asset	Percentage Held by Top 1 Percent of Wealth Holders
Total Assets	24.1
Real estate	15.1
Corporate stock	56.5
Bonds	60.0
Cash	13.5
Debt instruments	52.7
Life insurance	7.0
Trusts	89.9
Miscellaneous	9.8

Source: *Statistical Abstract of the United States,* 1980, p. 471.

One important cause of the unequal distribution of wealth is *inheritance,* or the process by which one generation passes wealth on to the next after death. Originally this wealth may have been created by luck, by refraining from consumption (saving), or by superior entrepreneurship. Wealth continues to be passed from one generation to the next because of several factors. First, the children of the wealthy, in addition to inheriting property, typically receive better education and training and develop important social contacts. Second, the children of the wealthy tend to marry others who are likely to inherit wealth. Third, the wealthy may pass on a genetic inheritance to their heirs—such as inherited entrepreneurial ability or intelligence.

Empirical studies of the effects of inheritance on the overall distribution of income fail to uncover a significant role for inherited wealth in the United States. The share of income from wealth has been declining, and even for high-income families (those earning $50,000 and above in 1979), income from wealth accounted for only 10.7 percent of total income.[5] One study finds that inherited wealth accounts for only 2 percent of the overall index of inequality in the United States.[6]

---

4. To show how human-capital investment decisions are made, assume an investment in an 8-year medical-degree training program costs $100,000. Once the training is complete, it promises to raise annual earnings $15,000 each year above what they would have been without additional training. In making this decision, the present value of the extra income ($15,000 in the ninth year, $15,000 in the tenth year, and so on until retirement from practice) must be calculated by converting each year's earnings to a present value. If the sum of the present values for each year's earnings exceeds the $100,000 cost, this human-capital investment is profitable.

Alternatively, one could calculate the rate of return that equates the cost and the present value. If this rate of return exceeds the rate of interest at which the $100,000 could be borrowed, then the investment is a profitable one.

5. *Statistical Abstract of the United States, 1981,* p. 443.

6. Alan S. Blinder, *Toward an Economic Theory of Income Distribution* (Cambridge, Mass.: MIT Press, 1974).

Although inherited wealth may not have a large direct effect on the distribution of income, it can have a substantial indirect effect that is difficult to measure. Inherited wealth may carry with it larger endowments of human capital in the form of better education, social contacts, and travel experiences, as mentioned earlier. These advantages are called ''fortunes'' by Nobel-Prize-winning English economist James Meade. Those who are fortunate enough to inherit these fortunes (wealth, education opportunities, abilities) have the opportunity to earn not only substantial income from wealth but also substantial labor income from their fortunate human-capital situation.

STUDIES OF THE CAUSES OF INEQUALITY

Considerable empirical work has been devoted to estimating the contribution of each of the inequality-creating factors—human-capital investments, luck, ability, inheritance, discrimination, occupational differences—to observed inequality. As is often the case, there is no universal agreement on the relative importance of each factor. Most researchers, however, agree that human-capital investments account for a substantial portion of observed inequality. For example, a prominent researcher in this field, Jacob Mincer, finds that human capital accounts for one half of the total inequality. Other researchers may disagree on the exact percentage, but there is agreement that differences in human capital explain much of the observed income differences among households.

A major dispute among economists is whether investment in schooling and training leads to higher earnings or whether individuals with more ability or more fortunate family backgrounds simply happen to be those with more schooling and training. In other words, what is the effect of human-capital investment on inequality if ability and family background are held constant? Estimates vary widely: some researchers find that ability or family environment have only a small independent effect (Zvi Grilliches and William Mason, James Morgan and Martin David) while others (Samuel Bowles) find that family environment has a substantial independent effect on inequality.

If ability and family environment explain a major portion of observed inequality, then inequality is in effect preordained. If one is not born with ability or into a favorable family environment, then one does not have the option of choosing between higher incomes now and higher income in the future, as human-capital theory suggests. Further research on this issue may ultimately determine how these effects should be sorted out.

Schooling and Screening

One explanation for why ability may have a relatively small independent effect on differential earnings is that employers use formal schooling as a screening device. Michael Spence and Nobel Laureate Kenneth Arrow maintain that the amount of formal schooling an individual has signals to employers that that individual is likely to possess sought-after traits. Lack of schooling credentials also serves to filter out for prospective employers individuals who are likely to be less productive. As long as schooling simply serves to screen employees for potential employers, the effect of ability should be modest. Employers will accept college graduates for positions with good career prospects and will not spend that much effort trying to distinguish among college graduates on the basis of ability.

The screening approach deviates from traditional human-capital theory, which argues that individuals with more schooling and training earn more because they are more productive. Screening theory suggests that schooling simply serves as a filter to admit some to high-paying jobs while excluding others who lack schooling credentials.[7]

Discrimination

The effect of discrimination on the distribution of income is also an important empirical issue. Is a substantial portion of observed inequality by

---

7. Signaling theory is treated in Michael Spence, ''Job Market Signaling,'' *Quarterly Journal of Economics* 87, 3 (August 1973): 355–74; Kenneth Arrow, ''Higher Education as a Filter,'' *Journal of Public Economics* 2, 3 (July 1973): 193–216.

race and sex the consequence of discrimination? For the postwar period as a whole, the average income of nonwhite households was slightly less than 60 percent that of white households. The postwar trend in the ratio of nonwhite to white incomes has been upward, beginning at 51 percent in 1947 and rising to an average of about 60 percent in the late 1970s. The severe economic downturn of the late 1970s caused a slight reversal of the upward movement.

There are also substantial differences in the average incomes of males and females. Women who work full time have had an average income equal to 60 percent of the incomes of their male counterparts since the late 1950s. Although the ratio of nonwhite to white earnings has increased since 1947, the female/male income differences have persisted. The relative position of average female earnings has actually worsened since the mid-1950s during a period when other (black/white, North/South) earnings differentials were improving. Figure 3 shows income differences by race and sex for the years 1965, 1975, and 1978.

The fact that whites earn, on average, more than nonwhites or that males earn, on average, more than females does not prove by itself that discrimination is present. Discrimination occurs when the entry of qualified individuals to jobs and occupations is blocked or when workers of equal skills and qualifications performing the same tasks are treated differently on the grounds of race, sex, or creed. Average differences in earnings may be the consequence of differences in natural ability, human capital, drive, and ambition, not of labor-market discrimination. How much is due to discrimination?

Studies of the effects of discrimination on black/white earnings differences conclude that about one half of observed differences in earnings can be attributed to schooling differences. Thus, a major cause of earnings differences is the disparity between the quantity and quality of schooling received by the different races. The most effective means, therefore, of reducing nonwhite/white earnings differentials is to provide equal access to quality education irrespective of race. If one eliminates the effects of other factors such as age, skills, and region, then perhaps one fourth of the observed wage differential can be attributed to la-

Figure 3
Income Differentials by Sex and Race

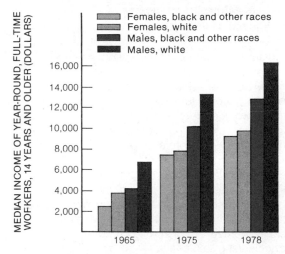

This figure illustrates that substantial differences in the income of blacks and whites and in the incomes of males and females are still present in the United States.

Source: U.S. Bureau of the Census.

bor-market discrimination.[8] Calculations of the effects of discrimination on wages are inexact because, typically, the discrimination effect is the difference that remains after all other factors that affect earnings—genetic factors, human capital, IQ, and so on—are accounted for. The researcher can never know whether the estimate overstates or understates the effect of discrimination.

Labor-market discrimination according to sex and race does not typically assume the form of discriminating between two workers (of different race or sex) performing the same job. In fact, there are federal laws guaranteeing equal pay for equal work (see Example 3). More often discrimination occurs when nonwhites and women are channeled into occupations regarded as "suitable" for nonwhite or female employment. As a consequence, these "suitable" professions—say, nursing and school teaching for women or bus

8. The results of extensive empirical research conducted in the 1960s and early 1970s on the impact of job discrimination on earnings are summarized in Bradley Schiller, *The Economics of Poverty and Discrimination* (Englewood Cliffs, N.J.: Prentice-Hall, 1973), chap. 10.

Example   3

Occupational Distributions of Women and Blacks

The table in the column at the right supplies statistics on the occupational distribution of women and nonwhites for selected occupations. Although women account for 41.7 percent of the total labor force, women are disproportionately concentrated in sales, clerical work, services, and private household work—professions that rank low in relative earnings. Nonwhites account for 11.3 percent of the labor force, but they are concentrated in occupations like bus driving, manual labor, and private household work—also occupations noted for low relative earnings. In the industrial professions, women and nonwhites tend to be packers, dry-cleaning attendants, and textile operatives, rather than higher-paying workers like artisans, butchers, and precision machine operators. The table also shows that women and nonwhites account for a very small percentage of dentists and craft workers.   ✖

Source: *Statistical Abstract of the United States, 1980,* pp. 418–20.

Occupation	Percent Female	Percent Nonwhite
Total employment	41.7	11.3
Professional and technical workers	43.3	8.9
Dentists	4.6	4.6
Physicians	10.7	9.5
Pharmacists	24.4	9.6
Registered nurses	96.8	11.4
Public-school teachers	70.8	10.1
Managers and administrators	24.6	5.4
Sales clerks, retail	70.7	6.9
Clerical workers	80.3	11.0
Secretaries	99.1	6.6
Telephone operators	91.7	16.8
Craft workers	5.7	7.9
Operatives	39.9	15.1
Dressmakers	95.4	13.8
Laundry operatives	65.9	24.9
Butchers and meat cutters	6.8	7.3
Packers and wrappers	63.7	19.2
Precision machine operators	13.3	8.9
Transport equipment operatives	8.1	14.5
Bus drivers	45.5	19.6
Taxicab drivers and chauffeurs	13.4	28.0
Laborers	11.3	17.4
Service workers	59.2	18.5
Private household workers	97.6	33.1

---

driving for black males—become *crowded,* and the relative earnings of these professions are driven down. If there were fewer formal and informal restrictions on the occupational choices of women and blacks, then public-school teaching, bus driving, and nursing would be less crowded and relative earnings in these professions would be less depressed.

HOW UNEQUAL IS U.S. INCOME DISTRIBUTION?

The Effect of Taxes

In the United States, the distribution of money income among households is not changed substantially by the tax system. For the vast majority of American households, the tax system (federal, state, and local) is roughly proportional. In other words, a household earning $15,000 per year will pay roughly the same percentage of its income in taxes as the household earning $50,000. (This conclusion will be explained in the next chapter.)

Figure 4, which is based on Table 4, shows the effect of income and payroll taxes on the U.S. distribution of income in 1972. The Lorenz curve before income and payroll taxes is shown as curve *B,* and curve *A* shows the Lorenz curve after taxes. Income and payroll taxes do equalize the distribution of income slightly: the share of the lowest 20 percent rises from 5.4 percent to 6.2 percent, and the share of the top 20 percent falls from 41.4 to 38.0 percent. These changes are relatively minor, however.

International Comparisons

Figure 5 compares the Lorenz curves of Brazil, the United States, Sweden, and Taiwan. Brazil is an example of a country with a highly unequal

Table 4
U.S. Lorenz Curves, Before and After Income and Payroll Taxes, 1972

Quintile	Before Taxes		After Taxes	
	Share of Income (percent)	Cumulative Share (percent)	Share of Income (percent)	Cumulative Share (percent)
Lowest fifth	5.4	5.4	6.3	6.3
Second fifth	11.9	17.3	13.3	19.5
Third fifth	17.5	34.8	18.3	37.8
Fourth fifth	23.9	58.7	24.1	61.9
Highest fifth	41.4	100.0	38.0	100.0

Source: Edgar K. Browning, "The Trend Toward Equality in the Distribution of Net Income," *Southern Economic Journal* 43, 1 (July 1976): 914.

distribution of income. Sweden and Taiwan are at the other extreme—their inequality in the distribution of income is considered to be relatively mild. The data show that Sweden, with a reputation for equality, is at about the same position as Taiwan but with more inequality at the lower end of the income distribution and less inequality at the upper end. The pattern of distribution in the United States is clearly closer to Sweden than to Brazil.

Figure 4
The Effect of Payroll Taxes on the U.S. Distribution of Income, 1972

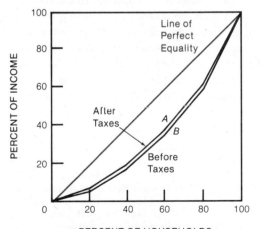

PERCENT OF HOUSEHOLDS

Income and payroll taxes have only a minor equalizing effect on the U.S. distribution of income.

Source: Based on Edgar K. Browning, "The Trend Toward Equality in the Distribution of Income," *Southern Economic Journal* 43,1 (July 1976): 914.

Figure 5
The Distribution of Income in Four Countries

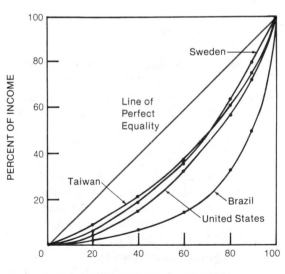

PERCENT OF HOUSEHOLDS

While Brazil has a highly unequal distribution of income, inequality in Sweden and Taiwan is relatively mild. The U.S. income distribution falls between these two extremes.

Source: The World Bank.

Figure 6
Age and Earnings of U.S. Males, 1978

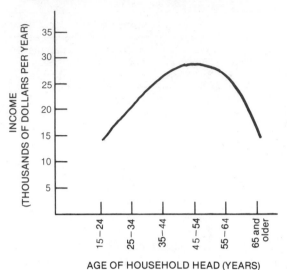

AGE OF HOUSEHOLD HEAD (YEARS)

Incomes tend to be low at the beginning of one's career, tend to rise until one's mid-fifties, and tend to drop off at retirement age.

Source: *Statistical Abstract of the United States,* 1981, p. 439.

Life-Cycle Effects

Income varies systematically during each person's lifetime. Incomes tend to be low at the beginning of one's career (say, age 20–24); earnings then rise until the person's mid-fifties and then drop off at retirement age. These trends in lifetime earnings are plotted in Figure 6. The appropriate measure of inequality, therefore, is the distribution of the *lifetime incomes* of households.

Because incomes vary over the life cycle, the degree of actual inequality will be overstated by the standard Lorenz curves already cited. Households at different stages in their earnings cycle are grouped together. Households with wage earners in their twenties or sixties will typically have lower incomes than those with wage earners in their thirties, forties, or fifties, even though their lifetime earnings may actually be identical.

Economist Morton Paglin has estimated that the U.S. lifetime Lorenz curve (the distribution of income adjusted for differences in age) shows

about 50 percent less inequality than the ordinary Lorenz curve. Other authors find that the correction for age should not reduce measured inequality by nearly as much as Paglin has estimated, but there is agreement that if age is held constant, the amount of inequality is reduced.[9]

The Unequal Distribution of Public Services

Household income consists of money income and **in-kind income.**

In-kind income consists primarily of benefits, such as free public education, school lunch programs, public housing, or food stamps, that the recipient is not required to pay for.

As already shown in Table 4, transfers of income through the tax system (taxing the more fortunate to finance money payments to the less fortunate) do not materially alter the distribution of income. What happens to the distribution of income when in-kind services are included? Figure 7 shows the 1972 Lorenz curve based on one researcher's effort to calculate the distribution of income after taxes, including receipts of public services like public education, government medical services, and other categories of income not captured in the official money income statistics. This calculation is by no means exact and requires numerous assumptions and qualifications, but it does show that the distribution of income becomes much more equal when all sources of income and in-kind benefits are included as income because the poor receive a larger share of public services than the rich. One reason why such calculations

9. Morton Paglin, in "The Measurement and Trend of Inequality: A Basic Revision," *American Economic Review* 65, 4 (September 1975); 598–609, reports that there is a significant trend towards a more equal distribution of income between 1947 and 1972 if the effects of age on the distribution of income are removed. Paglin's findings have been disputed by several authors, in particular by Sheldon Danziger, Robert Haveman, and Eugene Smolensky, in "The Measurement and Trend of Inequality: Comment," *American Economic Review* 67, 3 (June 1977): 502–13. For a survey of this literature, see Alan Blinder, "The Level and Distribution of Economic Wellbeing," in ed. Martin Feldstein, *The American Economy in Transition* (Chicago: The University of Chicago Press, 1980), pp. 450–53.

Figure 7
The Distribution of Income Before and After Taxes and Benefits

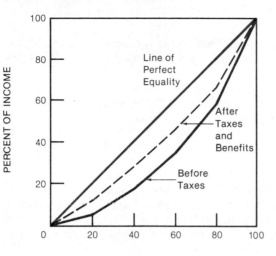

PERCENT OF HOUSEHOLDS

The distribution of U.S. income becomes much more equal when all sources of income and in-kind benefits are included as income.

Source: Based on Edgar K. Browning, "The Trend Toward Equality in the Distribution of Net Income," *Southern Economic Journal* 43,1 (July 1976): 914.

are inexact is that it is difficult to place an appropriate price tag on in-kind benefits. The recipient of a public service that costs $20 to produce (say, public health or public education) may value that service at less than $20 or may even place a zero value on the service. Calculations of the effect of the in-kind benefit must be based upon the cost of supplying the service because there is no way of knowing the value that the recipient places on the service.[10]

WHAT IS A JUST DISTRIBUTION OF INCOME?

Philosophers have debated the distribution of income for centuries. Is it fair to have extremes of wealth and poverty? What is a just distribution of income? Are unequal rewards required in order

10. Alternate calculations showing a smaller effect of in-kind services have been prepared by Timothy Smeeding, "On the Distribution of Net Income: Comment," *Southern Economic Journal* 46, 1 (January 1979): 932–44.

to bring out extra effort and talents? The issue of *distributive justice* is largely an ethical issue. Economists are in a better position to describe the economic consequences of different distributions of income than to judge whether one distribution of income is better than another. Over the years, different philosophies of distributive justice have been formulated. Some argue for more equal distributions of income than others.

Natural Law and the Leaky Bucket

According to the natural-law philosophers of the 17th century, each individual has the right to the fruits of his or her labors. In terms of modern economic theory, this philosophy translates into the marginal productivity theory of income distribution. According to this theory, the owners of the factors of production will receive a price that equals the marginal revenue product *(MRP)* of the factor. Under this system, those who are more productive (those who have high *MRPs* because of special skills or hard effort) will receive more than those with low *MRPs*.

Critics can point out with some justification that marginal productivity theory will lead to inequities. Some individuals will inherit factors with high *MRPs*; some will be fortunate enough to be born to rich or brilliant parents; those who are lucky will receive high rewards. Socialist theorists argue that these inequities will be diminished under socialism, where private property is abolished. In such a society, nonlabor factors of production belong to society as a whole; there is no inheritance of property; all individuals have equal access to educational opportunities.

The major advantage of distribution according to marginal productivities is that the owners of factors of production are encouraged to raise the marginal productivity of their factors. Individuals are encouraged to invest in human capital; owners of capital are encouraged to save to acquire more capital; entrepreneurs are encouraged to assume risks. If factors of production were not paid in accordance with marginal productivity, there would be a tendency to reduce effort, to acquire less human and tangible capital, and to take fewer risks. The end result would be that the economy would earn less income in total.

Equality and Efficiency: How Big is the Trade-Off?

In the United States, the instrument that is potentially most effective in redistributing income from the fortunate to the unfortunate is the income-tax system. How will the fortunate respond to substantial increases in their income-tax rates? As already noted in this chapter, the redistributive role played by income and payroll taxes in the United States is not large. What would happen to total income if tax rates were raised even more for the purpose of redistributing income?

In a 1979 study of the Brookings Institution of Washington, D.C., economist Jerry Hausman found that the current tax system does significantly reduce the supply of labor. If there were no taxes at all, men would work about 8 percent more. The top 20 percent of male earners would

increase their hours of work by 13 percent. Women would be even more strongly affected by taxes.

Just as one can estimate the deadweight loss from monopoly, so can one estimate the deadweight loss due to taxes. The deadweight losses are the dollars that people will not earn because the tax system discourages them from working more hours or working harder. Hausman concludes that this deadweight loss would be lower if everyone paid the same percentage of income to taxes because those in higher income brackets pay progressively more and thus reduce hours worked and effort proportionally more than those earning less income.   ✕

For this reason, most economists agree that there is a trade-off between more equality and more income. If income is redistributed from those who possess high-priced factors of production to those less fortunate (by means of a high tax on the fortunate, for example), the efficiency of the economy would decline, and less income would be available for society as a whole. Economist Arthur Okun describes the equity/efficiency trade-off using the analogy of a leaky bucket.[11] Redistributing income from the fortunate to the unfortunate is like transfering water from one barrel to another with a leaky bucket. In the process of making the transfer, water (income) is lost forever. If the leak is a slow one, then the costs to society of the redistribution are small. If the leak is large, then the losses of total income will be substantial. Society must decide whether the costs of greater equality are worth the price.

The Utilitarian Case for Equality

Natural-law philosophy and the marginal-productivity theory of income distribution support an

unequal distribution of income. Inequality allows individuals to reap the fruits of their efforts and raises economic efficiency. At the other end of the spectrum is the argument that equal income distribution will maximize the utility of society.

The law of diminishing marginal utility supplies the basic rationale for the *utilitarian theory* of income distribution. If people are basically alike (if they have the same tastes, obtain the same satisfaction from the same amount of income, and so on), then the total utility of society will be greatest when income is distributed equally because everyone is subject to the law of diminishing marginal utility. If Jones were rich and Smith were poor, Jones would be getting much less utility from his last dollar than Smith. If income were shifted from Jones to Smith, Smith's utility would increase more than Jones's would be reduced. Therefore, the reduction in equality would increase the total utility of society. If indeed everyone is alike, then the total utility of society would be greatest when income is distributed perfectly equally among individuals.

The obvious criticism of this case for equality is that people are indeed different. Some care little for money and worldly goods; others care a great deal. Therefore, it is not at all certain that the rich person gets less marginal utility from his

---

11.   Arthur Okun, *Equality and Efficiency: The Big Trade-off* (Washington, D.C.: The Brookings Institution, 1975).

or her last dollar than does the poor person. Modern economists agree that because one cannot make interpersonal utility comparisons of this sort, one cannot argue scientifically that the total utility of society is greatest when income is equally distributed.

Rawlsian Equality

A different argument for equality has been proposed by Harvard philosopher John Rawls.[12] Rawls maintains that inequality and injustice result from the fact that people already know too much about their endowments of resources and abilities when entering into bargaining concerning their economic, social, and political rewards. Economic, social, and political contracts determine the distribution of income and privileges. Those who know that they are better endowed with economic resources, social contacts, and political influence would be unwilling to enter into contracts (such as highly redistributive taxes) that give away these advantages and make them the equal of others less advantaged. The rational self-interest of the privileged will not allow a social consensus to emerge. According to Rawls, if everyone were operating behind a veil of ignorance about their endowments and fortunes, rational, self-interested individuals would act as risk avoiders and would agree on two basic principles of justice. 1) They would agree on the principle of equal liberty. 2) They would agree that social and economic inequalities should fulfill two conditions: any inequities must be to the greatest expected benefit of the least advantaged, and all offices and positions must be open to all under conditions of fair equality of opportunity.

Why would individuals operating behind Rawls's veil of ignorance agree unanimously on these principles? Not knowing how they would fare (not knowing their advantages and disadvantages in advance), individuals would opt to take the least risky position, or the maximin (best of the worst outcomes) position. In Rawls's system, there would be a strong tendency towards an equal distribution of income because risk aversion would require individuals in the initial situation to be concerned about the welfare of those occupying low positions in the income distribution because people couldn't be sure that they wouldn't end up in the low position. The actual distribution of income will differ from this ideal model because individuals do indeed know their relative economic and social positions. Rawls presents an ideal towards which he believes society should strive.

Critics of Rawls's notion of distributive justice argue that there is no guarantee that individuals placed in Rawls's original position would indeed reach a consensus on Rawls's two principles of social justice. Even in the original position, there would be some risk lovers who would dissent, believing that they could benefit at the expense of another. Moreover, Rawls's critics note that he ignores the problem of the efficiency/inequality trade-off. If the trade-off is substantial, a scheme that concentrates on protecting the least-advantaged could lead to a considerable loss of efficiency.

POVERTY

The causes of poverty are the same things that cause inequality in the distribution of income. The poor are poor because of their limited endowments of ability and skills, their limited amount of human capital, bad luck, discrimination, and (some might even argue) conscious choice. The poor are poor because their capacity to earn a "sufficient" income is for some reason impaired.

Defining poverty is not an easy task, because establishing poverty levels of income requires important judgments on the part of the analyst. There will always be disagreement over what constitutes a poverty income. Some analysts define poverty in terms of the amount of income necessary to provide a family of a certain size with the minimum essentials of food, clothing, shelter, and education. This approach provides an *absolute measure* of poverty. An absolute measure of poverty establishes a specific income level for a given sized household below which the household is judged to be living in a state of poverty. But is an absolute measure appropriate? Poverty can, after all, be relative. One's sense of poverty de-

---

12. John Rawls, *A Theory of Justice* (Cambridge: Harvard University Press, 1971); and "Some Reasons for the Maximin Criterion," *American Economic Review* 64, 2 (May 1974): 141–46.

Table 5
Persons Living in Households Below Poverty Levels, 1959 to 1980

Year	Number of Persons Below Poverty Level (millions)	Percentage of Population	Poverty Income for Household of 4 (dollars)
1959	39.5	22.4	2,973
1960	39.9	22.2	3,022
1965	33.2	17.3	3,223
1966	28.5	14.7	3,317
1968	25.4	12.8	3,553
1970	25.4	12.6	3,968
1972	24.5	11.9	4,275
1974	24.3	11.6	5,038
1976	25.0	11.8	5,815
1978	24.5	11.4	6,662
1979	25.3	11.6	7,412
1980	27.3	13.0	8,414

Source: *Statistical Abstract of the United States, 1981*, p. 446; *Christian Science Monitor*, April 23, 1982, p. 22.

pends upon the incomes of others in the community. If one's income is 10 percent of everyone else's, one may feel poor even if one's income is above that required to purchase the minimum essentials. A second approach to poverty, therefore, is to measure it in relative terms. A *relative measure,* for example, might classify a household as poor if the household's income is 25 percent of an average household's income.

The choice of a poverty definition will determine to a great extent the number of poor and the rate at which poverty is perceived as being eliminated. If the absolute standard is selected, rising real living standards will push more and more families above the poverty line. If, however, the relative standard is used, poverty can be eliminated only by equalizing the distribution of income. If the rich and the poor both experience equal percentage increases in income, the poor will not have improved their relative position. As economist Alan Blinder writes about relative poverty standards: "Under this definition, the War on Poverty would be unwinnable by definition, and the Bible would be literally correct: ye have the poor always with you."[13] For this reason, the discussion of trends in poverty that follows empha-

13. Alan Blinder, "The Level and Distribution of Economic Well-Being," p. 456.

sizes the official absolute poverty standards of the U.S. government. What Americans consider poor, however, would not necessarily be considered poor by some other countries.

Trends in Poverty

Table 5 lists the official statistics on the number of persons below poverty levels in the United States for the period 1959 to 1980. According to the absolute poverty standards of the U.S. government, the number of persons in households below the poverty level has declined from 39.5 million to 27.3 million between 1959 and 1980. As a percent of the U.S. population, the figure has declined from 22.4 percent to 13.0 percent. Progress has been uneven, however. Large percentage declines were experienced in the 1960s; the number of people below the poverty level has remained roughly the same since 1970, rising temporarily with the severe recessions of 1980 and 1982.

The figures in Table 5 refer only to reported money income. Economists have noted a tendency for the money incomes of the poor to be underreported because of the prevalence of moonlighting and unreported tips. Money income figures do not include in-kind services received by the poor but do include government cash trans-

Table 6

The Percentage of Persons Below Poverty Before and After Government Antipoverty Programs, 1976

Classification	All Households	White Households	Nonwhite Households
Income before taxes and cash payments	27.0	24.7	43.8
Income after cash payments	13.5	11.4	28.9
Income after cash and in-kind payments	8.1	7.1	15.9

Source: Congress of the United States, Congressional Budget Office, Background Paper No. 17, *Poverty Status of Families Under Alternate Definitions of Income,* June 1977.

fers, such as welfare payments and unemployment insurance. Yet government antipoverty programs emphasize in-kind benefits more than cash transfers. The government currently spends $3 in noncash benefits for every $2 in cash payments.

What effects do government cash and noncash antipoverty programs have on the number of persons living below the poverty line? Table 6 reports the number of persons living below poverty levels in 1976 before and after government antipoverty programs. These figures differ from those in the previous table because they consider households to be unrelated individuals as well as those living in families. These figures show that the percentage of Americans living below the poverty line would be much higher in the absence of government cash-transfer programs. Cash payments reduce the number of persons below the poverty line by roughly 50 percent. If in-kind transfers are included, government programs reduce the number living below poverty by more than two thirds. Without cash payments, 27 percent of the American population and almost 44 percent of the nonwhite U.S. population would be below the poverty line. The inclusion of government in-kind services further reduces the incidence of poverty. If both cash payments and in-kind benefits are included in income, the percentage of those living below poverty levels falls to 7.1 percent of the white population and 15.9 percent of the nonwhite population.

Who Are the Poor?

Table 7 provides a statistical profile of poor families. The poor tend to be disproportionately

Table 7

Characteristics of Poverty

Characteristic	Percentage of Persons Below Poverty Levels, 1979
By race	
White	6.8
Black	27.6
Spanish origin	19.7
By size of family	
2 persons	7.9
4 persons	8.5
5 persons	11.1
7 or more persons	24.2
By education of family head	
less than 8 years	23.0
8 years	12.8
1–3 years high school	13.8
4 years high school	6.6
1 or more years college	3.1
Sex of family head	
Male	68.1
Female	31.9
By age of family head	
15–24 years	18.7
25–44 years	9.8
45–54 years	6.8
55–64 years	6.0
65 or more years	9.1
Location	
Central cities	12.7
Suburbs	5.4
Outside metropolitan areas	10.8

Source: *Statistical Abstract of the United States, 1981,* pp. 446–452.

Example 5

Are Students Poor?

Professor Eugene Smolensky of the University of Wisconsin at Madison, a noted expert on the economics of poverty, gives a striking example of the effect of government services on the distribution of income. He calculates that students attending the University of Wisconsin receive in their four years a subsidy from the state of $20,000. The $20,000 figure comes from the difference between the cost of supplying four years of college education and the tuition and fees each student pays. University of Wisconsin students are therefore granted a gift of $20,000, which, according to Smolensky, places them in a privileged position in the distribution of lifetime income. With this free $20,000, they can accumulate human capital that will yield (according to Smolensky's calculation) an annual rate of return on investment of about 9 percent. A college graduate's income at age 22 (right after graduation) will be somewhat less than a high-school graduate who had gone to work four years earlier. But the college graduate quickly surpasses the high-school graduate. The high-school graduate's income peaks at age 45, whereas the college graduate's income keeps on rising to age 65.

Are college graduates entitled to cheap housing because they are poor? Smolensky's answer is no. Smolensky proposes that everyone should be given the $20,000, both those who want to go to college and those who want to work right after high school. This universal gift would put everyone on an equal footing.

Source: *The Milwaukee Journal,* September 17, 1980.

black and of Hispanic origin. They tend to live in large families; the family head tends to have little education, to be young, and to be female. The poor tend to concentrate in central cities and in rural areas. Contrary to popular myth, a majority of the poor (61.8 percent) are working poor; not all the poor receive cash assistance. In 1979, only 64 percent of the poor received some form of cash assistance from government antipoverty programs.

SOLUTIONS TO THE POVERTY PROBLEM

Income Maintenance

One ready solution to the problem of poverty is to raise the incomes of the poor. The two mechanisms used to accomplish this effect—voluntary charitable contributions and government cash-assistance programs—require a transfer of income from those above the poverty line to those below it. If society has determined to carry out this redistribution (and has determined that voluntary contributions alone cannot do the job), then the manner in which it is done will affect the efficiency of resource utilization. First, the redistribution from the rich to the poor may discourage work effort on the part of the rich and thus reduce the size of the income pie available for redistribution. Second, if the assistance to the poor discourages their work effort, the size of the income pie will be further reduced.

The Current Welfare System. In the United States, the current welfare-assistance program follows the basic principle that public assistance should be granted primarily on the basis of demonstrated need. For this purpose, a series of government programs have been established—such as Aid to Families with Dependent Children (AFDC), Food Stamps, public housing, and Medicaid—whereby the amount of public assistance is typically based upon family income. Under such programs, welfare authorities first determine what resources the family has (totaling the earnings of the family head, contributions from relatives, and so on). Public assistance is then granted on the basis of the need perceived by the welfare authority. The higher the resources of the family (its income from all sources and its savings), the less public assistance it is supposed to receive. The welfare family is, therefore, discouraged by this system from increasing its earnings because addi-

Table 8

A Hypothetical Negative Income Tax (with a guaranteed income of $6,000 and a tax rate of 50 percent)

Earnings (dollars)	Amount of Negative Income Tax Received (dollars)	Total Disposable Income = Earned Income + Tax Receipt (dollars)
0	6,000	6,000
3,000	4,500	7,500
6,000	3,000	9,000
9,000	1,500	10,500
12,000	0	12,000

tional earnings—if detected by welfare authorities—will cause a reduction in public assistance. If the trade-off is a $1 loss of public assistance for every $1 of extra income, the incentive to earn extra income would be negligible.

The *disincentive effects* of current public-assistance programs have been noted by economists and politicians alike, and proposals have been made to build better incentives into the existing system. In particular, it has been proposed to Congress that welfare recipients be permitted to keep a specified percentage of extra earnings without a reduction in existing public-assistance benefits.

A second drawback of the current public-assistance system is that the documentation of needs and resources is very costly in terms of society's resources, requiring an army of welfare workers to staff the program. Dollars that could have been devoted to public assistance are diverted into the bureaucratic costs of operating the system.

The Negative Income Tax.   Economists have proposed that the current system be replaced by a *negative income tax* (NIT). A negative income tax would work as outlined in Table 8. First, the government would set a floor below which family incomes would not be allowed to fall. For purposes of illustration, Table 8 sets this floor at $6,000 for a family of four. Second, the government would set a negative tax rate. In our example, this negative tax rate is 50 percent.

Families of four who earn less than the $6,000 floor would be guaranteed an income of $6,000. If the family earned zero income, it would receive a negative-income-tax payment of $6,000. But what about the family that earns between $0 and $6,000? If a family that earned $3,000 were to receive a negative income tax of $3,000 to bring it up to the $6,000 floor, it would be no better off than the family that has zero income, in which case there would be little incentive to earn income. This is where the 50 percent tax rate comes in. If a 50 percent negative tax rate were in effect, benefits would be reduced by $0.50 for every extra dollar earned. In this case, the family earns $3,000, and its benefits are reduced by one half of the $3,000 earnings from $6,000 to $4,500. The total income of the family will therefore be $3,000 plus $4,500 or $7,500. By earning the $3,000, the family has been made better off compared to not working. The benefits of a family that earned double the guaranteed income— $12,000—would decrease at the rate of $0.50 for each extra dollar earned, or by $6,000, so the $6,000 benefits would be reduced by $6,000. The family earning $12,000, therefore, will receive no negative-income-tax payment from the government. Its income will consist of its earnings of $12,000 plus a zero negative-income-tax payment. In this example, the $12,000 income is called the *break-even income*. At $12,000 and above, the family's total income will equal its own earnings minus the income tax for that level.

Figure 8 shows what happens to disposable income as earned incomes increase from $0 to $17,000.

The negative-income-tax scheme offers two advantages over the existing system. First, it preserves work incentives up to the break-even income level by allowing low-income families to keep a prescribed portion of earnings. Second, it promises to do away with the costly bureaucracy of the existing welfare system. Administration of the negative income tax would be carried out by the same authority—the Internal Revenue Service—that administers the current personal-income-tax system.

The basic disadvantage is that work incentives will depend on the negative tax rate. A 50 percent negative tax rate means that families will be able

Figure 8
The Workings of the Negative Income Tax

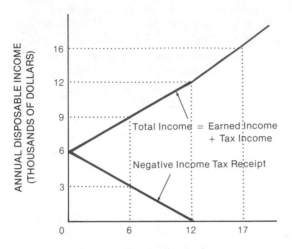

ANNUAL EARNINGS
(THOUSANDS OF DOLLARS)

This figure illustrates the workings of a hypothetical negative income tax. Here, the negative tax rate is set at 50 percent and a floor income is set at $6,000, below which no family income would be allowed to fall. A family with $0 income would receive $6,000 in benefits. Any family that earned more than $0 would have their $6,000 benefits reduced by $0.50 for every dollar earned. For example, a family earning $3,000 would receive $6,000 − (0.50 × $3,000) or $4,500 in addition to the $3,000 they earned. Up to an income of $12,000, families would still receive some benefits in addition to their income (benefits equal to $6,000 minus $0.50 times the amount of income earned). At an income of $12,000, however, families would receive no benefits in addition to their income because the $6,000 would be reduced by 0.50 × $12,000, or by $6,000 ($6,000 − $6,000 = $0). Beyond an income of $12,000, families would pay taxes. For example, a family earning $17,000 would pay taxes on the $5,000 difference between $17,000 and $12,000. If the tax rate were 20 percent, the family earning $17,000 would pay $1,000 in taxes (0.20 × $5,000) and would have a disposable income of $16,000.

---

to keep only one half of their earnings below the break-even point. Incentive effects can be raised by lowering the tax rate—say, to 25 percent, but this lowering of the rate raises the break-even income level to $24,000—well above any conceivable poverty level. To insure strong incentives requires low tax rates and negative-income-tax payments to those who are obviously not poor. Empirical studies show that 50 percent is about

the highest tax rate an NIT program could impose without significant disincentives.

The idea of a negative income tax has widespread support among economists. Two U.S. Presidents—Presidents Nixon and Carter—proposed NIT programs, but to date a negative-income-tax program has not been adopted.

Long-Run Solutions

Income-maintenance programs—be they of the negative-income-tax or assistance-according-to-demonstrated-need variety—offer only a short-run solution to the poverty problem. The long-run solution of poverty requires an attack on the fundamental sources of poverty—limited human capital and discrimination—that are responsive to government action. Income-maintenance programs may assist the children of the poor by providing the money resources to maintain health and fund the acquisition of training and education. Income-maintenance programs may perpetuate the poverty problem if they discourage work effort. To provide a long-run solution to the problem of poverty, government policy should aim at eliminating job-market discrimination and discrimination in the delivery of education to individuals according to color and sex. Moreover, government policy should encourage the children of the poor to invest in human-capital resources. The problem is how to devise a policy that does not defeat itself by reverse discrimination or by making the trade-off between equity and efficiency too costly. The intended effects of legislation can often differ dramatically from the actual effects.

This chapter examined the causes of inequality in the distribution of income and directed attention to the role of government in the redistribution of income to the poor. The next four chapters will be examining a variety of microeconomic issues but will focus on the role of government in the economy and the relationship between political and economic systems.

Summary

1. The distribution of income among households is determined first in factor markets. House-

hold income is the sum of the payments to the factors of production that the household owns. The government may change this distribution of income through taxes and the distribution of public services. The Lorenz curve measures the degree of inequality in the distribution of income. It shows the cumulative percent of all income earned by households at successive income levels. If the Lorenz curve is a straight 45-degree line, income is distributed perfectly equally. The more the Lorenz curve bows away from the 45-degree line, the more unequal is the distribution of income. The U.S. distribution of income has become more equal since 1929.

2. The sources of inequality are: different abilities, chance and luck, discrimination, occupational differences, different amounts of human capital investment, and property inheritance.

3. Differences in schooling may affect earnings because employers use educational credentials to screen and select job candidates for high-paying careers. Although earnings differentials between whites and nonwhites have been reduced in recent years, earnings differentials between males and females have not been reduced.

4. The distribution of income appears to be more equal when one makes adjustments for taxes, in-kind services, and life-cycle effects.

5. There are different views on what constitutes distributive justice. Marginal utility theory calls for a distribution of income according to the marginal productivity of the resources owned by households. The utilitarian school believes an equal distribution of income maximizes total utility. John Rawls calls for a distribution of income that maximizes the utility of the least-fortunate members of society.

6. Poverty can be measured either in absolute or relative terms. The absolute measure is based on an estimate of the minimum income necessary to allow a household to buy the minimum essentials. The relative poverty concept measures poverty in terms of the household's location in the income distribution. According to government absolute measures of poverty, the number of those living below the poverty line has declined substantially since

the 1950s. Currently, the almost 27 million Americans classified as poor account for about 13 percent of the American population. There has been little progress in the 1970s towards further reductions in the number of Americans living below the poverty line as measured by money income. If in-kind payments are included in income, slightly more than 7 percent of Americans are living below the poverty line. Poor Americans tend to be nonwhite, poorly educated, members of households headed by females and tend to be either very young or very old.

7. Income-maintenance programs are a short-run solution to the problem of poverty. The long-run solution is to raise the income-earning capacity of the children of the poor.

Key Terms

Lorenz curve
wealth
in-kind income

Questions and Problems

1. Draw a Lorenz curve for absolute equality. Draw a Lorenz curve for absolute inequality. Explain in words what the absolute-inequality Lorenz curve means.

2. "If all people were the same, the Lorenz curve would be a 45-degree line." Evaluate this statement.

3. "The fact that a woman earns on average two thirds of what a man earns proves beyond a shadow of a doubt that there is sex discrimination." Evaluate this statement.

4. There are two views of the causes of poverty. One school says that the poor are poor through no fault of their own. The other says that the poor are poor through choice. Give arguments for each position.

5. How does screening theory explain the apparently poor correlation between ability and inequality?

6. Contrast the utilitarian view of distributive justice with the Rawlsian view.

7. Explain why measured Lorenz curves that use disposable income before and after taxes may not give an accurate picture of the distribution of real income.

8. Would the work incentives be greater with a 25 percent negative-income-tax rate or a 50 percent NIT rate? Rework Table 8 and Figure 8 in the text to illustrate your answer.

IV

Microeconomic Issues

20

Public Finance

Chapter Preview

The distinguishing feature of economic behavior in the private sector is private ownership of the factors of production. Preceding chapters have described how private firms and private owners of the factors of production behave in different market environments. The private sector, however, does not account for all economic activity. A significant amount of economic activity is carried out by the *public sector,* or local, state, and federal governments. Public-sector economics is the study of the resource-allocation activities of government. One branch of public-sector economics is **public finance**.

Public finance is the study of government revenues and expenditures at all levels of government—local, state, and federal.

This chapter will study government expenditure and taxation and will examine the effects of government spending and taxation on private economic activity.

THE SCOPE OF GOVERNMENT ECONOMIC ACTIVITY

In 1981, the government purchased 20 percent of all goods and services produced by the economy. In an economy that produced some $2.9

Table 1
Exhaustive Expenditures and Transfer Payments of Government in 1981

Government	Purchases of Goods and Services, including Interest Payments (billions of dollars)	Transfer Payments (billions of dollars)	Total Expenditures for Goods and Services and Transfers (billions of dollars)
Federal government	298	280	578
State and local governments	338	42	380
All government	636	322	958

Note: GNP in 1980 = $2,627.4 billion. Purchases of goods and services include net interest payments. Federal transfers exclude grants to state and local governments.

Source: *Economic Report of the President,* January 1982, pp. 321–22.

trillion worth of goods and services, government purchases added up to $590 billion. The two types of government expenditures are **exhaustive expenditures** and **transfer payments**.

Exhaustive expenditures are government purchases of goods and services that divert real economic resources from the private sector making them no longer available for private use.

Exhaustive expenditures in 1981 accounted for two thirds of total government spending. The remaining government expenditures are government transfer payments.

Transfer payments transfer income from one individual or organization to another.

Government transfer payments do not change the amount of economic resources that the government consumes. For example, the social-security program transfers income from currently employed workers to retired or disabled workers and their families. Transfer payments affect the distribution of income among families but do not change the amount of goods and services exhausted (consumed) by government. Transfer payments may affect economic activity by changing the distribution of income and economic incentives.

As Table 1 reports, total government expenditures currently account for one third of gross national product *(GNP)*. The ratio of total government expenditures to gross national product is a common measure of the economic scope of government.

The average citizen's impression of the scope of government is formed by the share of personal income that he or she must pay to the government in personal tax payments—such as income taxes, inheritance taxes, or social-security contributions. In 1980, government collected $339 billion in personal income taxes, which amounted to 16 percent of total personal income earned in that year. In addition to personal tax collections, governments collected $112 billion from sales and excise taxes and $190 billion in social-security taxes and insurance. Together, all these taxes add up to about 30 percent of personal income.

Trends in Government

Government revenues and expenditures have been increasing at a rapid pace. Figure 1 shows the enormous acceleration of total government expenditures and transfer payments since 1929. Dollar figures exaggerate the growth of government because of the general rise in prosperity and prices; we would expect government revenues and expenditures to rise along with the general economy. The more relevant yardstick of the changing role of government is the ratio of total government spending to total economic activity, or GNP (see Figure 2). In 1890, government expenditures accounted for 6.5 percent of GNP, but by 1980, this ratio had risen to 33 percent.

The economic role of government, especially of the federal government, has increased dramatically over the past half century for at least five reasons:

Figure 1
Total Government Expenditures, 1929-1981

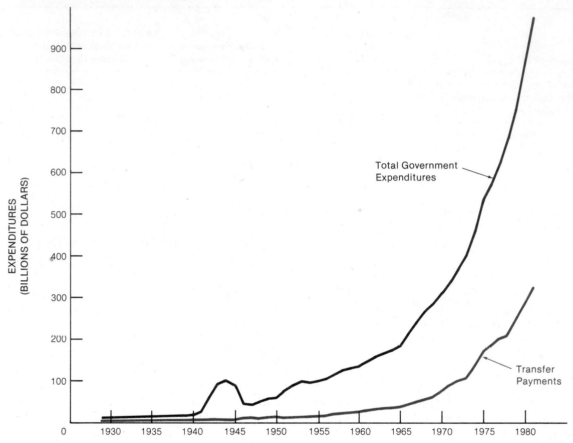

Total government expenditures and transfer payments have increased at an accelerating rate since 1929.
Source: *Economic Report of the President,* 1982, pp. 255, 320.

---

1. The United States, as one of the world's two major military superpowers, has had to devote an increasing share of its economic resources to national defense. On the eve of the Second World War, national defense expenditures accounted for 1.3 percent of GNP. At the peak of the Vietnam conflict, national defense accounted for almost 9 percent of GNP, falling thereafter to 5 percent of GNP.
2. Since 1929, government, especially the federal government, has increasingly taken responsibility for the health, education, and income security of the American population. Prior to the Great Depression of the 1930s, it was primarily the responsibility of the individual to provide for family health, income security, and retirement

needs. Educational needs were provided for by the local community, and private charitable organizations cared for the needy. Since the 1930s, this attitude has steadily eroded. In 1929, prior to the establishment of the social-security program, government social-welfare programs cost $3.9 million, a minute fraction of 1 percent of GNP. Today, government expenditures for health, education, and welfare account for almost 10 percent of GNP. Responsibility for health, education, and welfare has been transfered from the family and private charitable organizations to government.
3. The more modern and complex an economy becomes, the more government services it requires. Urban societies require more government services—sanitation, traffic control, water sup-

Figure 2
Total Government Spending as a Percent of GNP, 1890-1980

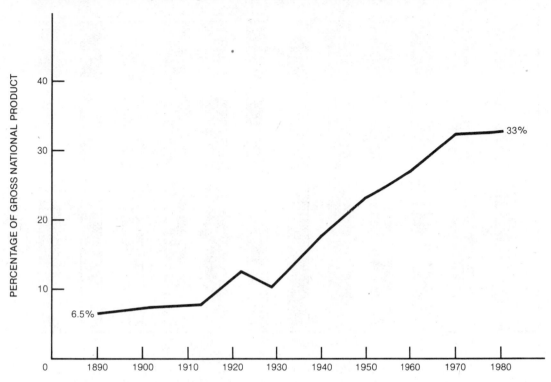

The ratio of total government expenditures to total economic activity (or GNP) is a better measure of the changing role of government than measures of government spending alone.

Source: *Economic Report of the President,* 1982, pp. 254-320.

plies—than rural societies. Congested areas require more police protection than low-density communities. Modern industrial societies require a more complex legal system.

4. Another explanation for the relative growth of government lies in the costs of supplying government services. Unlike manufacturing or agriculture, which have experienced substantial increases in productivity, efficiency gains in the government sector have been slow. It is easier to increase productivity in the private sector than it is in the public sector where *services*—such as school teaching, police protection, judicial services, and general record keeping—rather than *goods* are being provided. Because of slow productivity growth, price increases have been more rapid in the public sector than in the private sector. Since 1950, the prices paid by government to purchase goods and services have risen almost 60 percent faster than retail prices.

5. Because of the power of special-interest groups and lobbyists, democratic societies have been gradually increasing their support of government spending (see the chapter after next for further discussion).

**Shares of Federal,
State, and Local Governments**

Government economic activities are distributed among federal, state, and local governments. Each society must determine at what level of government a given public service should be provided. Should roads be built by federal or local government? Should the municipalities, the

Figure 3
State and Local Expenditures versus Federal Expenditures, 1930-1980

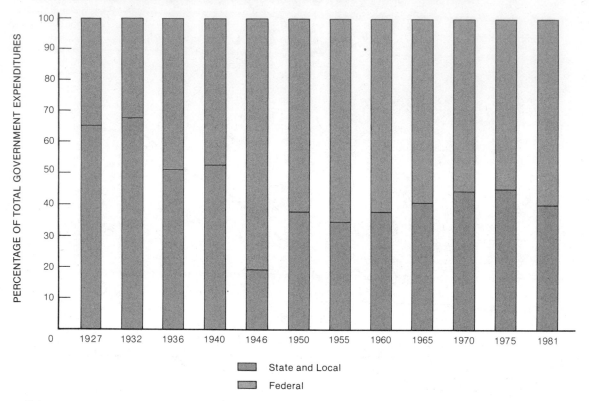

This graph shows that the dominance of federal over state and local spending is a fairly recent phenomenon.
Note: Federal expenditures do not include grants in aid to state and local governments.

Source: *Economic Report of the President,* 1982, pp. 321-23; *Historical Statistics of the United States,* vol. 2, pp. 1124-29.

states, or the federal government supply public education? There has been intense debate over issues like these since the founding of this country. Some citizens fear that the federal government is too removed from the people it represents and from local conditions and sentiments and that it has acquired too much economic power. They view the states as having too little power in relation to the federal government. Others consider the federal government to be the most efficient and rational supplier of government services and the best enforcer of national standards and legislation.

In 1980, the federal government accounted for 59 percent of all government expenditures, while state and local government accounted for 41 percent. Figure 3 shows that the dominance by federal government is a fairly new phenomenon. In 1930, state and local government accounted for 76 percent of government expenditures, while the federal government accounted for only 24 percent. As late as 1940, state and local government still accounted for about one half of all government revenues and expenditures. Since 1955, state and local government has been growing in importance—from 34 percent to 41 percent of total government. Proposals by President Reagan in 1982 for The New Federalism—turning more fiscal responsibilities over to the states—may accelerate this antifederal trend in the future if enacted.

Table 2
Tax Revenues for Selected Countries, 1977

Country	Tax Revenue (billions of dollars)	As Percent of GDP	Tax Revenue per Capita (dollars)
United States	556.0	30.3	2,564
Australia	29.7	29.7	2,110
Austria	18.9	39.3	2,507
Belgium	34.0	42.9	3,456
Canada	66.0	32.0	2,831
Denmark	19.5	42.0	3,822
Finland	12.4	41.2	2,625
France	151.0	39.6	2,845
Germany, F.R.	196.2	38.2	3,196
Greece	7.4	28.1	794
Italy	73.6	37.6	1,304
Japan	158.5	22.2	1,392
Netherlands	49.3	46.3	3,557
New Zealand	4.9	34.5	1,560
Norway	17.0	47.5	4,204
Portugal	4.4	27.2	453
Spain	26.0	22.5	710
Sweden	41.8	53.4	5,061
Switzerland	19.1	31.5	3,018
United Kingdom	89.4	36.6	1,599

Note: Covers national and local taxes and social security contributions. GDP = Gross domestic product.

Source: Organization for Economic Cooperation and Development, Paris, France, *Revenue Statistics of OECD Member Countries,* 1978.

An International Perspective

Government has become a $600 billion business and employs 15 out of every 100 workers in the economy. Is the economic role of government in the United States relatively larger than in other countries? As noted earlier, a convenient measure of government size is government tax revenues as a percentage of GNP. According to this measure, Table 2 shows that the U.S. government does not stand out as extraordinarily large or small. In fact, relative to the highly industrialized countries of Western Europe, the economic role of U.S. government appears to be moderate, despite the generally heavier U.S. defense burden.

The government's share of economic activity appears to rise with economic development. Low-income countries like Turkey, Portugal, and Spain have small shares of government, while the more advanced economies like Sweden, Denmark, the United Kingdom, Belgium, and Austria have large shares of government. For its level of economic development, the United States has a relatively low amount of government economic activity that is comparable to low-income countries like Chile, Italy, Ireland, and Brazil.

COST/BENEFIT ANALYSIS OF GOVERNMENT ACTIVITY

The single rule that guides the private sector's economic decision making has been repeated over and over again in this book: *Any economic activity should be carried out as long as its marginal revenue exceeds or equals its marginal cost.* The profit-maximizing firm expands its production to the point where marginal costs and marginal revenues are equal. The business firm carries out investment projects as long as the rate of return exceeds the interest rate.

Private decision making usually follows the logic of cost/benefit analysis. In principle, cost/

benefit analysis could play the same role in public decision making as it does in private decision making.

> *Cost/benefit analysis in the public sector requires the assessment of the costs and benefits of public-expenditure programs. Economic efficiency requires that a public-expenditure project be carried out as long as its marginal social benefit equals or exceeds its marginal social cost.*

The public-sector cost/benefit rule is similar to the private-sector profit-maximization rule. Instead of comparing a firm's marginal benefits and marginal costs, the marginal benefit *to society* is compared to *society's* marginal cost. A government project that yields $10 million in benefits while costing $5 million is worth undertaking according to this rule. A project that yields $50 million in benefits while costing $200 million should not be undertaken.

> *The optimal amount of government spending is that amount at which the marginal social costs and marginal social benefits of the last public expenditure program are equal.*

Government cost/benefit analysis is often difficult to apply. The major problem is how to assess the social costs and benefits of different government expenditure programs. If a dam is to be built that will benefit down-river communities with better flood control and cheaper electricity but will displace long-time residents or threaten an endangered species of fish with extinction, what cost/benefit price tags should be placed on the project? The private firm can readily assess its private costs and benefits, but in society at large there will often be substantial differences of opinion on costs and benefits.

Cost/benefit analysis also ignores questions of income distribution or equity. The benefits of a government program may go to one group and the costs may be imposed on another group. Unless the people who pay the costs are somehow compensated—which seldom occurs—the government program entails some redistribution of income.

Despite its problems, there has been an increasing trend towards the use of cost/benefit analysis in government. Many major government programs—such as dams, new highways, and labor-training programs—are being assessed in terms of costs and benefits.

A Substitute for the Market Test

In the private sector, the market provides safeguards to prevent costs from exceeding benefits. If private firms produce a product whose benefit to society (as reflected in its market price) is less than its cost, the firm will incur losses. In the long run, it will either go out of business or switch to producing products that yield a benefit equal to or greater than cost. This process is called the **market test.**

> *The **market test** is the process that ensures that goods and services in the private sector yield a benefit equal to or greater than their cost.*

Public goods are not subject to this market test. There is no guarantee that public expenditures will yield benefits equal to or greater than cost. One can argue that voters in a democratic society can always vote the politicians out of office or fire public officials who make unwise expenditures. However, if these decisions are made at high levels—say, in Washington—it is difficult for voters who cast their ballots every two or four years to voice by means of the ballot box their disagreement with specific government expenditures.

Publicly produced goods cannot satisfy everyone. In private markets, consumers buy what they want, for the most part. But as voters, people have to take the good with the bad. For example, a voter may support his or her congressional representative's position on defense spending but may oppose the representative's position on social security.

Should Programs Be Local or National?

At lower levels of government, however, the ballot box can often provide the market test on public expenditures. In municipal elections, voters are often asked to vote on specific expenditure projects (whether or not to issue bonds to build a new school, whether to raise police officers' salaries). At the local level, households can vote for public services "with their feet." Different communities offer different mixes of public expenditures. One community offers good schools but high property taxes. Another community offers low taxes but poor schools. Young couples with school-age children may choose to settle in the community with good schools; older couples or couples without children may settle in the community with low taxes and poor schools. In this manner, communities will provide the mix of public services that its residents desire.

The case for decentralization of public expenditures to the level of local government is persuasive but leaves important questions unresolved. By giving more responsibilities to the states and localities, government-spending decisions will be made by those in closest touch with local needs. The New Federalism Program of President Reagan proposes to turn certain major programs previously run by the federal government back to the states. Criticisms of increased state and local responsibility focus on the supposedly lesser competence and training of state and local bureaucrats and on the greater corruption at the local level.

Certain government programs can only be national in scope. The nation must have a uniform legal system. National defense can only be provided for the nation as a whole. Many government expenditure projects transcend state and local boundaries, such as the interstate highway system or a dam that affects several states. A whole range of public expenditures must be carried out above the local or even state level. Where the boundary is to be drawn between the various levels of government is a question that cannot be resolved by simple economic analysis.

PRINCIPLES OF TAXATION

To finance its expenditures, government—whether local, state, or federal—must have revenues. Taxation is the major source of general government revenue in the United States (see Table 3). Sales and charges for government products and services account for only a minor portion of government revenues. As Table 3 reports, 61.6 percent of government revenue is derived from taxes (income, sales, and property taxes), and 20.4 percent is derived from social-insurance con-

Table 3

Sources of Local, State, or Federal General Government Revenue, 1980

Source of Revenue	Percent of Total
Taxes	61.6
Individual income	30.7
Corporate income	8.4
Sales taxes	12.0
Property and other taxes	10.5
Social security, employee retirement, unemployment-insurance	20.4
Charges	15.3
Utilities and liquor stores	2.7
Total	**100.0**

Source: *Statistical Abstract of the United States,* 1981, p. 277.

tributions (primarily social security and unemployment insurance). The remaining 18 percent of government revenue is obtained through charges for products and services sold to buyers (postal services, tuition in state-run schools, public hospitals, government-run utilities, licenses, state liquor-store sales, and so on).

Distributing the Burden

Taxes have been with us since recorded history began, as has the debate over what constitutes a fair tax system. If people believe that taxes are unfairly levied, they will seek to evade taxes and will otherwise engage in taxpayer revolts. In some countries, tax evasion is an accepted social practice (see Example 1). In other countries, tax evasion is regarded as immoral. Public reaction depends upon whether the tax system is perceived as fair.

Over time, two principles of fairness have emerged. The first is the principle that the tax burden should be distributed according to benefits received. The second and opposing principle is that the tax burden should be distributed according to the ability to pay.

The Benefit Principle. The *benefit principle* of taxation states that those who benefit from the public expenditure that a tax finances should pay the tax. According to this principle, the persons

Example 1

Tax Evasion in Other Countries

Almost all countries—even the Soviet Union—have underground economies that generate earnings that are not taxed. The magnitude of underground untaxed earnings appears to depend upon tax rates. Swedish workers pay tax rates twice those of comparable American workers. As a consequence, Swedish workers enter the underground economy of bartered labor, work for cash only, and use other arrangements to avoid records of income earned. Despite efforts by Swedish authorities to discourage such activities, otherwise law-abiding Swedes are simply unwilling to pay the high tax rates required by Sweden's welfare state.

In Italy—a country with a cherished historical tradition of tax evasion—the underground economy is so large that economic planners must include it in their economic plans. It is estimated that one third of Italian workers are secretly employed, and income from underground labor is estimated at around 10 percent of GNP. Small firms are able to remain competitive in overseas markets by us-

ing hidden labor. Italian authorities fear that a crackdown on hidden labor would put too many people out of work and seriously damage the economy. Most Italian companies keep two books—one that records actual transactions and another prepared for tax authorities.

In Thailand, it is estimated that only 10 percent of the work force files tax returns. Virtually all products are exchanged under the table. Auto sellers offer cars at 10 to 30 percent off if the buyer pays cash and forgets about the deal. No one can even estimate the percentage of tax revenues lost to tax evasion.

Tax evasion is also practiced in the United States. Many taxpayers are tried and convicted for tax evasion, but the remarkable feature of the U.S. tax system is the relatively small magnitude of illegal tax evasion relative to other countries where tax evasion is a national pasttime.

Source: "Cheating on Taxes—A Worldwide Pursuit," *U.S. News and World Report,* October 22, 1979.

---

who benefit from a new state highway, from a new airport, or from a flood-control project—all financed from tax revenues—should be the ones to pay. If community members are not willing to pay for a public project—for example, if citizens vote against a flood-control project in their community—they are indicating that they do not consider the project's benefits to outweigh its costs. If all taxes were levied on the principle that the beneficiaries bear the full burden of the tax (and if the beneficiaries were given the opportunity to vote on each public expenditure), benefits of projects undertaken would exceed costs. One example of a benefit tax is a tax on gasoline that is used to finance highway construction. In many communities, special taxes are assessed for specific road repairs, streetlighting, and sidewalks.

One disadvantage of the benefit principle is that it is often difficult to identify the beneficiaries of different government expenditures. While it is obvious that automobile drivers benefit from public highways and that residents of New York City benefit from public expenditures on the New York subway system, it is often difficult to determine

who benefits and by what amount in the case of other public expenditures. Who benefits from national defense? Who benefits from police protection and from the legal system? Do the poor benefit more than the rich? Or is it the other way around? Who benefits most from the conduct of foreign policy? In order to apply the benefit principle, one must first know who is the beneficiary.

The Ability-to-Pay Principle. The second approach to fairness in the tax system is to tax on the basis of *the ability to pay*. This principle maintains that those better able to pay should bear the greater burden of taxes whether or not they benefit more from the resulting government expenditure. According to the principle, the rich may benefit less from public education and from publicly financed hospitals because they use private hospitals and send their children to private schools, but because they are better able to pay than the poor, they should bear a heavier burden.

A tax system that adopts the ability-to-pay principle must have both **vertical equity** and **horizontal equity.**

Vertical equity exists when those with a greater ability to pay bear a heavier tax burden.

Horizontal equity exists when those with equal abilities to pay pay the same amount of tax.

If vertical equity is lacking, then taxes are not being paid on an ability-to-pay basis. If horizontal equity is not present, then the ability-to-pay principle is being violated because taxpayers with equal abilities to pay are being treated differently.

Like the benefit principle, the ability-to-pay principle leaves important questions unresolved. How is ability to pay to be measured? If one uses income as an indicator, how does one adjust for differences in family size, catastrophic medical expenses, and families that are sending three children to college at once? If one uses money income as the measure, how does one account for nonpecuniary income arising from differences in leisure and work conditions? If one defines ability to pay in terms of family wealth rather than income, should the tax be levied on the basis of the value of stock, bonds, and real estate that a family owns? What about the elderly couple that owns a $1 million home, but has very little income?

Types of Taxes

A key feature of any tax system is whether taxes are used to redistribute income. An important ingredient of the redistributive impact of a tax system is the fraction of income each taxpayer must pay. A tax can be either a **proportional tax,** a **progressive tax,** or a **regressive tax**.

A proportional tax is one where each taxpaying unit pays the same percentage of its income as taxes.

A progressive tax is one where the higher is the income, the larger *is the percentage of income paid as taxes.*

A regressive tax is one where the higher is the income, the smaller *is the percentage of income paid as taxes.*

An example of a progressive tax is the federal income tax. In 1981, a married couple with $10,000 in taxable income paid $1,053 in taxes; a married couple with a $20,000 income paid $3,191; a married couple earning $40,000 paid taxes of $10,109. Taxes were about 10 percent of income for those with a $10,000 taxable income but more than 25 percent for those with a taxable income of $40,000.

An example of a regressive tax would be the sales tax because the wealthy spend a smaller portion of their income than poor people. For example, suppose the family with $40,000 of taxable income spends $20,000 and saves the rest, while the family with $10,000 taxable income spends the full $10,000. Each pays a 5 percent sales tax; the wealthy ($40,000) family pays sales taxes of $1,000, or 1/40th of its income, while the poor ($10,000) family pays sales taxes of $500, or 1/20th of its income. Although the poor family spends fewer dollars on sales tax, it spends a larger percentage of its income.

The people who believe that high-income families should pay a larger percentage of their income in taxes favor a progressive tax system. The supporters of a proportional tax system don't think the wealthy—who pay more taxes anyway when rates are constant—should pay a larger percentage of their income as taxes than the less affluent.

THE U.S. TAX SYSTEM

Society must decide for itself who should bear the burden of taxes. Society must resolve whether taxes are to be levied according to the ability-to-pay or the benefit principle and whether the tax system should be proportional, progressive, or regressive. Once these decisions are made, tax authorities must devise a tax system that fulfills these goals. At first glance, it seems simple. If society wants the rich to pay 40 percent of their income and the poor to pay 10 percent, then income-tax rates need only be set at 40 percent and 10 percent for these two groups. Right? Or, if society decides that cigarette manufacturers and big oil companies should pay a heavy share of taxes, then it must simply levy a tax on each carton of cigarettes and on each barrel of oil. Right?

The Incidence of Taxation

In reality, the individual or company that is being taxed is not necessarily the one who ends up actually bearing the full burden of the tax. In many cases, the **incidence of a tax** can be shifted to someone else.

*The **incidence of a tax** is the actual distribution of the burden of tax payment.*

For example, when a $1 tax is placed on each carton of cigarettes, cigarette manufacturers may reduce the supply of cigarettes to the market. When the price of cigarettes rises, the manufacturer has shifted the tax forward so that the consumer is paying at least part of the tax in the form of a higher price. If the price rises by $0.80 as a consequence of the $1 tax, then 80 percent of the tax has been shifted to the consumer, in which case most of the tax burden is borne not by the manufacturer but by the final consumer.

*A **tax is shifted to the consumer** when the consumer of the product being taxed pays a portion of the tax by paying a higher price for the product.*

Taxes can be shifted to suppliers of factors as well. If employers respond to the social-security payroll tax by reducing their demand for labor, the wage rate falls and the tax has been shifted from the employer to the supplier of labor: the employee. If a $50 monthly payroll tax for each employee causes wages to fall by $25, then the employer has shifted 50 percent of the tax to employees.

Virtually any tax—an income tax, a sales tax, a wealth tax, an inheritance tax, or a tariff on foreign goods—can be shifted. Some taxes can be shifted almost entirely to others; other taxes must be completely paid by the individual or organization that nominally pays the tax. An increase in income-tax rates may persuade physicians to reduce their patient load. If physicians generally reduce their supply of labor, physicians' fees (prices) rise. Who has paid the tax? Surprisingly, the patient pays a portion of the tax in the form of higher doctors' bills. If the government places

a tax on imported cars, who pays? If automobile prices rise, purchasers of cars pay in the form of higher automobile prices.

To determine whether a tax system is progressive, regressive, or proportional, one must first determine the incidence of taxation. If the rich are taxed at highly progressive rates, yet shift their taxes to the poor, then progressive taxation is only an illusion.

Federal Taxes

More than 90 percent of federal tax receipts are from taxes that are related to income. Individual income taxes account for 45.6 percent of federal revenues; social-security contributions account for 31.0 percent, and corporation income taxes account for another 13.8 percent.

The Federal Individual Income Tax. The major source of federal tax revenues is the individual income tax. Individual income-tax liabilities are determined by applying a tax schedule to taxable income.

In the United States (for income earned in 1981), taxes were 0 percent (no taxes) on taxable income below $3,400 for a married couple filing a joint return. Graduated income-tax rates varied from 14 percent of taxable income to 70 percent, but the maximum tax on income from labor (personal service income) was set at 50 percent. The maximum tax on unearned income (interest, dividends, profits) was set at 70 percent. For example, a married couple with a taxable income of $20,000 paid in 1981 a tax of $3,191, or 16 percent of taxable income. On a $60,000 taxable income, a married couple paid 33 percent of their taxable income.

In 1981, Congress passed the Economic Recovery Act, which made substantial changes in the federal income tax. The Economic Recovery Act was to be implemented between October 1981 and July 1983 and calls for the reduction of individual income-tax rates from the 1980 range of 14 percent to 70 percent to the new range of 11 percent to 50 percent. The overall rate reduction is approximately 25 percent. The law also reduced the maximum tax on unearned income from 70 percent to 50 percent, so that all forms of in-

Example 2

Reaganomics and Taxes

The Reagan Administration has emphasized the disincentive effects of high marginal tax rates. In 1981, the President's Economic Recovery Act was passed by Congress—an act that will lower substantially the marginal tax rates of American taxpayers between 1982 and 1984. From 1985 on, tax rates will be indexed to the U.S. inflation rate to prevent taxpayers from being pushed into higher tax brackets by inflationary increases in taxable income.

What is unusual about the timing of the Reagan tax cut is that it was adopted during a period of rapid inflation. Conventional wisdom would not call for lower taxes during inflations for fear that the additional consumer spending would worsen inflation. The Reagan tax cut, however, was based upon the notions of "supply-side" economists.

Reagan's advisors argued that a tax reform that substantially lowers the marginal tax rates of taxpayers and of businesses will cause a substantial increase in economic output. With more available income, people will work harder and more effectively and risks will be incurred more willingly, according to these advisors. The increased output will lessen inflationary pressures as more goods are placed on the market.

The Economic Recovery Act may ultimately be amended significantly by a Congress worried about a $150 billion federal deficit. If it survives intact, it remains to be seen over the next few years whether the "supply-siders" are correct in their vision that large increases in output can be obtained by lowering marginal tax rates.

---

come would be subject to the same maximum rate.[1]

The effect of highly progressive tax rates is softened by the numerous deductions and exemptions from taxable income allowed by law. These deductions and exemptions are often called *tax loopholes* and have aroused the fury of tax reformers over the years. Items excluded from taxable income reduce individual tax liabilities in three ways: 1) by deducting some forms of income from taxable income, 2) by deducting certain expenditures from taxable income, and 3) by deducting personal exemptions from taxable income.

Some forms of income are not included in reported income. The first $400 of dividends are exempted. Interest paid on bonds of local and state government (so-called *tax-exempt bonds*) is also excluded from income. Interest earned on *all-saver certificates* under the 1982 tax law is not included in taxable income. Transfer payments are not counted as a part of income. Certain contributions to retirement programs (Individual Retirement Accounts and Keogh Accounts) are not counted in taxable income.

The most important exclusion from taxable income is 60 percent of a **realized capital gain.**

A realized capital gain is income gained when property is sold at a higher price than its purchase price. According to current tax laws, the capital gain is long-term if the asset is held longer than one year.

If someone sells stocks, bonds, or real property that have been owned for at least one year for a profit, only 40 percent of this profit must be included as income. The preferential treatment of capital gains means that the highest tax rate on capital-gains income (as of 1982) is 20 percent (40 percent of the capital gain times 50 percent, the maximum tax rate).

The government allows taxpayers to deduct *certain expenditures* (taxes paid to state and local government, medical expenditures, interest payments, charitable contributions, fire and theft losses, and child-care costs for working mothers)

---

1. In the early 1950s, the maximum tax rate (on incomes of $200,000 and above) was 92 percent. Since then maximum rates have been lowered.

from taxable income. These deductions are called *itemized deductions*. There are two rationales for itemized deductions. The first is that adjustments should be made for special and unusual circumstances that affect one's ability to pay taxes. The family that has had catastrophic medical expenses or the family that has lost its home to fire has a reduced ability to pay income taxes. Other deductions are designed to encourage certain expenditures: the itemized interest deduction encourages home ownership; deductions for charitable contributions encourage voluntary giving to worthy charities; deductions of taxes paid to local and state governments protect taxpayers against excessively high tax rates from the combination of all government taxes and give state and local governments the opportunity to gather revenues.[2]

Personal exemptions can also be deducted from taxable income. Each family member is allowed a personal exemption of $1,000, and extra exemptions are allowed for those over 65 and for the blind. A family of four with one family member over 65 would have 5 personal exemptions and would subtract $5,000 from its income (5 times $1,000). The major function of personal exemptions is to differentiate among families of different sizes and circumstances that have the same income.

Taxable income is what remains after all deductions and exemptions are subtracted. The tax schedule is applied to taxable income, not to actual income. If substantial subtractions are made, the difference between income and taxable income can be great.

Deductions from taxable income cause an erosion of the tax base. Figures for 1976 (Table 4) show the effect of each type of exclusion on the tax base. After all exemptions and deductions, taxable income is only about 48 percent of personal income. Deductions erode the tax base by about one half.

The **effective tax rate** measures the ratio of tax liability to adjusted gross income (adjusted gross income is essentially personal income minus

2. Not all taxpayers itemize deductions. Individuals who do not have large itemized deductions are permitted to deduct a *standard deduction,* which currently is set at 10 percent of adjusted gross income (or at a maximum of $3,400 for a married couple).

Table 4

Relationship Between Personal Income and Taxable Income, 1976

Income	Amount (billions of dollars)	Percent of Personal Income
Personal income	1,380.9	100.0
minus		
Exclusions	−377.0	−27.3
equals		
Adjusted gross income	1,003.9	72.7
minus		
Itemized deductions	−207.0	−15.0
minus		
Personal exemptions	−128.2	−9.3
equals		
Taxable income	668.7	48.4

Source: Tax Foundation, *Facts and Figures on Government Finance,* 27th biennial ed., 1979, p. 108.

personal business expenses, contributions to retirement programs, and moving expenses).

*The **effective tax rate** is the percent of the actual tax payment to adjusted gross income. Effective tax rates show the effect of deductions and exclusions on tax rates.*

The effective tax rate is reduced by each deduction made from taxable income. Effective tax rates for different earnings levels are given in Table 5. Effective tax rates for a four-person family range from 4.5 percent for an adjusted gross income of $10,000 to 50.4 percent for an income of $1 million. Although the nominal tax rates call for a $50,000 tax (50 percent) on $100,000, the *effective tax rate* on a $100,000 income after the erosion of the tax base is 32.9 percent.

Social Security and Payroll Taxes. Since it was founded in 1935, the social-security system has been financed by a payroll tax, half of which is paid by the employer and half of which is paid by the employee. Unlike the individual income tax, where deductions exempt low-income families from paying the tax, social-security payroll taxes are paid starting with the first dollar of earn-

Table 5

Effective Tax Rates for a Married Couple with Two Dependents, 1978

Income Level (dollars)	Effective Tax Rate (percent)
10,000	4.5
15,000	9.2
25,000	13.8
50,000	22.2
100,000	32.9
250,000	44.1
500,000	49.8
1,000,000	50.4

Source: Tax Foundation, *Facts and Figures on Government Finance*, 20th ed., 1979, p. 105.

ings. In 1982, the payroll tax was 13.4 percent of the first $32,400 of earnings with the employer paying one half of the tax. For example, a worker earning $15,000 per year paid $1,005 in payroll taxes (the employer paid the same sum). Because the tax is imposed only on the first $32,400, an employee earning $500,000 would pay the same tax as one earning $32,400. For this reason, the social-security payroll tax is a regressive tax. In 1979 (when the payroll tax was a smaller percent of a smaller maximum income), for example, a typical employee earning $10,000 paid a payroll tax of 12.3 percent (and a personal income tax of 3.7 percent); while an employee earning $50,000 paid a payroll tax of 5.6 percent and an income tax of 21.7 percent.

Not all workers belong to the social-security system. Federal employees and some state-government employees have their own retirement programs, as do railroad workers.

Social-security payroll taxes finance the social-security retirement, health, and disability programs. The medicare program that subsidizes medical care for the elderly is part of the social-security system. Retirement benefits depend upon average monthly earnings during the years the worker paid into the program. According to 1976 benefit schedules, a worker retiring at age 65 would receive $108 per month if his or her average earnings had been $76 per month, and would receive $516 if his or her earnings had averaged

$1,000 per month. The poor worker receives retirement benefits greater than what earnings were while working, while the retired worker who had higher earnings ($1,000 per month) receives about one half of previous earnings. The fact that poor workers can draw monthly benefits in excess of their monthly contributions is felt to soften the regressive nature of contributions to the system.

Corporation Income Taxes. Corporations are subject to a federal tax on their profits. Corporation income tax rates in 1982 started at 16 percent for corporations with earnings of $25,000 per year, rose to 19 percent for the next $25,000, and then rose to a maximum of 46 percent on earnings in excess of $100,000. Like the individual income tax, the corporation income tax has provisions that erode the tax base. The major loopholes are the *investment tax credit* (which enables corporations to deduct up to 10 percent of the value of new capital equipment directly from their tax liabilities), fast depreciation write-offs, and special treatment for the minerals industry. Proposed changes in tax laws would permit corporations with losses to, in effect, transfer these losses to profitable corporations so that they can reduce their tax liabilities. Economists have estimated that the average effective tax rate for corporations is little more than 35 percent. The effective tax rate varies considerably by industry.[3]

Corporate profits that are distributed to stockholders as dividends are taxed twice. The profits are taxed once as corporate income and taxed again as "unearned" income when stockholders receive their dividends (see the chapter on business organization for a more detailed discussion of the effects of double taxation). Many public-finance specialists have argued against the double taxation of corporate dividends, and some propose that there be one tax on income because the double taxation of dividends discourages the paying out of dividends.

Excise, Customs, and Gift Taxes. A small proportion of federal tax receipts (about 7.5 percent) is gathered from **excise taxes, customs duties,** and **gift taxes.**

3. George Break and Joseph Pechman, *Federal Tax Reform: The Impossible Dream?* (Washington, D.C.: Brookings Institution, 1975), p. 91.

Excise taxes are per-unit taxes on the production or sale of specific goods or services.
Customs duties are taxes on the transfer of certain goods from one country into another.
Gift taxes are taxes on the transfer of property from one owner to another.

Federal excise taxes are levied on a wide range of goods and services including alcohol, cigarettes, gasoline, tires, firearms, telephones, airline tickets, and trucks.

State and Local Taxes

State and local governments must also finance their expenditures, but taxpayers are more heavily burdened by the federal income tax. Moreover, state and local governments must be careful not to tax their constituents markedly more than neighbor governments for fear of losing population and industry. One reason for allowing taxpayers to deduct tax payments to state and local governments from taxable income on their federal tax returns is to give state and local governments the opportunity to raise revenues without exhausting the taxpaying capacity of their citizens. It has even been proposed (but never implemented) that the federal government give a tax credit (of, say, 50 percent) on taxes paid for state income taxes. Under such circumstances, for every $100 in state taxes, one's federal income tax would be reduced by $50.

Unlike the federal government that relies heavily on income taxes for its revenues, state and local governments obtain only 11.8 percent of their revenue from individual and corporate income taxes. Property and sales taxes yield 36.1 percent of revenue. Payroll taxes for employee retirement and unemployment compensation contribute another 9.6 percent. The major single source of revenue is revenue from the federal government for public welfare, highways, education, and unemployment compensation, which accounts for 18.7 percent of state and local revenues.

The federal government is a major financier of state and local programs. The manner in which federal assistance is handled has been a controversial issue over the years. Those disturbed by the growing importance of Washington maintain that the federal government should provide money to state and local governments with no strings attached. The argument is that the federal government has preempted state and local governments by imposing heavy federal taxes, leaving the taxpayer with limited capacity to pay state and local taxes. This no-strings approach is called *revenue sharing*. It is argued that revenue sharing would allow state and local governments to make their own decisions on how to spend money. State and local governments, the advocates of revenue sharing maintain, are better judges of where the money is really needed. At present, only 1.8 percent of state- and local-government revenues are from revenue sharing. Federal funds are granted primarily as grants-in-aid for specific programs. In other words, federal money is granted for a specific purpose, and the states are obligated to spend the money as instructed by the federal government.

Is the U.S. Tax System Progressive?

The U.S. tax system consists of different taxes at the local, state, and federal level. The federal tax system relies primarily on individual income taxes, corporation income taxes, and payroll taxes. State and local governments use sales and property taxes to raise their revenues. The federal individual income tax is progressive: effective tax rates are higher the higher is the income of the taxpayer. Social-security payroll taxes are regressive: families with low wages pay a higher percentage of their income. Sales taxes are generally considered regressive because the poor spend a larger percentage of their income on the items taxed than do the rich.

When all these taxes are combined, is the overall U.S. tax system regressive, proportional, or progressive? Is the progressivity of the federal individual income tax strong enough to outweigh the regressivity of payroll taxes and sales taxes? To answer this question, economists must first determine the incidence of taxation.

It is very difficult to estimate the incidence of taxation. Economists who have worked on this question disagree substantially on the distribution

Figure 4
Two Views of the Tax Burden

(a) Pechman-Okner, 1970

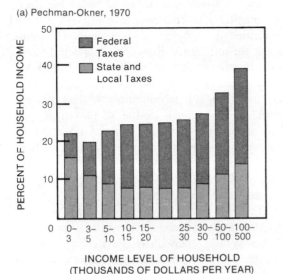

(b) Browning-Johnson, 1972

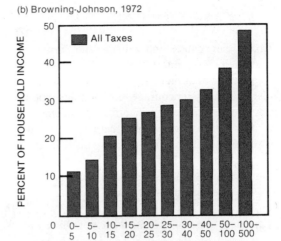

Browning and Johnson's findings indicate that the U.S. tax system is more progressive than Pechman and Okner's findings suggest. Both studies assumed that the most progressive tax incidence conditions applied.

Sources: Joseph A. Pechman and Benjamin Okner, *Who Bears the Tax Burden?* (Washington, D.C.: Brookings, 1974), p. 64; Edgar K. Browning and William R. Johnson, *The Distribution of the Tax Burden* (Washington, D.C.: American Enterprise Institute, 1979).

of the burden of taxes among different income groups.

In a major study of taxes, Joseph Pechman and Benjamin Okner concluded that the U.S. tax system is basically proportional. According to their study, only the very poor (those in the bottom 5 percent of the income distribution) and the very rich (those in the top 5 percent) do pay a higher proportion of their incomes in taxes. But for other families, the percentage of income paid in taxes is basically uniform. The Pechman and Okner results are shown in panel (a) of Figure 4.[4]

A study by Edgar Browning and William Johnson disputes the conclusions of Pechman and Okner.[5] Browning and Johnson find that the overall tax system is highly progressive, as shown in panel (b) of Figure 4. Families in the bottom 10 percent of the income distribution pay 10.7 per-

cent of their income as taxes, while families in the top 10 percent pay 46.4 percent of their income.

Why is it that these two studies come to such different conclusions? The basic point of disagreement is the incidence of sales taxes. Browning and Johnson argue that the transfer payments received by the poor (social security, welfare, and so on) are raised almost automatically when prices rise because transfer payments are adjusted for inflation. If a sales tax causes prices to rise, the price increase will not be passed on to the poor because the poor's incomes will rise along with the price. Therefore, sales taxes are not regressive as had been thought but are actually progressive because they are shifted primarily to the rich.

The difference of opinion over the burden of the tax system is an explosive issue. If the tax burden is indeed heavier on the poor than on the rich, tax reformers could argue that the rich should be taxed more heavily. On the other hand, if the current tax system is as progressive as

4. Joseph Pechman and Benjamin Okner, *Who Bears the Tax Burden?* (Washington, D.C.: Brookings Institution, 1974).
5. Edgar K. Browning and William R. Johnson, *The Distribution of the Tax Burden* (Washington, D.C.: American Enterprise Institute, 1979).

Browning and Johnson find, then society may be content with the existing system.

TAXES AND EFFICIENCY

Taxes can cause individuals and firms to change their economic behavior. Tax laws that give favorable treatment to capital gains and tax dividends doubly encourage corporations not to pay dividends. Increases in effective income-tax rates may cause high-income earners to reduce their supply of effort. High property taxes in areas with good schools will affect relocation decisions. Sales taxes may reduce supply and cause prices to rise. Few taxes are **neutral taxes.**

> A **neutral tax** is a tax that does not cause any change in private production, consumption, or investment decisions.

The goal of any economy is to obtain a maximum output from its limited resources. Economies would like to operate on their production-possibilities frontiers. If taxes cause output to be less than what could have been produced without the tax, then the tax has reduced the efficiency of the economy.

Some public-finance specialists favor a *neutral tax system* that leaves private economic actions unchanged. Others argue that a neutral tax system is impractical and that the tax system should be used to actively promote economic goals. If a government wishes to discourage alcohol consumption, for example, it should place a heavy tax on alcoholic beverages; if a government wishes to encourage home ownership, it should provide income-tax breaks to homeowners. If a government wishes to encourage marriages, it should place a heavier tax burden on singles.

Public-finance specialists agree that it is very difficult, if not impossible, to devise a neutral tax system. Any tax that individuals could reduce as a consequence of their actions is not neutral. If a tax is neutral, individuals cannot alter their tax liabilities by taking actions to reduce it. A $1,000 tax on each adult male between the ages of 20 and 55 would be a neutral tax because there is nothing the taxpayer can do to avoid or reduce the tax (outside of a sex-change operation). But such a tax would violate both the benefit principle and

the ability-to-pay principle and would not be widely accepted.

Taxes will continue to affect economic decision making. The challenge to politicians and tax authorities is to devise a tax system that minimizes the efficiency losses of nonneutral taxes while moving society in the direction of desirable social goals. If income taxes must be progressive, what tax system minimizes the loss of work effort? If government desires to encourage private homeownership, how can this objective be achieved in the least disruptive manner and with as little abuse as possible?

Taxes and Work Effort

Labor supply decisions are often affected by the tax system. Individuals, in deciding whether to work overtime, in deciding whether both husband and wife should work, or in deciding whether to play golf one or two days a week, examine their **marginal tax rate.**

> A **marginal tax rate** is the ratio of the increase in taxes to the increase in taxable income.

The distinction between average and marginal tax rates is important. Suppose Ann Smith is a physician who earns $150,000 annually and who pays an effective tax rate of 40 percent. Smith pays $60,000 a year in taxes and her average tax rate is 40 percent. If working a few more hours per week would increase her taxable income by $50,000 (from $150,000 to $200,000), her taxes would rise to $90,000. The $50,000 increase in taxable income would cause taxes to rise by $30,000. Her marginal tax rate, then, is the ratio of the increase in taxes ($30,000) to the increase in earnings ($50,000), or 60 percent.

Marginal tax rates are important because taxpayers tend to base their economic decisions on marginal tax rates rather than on average tax rates. For example, faced with a marginal tax rate of 60 percent, Smith may decide it is not worth the extra effort to earn an additional $50,000 of taxable income if she can only keep $20,000 of it. If she decides not to work the extra hours, economic efficiency has been reduced because the economy is producing fewer goods and services than it would have without the tax.

Some tax reformers favor a lowering of marginal tax rates to encourage greater work effort. The theory is that a lowering of marginal tax rates would give individuals a greater incentive to work extra hours, for homemakers to enter the work force, and for greater entrepreneurial risks to be taken. The proponents of lower marginal tax rates argue that the output of goods and services would increase without a change in the underlying resource base; that is, lower marginal tax rates would improve economic efficiency.

Tax Wedges

In addition to reducing work incentives, taxes reduce economic efficiency in a second way by driving a wedge between the prices consumers pay and the prices producers receive. For example, when a $1 per gallon sales tax on gasoline is imposed that is to be paid by the producer, the producer bases production decisions on the price of gasoline minus the $1 tax. For the producer's purposes, a $3 price per gallon yields only $2 per gallon after the tax. The consumer bases consumption decisions on the $3 retail price even though the producer is basing decisions on a $2 net price. The tax has driven a wedge between the two sides of the market. The end result is that producers will produce to the point where their net price (after the tax) equals their marginal cost. The price the consumer is willing to pay for a given quantity reflects the marginal benefit that the good provides to society and will be above the marginal cost of society's resources necessary for producing that quantity of the good.

Workability

In addition to being fair, a good tax system must be *simple* and *certain* and must have reasonable *compliance and collection costs*. A tax is *simple* if taxpayers can determine their tax liability without substantial costs. The tax system should not force people to bear large accounting and legal costs. A tax is *certain* if taxpayers are able to ascertain the tax consequences of their actions when they make their economic decisions. The rules of the game must be known by all, and changes in the rules of the game should not affect actions that have already been taken. The tax sys-

tem should not have high collection costs. A tax is inefficient if it costs almost as much to collect as the tax brings in.

FEDERAL TAX REFORM

Our system of federal taxation has evolved over the years through a series of tax reforms, legislative amendments, and court interpretations. The present tax system is a maze of regulations that supports the legion of professional accountants and tax specialists that are needed to advise the taxpaying public.

Can our existing system of tax collection be made significantly more efficient or equitable through tax reform? Public-finance specialists have recommended over the years a number of reforms of the existing system.[6]

Taxing Consumption, not Income

Currently, personal taxes are levied on personal income. The more one earns, the higher one's income-tax payments. Numerous distinguished economists and social thinkers—John Stuart Mill, Irving Fisher, Alfred Marshall, Thomas Hobbes, and Nicholas Kaldor—have supported taxing consumption rather than income for two reasons. First, supporters of this reform believe people should be taxed according to what they take out of production (consumption) rather than according to what they put in (saving). Society benefits from saving by gaining a larger stock of capital. Second, reformers argue that expenditures are a more accurate measure of a household's permanent spending power or ability to pay taxes than is income. Taxpayers could reduce consumption-tax payments by spending less (and saving more).

Consumption taxes are typically collected as sales taxes. The *value added tax* (or VAT) that is used in Europe is a prime example of a consumption tax. As already noted, sales taxes tend to be regressive, but must a consumption tax be regressive? Public-finance specialists argue that con-

6. For a collection of studies by public finance experts on tax reform, see: Michael J. Boskin, ed., *Federal Tax Reform: Myths and Realities* (San Francisco: Institute for Contemporary Studies, 1978).

sumption taxes, like income taxes, can be made progressive if society so desires. For example, taxpayers could report their income minus savings (which would equal their consumption) and then tax income minus savings using progressive tax rates.

Indexing Tax Rates to Inflation

In a progressive income tax system, as nominal incomes rise taxpayers are pushed into higher and higher marginal tax brackets. Since inflation tends to raise nominal incomes, many economists believe that progressive tax systems should be indexed to the rate of inflation. In a tax system indexed to the rate of inflation, the tax rate would fall as inflation rises. If the tax system is fully indexed, the after-tax real income of taxpayers would not decline as a consequence of inflation. The indexing of tax rates to inflation is a fairly simple reform. It is already in use in Canada and other countries. The Reagan Economic Recovery Act of 1981 currently calls for an indexing of the U.S. federal income tax to begin in 1984.

Integrating Personal and Corporate Income Taxes

As explained in an earlier chapter, corporations are useful devices for raising capital in a world of costly information and uncertainty. Many economists argue that taxing corporate income reduces the social gains obtained from this institutional innovation. The double taxation of corporate income through the double taxation of dividends dams up billions of dollars of investment funds inside corporate treasuries and thus encourages investment of retained earnings by the corporation itself. Eliminating the tax on corporate dividends would free these funds up for their best employment. The elimination of the corporate income tax would be opposed by many as a pro-business reform, but economists Martin Feldstein and Daniel Frisch have estimated the *social* loss due to the corporation income tax at $4 billion to $6 billion per year at 1976 income levels.[7]

7. Martin Feldstein and Daniel Frisch, "Corporate Tax Integration: The Estimated Effects on Capital Accumulation and Tax Distribution of Two Integration Proposals," *Discussion Paper 541* (Cambridge, Mass.: Harvard University Institute of Economic Research, 1980).

Taxing only Real Capital Gains

The current tax system—although it does give favorable treatment to realized capital gains—does not adjust for the effects of inflation. Stock purchased 10 years ago may have doubled in value, but if prices have doubled as well, the investor is no better off in terms of purchasing power. Presumably, inflation would reduce the incentive to invest and to take risks. If only *real* capital gains were taxed—that is, if capital gains were taxed only after adjustment for inflation—investors would have an added incentive to take risks.

Eliminating the Marriage Penalty

According to the current tax system, both husband and wife generally benefit by filing a joint income-tax return and splitting their income. When married couples split their income, they are taxed as if each of them had earned half of their combined income. Income splitting works to the advantage of a couple if one spouse earns considerably more than the other. If both partners earn about the same amount, they may pay more than if they were each single because of the so-called **marriage penalty.** The marriage penalty violates horizontal and vertical equity.

> The **marriage penalty** is the increase in taxes paid by a married couple over what their combined tax payment would be if they were filing as two singles. The marriage penalty results when their combined salary pushes them into a tax bracket with a higher tax rate than either of the two lower tax rates.

Because of the marriage penalty, one partner may find his or her earnings taxed at a very high marginal tax rate, and the couple may conclude that the partner should not work because earnings after taxes are small. Insofar as the supply of labor of secondary workers (such as married women) is highly elastic with respect to after-tax income, income splitting causes a loss of economic output.[8]

8. The 1981 Economic Recovery Act reduces the marriage penalty by allowing married couples filing joint returns to deduct 10 percent of $30,000 or 10 percent of the earned income of the spouse with the lower income, whichever is smaller.

This chapter examined how government collects revenues and spends income and the effects of taxes and government expenditures on private economic activity. The next chapter will explore the reasons why government activity may be necessary to correct certain failures in the private economy.

Summary

1. Public finance studies government expenditures and revenues. It examines the effects of government taxes and spending on private economic activity. Government expenditures are either exhaustive expenditures or transfer payments. Exhaustive expenditures divert resources to the public sector. Transfer payments affect the distribution of income in the private sector. Government expenditures of all kinds account for about 33 percent of GNP. Government spending rose from 10 percent of GNP in the late 1920s to 33 percent in the 1980s. Expenditures shifted away from local government to state and federal government. The relative size of government in the U.S. does not appear to be exceptionally large by international standards.

2. Cost/benefit analysis applied to government spending suggests that government spending should be carried to the point where marginal social benefits and marginal social costs are equal. Cost/benefit analysis could serve as a substitute for the market test that private goods must pass. Local programs stand a greater chance of passing the cost/benefit test.

3. There are two competing principles of fairness in taxation. One is that taxes should be levied according to benefits received. The other is that taxes should be allocated on the basis of ability to pay. If the ability-to-pay principle is used, the tax system should have both vertical and horizontal equity. Progressive tax rates rise with income, regressive tax rates fall with income, and proportional tax rates do not change with income.

4. Federal taxes rely most heavily on individual income taxes, payroll taxes, and corporation profits taxes. State and local governments use primarily sales and property taxes. Although tax rates on taxable income are highly progressive, effective tax rates are lower because of the exclusions and deductions (loopholes) allowed by law that erode the tax base by almost 50 percent. There is no agreement on how progressive the U.S. tax system is. Two major studies of this question are in sharp disagreement.

5. A neutral tax system is one that does not cause production, consumption, and investment decisions to change. In reality, neutral taxes are almost impossible to devise. Taxes do affect economic efficiency. The challenge is how to devise a tax system that moves the economy in a socially desired direction without severe losses of efficiency. A tax system should be simple and certain and should not involve large collection costs.

6. Proposals for federal income tax reform call for taxing expenditures not income, indexing marginal tax rates to the rate of inflation, integrating the personal and corporate income tax, taxing real capital gains, and reducing the effects of income splitting by married couples.

Key Terms

public finance
exhaustive expenditures
transfer payments
market test
vertical equity
horizontal equity
proportional tax
progressive tax
regressive tax
incidence of a tax
realized capital gain
effective tax rate
excise taxes
customs duties
gift taxes
neutral tax
marginal tax rate
marriage penalty

Questions and Problems

1. Explain how the market test for private spending balances costs and benefits and how cost/benefit analysis may substitute for the market test in the case of public spending.

2. Explain how "voting with one's feet" may make local-government spending more efficient than national-government spending.

3. Explain the different principles of fairness in taxation. Why can't the benefit principle simply be applied to all taxes?

4. What is meant by vertical and horizontal equity in a tax system?

5. Mr. Jones has a taxable income of $25,000. He pays a tax of $5,000. Ms. Smith has a taxable income of $50,000. How much tax would Smith have to pay for the tax system to be a) proportional? b) progressive? c) regressive?

6. "A tax on shoe sales that requires the dealer to pay a $2 tax on every pair of shoes sold should not be of concern to consumers because the dealer has to pay the tax." Evaluate this statement.

7. Define the following terms: a) *effective tax rate* and b) *erosion of the tax base*.

8. Explain double taxation of corporations.

9. Why is there a trade-off between equity and efficiency in any tax system?

10. When Jones's taxable income increases by $1,000, Jones's income tax increases by $200. What is Jones's marginal tax rate?

11. Explain why a consumption tax would likely result in a higher national saving rate than an income tax.

21

Market Failure: Energy and the Environment

Chapter Preview

This chapter will discuss the reasons for government intervention in the economy. Government intervention is usually justified as an attempt to deal with one of five problems that the market fails to deal with on its own: 1) monopoly power, 2) macroeconomic instability, 3) poverty, 4) externalities, and 5) the provision of public goods. Previous chapters examined government action in relation to monopoly, macroeconomic instability, and poverty. This chapter tries to accomplish four things: First, it restates the economics of externalities (introduced in an earlier chapter) and shows the circumstances under which government action is necessary. Second, it examines the most important case for government action—the provision of

public goods. Third, the chapter outlines the failure of the market to achieve voluntary cooperation or a fair income distribution. Finally, in describing the economics of nonrenewable resources, the chapter raises the question of whether government intervention is necessary to protect the interests of future generations who have to live with the energy resources left by the present generation.

EXTERNALITIES AND EFFICIENCY

An **externality** is present whenever there is a divergence between private costs (or benefits) and social costs (or benefits):

*An **externality** exists when a producer or consumer does not bear the full marginal cost or enjoy the full marginal benefit of an economic action.*

For example, a factory imposes external cleaning or health-care costs on the community by polluting its air or water. The unique feature of these costs is that they are not paid by the factory, but by economic agents external to the factory. The factory does not have to pay the cleaning and health-care costs it imposes on the community; they do not show up anywhere in the factory's accounting.

On the other hand, a consumer who pays for an education is not the only one who benefits from that education. Society benefits when individuals receive education because education provides a common culture and language and encourages scientific progress.

Social costs = private costs + external costs. Social benefits = private benefits + external benefits.

As noted in an earlier chapter, whenever externalities are present, perfect competition does not lead to economic efficiency.

Social efficiency requires that marginal social benefits and marginal social costs be equal, but private participants equate marginal private benefits with marginal private costs.

When externalities are present, the polluting competitive firm produces too much output because the firm produces that level of output at which private marginal costs and private marginal benefits are equal; it ignores the external costs of its actions. At the profit-maximizing level of output marginal social costs exceed marginal social benefits. Society as a whole would be better off if the factory reduced its output to the point where marginal social costs and marginal social benefits are equal.

Internalizing Externalities

When externalities are present, market transactions between two parties will have harmful or beneficial effects on third parties. The effects are external to the price system and are not the outcome of mutual agreement between all the interested parties.

Examples of the harmful effects of externalities are not hard to find. Pollution of the air and water by industry and by the private car impose substantial external costs on the community. Ocean fishing grounds tend to be depleted because of the failure of one commercial fishing business to consider the external costs it imposes on others by overfishing. Modern skyscrapers built with reflective glass impose external costs on neighboring buildings by raising their air-conditioning costs. The buffalo almost became extinct because of the overkilling on the part of individual buffalo hunters who failed to consider the external costs imposed on others by overkilling.

Economists agree that externalities cause departures from the social optimum, and they are generally agreed about the manner in which to solve the externality problem. The individual consumer or producer must include the internal costs or benefits in its calculations of private gain. The solution is to internalize, or put a private price tag on, externalities. This price must be paid by the one imposing the cost or received by the one imposing the benefit.

Internalization of an externality is the process of putting private price tags on external costs or benefits.

If an economic agent pays for the costs imposed on others or receives a price for the benefits that others experience, it will take into account such costs and benefits in private cost/benefit calculations. An externality can be internalized in three ways: 1) by redefining property rights, 2) by making voluntary agreements, or 3) by taxing or subsidizing the externality generator.

Redefinition of Property Rights. Property rights specify who owns a resource and who has the right to use that resource. Many externalities are caused by poorly defined property rights. Do firms or the community own the property rights to the air people breathe? Who owns the property rights to fish the seas? If the property rights for a resource are held by the community, but each person has free access to the resource, the resource

Cattle Grazing:
Externalities and Property Rights

Cattle grazing is an example of how externalities can be internalized by changing property rights. Before the establishment of private property rights for grazing land, cattle owners allowed the common grazing property to be overgrazed. No one owned grazing land (or could enforce property rights by keeping other cattle off their property); and individual cattle owners did not have to consider the costs they imposed on other cattle owners by allowing their cattle to wander and graze at will.

The barbed-wire fence gave cattle owners the technological and legal ability to enforce private-property rights. By keeping their fences repaired (and keeping others out with their six-shooters), owners of grazing land were able to restrict the use of their grazing land to their own cattle. If overgrazing occurred, the owners would bear the private costs of overgrazing. The barbed-wire fence internalized the externality. The individual owner of cattle now had the incentive to prevent grazing land from being ruined by overgrazing.

◤

will likely be exploited and abused. Fishing businesses will overfish ocean waters; factories will overpollute the air.

If private property rights for the resource could be established, the externality would likely disappear. For example, if one person in the community were somehow given ownership of the community's air, that person would have the legal right to charge the polluting factory for its use of the air. If one country held the property rights to the ocean's fishing grounds, it could charge fishing businesses from all countries for their use of the ocean.

As these examples show, it is not easy to eliminate externalities by changing property rights. Redefining property rights will not work when it is very costly to define or enforce property rights—as is the case for whales, which tend to be overkilled. How does one determine who owns the whales and how does one protect the owner's property rights? The case of pollution is another example of poorly defined property rights. If a car pollutes the air, it is impossible to redefine the property rights so that the owner of the car is the only person who breathes the polluted air. The ownership rights to clean air are too poorly defined to allow those with property rights to clean air to sue polluters.

Voluntary Agreements. Voluntary agreements between those that create the externality and third parties are a second means of internalizing externalities. The number of individuals involved in a voluntary agreement must be small in order to keep bargaining costs down and to prevent other parties from "riding free." With well-defined property rights, voluntary agreements negotiated through the legal system can internalize external costs.

The proposition that voluntary agreements can handle the externality problem is called *the Coase theorem,* after Ronald H. Coase of the University of Chicago. Basically, Coase argues that external costs and benefits can be internalized by negotiations among affected parties.

Coase gives the example of a rancher whose cattle occasionally stray onto a neighboring farm and damage the neighbor's crops. If the rancher were legally liable for the damage to the farmer, then private bargaining would result in a deal between the rancher and the farmer in which the farmer would be paid for the increased cost of growing crops imposed by the straying cattle. These extra costs would induce the rancher to reduce the size of the herd (or build better fences) and the potential externality would disappear. Likewise, efficiency would still result even if the rancher's cattle had the legal right to stray onto the farmer's land.

The farmer in this case would make a deal in which the rancher would agree to reduce the size of the herd or build a fence in return for a cash payment from the farmer. Again, when a price tag is placed on the externality, it disappears.

There is some evidence that economists have underestimated the ability of negotiated voluntary

Example 2

Different Methods of Controlling Pollution

Economists over the years have tended to favor pollution taxes as a way to internalize pollution externalities. Such pollution taxes could be quite flexible: the tax could be adjusted upward or downward to lower or raise pollution; administration would be relatively simple; markets responding to the laws of supply and demand would allocate resources; market prices and costs would still provide valuable information about private benefits and costs.

A pollution tax would ideally be implemented as follows: the pollution tax would be set to equal the marginal external cost per unit of output. If the polluting steel factory imposed $10 of external costs per ton of steel, a pollution tax of $10 per ton would be charged. The steel company's marginal private costs (including the tax) would then equal approximately the marginal social cost, and the steel company would be motivated to behave efficiently.

In the real world quantity standards are the method typically used to control pollution, as in the case of pollution-emission standards for automo-

bile pollution. Economists argue that pollution standards are not efficient. If every producer is forced to meet an arbitrary standard to reduce pollutants, the producers that are more efficient in reducing pollution will have to cut back on pollution the same amount as the relatively inefficient firms. Firms that are efficient at reducing pollution should reduce pollution more than the firms that are inefficient at reducing pollution in order to save scarce resources that the economy can use elsewhere.

A new idea advanced during the late 1970s by economists in the Environmental Protection Agency is to sell "rights to pollute." First, the government would establish the total volume of pollutants that could be safely emitted into the atmosphere in a particular region. It would then auction off the rights to emit this volume of pollutants to the highest bidders. By forcing firms to buy rights to pollute, external costs would be internalized, and the polluting firms would tend to produce an optimal amount of pollution.

---

agreements to solve externality problems. Nobel laureate, James Meade, used honey and apples as a classic example of externalities. The production of honey is stimulated by apple blossoms; the pollination of apple blossoms is facilitated by bees. Steven S. Cheung of the University of Washington discovered in his research that not even this seemingly clear-cut example is perfect.[1]

Cheung investigated the nectar and pollination business and found that they are bought and sold in the marketplace. He found, in the State of Washington where it is a lively business, that the beekeeper's fee for pollination is smaller the greater is the expected yield of honey because pollination improves honey production.

This example illustrates the Coase theorem that if small numbers are involved and bargaining costs are small the market will internalize the externality.

1. Steven S. Cheung, "The Fable of the Bees: An Economic Investigation," *Journal of Law and Economics,* April 1973.

Government Taxes and Subsidies. The third way for an externality to be internalized is for the government to impose corrective taxes or subsidies. When market transactions impose external costs, the volume of the transactions will exceed what is efficient because private agents ignore the costs imposed on others. If an appropriate tax is placed on the externality-generating action, the economic agent must take into account the costs imposed on others and will, accordingly, reduce the amount of activity to the point where marginal social costs equal marginal social benefits (the efficient level). When market transactions are accompanied by external benefits, the volume of transactions will fall short of the efficient level. In this case, a government subsidy will encourage the activity to increase to the efficient level.

This third approach to internalization is appropriate when private bargaining costs are too high and voluntary agreements cannot be reached. When the government steps in with corrective taxes or subsidies, the government takes on the bargaining costs of the private parties. If the externality affects many people, it is cheaper to use collective or government action to internalize the externality. If external costs are imposed on thousands of individuals, voluntary agreement among the affected parties is unlikely.

Externalities do not automatically require government action, however. Making collective decisions is costly in and of itself, and society must weigh the costs and benefits of government action. For example, a small externality is involved in the choice of what color shirt or tie to wear; outrageous dress may offend some people. Yet society cannot afford to use collective action to deal with all trivial external costs or benefits. On the other hand, the emission of highly toxic fumes by factories imposes substantial social costs that require government action.

Both government action to correct externalities and externalities themselves can impose costs on individuals. Both the market mechanism and government action have advantages and disadvantages. There are, therefore, few hard and fast rules on whether the government or the market should solve the problem. It is necessary to weigh the advantages and disadvantages in each particular instance. There will always be room for controversy.

Some examples of externalities that probably require some government action would be automobile pollution, the abuse of scenic beauty, and the killing of whales and fish. In these cases the costs of negotiating and enforcing private contracts exceed the potential gains. Some examples of potential externalities that may not require government action would be honey and apple production or localized pollution. In the case of localized pollution (air or noise), people can be compensated indirectly by moving (voting with their feet). The worker who lives near the paper mill receives a compensating wage differential; the residents near the airport have lower home costs.

Optimal Pollution

The three economic solutions to externalities all call for the internalization of externalities. As long as economic agents must pay for the full marginal social costs of their actions, economists feel that they will allocate resources efficiently. In other words, the factory should be allowed to pollute as long as it bears the external costs it imposes on others.

Many critics feel that it is irresponsible to speak of an optimal amount of pollution. They argue that all pollution is bad and should, therefore, be banned.

The economist's response is that there must be a balancing of marginal social costs and marginal social benefits. The polluting steel mill may impose an external cost of $10 per ton in addition to its private marginal cost of $80 per ton. But if a ton of steel yields marginal social benefits of $90 per ton, economists would argue that the last ton of steel should be produced, even with its pollution costs. As long as all external costs are accounted for, society should be allowed to equate marginal social costs and benefits.

Measuring external costs is difficult. For example, advocates of nuclear power claim the radiation dangers are small. Opponents argue that nuclear power imposes enormous external costs. The inability to resolve this issue makes it impossible to determine the optimum level of pollution.

PUBLIC GOODS

Why is it necessary for government to allocate any resources? Why can't a competitive economy provide optimal quantities of all the goods and services society demands? Public goods and services that are provided by the government—like public schools, public parks, public roads and bridges, national defense, police protection, or public health services—are generally made available to the public at no explicit charge and are financed by taxes (although in some instances, government charges for government services, as in the case of postage or admission fees to public parks). Governments must decide whether or not to provide **public goods.**

Public goods are goods or services characterized by 1) nonrival consumption and 2) nonexclusion.

Nonrival Consumption

If a dam is built that protects a particular geographic area from flooding, everyone who lives in

Rivalry and Nonrivalry: Cars, Fire Stations, and Libraries

Nonrival consumption depends very much on the physical contiguity of the consumers. If Jones and Smith are neighbors, they could conceivably use the same car for work or shopping as long as they do not have to shop or work at the same time in different places. In this particular case, Smith and Jones are nonrival consumers of the car. In the case of a shared car, it would be unusual for Smith and Jones to avoid rivalry. A library is an example of nonrival consumption of a common good. Strictly speaking, when one person checks out a book, that book is not available to others. But the probability of two people wanting the same book at the same time is small. The probability is higher for recent best sellers, which are loaned out for shorter periods. For most other books, from the viewpoint of probable use, a library offers nonrival consumption to a large collection of diverse people. The same is true of a fire station. While fire-fighters cannot put out two fires at once, it is unlikely that fires will occur at the same time. ✖

the protected area benefits. Moreover, the fact that one person's house is protected by the dam does not reduce any other house's protection. A radio program is another "good" that is characterized by **nonrival consumption.** One person can listen to a program without reducing the amount of the program any other listener enjoys. All listeners are nonrival consumers.

> *A good is characterized by **nonrival consumption** if its consumption by one person does not reduce its consumption by others, given the level of production.*

The classic example of nonrival consumption is national defense. If the government builds an antimissile system that substantially reduces the likelihood of nuclear attack by a foreign nation, everyone in the protected geographical area enjoys the benefits. The protection of one person's life and property does not reduce the protection enjoyed by others.

Nonrival consumption does not mean that everyone benefits to the same degree. A pacifist may not like the national defense effort; nor would an enemy spy. A family with a large estate may benefit more from flood control than one living in a wooden shack.

Most goods and services that are exchanged in markets are characterized by **rival consumption.**

> *A good is characterized by **rival consumption** when the consumption of the good by one person lowers the consumption available to others, given the level of production.*

Food and drink, cars, houses, shoes, dresses, and medical services are rival in consumption. Some goods can be either rival or nonrival depending on the circumstances. Uncrowded movies or sporting events are nonrival. One person can enjoy an uncrowded movie without reducing another person's consumption, but a crowded movie or sporting event is rival, because each additional spectator displaces another possible spectator. The problem of rationing the available supply of most rival goods is solved by charging prices; those who consume the rival good place a higher value on it than those who do not consume the good.

Nonexclusion

The second characteristic of pure public goods is **nonexclusion,** or the extreme cost required to exclude people from using the good (once it has been produced). National defense and flood control are classic examples. It is virtually impossible to exclude any person in the protected area from enjoying the benefits of the good; **exclusion costs** are prohibitive.

Exclusion costs are the costs of defining and enforcing private property rights in some good, or the cost of preventing those who do not have property rights in the good from enjoying the good.

*A good is characterized by **nonexclusion** if the exclusion costs are so high that it is not possible (or practical) to exclude people from using the good.*

Nonrivalry should not be confused with nonexclusion. An uncrowded movie theater is nonrival in consumption, but nonpayers can be prevented from consuming a movie by not allowing them to enter the theater.

Identifying a public good can be difficult. Nobel laureate Paul Samuelson used the lighthouse as an example of pure public goods, since any one ship's use of the light does not detract from any other ship's use (nonrivalry) and since it is difficult for the lighthouse to exclude nonpaying ships from using the light (nonexclusion). Economist Ronald R. Coase, however, found that in England lighthouses were for many years privately owned and operated.[2] From 1700 to 1834 the number of privately operated lighthouses increased, so the business was obviously profitable. Instead of being unable to provide this public good, the private market in lighthouses appeared to be thriving. Lighthouse owners were paid by the ship owners at the docks according to the tonnage of the ship. The economists did not realize that usually only one ship is near the lighthouse at a time; the light could be turned off if the ship did not fly the flag of a fee-paying vessel. Thus, exclusion costs were not high.

Most private goods are rival in consumption and have low exclusion costs so that nonpayers can be excluded from consuming them. Some goods, however, are rival in consumption and also have high exclusion costs. One example is crowded city roads during rush hour; to exclude some users would require building expensive toll gates. Park benches are another example. Goods with high exclusion costs, be they rival or nonri-

2. Ronald R. Coase, "The Lighthouse in Economics," *Journal of Law and Economics,* October 1976.

val, are normally provided through the government.

Nonrival Goods with High Exclusion Costs. The private provision of public goods is dependent upon the voluntary contributions of beneficiaries. Since those who benefit cannot be excluded from its use whether or not they are paying for it, people need not pay. People who attempt to enjoy the benefits of the good without paying are **free riders.**

*A **free rider** is anyone who enjoys the benefits of a good or service without paying the cost.*

When some of the beneficiaries are free riders, the private revenues voluntarily contributed to pay for a public good will be less than the social benefits the good generates—in which case, the good will not be produced or will be underproduced by the private market.

Nonrival Goods with Low Exclusion Costs. For many nonrival goods, however, exclusion costs are not excessive and there is some rivalry in consumption. Some nonrival goods have low exclusion costs. Some people feel that private markets may not provide enough movies, pay TV, or sporting arenas. For example, in a world of diverse tastes, any price charged for pay TV will exclude some people from the market. If it costs society nothing to add one more user (because of nonrivalry), it seems wasteful to exclude that user.

Viewers can consume ordinary TV and radio as much as they like (once they have a receiver); the private market ingeniously finances private TV and radio by advertising. An alternative procedure for radio and TV production would be to ban advertising, set up a public TV monopoly, and let everyone pay the costs in taxes.

The problem of publicly providing nonrival goods with low exclusion costs is that the good must somehow be paid for. Is it fair for people who hate baseball games to be forced to pay for entertaining those who love baseball games? Charging a toll on an uncrowded bridge leads to economic inefficiency because some users are excluded even though they do not keep others from using the bridge. Without the toll, however, non-users would be forced to pay for the bridge in taxes.

Why is it that toll bridges are publicly owned while movies and sporting events are privately produced? The justification for public ownership of bridges is that a private owner would have a monopoly position and could charge monopoly prices.

MARKET FAILURE

A public good is a classic example of a **market failure.**

*A **market failure** occurs when the price system fails to produce the quantity of the good that would be socially optimal.*

Voluntary Cooperation

The free-rider problem confounds the production of public goods. Suppose a dam costing $2,000 will protect a community of 10 people from flooding and that the flood protection of the dam is worth $400 to each person. The total value of the dam is $4,000; it is worth building because it costs only $2,000. Building the dam by charging $200 to each person would clearly benefit everyone.

Voluntary agreement among the 10 people may be difficult. Any one might realize that if the other 9 build the dam without his or her contribution, he or she could still enjoy the benefits. Such free riders attempt to enjoy the benefits of the dam without paying their share of the costs. In this example, will the dam be built? If 6 people behave as free riders, the dam will not be built by voluntary agreement; the non-free-riders can raise only $1,600. If only 4 people behave as free riders the dam will be built.

Voluntary agreements will work if the amount of free riding is not excessive. Voluntary cooperation is more likely the smaller is the group, the more often collective decisions are made, and the greater is the individual gain from adopting cooperative behavior.

Examples of cooperative behavior abound. Dams are built by municipalities; public grounds in subdivisons are landscaped; most people obey the law; volunteers work to improve the community. But if the group is large, if collective decisions are made infrequently, and if the individual gains to cooperation are small, free riding will be more prevalent.

Income Redistribution

Externalities and public goods provide a rationale for government action. An earlier chapter noted that government is also active in the area of income redistribution. Why is income redistribution not handled by the market through private charity and voluntary giving? Surprisingly, the voluntary charitable giving is subject to many of the same problems as public goods.

Most of us feel better off when the position of poor people improves. Because human beings are affected by motives of altruism, one person's welfare is affected by the well-being of others. The welfare of those with strong altruistic feelings towards the poor will be improved by a redistribution of income in favor of the poor. Again, however, voluntary contributions cannot be relied upon because of the free rider problem.

Imagine that 50 million upper-income (non-poor) people want to help 1 million poor people. If each of the 50 million nonpoor were willing to give $100, then $5,000 could be transferred to each poor person, and the poverty problem would be reduced. Everyone would be better off. The nonpoor would have assisted the poor in a substantial way, satisfying their altruistic motives, and the poor would each be $5,000 richer. Why is it unlikely for a voluntary program of income redistribution of this magnitude to come about? Each person realizes that giving $100 has no impact whatsoever on the poverty problem, as $100 spread over 1 million people amounts to one cent per hundred people; the individual has no incentive to contribute. Only if the individual knows that all 50 million are going to contribute (that there will be no free riders) will there be any noticeable effect on poverty. In this situation, the free riders will not contribute because they will believe it is likely that virtually everyone else will be a free rider. Government is left with the responsibility for income redistribution.

Another reason for government involvement in income redistribution is that it is impossible to take out private insurance policies against being poor. Consumers can buy fire insurance, life insurance, health insurance, or car insurance, but they cannot buy "poverty" insurance. The absence of poverty insurance is a market failure. One can think of being poor as an unfortunate event, just like a fire or accident. Private insurance companies do not offer policies against being poor for two reasons.

Moral Hazard. The person who takes out poverty insurance has less of an incentive to avoid being poor. In the insurance business, *moral hazard* is the problem insurance companies face when those who have bought insurance alter their behavior to increase the probability of collecting insurance. For example, property owners who have fire insurance may become careless or even set fires. Similarly, a person with poverty insurance may become lazy or careless about working to earn income.

Adverse Selection. Those who feel their chances of being poor are low probably would not buy poverty insurance. Hence, those who buy will be mainly those people that are most likely to be poor. *Adverse selection* is a problem that occurs when those who buy insurance are more likely to collect it than the average population. Because only those likely to be poor will buy, poverty insurance rates will be quite high, and the business of poverty insurance will be privately unprofitable.

Yet all sorts of random events such as bad health, technological progress, accidents, and changes in tastes can cause poverty. Since private insurance is impractical, government redistribution programs can act as an insurance program for the nonpoor.

The Information Problem

The problem of externalities and public goods are ultimately problems of information. If everyone had perfect information, bargaining and transaction costs would be minimal or zero. With perfect information, free riders could be identified and property rights could be defined as finely as one wished (even to the point of assigning property rights to fish in the ocean).

In a world of imperfect information, many difficulties arise in applying the theory of externalities or public goods. There are usually several policy options that can be followed; it is easy to make mistakes in identifying the externality or public good. There are enormous controversies over nuclear power and depletion of the ozone layer, for example. It is difficult to measure external costs and benefits for the purpose of establishing appropriate taxes or subsidies; externalities may be more apparent than real. In short, the information costs that are implicit in any externality also make it difficult to apply government solutions to the market failure.

EXHAUSTIBLE RESOURCES

Externalities and public goods are likely to lead to market failure, and government action is seen as one way to deal with externalities. Some argue that the problem of exhaustible resources is another example of potential market failure. In their view, private resource allocation could lead to the too-rapid depletion of an **exhaustible resource.** Is government action also required to prevent the exhaustion of the globe's nonrenewable resources?

*An **exhaustible** (or nonrenewable) **resource** is any resource of which there is a finite stock in the long run because the stock is fixed by nature.*

A firm that produces a **renewable resource**—such as timber or livestock—does not behave differently in substance from the competitive and monopolistic firms described in previous chapters. Additional quantities of the renewable resource can be produced if the firm is willing to bear the additional cost. For example, there is not a fixed supply of timber that will be exhausted at some point in the future. By incurring the marginal costs of planting saplings, fertilizing them, and protecting them from disease, timber producers can increase or renew stocks of trees.

*A **renewable resource** is any resource of which the stock is not fixed in the long run.*

The firm that produces renewable resources follows the standard profit-maximizing rule: in each period it produces that quantity of output at which the marginal revenue from the last unit of output equals its marginal cost. If the firm follows this simple rule, its profits will be maximized over the years. Unless externalities or monopolies are present, there will be social efficiency.

Consider a firm that supplies an exhaustible resource—the stock of which is fixed by nature. The firm cannot increase its stock of the exhaustible resource. Instead, the firm must decide how to allocate its fixed stock of the nonrenewable resource over time. The firm that extracts natural gas from a fixed reservoir must decide how much to supply to the market this year, next year, 5 years from now, and 20 years from now.

The nonrenewable-resource firm faces an opportunity cost not present for renewable-resource firms. In the case of renewable resources, the decision to supply x units this year does not mean that these x units cannot be supplied again (another tree can be planted). In the case of nonrenewable resources, every unit supplied this year will be one unit not available for subsequent years. Equivalently, units supplied next year will not be available this year.

Suppliers of exhaustible resources face an additional opportunity cost: units supplied today will never be available in the future.

Because supplies of nonrenewable resources must be traded off between current and future consumption, suppliers of nonrenewable resources must make an *intertemporal* (across time) comparison of the costs and benefits of supplying the resource today versus supplying it tomorrow.

Suppose a crude-oil firm can extract crude oil from a reservoir containing 1,000 barrels at a zero marginal cost (the oil simply rises by itself to the surface). For simplicity, suppose also that the firm must sell its entire stock of 1,000 barrels within a two-year period. The market rate of interest is 10 percent.

How will this firm allocate its stock of crude oil between the two years? If the price of crude oil today is $20 per barrel, and the price expected next year is $21.50, the firm should sell all 1,000 barrels this year. By selling now, the firm gets $20 per barrel that can be invested at 10 percent interest; in one year, the firm will have $22 per barrel ($20 $\times$ 1.1). Each barrel the firm sells next year will yield only $21.50; so the firm is better off selling now. If next year's price were to be greater than $22, the firm's best course of action would be to wait to sell all 1,000 barrels next year. *If the price rises at the same rate as the interest rate (in this case, by 10 percent per annum), the firm would be indifferent as to whether it sold its stock of the nonrenewable resource this year or next year.*

Turning from the exhaustible resource firm to the market, suppose a perfectly competitive market consists of a large number of price-taking firms (see Figure 1). The stock of the exhaustible resource owned by all the firms together is fixed (at 30 units), and firms must sell their entire stock within a two-year period (either in period 0 or period 1).

In Figure 1, the horizontal axis is 30 units long because only 30 units of the resource are available; what is supplied in period 0 will not be available for period 1. The period 0 demand curve is a standard demand curve read from left to right, but the period 1 demand curve is unusual because it must be read backwards; it should be read from right to left. Both demand curves indicate what quantities will be demanded in each period at various prices. Because only 30 units are available, once period 0's supply is set, whatever remains of the 30 units is what is available for period 1.

If 20 units were sold in period 0 and 10 units were sold in period 1, Figure 1 indicates that the period 0 price would be $6 per unit (point *a*) and the period 1 price would be $11 per unit (point *b*). Would the individual firms be content with this outcome? No. Each unit sold in period 0 and invested at 10 percent interest would be worth only $6.60 in period 1; whereas each unit sold in period 1 yields $11. Clearly, firms would want to supply less than 20 units in period 0 and more than 10 units in period 1.

An equilibrium would be attained when the period 0 price equals the present discounted value

Figure 1
Market Equilibrium for an Exhaustible Resource in Two Periods

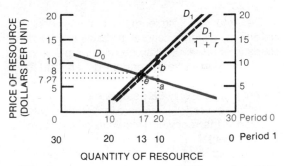

QUANTITY OF RESOURCE

This figure represents a competitive market composed of a large number of perfectly competitive firms. The firms in the market together have a fixed supply of 30 units of the nonrenewable resource, and these 30 units must be used either in period 0 or period 1. The market demand curves are D_0 for period 0 and D_1 for period 1. Firms will contrast the price received in period 0 with the present discounted value of the price received in period 1. $D_1 \div 1.1$ is the present discounted value of the period 1 demand curve when the interest rate is 10 percent. When the available supply is allocated between periods 0 and 1, the prices in the two periods are established. As long as the period 0 price is less than the present value of the period 1 price (as it is when period 1 quantity is 20 and period 1 quantity is 10), firms will reallocate supplies from period 0 to period 1. Equilibrium will be reached when quantity is 17 in period 0 and 13 in period 1 and when price is $8 in period 0 and $7.27 in period 1. The ratio of the price in period 1 to the price in period 0 will be 1 plus the interest rate, or 1.1, in equilibrium.

Figure 2
Real U.S. Crude Oil Prices, 1880–1977

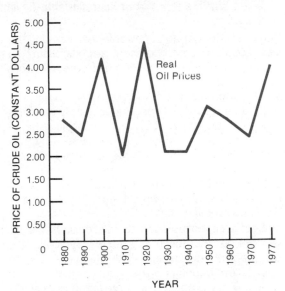

YEAR

Since 1880, overall *real* U.S. crude oil prices have neither increased nor decreased significantly.

Sources: U.S. Bureau of Mines, U.S. Bureau of Labor Statistics.

---

of the period 1 price, or when the period 0 price equals the period 1 price divided by 1.1. At this point, there would no longer be an incentive for firms to switch supplies from one period to the other. The dashed demand curve in Figure 1 shows the period 1 prices divided by 1.1 and represents the present discounted values of the period 1 prices. The quantity where the dashed curve intersects the period 1 demand curve (at point *e*) is the equilibrium quantity. The quantity corresponding to point *e* is 17 units in period 0 and 13 units in period 1. In Figure 1, the period 0 price for 17 units is $7.27, and the period 1 price for 13 units is $8. The present discounted value of $8 is $7.27 at a 10 percent rate of interest. At these prices, firms no longer have an incentive to shift supplies from one period to the other.

When marginal costs are zero and the market is perfectly competitive, the price of an exhaustible resource will rise at the same rate as the interest rate.[3]

If period 1's demand increases between periods 0 and 1, D_1 would shift up, as would its discounted present value. The new equilibrium would be reached at higher prices in both periods, but with period 0's supply reduced. In equilibrium, the present value of period 1's price would still equal period 0's price. The anticipation of an increase in demand in some future period will tend to redistribute supplies of exhaustible resources from the present to the future.

Technology and Exhaustible Resources

Figure 1 delivers a reassuring message: competitive markets deal automatically with the rising

---

3. Another important condition underlies this conclusion; namely, that technology is held constant. The importance of this assumption will be discussed later in the chapter.

When Will We Run Out of Nonrenewable Resources?

Will we run out of nonrenewable resources by the year 2000 as some doomsday experts claim? By using exhaustible resources now, are we condemning future generations to poverty and starvation? The prospect of running out of crucial nonrenewable resources appears especially alarming if one divides known reserves of specific exhaustible resources—such as oil or copper—by current annual consumption of the resource (or worse still by projections of the growth of consumption). Such exercises indicate that supplies of oil, copper, zinc, and about everything else will run out in our children's lifetime.

Before accepting such alarmist conclusions, let us consider the notion of reserves. Typically, engineers and geologists use the term *reserves* to refer to the quantity of the resource that can be economically produced with prevailing prices and technology. When prices rise and technology improves, reserves tend to increase. For example, known world reserves of oil were 75 billion barrels in 1950. By 1979, world reserves had risen to 679 billion barrels—a 905 percent increase. This enormous increase in reserves was caused by the discovery of new deposits and technological improvements that allow higher recovery rates in established fields.

The American Petroleum Institute estimates that the original oil in place in all oil fields in the United States is about 450 billion barrels. Of this amount, 115 billion barrels have been produced, and there are 30 billion barrels of known reserves. Experts currently expect only 32 percent recovery of oil already discovered. American oil reserves would be doubled if the recovery rate were to rise from 32 to 40 percent.

The rapid increase in known world reserves is characteristic of most nonrenewable resources. Manganese reserves have increased 27 percent, zinc 61 percent, lead 115 percent, copper 179 percent, bauxite 279 percent, chromite 675 percent, iron 1,221 percent, potash 2,360 percent, and phosphates 4,430 percent from 1950 to 1970.

The accompanying table shows the number of years known reserves of exhaustible resources will last at prevailing consumption rates. Known reserves will last from 9 years (gold) to 481 years (phosphorus). Using the U.S. Geological Survey's estimates of ultimate recoverable resources, we find that the various resources will last from 102 years (gold) to 68,066 years (aluminum). Using the amount of the resource estimated to be in the earth's crust, we find that resources are virtually inexhaustible—lasting millions of years.

scarcity of exhaustible resources. The annual growth rate of the prices of exhaustible resources should tend to equal the market rate of interest in the long run. In other words, the natural rise in the prices of nonrenewable resources should discourage their consumption. Moreover, if increasing scarcity is expected, supplies of the nonrenewable resource will be shifted to the future.

Figure 2 on the preceding page shows the long-run trend in the real price of a barrel of oil since 1880. The prices in Figure 2 are the ratio of the resource price to consumer prices in general. As the reader can readily see, over the whole period there is no trend in the real price of oil resources. Since 1800 there has been a distinct downward trend in the real price of such exhaustible resources as copper, aluminum, and pig iron. Why have the real prices of exhaustible resources not risen as the theory predicts?

The theory of exhaustible resources developed above makes two important assumptions:

1. The marginal cost of extracting the resource is zero.
2. The technology of resource extraction, discovery, and recovery is fixed.

If either of these two assumptions fails to hold, it is possible for exhaustible-resource prices to move contrary to the predictions of the theory.

Marginal Extraction Costs. As shown in Figure 1, when marginal extraction costs are zero, firms will allocate supplies between the two periods so that the period 0 price equals the present value of the period 1 price. When positive marginal extraction costs are introduced, this equilibrium condition changes as follows:

	Years of Potential Consumption if Known Reserves are Divided by Annual Consumption	Years of Potential Consumption if Ultimate Recoverable Resources are Divided by Annual Consumption	Years of Potential Consumption if Amount Estimated in Earth's Crust is Divided by Annual Consumption (millions)
Copper	45	340	242
Iron	117	2,657	1,815
Phosphorus	481	1,601	870
Molybdenum	65	630	422
Lead	10	162	85
Zinc	21	618	409
Sulphur	30	6,897	N.A.
Uranium	50	8,455	1,855
Aluminum	23	68,066	38,500
Gold	9	102	57

When a particular resource threatens to become scarce in supply, its relative price would be expected to rise. Rising relative prices would discourage consumption; therefore it is not appropriate to assume that current consumption rates would continue into the future if the resource were threatened with depletion. ✂

Sources: William Nordhaus, "Resources as a Constraint on Growth," *American Economic Review* 64, 2 (May 1974): 23; *Handbook of Economic Statistics,* 1980; James Griffin and Henry Steele, *Energy Economics and Policy* (New York: Academic, 1980), pp. 311–12; Julian Simon, *The Ultimate Resource* (Princeton: Princeton University Press, 1981), p. 34.

$$P_0 - MC_0 = \frac{P_1 - MC_1}{1 + r}$$

where P_0 = the price in period 0, P_1 = the price in period 1, MC_0 = marginal extraction costs in period 0, MC_1 = marginal extraction costs in period 1, and r = the interest rate in decimal form. Firms seek to equate the present value of price minus marginal costs in period 1 with the price minus marginal cost in period 0. To illustrate, consider what would happen in Figure 1 if the marginal cost is expected to rise from zero in period 0 to $0.25 per barrel in period 1. Each firm would receive (after deducting the marginal cost) $7.27 on the last barrel sold in period 0 and $7.75 ($8 − $0.25) on the last barrel sold in period 1— the present value of which equals only $7.05. The firm would, therefore, sell more in period 0 and less in period 1 until the period 0 price equals the present value of the period 1 price minus the mar-

ginal cost. *When marginal cost is greater in period 1 than in period 0, the price rises by more than the rate of interest.*

In the case where marginal cost is declining over time (say, due to improvements in extraction methods), the price would rise by less than the market rate of interest. If marginal costs are 0 in period 1 and $0.25 in period 0, the price will rise by less than the interest rate.

If marginal costs are rising over time, the price of an exhaustible resource can rise more rapidly than the interest rate. If marginal costs are falling over time, the price can rise more slowly than the interest rate.

Technological Advances. If technological advances occur that allow exhaustible-resource producers to increase their recovery rates, prices would not be expected to rise at the rate of interest. In fact, if technological advances are large, exhaustible resource prices can fall.

Consider a resource firm that develops a new technology that will allow it to recover more of the exhaustible resource in period 1 than in period 0. Suppose an oil company with existing technology can recover one out of every two barrels under ground and has a total of 200 barrels under ground. A new technology that will be available in period 1 allows it to recover 1.5 barrels from every two barrels underground. For every barrel sold in period 0, the firm passes up the opportunity to sell 1.5 barrels (with the new technology) in period 1. As a result, more supplies will be shifted to period 1, thereby lowering the period 1 price and raising the period 0 price.

Technological advances that are scheduled to take place in the future cause supplies of exhaustible resources to be shifted to the future, thereby raising current prices and lowering future prices.

Backstop Resources. If a **backstop resource** exists, the pattern of pricing of the nonrenewable resource over time is affected.

*A **backstop resource** is a close substitute for an exhaustible resource that is available in virtually unlimited supply but at a higher cost.*

Examples of backstop resources are solar energy as a backstop for conventional energy and shale oil and tar sands as backstops for conventional crude oil.

What effect does the availability of a backstop fuel—such as shale oil—have on the allocation of crude oil and oil prices over time? Suppose that shale oil is available in virtually unlimited supply at a price of $40 per barrel. The backstop fuel sets a price limit of $40 per barrel on conventional crude oil because consumers would switch to shale oil if the crude oil price went above $40. Until the $40 backstop price is reached, the price should increase by the rate of interest. Once the backstop price is reached, however, the price will then remain constant.

The advantage of the backstop resource is that it allows greater consumption of the nonrenew-

able resource in the present at lower prices than would be possible without the backstop resource. With the backstop resource, supplies of the nonrenewable resource need cover demands only up to the backstop price. As a result, more of the resource can be consumed now and in the near future with the knowledge that the distant future will be taken care of by the alternate resource.

The Price System and Exhaustible Resources

As demonstrated in this chapter, natural market forces should cause nonrenewable resources to be allocated efficiently over time. Suppliers of nonrenewable resources must consider the opportunity costs of selling resources today and thereby raising their scarcity tomorrow. Unless rapid technological progress increases the supply of recoverable nonrenewable resources, their prices will tend to rise at the rate of interest. Suppliers must always weigh the returns from exploiting the resource now against waiting for the resource to become more scarce (and thus sell for a higher price) tomorrow.

The major threat to the rational use of nonrenewable resources is interference in the pricing of resources. If prices are controlled—for example, if price ceilings are placed on oil or natural gas—then resource firms will have to make resource-allocation decisions on the basis of prices that do not correctly reflect scarcities today and tomorrow. In other words, price controls could result in too little being allocated to present consumption and too much being allotted to future consumption.

This chapter discussed some of the possible arguments for government action. Externalities, public goods, and income distribution represent legitimate cases of market failure. The next chapter will explore the question: If government action is needed, how does government work in a world of limited information, majority rule, and self-interest?

Summary

1. Externalities occur when marginal social costs (or benefits) do not equal marginal pri-

vate costs (or benefits). Social efficiency requires that marginal social benefits and marginal social costs be equal, but private market participants equate marginal private benefits with marginal private costs. Externalities can be internalized by redefining property rights, by making voluntary agreements, or by taxing or subsidizing the externality generator.

2. Pure public goods have two characteristics: a) the consumption of the good is nonrival among all users; b) no one can in practice be prevented from using the good (nonexclusion).

3. Market failures occur when the price system fails to produce the quantity of the good that would be socially optimal. Market failures can be total (the good is not produced at all) or partial (the good is underproduced). Examples of market failures are pure public goods, externalities, and income distribution.

4. Firms that produce nonrenewable resources must determine how to allocate the available fixed supply over time. When marginal extraction costs are zero, when the industry is perfectly competitive, and when there is no technological progress, they will allocate the resource so that the present discounted values of the prices in each period are the same. Prices will rise at the rate of interest. If increasing scarcity is anticipated in the future, supplies of the nonrenewable resource will be reallocated from the present to the future. The prices of nonrenewable resources in general have not risen in real terms because of declining marginal extraction costs and rapid technological progress. Natural market forces should cause the efficient allocation of nonrenewable resources over time.

Key Terms

externality
public goods
nonrival consumption
rival consumption
nonexclusion
exclusion costs
free rider
market failure
exhaustible resource
renewable resource
backstop resource

Questions and Problems

1. Factory A produces 1,000 tons of sulphuric acid. It costs A $10,000 to produce 1,000 tons. As a consequence of producing 1,000 tons of sulphuric acid, people in the community must increase their medical payments by $5,000; they lose $4,000 in wages by being sick; their dry-cleaning bills increase by $1,000. What are the private and social costs of the 1,000 tons of sulphuric acid?

2. Explain how the external costs calculated in the previous example might be internalized. Will this internalization be handled differently when there are three people who are hurt by the factory from when 300,000 people are hurt? In which case is government action more likely?

3. Most everybody thinks we need national defense. Why is it therefore difficult to get people to pay voluntarily their share of national defense? Why is there no problem in getting people to pay for shoes?

4. Explain why two people are nonrival consumers of a big city expressway if they are driving at 3:00 A.M. but are rival consumers when driving at 5:00 P.M.

5. Why is there a moral-hazard problem in the sale of private unemployment insurance? Why would this moral-hazard problem not be present in the case of life insurance?

6. Is there an adverse selection problem with auto accident insurance? Does this problem justify the common requirement that everyone buy liability insurance?

7. An oil producer has 100 barrels of oil that must be sold within a two-year period. The interest rate is 20 percent and the price of crude oil expected next year is $35 per barrel. At which prices would the oil producer sell all the oil this year? At which prices would oil producers sell all the oil next year? If the oil producers expects an improvement in technology to increase the recovery rate by 10 percent next year, how will this affect the decision?

22

Public Choice

Chapter Preview

The two preceding chapters explored how governments raise revenues to finance their expenditures and why governments might be needed to allocate resources in the case of market failures. This chapter will examine how a government allocates its resources—or makes its expenditures—in a way that reflects the preferences of the different individuals that compose the society. This question is especially important in a democratic republic where individual choices do matter.

Research in the area of *public-choice theory* has contributed to a greater understanding of the circumstances that determine government successes and failures. This chapter is devoted to the economics of public choice.

UNANIMITY: THE IDEAL WORLD

A market failure creates a role for government action. Public choices must be made. The attitude that was popular for many years was that if the market failed to function efficiently, the government should step in to fill the gap and that even imperfect government action was better than doing nothing. It is entirely possible, however, for government action to make a bad situation even worse. Public-choice economists consider how public decisions can be made that will contribute to economic efficiency.

In an ideal world, government would work so well that everyone would be unanimous in their approval of government action and public choices.

The criterion of a perfect government is similar to that of a perfectly working price system. The price system is considered efficient (perfect) when it is impossible to make anyone better off without hurting someone else. An efficient economic system is making as large a pie as possible; in an efficient system, to give one person a larger piece is to give someone else a smaller piece. An *inefficient* economic system is one in which the pie could be made larger. In a sense, unanimity is at the base of an evaluation of a good price system. When two people engage in an exchange, they are both made better off: they are unanimous in agreeing to the deal.

The turn-of-the-century Swedish economist, Knut Wicksell, has suggested that the analog to the private market in questions of public choice is unanimity.

Consider a hypothetical community that has no information costs or bargaining costs. Everyone knows everything about everyone else. In such a community, unanimous collective decisions are no longer difficult. Consider the adoption of a flood control project. In the real world flood control is a pure public good because no one can be excluded from its benefits. The market will fail to provide it; the community must, therefore, decide how much flood control to produce. In our imaginary community, each person's demand schedule for flood control is known to everyone else. Suppose the community consists of individuals A, B, and C. Figure 1 shows their three demand schedules. The demand curve D_A shows person A's marginal valuation of flood control at different amounts of flood control. (Assume that the quantity of flood control is measured in terms of the height of a dam. A higher dam provides a larger "quantity" of flood control.) For example, the 100th foot of a dam is worth $1 to person A. If the community provides a 100-foot dam, the same amount of flood control is available to A as is available to B or C. According to the three demand schedules, A's marginal valuation of the 100th foot of a dam is $1, B's valuation is $5, and C's valuation is $6. The community's total marginal valuation of the 100th foot of a dam is thus $12. The total demand curve is the vertical summation of each of the individual demand curves.

Figure 1
Unanimity: Ideal Benefit Taxes

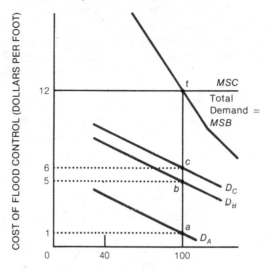

QUANTITY OF FLOOD CONTROL
(HEIGHT OF DAM IN FEET)

Here is an ideal three-person community where the demand curves of A, B, and C for the nonrival good, flood control, are known to all. The total demand for flood control is the vertical sum of the three individual demand curves because, with a nonrival good, providing one person with flood control provides all with flood control. The marginal social cost *(MSC)* of flood control is $12; the height of the demand curve measures the marginal social benefit *(MSB)* of flood control. The optimum occurs where 100 units of flood control are provided, because *MSC* equals *MSB* at 100 units. With the individual demand curves known to all, benefit taxes of $1, $5, and $6 (per unit of flood control) imposed on A, B, and C would lead them to unanimously choose 100 units of flood control.

The demand curve for a nonrival (public) good differs from the demand curve for a rival (private) good. The market demand curve for a nonrival good is the **vertical** *summation of each individual's demand curve. (Recall for contrast that the market demand curve for a rival good is the* **horizontal** *summation of all the individual demand curves.)*

The ideal quantity of flood control in Figure 1 is a 100-foot dam because the marginal social cost *(MSC)* of flood control is $12, which we assume to be constant for simplicity. The optimal quantity of flood control is a 100-foot dam because at that amount of flood control, marginal social benefits equal marginal social costs.

In our hypothetical community, optimality (unanimity) can easily be attained. The ideal government knows the demand schedules of all concerned and simply taxes people according to each person's marginal valuation. Thus A pays a price of $1 per unit of flood control; B and C pay the higher prices of $5 and $6 per unit of flood control. The prices paid by each individual exactly match the benefits they receive. If such taxes were imposed on each person, each would vote for a 100-foot dam's worth of flood control. All members of the community would vote unanimously for a 100-foot dam.

This voluntary-exchange view of collective action assumes governments have more information than they actually have. If the individual demand schedules for a public good are not known, some voting process other than unanimity would have to be used.

The costs of discovering the government expenditure and tax program that would bring about unanimous approval of all members of the population are prohibitive; hence, it is necessary to accept some principle of collective action short of unanimity. When the community departs from the unanimity principle, how efficient is public choice?

MAJORITY RULE

The most popular method of making political decisions is majority rule. In the three-person community considered above, any proposal for flood control would require only 2 yes votes to be carried out.

For simplicity, assume that the $12 marginal cost per unit of flood control is divided equally among the three persons. The "tax price" of flood control would then be $4 per person per unit of flood control. The total tax liability of each individual would depend on the number of units the community chooses to produce.

Figure 2 illustrates the majority voting process. With a tax price of $4 per person, A prefers a 40-foot dam, B prefers a 120-foot dam, and C prefers a 140-foot dam. If any dam lower than 40

Figure 2
Marjority Rule

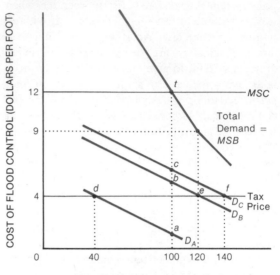

QUANTITY OF FLOOD CONTROL
(HEIGHT OF DAM IN FEET)

This figure represents the same three-person community portrayed in Figure 1, except that now majority rule reigns and the individual demand curves are not known socially. For simplicity, suppose that the $12 per unit cost of flood control is shared equally by all so that the tax price is $4 per unit of flood control per person. At this price A will want 40 units, B will want 120 units, and C will want 140 units of flood control. B is the median voter; under majority rule the median voter determines the outcome. Thus, 120 units of flood control will be provided. This quantity is inefficient because the marginal social benefit of the 120th unit is only $9 (compared to the marginal social costs of $12).

feet is proposed, which is the dam height desired by the person who desires flood control the least, all three members would favor flood control. But B and C would realize that such a proposal is very costly to them. At a tax price of $4, B and C want a 120-foot and a 140-foot dam, respectively. To them a 40-foot dam is far too small for the price. If a 100-foot dam (the optimal height) is proposed, A (who wants only a 40-foot dam) would vote against the proposal, but B and C would favor it over a 40-foot dam. However, B and C would still realize that a 100-foot dam is not enough flood control for the price. The median voter, B, wants a 120-foot dam. B and C will press for higher and higher levels of flood control until this median voter is satisfied. If a 120-foot dam is proposed, A will vote against it, but both B and C will vote for it. If a dam higher than 120 feet is proposed, A and B will vote against it. Thus the median voter (B) gets his or her wish: a 120-foot dam. Using the principle of majority rule, the spending proposal of providing a 120-foot dam costing a total of $1440 (= $12 × 120 feet) will defeat all other proposals. Each voter will be assessed $480 to pay for flood control.

Under majority rule the median voter determines the outcome. The median voter's preferences count most because precisely half of the remaining voters prefer less of the public good and half prefer more.

Three important conclusions follow from the decisive role of the median voter in simple, direct voting under majority rule:

1. *Social choices need not respond to individual wants.* Many people are dissatisfied with how the government reacts to the individual because the votes of those in the minority (or 49 percent of the voters on some issues) do not count. The most disgruntled members of our society are those whose preferences are almost always in the minority.

2. *Majority-voting rules may not reflect the relative intensity of preferences.* Since the median voter determines the outcome, a change in the intensity of anyone else's preferences has no impact. Shifting the demand curve of A downward and C upward in Figure 2 would have no impact on the outcome. The intensity of A's preferences and C's preferences are irrelevant. Only the median voter's preference intensities count. This system is in sharp contrast to the market for private goods where dollar votes for goods duly register the intensity of each person's preferences.

3. *Majority voting need not be efficient.* In Figure 2, majority rule led to a 120-foot dam, which is higher than the 100-foot dam an efficient economy would provide. Although the intensity of preferences of nonmedian voters is irrelevant, as we just saw, the intensity of preferences of nonmedian voters affects marginal social benefits. In Figure 2, too much of the public good is produced. Whether too much or too little is produced

depends on the distribution of demands around the median voter.

LOGROLLING AND PARADOX

In our example of majority rule the policy that was adopted was supported by the majority of voters. When more than one issue is involved, **logrolling** or "pork-barrel politics" can result in the approval of policies that are actually opposed by a majority. Majority voting may paradoxically lead to several inconsistent outcomes.

Logrolling is the trading of votes to secure a favorable outcome on decisions of more intense interest to each voter.

Multiple Decisions

One characteristic of majority rule is that intensities of preferences do not matter. The vote of a person who is passionately against some measure and the vote of one who is only marginally in favor of the measure are given equal weight in deciding the final outcome. On a single issue, the difference in preference intensity has no effect on the outcome. But the political process involves not just one decision but a stream of decisions that are both complex and simple. The person who is only mildly in favor of one proposal might trade his or her vote with a person strongly against the proposal in exchange for a similar trade when their positions are reversed.

Consider three farmers, A, B, and C. Suppose B and C could each use a separate access road to the main highway. Farmers B and C would each gain $7 from an access road that costs $6 to the community. The $6 cost is equally shared by all three farmers ($2 each). Table 1 describes the net benefits (+) or costs (−) to each farmer from building these access roads at the public expense.

Since the $6 cost is shared equally, building a road has a $2 cost per farmer. Roads built for B or C do not benefit A at all. But a road built for B gives B a net benefit of $5, as the gains from the road are worth $7 and B's share of the cost is only $2. If a road is built for C, B is in the same position as A, but C gains a net benefit of $5.

According to majority rule, if an access road for B is proposed, farmers A and C will vote

Table 1
Building Access Roads for Farmers B and C: Benefits Exceed Costs

Beneficiaries	Net Benefit (+) or Cost (−) of Access Road for B	Net Benefit (+) or Cost (−) of Access Road for C
A	−$2	−$2
B	+$5	−$2
C	−$2	+$5
Society	+$1	+$1

In this example, access roads cost $6; these costs are shared equally by each farmer ($2 each). But each access road is worth $7 to the affected farmer. Building both roads is socially efficient in this case because total benefits ($14) exceed costs ($12). Under simple majority rule without logrolling, neither road is built because the *number* of voters benefiting does not exceed the number of voters who do not benefit. But if Farmers B and C link their votes (if both vote for both roads), then both roads can be built and society benefits.

against it; similarly, an access road for C will be defeated by A and B. Majority rule without logrolling causes the defeat of such special-interest legislation.

But farmers B and C will each perceive that they can gain by voting for the other farmer's access road. If farmers B and C link their votes, both roads will be built, and farmer A will have to shell out $4 in taxes. Farmers B and C each gain $3 (= $7 − $4), which is their net gain from building both roads.

Whether logrolling increases or decreases economic efficiency depends on the circumstances. In this example, building both roads has a net social benefit of $2. Each road costs $6; each road brings benefits of $7. Thus, from a purely social point of view, it is worthwhile to build the two roads. Hence, logrolling in this case is a good thing because without logrolling the roads would not have been built.

But logrolling can also result in inefficiencies. If each road brings in net benefits of only $5 each to farmers B and C instead of $7 each, farmers B and C, if they link their votes, must each pay out $4 ($2 for each access road) and A must contribute $4 ($2 per road). Since the benefit to B and C ($5 each) exceeds their cost ($4 each), it is still worthwhile to them to logroll. But now the net social benefit is −$2 rather than +$2. The new net benefits and costs are shown in Table 2.

The example described in Table 2 demonstrates that majority rule with logrolling can result in policies that lower the size of the total economic pie. Indeed, for this reason some political scientists have recommended political reforms that eliminate logrolling opportunities.[1]

The Voting Paradox

Even in simple majority-rule voting situations without logrolling, a definite outcome may not emerge. The real world is filled with examples of many policy inconsistencies. Governments pass minimum-wage laws that create unemployment and then create job-training programs to put people to work. The government raises the cost of food to the poor through farm price supports and then hands out food stamps to the poor. Governments subsidize college students (who tend to be from affluent families) and then enact policies that benefit middle-income or poor families.

This inconsistency can be explained using an example. Suppose three voters (A, B, and C) must vote on three policies (policy a, policy b, and policy c). Policy a redistributes income to voter A, policy b redistributes income to voter B, and policy c redistributes income to voter C. Table 3 describes how voters A, B, and C rank these various policies. Naturally, the first choice of each voter is the policy that benefits him or her. But each voter also has preferences for the other policies as well. Voter A, for instance, might like voter C more than voter B. Hence, policy c is A's

1. Dennis C. Mueller, *Public Choice* (Cambridge: Cambridge University Press, 1979), pp. 49–51.

Table 2
Building Access Roads for Farmers B and C: Costs Exceed Benefits

Beneficiaries	Access Road for B	Access Road for C
A	− $2	− $2
B	+ $3	− $2
C	− $2	+ $3
Society	− $1	− $1

In this case, access roads still cost $6 each and cost is still shared equally by all three farmers. But each access road is worth only $5 to the affected farmer. Building the roads is socially inefficient in this case. Under simple majority rule without logrolling neither road is built, but when Farmers B and C link their votes both roads are built even though the benefits to the two farmers do not exceed the costs to society.

second choice and policy b is A's third choice. Table 3 shows that voter B prefers policy a to policy c, and that voter C prefers policy b to policy a.

Notice that in Table 3 every policy is one person's first choice, another's second choice, and a third person's third choice. The table is therefore perfectly symmetrical in this respect. Only two issues are voted on at a time. In a contest between policies a and b, voter C determines the outcome because A and B vote for their own policies. Since voter C prefers b to a, policy b wins.

Table 4 shows the three possible contests and outcomes. In each of the three possible contests, a different policy wins. No one policy wins more than one contest. If someone witnessed only the first two contests and saw that b was preferred to a and that a was preferred to c, logic would suggest to that person that b should be preferred to c. However, the third row of Table 4 shows that in fact c is preferred to b. Majority rule has resulted in an inconsistent outcome. This inconsistency is the *paradox of voting*. If one reverses the second and third choices of just one of the voters, the paradox disappears, however.

THE POLITICAL MARKET

The political market consists of voters, politicians, political parties, special-interest groups, and the bureaucracy. How do each of these affect the public choices made by democratic governments?

Voters

It is common after an election for journalists and television announcers to bemoan the difficulty of motivating people to vote. The decline in voter turnout between the U.S. elections in 1960 and 1972 and the continued decline in the 1980 election indicates to some far too much apathy on the part of voters.

What motivates a voter to vote? Objectively, there is a marginal cost (in time and effort) of going to vote. The probability of any single person's vote deciding an election is close to zero. According to one study, most people vote out of a sense of obligation and duty, but an important determinant of voter turnout is the cost of going to the polls and the closeness of the election. If

Table 3
Policy Rankings

Policy	Voter A	Voter B	Voter C
a	1st choice	2nd choice	3rd choice
b	3rd choice	1st choice	2nd choice
c	2nd choice	3rd choice	1st choice

Table 4
Possible Contests and Outcomes

Contest	Winning Policy
a vs. b	b
a vs. c	a
b vs. c	c

people expect a close election, the chances of voting are larger.[2]

The evidence suggests that people do make a cost/benefit calculation when they decide whether or not to vote. The benefit voters enjoy is the knowledge that they have performed their duty as a citizen; this benefit increases the closer the election is supposed to be.

Do people make informed decisions when they do go to the polls? Anthony Downs calls the lack of information on the part of the voting public **rational ignorance.**[3]

> ***Rational ignorance*** *is a decision not to acquire information because the marginal cost of acquiring the information exceeds the marginal benefit of having the information.*

The chapter on information costs explained that people gather information about choices as long as the extra benefits of information gathering exceed the extra cost. The cost of acquiring information about public choices is greater than the cost for private choices because public programs are more complicated than most private goods and the link between the act of voting and the benefits received is very uncertain. Hence, most people will know much more about private choices than about public choices. This ignorance is rational because it is a response to the costs of information.

Special-Interest Groups

The major implication of rational ignorance is that voters will know much more about legislation that affects them than about legislation that affects someone else. *Special-interest groups* are minority groups with intense preferences about specific government policies. Dairy farmers will be very well-informed about milk-price supports; many consumers may not know they exist. The benefits to dairy farmers from higher milk-price supports are enormous; the costs to the typical voter of

these supports are comparatively small. To the individual voter, the cost of finding out about the milk-price-support program exceeds the increase in the price caused by the program. Thus, the dairy farmers will have intense preferences for milk price supports, and the rest of the public will be nearly indifferent. This is just the type of situation where logrolling and vote trading among politicians can result in special-interest legislation that is economically inefficient.

Politicians and Political Parties

President John F. Kennedy was fond of quoting the typical mother who wanted her offspring to grow up to be President, but who did not want a politician in the family. For reasons imbedded deeply in human psychology, people expect politicians to behave on a higher or more altruistic level than the average person. When they act just like anyone else does, people are disappointed in their low moral character.

The successful politician is a political entrepreneur. Politicians, through voting and logrolling, determine government policies. Like a business entrepreneur who stays in business by offering consumers what they want, the political entrepreneur can only stay in business by offering a platform of positions that will attract enough votes at election time. The politician earns his or her living by getting reelected. The rewards of reelection are many: popularity, power, prestige, and increased income opportunities. The public-choice economist assumes that politicians are more interested in votes than in serving the public interest. Even if they are completely unselfish, politicians cannot serve society unless they are reelected.

Remembering that voters are rationally ignorant about the complex of policies a particular politician supports, a vote-maximizing politician can put together a package of policies consisting of special-interest legislation that benefits a minority but hurts the majority. Each member of the minority will benefit enormously while each member of the majority will be hurt only a trivial amount. By preparing a package of such policies, the politician can attract enough support from a coalition of minority groups to actually win. The politician who opposes all the special-interest leg-

2. O. Ashenfelter and S. Kelly, Jr., "Determinants of Participation in Presidential Elections," *Journal of Law and Economics* 18 (December 1975): 695–733.

3. Anthony Downs, *An Economic Theory of Democracy* (New York: Harper & Row, 1957).

islation might be looking for a job after the next election.

The central problem of public choice in our society is that the benefits of government policies are highly concentrated while the costs are highly diffused.

Restricting Japanese car imports makes the American automobile manufacturer and worker better off in an obvious way. The costs of import restrictions, however, are distributed over the entire population in such a subtle fashion that the public cannot distinguish between the increase in the price caused by the policy and, say, inflation. The French economist, Frederick Bastiat, referred to this as *what is seen* and *what is unseen*. What is seen is the fact that farmers are better off with price supports; what is unseen is that the price of dairy products is a few cents higher to everyone. The consumer does not know how much of the price paid for a TV set is due to the U.S. tariff on imported TV sets. American TV manufacturers and assembly workers, however, are very aware of the protection.

All government policies do not make the public worse off. The same political process that provides valuable pure public goods may result in inefficient levels of public goods (which may be unavoidable) and costly special-interest policies.

Bureaucrats

Aside from assorted lobbyists and pressure groups, the final actor on the political stage is the much-maligned *bureaucrat*. Basically, a bureaucracy is needed to run the government programs enacted by politicians. The bureaucrats tend to be the experts (social scientists, lawyers, accountants) who execute the programs.

Many observers have pointed out that bureaucracies tend to produce budgets that are too large. In market firms, profits provide the incentive to minimize costs. In bureaucratic firms, there are few incentives to minimize costs—instead bureaucrats may maximize "personal profits" in the form of plush offices or European trips. Large budgets cannot be monitored because of rational ignorance on the part of the politicians that approve the budgets. Legislators, who must be con-

cerned with thousands of different programs, get the bulk of their information from the very bureaucracies they are trying to oversee. The bureaucrat has an enormous information advantage over the typical legislator. Since the bureaucrat is interested in expanding the budget and since the legislator is not too interested in cutting out the program completely (due to the importance of special interests), the budget will tend to be larger than necessary.

Competition Among Local Communities

Although voting at the ballot box is one form of voting, Charles Tiebout also believes voters can "vote with their feet." Charles Tiebout hypothesized that households are not frozen in particular localities but, instead, can shop around to seek out the bundle of public goods and taxes that most closely approximates their demands for local public goods, such as parks, police protection, roads, zoos, and schools.[4] Consumers have some discretion over their consumption of public services. The competitive aspects of the provision of public services by different cities or states may stimulate local officials to try to minimize costs and to respond to consumer tastes.

THE SCOPE OF GOVERNMENT

Economic analysis suggests that some government resource-allocation activities may be carried too far while others are not carried far enough. Recent popular and political opinion, as indicated by the election of Ronald Reagan as President, has tended to support the view that government is too large.

Opponents of large government criticize the combination of special interests, logrolling, and rational ignorance on the part of both the public and our representatives. Public spending on supporting particular groups or industries—such as agriculture or the Chrysler corporation—is criticized as not being in the "public interest."

Anthony Downs has pointed out that rational ignorance is also responsible for government being too small. According to Downs, the voter

4. Wallace E. Oates, "On Local Finance and the Tiebout Model," *American Economic Review* 71 (May 1981): 93–98.

will usually underestimate the *benefits* (not just the costs) of fully justifiable government expenditures because they are remote and uncertain. In Down's view, a fully informed voter would vote for larger budgets, but voters are not so informed because of private information costs. John Kenneth Galbraith has also argued that private advertising makes people more aware of private needs than public needs.

Many public-choice economists believe that government has grown too large. James Buchanan argues that constitutional limits must be imposed on democratic governments in order to constrain their inherent tendencies to overexpand:

> Modern America confronts a crisis of major proportions in the last decades of the twentieth century. In the seven decades from 1900 to 1970, total government spending in real terms increased forty times over, attaining a share of one-third in national product. These basic facts are familiar . . . The point of emphasis is that this growth has occurred, almost exclusively, within the predictable workings of orderly democratic procedures.[5]

GOVERNMENT FAILURE

Modern public-choice theory suggests that, regardless of the size of government, there are substantial government failures involved in the way public choices are made. The preferences of everyone, from the lowest worker to the captain of industry, should be duly registered when public choices are made. Public-choice economists have proposed a variety of reforms to accomplish this objective, including the following:[6]

1. Members of Congress should be determined by a process of random selection from the general public.
2. A three-fourths majority should be required for some types of legislation (particularly obvious special-interest legislation, such as tariffs, price supports, minimum-wage laws, and loans to bankrupt-prone firms).
3. Decisions on major proposals should be made by direct majority voting by the general public.
4. All expenditure programs should be linked to a visible tax increase.

These reforms attempt to address the problems of rational ignorance, logrolling, and the overrepresentation of special interests.

This chapter examined how government works. The self-interest of politicians and bureaucrats combined with limited information can often result in poor public policies. This chapter looked at only one political-economic system: democratic capitalism; the next chapter will look at other economic systems.

Summary

1. The government must make resource-allocation decisions because the market fails to efficiently allocate public goods. In an ideal world, all government actions would have the unanimous support of all citizens. Unanimous collective decisions, however, require perfect information and zero bargaining costs. Governments would price public goods according to each individual's marginal valuation of the good, and each individual would vote for the proposal.
2. Unanimity is virtually impossible in the real world. The most popular alternative in democratic societies is majority rule. Under majority rule, the median voter decides on public goods. Social choices, therefore, do not reflect the relative intensities of preferences of different voters. Majority rule does not guarantee that the socially optimal amount of the public good will be produced.
3. Majority rule makes possible logrolling and pork-barrel politics in situations involving more than one decision. By forming vote-trading coalitions, beneficiaries of public goods can create majorities that would not have been possible otherwise. Majority voting can also lead to the paradox of voting.

5. James M. Buchanan, *The Limits of Liberty* (Chicago: The University of Chicago Press, 1975), p. 162. Chapter 9 of Buchanan's book contains compelling reasons why governments can get too large.
6. The proposals are given in E. Browning and J. Browning, *Public Finance and the Price System* (New York: Macmillan Publishing Co., 1979).

4. The political market consists of voters, politicians, political parties, special-interest groups, and the bureaucracy. Voters use personal cost/benefit analysis in their voting decisions; they vote when the perceived costs are low and the perceived benefits are high. Voting decisions are characterized by *rational ignorance*. The costs to most voters of acquiring information on complex public issues are high and the benefits are low. For special-interest groups, however, the benefits are high relative to the costs of acquiring information. Politicians must adopt policies that will improve their chances of reelection. Rational ignorance and the fact that the public does not see the effects of many government policies encourage special-interest legislation.

5. Economic analysis indicates that the government undertakes many programs for which the marginal social benefits do not exceed the marginal social costs or fails to undertake many programs for which the marginal social benefits do exceed the marginal social costs.

6. Public-choice economists have offered suggestions on how to improve public choices. These suggestions attempt to solve the problems of rational ignorance, logrolling, and overrepresentation of special interests.

Key Terms

logrolling
rational ignorance

Questions and Problems

1. What factors limit unanimity on political decisions?

2. Some politicians have been observed to switch their positions in the course of political contests (for example, between the primary and the general election). Is this fact consistent with the theory of the role of the median voter in majority rule elections? Why or why not?

3. If people are rational, how can public choice result in government actions with benefits that are less than the costs?

4. In 1981, the United States spent $225 billion on income security programs. Social security absorbed $145 billion, and federal expenditures to finance assistance for housing, food, nutrition, and other aid to needy families amounted to $43 billion. Do you think the political process is working to the advantage of the needy or of the average person who retires? Explain.

5. Do you think government will be more or less efficient than competitive enterprise? Will it be more or less efficient than private monopoly? Explain.

6. Do you think lobbying promotes or reduces the general welfare? Explain.

7. How would you reform the political process to make majority rule work better?

8. "The more localized are public goods, the more likely it is that unanimity can be achieved in public choices." Evaluate this statement.

23

Comparative Economic Systems

Chapter Preview

Most of this book has been devoted to the American economy, but no two economies are exactly alike. In many ways, the study of the American economy provides a useful introduction to economics. The American economy uses primarily the market forces of supply and demand to solve the economic problem of *what, how,* and *for whom.* Although the economic role of government appears to be large to most of us, in proportion to the huge size of the American economy, it is still smaller than in most other countries. Although the government does redistribute income through taxes and the allocation of government services, the redistributive role of American gov-

ernment is still less than in most other developed countries.

The American economy comes about as close as possible in our modern world to being a textbook example of a capitalist market economy. Some economies, however, rely more on government planners to allocate resources than they do on markets. In some economies, there is virtually no private ownership of land or capital. In other economies, substantial differences between the rich and poor are eliminated by government action. In some countries, consumers have a great say in determining what will be produced; in others, government officials assume this responsibility. Each country solves the economic problem using its own particular type of **economic system.**

*An **economic system** is the set of ownership, resource-allocation, incentive, and decision-making arrangements that a society uses to solve the economic problem.*

This chapter will examine the functioning and evaluate the performance of the economic system that prevails in the Soviet Union as the major alternative to the capitalist economic system that prevails in the United States.

HOW ECONOMIC SYSTEMS DIFFER

Economies differ according to a large number of attributes. An economic system cannot be defined or categorized on the basis of one characteristic alone. Typically, economic systems are differentiated according to four dimensions:

1. Ownership of resources.
2. Allocation of resources.
3. Incentives.
4. Level of decision making.

Ownership of Resources

Who owns the factors of production is an important identifying trait of an economic system. The factors of production may be owned primarily by society (or by a government that is supposed to represent society), by private individuals, or by a combination of the two.

Allocation of Resources

Goods and the factors of production can be allocated by the forces of supply and demand or they can be allocated by government planners. How resources are allocated will determine how a society solves the what and how problems. In some economic systems, individual firms decide what and how to produce, and in others government officials give orders to enterprises.

Incentives

Most economic systems use one of two basic mechanisms for motivating the participants in the economic system to carry out their economic tasks. The first mechanism is to provide *economic incentives* to motivate people. The other alternative is to provide *moral incentives* (medals, adulation in the press) or even *threats* to induce individuals to work and produce.

Level of Decision Making

Different economic systems make economic decisions at different levels. The individual participants in the economic system (households and individual firms) may make their own decisions (a decentralized arrangement) or their decisions may be made for them at higher levels (a centralized arrangement). When resource allocation decisions are made by government officials, they may be made at the local, regional, or national level.

CAPITALISM VERSUS SOCIALISM

Using the four characteristics of an economic system, **capitalism** and **socialism** can be defined more exactly.

***Capitalism** is an economic system characterized by private ownership of the factors of production, market allocation of resources, the use of economic incentives, and decentralized decision making.*

Socialism exists in two variants: **planned socialism** and **market socialism.**

***Planned socialism** is an economic system characterized by state ownership of the factors of production (other than labor), the use of moral as well as economic incentives, resource allocation by economic plan, and centralized decision making.*

***Market socialism** is an economic system characterized by state ownership of the factors of production, the use of primarily economic incentives, market allocation of resources, and decentralized decision making.*

No real-world economy fits exactly into any one of these three abstract molds. In all economies, there is a mixture of private and public ownership, administrative and market allocation, economic and moral incentives, and centralized and decentralized decision making. However, in most economies, the major traits of one particular economic system will dominate. For example, the American economy is considered a capitalist economy because private ownership, market resource allocation, economic incentives, and decentralized decision making dominate. The Soviet economy is a planned socialist economy because public ownership, resource allocation by plan, and centralized decision making dominate in that economy.

Examples of market socialism—economies where resources are publicly owned, yet where allocation occurs by way of the market—are harder to find in the contemporary world. Yugoslavia is a notable current example of market socialism, and Hungary is experimenting with different forms of market socialism.

This book has already provided a thorough introduction to one economic system—capitalism—in its presentation of the American economic system. The functioning of the major alternative to the capitalist system—planned socialism—is best illustrated by an analysis of the Soviet economy. Of course, one cannot directly generalize from the Soviet and American economies to the abstract economic systems they represent. The Soviet and American economies are quite different in other respects than their economic system. After all, the Soviet economy, despite its impressive military power, is still a much more backward economy than the United States. When the Soviet Union began its industrialization drive in the 1930s, it was one of the poorest countries of Western Europe and remains so today despite considerable economic growth. Nevertheless, the Soviet Union is a country much like the United States in the richness of its resources and in its position as an economic and political power in its sphere of influence.

THE SOVIET ECONOMY

It is not possible to understand how the Soviet economy works without understanding the ideology and political system of the Soviet Union. For deep-rooted ideological reasons and because of perceived negative experiences with the market in the 1920s, the leadership of the Soviet Union has been and remains deeply distrustful of resource allocation by the forces of supply and demand. The leadership of the Soviet communist party believes it is the responsibility of the party (and the state) to decide what is to be produced, how it is to be produced, and for whom. The purpose of the 1917 revolution in Russia was to place the communist party in charge of resource allocation.

Soviet leaders believe that the communist party knows what is best for society at large and that the market leads only to anarchy. Therefore, they believe it is essential for the party, not the market, to resolve the economic problem.

The communist party begins the process of solving the economic problem by setting economic priorities. These priorities are handed down to government and industry officials by government planners in the form of general instructions. These instructions presumably set general goals for major industries, announce major changes in economic policy, set targets for Soviet agriculture, and detail the defense budget.

In the Soviet Union, the main planning body is *Gosplan* (the State Planning Agency), and Gosplan is directly responsible to the highest officials of the communist party. The Industrial Ministries participate in the planning process by assisting in the preparation of detailed plans for the enterprises that they control. Together, Gosplan and the Industrial Ministries make up the planning apparatus of the Soviet Union.

Soviet planners translate the priorities of the communist party into actual directives and orders for each enterprise in the Soviet Union. As there are currently several hundred thousand such enterprises in an economy that produces a gross national product (GNP) of more than $1 trillion, this task is not easy.

Balancing Supplies and Demands

In the 1930s, there was a lively debate among economists about the feasibility of a planned socialist economic system. The sceptics in this "socialist controversy"—Friedrich von Hayek and Ludwig von Mises—argued that a modern economy, comprised of thousands of enterprises, millions of consumers, and producing millions of distinct products, could not conceivably be planned in a satisfactory manner. The job of balancing supplies and demands would simply be too large even in a world of high-speed computers. But the Soviet economy—despite the dire predictions of Hayek and Mises—has survived as a centrally planned economy for more than 50 years. How have Soviet planners managed to plan an increasingly complex economy?

The planning method developed by the Soviets in the 1930s (and still used in virtually the same form today) is called **material-balance planning.**

Material-balance planning is a system of resource allocation in which centralized planning is restricted to controlling the output levels of only the most important industrial commodities that the economy produces and in which the production of other less important commodities is controlled at lower levels in the planning hierarchy.

Commodities such as electricity, steel, concrete, coal, oil, motor vehicles, cotton textiles, industrial chemicals, and machine tools determine the direction of the economy and are therefore planned and allocated from Moscow. Other less important commodities—such as services, garments, and toys—are planned, but they are managed at lower planning levels. Only those enterprises that have been granted permission by the highest planning authorities are permitted to use the basic industrial commodities. Other less important commodities are planned by the ministries or by regional or even local authorities. Some commodities are not planned at all; in rare cases, some commodities are even allocated by the market. The notion of dealing centrally with only the most important industrial commodities derives from practical necessity and from the theory that the communist party could control the whole economy by controlling its most important industrial commodities.

For each of the several thousand commodities that are planned by Gosplan, Gosplan must determine a **material balance.** For example, Gosplan knows from its preliminary production targets that 500 million tons of coal are to be produced in the coming year. It also knows that there are existing contracts to export 50 million tons of coal. A do-

mestic supply of 450 million tons then remains. On the demand side of the market, Gosplan knows (largely on the basis of past experience) the coal requirements of each industry that are necessary to meet their anticipated production targets and also the coal requirements of the housing sector. Thus, Gosplan can estimate the anticipated demand for coal during the coming year.

*The **material balance** is a comparison of the anticipated demands and supplies of a critical good by administrative means.*

Gosplan must draw up a material balance for each critical commodity—for steel, for cement, for sulphuric acid, for trucks, and so on. Once Gosplan has listed all the anticipated supplies and demands, it must make sure that there is an overall balance. Gosplan may find, for example, that the anticipated demand for coal exceeds the anticipated supply of coal.

In capitalist economies, imbalances between supply and demand are corrected by spontaneous changes in relative prices. If there is an excess demand for coal and an excess supply of steel, coal prices will rise and steel prices will fall. In this way, capitalist economies can equate supplies and demands. Soviet material-balance planning corrects imbalances by making administrative changes in planned supplies and demand. If there is an excess demand for coal, planners can either raise production targets for coal or reduce the planned allocations of coal. In the Soviet Union, there is rarely an excess supply of any critical commodity. The problem planners typically must correct is excess demand. Responding to excess demands by raising production targets could disrupt other balances. Gosplan, therefore, has typically corrected imbalances by reducing planned allocations (by reducing demand) and not by increasing supply.

Setting Priorities. Gosplan does not reduce material allocations in a haphazard manner. It will not, for example, say that every firm must take a 10 percent cut in coal allocations if it is necessary to reduce the demand for coal by 10 percent. Instead, Gosplan will follow a strict **priority principle.**

*The **priority principle** is that the industries most important to the communist party will be the last to take cuts in supplies. Historically, light industry, which produces goods for the consumer, has been the low-priority industry. Therefore, when cuts have had to be made, they are absorbed by light industry and, ultimately, by the consumer.*

There are two reasons for the strict observance of the priority principle over the years. The first is that the Soviet leadership has consistently favored heavy industry over light industry because heavy industry provides military hardware and because heavy industry is supposed to provide the basis for the future communist society. The second reason is that it is better to avoid plan shortfalls in heavy industry than in light industry. If steel, oil, or coal targets are not met, these shortfalls will disrupt the entire plan. If the plan for men's suits or children's shoes is not met, the overall impact on the plan will be limited.

Executing the Plan.   After intense negotiation and tough bargaining among all interested parties—the communist party, Gosplan, the ministries, regional authorities, and enterprise managers—Gosplan prepares a balanced operational economic plan for the U.S.S.R. economy. This national economic plan is then submitted to the Soviet government for final approval, after which the economic plan becomes the law of the land. It is then the responsibility of every Soviet citizen and every Soviet enterprise to fulfill the tasks set out in the national plan.

Each enterprise receives a detailed enterprise plan—a thick document—that tells it what commodities it must produce, how many employees to have on the payroll, what materials it is to receive, what new machinery to install, what bank credits to draw on, and so on down to the finest details of enterprise operation. The enterprise director is responsible for fulfilling this enterprise plan.

Surprisingly, the national economic plan is only the first phase in the resource-allocation process. Plan targets are never fulfilled in their entirety. In the course of plan fulfillment, it may become evident that some targets cannot be achieved or that not all promised supplies can be delivered. Again, administrative decisions about what parts of the plan will be fulfilled and what targets must be set aside are made according to the priority principle. There is no formal process for making such decisions. What is evident from Soviet economic history is that a strict priority principle has been observed, whereby low-priority branches bear the burden when resources are juggled. When the plan is announced with great fanfare, ambitious increases in consumer goods are typically called for, but when the plan is completed, the shortfalls are concentrated in the consumer-goods area.[1]

Soviet Managers

Official accounts of Soviet planning portray the Soviet manager as an unimportant actor in the resource-allocation process. After all, the economic plan provides the manager with a detailed set of instructions concerning what is to be produced and how it is to be produced. It would appear that all the Soviet manager has to do is to follow these instructions. Nothing could be further from the truth. Because the Soviet manager is given so many instructions—many of which are contradictory—he or she has considerable discretionary authority in the conduct of the enterprise's business. The fact that the enterprise manager is the one who decides what plan directives to follow and which directives to ignore makes the enterprise manager an important participant in the resource-allocation process.

Soviet managers—just like American managers—want to be successful, and to be successful, they too must please their bosses. The manager's boss is his or her immediate superior (perhaps a regional minister, or, if it is a large firm, it may even be the national minister). The immediate superior is then responsible to his or her superior, and so on up the hierarchy. Eventually, everyone is responsible to the communist party.

Over the years, Soviet managers have learned that success is measured by one's ability to fulfill

---

1.   It is difficult to pin down the record of plan fulfillment. During the course of a plan, plan targets are continuously revised so that at the end of the plan, party officials can announce the plan's success.

Pollution in the U.S.S.R.

Many people associate pollution with market failure and social selfishness. Capitalist societies, where businesses are interested in maximizing profits, appear to be a fertile breeding ground for pollution. However, pollution is not unique to capitalism; it is also present in planned socialist societies, such as the U.S.S.R. In the Soviet Union virtually all firms are government-owned and are directed by the orders of the government planners. Government planners, who are in a position to internalize externalities, fail to eliminate pollution because it is costly for enterprise managers and industrial ministers to eliminate pollution. Government enterprises are judged on the basis of how much they produce. Industrial ministries are judged on the basis of how much enterprises under their jurisdiction produce. To devote resources to pollution reduction means producing less output today; yet Soviet society rewards production today, not the social benefits society may receive from a cleaner environment tomorrow. ◢◣

those plan targets that one's superiors regard as most important. The relative importance of different plan targets has changed over the years—one year cost reduction targets are important; the next year the labor-productivity plan is more important—but what remains constant is that one's success as a manager is judged primarily on the basis of one's ability to fulfill output targets. All other targets are secondary in comparison to the output target. Therefore, it is not surprising that Soviet managers have devoted most of their attention to making sure that they meet output targets.

The use of output targets as the criterion for judging managerial success has led to paradoxical economic behavior on the part of the Soviet manager. Rational Soviet managers are led by their own incentive system to engage in activities that reduce output and waste economic resources. From the viewpoint of the Soviet manager, an ideal plan is one that gives the manager more resources than are necessary to produce an output well below the enterprise's capacity. Under these circumstances, the manager knows that the plan targets can be met with little risk of failure. The worst thing that can happen is that the manager gets a plan that supplies few resources and requires the production of an output beyond the capacity of the enterprise. It is in managers' best interests to provide false or misleading information to their superiors—to overstate their input requirements and to understate their output capacities. During the Stalin years, managers who failed to meet output targets were branded as capitalist saboteurs and sent to Siberia or summarily executed. Although contemporary penalties for such failures are by no means so drastic, the search for managerial success continues.

When the manager receives the ideal plan of ample resources and small outputs requirements, one might expect that the manager would like to impress his or her superiors by overfulfilling the targets. On the contrary, however, the manager who reports an impressive degree of overfulfillment would risk receiving a much more ambitious set of targets next year. Soviet managers fear the *ratchet effect,* whereby planners respond to plan overfulfillment by "ratcheting up" plan targets for the next year. Soviet managers therefore avoid impressive plan overfulfillment, preferring to overfulfill the output plan by a modest margin.

The difficulty of exactly defining the desired mix of output encourages the Soviet manager to engage in other kinds of opportunistic behavior. If the manager is told to produce 10 million rubles worth of children's shoes, the easiest thing to do is to produce all shoes of the same size and color and flood the market with goods the consumer does not want. If the manager is told to produce a specific mix of sizes and colors, he or she may skimp on materials and produce defective shoes, technically fulfilling the output targets.

The manager will hesitate to innovate because the risks of trying new things will be large, and the perceived benefits will be small. New production technologies may disrupt existing supply channels, construction delays may endanger fulfillment of the all-important output plan. Planners might not recognize that a better product is being produced or that output is being produced more efficiently.

MARKET ALLOCATION IN THE SOVIET UNION

Although most industrial commodities and investment goods are allocated by the administrative orders of planners and party officials, market-resource allocation does play a reasonably important role in the Soviet economy. The major areas of market-resource allocation are in the buying and selling of consumer goods, labor, and underground commodities.

Consumer Goods

The amounts and qualities of consumer goods produced in the Soviet Union are planned by government and party officials, although enterprise managers do have some leeway to determine what will be produced. In the whole process of determining what to produce, the consumer has remarkably little say. Soviet consumers must spend their income on those goods that the state and enterprise managers have decided to produce. Once produced, consumer goods are, with important exceptions, allocated to consumers much as they are allocated in capitalist countries. Soviet consumers make up their own minds as to what they want to buy with their earned income, and the state generally attempts to set prices to equate supplies and demands. In terms of supply and demand curves, consumer goods are allocated as in Figure 1. The supply of good X is completely inelastic; the demand curve is no different from the demand curves drawn in earlier chapters. If the state, which sets virtually all prices in the Soviet Union, fails to set the price at equilibrium, there will be either a shortage or a surplus. Surpluses are not unknown, especially for shoddy or defective merchandise that accumulates unsold in Soviet stores. Shortages are more common, but Soviet pricing authorities have learned that if shortages are too widespread consumers will find that they cannot use their earnings to buy what they want and will lose interest in higher earnings. This loss of incentives can harm the econ-

Figure 1
Retail Pricing in the Soviet Union

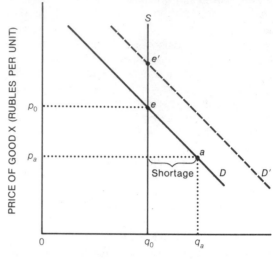

In the Soviet Union, the supply of consumer goods is basically determined by planners without reference to price. Thus, the supply curve is virtually vertical (perfectly inelastic). The demand curve, however, obeys the law of demand and is downward-sloping.

For many products, Soviet authorities attempt to set retail prices at the equilibrium price (at p_0). Other products, however, are priced below equilibrium (at p_a, for example) for reasons of income distribution and social control. An important feature of the Soviet system is that increases in demand (an increase from D to D') do not lead to increases in quantity supplied.

omy; therefore, in general, the Soviets have attempted at least in recent years to keep prices of consumer goods near equilibrium levels.

The rule of pricing consumer goods to equate supply and demand is broken in many instances. Housing, automobiles, high-quality merchandise imported from the West, and other prestige items are typically sold at prices too low to equate supply and demand. Housing rents are maintained at ridiculously low levels both for purposes of income distribution (Socialists believe no one in a Socialist society should be denied housing for reasons of income) and for reasons of social control. If prized apartments are allocated not by price but by political authorities or plant managers, then authorities have another tool for controlling and motivating the population. The same can be said of private automobiles, access to French or West German goods, and seaside resorts. Government officials allocate such goods as rewards for good workers and the party faithful.

Labor

With some exceptions, Soviet citizens can select their own occupations and places of employment. One exception is that college graduates are assigned their first job and must remain in these jobs for a prescribed period of time. Authorities also limit the number of people who are allowed to move to major urban centers like Moscow and Leningrad. Otherwise, the Soviet labor force makes its own decisions about where to work.[2]

Planning authorities determine the demand for labor in different occupations and in different industries. To insure that these demands will be met, industrial wages are set to equate supply and demand. As a result, occupations in undesirable locations or dangerous, unpleasant, or dirty jobs are paid more than others. In fact, Soviet wage differentials appear to be much like those in the United States or other capitalist countries. Workers in the Far North who work under extreme weather conditions earn wages 2 to 3 times those in central U.S.S.R. The Soviet economy most resembles a capitalist economy in the area of labor allocation. The Soviets have learned that incentives will be low if occupational choice is not relatively free. People cannot be ordered around from one job or occupation to another like steel and cement. A relatively free labor market is the price that must be paid to maintain worker incentives.

The Second Economy

Karl Marx had hoped that the creation of a socialist state would create a ''new socialist man''—a new type of individual who would place the interests of society above personal self-interest (see Appendix to this chapter). As we have shown, however, the Soviet labor market operates much like a capitalist market. Recent research shows that a substantial unplanned sector of the Soviet economy—called the ''second economy''—may be as important in the Soviet Union as it is to Western capitalist economies. In capitalist economies, the underground economy supplies goods and services and serves as a device for evading taxes. In the U.S.S.R., the underground economy specializes in supplying goods and services planners are incapable of or unwilling to supply.

There is no way to measure the relative size of the Soviet second economy. Newspapers report spectacular court proceedings in the Soviet Union that unearth self-made Soviet millionaire entrepreneurs. Emigrants from the Soviet Union also report a wide range of second-economy activities: physicians have large earnings from private practices (which are not allowed by law); materials from state enterprises are diverted into the production of high-quality consumer goods; important positions in the communist party are sold by party officials. Scarce supplies are made available to industrial firms by under-the-table deals between enterprises. In fact, in the Soviet Union, a recognized profession is that of the *expeditor*—the individual who arranges for industrial materials outside of normal supply channels.

The activities mentioned above are illegal activities, but there is one form of legal private economic activity that is openly tolerated by Soviet officials: the collective farm market. Farmers in socialist agriculture are allowed to keep small plots of land for their own cultivation or for sale if they decide. The products from these private plots are sold in collective farm markets at prices determined by the forces of supply and demand. Collective farm markets can vary from a large organized outdoor market in a large city to a peasant woman selling apples on a street corner. The output of private agriculture—which comes from land that is only 1 percent of total cultivated acreage—accounts for a large proportion of the Soviet consumption of meat, dairy, and vegetable products. The role of these farm markets is so important in feeding the Soviet population that party authorities have no choice but to accept it.

---

2. This was not always the case. During the early years of the Soviet regime (1918–1921), labor was treated pretty much like military conscripts (this was, after all, the time of the Russian civil war), and the state told people where they were to work and whether or not they could quit their jobs. The same was true during the Second World War, when there were severe penalties for tardiness or changing jobs without permission. But with these exceptions, Soviet citizens have been relatively free in their choice of occupations.

SOVIET ECONOMIC PERFORMANCE

The preceding section described briefly how the Soviet economy solves the *what, how,* and *for whom* problems. This description of the Soviet economy suggests that there are certain weak points. Material-balance planning is a clumsy and cumbersome process that aims more at finding balances of supplies and demands than at finding the best way to combine inputs. Managers are more interested in meeting output targets than in combining resources in the most efficient manner. Managers are not motivated by the incentive system to take risks.

Market economies also have their own weaknesses. When firms possess monopoly power, output is restricted below the social optimum. When externalities are present, only private costs and benefits will be considered. Capitalism may lead to an income distribution that many people may regard as unfair.

Assessing how well one existing economy performs relative to another is a tricky business. It is even more difficult to determine how well a theoretical economic system should perform relative to another. One conceptual problem confounds such comparisons: by whose standards should one judge economic performance? By the standards of the Soviet communist party, Soviet economic performance may be regarded as satisfactory. By standards that place more emphasis on living standards, Soviet performance is less satisfactory. Value judgments must be made to draw conclusions concerning economic performance, and there is no scientific way to prove that one person's (or one group's) judgments are better than any other's.

The various criteria that are typically used to evaluate economic performance include: economic growth, economic efficiency, economic stability, military power, and income distribution. Once the performance of the Soviet economy in each area has been evaluated, it is then up to the individual reader to decide just how well or how poorly the Soviet economy has performed.

Economic Growth

From the viewpoint of the Soviet leadership, rapid economic growth has always been an im-

Table 1
Annual Rates of Economic Growth: U.S.S.R., United States, and Major Capitalist Economies

Country	Growth Rate (percent)
U.S.S.R.	
1885–1913	3.3
1928–1940	5.4
1950–1981	4.8
1928–1981	5.0
United States	
1834–1929	4.0
1929–1981	3.0
United Kingdom (1855–1980)	2.2
France (1831–1980)	2.5
Belgium (1900–1980)	2.3
Netherlands (1860–1980)	2.6
Germany (1850–1980)	2.9
Denmark (1865–1980)	3.1
Japan (1874–1980)	4.6
Canada (1870–1980)	3.6

Source: Paul Gregory and Robert Stuart, *Soviet Economic Structure and Performance,* rev. ed. (New York: Harper and Row, 1981), p. 335, 337.

portant goal for several reasons. Rapid economic growth lays the economic foundation for communism; it allows the Soviet Union to catch up and overtake its capitalist enemies; economic growth, particularly of heavy industry, makes possible a strong military. Moreover, the Soviet leadership has consistently claimed that the superiority of the Soviet economic system would be demonstrated by its ability to grow more rapidly than the declining and decadent capitalist West.

Table 1 supplies data on the long-term economic growth of the U.S.S.R. and of the major capitalist countries. These data show that the Soviet economy has indeed grown rapidly since the initiation of its industrialization drive in 1928, more rapidly in the long run than any major capitalist country with the exception of Japan. The data also show that the Soviet growth rate has been declining over the past two decades; Soviet economic growth is now no more rapid than the average growth of capitalist countries. Soviet ambitions to overtake the United States economy must, therefore, be put aside unless a means can be found to revive the ailing Soviet growth rate.

The most rapid Soviet growth took place in the early 1950s after the death of Stalin when the new leadership found itself in a position to loosen the more restrictive features of the Stalin dictatorship. This upsurge in growth, however, did not lead to growth that was more rapid than the fast-growing capitalist countries like West Germany and Japan.

The declining growth rate troubles the Soviet leadership. It forced them to experiment in the mid-1960s with modest economic reforms—reforms that gave slightly more authority to managers and gave consumers more of a voice in the choice of consumer goods. These modest reforms failed to produce the desired result and have largely been abandoned. It has also forced them to expand their trade with the West.

Economic Efficiency and Productivity

There is no direct statistical measure of how efficiently an economy utilizes its available resources—of how close it is to its production-possibilities frontier—but there is a great deal of indirect evidence of economic inefficiency in the Soviet economy. The perverse behavior of Soviet managers in response to output targets, the extent to which economic activities are forced into the second economy, and the cumbersome material-balancing system have already been described. Moreover, the practice of pricing many goods below equilibrium has caused an unproductive use of time because of the vast amount of time spent in lines.[3]

Soviet productivity growth (the growth of output per unit of input) is average or below average when compared to the Western world. The Soviet Union was a technologically backward country in 1917, and an objective of the Soviet leadership has been to catch up with Western technology. But Soviet productivity growth has not exceeded productivity growth in the capitalist West. The technology gap thus remains quite large.

Earlier, it was noted that long-term Soviet growth has been rapid but that productivity growth was at best average. This combination of facts suggests that Soviet economic growth is explained primarily by the growth of labor and capital inputs. Output per unit of inputs has not increased at a significant rate.

Military Power

The Soviet leadership came to power in a militarily weak country surrounded by capitalist foes, and the leadership had strong pretensions of initiating a world communist revolution to convert the world from capitalism to Marxist ideals. For these reasons, the goal of military power—to maintain and expand communist power—has always been important to the Soviet leadership.

In this area of economic performance, there can be little doubt of Soviet successes. Although the overall size of Soviet gross national product is roughly 60 percent that of the United States, Soviet military power exceeds or rivals that of the United States, as illustrated by comparisons of defense capital stock (such as personnel, tanks, bombers, or missiles).

The costs of achieving military parity with or superiority to the United States have been high. The best Soviet material and human resources have been devoted to defense and have been diverted from the production of industrial capital or consumer goods. The U.S. intelligence community estimates that some 14–16 percent of Soviet GNP is devoted to defense, whereas in the United States the percentage is 4 to 5 percent. Obviously, such large military outlays hinder the attainment of other goals—such as reviving the declining Soviet growth rate or raising Soviet living standards.

Economic Stability

The Soviet press and economic textbooks emphasize the great economic instability of capitalism. *Pravda* (the official newspaper of the Communist party) gleefully announces the latest

---

3. Even official Soviet sources admit to low output per unit of input. Soviet industrial workers produce about one half as much as their American counterparts. American estimates show that the Soviet economy produces about 60 percent as much output from one unit of input (whether labor, capital, or land) as does the American economy. Comparisons of Soviet productivity with that of Western Europe also show Soviet productivity to be well below that of most European countries but about equal to that of Italy. By themselves, such figures do not demonstrate that the Soviet economic system is less efficient than its capitalist counterpart. Many factors other than the economic system determine efficiency.

American or British figures on unemployment and inflation. The sad lot of the capitalist worker is emphasized: the ever-present threat of losing one's job. In contrast to the anarchy of the market, Soviet officials emphasize the greater economic stability of their economic system. Unemployment, they declare, was liquidated in 1929. Everyone is guaranteed a job; no one is denied suitable housing because of low income. All workers are protected from cradle to grave by free health services and by state pensions. Education is free. Moreover, Soviet consumers are protected from the ravages of inflation by the state's control of consumer prices. In fact, official Soviet price indexes show that prices are lower in the Soviet Union today than they were in 1950—a remarkable claim in a world of double-digit inflation.

Considerable Western research has been devoted to testing these Soviet claims, and this research shows that there is indeed unemployment and inflation in the U.S.S.R. Inflation takes several forms: first, it takes the form of *repressed inflation* when people must stand in line longer (for often nonexisting goods) rather than pay a higher price. Although repressed inflation is less prevalent than it was in earlier years, it is still an important factor. Second, inflation can take the form of price increases that are hidden from view by the official statistics. The official figures are 'fudged in a number of ways to understate inflation. Third, the inflation can spill over into the second economy, where the rate of inflation cannot be readily measured. Nevertheless, most Western studies show that both inflation and unemployment are much less severe than in most capitalist countries. The unemployment rate may be around 1.5 percent, while the inflation rate may be between 2 and 3 percent.

This result is not unexpected. Soviet industrial wages have been allowed to increase at rates equal to the rate of growth of labor productivity. Workers are guaranteed jobs whether they are redundant or not. Yet the Soviets have had to pay a price for this economic stability. Soviet workers know they cannot be fired unless they engage in extreme misconduct, and even then Soviet managers have little to gain by letting bad workers go. The price of stability in official price indexes has been greater hidden inflation and the direction of economic activity into the second economy where prices are not controlled. In general, one can say

that greater economic stability has been purchased at the price of lower economic efficiency.

Income Distribution

During the Soviet industrialization drive of the 1930s, income distribution for Soviet workers was more unequal than for their American counterparts. The gap between the pay of skilled and unskilled workers was immense. The cause of these differentials was probably more economic than ideological. The Soviet economy was plagued by a shortage of skilled and educated workers. Many technicians had fled abroad, and the children of the working class did not possess the needed educational credentials. The large wage differentials were required to equate the supply to the extraordinary demand for skilled workers.

By the mid-1950s, the Soviet educational establishment had succeeded in graduating an impressive number of technically skilled and educated workers and employees. In recognition of this fact, substantial reforms in the system of industrial wages were begun in 1956 and completed in the mid-1960s. As a consequence of these reforms, wage differentials between skilled and unskilled workers were reduced, so that today wage differentials are smaller than in most capitalist countries.

The overall distribution of income in the Soviet Union is hard to estimate because Soviet statistical authorities do not readily publish information on the earnings of the ruling elite. Moreover, Soviet citizens' claims on economic resources are not determined entirely by income because the elite often receives more highly priced goods free of charge—such as chauffeur-driven cars, free vacations, or travel to the West—and those would not show up in income statistics.

Even with these reservations, it is safe to say that the distribution of income in the U.S.S.R. is much more equal than it is in the United States. Surprisingly, the same conclusion cannot be drawn from comparisons of the U.S.S.R. income distribution with capitalist countries in which the state plays a large redistributive role (Table 2). The main reason for the more equal Soviet distribution compared to U.S. distribution is the absence of income from land and capital in the Soviet Union.

Table 2
Soviet and Western Income Distributions

Country	Ratio of Income of Top 10 Percent to Income of Bottom 10 Percent
Soviet Union, 1966	3.5
United Kingdom, 1969	3.4
United States, 1968	6.7
Italy, 1969	5.9
Canada, 1971	6.0
Sweden, 1971	3.5

Source: P. J. D. Wiles, *Economic Institutions Compared* (New York: Halsted Press, 1977), p 443.

OTHER ECONOMIC SYSTEMS

The American and Soviet economies are only two of the many types of economic systems that exist in theory and in practice.

In Yugoslavia, a form of market socialism is practiced whereby workers make decisions about enterprises, although they elect a manager to conduct the day-to-day business of the firm. The state maintains ownership of the capital and land on which the enterprise operates and charges the workers a fee for their use. Worker-managed enterprises are not given output or input targets but are allowed to make most of their own decisions concerning *how, what,* and *for whom.* The state and communist party exercise influence largely through the banking system, by setting rules on the distribution of enterprise profits, and by imposing some price controls. Yugoslavia is probably the closest representative to market socialism in the world today.

Other countries are interesting blends of socialism and capitalism. In recent years, China has experimented with a greater use of market allocation. Hungary is currently experimenting with the process of introducing more free-market forces into what was once basically a planned socialist economy. Obligatory output and input targets are gradually being abandoned; more prices are being freed from price controls by the state to be determined by supply and demand; more and more decisions are being made by the enterprises

themselves. The Hungarian experiment is more than 15 years old, but it remains to be seen whether a planned socialist economy can be successfully converted into a market socialist economy.

Equally interesting experiments are being conducted in capitalist economies. In West Germany and Scandinavia, experiments are underway on worker participation in enterprise decision making. These countries have begun requiring seats for worker representatives on corporate boards of directors to insure that the company does not neglect the interests of its workers. These experiments in worker participation in capitalist enterprises provide interesting test cases for the protection of private property that capitalist legal systems typically provide. One question to be resolved is whether participating workers can require companies to act in a way that reduces the value of the owner's (stockholders') property.

Other capitalist countries are experimenting (and have been experimenting for almost a century) with methods for reducing the economic insecurity of capitalist workers and employees. Benefits such as unemployment compensation, free medical care, protection from firing, generous retirement benefits, and maternity leaves are now common in most capitalist countries. These measures have proven to be very costly, and they have had to be financed by higher taxes. It remains to be seen whether the efficiency losses due to extremely high taxes on high-income individuals will be accepted in the long run.

The expansion of public ownership in capitalist countries is another interesting feature of capitalist economies. In many European countries, socialist political parties compete with conservative parties for political power, and a common plank in the socialist platform is the nationalization of important industries. In England, labor (socialist) governments have nationalized a wide range of industries—such as steel, transportation, coal, and oil—often for the sake of preventing the industry from going bankrupt. The victory of a socialist government in France in 1981 will likely lead to more nationalization of industries in France.

This chapter has examined how planned economies solve the economic problem, using the Soviet Union as an example of a planned economy but pointing out the great diversity of resource-allocation arrangements that exist in today's world. The appendix to this chapter will discuss the principles of Marxist economics.

Summary

1. No two economic systems are alike. Economic systems are multidimensional. They differ in their ownership of resources, their allocation of resources, their production incentives, and their decision making.
2. Capitalism is an economic system with private ownership, economic incentives, market allocation, and decentralized decision making. Socialism exists in two variants: Planned socialism features state ownership, the use of moral as well as economic incentives, plan rather than market allocation, and centralized decision making. Market socialism features public ownership, economic incentives, market allocation, and decentralized decision making.
3. The Soviet Union is the best example of planned socialism. In the Soviet economy, the communist party decides what is to be produced and the planning agencies construct an economic plan that implements these instructions. Supplies and demands are equated by administrative orders, not by the price system. Each participant in the economy is obligated to fulfill the plan. Each enterprise receives a detailed plan that gives it detailed instructions on what, how, and for whom. Soviet managers are given a large number of often conflicting targets. They decide which targets to fulfill on the basis of the priority principle.
4. There are important elements of market allocation in the Soviet Union. Consumer goods, once produced, are allocated primarily through the market, although there are significant exceptions. Labor is allocated primarily through the market, and the "second (underground) economy" operates strictly through the market.
5. Soviet economic performance must be judged in terms of economic growth, economic efficiency, income distribution, economic stabil-

ity, and military power. After a period of rapid economic growth, economic growth has been declining in recent decades. Soviet productivity growth has failed to reduce the technology gap the Soviets inherited. The Soviet distribution of income is more equal than the U.S. income distribution, but is close to that of the capitalist welfare states. Soviet achievements have been greatest in the military sphere.
6. A large number of economic systems fall between the two extremes of capitalism and socialism represented by the United States and the Soviet Union. Yugoslavia is an example of market socialism. Hungary is an example of a planned socialist economy in the process of transition to market socialism. The major experiments being conducted by the capitalist economies are experiments in worker participation, nationalization, and efforts to reduce the economic instability of capitalism.

Key Terms

economic system
capitalism
planned socialism
market socialism
material-balance planning
material balance
priority principle

Questions and Problems

1. Explain how capitalism differs from socialism in terms of the four characteristics of an economic system.
2. Compare the ways in which the Soviet economy and a capitalist economy deal with a shortage of a particular industrial commodity.
3. What are the causes of an underground economy in the Soviet Union?
4. Why is Soviet long-term growth rapid by international standards while Soviet productivity has grown at only an average rate?

23A

Marxist Economics

Appendix Preview

Every economic system must resolve the economic problems of *what, how,* and *for whom.* To this point, this book has examined how capitalism deals with the economic problem. Writers of the radical-socialist tradition maintain that capitalism cannot satisfactorily solve the economic problem because capitalism is subject to basic internal contradictions that cannot be remedied through reform of the capitalist economic system. Marxists believe that capitalism will be replaced by a superior socialist economic order.

Supporters of the Marxist tradition include revolutionary activists, abstract socialist theorists, Soviet party ideologists, proponents of worker management, and many others. Their ideas are often quite different but are united by one common thread: the belief that private ownership of capital is wrong. In the Marxist view, private ownership leads to the concentration of economic and political power in the hands of the capitalist class, to the exploitation of workers, and to class conflict.

Radical economics represents an important current in social and economic thought. Today, approximately one third of the world's population lives in countries that profess ideological allegiance to Marxism. Many of the third-world countries—whose economic and political systems are still in flux—must choose between capitalism

and socialism. The major military challenge to the United States comes from a communist country, the U.S.S.R. The communist parties of France and Italy represent important political forces in their countries. A number of African and Latin American countries call themselves *Marxist.* This appendix will explain radical economic theory as envisioned by Karl Marx.

KARL MARX

Karl Marx (1818–1883) and his collaborator and financial backer, Friedrich Engels (1820–1895), mounted the most serious intellectual challenge to capitalism. The culmination of this challenge is Marx's three-volume work, *Capital (Das Kapital* in German). In *Das Kapital,* Marx explains why he believed capitalism to be an inherently unstable economic system with an inevitably limited life span.

THE MATERIALISTIC CONCEPTION OF HISTORY

Marx's **materialistic conception of history** is crucial to understanding Marx.

*Reduced to its most basic idea, **the materialistic conception of history** declares that economic (material) factors determine all social, political, and cultural experiences.*

The Mode of Production

Marx believed that at any point in time, there is a dominant *mode of production*. (*Mode of production* is Marx's term for economic system.) One mode of production is slavery, where production is based upon the ownership of labor by slave owners. Another mode of production is serfdom, where the dominant factor of production—land—is owned exclusively by landlords. Another mode of production could be capitalism, where capital is owned by capitalists who hire labor.

Within any dominant mode of production, new economic and social relationships will begin to emerge. In feudal societies, hired labor began to take its place alongside serfs, and capitalists began to manage production alongside the dominant landlord class. According to Marx, each mode of production contains the seeds of its own destruction, because it tends to create new modes of production that will conflict with the old. Capitalism replaced serfdom because hired labor and capitalist production was superior to the serf order. Capitalism, like the systems before it, carries the seeds of its own destruction. Class conflict between the worker and the capitalist, in Marx's view, will inevitably cause the overthrow of capitalism.

Class Conflict and Qualitative Change

Every mode of production has class conflict. In serfdom, the conflict was between the land-owning and capitalist classes. In capitalism, the conflict is between the worker and the capitalist classes. Eventually, the class struggle becomes so intense that a *qualitative change* occurs (usually accompanied by violent revolution or war), and a new dominant mode of production replaces the old. Qualitative changes are inevitable because societies are destined to evolve from lower to higher modes of production. Feudalism was bound to replace slavery, capitalism was bound to displace feudalism, and socialism will eventually replace capitalism. The engine of change is the conflict between classes.

The Dialectic

The process of inevitable change through the conflict of opposing forces is the foundation of Marx's theory of **dialectical materialism.**

Dialectical materialism states that class conflict will necessarily force societies to evolve from lower-order to higher-order economic systems.

According to Marx, the victory of capitalism over feudalism in the 17th and 18th centuries was a qualitative step forward for society. Two landmarks signaled the emergence of capitalism. The first was the initial accumulation of capital by the emerging capitalist class—a process Marx called *primitive capitalist accumulation*. Rather than acquiring capital through patient saving and sacrifice, primitive capitalist accumulation resulted from expropriation by the strong of the property of the weak. Through primitive capitalist accumulation, capital came to be controlled exclusively by the capitalist class. The second indicator of the emergence of capitalism was the formation of a free labor force. When the capitalist class gained control over the means of production, laborers were separated from the factors of production (land, tools, livestock) and were left with only their labor to sell. The capitalist, who now controlled the means of production, hired labor and established capitalist factories. At this point, the basic class conflict of capitalism was born: the conflict between the working class and the capitalist. A new social order was created in which all social, political, and religious institutions served the interests of the capitalists.

LABOR THEORY OF VALUE

The downfall of capitalism is preordained by its tendency towards ever-worsening economic crises, unemployment, and declining profits. According to Marx's **labor theory of value,** the value (price) of every commodity is ultimately determined by the amount of labor used to produce it.

Marx's **labor theory of value** *states that the value of a commodity (C) equals the sum of direct labor costs (v), indirect labor costs (c), and surplus value (s).*

$$C = c + v + s$$

In this equation, fixed capital expenditures *(c)* are outlays for plant, equipment, inventories, and materials. The *v* stands for wage costs, called "variable capital" by Marx. The *s* denotes *surplus value,* Marx's term for profits.

Surplus Value

Surplus value is the root cause of the class conflict. The feature that distinguishes labor from other factors of production is that capitalists can compel workers to produce **surplus value.**

Surplus value is the value of any labor over and above the amount of labor the worker would have to work to meet subsistence needs.

Employers do not have to pay workers the full value of their production—only enough to allow them to subsist. A worker may have to work 8 hours to produce enough output for subsistence needs; yet, the employer can force the worker to create a surplus by working 12 hours—4 hours more than required for subsistence.[1]

Fixed capital, though essential to production, cannot create surplus value; only labor can create surplus value. Workers are exploited because their surplus value produces profits for the capitalist class. Exploitation is the basic source of class conflict. Surplus value plays a central role in Marxian theory because the capitalist's desire to maximize profits is the driving force behind capitalism.

Unemployment

Workers are prevented from receiving a share of the surplus value because of unemployment.

1. Marx was unclear about how subsistence should be defined—whether it was physical subsistence or some socially accepted norm of existence. Scholars and ideologists after Marx have long debated this particular point.

Marx believed that wages would hover at subsistence even when workers worked longer than subsistence requires because capitalism naturally produces a large amount of unemployment. The major cause of unemployment in Marx's view is the replacement of workers by machines. Massive unemployment keeps wages from rising above subsistence: if an employed worker is unwilling to work at the subsistence wage, a number of unemployed workers would be more than happy to take his or her place.

Marx believed that in the long run capitalist profits would eventually decline. According to Marx's "law" of declining profit rates, as an economy becomes more capital-intensive and less labor-intensive, the profit rate falls. Marx believed that competition compels capitalists to become more capital-intensive because capitalists are forced by competition to introduce cost-saving innovations. When one capitalist firm introduces a labor-saving technology and attracts its competitors' customers through lower prices, its profits increase temporarily. These extra profits, however, are short-lived as competitors eventually introduce the same cost-saving techniques and new firms enter the market. Excess industry profits are eliminated, and capital has been substituted for labor.

According to Marx, the inherent tendency for capitalists to substitute capital for labor, even though labor is the sole source of surplus value, will have disastrous long-run consequences for capitalism.

As the profit rate falls, the internal contradictions of capitalism become apparent. In an effort to halt the decline in profits, capitalists will try to increase the exploitation of their workers by raising surplus value, and the class conflict intensifies. The declining rate of profit will cause mass business failures, and bankrupt small capitalists will join the ranks of the unemployed.

Marx predicts that the economy will then begin to suffer overproduction and disproportions. Workers will be kept at subsistence incomes, capitalists will not be willing to increase their spending on luxury goods. Moreover, the ranks of the capitalists will thin as monopolists drive smaller capitalists out of business. Yet all the while, the productive capacity of the economy will be growing. Aggregate demand will fall chronically short of aggregate supply and recessions and depressions will become commonplace.

At this point, the stage is set for the qualitative change from capitalism to socialism. The workers, unable to bear their economic misery any longer, will unite against the weakened capitalist class and a violent world revolution will install a new socialist order. Capital becomes the property of the working class, who take control of government.

THE NEW SOCIALIST STATE

Marx and Engels had surprisingly little to say about what happens after the socialist revolution installs the first socialist state. Marx felt that the new socialist society would go through two phases, later called *socialism* and *communism* by V. I. Lenin. During the first transitional phase, elements of the old capitalist order would remain; the powers of the new socialist state—called the *dictatorship of the proletariat* by Marx—would have to be directed against these capitalist forces. During this transitional phase, a strong state would be required to direct the class struggle against capitalist elements and to build up society's productive capacity. Scarcity would still be present, and the old capitalist system of rewarding labor would be continued. Marx's formula for distribution during this first phase was "to each according to his contribution."

Eventually, a stage of abundance would be reached. At this point, full communism would be established, the state would wither away, and there would be enough to go around for everyone. There would no longer be any class struggle because there would be only one class, the class of workers. Work would cease to be a chore, and distribution could now proceed according to the formula: "from each according to his ability, to each according to his needs."

Summary

1. Karl Marx viewed capitalism as an unstable economic system, destined to be replaced by socialism through a violent socialist revolution.

2. Marx believed labor alone creates surplus value but that replacing labor with capital causes the profit rate to fall. When profits fall, the capitalist class increases worker exploitation, economic crises become more severe, and the capitalist system breaks down.

3. The breakdown of capitalism is inevitable because the capitalist system is based upon class conflict between the working class and the capitalists.

Key Terms

materialistic conception of history
dialectical materialism
labor theory of value
surplus value

Glossary

accounting profits revenues minus explicit (accounting) costs **(8, 18).**

aggregate production function the relationship between the total output produced by the economy and the total labor, capital, and land inputs used by the economy **(15).**

allocation the apportionment of resources for a specific purpose or to particular persons or groups **(2).**

arbitrage buying in a market where a commodity is cheap and reselling it in a market where the commodity is more expensive **(13).**

average fixed cost *(AFC)* fixed cost divided by output **(8).**

average revenue *(AR)* total revenue divided by output **(10).**

average total cost *(ATC)* total cost divided by output, or the sum of average variable cost and average fixed cost **(8).**

average variable cost *(AVC)* variable cost divided by output **(8).**

backstop resource a close substitute for an exhaustible resource that is available in virtually unlimited supply but at a higher cost **(21).**

bankruptcy the state of a corporation that cannot pay its bills or its interest obligations **(7).**

barrier to entry any advantage that existing firms hold over firms that might seek to enter the market **(12).**

benefit (see **external benefit, private benefit, social benefits**)

bonds IOUs of a corporation that bind the corporation to pay a fixed sum of money (the *principal*) at maturity and also to pay a fixed sum

*The number of the chapter in which each term is defined appears in parentheses.

of money annually until the maturity date (the *interest* or *coupon payment*) **(7)**.

budget line all the combinations of goods the consumer is able to buy given a certain income and set prices. The budget line shows all the choices of consumer goods available to the consumer **(6A)**.

capital the equipment, plants, buildings, and inventories that are available to society **(2)** (see also **human capital**).

capital gain the increase in the market value of any asset above the price originally paid. The capital gain is realized when the asset is sold **(7)** (see also **realized capital gain**).

capitalism an economic system characterized by private ownership of the factors of production, market allocation of resources, the use of economic incentives, and decentralized decision making **(3, 23)**.

cartel an arrangement that allows the participating firms to operate the industry as a shared monopoly **(12)**.

centralized market a market in which all buyers and sellers of a particular product make their transactions in one location **(13)**.

ceteris paribus fallacy the false attribution of the effects of changes in one set of variables to changes in another set of variables **(1)**.

circular-flow diagram summarizes the flows of goods and services from producers to households and the flows of the factors of production from households to business firms **(3)**.

coefficient of the price elasticity of demand (E_d) the absolute value of the percentage change in quantity demanded divided by the percentage change in price. The coefficent measures the percentage change in quantity demanded per 1 percent change in price **(5)**.

collective bargaining the process whereby a union bargains with management as the representative of all union employees **(17)**.

common stock confers voting privileges but no prior claim on dividends. Common stock dividends are paid only if they are declared by the board of directors in any given year **(7)**.

comparative advantage (see **law of comparative advantage**)

compensating wage differentials the higher rewards (wages or fringe benefits) that must be paid workers to compensate them for undesirable job characteristics **(16)**.

competing ends the different purposes for which resources can be used **(2)**.

competition (see **perfect competition, monopolistic competition**)

concentration ratio the percentage of industry sales (or output or labor force or assets, as the case may be) accounted for by the x largest firms **(12)**.

conglomerate merger occurs when one company takes over another company in a different line of business **(14)**.

conscious parallelism occurs when the actions of producers can be coordinated within certain ranges without formal or even informal agreements. Oligopolists use their understanding of the industry to make their own decisions and anticipate the behavior of other oligopolists **(12)**.

constant-cost industry a relatively small industry that can expand or contract without significantly affecting the terms at which factors of production used in the industry are purchased. The long-run industry supply curve for such an industry is horizontal **(9)**.

constant returns to scale present when a given percent change in all inputs results in the same percent change in output **(8)**.

consumer equilibrium occurs when the consumer has spent all income and the marginal utilities per dollar spent are equal on each good purchased ($MU_A/P_A = MU_B/P_B$). At this point, the consumer is not inclined to change purchases unless some other factor (such as prices, income, or consumer preferences) changes **(6)**.

consumer surplus the excess of total consumer benefit that a good provides over what the consumers actually have to pay **(6)**.

convertible stock a hybrid between a stock and a bond. The owner of convertible stock receives fixed interest payments but has the privilege of converting it to common stock at a fixed rate of exchange **(7)**.

corporation a form of business enterprise that is owned by a number of stockholders. The corporation has the legal status of a fictional individual and is authorized by law to act as a single person. The stockholders elect a board of directors that appoints the management of the corporation, usually headed by a president. Management is charged with the actual operation of the corporation (7).

cost (see **explicit cost, implicit cost, external cost, opportunity cost, private cost, social costs**)

craft union a union that represents workers of a single occupation (17).

credit markets markets for borrowing and lending (18).

cross-price elasticity of demand the percentage change in demand of one product divided by the percentage change in the price of a related product (5).

customs duties taxes on the transfer of certain goods from one country into another (20).

deadweight loss a loss to society of consumer surplus or producer surplus that is not offset by anyone else's gain (11).

decentralized market a market in which buyers and sellers of a particular product make their transactions in a variety of different physical locations (13).

demand the relationship between the amount of the good or service consumers are prepared to buy at a given price and the price of the good or service (4) (see also **law of demand**).

depreciation the wearing down of the economic value of capital goods as they are used in the production process (18).

derived demand factor demand that results from the demand for the goods and services the factor of production helps produce (15).

dialectical materialism the view that class conflict will necessarily force societies to evolve from lower-order to higher-order economic systems (23A).

diseconomies of scale are present when an equal percentage change in inputs leads to a smaller percentage change in output (8) (see also **economies of scale, constant returns to scale**).

economic equity the fair distribution of resources (11).

economic profits the excess of revenues over total *opportunity costs* (which include both actual payments and sacrificed alternatives); profits in excess of normal profits (8, 18).

economic rent the excess of the payment to the factor over its opportunity cost (18).

economics the study of how scarce resources are allocated among competing ends (2); the study of how people choose to use their limited resources (land, labor, and capital goods) to produce, exchange, and consume goods and services (1).

economic system the set of organizational arrangements and institutions that are established to solve the economic problem (2); the set of ownership, resource-allocation, and decision-making arrangements that society establishes to solve the economic problem (23).

economies of scale are present in the production process when large output volumes can be produced at a lower cost per unit than small output volumes (7); are present when equal percentage changes in the use of inputs lead to larger percentage changes in output (8).

effective tax rate the percent of the actual tax payment to adjusted gross income; shows the effect of deductions and exclusions on tax rates (20).

efficiency is present when society's resources are so organized that it is impossible to make someone better off by any reallocation of resources without hurting someone else (11); results when no resources are unemployed and when no resources are misallocated (2).

elasticity of demand (see **cross-price elasticity of demand, income elasticity of demand, perfect elasticity of demand, perfect inelasticity of demand, price elasticity of demand**)

elasticity of supply (see **perfect elasticity of supply, perfect inelasticity of supply, price elasticity of supply**)

employee association an organization that represents employees in a particular profession (17).

entrepreneur one who organizes, manages, and assumes the risks for an enterprise (2).

equilibrium (see **consumer equilibrium**)

equilibrium (or *market-clearing*) **price** the price at which the quantity demanded by consumers equals the quantity supplied by producers (3, 4).

equity (see **economic equity, horizontal equity, vertical equity**)

excise taxes per-unit taxes on the production or sale of specific goods or services (20).

exclusion costs the costs of defining and enforcing private property rights in some good, or the cost of preventing those who do not have property rights in the good from enjoying the good **(21)**.

exhaustible (or *nonrenewable*) **resource** any resource of which there is a finite stock in the long run because the stock is fixed by nature **(21)**.

exhaustive expenditures government purchases of goods and services that divert real economic resources from the private sector, making them no longer available for private use **(20)**.

explicit cost (or *accounting cost*) a cost incurred when an actual payment is made **(8)** (see also **implicit cost**).

external benefit the benefit enjoyed by someone other than the firm producing the good **(11)**.

external cost the cost borne by someone other than the firm producing the good **(11)**.

externality exists when a producer or consumer does not bear the full marginal cost or enjoy the full marginal benefit of an economic action **(21)**.

factor (or *input*) **market** the market in which firms purchase the land, labor, and capital inputs required to produce their output **(15)**.

factors of production land, labor, capital, and entrepreneurship **(2)**.

fallacy (see **false-cause fallacy, fallacy of composition, ceteris paribus fallacy**)

fallacy of composition the false belief that what is true for each part taken separately is also true for the whole, or that what is true for the whole is true for each part considered separately **(1)**.

false-cause fallacy the false belief that, because two events occur together, one event has caused the other **(1)**.

fixed cost the cost that does not vary with the level of output **(8)**.

focal point an obvious benchmark by which price or output could be coordinated by firms in an industry without an explicit agreement **(12)**.

fraud an act of deceit or misrepresentation **(13)**.

free good a good of which the amount available is greater than the amount people want at a zero price **(2)**.

free rider anyone who enjoys the benefits of a good or service without paying the cost **(21)**.

functional distribution of income the distribution of income among the four broad classes of productive factors: land, labor, capital, and entrepreneurship **(15)**.

futures market a market in which buyer and seller agree now on the price of a commodity to be delivered at some specified date in the future **(13)**.

game theory a way to analyze strategic decision making when the consequences of one decision maker's decisions are dependent upon (and potentially adversely affected by) the decisions of other decision makers **(12)**.

gift taxes taxes on the transfer of property from one owner to another **(20)**.

hedging the temporary substitution of a futures market transaction for an intended spot or cash transaction **(13)**.

horizontal equity exists when those with equal abilities to pay pay the same amount of tax **(20)**.

household production work in the home, including such activities as meal preparation, child rearing, and cleaning **(16)**.

human capital the accumulation of past investments in schooling, training, and health care that raises the productive capacity of people **(2)**.

immediate run a period of time so short that the quantity supplied cannot be changed at all. In the immediate run—sometimes called the *momentary period* or *market period*—supply curves are perfectly inelastic **(5)** (see also **long run, short run**).

implicit cost cost incurred when an alternative is sacrificed **(8)** (see also **explicit cost**).

incidence of a tax the actual distribution of the burden of tax payment **(20)**.

income (see **functional distribution of income, personal distribution of income**)

income effect occurs when a fall in the price of a good makes more income available for purchasing all goods and services, including the one whose price has fallen **(6)** (see also **substitution effect**).

income elasticity of demand the percentage change in the demand for a product divided by the percentage change in income, holding all prices fixed **(5)**.

increasing-cost industry an industry in which, as

the number of firms expands, the factor prices of resources are bid up; an industry in which, as the number of firms contracts, the prices of these factors fall; the long-run industry supply curve for such an industry is upward-sloping (**9**).

indifference curve a graph of all the alternative combinations of two goods that yield the same total satisfaction and among which the consumer would be indifferent (**6A**).

industrial union a union that represents employees of an industry or a firm regardless of their specific occupation (**17**).

inefficiency is present when resources can be reallocated to make someone better off without making someone else worse off (**11**).

inferior good a good the demand for which will fall as income rises (**4**).

information costs the costs of acquiring information on prices and product qualities (**13**).

in-kind income consists primarily of benefits, such as free public education, school lunch programs, public housing, or food stamps, for which the recipient is not required to pay (**19**).

interest the price of credit, usually a percentage of the amount of money borrowed (**3**).

interest income income earned from the direct or indirect ownership of capital (**18**).

interest rate measures the cost of borrowing over a specified period of time (**18**) (see also **real interest rate**).

intermediaries (or "*middlemen*") buy in order to sell again or simply bring together buyers and sellers (**13**) (see also **financial intermediaries**).

intermediate goods goods that are completely used up in the production of another good; the value of intermediate goods is reflected in the price of the final goods (**3**).

internal labor market the hierarchy of labor—from general laborers to top-level executives—within the firm itself (**16**).

investment additions to the stock of capital (**2**).

kinked demand curve an oligopolistic firm's demand curve when other firms match the firm's price decreases but do not match the firm's price increases (**12**).

labor the physical and mental talents that human beings contribute to the production process (**2**).

labor market an arrangement (either a formal contract or an informal agreement) whereby buyers and sellers of labor services come together to agree on working conditions (such as compensation, fringe benefits, and hours of work) (**16**).

labor shortage occurs when the number of workers firms wish to hire at the prevailing wage rate exceeds the number willing to work at that wage rate (**16**).

labor surplus occurs when the number of workers willing to work at the prevailing wage rate exceeds the number firms wish to employ at that wage rate (**16**).

labor theory of value Marx's view that the value of a commodity equals the sum of direct labor costs, indirect labor costs, and surplus value (**23A**).

labor union a collective organization of workers (**17**).

land any part of nature's bounty—including minerals, forests, land, water resources, or oxygen (**2**).

law of comparative advantage people or countries specialize in those activities in which they have the greatest advantage or the least disadvantage compared to other people or countries. Equivalently, people or countries specialize in those activities in which they have the least disadvantage compared to other people or countries (**3**).

law of demand there is a negative (or inverse) relationship between the price of a good and quantity demanded, holding other factors constant (**4**).

law of diminishing marginal rate of substitution as more of one good is consumed, the amount of the other good that the consumer is willing to sacrifice for one more unit of the first good declines (**6A**).

law of diminishing marginal utility as more of a good or service is consumed during a given time period, its marginal utility declines, holding the consumption of everything else constant (**6**).

law of diminishing returns as ever larger quantities of a variable factor are combined with fixed amounts of other factors, the marginal physical product of the variable factor will eventually decline (**2, 8, 15**).

law of increasing costs as more of a particular

commodity is produced, its opportunity cost per unit will eventually increase (2).

leisure time spent in any activity other than work in the labor force or work in the home (16).

loanable funds the amount of lending from all households, governments, and businesses, or the bank credit made available to borrowers in credit markets (18).

logrolling the trading of votes among two or more voters to secure a favorable outcome on decisions of more interest to each voter (22).

long run a period of time long enough for new firms to enter the market, for old firms to disappear, and for existing plants to be expanded (5); a period of time long enough to vary all inputs (8) (see also **immediate run, short run**).

long-run average cost *(LRAC)* **curve** shows the minimum average cost for each level of output when all factor inputs are variable and when factor prices are fixed (8).

Lorenz curve shows the percentage of all income earned by households at successive income levels. The cumulative share of households (ranked from lowest to highest incomes) is plotted on the horizontal axis, and the cumulative share of income earned by the cumulative percent of households is plotted on the vertical axis (19).

lump-sum tax a tax that does not vary with any indicator of the firm's performance; that is, it does not vary with the firm's output, profit, or employment (11).

luxuries those products that have an income elasticity of demand greater than 1 (5).

macroeconomics the study of the economy in the large; deals with the economy as a whole rather than with individual markets and individual consumers and producers (1).

managerial coordination the allocation of factors of production by a manager or central planner (7).

marginal analysis a strategy for decision making that examines the consequences of making relatively small changes from the current state of affairs (1).

marginal cost *(MC)* the addition to total cost (or equivalently to variable cost) of producing one more unit of output (8).

marginal factor cost *(MFC)* the extra cost to the firm of using one more unit of a factor of production (15).

marginal physical product *(MPP)* the increase in output that results from increasing a factor of production by one unit, holding all other inputs constant (8, 15).

marginal rate of substitution *(MRS)* how much of one good a person is just willing to give up to acquire one unit of another good (6A).

marginal revenue *(MR)* the increase in revenue brought about by increasing output by one unit (9).

marginal revenue product *(MRP)* the extra revenue generated by increasing a factor of production by one unit (15).

marginal revenue schedule the relationship between marginal revenue and the quantity of output (10).

marginal tax rate the ratio of the increase in taxes to the increase in taxable income (20).

marginal utility the increase in utility that a consumer experiences when consumption of a good or service (and that good or service alone) is increased by one unit (6) (see also **law of diminishing marginal utility**).

market an established arrangement by which buyers and sellers come together to exchange particular goods or services (2, 4).

market demand curve the demand curve of all consumers of a particular product (4); shows the total quantities demanded by all consumers in the market at each price and is the horizontal summation of all individual demand curves in that market (6).

market failure occurs when the price system fails to produce the quantity of the good that would be socially optimal (21).

market socialism an economic system characterized by state ownership of the factors of production, the use of primarily economic incentives, market allocation of resources, and decentralized decision making (23).

market test the process that ensures that goods and services in the private sector yield a benefit equal to or greater than their cost (20).

markup pricing the setting of prices at a given percentage above average cost (10).

marriage penalty the increase in taxes paid by a married couple over what their combined tax payment would be if they were filing as two singles (20).

material balance a comparison of the anticipated demands and supplies of a key commodity **(23)**.

material balance planning a system of resource allocation in which centralized planning is restricted to controlling the output levels of only the most important industrial commodities that the economy produces and in which the output of other less important commodities is controlled at lower levels in the planning hierarchy **(23)**.

materialistic conception of history that economic (material) factors determine all social, political, and cultural experiences **(23A)**.

merger (see **conglomerate merger**)

microeconomics the study of the economic decision making of firms and individuals in a market setting; the study of the economy in the small **(1)**.

"middlemen" (see **intermediaries**)

midpoints formula the coefficient of the price elasticity of demand equals the percent change in quantity demanded divided by the percent change in price, where the percent change in quantity demanded is the change in quantity demanded divided by the average of the two quantities and where the change in price is the change in price divided by the average of the two prices **(5)**.

minimum efficient scale the lowest level of output at which average costs are minimized **(8)**.

money anything that is widely accepted in exchange for goods and services and that can be used for paying debts and taxes **(3)**.

money price a price expressed in monetary units (such as dollars, francs, etc.) **(3)**.

monopolistic competition a type of market structure in which 1) the number of sellers is large enough so that each seller acts independently of the others, 2) the product is differentiated from seller to seller, 3) there is free entry into and exit from the industry, and 4) sellers are price searchers **(7, 10)**.

monopoly (see **pure monopoly, shared monopoly**)

monopoly rent seeking the efforts of anyone trying to turn a competitive industry into a monopoly in order to gain the monopoly profits, or "rent" **(11)**.

monopsony a market in which there is only one buyer **(15)**.

mutual interdependence characteristic of an industry in which the actions of one firm will affect other firms in the industry and in which these interrelationships will be recognized **(12)**.

natural monopoly a firm whose long-run average costs decline over the range of output that the industry would produce **(14)**.

natural selection theory if business firms do not maximize profits, they will be unable to compete with other firms and will be driven out of the market **(7)**.

necessities those products that have an income elasticity of demand less than 1 **(5)**.

negative (inverse) relationship exists between two variables if an increase in the value of one variable is associated with a reduction in the value of the other variable **(1A)**.

neutral tax a tax that does not cause any change in private production, consumption, or investment decisions **(20)**.

nominal rate of interest the rate of interest expressed in terms of today's dollars **(3)**.

noncompeting groups groups of labor suppliers that are differentiated by natural ability and abilities acquired through education, training, and experience to the extent that they do not compete with one another for jobs **(16)**.

nonexclusion characteristic of a good for which the exclusion costs are so high that it is not possible (or practical) to exclude people from using the good **(21)**.

nonprice competition any action other than the lowering of prices that differentiates one product from the competition and delays the disappearance of economic profits **(10)**.

nonrival consumption characteristic of a good the consumption of which by one person does not reduce its consumption by others, given the level of production **(21)**.

normal good a good the demand for which increases as income rises **(4)**.

normal profit the return that the time and capital of the entrepreneur would earn in the best alternative employment and that is earned when total revenues equal total opportunity costs **(8)**; the profits that are required to keep resources in that particular business **(18)**.

normative economics the study of what *ought to be* in the economy **(1)**.

oligopoly a type of market in which 1) there are only a few mutually interdependent sellers but many buyers, 2) homogeneous or differentiated products may be produced, 3) there are significant barriers to entry, and 4) sellers are price searchers able to exercise some control over price (**7, 12**).

opportunity cost the loss of the next best alternative (**2**); the value of the best forgone alternative (**8**).

partnership a business enterprise that is owned by two or more people who make all the business decisions, share the profits of the business, and bear the financial responsibility for any losses (**7**).

perfect competition a type of market structure in which 1) there is a large enough number of buyers and sellers that no single buyer or seller has a perceptible influence on the market price, 2) each seller and buyer has perfect information about prices and product quality, 3) the product being sold is homogeneous, 4) there are no barriers to entry into or exit from the market, and 5) all firms are price takers (**4, 7, 9**).

perfect elasticity of demand demonstrated by a horizontal demand curve, where quantity demanded is most responsive to price (**5**).

perfect elasticity of supply demonstrated by a horizontal supply curve, where quantity supplied is most responsive to price (**5**).

perfect inelasticity of demand demonstrated by a vertical demand curve, where quantity demanded is least responsive to price (**5**).

perfect inelasticity of supply demonstrated by a vertical supply curve, where quantity supplied is least responsive to price (**5**).

perfect market (see **perfect competition**)

personal distribution of income the distribution of income among households, or how much income one household earns from the factors of production it owns relative to other households (**15**).

planned socialism an economic system characterized by state ownership of the factors of production (other than labor), the use of moral as well as economic incentives, resource allocation by economic plan, and centralized decision making (**23**).

positive economics the study of *what is* in the economy (**1**).

positive (or **direct**) **relationship** exists between two variables if an increase in the value of one variable is associated with an increase in the value of the other variable (**1A**).

preferences people's evaluations of goods and services independent of budget and price considerations (**6**).

preferred stock confers a prior claim on dividends but no voting privileges (dividends must be paid before paying common stock dividends but after meeting interest obligations) (**7**).

present value the most anyone would pay today in order to receive money in the future (**7**); the most anyone is willing to pay today for an asset in order to be able to receive a stream of returns from that asset in the future (**18**).

price (see **money price, relative price**)

price discrimination exists when the same product or service is sold at different prices to different buyers (**10**).

price/earnings ratio (*PE*) the stock price divided by the earnings per share of stock (**7**).

price elasticity of demand a measure of the responsiveness of quantity demanded to a change in price; the percentage change in the quantity demanded divided by the percentage change in price (**5**).

price elasticity of supply a measure of the responsiveness of quantity supplied to a change in price; the percentage change in the quantity supplied divided by the percentage change in price (**5**).

price leader a firm whose price changes are consistently imitated by rival firms (**12**).

price searcher *in a factor market:* a buyer of inputs whose purchases are large enough to affect the price of the input (**15**); *in a product market:* a seller with the ability to control the price of the goods it sells (**10**).

price system the entire set of millions of relative prices that provides information to buyers and sellers (**3**).

price taker *in a factor market:* a buyer of an input whose purchases are not large enough to affect the price of the input (**15**); *in a product market:* a seller that does not have the ability to control the price of the goods it sells (**10**).

principle of substitution practically no good is irreplaceable in meeting demand because users are able to substitute one product for another to satisfy demand **(3)**.

priority principle industries most important to the communist party will be the last to take cuts in supplies **(23)**.

private benefit the benefit enjoyed by the firm producing a good **(11)**.

private cost the cost borne by the firm producing a good **(11)**.

producer surplus the excess of what producers receive over the minimum value the producer would have been willing to receive **(9)**.

production function indicates the maximum amount of output that can be produced from different combinations of labor, capital, and land inputs **(8, 15)**.

production-possibilities frontier *(PPF)* shows the combinations of goods that can be produced when the factors of production are utilized to their full potential; reveals the economic choices open to society **(2)**.

profit maximization the search by firms for the product quality, the output, and the price that give the firm the highest possible profits **(7)**.

profit-maximization rule a firm will maximize profits by producing that level of output at which marginal revenue equals or exceeds marginal cost **(9)**.

profits (see **accounting profits, economic profits, normal profit**).

progressive tax a tax where the higher is the income, the larger is the percentage of income paid as taxes **(20)**.

property rights the right of an owner to use and exchange property **(3)**.

proportional tax a tax where each taxpaying unit pays the same percentage of its income as taxes **(20)**.

proprietorship (see **sole proprietorship**)

public finance the study of government revenues and expenditures at all levels of government **(20)**.

public goods goods or services characterized by 1) nonrival consumption and 2) nonexclusion **(21)**.

pure economic rent the price paid to a productive factor (such as land) that is completely inelastic in supply **(18)**.

pure monopoly a type of market structure in which 1) there is only one seller, 2) the seller's product has no close substitutes, 3) the seller

is protected from the entry of competitors by barriers to entry, and 4) the seller is a price searcher that can control the price **(7, 10)**.

quantity demanded the amount of a good or service consumers are prepared to buy at a given price **(4)**.

quantity supplied the amount of a good or service offered for sale at a given price **(4)**.

quasi rent a payment over and above the short-run opportunity cost necessary to induce the owners of the resources to offer their resources for sale or rent in the short run **(18)**.

rate of return of a capital good that rate of interest which makes the present value of the stream of marginal revenue products for each year of the good's life equal to the cost of the capital good **(18)**.

rational ignorance a decision not to acquire information because the marginal cost of acquiring the information exceeds the marginal benefit of having the information **(22)**.

real interest rate the nominal interest rate minus the anticipated rate of inflation **(3, 18)**.

realized capital gain income gained when property is sold at a higher price than its purchase price **(20)**.

regressive tax a tax where the higher is the income, the smaller is the percentage of income paid as taxes **(20)**.

regulatory lag occurs when government regulators adjust rates some time after operating costs and the rate base have increased **(14)**.

relative price a price expressed in terms of other commodities **(3)**.

renewable resource any resource of which the stock is not fixed in the long run **(21)**.

rent (see **economic rent, pure economic rent, quasi rent**)

resource (see **backstop resource, exhaustible resource, renewable resource**)

return (see **rate of return**)

rival consumption the characteristic of a good the consumption of which by one person lowers the consumption available to others, given the level of production **(21)**.

roundabout production the production of goods that do not immediately meet consumption needs; the production of intermediate goods **(3)**.

rule of reason "monopolies are in violation of the Sherman Act if they engage in unfair or illegal business practices, not because they are a monopoly *per se*" (**14**).

scarce good a good the amount of which available is less than the amount people would want if it were given away free of charge (**2**).

scientific method the process of formulating theories, collecting data, testing theories, and revising theories (**1**).

screening the process used by employers to raise the probability of selecting the most qualified workers on the basis of observable worker characteristics (**16**).

shared monopoly an oligopoly in which all the firms in the industry coordinate price and output by some means; in its extreme form, the industry behaves like one gigantic firm (**12**).

shortage results if at the current price the quantity demanded exceeds the quantity supplied; the price is too low to equate the quantity demanded with the quantity supplied (**4**).

short run a period of time long enough for existing firms to produce more goods but not long enough for existing firms to expand their capacity or for new firms to enter the market. Output can be varied only by varying the variable inputs (of labor and raw materials) and only within the limits of existing plant capacity (**5, 8**).

shutdown rule if the firm's revenues at all output levels are less than variable costs, it minimizes its losses by shutting down; if there is at least one output level at which revenues exceed variable costs, the firm should not shut down (**9**).

signaling the process by which credentials (such as educational degrees, grades, specific experience, or references) are used to differentiate among prospective employees (**16**).

slope the ratio of the change in *x* to the run in *y* (**1A**).

social benefits private benefits plus external benefits (**11**).

social costs private costs plus external costs (**11**).

socialism a society characterized by collective ownership of property and government allocation of resources (**3**) (see **market socialism, planned socialism**).

sole proprietorship a form of business that is owned by one individual who makes all the business decisions, receives the profits, and bears the financial responsibility for losses (**7**).

speculators those who buy or sell in the hope of profiting from market fluctuations

spot (or **cash**) **market** a market in which agreements between buyers and sellers are made now for payment and delivery of the product now (**13**).

stock (see **common stock, convertible stock, preferred stock**)

strike occurs when all unionized employees cease to work until management agrees to specific union demands (**17**).

substitution (see **principle of substitution**)

substitution effect occurs when the fall in the price of a good motivates consumers to substitute that good for other goods (**6**).

supply the relationship between the amount of a good or service offered for sale at a given price and the price of the good or service (**4**).

surplus results if at the current price the quantity supplied exceeds the quantity demanded; the price is too high to equate the quantity demanded with quantity supplied (**4**) (see also **consumer surplus, producer surplus**).

surplus value the value of any labor over and above the amount of labor the worker would have to work to meet subsistence needs (**23A**).

tangent a straight line that touches the curve at only one point (**1A**).

tax (see **customs duty, excise tax, neutral tax, progressive tax, proportional tax, regressive tax**)

theory isolates those factors that may be crucial determinants of the phenomenon being explained (**1**).

total cost (*TC*) the total of the variable and fixed costs of producing each level of output (**8**).

total revenue (*TR*) the price of the commodity multiplied by the quantity sold (**5**).

total revenue test 1) if price and total revenue move in different directions, demand is elastic; 2) if price and total revenue move in the same direction, demand is inelastic; 3) if total revenue does not change when price changes, demand is unitary elastic (**5**).

transactions costs the costs associated with bringing buyers and sellers together (**13**) (see also **information costs**).

transfer payments transfers of income from one individual or organization to another **(20).**

trust a combination of firms that come together to act essentially as a monopolist; the firms set common prices, agree to restrict output, and punish member firms who fail to live up to the agreement **(14).**

union (see **craft union, industrial union, labor union**)

utility the satisfaction that people enjoy from consuming goods and services **(6).**

variable cost *(VC)* the cost that varies with the level of output **(8).**

vertical equity exists when those with a greater ability to pay bear a heavier tax burden **(20).**

wage/employment trade-off the situation confronted by any labor union that faces a downward-sloping demand curve: higher wages can be obtained only by sacrificing the number of jobs; lower unemployment can be obtained only by sacrificing higher wages **(17).**

warranty a guarantee of the integrity of a product and of the seller's responsibility for the repair or replacement of defective parts **(13).**

wealth the value of one's total assets minus the value of one's liabilities **(19).**

X-inefficiency the organizational slack that results from the lack of competition in monopolies; results in costs that are higher than necessary **(11).**

Suggested Readings

CHAPTER 1

Friedman, Milton. *Essays in Positive Economics*. Chicago: University of Chicago Press, 1953.

Kohler, Heinz. *Scarcity and Freedom*. Lexington, Mass.: D.C. Heath, 1977, part 1.

McCloskey, Donald. *The Applied Theory of Price*. New York: Macmillan, 1982, pp. 1–6.

Mundell, Robert A. *Man and Economics*. New York: McGraw-Hill, 1968, chap. 1.

CHAPTER 2

Franklin, Raymond S. *American Capitalism: Two Visions*. New York: Random House, 1977, chap. 1.

Heilbroner, Robert L. *The Making of Economic Society*. Englewood Cliffs, N.J.: Prentice-Hall, 1962, chap. 1.

Mundell, Robert A. *Man and Economics*. New York: McGraw-Hill, 1968, chaps. 1 & 2.

North, Douglass C. and Roger LeRoy Miller. "The Economics of Clamming and Other 'Free' Goods." In *The Economics of Public Issues*, 5th ed. New York: Harper and Row, 1980, pp. 152–56.

CHAPTER 3

Hayek, Frederick A. "The Price System as a Mechanism for Using Knowledge." In *Comparative Economic Systems: Models and Cases*, 4th ed, ed. Morris Bornstein. Homewood, Ill.: Richard D. Irwin, 1974, pp. 49–60.

McKenzie, Richard B. and Gordon Tullock. *Modern Political Economy*. New York: McGraw-Hill, 1978.

Neuberger, Egon. "Comparative Economic Systems." In *Perspectives in Economics: Economists Look at Their Field of Study*, eds. Alan A. Brown *et al*. New York: McGraw-Hill, 1971, pp. 252–66.

Radford, R. A. "The Economic Organization of a P.O.W. Camp." In *Economica* 12 (November 1945): 189–201.

Smith, Adam. *The Wealth of Nations*. ed. Edwin Cannan. New York: The Modern Library, 1937, book 1.

CHAPTER 4

Kohler, Heinz. *Intermediate Microeconomics: Theory and Applications*. Glenview, Ill.: Scott, Foresman, 1982, pp. 188–192.

Leftwich, Richard H. and Ansel M. Sharp. *Economics of Social Issues*, 3rd ed. Dallas: Business Publications, Inc., 1978, chap. 2.

Manne, Henry G. "The Parable of the Parking Lots." In *The Public Interest* 23 (Spring 1971): 10–15.

North, Douglass C. and Roger LeRoy Miller. *The Economics of Public Issues*, 5th ed. New York: Harper and Row, 1980, chap. 1.

Stigler, George. *The Theory of Price*, rev. ed. New York: Macmillian, 1952, chaps. 1 & 3.

CHAPTER 5

Kohler, Heinz. *Intermediate Microeconomics: Theory and Applications*. Glenview, Ill.: Scott, Foresman, 1982, pp. 94–105.

Mansfield, Edwin. *Microeconomics: Theory and Applications*. New York: W. W. Norton, 1979, chap. 4.

CHAPTER 6

Mansfield, Edwin. *Microeconomics: Theory and Applications*. New York: W. W. Norton, 1979, chap. 3.

Stigler, George. *The Theory of Prices*, rev. ed. New York: Macmillan, 1952, chaps. 4–5.

Walsh, Vivian Charles. *Introduction to Contemporary Microeconomics*. New York: McGraw-Hill, 1970, chaps 4–5.

CHAPTER 7

Alchian, Armen and Harold Demsetz. "Production, Information Costs, and Economic Organization." *American Economic Review* 57, 5 (December 1972): 777–95.

Coase, Ronald H. "The Nature of the Firm." *Economica* 4 (1937): 386–405.

Knight, Frank H. *Risk, Uncertainty, and Profit*. New York: Harper Torchbooks, 1957.

CHAPTER 8

Kohler, Heinz. *Intermediate Microeconomics: Theory and Applications*. Glenview, Ill.: Scott, Foresman, 1982, chap. 10.

Scherer, Frederick. *Industrial Market Structure and Economic Performance*, 3rd ed. Boston: Houghton Mifflin, 1980, chap. 4.

CHAPTER 9

Kirzner, Israel. *Competition and Entrepreneurship*. Chicago, University of Chicago Press, 1973.

Mansfield, Edwin. Microeconomics: Theory and Applications. New York: W. W. Norton, 1979, chap. 8.

Weiss, Leonard. *Case Studies in American Industry*. New York: John Wiley, 1971, chap. 2.

CHAPTER 10

Chamberlin, Edward H. *The Theory of Monopolistic Competition*, 6th ed. Cambridge: Harvard University Press, 1980.

Kitch, Edmund W. *et al.* ''The Regulation of Taxicabs in Chicago.'' *Journal of Law and Economics* (October 1971), pp. 285–350.

North, Douglass C. and Roger LeRoy Miller. *The Economics of Public Issues,* 5th ed. New York: Harper and Row, 1980, chap. 2.

Smith, Adam. *The Wealth of Nations,* ed. Edwin Cannan. New York: The Modern Library, 1939, chap. 7.

CHAPTER 11

Galbraith, John Kenneth. *Economics and the Public Purpose*. Boston: Houghton Mifflin, 1973, parts I-III.

Harberger, Arnold. ''Monopoly and Resource Allocation.'' *American Economic Review* 44 (May 1954): 77–87.

Kamien, Morton, and Nancy Schwartz. ''Market Structure and Innovation: A Survey.'' *Journal of Economic Literature* 8, 1 (March 1975): 1–38.

Mansfield, Edwin. *Microeconomics: Theory and Applications*. New York: W. W. Norton, 1979, chap. 10.

Schumpeter, Joseph. *Capitalism, Socialism, and Democracy,* 3rd ed. New York: Harper and Row, 1950.

Tullock, Gordon. ''The Welfare Cost of Tariffs, Monopolies, and Theft.'' *Western Economic Journal* 5 (June 1967): 224–32.

CHAPTER 12

Adams, Walter, ed. *The Structure of American Industry,* 4th ed. New York: Macmillan, 1971, pp. 77–78.

Bain, Joe S. *Barriers to New Competition*. Cambridge, Mass.: Harvard University Press, 1965.

Caves, Richard. *American Industry: Structure, Conduct, Performance*. Englewood Cliffs, N.J.: Prentice-Hall, 1981.

Galbraith, John K. *American Capitalism,* rev. ed. Cambridge: The Riverside Press, 1956.

Koch, James V. *Industrial Organization and Prices,* 2nd ed. Englewood Cliffs, N.J.: Prentice-Hall, 1980, p. 181.

Scherer, F. M. *Industrial Market Structure and Economic Performance,* 2nd ed. Boston: Houghton Mifflin, 1980, p. 67.

Williamson, Oliver. *Markets and Hierarchies: Analysis and Antitrust Implications*. New York: The Free Press, 1975, p. 234.

CHAPTER 13

Akerlof, George. ''The Market for 'Lemons': Quality, Uncertainty, and the Market Mechanism.'' *Quarterly Journal of Economics* 84 (August 1970): 488–500.

Hayek, F. A. ''The Use of Knowledge in Society.'' *American Economic Review* 35 (1945): 510–30.

Heyne, Paul and Thomas Johnson. *Toward Understanding Microeconomics*. Chicago: SRA, 1976, chap. 8.

Kohler, Heinz. *Intermediate Microeconomics: Theory and Applications*. Glenview, Ill.: Scott, Foresman, 1982, chap. 10.

Stigler, George. ''The Economics of Information.'' *Journal of Political Economy* (June 1961), pp. 213–25.

CHAPTER 14

Baumol, William J. ''Reasonable Rules for Rate Regulation: Plausible Policies in an Imperfect World.'' In *The Crisis of the Regulatory Commissions,* ed. Paul MacAvoy. New York: W. W. Norton, 1970, pp. 187–206.

Mansfield, Edwin. *Monopoly Power and Economic Performance,* 3rd. ed. New York: W. W. Norton, 1974, pp. 57–68.

Singer, Eugene. *Antitrust Economics*. Englewood Cliffs, N.J.: Prentice-Hall, 1968, chap. 2.

Swartz, Thomas R. and Frank J. Bonello, eds. *Taking Sides: Clashing Views on Controversial Economic Issues*. Guilford, Conn.: Duskin Publishing Group, 1982, pp. 58–73.

Weidenbaum, Murray L. *Business, Government and the Public,* 2nd ed. Englewood Cliffs, N.J.: Prentice-Hall, 1981.

White, Lawrence J. *Reforming Regulation: Processes and Problems*. Englewood Cliffs, N.J.: Prentice-Hall, 1981.

Williamson, Oliver. *Markets and Hierarchies: Analysis and Antitrust Implications*. New York: The Free Press, 1975.

CHAPTER 15

Kohler, Heinz. *Intermediate Microeconomics: Theory and Applications*. Glenview, Ill.: Scott, Foresman, 1982, pp. 213–20.

North, Douglass C. and Roger LeRoy Miller. *The Economics of Public Issues*. New York: Harper and Row, 1980, chap. 3

Stigler, George. *The Theory of Price*, rev. ed. New York: Macmillan, 1952, chap. 11.

CHAPTER 16

Addison, John T. and W. Stanley Siebert. *The Market for Labor: An Analytical Treatment*. Glenview, Ill.: Scott, Foresman, 1979.

Becker, Gary. *Human Capital,* 2nd ed. New York: National Bureau of Economic Research, 1975.

Doeringer, Peter and Michael Piore. *Internal Labor Markets and Manpower Analysis*. Lexington, Mass.: D.C. Heath, 1971.

Dunlop, John T. and Walter Galenson, eds. *Labor in the Twentieth Century*. New York: Academic Press, 1978.

Ehrenberg, Ronald G. and Robert S. Smith, *Modern Labor Economics: Theory and Public Policy*. Glenview, Ill.: Scott, Foresman, 1982.

Welch, Finis. *Minimum Wages: Issues and Evidence*. Washington, D.C.: American Enterprise Institute, 1978.

CHAPTER 17

Barbash, Jack. "The Labor Movement After World War II." *Monthly Labor Review,* November 1976.

Bowen, William G. and Orley Ashenfelter, eds. *Labor and the National Economy,* rev. ed. New York: W. W. Norton, 1975.

Ehrenberg, Ronald G. and Robert S. Smith. *Modern Labor Economics: Theory and Public Policy*. Glenview, Ill.: Scott, Foresman, 1982, chap. 12.

Freeman, Richard B. and James L. Medoff. "The Two Faces of Unionism." *Public Interest* 57 (Fall 1979): 69–93.

Paisley, C. J. "Labor Unions and Wages: A Survey." *Journal of Economic Literature* 18 (March 1980): 1–31.

CHAPTER 18

Heyne, Paul and Thomas Johnson. *Toward Understanding Microeconomics*. Chicago: SRA, 1976, chap. 2, 13.

Knight, Frank. *Risk, Uncertainty and Profit*. New York: Harper Torchbooks, 1957.

Schumpeter, Joseph. *Theory of Economic Development*. Cambridge, Mass.: Harvard University Press, 1949.

CHAPTER 19

Blinder, Alan S. *Toward an Economic Theory of Income Distribution*. Cambridge, Mass.: MIT Press, 1974.

Blinder, Alan S. "The Level and Distribution of Economic Well-Being." In *The American Economy in Transition*. ed. Martin Feldstein. Chicago: The University of Chicago Press, 1980, pp. 450–53.

Friedman, Milton. "Choice, Chance, and the Personal Distribution of Income." *Journal of Political Economy* 61, 4 (August 1953): 277–90.

Kohler, Heinz. *Scarcity and Freedom*. Lexington, Mass.: D.C. Heath, 1977, pp. 339–80.

Lloyd, Cynthia B., ed. *Sex, Discrimination, and the Division of Labor*. New York: Columbia University Press, 1975.

Okun, Arthur. *Equality and Efficiency: The Big Trade-off*. Washington, D.C.: The Brookings Institution, 1975.

Paglin, Morton. "The Measurement and Trend of Inequality: A Basic Revision." *American Economic Review* 65, 4 (September 1975): 598–609.

Rawls, John. *A Theory of Justice*. Cambridge: Harvard University Press, 1971.

Rawls, John. "Some Reasons for the Maximin Criterion." *American Economic Review* 64, 2 (May 1974): 141–46.

Schiller, Bradley. *The Economics of Poverty and Discrimination*. Englewood Cliffs, N.J.: Prentice-Hall, 1973, chap. 10.

CHAPTER 20

Boskin, Michael J., ed. *Federal Tax Reform: Myths and Realities*. San Francisco: Institute for Contemporary Studies, 1978.

Break, George and Joseph Pechman. *Federal Tax Reform: The Impossible Dream?* Washington, D.C.: Brookings Institution, 1975, p. 91.

Browning, Edgar K. and William R. Johnson. *The Distribution of the Tax Burden*. Washington, D.C.: American Enterprise Institute, 1979.

Musgrave, Richard A. and Peggy B. Musgrave. *Public Finance Theory and Practice,* 3rd ed. New York: McGraw-Hill, 1980.

Pechman, Joseph and Benjamin Okner. *Who Bears the Tax Burden?* Washington, D.C.: Brookings Institution, 1974.

CHAPTER 21

Cheung, Steven S. "The Fable of the Bees: An Economic Investigation." *Journal of Law and Economics,* April 1973.

Coase, Ronald H. "The Lighthouse in Economics." *Journal of Law and Economics,* October 1976.

Coase, Ronald H. "The Problem of Social Costs." *Journal of Law and Economics,* October 1960.

Griffin, James A. and Henry B. Steele. *Energy Economics and Policy*. New York: Academic, 1980.

Heyne, Paul and Thomas Johnson. *Toward Understanding Microeconomics*. Chicago: SRA, 1976, chap. 14.

Krutilla, John V. and Anthony C. Fisher. *The Economics of Natural Environments*. Baltimore: John Hopkins, 1975.

Ruff, Larry E. "The Economic Common Sense of Pollution." *The Public Interest* 18 (Spring 1970): 69–85.

Simon, Julian. *The Ultimate Resource*. Princeton: Princeton University Press, 1981, p. 19, appendices A2–A5.

CHAPTER 22

Browning, E. and J. Browning. *Public Finance and the Price System*. New York: Macmillan, 1979.

Buchanan, James M. and Gordon Tullock. *The Calculus of Consent*. Ann Arbor: University of Michigan Press, 1962.

Buchanan, James M. *The Limits of Liberty*. Chicago: The University of Chicago Press, 1975, p. 162.

Downs, Anthony. *An Economic Theory of Democracy*. New York: Harper and Row, 1957.

Mueller, Dennis C. *Public Choice*. Cambridge: University Press, 1979, pp. 49–51.

CHAPTER 23

Bornstein, Morris, ed. *Comparative Economic Systems: Models and Cases,* 4th ed. Homewood, Ill.: Richard D. Irwin, 1979.

Gregory, Paul R. and Robert C. Stuart. *Comparative Economic Systems*. Boston: Houghton Mifflin, 1981.

Gregory, Paul R. and Robert C. Stuart. *Soviet Economic Structure and Performance*. New York: Harper and Row, 1982.

Grossman, Gregory. *Economic Systems*. Englewood Cliffs, N.J.: Prentice-Hall, 1967.

Nove, Alec. *The Soviet Economic System*. London: Allen and Unwin, 1977.

Index